ADDISON AND STEELE: THE CRITICAL HERITAGE

THE CRITICAL HERITAGE SERIES

GENERAL EDITOR: B. C. SOUTHAM, M.A., B.LITT. (OXON.)
Formerly Department of English, Westfield College, University of London

For a list of books in this series see the back end paper

ADDISON AND STEELE

THE CRITICAL HERITAGE

Edited by
EDWARD A. BLOOM
Professor of English
Brown University
and
LILLIAN D. BLOOM
Professor of English
Rhode Island College

reviewed
TLS. 25 July 1980 p 849
oTHES

ROUTLEDGE & KEGAN PAUL
LONDON, BOSTON AND HENLEY

First published in 1980
by Routledge & Kegan Paul Ltd
39 Store Street,
London WC1E 7DD,
Broadway House,
Newtown Road,
Henley-on-Thames,
Oxon RG9 1EN and
9 Park Street,
Boston, Mass. 02108, USA
Printed in Great Britain by
Redwood Burn Ltd, Trowbridge & Esher
Copyright Edward A. Bloom and Lillian D. Bloom 1980

British Library Cataloguing in Publication Data

Addison and Steele, the critical heritage.–

(Critical heritage series).
1. Addison, Joseph – Criticism and interpretation–
    Addresses, essays, lectures
2. Steele, Sir Richard – Criticism and interpretation–
    Addresses, essays, lectures
I. Bloom, Edward A.   II Bloom, Lillian Doris
III. Series
H241'.5.09   PR 3301   80–40048
ISBN 0 7100 0375 7

General Editor's Preface

The reception given to a writer by his contemporaries and near-contemporaries is evidence of considerable value to the student of literature. On one side we learn a great deal about the state of criticism at large and in particular about the development of critical attitudes towards a single writer; at the same time, through private comments in letters, journals or marginalia, we gain an insight upon the tastes and literary thought of individual readers of the period. Evidence of this kind helps us to understand the writer's historical situation, the nature of his immediate reading-public, and his response to these pressures.

The separate volumes in the *Critical Heritage Series* present a record of this early criticism. Clearly, for many of the highly productive and lengthily reviewed nineteenth- and twentieth-century writers, there exists an enormous body of material; and in these cases the volume editors have made a selection of the most important views significant for their intrinsic critical worth or for their representative quality—perhaps even registering incomprehension!

For earlier writers, notably pre-eighteenth century, the materials are much scarcer and the historical period has been extended, sometimes far beyond the writer's lifetime, in order to show the inception and growth of critical views which were initially slow to appear.

In each volume the documents are headed by an Introduction, discussing the material assembled and relating the early stages of the author's reception to what we have come to identify as the critical tradition. The volumes will make available much material which would otherwise be difficult of access and it is hoped that the modern reader will be thereby helped towards an informed understanding of the ways in which literature has been read and judged.

B.C.S.

For Donald F. Bond

'A Faithful Friend is a strong Defence;
and he that hath found such an one, hath found a Treasure.'
Spectator 68

Contents

vii

CONTENTS

VI Addison the Dramatist

VII Addison the Man and Writer

CONTENTS

Preface

For more than a hundred years literary myth has coupled
the names of Addison and Steele. If the one is mentioned,
the other soon follows. The immediate question is why.
Perhaps the answer to this gemini-like identification lies
in the fact that the two greatest periodicals of the eighteenth century emerged from their joint effort, however
uneven the effort was. Perhaps too the answer arises in
part from a pathetic journalistic episode. Friends and
political allies for so long, they became embroiled during
the last years of Addison's life in a paper war that deni-
grated the integrity of both. For all the linking of
their names, their personalities and talents differed. In
their own lifetime and well into the next century their
reputations moved in contrary directions. Addison's fame
seemed unstoppable despite the onslaughts of John Dennis
and Alexander Pope. Steele's notoriety centred in rough-
and-tumble controversy, sinking - as the years passed -
into virtual invisibility.

This volume highlights the separate identities of the
two men. It also documents their reputations by concentrating largely upon eighteenth-century criticism. Steele,
for example, is either attacked or defended for reasons
largely factional. Even those who answered yea or nay to
his comedies and dramatic criticism were conscious of his
party commitment. The eulogies following his death were
cast in a Whiggish mould, as much panegyrics upon Walpole
as upon the deceased. Almost non-existent through the
second half of the century, Steele re-entered the critical
scene in 1836 when Coleridge and his friend Thomas Allsop
spoke and wrote sympathetically of him. From that time on,
those who enjoyed the polemicist and dramatist, emphasized
his feeling heart, his sentimental wit and harmless peccadilloes.

Addison's glory focused on the man, the author of

'Cato', and the prose stylist. Indeed, his glory stemmed
- as legend had it - from a fount of moral purity and
verbal elegance, expressed without self-consciousness and
seemingly as part of popular idiom. He was never forgotten during the eighteenth century, his nobility developing
a patina of its own as the century advanced. His sanctifi-
cation achieved its most eloquent statement in Macaulay's
1843 review of Lucy Aikin's two-volume biography. Without
quarrelling with the gentleman-critic in the 'Edinburgh
Review', Thackeray in 1853 trod lightly upon Victorian
propriety and taste. In his 'English Humourists of the
Eighteenth Century', he brought Addison and Steele
together. More important, he did not depreciate one to
elevate the other. On the contrary, he compared them,
pointed out their particular talents, and praised both for
their unique literary gifts.

The organization of this book is tripartite. The first
three sections deal with Steele the man, the pamphleteer,
and the dramatist. Then he and Addison meet in sections IV
and V not primarily as personalities but as the authors of
the 'Tatler' and 'Spectator'. The last two sections of the
book deal with Addison's fame as a dramatist, then as the
artist whose genius is inseparable from the human being.
Within the volume the selections - a few eccentric, many
more insightful - represent the history of two men's reputations from 1702 to 1853. What followed thereafter - the
turns and twists, the rise and fall of these same reputations - are discussed or presented in the Introduction and
Bibliography.

Introduction

Between 1709 and 1729 the literature which raged about
Steele often made no distinction between the man and the
polemicist. Even his association with the Drury Lane
Theatre as governor was centred in controversy and tinged
by factional loyalties. But several years before then –
indeed by the spring of 1709 – he came within range of
Tory consciousness as a potential menace. Consequently,
every piece of writing signed by or attributed to him was
interpreted as a possible handle for party use. And the
Steele-Watchers, synonymous with those Tories working for
Harley and St John, were very nearly right.

For five years – from May 1709 to the summer of 1714 –
Steele remained an outsized target, his enemies indifferent to his literary achievement. Swift, for example,
identified him as the 'Author of two tolerable Plays, (or
at least of the greatest part of them) which, added to the
Company he kept, and to the continual Conversation and
Friendship of Mr. *Addison*, hath given him the Character of
a Wit.'(1) Swiftian sarcasm in this instance was almost
gentle, at least when measured against other descriptions
of Steele as a scribbler, a tool of faction, a Grub Street
hireling, an ingrate, a republican, and ultimately a
traitor.

The constant in his life was a series of paper wars.
The first, whether we end it with his expulsion from the
Commons in March 1714 or the collapse of the Tory ministry
some five months later, saw the publication of the great
periodicals: the 'Tatler', 'Spectator', and 'Guardian'.
During this same period Steele advanced in the Whig party
from apprentice pamphleteer to number one propagandist.
The tussle began with Mrs Manley's 'New Atalantis' which
appeared on 26 May 1709, just a month and a half after the

'Tatler' came to London. Her fiction, frankly political, praised the Tories and Anne's new favourites - Harley, Peterborough, and Mrs Masham - and offered some 'faint representations, some imperfect pieces of painting, of the heads of that party that have misled thousands'.(2) Surely in so formidable a Whiggish assembly Steele had minor standing. Nonetheless, in her portrait of him as Monsieur le Ingrate, a blackened grotesque, she could settle personal scores and deny him, as Gazetteer and Bickerstaff, any moral credibility or political sense. The portrait was successful, setting a pattern for anti-Steele invective, a *vituperatio hominis* that reached a scatological climax in 1713-14.

Given his personality (the sinner self-canonized), his Whiggish ambitions, and his ineluctable need for money, Steele would have in time triggered off a paper war. The publication of the 'Tatler' merely hastened the first skirmish. Its party slant was anticipated even before distribution. Thus Lady Elizabeth Hervey wrote to her husband: 'This is all the news I know, except this in-closed paper, which I heard Lord Sun: commend mightily, so I have teazed Mr. Hopkins till he got it for me, for tis not published, tho' it is printed, Mr. Manruing and one or two more is named for the authors of it.'(3) From the beginning, then, the journal was linked with men bla-tantly Whig and within a week or two Steele was identi-fied as Bickerstaff.

The attacks on the journal and Steele were sporadic in 1709. In October of that year Mrs Manley found the 'Tatler's' satire deficient, its blandness a cover for every weakness that sapped national 'Greatness', 'Virtue', and 'Glory'. Shortly thereafter a broadside, called 'The Character of the Tatler', was printed.(4) Indebted to Mrs Manley's personalized criticism of Steele, it moved between belittling gibes at 'Abednego Umbra' and serious denunciations of the hireling propagandist. Pragmatically it devoted itself to the dispersal of the 'Tatler's' audience; it therefore sneered at and scolded the periodi-cal for pretending literary integrity when it was a grubby adjunct of party.

Such attacks left only faint marks on the thickening skin of Steele, if only because they were so few. By August 1710, however, all that was changed. In fact, his whole world was changed. The Godolphin ministry had been dismissed; a Whig defeat in the parliamentary election scheduled for early autumn was a certainty. Harley, now Lord Treasurer, who had been derided by Bickerstaff as Hanno and Polypragmon, was ready to spend thousands of pounds to rid the political arena of Steele's journal.

The 'Examiner' had been launched, and for the Tories it
decided the rules of warfare. With its fifth number it
abused the 'Tatler's' news reporting. After its campaign
opened on 24-31 August 1710, it never lost sight of the
man it would gladly smash at any time and in any way.

The assault, begun by Mrs Manley, was cruelly extended
by the 'Examiner'. To one Whig observer, the scheme was
to 'Build Scandal on Fiction, and assert boldly and abu-
sively without Shame or Conscience'.(5) Specifically the
scheme aimed to excoriate Steele in order to discredit his
political writing. In a jingling ballad 'The Loyal
Calves-Head-Club' (1710) he was found guilty by association and the 'Tatler' was defined as the mouth-piece of
the Kit-Cats, 'Hard-mouthed Sots' and republicans all, who
would 'advance *their* Canting State' by any lie or 'Plot'.
Again in 1710, 'A Condoling Letter to the Tattler' speared
the journalist with familiar epithets: Steele the spend-
thrift, Steele the hypocrite, Steele the inmate of a
sponging-house, Steele the madman whose frenzy could be
neither condoned nor condoled.(6)

Under the date of 3 October 1710 the Tory 'Moderator'
hinted the demise of 'the Ingenious Isaac Bickerstaffe ...
much lamented by the Gentlemen of the *Kit-Kat-Club* and all
true *Republican Spirits*, for his hearty Zeal to the good
old Cause, his universal Learning, and particular Skill in
the Laws of the Land.' The author of the 'Moderator' knew
this: within the first few days of October Steele had promised Harley the death of the 'Tatler' in order to retain
his post in the Stamp Office. The demise itself on 2
January was celebrated by the 'Friendly Couriere,' a dis-
cursive periodical which lasted for all of one number.(7)

The Spectatorial days between March 1711 and December
1712 were almost irenic for Steele. But even then he did
not quite disappear as a target. The Tories never assumed
that he could be silent for long and they questioned the
non-political intention of the 'Spectator' just because he
was associated with it. In early April and in response to
the third number, Mr Spectator was warned - as Bickerstaff
had been warned - that he was being watched, investigated
and 'spied' upon.(8) Almost a year later there was a
flurry of journalistic activity as Tory journalists -
William Wagstaffe, Oldisforth, and Swift - hooted at
Steele for reprinting Fleetwood's Whiggish Preface to his
'Four Sermons'. Mr Spectator was mocked as Dick Hotspur
and a projector of republican adventures. He was laughed
at as only one of a factional 'Fraternity', a 'Dealer in
Words', and a purveyor of Whiggish tomfoolery.(9) Near
the end of that year, in November, Steele was cudgelled in
a verse pamphlet called 'The British Censor'. Despite its

literary pose, it presented little that was new except the
image of a journalistic Maecenas doling out favour and
'extorting blind Obedience'. Ironically, Steele never
commanded any authority except when he wore the mask of
Bickerstaff or gambled on his chances of evading martyrdom in the last year of the Queen's ministry.

'The British Censor' was bad poetry but ripping *ad
hominem* criticism. In 1712, however, its victim refused
to be victimized. Too many other things - exciting and
potentially fruitful - were happening all about him.
Arthur Maynwaring had just died and Addison stepped into
his place as unofficial director of Whig propaganda,
gathering together a journalistic tribe, feeding them
information and a point of view, dispensing employment as
rewards. Receptive to anyone's gift of rhetoric, he
determined to use the former Gazetteer as 'a Brother-
Scribler' and the most audible of Whig propagandists.
By August 1713 and without much urging, Steele was ready
to serve his party as pamphleteer and Member of Parliament. For all the duality of function, he had a single
goal. As one opponent put it, 'he does not question overturning the Ministry, and doing that before the first
Sessions of Parliament is over, which my Lord Wh--on and
S--rs have been foil'd at, for Three Years together'.(10)

To chisel away at ministerial strength, Steele raised
the Dunkirk issue in 'Guardian' 128. Tory reaction was
swift and torrential. The 'Examiner' dismissed him as an
'Ingrate' and a 'contemptible Wretch', his position as a
'Lye' and a 'Libel'. And in 'The Honour and Prerogative
of the Queen's Majesty Vindicated' (No. 12), Defoe heaped
together epithets as so many stones to hurl against the
'traytor', 'renegade', 'counterfeit', 'bully', and
'Judas'. This merely set the tone for what was to come.
And coming almost immediately was 'A Second Whigg-Letter
from William Prynn to Nestor Ironside', a clumsy drama-
tization of Defoe's innuendo that the 'Guardian's' statement tended to sedition. (11)

The retort to such verbal gibes appeared in 'The Importance of Dunkirk Consider'd' and in a candidly partisan
journal, the 'Englishman'. By the autumn and winter of
1713 the Tories engaged their best writers - disputatious
and punitive - in all-out warfare against Steele. Swift,
for example, produced 'The Importance of the Guardian Considered'. William Wagstaffe probably wrote 'The Character
of Richard Steele', which proved to be the most popular,
certainly the most devastating, anti-Steele pamphlet of
the year. It went through four editions, steadily hoping
to reduce 'Old *Ironsides* to so low a Condition, that perhaps he may be glad to put an End to this long and Bloody
War'. (12)

As invective followed invective, Steele marched virtu-
ously militant into 1714. Because his new pamphleteering
probe against the ministry - 'The Crisis' - had been
advertised for so long and he had already 'got into the
Fire,' as Swift taunted him on 6 or 7 January, he could
not 'easily retire'. In truth he could not retire at all,
and so on 19 January he masked himself in that pamphlet as
a professional liberator, warning his audience of imminent
authoritarian dangers. Again the Tories rose to the bait.
Mrs Manley introduced 'A Modest Enquiry into the Reasons
of Joy Expressed by a Certain Sett of People, upon the
Spreading of a Report of Her Majesty's Death'. Steele
did not respond to it or to other pamphlets seemingly
myriad. He shrugged off the scatological farce of 'A
Letter from the Facetious Doctor Andrew Tripe'. He listened indifferently to mockery of 'The Publick Spirit of
the Whigs', in which Swift hoped to hurl his opponent into
oblivion as an insinuating 'Politician', a 'child of
Obscurity', a pedant and maxim-monger 'grossly defective
in Truth, in Sense, or in Grammar', and ultimately a
'CREATURE' stripped of humanity.
    Steele, however, had learned experientially that he
could not be vilified or jeered into insignificance. He
knew that the Tory-dominated Commons would vote his expulsion and paradoxically establish both his political
worth and fame. On 18 March he was found guilty of writing certain *scandalous and seditious Libels* designed
*to alienate the Affections of her Majesty's good Sub-
jects, and to create Jealousies and Divisions among
them*.(13) The verdict did not dampen his party commitment. He continued to write anti-Tory pamphlets through
the rest of the year and ministerial writers, such as the
pseudonymous John Lacy, continued to attack him, although
without their customary virulence or enthusiasm. The
lacklustre quality of the paper war after March may be
attributed to the visibly sinking fortunes of the Oxford-
Bolingbroke government, which none saw more clearly than
the Tories themselves. Swift thus wrote to Bolingbroke
on 7 August: 'Your machine of four years modelling is
dashed to pieces in a moment: And, as well by the choice
of Regents, as by their proceedings.' By the 30th of
that month, Mrs Manley complained to Oxford: 'I have
nothing but a starving scene before me, new interests to
make without any old merit, Lord Mal-- and all his accomplices justly enraged against me. Nothing saved out of
the general wreck'.(14)
    Never again was Steele politically assaulted as he was
before his expulsion from the House. His 'Declaration'
pamphlets created some excitement when Tory rebuttals

appeared, but the excitement was soon dissipated. In 1719
he and Addison engaged in a contretemps over the peerage
bill. But it was a quarrel far more sad than angry, productive only of the 'Plebeian' and the unfinished 'Old
Whig'. The exchange of insults ended a friendship which,
although strained since 1717, had for almost a generation
survived the annoyances and disputes that must inevitably
arise from contrary dispositions.(15)

Whatever praise Steele received during his lifetime was
usually partisan or muddied by controversy. Even the two
elegies written in 1729 had a political flavour, which
celebrated Walpole almost as much as they did Steele.
Benjamin Victor thus interrupted his lament to boast of
the journalist's triumph over Harley and of his loyalty to
Sir Robert.(16)   Joseph Mitchell went so far as to call
his elegiac stanzas 'The Monument' in the hope that the
Lord Treasurer would push through a plan to memorialize
Steele in the Abbey. The plan, however, came to nothing
and 'The Bard, the Patriot, Soldier, and the Sage' was
remembered by two inept versifiers. So different had been
the literary reaction to Addison's death that Mitchell
blurted out a series of rhetorical questions.

> But are the *Muses* all, at once, struck dumb?
> Yet unadorn'd remains the silent Tomb?
> Is POPE confounded with uncommon Woe?
> No more does YOUNG's high Inspiration flow?
> Quite is the laurel'd EUSDEN's Lyre unstrung?
> And TICKELL's Harp on rueful Willows hung?
> Ungenerous Tribe!

In 1731 an anonymous 'Memoirs of the Life and Writings
of Sir Richard Steele' was distributed. Thirteen years
later Corbyn Morris made passing reference to a martyred
Steele, 'a Gentleman endeared to the Nation by the Humanity and Politeness of his Writings', who was persecuted
for the 'Crime' of patriotism.(17) By the second half of
the eighteenth century, however, his reputation as a personality and pamphleteer seemed to have died with him.
Like the issues which provoked them, the pamphlets were
but ephemera. Once the causes and the crises had been
forgotten, so too their literature and author. Paradoxically, while the great periodicals were acknowledged in
the eighteenth century to be essentially Steele's, it was
Addison as prose stylist who was celebrated in the second
half of that century. With the emergence of a new romantic temper Coleridge and his disciple Thomas Allsop helped
to resurrect the name and genius of Steele. They were
adamantly certain, albeit on subjective grounds, that he

was Addison's superior, that his essays were rendered dis-
tinctive by 'their pure humanity springing from the
gentleness, the kindness of his heart'. Thackeray, as we
shall see, emphasized the same qualities.

In a 'Quarterly Review' article for March 1855 (expanded three years later as one of his 'Historical and Biographical Essays') John Forster wrote of Steele to balance
the record so slanted in Addison's favour by Macaulay.
Less than a decade after Forster's appreciation - by
1865 - Henry R. Montgomery offered a two-volume biography
that was equally sympathetic. Aitken's 'Life' in 1889
aimed to pinpoint the personality through an analysis of
the public response aroused by the man in his varying
occupations: military officer, tract writer, dramatist,
party pamphleteer, Whig polemicist and Whig dissident,
member of parliament, theatre manager, inventor. By 1899
Austin Dobson became an apologist for his subject.

> And if Steele has suffered from scandal and misrepre-
> sentation [of faction], he has also suffered from his
> own admissions. The perfect frankness and freedom of
> his letters ... leave upon many, who do not suffi-
> ciently bear in mind their extremely familiar charac-
> ter, an ill-defined impression that he was over-
> uxorious, over-sentimental. But a man is not neces-
> sarily this for a few extravagant *billets-doux*.(18)

Inevitably Dobson fell back upon Berkeley's first-hand
knowledge of Steele's 'love and consideration for his
wife, of the generosity and benevolence of his temper, of
his cheerfulness, his wit, and his good sense'. This
same image, so long submerged, leaped into the first
quarter of the twentieth century with only slight alteration. The weaknesses that the Victorians were forced to
rationalize had by the time of Dobrée's 'Essays in Biography' been elevated into near-virtues. Sir Richard,
in short, had become the lovable irresponsible, a Skim-
pole not gone bad, whose rashness and prodigality were
motivated by joy and candid good will. Quite obviously
the passage of time, the shifts of taste, the subjective
standards of both his opponents and admirers have seriously dulled the tones of his portrait. But slowly
through the application of modern scholarly techniques
and the findings of Rae Blanchard, Bertram Goldgar, and
Calhoun Winton the one-time 'wretched Trooper' is being
restored to realistic focus. (19)

II

Of Steele's four plays only 'The Lying Lover' was a theatrical failure in the eighteenth century. Opening at the Drury Lane Theatre on 2 December 1703, it had a moderately good first run. It then vanished from the stage and its author's mind. It had an unexplainable revival for four nights in the spring of 1746, after which it disappeared apparently forever. On the other hand, his remaining plays - 'The Funeral', 'The Tender Husband', and 'The Conscious Lovers' - all became a part of repertory, at least until the last few years of the century. Certainly 'The Conscious Lovers' was talked about longer and more vehemently than the others. Thus Mrs Inchbald in 1808 acknowledged that its effectiveness 'has since been much obscured by imitations which have surpassed the original; but to Steele are due the honours of originality, and of teaching an audience to think and to feel, as well as to laugh and applaud, at the representation of a comedy.' Ironically, the concept of 'the fine Gentleman', for which Steele was attacked in 1722 and 1723, did not sufficiently satisfy the moral palate of most Victorian spectators. Foreshadowing that judgment, Mrs Inchbald found in Bevil and Indiana 'a degree of languor', and in Cimberton evidence that the dramatist 'has at times degraded his muse to comply with the degraded taste of the auditors of that period'.(20)

The fact remains that in the eighteenth century three of the plays had healthy lives, enjoying different degrees of debate or discussion. The first of them, 'The Funeral' (1701), which Steele wrote to assuage his creditors and 'to enliven his Character' after 'The Christian Hero', had its detractors and supporters. Even those who were to fault the comedy did so with a semblance of restraint: ''Tis a dangerous Matter to talk of this Play; the Town has given it such applause.' Still the author of 'A Comparison between the Two Stages' (1702) argued that the improbability of plot and a wanton reliance upon contrivance had reduced 'this so celebrated Comedy to the indignity of the vilest Farce' (see No. 16). By 1713 praise had drowned out detraction, its admirers stressing 'The Funeral's' sensitive call to the *humanitas* shared by all theatregoers. So Sir Richard Blackmore in the 'Lay-Monastery' maintained: 'Every one will own, that in this Play there are many lively Strokes of Wit and Humour; but I must confess I am more pleas'd with the fine Touches of Humanity in it, than with any other Part of the Entertainment.'(21)

More surprising than the attention given to Steele's

first play was the durability of 'The Tender Husband'.
From its first appearance in 1705 until 1794 it was acted
at least 165 times in London. One of these performances
was attended by Pamela, who conveyed her reaction to Lady
Davers in a derogatory review-letter. Motivated as always
by her sense of the expedient, Richardson's heroine was
particularly offended by the first scene.

> Mr. Fainlove, alias Mrs. Lucy, undertakes the task, in
> hopes to live with Mr. Clerimont, in case of a divorce
> from his wife; or to be provided for, in case the plot
> does not succeed; which makes it apparent, that, to say
> nothing of his morality, poor Lucy has not met with a
> generous man in Mr. Clerimont; since, after the for-
> feiture of her honour, she was still to do a more in-
> famous job, if possible,. to procure for herself a pro-
> vision from him.

Notwithstanding the literary sanctity surrounding the
names of Addison and Steele, Pamela was 'grievously disappointed' not merely by the opening of the play but by
its sordid morality throughout and its violation of
'*probability*'.(22) Her severity, oddly enough, did not
foreshadow the spirit of the Victorians who in 1841
enjoyed Richard Brinsley Peake's stylized adaptation of
'The Tender Husband'.
  Between 1715 and 1722 Steele became involved in yet
another quarrel whose intensity almost matched the earlier
political flyting. Since October 1714 he had been a lic-
ensed partner in the Theatre Royal in Drury Lane. Then,
from the following January, he served as governor of the
theatre under a life-patent granted by the King as partial
payment for his dedication to the Hanoverian cause. The
appointment, like almost every other public event of his
life, was both supported and denounced. According to Lady
Cowper, who had followed the theatrical criticism in the
'Tatler' and 'Spectator': 'It were to be wished our Stage
were Chaster, and I cannot but hope, now that it is under
Mr. Steele's Direction, that it will mend.' But to Defoe
the King's choice was an abomination. He singled Steele
out as the person who, 'by recommending the Play-Houses,'
did more 'to promote the present Madness of the Age ...
than all the Agents Hell ever employed before.'(23)
Defoe, however, was tilting against windmills, his words
scattered into oblivion.
  Steele's control of the theatre was not challenged
until 1717, when the Duke of Newcastle was made Lord
Chamberlain. From then until the winter of 1719-1720 when
overt hostilities broke out, there was continuous sniping

between the governor and his managers - Cibber, Wilks, and
Booth - on one side and the young, somewhat impetuous Lord
Chamberlain on the other. At the centre of the crisis,
complicated by political considerations, was a conflict
over authority: whether the players should be ruled by
Newcastle as Chamberlain of the King's Household or Steele
as governor of the Royal Company of Comedians. The pamphlet war began not with a pamphlet but with Cibber's dedicatory epistle to the governor prefixed to the printed
'Ximena' (September 1719). The epistle fulsomely recognized Steele's contributions to the reformation of a one-
time licentious theatre. 'Nothing but a Genius so universally rever'd could, with such Candor and Penetration, have
pointed out its Faults and Misconduct; and so effectually
have redeem'd its Uses and Excellence from Prejudice and
Dis-favour.' As if this were insufficient, Cibber limned
his friend as a forgotten martyr who spent his talent without stint on behalf of King and country. It was not long
after 'Ximena' was published that Newcastle took his first
formal action against the governing body of the Drury Lane.
Specifically, he silenced Cibber in December.

Angered at the action taken against one of his managers,
Steele did what he usually did when he felt threatened. He
brought his arguments to the public, this time in a periodical begun on 2 January 1720 and in whose pages he wore
the mask of Sir John Edgar. The covert intention of the
'Theatre' was to protect 'the separate ministry' of the
playhouse's managerial group and to fend off through the
weight of popular support any further action by the Lord
Chamberlain. Certainly the periodical was widely read.(24)
Still that fact did not deter Newcastle from successfully
urging the revocation of Steele's Drury Lane license, his
authority as governor suspended, and his salary withheld.

Seemingly the dispute had peaked, but in actuality it
was exacerbated not merely by further manoeuvres of the
Lord Chamberlain but also by the presence of John Dennis,
still smarting over what he believed to be the Drury Lane's
delayed and badly scheduled production of his play 'The
Invader of his Country'. In four letters called 'The
Characters and Conduct of Sir John Edgar', he offered
typical *ad hominem* criticism of Steele and pointed with
alarm to the dangers implicit in the idea of a 'separate
ministry', which he saw as a reality productive of nothing
but a self-seeking, absolutist anarchy.(25)

Whenever Dennis wrote, someone responded. So in a
rather mindless pamphlet, an anonymous writer addressed
himself directly to the critic: 'For lookee, Mr. *Tremen-
dous*, I think it very ill done of any one to fall foul of
poor Maister *Edgar*, now he is under Misfortunes; but I

shall see him stand upon his own Legs again for all this,
and make out something of a Latin Motto, that I have heard
People talk of, that Ends with - *pondere virtus*.'(26) The
paper war was fully launched, with the supporters of
Dennis outnumbering those of Steele. A 'Sir Andrew Artlove' wrote in successive numbers of 'Applebee's Original
Weekly Journal' (13-27 February 1720) three letters entitled 'A Full Consideration and Confutation of Sir John
Edgar'. Even more vigorously anti-Steelean was a mock-
heroic prose pamphlet, 'The Battle of the Authors lately
Fought in Covent-Garden, Between Sir John Edgar, Generalissimo on one Side, and Horatius Truewit, on the other'.
But the most persevering of Steele's detractors was the
author of the 'Anti-Theatre' who twice-weekly masked himself as 'Sir John Falstaffe' to harass his 'Adversary ...
with such Weapons as Men of Learning commonly use against
one another'.

Steele swiped at his opponents off-handedly. He had
neither time for nor interest in them. Instead he concen-
trated his energies, writing the relentless issues of the
'Theatre' and composing a pamphlet in which was spelled
out 'The State of the Case between the Lord-Chamberlain of
His Majesty's Household, and the Governor of the Royal
Company of Comedians'. Published on 29 March, it provoked
an almost immediate response. By 7-9 April the state of
the case was 're-stated in Vindication of King George, and
the most Noble The Duke of Newcastle'. In this tract
Steele's argument is tossed aside as worthless, no more
tolerable than Steele himself.

> I never knew a man truly brave, make such *Thrasonic*
> boasts of his courage; nor a man truly virtuous, make
> such a noise with his honesty; nor a man truly reli-
> gious, crying up his sanctity at the corner of the
> streets, and on the tops of houses; for these are the
> refuges of the *Faux-braves*, Knaves, and Hypocrites.

Within a year - again in the spring - Steele was
returned to the governorship of the Theatre Royal in
Drury Lane. The way was now open for the production in
November 1722 of 'The Conscious Lovers' and a whole new
debate over the merits and demerits of the fine gentleman
as a comic hero, of the worth of sentimental over satiric
comedy. The play, which took so long in being born,
achieved instant success in its first run of eighteen
successive performances. Steele and his company had for
some time advertised its innovative qualities. What was
new about it was less its use of pathos and decorous language than its creation of a hero who, functioning as a

model of propriety, also amused and charmed a sophisticated audience. Bevil Jr. was, in short, the moral anti-
thesis of the gallant who moved through the comedies of
Etherege, Wycherley, and Congreve.

The debate over 'The Conscious Lovers' engaged both
Steele and Dennis. It was actually initiated by Steele,
who had often insisted that the plays of Etherege tended
'to corrupt Chastity of Manners, and introduce a wrong
Taste'.(27) Without waiting to read or see Steele's
drama, Dennis brought out 'A Defence of Sir Fopling
Flutter' (2 November 1722; see No. 24). In that pamphlet
he reasoned in terms of comic theory, arguing for the
ridiculous as the quintessence of comedy and the employment of characters whose absurdities served as admonitions to viewers.

Nor did the play fare well in newspaper reviews. The
'St James's Journal' tried for neutrality but Mist's
'Weekly Journal' and the 'Freeholder's Journal' were
denunciatory. Steele's followers had read and heard
enough; they now rose to defend the author and his play.
On 29 November Victor published 'An Epistle to Sir Richard
Steele, On his Play, call'd The Conscious Lovers' (No. 26),
in which he was less concerned with dramatic theory than
with the annihilation of Dennis and his 'malapert Way of
Detraction'. More direct than Victor about the issues
was the anonymous author of 'Sir Richard Steele, and his
New Comedy call'd The Conscious Lovers'. Championing the
propriety of 'Virtuous Characters' and pathos in comedy,
he nevertheless left himself a small way out, a tiny
cavil useful for escape. If 'The Conscious Lovers' 'be
not in the strictest Sense throughout a Comedy, it is an
Entertainment superior to it'.

Angered as much by the success of the play as by its
proponents, Dennis struck again on 24 January 1723.
Whereas 'A Defence of Sir Fopling Flutter' damned the concept of the conduct-book hero, the 'Remarks on a Play,
Call'd, The Conscious Lovers' (No. 28) denied that pathos
is compatible with the comic spirit. His conclusion is
devastatingly direct: Steele's play, whatever mutation it
might be, was no comedy. Limping after what Dennis considered to be the last word on the subject was the longest
of the pamphlets written against the play. 'The Censor
Censured' is an 88-page dialogue between Sir Dicky Marplot
and Jack Freeman. It contributed no substance to the
quarrel, but its very length attested to the sustained
critical interest in Steele's final play.

Indeed, the comedy continued to attract such attention
for a good part of the eighteenth century. Victor wrote
once more on the contretemps, denigrating in 1761 the

long-forgotten position of Steele's antagonist. 'The
learned Mr. *Dennis*, the celebrated Critic of his time, was
then in the Decline of Life; and as his Subsistence could
only arise from his Attacks on Merit, the Author of ['The
Conscious Lovers'] could not escape him.'(28) In the next
year the 'Gentleman's Magazine' printed 'A Letter to Sir
Richard Steele, on his Play of the Conscious Lovers:
Written at the time of Exhibition but never before published'. Thereafter the play fell more or less into a
critical limbo. It had established a mode now beyond
theatrical dispute and ironically it had been surpassed by
several of its imitators. In the twentieth century all of
Steele's comedies have aroused academic interest: Shirley
Strum Kenny, for example, has expertly edited them (1971),
and John Loftis has published a sensitive description of
'Steele at Drury Lane' (1952).

III

If the 'Tatler' was suspected of being a party paper even
before its distribution, the suspicion became fact shortly
after 12 April 1709. Indeed, there was little that Steele
could do to prevent the translation, for the Godolphin
ministry, with its Junto affiliation, confronted awesome
difficulties. And, good Whig that he was, he used his
periodical almost immediately to support the coalition
government. In the fourth number, for example, he sketched the parable of Felicia, an island in America equat-
able with Britain under its current leadership, astute
and virtuous. Nor was this all. Before its second week
ended, the journal set forth King William as its own myth
figure and Marlborough as its talismanic hero. The word
Whig was never mentioned but it hovered over the 'Tatler'
as an aura surprisingly perceptible to every Englishman.
    The Tories tracked the adventures of Isaac Bickerstaff.
No one questioned his commitment to party. But how and
when it would be expressed remained anyone's guess. For
almost a year and a half anti-ministerial propagandists
were prepared to pounce, but they were for the most part
caught either unaware or with very little room in which
to manoeuvre. They could not foresee in 1709 the trans-
parent and variable fictions through which Steele set
forth but never labelled his political values. They
could not second-guess the topics on which he chose to be
expansive or terse. What was the rationale, they won-
dered, by which he thought it journalistically wise to
spend four essays on a five-months-old controversy between the high-flying Offspring Blackall, Bishop of

Exeter, and the Whig clergyman Benjamin Hoadly. And they
must have bitten their pens in frustration when they real-
ized that Bickerstaff in a gesture of forbearance smiled
away the Sacheverell incident, the most volatile in the
first decade of the century, as a prank designed to amuse
bored ladies who, during the trial, devoured 'many cold
Chickens ... for the Good of the Country.'(29)

Prior to the fall of the Godolphin ministry, the shots
fired at the 'Tatler' were random. As we have seen, Mrs
Manley objected to what she regarded as its flaccid satire, 'The Character of the Tatler' to 'Seignior *Chalybo*;
Captain *S---l*, that mighty Wit, who surpasses all Mens
Understanding, and knows Nobody, even not himself'. Such
criticism could frighten only its authors, not Steele.
When the ministry changed, however, Isaac Bickerstaff was
stalked with furious vigour. The 'Examiner' in its fifth
number moved against the 'Tatler', concentrating on its
news coverage generally and its report of the battle of
Balguer for specific annihilation. With the innuendo,
'We had lately News of a great Action in *Spain*, where for
Years the War has been carry'd on very calmly', the Tory
persona accused the journal of fabricating current events
or overplaying their importance to conceal the undeniable
reality of a vanquished ministry. The 'Examiner' for
24-31 August was not yet finished with its Whig rival.
Putting aside insinuation for mock-aesthetic seriousness,
the Tory paper set up parallel columns in which statements
describing the Spanish battle were drawn from the 'Tatler'
and the 'Gazette'. The columnar structure had a dual purpose: to suggest first that Bickerstaff and the Gazetteer
shared privileged information for their unique profit; and
secondly, to prove that there was no creative difference
between the periodical and the newspaper. Nor could there
be since they were aborted from a single malodorous identity and shared a nonsensical pomposity. Thus, said the
'Examiner's' persona, they 'move together in an amicable
Way, Hand in Hand, and like the *Two Kings in the Rehearsal*, smell to the same *Nosegay*' (see No. 32).

As long as the 'Tatler' continued to be printed, it
was an object of attack and some slight praise. The
'Examiner' pursued a hit-and-run course, and it attracted
a host of lesser 'executioners'. Among the many accusa-
tions which 'A Condoling Letter to the Tattler' (No. 33)
hurled at Bickerstaff in September 1710 was his arrogant
assumption of journalistic power, his 'Crime of Usurpation' in appropriating the role of censor for himself.
If the abuse in the summer and autumn of 1710 was politically motivated, so too was the applause. The Whiggish
Lord Cowper in 'A Letter to Isaac Bickerstaff' (No. 34)

stressed the 'Tatler's' wit (and implicitly its statesman-
ship) which were manifested 'not by Argument, but Example,
by numerous Sketches and some finish'd Pieces drawn with
irresistible Strength and Beauty'. Similarly, in 'A
Character of Don Sacheverellio' - somewhat belatedly - the
anonymous pamphleteer urged that the 'Tatler's' talent in
exposing social hypocrisy be extended to that of political
fraud disguised as religious principle.

Only after the periodical printed its last sheet on 2
January 1711 was there an attempt to divorce its Whiggism
from the literary genius which informed it. By May of
that same year John Gay, sensitive to the 'Tatler's' political alliances, wrote of the courage with which it 'ventured to tell the Town that they were a parcel of fops,
fools, and coquettes; but in such a manner as even pleased
them, and made them more than half inclined to believe
that [Bickerstaff] spoke truth'. (30) Two years later,
Henry Felton was prepared to recommend the 'Tatler' as a
pedagogical tool which orders the little things of 'common
Life with so much Judgment, in such agreeable, such lively
and elegant Language', that one learns not only manners
but an easy style in writing.(31)

Some time in the spring of 1729, when Steele was mortally ill, Joseph Mitchell compared Socrates' Athenian
disciples with Bickerstaff. The latter fortuitously 'by
the Help of Printing, was saved the Fatigue of travelling
abroad in bad Weather'. His facility in staying warm and
dry did not alter the truth that 'His Penny-papers some
time supplied the Place of the Ancient Cart, with great
Honour: People bought the best Instruction and Entertainment, on easy Terms'.(32) Despite such a tribute, too
fulsome to be credible, the 'Tatler's' reputation from
1711 onwards was eclipsed by that of the 'Spectator',
which - like the earlier journal - was thought to be
largely the handiwork of Steele. Not that Addison's
association with the Spectatorial venture was kept secret.
John Gay was sufficiently aware of it to hope that the
'known Temper and prudence' of the one would prevent 'the
other from ever lashing out into Party, and rendering that
Wit, which is at present a common good, odious and
ungrateful to the better half of the Nation'.(33)

What was unknown, of course, was the extent of Addison's involvement. Steele announced it finally in 'Spectator' 555 but his credibility was challengeable. Only
with Tickell's edition of 'The Works' in 1721 did the
identity of the Addisonian essays become fixed. Not
unexpectedly, Steele had often been made the scapegoat for
pieces written by his collaborator. And this applied to
essays as much apolitical as political. So it was that

William Wagstaffe, a serious doctor and a Tory droll,
parodied the 'Spectator's' ballad criticism. Almost at
the end of his guffaws, he addressed the last of his jeers
in Latin verse not to Addison but to Steele, who liked to
pose as the gentleman from Llangunnor.

> Tu, Taffi, aeternum vives, tua munera Cambri
> Nunc etiam celebrant, quotiesq; revolvitur Annus
> Te memorant, Patrium Gens tota tuetur Honorem,
> Et cingunt viridi redolentia tempora Porro.(34)

The greatness of the 'Spectator' was first predicted
by Gay, who was himself awed by its early numbers, by the
journal's fusion of irrepressible spontaneity and real
wisdom. 'We had,' he wrote in 'The Present State of Wit',
'no manner of notion how a diurnal paper could be continued in the spirit and style of our present 'Spectators':
but, to our no small surprise, we find them still rising
upon us, and can only wonder from whence so prodigious a
run of Wit and Learning can proceed.' The time was not
yet right for such prophecy. More familiar rather were
the observations of Tory pamphlets like 'A Spy upon the
Spectator' (No. 37) and 'The Spectator Inspected', both
scribbled and printed in 1711. The latter pamphlet, particularly, out-examined the 'Examiner' in the vitriol it
spewed against the journal.

> What is more odious in England than the Name or Memory
> of an Usurper or Tyrant? What can be a greater Usur-
> pation, upon the Magistracy and Government of the chief
> City of the best constituted Nation in the Universe,
> than for a fantastical, splenetick discontented
> Wretch to assume to himself the Authority of a Censor,
> to expose every thing that disagrees with the humour
> which happens to be uppermost, while he is writing for
> his daily bread? What can be a greater Tyranny upon
> the Subject, than to have a constant Spy upon their
> actions, to publish, in a false light, family conversa-
> tions, harmless mirth, and other trivial incidents,
> which would never be thought faults, if they were not
> by his Talent improv'd into such; and that sometimes
> to such a degree as to be made occasions of withdraw-
> ing Parents affections from their Children, and Child-
> rens obedience from their Parents? What can be more
> supine and indolent in any Government, than to suffer
> an itinerant scrap to be cry'd every day, about the
> streets, for the propagation of Loosness and Libertin-
> ism?

Such a flailing assault, hysterical in its charges of the
'Spectator's' immorality, urged the government to take the
last necessary step and suppress the paper by official
action.
    The government fortunately restrained itself, and the
first series ended with number 555 on 6 December 1712.
The Tories hoped, in fact, that the periodical would be
forgotten as soon as any out-dated paper. Their hopes,
however, were futile. The 'Spectator' was revived, its
second series beginning in June 1714. Almost immediately
thereafter 'A Letter from Will Honeycomb' advised the
'Examiner' to be watchful of its natural enemy, to use
'the Rod for the Fool's Back' when the Fool 'dares again
to affront his Superiors'.(35) Even after 20 December
1714, when the 'Spectator' was no more, a Tory pamphleteer assumed the right to the last word. In 'A Letter to
the late Author of the Spectator' he equated the paper and
faction, sarcastically announcing his pleasure 'to see
these TWO Gentlemen well rewarded, and all others that
have been honest in the WORK of Times'.
    By 1716 Blackmore's 'Essay upon Wit' (No. 40) favour-
ably judged the 'Tatler' and 'Spectator' on literary merit
alone and set the tone for what was to come. Some disaffected notes were sounded, but they made their little
squeak and were heard no more.(36) During the last forty
years of the eighteenth century and on through most of the
nineteenth the 'Spectator' had a near-unassailable aesthetic worth and a certain utility as well. Its essays
were made to function as a series of lectures on rhetoric
and conduct, with Addison the moralist and prose stylist
to be emulated. If Steele stood full centre on the Spectatorial stage between 1711 and 1714, he soon thereafter
yielded his place to the 'Gentleman' responding to the
'Muse CLIO'.(37) But no matter who received star billing,
the 'Spectator' was a work not merely to be read but to
be carried about ostentatiously. And why? asked Jane
Austen with mock rhetorical indignation: 'the substance
of its papers so often consisting in the statement of
improbable circumstances, unnatural characters, and
topics of conversation, which no longer concern anyone
living; and their language, too, frequently so coarse as
to give no very favourable idea of the age that could
endure it.'(38)

IV

Addison spent most of a relatively short life yearning
for praise and avoiding controversy. In 1713 he received

the accolades he needed but paid dearly for them during
the storm blown up by the production of 'Cato'. The history of his dramatic contributions is quintessentially the
history of that one play. Whatever else may be said about
it, the tragedy was the most successful and talked-about
theatre event of Queen Anne's reign. The explanation for
its renown lies less in its intrinsic value than in what
its many viewers saw as political meaning.

But its meaning remains as clouded today as in 1713.
Certainly when it was first conceived, it was apolitical.
Addison had completed a rough draft of the four acts
before he left Magdalen in 1699. Working on these off and
on during his grand tour, he was able to show them to
Colley Cibber and Steele by 1703 or the year after. Both
men encouraged him to finish the drama but this took even
longer than its inception and intermittent polishing.
The dramatic project was never a secret so that sometime
between 1704 and 1713 a 'Mr Webster of Christ Church,
Oxon' versified a college plea:

> And thou, O Addison, no more detain
> The free-born Cato, struggling in his chain;
> 'Tis liberty he loves; disclose thy vast design,
> And let us see that every Muse is thine.(39)

Only in the spring of 1713, undoubtedly upon the prodding
of some Whigs who anticipated the fall of the Harley-St
John ministry, did Addison write a last act for 'Cato'
with remarkable speed. Steele, relying on his memory,
noted that 'the fifth Act was written in less than a
Week's time'.(40)

The debate over 'Cato' concerns authorial purpose,
whether or not it was intended to be a party play. For
more than two centuries some have argued against its
political impetus. On the other hand, there are those
who use Lady Mary Wortley Montagu's critique of the play
before production to argue that several of the lines on
liberty were deliberately superimposed on the dialogue
and given a Whiggish colouration.(41) What cannot be
denied is that Addison rarely did anything without first
taking his sights on practical considerations. If he
added lines extolling the necessity of political freedom,
he had in mind his party's consistent attacks on Tory
'tyranny'. If 'the love part was flung in after' the
play was first conceived, it was 'to comply with the
popular taste'.(42)

However much Addison yielded to expedience in the
final presentation of 'Cato', he also wrote a drama which
was a paean to political liberty and hardly served the

needs of one faction over another. He himself wished to
squash the idea of its partisanship. He therefore
approached Pope, whose friends at that time cut across
party lines; he desired, wrote Pope, 'to have my sincere
opinion of it, and left it with me for three or four days.
I gave him my opinion sincerely, which was that "I thought
he had better not act it, and that he would get reputation
enough only by printing it." This I said as thinking the
lines well writ, but the piece not theatrical enough.'
So matters stood for a short time while people like Lady
Mary Wortley Montagu pushed for production and Steele
promised to pack the theatre with a congenial first-night
audience. Addison apparently responded to their pressure
but almost immediately upon completing 'Cato', he returned
to Pope and asked him 'to show it to Lord Bolingbroke and
Lord Oxford, and to assure them that he never in the least
designed it as a party-play'.(43)

Addison, in short, contrived it both ways, satisfying
Whigs and Tories alike. Steele's friends applauded every
line in which the word 'liberty' was mentioned. At the
same time several of the Queen's ministers were ostentatiously present at the first performance on 14 April. The
incident, an exercise in factional manoeuvring, was described to John Caryll by Pope. 'I believe,' he wrote,
'you have heard that after all the applauses of the opposite faction, my Lord Bullingbrooke sent for Booth who
played Cato, into the box, between one of the acts and
presented him with 50 guineas; in acknowledgment (as he
expressed it) for his defending the cause of liberty so
well against a *perpetuall dictator*: the Whigs are unwilling to be distanced this way, as 'tis said, and therefore design a present to the said Cato very speedily.'
Addison carried it off. He pleased the Whigs and gave no
offense to the Tories. But he never achieved what Cibber
later claimed for the play, specifically its capacity to
turn two factions into a patriotic whole.(44)

The political ambiguity of the play startled and
attracted theatrical audiences; it also provoked a paper
war as pamphleteers strove to fix its meaning, according
to party allegiance. In its issue of 27 April-1 May 1713
the 'Examiner', never naive about Addisonian loyalty,
muted its real suspicions and instead loudly applauded
'the Excellent Author of CATO, who has convinc'd us, in
so happy a Manner, that the Affections may be moved, and
the Passions actuated, by a Distress arising from a Principle of Honour as well as Love' (No. 45). This piece in
its turn provoked the 'Flying Post' (30 April-2 May) to
derogate the bland magnanimity of the 'Examiner' and to
insist that 'Cato' was a political allegory whose lessons

were sanctioned by every true-blue Whiggish Englishman
(No. 46).

Although the party lines were drawn, they soon became
blurred by a succession of pamphleteers anxious to discuss
the tragedy as a tragedy. George Sewell, oddly enough a
member of the Tory stable of hacks, at some time prior to
June 1713 presented a plodding series of 'Observations
upon Cato' (No. 48). His eulogy was followed by one perhaps even more eulogistic, Charles Gildon's 'Cato
Examin'd' (No. 47). Neither pamphlet is important in
itself but together they prompted Dennis, prodded a bit
further by the bookseller Lintot, to finish his splenetic
but insightful 'Remarks upon Cato' (No. 49) by 19 June.
He saw them printed before mid-July. He thought the tragedy a composite of 'Faults and Absurdities', its seeming
profundity only the product of Artifices'. That it had
become a *succès d'estime* infuriated him. Rage, however,
did not cloud his vision and so exactly did he detail
'Cato's' inadequacies that Johnson could write some
sixty-eight years later: Dennis 'found and shewed many
faults: he shewed them indeed with anger, but he found
them with acuteness, such as ought to rescue his criticism
from oblivion.'(45)

But in 1713 there were those who would make the 'sower
undistinguishing' critic a scapegoat, his carcass thrown
to scavengers. In 'The Narrative of Dr. Robert Norris,
concerning the Strange and Deplorable Frenzy of Mr. John
Denn--', a rudimentary fiction presented a staring,
raving critic, sputtering 'between his Teeth the Word
'Cator', or 'Cato', or some such thing'. As disorderly as
the man himself was his room, on whose walls were 'pinned
a great many Sheets of a Tragedy called 'Cato', with notes
on the Margin with his own Hand. The Words *Absurd, Monstrous, Execrable,* were everywhere written in such large
Characters' that they were visible to the attending physician without his spectacles. As the raucous narrative
concluded, the lunatic critic is left a lonely figure,
abandoned by all with sense and even by his money-grubbing
genius Bernard Lintot.

Surrounding the criticism of 'Cato' were the factional
responses to the play. They divided upon the identification of the dramatis personae and their living equival-
ents. To the Whigs Marlborough and Cato were one in that
they embodied the concepts of liberty, courage, and fortitude in adversity. Indeed, Addison's political colleagues
made even more specific equations: Juba represented the
Emperor of Germany, Syphax Prince Eugene; the villainous
Lucius and Sempronius personified Oxford and Bolingbroke.
The Tories, on the other hand, were content to prove only

that there was a resemblance between the tyrannical Caesar
and the grasping Marlborough, who manoeuvred in vain to
become Captain General for life. Typical of these interpretations were the Whiggish 'Key or Explanation to the
History, and Play of Cato' and the Tory 'Comparison Between Cato and Caesar'. Cleverest of all was the sardonic
'Mr. Addison turn'd Tory: Or, The Scene Inverted: Wherein It is made [to] appear that the Whigs have misunder-
stood that Celebrated Author in his applauded Tragedy,
Call'd Cato, And that the Duke of M——'s Character, in
endeavouring to be a General for Life, bears a much
greater Resemblance to that of Caesar and Syphax, than
the Heroe of his Play.'

Certainly the paper war did not hinder the theatrical
success of 'Cato'. After its initial run that began on
14 April 1713 at the Drury Lane, it was brought to Oxford
University, where both the dramatist and the tragedy were
audibly revered by a student group with literary and political aspirations. In its first season (1712-13) the
tragedy was presented in London some twenty times. In the
next two seasons it was staged less frequently but frequently enough and always before large audiences.(46) The
1715-16 season saw six performances; but a new argument
exploded when 'Cato' vied first with the printed version
of Deschamps's 'Caton d'Utique' and in late spring with
John Ozell's translation acted on a London stage. The
controversy between the two 'Catos' was hinted even prior
to the theatrical competition. The French play had been
printed in Paris early in 1715; almost immediately it
circulated in London and was read in the fashionable end
of town. Having been given a copy, the persona of the
'Grumbler' (No. 50), thus, found that he had not reached
the conclusion of the third act 'when his Patience began
to fall, and his Expectations sank to nothing'. He did
not wish so much to deprecate the French effort as he
wanted to exalt the English: the former is 'as much beneath Criticism, as the English 'Cato' is above it.' Upon
publication of Ozell's translation and its opening at the
Lincoln's Inn Fields Theatre on 14 May 1716, the argument
over the merits of the two plays was carried forward by an
indefatigable George Sewell, who in his 'Vindication'
answered the censorious author of 'A Parallel betwixt
[Ozell's "Cato of Utica"] and the Tragedy of Cato written
by Mr. Addison'. The debate was won easily by Sewell, if
only because he had the advantage of defending the better
play.(47)

After 1713 'Cato' became a repertory piece, its popularity during the first half of the century remarkable.
It was performed every season until that of 1750; the

1730s in particular witnessed a stunning proliferation of
revivals. The applause continued but so also did the mut-
tering. In the 'Criticks' (24 March 1718) the tragedy was
regarded as inferior to 'The Campaign', Addison's 'most
notable Production'. Ironically the doubts which were
provoked about 'Cato' in 1718 and 1719 originated in
moralistic anxiety. Ambrose Philips, writing in the
'Free-Thinker' on 11 April 1718, demanded that a dramatic
and epic fable should effect national improvement. With
this single criterion fixed in his mind, he had necessarily to condemn Addison's tragedy. 'I leave every judicious
and candid Spectator to determine, whether the setting
Self-Murther in that dazzling Light, it appears in upon
the Stage, in the Person of *Cato*, does not tend ... to
abate our Horrour for it.' According to Philips, 'Cato'
sapped English pluck and undermined a code of morality
responsible for his country's glory.

A still stranger piece is one which appeared in 'The
Occasional Paper' for 1719. Here Addison's tragedy is
placed within a widening attack upon the stage as a force
'calculated and design'd to fill the Mind with false
Notions of Honour, and wrong Sentiments of Things; to
corrupt the Imagination, to fire the Passions of unexperi-
enc'd Youth, to wear out Impressions of Virtue, and to
dispose, by Degrees, to every Evil.' Whoever was responsible for this statement found 'Cato' morally sound. And
yet that quality was its source of danger:

> Being produc'd but very rarely, it only serves to do
> Mischief; by drawing in the better and soberer Part of
> the Town, to those Diversions, which, in the common
> Course of them, are the most pernicious things in the
> World. And for my own Part I can't help wishing, that
> either all Dramatick Entertainments were like 'Cato',
> and those of that sort; or else that there were none
> such: for then I hope in a little Time there would be
> none at all: Every thing of this kind, when ill
> applied, makes those publick Representations greater
> Instruments of Mischief.(48)

It is a relief to turn from the spectre of Jeremy
Collier and the eccentricity of such criticism to Voltaire
on 'Cato'. He viewed it historically, recognizing wherein
it excelled or failed and why. 'The first *English*
Writer,' he declared, 'who compos'd a regular Tragedy, and
infus'd a spirit of elegance thro' every part of it, was
the illustrious Mr. *Addison*.' Not blindly adulatory,
Voltaire accounted for the offensive love scenes as the
author's desire to satisfy dramatic convention and the

voracious amatory interests of those ladies who frequented
the theatres; 'and from an endeavour to please quite
ruin'd a master-piece of its kind'.(49)
    'Cato' remained persuasive throughout the century, whether
it was seen in a theatre or read in a closet. There were
some twenty-six English editions in that period and the
Continent was not far behind its island neighbour. The
Italians issued four translations, the Germans two, the Dutch
three, the Poles one, the French five. In 1764 an English-
Latin version appeared, with the love scenes omitted. For
some people it continued the call to freedom during political crisis. During the troubled summer of Forty-Five,
Horace Walpole confessed to George Montagu on 1 August
that he was 'laying in scraps of 'Cato', against it may
be necessary to take leave of one's correspondents à *la
Romaine*, and before the play itself is suppressed by a
lettre de cachet to the booksellers.' Almost two generations earlier 'Cato' began its long history of reassuring
large audiences. From 1713 until 1797 it was staged 234
times. But by the time of the Regency it had become what
Pope said it always was: a closet drama. And not even
the Victorian adoration of its author could make it anything else. Surprising, however, was the courage of
William Steere who, perhaps remembering the burlesques of
'Cato' by Gay and Fielding, published in 1860 'Billing's
Gate: A Tragedy', a daring parody of Addison's drama
whose moral loftiness sometimes overreached its own blank
verse.(50)

V

In his own lifetime Addison very nearly escaped the mockery and attack that provided an ambience for Steele's
ambition. Early in his career - in 1705 when he was more
or less a political novice visibly dependent on patronage
- his 'Remarks on Italy' was mocked in a 'Table of all the
accurate Remarks and surprising Discoveries of the most
learned and ingenious Mr. Addison in his Book of Travels'.
The pamphlet coldly tabulated the many platitudinous or
infelicitous statements presented in the Addisonian work,
so that the 'Remarks on Italy' appeared to be a swollen
mass of clichés ineptly and hypocritically concealed by
pretentious prose. But the jeers were unheard by Addison,
who in that same year heard only the extravagant praise
of 'The Campaign' and its promise of lucrative employment.
    Certainly the poem was motivated in part by political
expedience; in fact necessity would be a more precise
term. But Defoe exaggerated the case when in 'The Double

Welcome' he crudely intimated the impetus for Addison's
Virgilian song: 'Maecenas has his modern Fancy strung,/
And fix'd his pension, first, or he had never sung.' The
hyperbole of Defoe's accusation was matched or perhaps
surpassed by the encomia of William Harrison, Le Clerc,
Blackmore, and later by Cobden, all of whom noted the
poet's 'epic' strength.

> When You display undaunted *Churchill*'s Soul
> Teaching the furious Tempest where to roll;
> Dealing destruction round the dreadful Plain,
> Unmov'd - except with Pity for the Slain;
> On whose commands Defeat and Death depends,
> Whose every Standard Victory attends.(51)

In his own day, Addison was celebrated as the 'great Bard,
of sweetest strains,/Who sung the Hero on the deathless
plains'.(52)

Just about everything he wrote between 1705 and 1719
seemed to be touched with literary glory. If any of it
offended his contemporaries or chastised too loudly some
of 'the wittiest men of the age', it was Steele who bore
the brunt of the complaint, who was 'traduced and calum-
niated'.(53) Addison himself seemed to stand above critical reproach. Even his failures either had their vocal
admirers or were quickly re-evaluated. On 14 September
1710, for example, he surrendered to the urging of Arthur
Maynwaring, who 'could not suffer [the 'Examiner's'] insolence to pass, without animadversion'. Addison undertook,
somewhat reluctantly, to issue the 'Whig-Examiner' as a
rebuttal to the Tory periodical. From the start he candidly asserted that his paper was both defensive and
righteous, designed 'to give all persons a rehearing, who
have suffered under any unjust sentence of the "Examiner".
As that author has hitherto proceeded, his paper would
have been more properly entitled the "Executioner". At
least, his examination is like that which is made by the
rack and wheel.'(54)

But for all its vigorous intention, the journal could
not endure: it lacked the excitement of new ideas; it had
the defeatist tone of a doomed cause. The Whig command,
desperate in its journalistic need, capitulated to the
fact that the most poised and elegant writer in its stable
wanted the editorial belligerence necessary for party
journalism in a crisis year. He was therefore relieved of
his assignment, one that both Maynwaring and Oldmixon took
up when they published the 'Medley' from 5 October 1710 to
6 August 1711. The 'Whig-Examiner', unable to make head-
way in its argument with the opposition, died after only

five numbers. Still Gay, remarkably fair-minded in his
judgment of partisan writing, could assert that the 'Whig-
Examiner' was done 'with so much fire, and in so excellent
a style, as put the Tories in no small pain for their favourite hero'.(55) The endorsement undoubtedly pleased
Addison, but as a political realist he knew his journal
was beyond salvage in a paper war that demanded blatant
irony and invective, scurrilous heat and fibre.

Another qualified failure was 'The Drummer', whose
initial run of only three nights in March 1716 was an
unexpected disappointment. Steele confessed that despite
his own partiality it 'made no great Figure on the Stage,
tho exquisitely well acted'. And when he brought out a
second edition of the comedy in 1722, he went no further
than to recommend it 'as a Closet-piece, to recreate an
intelligent Mind in a vacant Hour'.(56) Steele, however,
was deceptively circumspect. He knew that the comedy had
been revived in February 1722 for seven successful nights.
The author of the 'Freeholder's Journal', a first-nighter
at the Lincoln's Inn Fields Theatre, isolated the source
of the play's sudden glory. The taste for sentimental
drama having been carefully nurtured in theory and performance, 'The Drummer' was applauded by a newly educated
audience as 'so chast a play ... without any prophane Wit,
or ambiguous Obscenity'.(57) As the century advanced, the
moral emphasis of the theatre advanced with it. Consequently, the 'piece', which began so dismally, was acted
about ninety-five times between 1729 and 1790.

Addison himself had few doubts about his literary immortality. He therefore 'bequeathed' his writings to
James Craggs the younger but allowed the onerous task of
editing to fall upon Thomas Tickell. 'I have,' wrote
Addison to Craggs, 'left the care of them to one, whom,
by the experience of some years, I know well qualified to
answer my intentions.'(58) These arrangements planned
and executed, Addison devoted himself to choosing and
'collecting' his works for publication. He revised 'The
Campaign' and several of the 'Spectator' essays. His own
effort was scrupulous, his editor devoted to his mission.
By 1721 Tickell brought out a handsomely printed four-
volume edition of his patron's poetry and prose. Two
years later Addison was given four pages in 'The Poetical
Register', which acknowledged that in his 'Writings ...
there appears an uncommon Beauty; an Elegance of Style;
an Improvement of Diction; a Strength of Reason; an Excellency of Wit; and a Nobleness and Sublimity of Thought,
equall'd by few, if any of our Modern Poets.'

Virtually every public event that moulded the last
decade of Addison's life was celebrated in print. An

occasional dissident voice was heard, Mrs Manley's a
little shriller than most. It is also probably true that
Pope circulated the Atticus lines before 1719.(59)
Although Addison must have admired the brilliant satire,
he could not help being hurt by the exposure of flaws
that, while exaggerated, he himself had either to admit or
bury beyond consciousness. Still the reactions of Mrs
Manley and Pope were the exception rather than the rule.
What his contemporaries saw and what too many modern critics gloss over is his political integrity. Swift, for
example, congratulated Addison on becoming Secretary of
State. His letter of 9 July 1717 avoided any suggestion
of mere studied civility.

> I examine my Heart, and can find no other Reason why I
> write to you now, beside that great Love and Esteem I
> have always had for you. I have nothing to ask you
> either for any Friend, or for my self. When I con-
> versed among Ministers I boasted of your Acquaintance,
> but I feel no Vanity from being known to a Secretary
> of State. I am only a little concerned to see you
> stand single, for it is a prodigious singularity in
> any Court to owe ones Rise entirely to Merit.(60)

As an adept politician, Addison made compromises, but
only where principle was not involved. He rejected the
possibility of ever being a 'renegado', as his friend
Steele became, most overtly in his 'Letter to the Earl of
O———d, concerning the Bill of Peerage'. And again unlike Steele, he preferred to give up 'an employment
rather than hold it under the Tories, which by a little
compliance he might have done'.(61) He abhorred the
thought of bribery and adamantly refused a 'token of
esteem' from the South Sea Company. He may have encouraged young poets to write of his accomplishments but on
the other hand they were avid for place and all very much
obligated to him for good will and offices. If he presided over a 'little senate', then the senators were
voluntarily prepared to abide by the rules of the
assembly.
   When Addison had no choice but to accept in 1714 his
appointment as secretary to Sunderland, Lord Lieutenant
of Ireland, Laurence Eusden transformed his patron's
disappointment through fulsome verse into a triumph.

> Boldly a tributary Verse I bring,
> Your Lawrels shade me, when to you I sing.(62)

In 1716 he married Charlotte, Countess of Warwick.

Customarily ignored by poets and statesmen, she now
received several congratulatory epistles. How she reacted
to them is difficult to tell since they complimented her
not for herself but for the mate she selected. Tickell
wrote one of these epithalamia and so did Leonard
Welsted (No. 57). The latter, particularly, paid no heed
to the new bride except as a vicarious source of praise
for her husband.

> Not *Edward*'s Star, emboss'd with Silver Rays,
> Can vie in Glory with thy Consort's Bays;
> His Country's Pride does Homage to thy Charms,
> And every Merit Crowds into thy Arms.(63)

The following year Addison became Secretary of State for
the Southern Department and Nicholas Amhurst, a tumultuous and Whiggish Oxonian, rose to the occasion. His poem
was an unabashed paean.

> From *Isis'* Laurel'd Banks, the Muse reveals
> A Joy which ev'ry honest *Briton* feels,
> Who sees his Country's and his KING's Commands
> Intrusted to your unpolluted Hands.

As the adulation became more and more 'nervous', Addison
became the saviour of his country and perhaps as significantly of his university, where 'No longer are the Muses
Learned Seats,/The Schools of Treason, and Seditious
Heats'.(64)
   His death in June produced a flutter of elegies in
prose and verse. Giles Jacob wrote 'Memoirs of the Life
of the Rt. Hon. Joseph Addison, Esq;'. Allan Ramsay composed 'Richy and Sandy' (No. 59), Cobden 'A Poem',
Amhurst 'Upon the Death of Mr. Addison'. All these were
printed in 1719 or 1720 but not before the 'Weekly Medley'
for 4 July began a long column of biographical fact with
the statement: 'Methinks I can never pay sufficient Veneration to the Ashes of Mr. Addison.' Edward Young addressed his pastoral elegy (1719) to Thomas Tickell as if the
protégé-editor had inherited the dead man's genius and
spirit.

>   ... bring
> And teach me thy departed friend to sing:
> A darling theme! once powerful to inspire,
> And now to melt, the Muses' mournful choir:
> Now, and now first, we freely dare commend
> His modest worth, nor shall our praise offend.

The contribution of Tickell himself (No. 60) was an
instance of belated grief. Not as delicate as Ramsay's
'Richy and Sandy' or as intellectually oriented as Cobden's pastoral, his elegy had the advantage of perspective. Written almost two years after the mourning was
finished, it tempered glorification with credibility,
grief with realism.

> Slow comes the verse, that real woe inspires:
> Grief unaffected suits but ill with art,
> Or flowing numbers with a bleeding heart.

The 'Elegy' was probably Tickell at his best for, to quote
Goldsmith, it 'is one of the finest in our language; there
is so little new that can be said upon the death of a
friend, after the complaints of Ovid and the Latin Italians in this way, that one is surprised to see so much
novelty in this to strike us, and so much interest to
affect.'(65)

The suspicion, even the hostility, directed against
Addison in the twentieth century infrequently surfaced in
either of the two preceding centuries. As we have seen,
for example, there was Mrs Manley's minuscule mutter.
Pope's Atticus lines were finally printed as part of the
'Epistle to Dr Arbuthnot' in 1735. Within a narrative
framework, Fielding gently scoffed at Addisonian self-
esteem. In Chapter 8 of 'A Journey from this World to
the Next' (1743), he had his fictional narrator enter into
Elysium, where he met Virgil, with Mr Addison clinging
tightly to the arm of the Latin poet. Virgil began the
conversation.

> 'Well, sir,' said he, 'how many translations have these
> few last years produced of my Aeneid?' I told him I
> believed several, but I could not possibly remember;
> for that I had never read any but Dr. Trapp's. 'Aye,'
> said he, 'that is a curious piece indeed!' I then
> acquainted him with the discovery made by Mr. Warburton
> of the Eleusinian mysteries couched in his sixth book.
> 'What mysteries?' said Mr. Addison. 'The Eleusinian,'
> answered Virgil, 'which I have disclosed in my sixth
> book.' - 'How!' replied Addison; 'you never mentioned
> a word of any such mysteries to me in all our acquain-
> tance.' - 'I thought it was unnecessary,' cried the
> other, 'to a man of your infinite learning: besides,
> you always told me you perfectly understood my mean-
> ing.' Upon this I thought the critic looked a little
> out of countenance, and turned aside to a very merry
> spirit, one Dick Steele, who embraced him, and told him

he had been the greatest man upon earth; that he
readily resigned up all the merit of his own works to
him. Upon which Addison gave him a gracious smile,
and, clapping him on the back with much solemnity,
cried out, 'Well said, Dick!'

Fielding's mildness would not do for Joseph Warton, whose
empathy with Pope permitted him to take on the poet's
enemies as his own. Addison therefore was labelled
villain, his malice extorting 'from POPE the famous
character of Atticus, which is perhaps the finest piece
of satire extant'.(66)
  The verbal sneers were meagre; only Pope's achieved
universality. On the other hand, the praise, loud and
consistent, reached a crescendo in Macaulay's essay (No.
70). Long before 1843, the applause was shared by the
prose stylist and the moralist who practised in life what
he urged in words. As early as 1716 his reputation as
an essayist was affirmed without question. In a letter
written presumably on 3 July of that year (although not
printed until 1748) William Melmoth singled out Addison
as one who captured that elusive quality of creative
grace: 'In a word, one may justly apply to him what Plato,
in his allegorical language, says of Aristophanes; that
the *Graces*, having searched all the world round for a
temple wherein they might for ever dwell, settled at last
in the breast of Mr. Addison.' Precisely forty years
later Warton was compelled to admit, indeed he did 'candidly own, that in various parts of his prose-essays, are
to be found many strokes of genuine and sublime poetry;
many marks of a vigorous and exuberant imagination.' Free
of Warton's personal animus, Vicesimus Knox (No. 66) also
pinpointed a split in Addisonian genius: 'Had not a
veneration for his name prevented critics from speaking
their real sentiments, though Addison would, as a moral
essayist, most justly have been called the Socrates, Plato,
or Xenophon of his age; yet he would never have been
esteemed the first of poets'.(67)
  Within the last forty years of the eighteenth century
and on into the next, people like Hugh Blair, Thomas
Wallace, and David Irving promoted Addison as a prose
writer whose style was worthy of imitation. Thus the
'Spectator', for example, became a pedagogical tool, a
classic that needed to be studied in grammar schools and
university study halls. In a series of lectures first
offered in 1760, Blair assured his pupils at the University of Edinburgh that Addison had perfected an English
prose, in which 'minute imperfections' very much like
'spots in the sun', would assist beginners to avoid

comparable mistakes. Again and again as he analysed
'Spectators' 411 to 414 he stressed the journal's lasting
appeal. It is, he promised his audience, 'a book which is
in the hands of every one, and which cannot be praised too
highly. The good sense, and good writing, the useful
morality, and the admirable vein of humour which abound
in it, render it one of those standard books which have
done the greatest honour to the English nation.'(68)
Blair, in short, established the tradition of seriously
examining the structural components, the language and the
imagery that constituted the elegance and deceptive ease
of Addisonian art.

Adding nothing substantive to what Blair had already
said and written, Wallace in 1796 did provide a historical
perspective. He argued that the essayist began a prose
revolution, created the first alteration in English style
since 1688, and achieved freedom from the techniques of
the schoolmen: 'the forced metaphor, the dragging clause,
the harsh cadence, and the abrupt close'. Although he
underestimated Addison's erudition and finesse in handling
the niceties of metaphysical distinction, Wallace recognized his sense of an audience that gave coherence to the
sheets of the 'Spectator'. There was, he pointed out, a
perfect reconciliation between subject and style on the
one hand and a reader's needs and capabilities on the
other.(69) Just about everyone in the eighteenth and
nineteenth centuries who analysed Addison's prose style
recognized its achievement of 'classical purity'. Nathan
Drake agreed. He went one step further to maintain that
by virtue of its unique yet 'elegant simplicity', it could
be neither copied nor taught to others. Posterity therefore had to be content with admiration alone.(70)

If certain critics were enthusiastic about his creative
talent, others marvelled not only at the wholesomeness of
his literary lessons but of a life that seemingly kept
pace with them. By 1759, through personal recollection,
Addison took on heroic proportions: the mortal man was
idealized and the dying Christian adulated. In Edward
Young's opinion,

> His compositions are but a noble preface; the grand
> work is his death: That is a work which is read in
> heaven: How has it join'd the final approbation of
> angels to the previous applause of men? How glori-
> ously has he opened a splendid path, thro' fame immor-
> tal, into eternal peace? How has he given religion to
> triumph amidst the ruins of his nature? And, stronger
> than death, risen higher in virtue when breathing his
> last.

So exuberantly pietistic was Young's appreciation of the
way in which Addison died that even Richardson, never nig-
gardly in his praise of Christian virtue, suggested caution. Responding to a manuscript version of the 'Conjectures', he wrote to Young on 18 December 1758:

> Let me ask, however great and noble what you say of Mr.
> Addison's death is, whether it may not bear shortening?
> Will it not be thought laboured? And when, from the
> different nature of diseases, some of them utterly
> incapacitating, and deliriums happening often, it is
> not, or may not be, discouraging to surviving friends,
> to find wanting in the dying those tokens of resigna-
> tion and true Christian piety, which Mr. Addison was
> graciously enabled to express so exemplarily to Lord W.
> (71)

For Richardson the issue was simple: no matter how intense
the religious exercise, it required the restraint of probability.
   Twenty-two years after publication of the 'Conjectures',
Johnson, no less pious than Young, looked judiciously at
the Addisonian record in order to re-assess the literary
performance and the personality responsible for it (No.
67). The 'Life', printed in 1781, stood forth as the
first objective portrait of the man and artist who was
more to be praised than blamed. And its judgment cannot
be significantly challenged after almost two centuries.
There was as always something old in the 'Life' and something new, but its tone - measured and surprisingly apolitical, critical and historically sensitive - gives it a
modern relevance. The 'Life' of Addison, unlike some of
the other Johnsonian biographies, will never become dated,
if only because the essayist has not gone the forgotten
way of John Pomfret, for example, or into the oblivion of
George Stepney, John Philips, and William Walsh, among
others.
   Along with many who preceded him, Johnson found Addison's poetry pleasant but thoroughly lacking in passion
and imagination. There was consequently 'in most of his
compositions a calmness and equability, deliberate and
cautious, sometimes with little that delights, but seldom
with any thing that offends'. 'Cato' he dismissed by way
of a long and hostile excerpt from Dennis's 'Remarks' on
the play. However indirectly harsh his judgment of the
dramatist, Johnson was in advance of his time when he gave
high marks to the aesthetician-critic, understanding the
delicacy required to adjust the profundity to the needs
of a popular audience. 'His purpose was to infuse

literary curiosity by gentle and unsuspected conveyance
into the gay, the idle, and the wealthy; he therefore presented knowledge in the most alluring form, not lofty and
austere, but accessible and familiar.' What refreshes
about Johnson's evaluation is less its appreciation of
Addison as a 'model of the middle style', but, more importantly, its rational respect for the man. Thus 'though his
station made him conspicuous, and his ability made him
formidable, the character given him by his friends was
never contradicted by his enemies: of those with whom
interest or opinion united him, he had not only the esteem
but the kindness; and of others, whom the violence of
opposition drove against him, though he might lose the
love, he retained the reverence.'
    Johnson's moderation did not take hold. For the most
part adulation abounded. Thomas Tyers in 1783 wrote 'An
Historical Essay on Mr. Addison' which was admittedly a
'rhapsody' and a panegyric 'of the Addisonian School'.
Even as he admired, he confessed his frustration - all too
conscious of the distance between himself and his subject.

> If Mr. Addison, the intended hero of this essay, had
> been the Plutarch of his own life (for Plutarch enters
> into a thousand interesting particulars and brings his
> hero into the closet) it must have made an entertaining
> volume; though the modesty and diffidence that accom-
> panied him thro' every scene of life, would have pre-
> vented him from enlarging on a multitude of things to
> his own glory and the disadvantage of others. For on
> many occasions he chose rather to hide himself than be
> seen, and to practice reserve than to open his lips
> (pp. 3-4).

Unperturbed by the biographical elusiveness of the man,
Nathan Drake in 1805 moved toward the apotheosis of
Addison. He presented him as the journalist whose talent
was a single-edged weapon to drive home religious, moral,
and social virtue. That he could actually 'effect so
much improvement, and ... acquire a kind or moral dominion
over his countrymen, must be ascribed, in a great measure,
to that suavity of disposition and goodness of heart so
visible throughout all his compositions, and which give to
his reproof and censure, his precepts and admonitions, the
air of parental affection and monitory kindness.'(72)
    The road paved with Addisonian glory from Drake to Mac-
aulay ran straight and uncluttered. Steele was occasionally introduced for comparative purposes but not often
enough to interfere with the ultimate transfiguration of
his collaborator in the Macaulay essay (No. 70).

Goldsmith, one of those who wrote about Steele, delineated him as self-victimized by a competitive intimacy with his friend. 'This was not owing so much to the evident superiority on the part of Addison, as to the unnatural efforts which Steele made to equal or eclipse him. This emulation destroyed that genuine flow of diction which is discoverable in all his former compositions.' A half century later, Hazlitt - very much like Coleridge - found Steele natural and innovative, preferable to a studied and contrived Addison. Hence the 'Tatler' surpassed the 'Spectator': 'it has more of the original spirit, more of the freshness and stamp of nature. The indications of character and strokes of humour are more true and frequent; the reflections that suggest themselves arise more from the occasion, and are less spun out into regular dissertations. They are more like the remarks which occur in sensible conversation, and less like a lecture.'(73)

Despite Hazlitt and his preference, which many of his contemporaries considered perverse, Addison won secular transcendence in Macaulay's prose. He moved through the pages of the 'Edinburgh Review' without flaw, his eminence increasing when he was measured against his contemporaries. Steele, for example, 'was a rake among scholars, and a scholar among rakes'. As a satirist, Addison irradiated his own supremacy:

He neither laughs out like [Voltaire] nor, like [Swift], throws a double portion of severity into his countenance while laughing inwardly; but preserves a look peculiarly his own, a look of demure serenity, disturbed only by an arch sparkle of the eye, an almost imperceptible elevation of the brow, an almost imperceptible curl of the lip. His tone is never that either of a Jack Pudding or of a Cynic. It is that of a gentleman, in whom the quickest sense of the ridiculous is constantly tempered by good nature and good breeding.

As Macaulay sketched in the details of the portrait, he himself became mesmerized by its splendour. He took pride in his opportunity to erase - to his own satisfaction - the one presumed blot on the Addisonian record. That is, he believed his tenuous proof that the slur against 'Little Dicky' was not a betrayal of friendship but merely a remark about a comedian named Henry Norris. In a letter to Macvey Napier, the critic barely restrained his jubilation: 'But I am still more pleased that the vindication of Addison from an unjust charge, which has been universally believed ever since the publication of the 'Lives

of the Poets', should thus be complete.'(74) To Macaulay
Addison was a precursor of the Victorians and possibly
among the best of them: practical in his idealism, kindly
in his righteousness, moral in his worldliness, humble in
his erudition.

Thackeray, who wrote ten years after Macaulay, did not
dispute the eulogy. And yet there is a hint of ambival-
ence in the novelist's awe of Addison's intellect and at
the same time a suspicion of the human being who 'walks
about the world watching [humanity's] pretty humours,
fashions, follies, flirtations, rivalries; and noting them
with the most charming archness'. What disturbed Thackeray was only intimated: the essayist's detachment and an
almost uncrackable good will. More to his liking,
although the comparison remained unstated, was Steele, the
natural man who lived among all sorts of people, enjoyed
them, and was enjoyed in return. Thackeray, however, was
very much the Victorian. While he could not admire Addison with Macaulay's single-mindedness, he exonerated
Steele with nineteenth-century condescension:

> Poor Dick Steele stumbled and got up again, and got
> into jail and out again, and sinned and repented; and
> loved and suffered; and lived and died scores of years
> ago. Peace be with him! Let us think gently of one who
> was so gentle: let us speak kindly of one whose own
> breast exuberated with human kindness.(75)

The Addisonian figure, whose worth increased with only
slight demur for almost two centuries, had inevitably to
topple. Bonamy Dobrée in 1925 began to do violence to the
image, deprecating the journalist as 'the First Victorian'. Dobrée's attitude is hardly arcane. His hostility
to the self-designated rectitude and complacency of the
Queen merged with and fostered his rejection of Addison.
The twentieth-century critic assumed the oracular stance
of his modernity: 'To us, in rebellion against the Victorian view, with more faith in the human being, and much
less in his ideals, approaching as we do indeed a nihil-
ism in values, a character such as Addison's must seem
unsatisfactory.'

The 'character' took on a multitude of vices, as
Dobrée depicted him with unalloyed contempt. Thus the
once-virtuous essayist revealed a sick need to patronize
and possess; to feel safe, that is, 'superior'. His
dwarfed soul was locked in an obsessive secrecy that at
one and the same time hid a conscious hypocrisy and
exhibited a committed prudence. What seemed at first to
be admirable - Addisonian constancy - even that proved

the mark of a fossilized mind and an enfeebled but lulling
prose style. Subjective and vengeful, the Dobrée portrait
became in fact a cartoon of villainy.

Surely the truth about the man and the artist lies
somewhere between Macaulay's adoration and Dobrée's venom.
It is true that behind Addison's correct exterior lurked
a not insignificant capacity for pique. Still he would
have been less than human if he did not hit back, however
covertly, at those whom he often befriended and who just
as often betrayed him. Surely he must have felt distaste
for the fawners who nagged at him for political doles.
And he could not have been indifferent to the gossip that
questioned his virility and made broad jokes about a
pallid marriage that earned him a countess and the magnificent Holland House. Although the privacy he cherished
was sometimes invaded by slander, he concealed whatever
he knew or felt about it. His austere façade that revealed few intimate feelings is undeniably awesome and it
makes certain readers uncomfortable. It is always easier
to respond positively to a personality that is expansive
and open - even in his vices - than to one that is withdrawn and reticent - even in his virtues.

Whatever we feel about the individual, we must or
should recognize his ethos as a man of letters. His
intellectual moderation expresses itself in language
suggestive of easy conversation, freed - as it must be -
of passion and metaphorical richness. He wrote, Johnson
justly said, 'on grave subjects not formal, on light
occasions not grovelling; pure without scrupulosity, and
exact without apparent elaboration.... Addison never
deviates from his track to snatch a grace; he seeks no
ambitious ornament, and tries no hazardous innovations.'
He wrote, in short, like a man who felt at peace in the
middle station, able to skirt the extremes of cold intel-
lectuality and undisciplined imagination. His was a
rhetorical art whose techniques of persuasion slyly hid
their brilliance and made their mark with tact and credible humility.

What should never be forgotten about Addison is that in
delicately structured essays he caught the quintessence of
his age as few other artists were able to do.

As a social thinker he exhibits both the weakness and
enlightenment of Augustan England. Although lacking
intellectual originality, he had a genius for embrac-
ing and communicating contemporary social issues, both
large and small. His literary concern with the fops
and their ladies was no less than his concern with
England's mercantile wars and Protestant succession.

He had a sure instinct for singling out ideas that were
much in men's minds and for explaining them in a style
that was at once plain and relaxed. His readers identified themselves with the point of view of his essays
even as he identified himself with the thinking of the
public which, paradoxically, he helped formulate.(76)

Notes

1   'The Importance of the Guardian Considered' (1713);
    see No. 13.
2   The portrait appears in 'The New Atalantis' (2nd ed.,
    1709), I, 187–93. For her statement of technique, see
    her letter to Harley, 12 May 1710, in Hist. MSS. Com.,
    'The Manuscripts of his Grace the Duke of Portland'
    (1897), IV, 541.
3   'Letter-Books of John Hervey, First Earl of Bristol',
    ed. Sydenham H. A. Hervey (1894), I, 249.
4   Mrs Manley's Dedication to Henry Duke of Beaufort in
    vol. II of 'The New Atalantis'. For 'The Character of
    the Tatler', see No. 31.
5   John Oldmixon, 'The Life and Posthumous Works of
    Arthur Maynwaring' (1715), p. 159.
6   For 'A Condoling Letter to the Tattler', see No. 33.
7   'Moderator' 42. The 'Friendly Couriere' was dated
    2 January.
8   The Preface to 'A Spy upon the Spectator' (1711); see
    No. 37.
9   See 'The Spectator', ed. Donald F. Bond (1965), No. 384
    and n.2. For an account of the pamphlets pro and con
    see 'Political State' (June 1712), III, 452–9, and
    John C. Stephens, Jr, Steele and the Bishop of St
    Asaph's Preface, 'PMLA', LXVII (1952), 1011–23.
10 [William Wagstaffe?], 'The Character of Richard
    St--le, Esq; with some Remarks. By Toby, Abel's Kins-
    man' (1713); also [John Arbuthnot?], 'An Invitation to
    Peace' (1714) (No. 5).
11 'Examiner' for 14–21, 21–24 August 1713. Defoe's pam-
    phlet was advertised in the 'Examiner' 10–14 August
    under the rubric 'This Day is Published'. 'A Second
    Whigg-Letter from William Prynn to Nestor Ironside'
    was being sold by the last week in September.
12 'An Invitation to Peace'.
13 The Whig account of the trial appears in 'The Case of
    Richard Steele, Esq;' (1714) (No. 6). It was subse-
    quently issued as 'A Full Account of the Proceedings
    in the last Session of Parliament, against Richard
    Steele' (1714).

14 'The Correspondence of Jonathan Swift', ed. Harold
    Williams (1963-5), II, 111. For Mrs Manley's letter,
    see Hist. MSS. Com. 'Portland', V, 491.
15 See Steele's statement of friendship for Addison in
    the Dedication to 'The Tender Husband' (1705).
16 On the Death of Sir Richard Steele, in 'Original
    Letters, Dramatic Pieces, and Poems' (1776), III,
    28-30 (No. 8). Victor also dedicated his elegy to
    Walpole.
17 'An Essay towards Fixing the True Standards of Wit,
    Humour, Raillery, Satire, and Ridicule' (1744), pp.
    xvi-xviii.
18 Austin Dobson, 'A Paladin of Philanthropy' (1899),
    p. 109.
19 Bonamy Dobrée, The First Victorian, in 'Essays in Bio-
    graphy 1680-1726' (1925); Winton, 'Captain Steele'
    (1964), and 'Sir Richard Steele, M.P.' (1970); Gold-
    gar, 'The Curse of Party' (1961).
20 'The British Theatre', XII, 5.
21 No. 9 (4 December 1713).
22 From vol. IV, Letter 15 of Pamela (4 vols, 1742) (No.
    18).
23 'The Diary of Mary Countess Cowper, Lady of the Bed-
    chamber to the Princess of Wales, 1714-1720' (1864),
    entry for 15 February 1715. Defoe, 'The Fears of the
    Pretender Turn'd into the Fears of Debauchery' (1715).
24 See 'The Letters of the Late Thomas Rundle ... to Mrs
    Barbara Sandys', introduction by James Dallaway
    (1789). 'The demand for [the 'Theatres'] was so
    great, that even his fiercest enemies bought them up,
    and enjoyed the author, while they persecute the man.'
25 Letters I and II appeared on or shortly before 5
    February 1720, Letters III and IV were published not
    later than March 1720 (see No. 21). Steele answered
    Dennis in 'Theatre', 11, 12.
26 'An Answer to a Whimsical Pamphlet, call'd The Charac-
    ter of Sir John Edgar' (1720).
27 Welsted, Preface to 'A Prologue occasioned by the Re-
    vival of a Play of Shakespear [Measure for Measure]'
    (1721). See Steele's Epilogue for the same 'Revival',
    in which he wrote:

        Else say, in Britain, why it should be heard
        That Etherege to Shakespear is preferr'd;
        Whilst Dorimant to crowded Audiences wenches,
        Our Angelo repeat to empty benches.

    From 'The Works of Leonard Welsted', ed. John Nichols
    (1787), pp. 76-80.

28 'The History of the Theatres of London and Dublin', II,
    99–101.
29 The religious debate was dramatized in 'Tatler' 44,
    45, 50, 51. For the periodical's treatment of Sachev-
    erell, see 142; also 140, 141.
30 'The Present State of Wit' (1711).
31 'A Dissertation on Reading the Classics, and Forming a
    Just Style', 2nd ed. ([1713], 1715) (see No. 36).
32 The Judgment of Hercules, in 'Poems on Several Occa-
    sions' (1729), I, 84–5.
33 'The Present State of Wit'.
34 'A Comment upon the History of Tom Thumb' (1711) (No.
    38).
35 'A Letter from Will Honeycomb to the Examiner, Occa-
    sion'd by the Revival of the Spectator' (1714) (No.
    39).
36 Charles Gildon, 'The Complete Art of Poetry' (1718)
    (No. 41); Robert Heron [John Pinkerton], 'Letters of
    Literature' (1785) (No. 43).
37 'Spectator' 555.
38 'Northanger Abbey' (1818), ch. V (No. 44).
39 Thomas Birch, 'A General Dictionary, Historical and
    Critical' (1734–41), I, 263, note F.
40 Dedication to 'The Drummer', as cited by Joseph
    Spence, 'Observations', ed. James M. Osborn (1966),
    sect. 154 n.
41 See, e.g., Robert Halsband, Addison's 'Cato' and Lady
    Mary Wortley Montagu, 'PMLA', LXV (1950), 1122–9 (an
    argument for the political intention of the play);
    Peter Smithers, 'The Life of Joseph Addison' (2nd ed.,
    1968), p. 269 (a contrary argument); John Loftis,
    'Politics of Drama in Augustan England' (1963), p. 57
    (a presentation of both sides).
42 Spence, sect. 154.
43 Spence, sect. 153; see also Swift, 'Journal to Stella',
    entry for 21 March 1713 (Letter 62).
44 'The Correspondence of Alexander Pope', ed. George
    Sherburn (1956), I, 175.
45 'Addison', in 'The Lives of the English Poets' (1781)
    (No. 67).
46 In 1713–14 'Cato' was presented a dozen times and in
    the following season eight.
47 The 'Grumbler', 20 May 1715 (No. 50); Sewell, 'A
    Vindication of the English Stage' (1716) (No. 52).
    The 'Parallel' was appended to Ozell's 'Cato of Utica'
    (1716) (No. 51).
48 Of Plays and Masquerades, in 'The Occasional Paper'
    (1719).
49 'Letters concerning the English Nation' ([1733],

1760), pp. 141-2.

50 See, e.g., Elizabeth Inchbald, 'British Theatre'
   (1808), vol. VIII; Richard Cumberland, 'British
   Theatre' (1817), vol. I; William Oxberry, 'The New
   English Drama' (1818-25), vol. XVII.

51 Smithers, 'The Life of Joseph Addison', pp. 98-9;
   Edward Cobden, 'A Poem on the Death of ...
   Joseph Addison, Esq.' (1720).

52 'A Letter from Mr. Jacob Bickerstaffe, Nephew to Isaac
   Bickerstaffe, Esq; Occasion'd by the Death of Queen
   Anne. To A Gentleman in Holland' (1714).

53 Dedication to 'The Drummer' (1722), in 'The Works of
   the Right Honourable Joseph Addison', ed. Richard
   Hurd (1856), V, 148.

54 For Maynwaring's influence on the 'Whig-Examiner', see
   Oldmixon, p. 158; the 'Whig-Examiner' 1.

55 'The Present State of Wit'.

56 See his Preface to 'The Drummer' (1716) and his
   Dedication to the second edition (1722). Until 1722
   very few knew of Addison's authorship. Giles Jacob in
   the 'Memoirs' (1719) wrote: 'Now I could never learn,
   upon the strictest Enquiry, that he had any Hand in
   that Piece; on the contrary, I am inform'd, that a
   Gentleman now living, and possess'd of a publick
   Employment is the Author of it.'

57 7 February 1722 (No. 53).

58 As cited in the Preface to Tickell's edition (1721).

59 For Mrs Manley on Addison, see 'The New Atalantis',
   7th ed. (1736), III, 218-19 (No. 55); Spence, sect.
   168.

60 'Correspondence', II, 277. For what Swift regarded
   as Addison's sell-out, see 'A Libel on D-- D-- and a
   Certain Great Lord' [1730], in 'The Poems of Jonathan
   Swift', ed. Harold Williams (1937), II, 479-86.

61 As reported by Berkeley, Hist. MSS. Com., 'The Appen-
   dix to the Seventh Report' (1879), VII, 238.

62 'A Letter to Mr. Addison, on the King's Accession to
   the Throne' (1714).

63 'To the Countess of Warwick on her Marriage with Mr.
   Addison' (c. 1716) (No. 57)

64 Nicholas Amhurst, 'A Congratulatory Epistle to ...
   Joseph Addison, Esq; Occasioned, by his being made One
   of His Majesty's Principal Secretaries of State'
   (1717) (No. 58).

65 Oliver Goldsmith, 'The Beauties of English Poesy'
   (1767), II, 79.

66 'An Essay on the Writings and Genius of Pope' (1756)
   (No. 62).

67 Letter 16, in 'Letters on Several Subjects by ... Sir

Thomas Fitzosborne [William Melmoth] (No. 61). See
also John Gilbert Cooper, 'Letters concerning Taste'
(1755) (No. 65).

68   'Lectures on Rhetoric and Belles Lettres' ([1760],
1783), Lectures 19, 20 (No. 64).

69   An Essay on the Variations of English Prose, from the
Revolution to the Present Time, in 'Transactions of
the Royal Irish Academy' (1797), VI, pt. 2, 41-70
(No. 68).

70   Essay 2, in 'Essays, Biographical, Critical, and
Historical, Illustrative of the Tatler, Spectator,
and Guardian' (1805).

71   'Conjectures on Original Composition' (1759) (No. 63);
'The Correspondence of Edward Young', ed. H. Pettit
(1971), pp. 482-3.

72   Essay 6.

73   Oliver Goldsmith, 'The Bee' (24 November 1759);
Hazlitt, Lecture 5, On the Periodical Essayists, in
'The English Comic Writers' (1819) (No. 69).

74   22 July 1843, in 'Selections from the Correspondence
of Macvey Napier' (1879), p.431.

75   'The English Humourists of the Eighteenth Century'
(1853) (No. 71).

76   Edward A. Bloom and Lillian D. Bloom, 'Joseph Addison's Sociable Animal' (1971), pp. 208-9.

Note on the Text

Copy-text and modern editions are identified in the head-
notes. The long 's' and typographical eccentricities
have been discarded. Accidentals have been corrected
silently. The original italics, punctuation, and spel-
ling have been preserved in each text, but only beginning
and concluding quotation marks have been retained around
cited material.

All translations of classical authors, unless otherwise noted, are drawn from the relevant volumes in the
Loeb Classical Library (Cambridge, Mass., Harvard University Press; and London, Heinemann).

The help of many libraries and their staffs has gone
into the making of this book. We wish now to record our
indebtedness and gratitude to the following: the Hunting-
ton Library, San Marino, Calif.; the Houghton Library of
Harvard University, Cambridge, Mass.; the Beinecke Library
of Yale University, New Haven, Conn.; the Bodleian
Library, Oxford; the British Library, London.

I Steele the Man

1. MARY DELARIVIERE MANLEY, 'SECRET MEMOIRS AND MANNERS OF SEVERAL PERSONS OF QUALITY, OF BOTH SEXES'. FROM 'THE NEW ATALANTIS'

May 1709

Mary Delariviere Manley (1663-1724) wrote 'The New Atalan-tis' to extol, among others, the Tories Harley and Peter-borough. At the same time she used her satirical fiction to attack the Marlboroughs, the Junto Whigs, and their followers. Her insinuations about Steele, factually true, reflect as much personal malice as political bias.

For variations on her name (e.g., Mary de la Rivière Manley), see Patricia Koster, Introduction to 'The Novels of Mary Delariviere Manley' (1971).

From the second edition (October 1709).

O let me ease my Spleen! I shall burst with Laughter; these are prosperous Times for Vice; d'ye see that black Beau, (stuck up in a pert Chariot) thick-set, his Eyes lost in his Head, hanging Eye-brows, broad Face, and tallow Complexion; I long to inform my self if it be his own, he cannot yet sure pretend to that. He's call'd *Monsieur le Ingrate*,(1) he shapes his Manners to his Name, and is exquisitely so in all he does; has an inexhaustible Fund of Dissimulation, and does not bely the Country he was born in, which is fam'd for Falshood and Insincerity; (2) has a World of Wit, and genteel Repartee: He's a Poet too, and was very favourably receiv'd by the Town, especi-ally in his first Performance, where, if you'll take my

Opinion, he exhausted most of his Stock; for what he has
since produc'd, seem but faint Copies of that agreeable
Original. (3) Tho' he's a most incorrect Writer, he
pleases in spight of the Faults we see, and own. Whether
Application might not burnish the Defect, or if those very
Defects were brightned, whether the genuine Spirit would
not fly off? are Queries not so easily resolv'd.

I remember him almost t'other Day, but a wretched
common Trooper; he had the Luck to write a small Poem, and
Dedicated it to a Person whom he never saw, a Lord that's
since Dead, who had a sparkling Genius, much of Humanity,
lov'd the Muses, and was a very good Soldier. He
encourag'd his Performance, took him into his Family, and
gave him a Standard in his Regiment.(4) The genteel Company that he was let into, assisted by his own Genius,
wip'd off the Rust of Education; he began to polish his
Manners, to refine his Conversation, and in short, to fit
himself for something better than what he had been used.
His Morals were Loose; his Principles nothing but Pretence, and a firm Resolution of making his Fortune, at
what rate soever; but because he was far from being at
Ease that way, he cover'd all by a most profound Dissimulation, not in his Practice, but in his Words; not in his
Actions, but his Pen; where he affected to be extreme
Religious, at the same Time when he had two different
Creatures lying-in of base Children by him.(5) The Person
who had done so much for him, not doing more, he thought
all that he had done for him was below his Desert; he
wanted to rise faster than he did. There was a Person who
pretended to the great Work, and he was so vain as to believe the illiterate Fellow could produce the *Philosopher's-Stone*, and would give it him. The Quack found him
a Bubble to his Mind, one that had Wit, and was sanguine
enough to cheat himself, and save him abundance of Words
and Trouble in the pursuit. Well, a House is taken, and
furnish'd, and Furnaces built, and to work they go; the
young Soldier's little ready Money immediately flies off,
his Credit is next stak'd, which soon likewise vanishes
into Smoak.(6) The Operator tells him, 'Twas not from
such small Sums as those he must expect Perfection; what
he had seen hitherto was insignificant, or minute, as one
Grain of Sand compar'd to the Sea-shore, in value of what
he might assure himself of in the noble pursuit of Nature,
that he would carry him to wait upon a Gentleman very
ingenious, who has spent more than ten times that Sum in
the Hands of the Ignorant, yet convinc'd of the Foundation, was ready to join with him for the Experience to go
on with a new Attempt. Accordingly *Monsieur* is introduced
to one, who was indeed a Friend to the Quack, but did not

absolutely confide in his Skill, tho' he still believ'd there was such a Thing as the *Philosopher's-Stone*; yet hearing how illiterate this pretended Operator was, he could not imagine he had attain'd that Secret in Nature, which was never purchas'd, (if ever purchas'd at all?) but with great Charge and Experience. This Gentleman had an airy Wife, who pretended to be a sort of a Director in the Laws of Poetry, believ'd her self to be a very good Judge of the Excellencies and Defects of Writing;(7) she was mightily taken with *Monsieur's* Conversation, pray'd him often to favour her that way. Being inform'd of the narrowness of his Circumstances, she gave him Credit to her Midwife, for assistance to one of his Damsels, that had sworn an unborn Child to him; the Woman was maintain'd 'till her lying-in was over, and the Infant taken off his Hands, *par la sage Femme*, for such and such Considerations upon Paper; he had no Money to give, that was before-hand evaporated into Smoke.(8)   Still the Furnace burnt on, his Credit was stretch'd to the utmost; Demands came quick upon him, and grew clamorous; he had neglected his Lord's Business, and ev'n left his House, to give himself up to the vain pursuits of Chymistry. The Lady who had taken a Friendship for him, upon the Score of his Wit, made it her Business to inform her self from her Husband, of the Probability of their Success; he gave her but cold Comfort in the Case, and even went so far as to tell her, he believ'd that Fellow knew nothing of the Matter, tho' there was a great City-Hall taken, and Furnaces order'd to be built, that they might have room enough to transmute abundantly. The Operator had perswaded the young Chymist to sell his Commission; which he was very busie about, and even repin'd that he met not a Purchaser as soon as he desir'd, for he thought every Hour's Delay kept him from his imaginary Kingdom; but it was to be fear'd, when he had put the Money into the Doctor's Hands, to be laid out in *Mercury*, and other Drugs, that were to be transmuted into *Sol*, (as small a Sum as it was) he would give him the Slip, and go out of the Nation with it. The Lady was good-natur'd, and detested the Cheat; she begg'd her Husband, that he would give her leave to discover it. He advis'd her against it, it might do 'em both a Mischief; but she insisted so much upon it, that he bid her to do what she would. The Lady was then in Childbed, among a merry up-sitting of the Gossips, *Monsieur* made one; his Genius sparkled among the Ladies, he made Love to 'em all in their Turn, whisper'd soft Things to this, ogled t'other, kiss'd the Hand of that, went upon his Knees to a fourth, and so infinitely pleas'd 'em, that they all cry'd he was the Life of the

Company. The sick Lady was gone to repose her self upon her Bed, and sent for *Monsieur* to come to her alone, for she had something to say to him. Vain of his Merit, he did not doubt but she was going to make him a passionate Declaration of Love, and how sensible she was of his Charms; he even fancy'd she withdrew, because possibly she was uneasie at those Professions of Gallantry he had been making to others. He approach'd the Bed-side with all the Softness and Submission in his Air and Eyes, all the Tenderness he well knew how to assume. The Lady desir'd him to take a Chair, and afford her an uninterrupted Audience in what she was going to say. This confirm'd him in his Opinion, and he was even weighing with himself, whether he should be Kind or Cruel, for the Lady was no Beauty, but lay all languishing in the becoming Dress of a Woman in her Circumstances. She entertain'd him very differently from what he expected. In short, she dis-cover'd the Cheat, and advis'd him to take care of him-self, to withdraw from that Labyrinth he was involv'd in, as well as he could: He was undone if he sold his Commis-sion, all the World would laugh him to Scorn, and he would hardly find a Friend to help him to another. A Thunder-bolt falling at the Foot of a frightful Traveller, could not more have confounded him than this did our Chymist. What! all his Furnaces blown up in a Moment, all evapora-ted into Smoke and Air; he could never believe it, the Plumes (elate and haughty as he appear'd before) sunk upon his Crest. Who would have believ'd there could have been such a shrinking of the Soul? Such a contractedness of Genius; such a poorness of Spirit; so abject a Fall from so tow'ring a Height. He was not able, in half an Hour's Time, to speak one Word; his Address was departed, he knew not what to say, only begg'd leave to retire. 'Twas necessary that he must go thro' the Chamber where the Ladies were, to go to the Stairs; he pull'd his Hat over his Eyes, without seeing 'em, and away he went. The Lady was satisfy'd with doing the friendly and honest Part, let him receive it how he would; the *Coquets* fell upon her with Violence, and ask'd her what she had done to *Monsieur*? What she had said to him had certainly be-witch'd him. Never was such an alteration, for they had easily seen his change of Countenance and Air. She defen-ded her self as well as she could, and they were forc'd to conclude the Entertainment without him.

The young Chymist was so base (as he afterwards told the Lady) to believe this only an Artifice of her Hus-band, to keep the Learned Doctor to himself, and deprive him of his share of Philosophical Riches; in his Thought he mortally hated the Discoverer, but his Eyes being open'd, and his Sight clear'd, he quickly saw the Fallacy as plain as the Sun at Noon. He was already undone, or very near it; they had contracted abundance of Debts; the Doctor was a sort of an insolvent Person, the Creditors knew that, and did not trouble their Heads about him. *Monsieur* was forc'd to abscond; all he could preserve from the Chymical-Shipwrack, was his Commission. This Lady engag'd her Husband to serve him in his Troubles, and sent him perpetual Advices when any Thing was like to happen to him; she prevented him several Times from being persecuted by the implacable Midwife; he us'd to term her his *Guardian-Angel*, and every Thing that was Generous and Humane.

But Fortune did more for him in his Adversity, than would have lain in her way in Prosperity, she threw him to seek for Refuge in a House, where was a Lady with very large Possessions; he marry'd her, she settled all upon him, and dy'd soon after.(9) He re-marry'd to an Heiress, who will be very considerable after her Mother's Decease, has got a Place in the Government, and now, as you see, sparks it in the *Prado*.

The Lady who had served him, lost her Husband, and fell into a great deal of Trouble; after she had long suffered, she attempted his Gratitude by the Demand of a small Favour, which he gave her Assurances of serving her in; the Demand was not above ten Pieces, to carry her from all her Troubles to a safe Sanctuary, to her Friends, a considerable distance in the Country; they were willing to receive her if she came, but not to furnish her with Money for the Journey: He kept her a long time (more than a Year) in suspence, and then refus'd her in two Lines, by pretence of Incapacity; nay, refused a second time to oblige her with but two Pieces upon an Extraordinary Exigency, to help her out of some new Trouble she was involv'd with.(10)

It is not only to her, but to all that have ever serv'd him, he has shew'd himself so ingrateful; the very Midwife was forced to sue him: In short, he pays nor obliges no body, but when he can't help it.

Notes

1   Richard Steele.
2   Steele was born in Dublin.
3   'The Funeral' was first performed in December 1701. It was followed by 'The Lying Lover' (December 1703) and 'The Tender Husband' (April 1705).
4   'The Procession' (1695) was dedicated to John Lord

Cutts. In 1695 Steele joined Lord Cutts's company,
the Coldstream Regiment, the Second Regiment of Foot
Guards.

5   Steele had one natural daughter, Elizabeth Ousley, and
in all likelihood another, 'Mrs Temperance'.

6   In the late 1690s Steele undertook an alchemical
experiment, along with John Tilly, Mrs Manley and
William Burnaby. The operator was Sir Thomas Tyrrel.

7   Mrs Manley was but the mistress of Tilly, Warden of
Fleet Prison.

8   Probably Elizabeth Tonson, the sister of Jacob Tonson
the younger, who was to become one of Steele's
publishers.

9   Steele married in 1705 Margaret Ford Stretch, a widow
of St Andrew's parish, Barbadoes. After her death in
December 1706, he married Mary Scurlock, probably in
September 1707.

10 It was in the summer of 1701 that Mrs Manley asked the
impoverished Steele to lend her money. He refused.

2. 'THE BRITISH CENSOR'

1712

This mock-heroic poem begins with an attack on the 'Spectator's' intellectual vapidity, particularly the essays
in criticism. It holds Steele responsible for the 'Spectator' and, to a lesser extent, Tickell. The poet seems
to have no awareness of Addison's involvement.

While thy most fruitful Labours pass about,
And fill with Rapture the judicious Rout,
While all the fashion's Things persuing thee,
A while Neglect their darling Chat and Tea;
Beaux, *Belles* (and all whom empty Thought befriend)
Assist thee, and thy plenteous Works commend:
Permit, oh mighty Man! among the Crowd,
A Swain unknown to sing thy Praises loud,
Transported with the Theam, I'm all on Fire,
Thy Sence I much, but more thy Confidence admire:
Thy Confidence - for sure 'tis that alone
Pleases the gaping and Admiring Town.

Say, it is only This, or Zeal for Truth,
That makes Thee kindly prompt each forward Youth:
Makes Thee in each mishap'd Performance find
Conspicuous Beauties, to which all Mankind,
(But thy sagacious Self) was wholy Blind?
Thy wond'rous Comments shew thee wond'rous Wise,
And Chevy-Chace exalts thee to the Skies!(1)

Two of Repute, (who once Judicious seem'd)
That Reverend Ballad ('tis confess'd) esteem'd;
They saw perhaps some beauteous Thoughts arise,
Where untaught Nature, with some small Surprize,
Do's start, and pleasing Images express,
In a mean, simple and unletter'd Dress:
But cou'd they e'er discry that lofty Sence,
That Majesty of Style, that Eloquence,
Which thou (more penetrating far than they)
Hast found so well, and dost so well Display!
But in Respect of thy prodigious Pen,
What Worth had *Sidney* or unlearned *Ben*?(2)
Poor bashful Souls! Wou'd ever they have dar'd,
The two chief Roman Bards t'have so compar'd?
Horace looks down with joyful Pride to see
Himself so favour'd and extoll'd by thee!
The *Mantuan* too (for Modesty renown'd)
Blushes to be with such Applauses crown'd!

[2 stanzas deleted]

Howe'er with Rev'rance, (as we safely can)
Let's view this mighty, formidable Man,
Observe by what Degrees he rose to Fame
And Spread o'er Britain his tremendious Name.

Once a *Cadet*, obscure and little known,(3)
(Now such a bright conspicuous Wonder grown)
His springing Parts he ventures to expose,
To thoughtless Bullets, and to blund'ring Foes.

Stop, stop, ye barb'rous Men! Suppress your Rage,
And spare the future Censor of an Age!(4)
Oh, be not to approaching Blessings blind,
Tho' Enemies to Him, regard Mankind!
Nor let to nether Shades that Soul be hurl'd,
Whose only Precepts must reform the World!

Behold Him now more free from dire Surprize
Contemplative become and mighty Wise!
Moulding his Thoughts in a religious Strain,

And growing Pious for the Sake of Gain.
Oh prudent Man! How vast is thy Applause,
Redounding from thy Patron and thy Cause;
In this clear Mirrour (thy Example) we
Each Modern Author's Image plainly see;
First on some unexpected theam They fall,
As Int'rest, not as Truth or Justice, call;
Then by a more surprizing Spell, with Ease,
Convert their Patrons to what Form they please;(5)
The Great (tho' worthless Peer) now Worthy grown,(6)
Glitters with Virtues that were not his Own;
The lewdest Rake good Christian do's commence,
Such is the wond'rous Power of Sacred Pence!

[1 stanza deleted]

    A Chymist now, whose vain Projection broke,
Was not his Sence in Part dissolv'd in Smoke?
But what is Sence? Sence in these Times may fail!
But, oh, Assurance must and will prevail!
With this, He's now a fam'd Reformer grown,
Correcting all Men's Manners, but his own:
So oft the Judge unjustly Sentence gives,
And doom's that Wretch who far less Guilty lives:
So the proud, cruel, stubborn priestly Tribe,
Submission, Peace and Charity, prescribe,
But if, Great Man, we must not hope from Thee,
The Wond'rous Charms that in Example be,
Let us some wond'rous Charm in thy Instructions see;
(To warn our vagrant Minds, and fix them right)
Which may like Lightning pierce, or Thunder fright.

    Where's then that Learning, Tow'ring Thought and
          Wit,
That do the glorious Name of Censor fit?
Let Words (Oh grave Instructor!) less abound,
And give Us more of Sence and less of Sound!
Thy Style still overflows thy various Theams,
Like floating Froth that on the Ocean Swims;
An equal certain Course do's ever run,
Constant as Time, or the returning Sun!

    What's florid Phrase? That Women may attain,
And the loose Juglers of the canting Strain;
'Tis powerful Truth, and solid Sence shou'd sway.
Man's list'ning Soul - and force it to Obey.

    But hold, all those are sure presumptious Fools,
Who dare affirm, thou wan'st instructive Rules.

All Things by Thee are clearly Understood,
From *Homer*, to the *Children in the Wood*.(7)
Maxims of Schools, and the grave Ayrs of *France*,
Ethics and Modes, Divinity and Dance;
Pain, Bliss, Hate, Friendship, Lamentation, Song,
To thy extended Province, all belong;
But Poetry is thy peculiar Care,
And here thy Judgment is - beyond Compare.
Thro' thy just Praise each arch Pretender shines,
With *Blackmore*'s easie, clear and nervous Lines.(8)
But *Tickell* is, (thy Theam's Sublimer Scope)
Of ev'ry Muse, and Grace the springing Hope.
Tickell (surprizing Object of thy Love!)
Who do's the just Reverse of *Denham* prove.(9)
(Deep, yet not clear, not gentle, and yet dull,
Raging, yet weak, o'erflowing, yet not full;)
Affected, stiff, pompous, with low Design,
Still bell'wing Peace in ev'ry Thund'ring Line!
Proceed bright Bard! With Nature's Laws dispence,
And bravely Scorn the servile Rules of Sense.
Proceed, I say, pursue illustrious Fame!
She's thine, thou grasp'st her now, the willing Dame,
And ever will, if Thou to him submit,
And by his Judgment regulate thy Wit,
What mayn't the coming Age expect to see,
When two such Worthies so combin'd agree,
One who like him Approves, one who Performs like Thee!
Pardon ye Critics, worthy Censor thou,
This small Digression (for thy Sake) allow;
Where (like your Friendships) I presume to joyn,
The Fame of so profound a Wit with Thine!

　　　Sages of old (by some reputed far
Wiser than 'Tatlers' or 'Spectators' are,
Who judging Rules from best Experience brought)
Science so vast and so stupendious thought,
So Difficult, that utmost human Art,
Cou'd scarce attain Perfection in one Part,
The *Grecian*, whom *Apollo*'s Self confest,
To be of Men, the wisest and the best.
What was th' Assurance he from Learning drew,
But this - Of knowing that he Nothing knew?
Did not the most (however wond'rous clear)
Still dark and dubious to Themselves appear?
But Thou more mighty than these mighty Dead,
Art Wit's, art Learning's, universal Head.
Like *Rome*'s chief Prelate do'st thy Lords dispence,
Like Him extorting blind Obedience;
And seem'st thy Self unerring to believe.
Flush'd with the dull Regard that Bigots give.

But tho' thou seem'st to Think so great a Store
Of Knowledge thine (more blest than Man before)
Which thou (by ought unbyass'd) dost bestow
So freely on the wond'ring Crowd below;
For Thy own Sake, not blindly Zealous be,
But deign to take this small Advice from Me.

The Praise of Fops and half-learn'd Fools decline,
Who Female-like, admire what e'er seems Fine;
Distrust thy Self, examine well thy Mind,
Nor solid Learning think with so much Ease to find.
Read o'er the Antients, and digest them well,
With Pains discover where they most excell.
Consider well their Merit, and their Fate,
And by what Means they rose so wond'rous Great.

But this Way's unpropitious and too hard,
True Sence and Virtue meet with small Reward:
Thou wilt not wreck thy Fortunes, or thy Brain,
But Prudently inclin'st to Ease and Gain.

Cease, Cease, my Muse, for thine's too hard a
        Task,
And do's more Skill and greater Labour ask,
Than thou can'st e'er contribute to remove   ⎫
Errors - or Plant right Notions, where Self-Love ⎬
Is fixt so firm, and where gull'd Fools approve. ⎭

F I N I S

Notes

1 'Spectator' 70, 74, written by Addison but attributed
   to Steele by contemporaries.
2 Both Ben Jonson and Sir Philip Sidney admired the
   ballad; see 'Spectator' 70.
3 Steele joined the Second Troop of Life Guards in June
   1692 as a trooper. In 1695 he moved to the Coldstream
   Regiment, becoming an ensign in 1697.
4 Isaac Bickerstaff, the persona of the 'Tatler'.
5 A reference to the 'Tatler's' attacks on Robert Harley.
   As one of the two Secretaries of State, Harley (1661-
   1724) was believed to have appointed Steele Gazetteer
   in 1707.
6 Thomas Earl of Wharton (1648-1715), praised, e.g., in
   'Tatler' 130.
7 'Spectator' 85, written by Addison and attributed to
   Steele by contemporaries.

8   Sir Richard Blackmore (d. 1729) as poet and critic is
    praised and cited in the 'Tatler' and the 'Spectator'.
9   Among Steele's contemporaries his signature letter T
    in the 'Spectator' was sometimes associated with
    Thomas Tickell (1686-1740). John Denham (1615-69) was
    best known for 'Cooper's Hill' and the musical elegy on
    Cowley.

3. WILLIAM WAGSTAFFE[?], 'THE CHARACTER OF RICHARD ST--LE,
ESQ; WITH SOME REMARKS. BY TOBY, ABEL'S KINSMAN...'

1713

An excerpt from the most popular anti-Steele pamphlet of
1713. It sought to undo the effectiveness of Steele's
position on Dunkirk and his new journal, the 'Englishman'.

Mr. St--le, *Sir*, having lately had a Welsh Estate left him
by his Wife's Mother, began to look upon himself as a
considerable Person in Land, as well as Sense, as is
Natural for those, who have been Indigent and Necessitous
all their Lives.(1) He was told by the *Minor Poets*, his
Companions at *Button*'s,(2) That a Man of his Sense must
undoubtedly advance himself by being in the Senate, and
that he knew the World, as *Dick* himself insinuates in his
Treatise upon Demolition, as well as any Man in *England*,
and had all the Qualifications requisite for a *Minister of
State*.(3) There was no great Occasion to press him to any
Thing of this Nature: He embraced it with all the Eagerness imaginable, but offered at first a sort of *Nolo
Episcopari*, that it might go down the more plausibly. He
considered wisely, that his Wit and Credit began to run
very low, that the Chief of his Assistants had deserted
him, that *C. Lilly* had lately refused to lend him Half a
Crown, *Jacob* dun'd him more than was consistent with good
Manners, and if he got into the *House* he could not be
Arrested.(4) What seduced him more, than all these Con-
siderations, was a Pension from the Party, double the
Income of the *Stamp-Office* at Present, and in Hand, for
Speaking in the *House*;(5) and he has amassed together a
Multitude of set Speeches, which he designs to get *Extem-
pore* for that Purpose. He is at this Time so elated, I

am told, that he has already promised several Places under
him, when he is *Secretary* or *Lord Treasurer*. Mr. *Button*
is an *Auditor* of the *Exchequer*, and Mr. *Bat. Pigeon* in the
Room of Sir *Clement, Master of the Ceremonies*. He has
declared publickly, he does not question overturning the
Ministry, and doing that before the first Sessions of
Parliament is over, which my Lord *Wh---on* and *S----rs*
have been foil'd at, for Three Years together.(6)

I need not tell you, *Sir*, how exulted he seem'd at
Stockbridge, and after what Manner he address'd the Bailiff and his Brethren.(7) There was nothing there to perplex him, but the Payment of a 300 l. Bond, which lessened
the Sum he carried down, and which an odd Dog of a
Creditor had Intimation of, and took this Opportunity to
recover. But, Alas! We may date the Ruin of the Man, and
the Loss of his Intellects from this Juncture; as soon as
he came to Town the *Political Cacoethes* began to break
out upon him with greater Violence, because it had been
suppressed, and He, who had lived so long upon the *Lucubrations* of others, was resolv'd at last to do Something.
Mr. *John Snow* has since received such Marks of his Favour
and Esteem, that he has appealed to him in the Dispute betwixt Himself and his Prince, *Whether it was expedient to
demolish* Dunkirk *or not,* and has chosen Himself and the
Bailiff of a petty Corporation to be Directors of Her
Majesty. To convince his Electors he can write, he has
Dedicated a Book to their *Bailiff*, and for their Civility
in attempting to choose him, has inflicted the Punishment
of Reading it, upon the Corporation....

This, *Sir*, is that Gentleman of Merit! that Hero of
good Sense! that Man of Charity and Publick Spirit! that
Censor of Great Britain! that *Venerable* Nestor!(8)

O, Ye Literati of *Button*'s Coffee-House! Ye Ladies of
St. *James*'s! Ye Milliners of the *Exchange*! Ye Upholster-
ers of the *City*! Ye Stock-Jobbers of *Jonathan*'s! Ye
Neighbours of Sir *Roger*, and Ye Family of the *Lizards*!(9)
Behold the Patron of Learning! the Encourager of Arts and
Sciences! the Dispenser of Morality and Philosophy! the
Demolisher of Tuckers and Hoop'd-Petticoats! the Terror of
Politicians! and the Debellator of News-Writers! dwindled
on a sudden into an Author below the Character of *Dunton!*
below the Politicks of *Ridpath!*(10) Ingratefully insulting his Queen, and committing Petty-Larceny upon the Reputation of a Great Man!(11) See the Man who talked like an
Oracle, who had all the Gay, the Delicate, the Humorous,
at his Command, calling Names, and daubing his Style with
the Language of a *Scavinger*!

O Tempora! O Mores! More Phlebotomy and fresh Straw.

For the Man in the Moon drinks Claret,
Eats Powder'd Beef, Turnip, and Carrot.

Is this that *Richard St--le* Esq; who published the
'Tatlers' and 'Spectators', who was believed to be one of
the most Accomplished Gentlemen in the World! It is
impossible! 'Tis some Impostor, some Enemy to that
Gentleman, some savage Miscreant, who had his Birth and
Education in a Place more Barbarous than *Carrickfergus*.
If Mr. *St--le, Sir,* was ever a Man of Parts, he is
strangely degenerated, and has undergone a greater Alteration on a sudden, than any in *Ovid*'s *Metamorphosis*,
though the following Account in my Opinion, may be as properly applied to *Apollo* and Mr. *Ironside*, as to the Person
spoken of by that Author, which for the Benefit of the
City Politicians, I shall leave in the Original.

-------- *Nec Delius Aures*
Humanam Stolidas patitur retinere figuram,
Sed trahit in spatium; villisq; Albentibus Implet;
Induiturq; Aures lente Gradientis Aselli. (12)

Our Author has given his Reputation such a Stab, that
I can scarcely think but he is in some Measure guilty of
self Murder, and as Dead as Dr. *Partridge*; or any other
Person he killed formerly. (13) If the Coroners Inquest
was to examine him, the *Welsh Estate* would in all Probability be in Danger, was it not for the *Salvo* of *Non
Compos*. It is a miserable Consideration, when a Man
exposes his Morals and Integrity to Sale, when he lets
his Wit by the Day, and Jades and Hackneys down his
Genius to supply his Luxury. I should have thought Mr.
St--le might have had the Example of his *Friend* before
his Eyes, who had the Reputation of being Author of the
Dis--------ry, till, by two or three unlucky After-Claps,
he proved himself incapable of writing it. (14)
But we ought to have another Opinion of our *Adviser
of Princes*, if we reflect on what he tells us in his
Importance, that an *Honest*, tho' a *Mean* Man, gives Her
Majesty to understand, That the *British Nation expects
the immediate Demolition of* Dunkirk: *Expects it,* says
he, *from the Duty they owe their Queen, from their Care
of the Preservation of Her Sacred Life, Her Crown and
Dignity, from the Honour and Integrity of Her Councils,
from the glorious Advantages of Her Arms, from the Faith
and Sincerity of Her Treaties, from the Veneration and
Regard due to Her from his Most Christian Majesty, and
from the Duty they owe themselves and their Posterity;
and is this Insolence and Ingratitude?*(15) If we had

Leisure to examine this Construction, it would open to us
a Field of Incongruity, but I shall rather give you the
true Reasons of the Expectations of himself and his Party,
abstracted from the false Meanings he has put upon them.
The Party then expects it from a particular Care of the
Dutch Trade, and from an Apprehension that *England* should
be too powerful, from the Duty they owe the *Dutch* and
their Posterity, from an Endeavour to blacken and asperse
the Peace, from a Jealousy that the present Ministry are
in the Interest of the Church, from an Uneasiness they are
under because of Her Majesty's Administration, and from a
Desire of seeing her Successor upon the Throne, and *is
this Insolence and Ingratitude!* ...
    You may blame me perhaps, for reminding Our Author of
his Debts, and I should justly think my self blameable,
were they not the Effects of his Luxury, his Vanity and
Ambition, and not of Accident or Misfortune. I could
easily excuse and pity a Man for being poor, but not when
he labours by his Vices to undo himself. Not when he endeavours to make a Figure, or become a *Senator* at the
Expence of his Creditors. Some *Civilians* look upon such
Chymists, who are Searchers only of the Philosopher's
Stone, as unfit to be tolerated in any Community, because
they reduce not only themselves and Families to Beggary,
but several other People; and certainly Spendthrifts and
Projectors of any Sort, are equally pernicious, and are so
far from having any Spice of *Publick Spirit*, so much
boasted of by some, that they are useless Members to the
Government they live under, and a Nuisance to the Publick.
Where is the *Publick Spirit* of such a Man who will be
bribed to recommend a *Barber*, a *Buffoon*, or a *Perfumer* to
the World, to carry on Intrigues, which a Man of Honour
would blush to hear of, and to *Pimp* in Print? Where is
his *Charity* and *Benevolence to Mankind*, who is squander-
ing away a handsome Competency among the *Illegitimate*, who
is running into every Body's Debt, and Paying Nobody?
Where is his *Disinterest* who votes for more than double an
Equivalent of the *Stamp Office*. *Are the Pursuits of
Avarice and Ambition contemptible to such an one? And is
this laying aside the common View by which the mistaken
World are actuated?*
    Pardon me, *Sir*, however merry I have been, I can con-
tain no longer: *Publick Spirit, Charity, Benevolence to
Mankind, and Disinterest*, are Virtues known to our *Mush-
room Patriot* by Name only, and it raises the Contempt and
Indignation of every honest Man, to hear a Person of the
vilest Principles, and the most mercenary Hireling, who
ever prostituted his Pen in the Defence of any Faction,
giving himself such an Air of Sanctity and Virtue? A Man

of such a *Publick and enlarged Spirit*, is as well qualified as any *Judas* (16) of them all, to betray his Friend,
his Benefactress or his Sovereign, if you bait with a
Bribe considerable enough to reach his Conscience: And
he may very well be careless what *Ideas* are affixed to
the Letters of his Name, when it is impossible for the
worst to Sully him....

Mr. *St--le*, in short, has neither an Head, nor a
Style, for Politicks; there is no one Political *Englishman* but contains either some notorious Blunder in his
Notions or his Language; and he seems himself so well
aware of this, that he is already run from his Purpose.
I should be glad to find any Signs of Conversion in him;
and I could wish he would follow the Example of *Midas*,
who after the Transformation of his Ears, was ashamed,
and endeavoured to cover his Ignominy from the World.

If I might Advise him, I should think it his best Way
to retire into *Wales*, and Live upon his Estate; for by
these Means he may keep his Circumstances within Bounds;
and when his Head is Cool and Purged of his Politicks, he
may now and then revisit and divert the Town, by publishing the Works of his Friends, and retrieve the little
Reputation he had gained by them. Whatever Hopes the
Party may have given him, or whatever Promises they have
made, he may depend upon it they will never answer. He
will prove their *Cully* and their *Tool*, and *ruined in the
End*; and if he persists in his Purpose, I dare engage, if
I can be sure of any Thing in Futurity, that I shall live
to see him in *Jayl*, or under the Hands of *Longbottom*, in
Bedlam; (17) and his Works exposed in that Neighbourhood
for Years together to the Inclemency of the Seasons. I
know not, I must confess, whether his Misfortunes will
deserve our Pity. Such a Fate will be the Genuine Product
of his Indiscretion and Ill Principles, and his Stupidity
a Curse upon his *Ingratitude*.

Neither Mr. *Baker.*, Mrs. *Baldwin,* or any other English
Publisher, ever obtained so great a Character, as the
Person we have been speaking of, or received more
Encouragement from People of Condition; And it would have
been as much a Crime, but a little Time since, to have
spoke against him, as now it is to speak for him. Some
Historians have observed, That *Alexander* was as Fortunate
in his Death, as in any Action of his Life; he died soon
after he had subdued the World, nor lived to Hazard the
Glory he had gained in any Rebellion, that might have been
formed against him. How Happy had it been for our *Politician* had he died in such a Manner; had he followed his
Friend Sir *Roger*, soon after he published his Death, and
left no 'Guardians', no 'Englishmen', behind him, as the

Monuments of his Ignorance and Indiscretion.... (18)

Notes

1 Elizabeth Scurlock died early in 1713 and because of
  her bequests her son-in-law could now call himself
  'Mr Steele of Llangunnor in the county of Carmarthen'.
2 The coffee house in Russell Street, Covent Garden.
  Established in 1712 or the next year, it survived
  Button's death in 1731 to close down in 1751.
3 'Guardian' 128 and 'The Importance of Dunkirk
  Consider'd'.
4 Addison was regarded as Steele's assistant in their
  periodical ventures. Charles Lillie, the perfumer,
  had helped Morphew in the publication of the 'Tatler'.
  A friend of Steele, he is mentioned several times in
  the 'Spectator'. The younger Jacob Tonson was involved in the printing of the 'Tatler' and 'Spectator'.
5 Appointed a Commissioner of the Stamp Office at £300
  annually, Steele resigned the post in late spring
  1713.
6 Thomas Earl of Wharton and John Lord Somers (1651-
  1716), Lord Chancellor of England.
7 'The Importance of Dunkirk Consider'd' is addressed
  to 'Mr. John Snow, Bailiff of Stockbridge'.
8 Nestor Ironside, the 'Guardian's' persona.
9 St James's Coffee House, near St James's Palace, was
  established in 1705 and frequented by Addison and
  Steele. The Royal Exchange [II], replacing its predecessor destroyed in the Great Fire, was itself
  burned down in 1838. It served as a meeting place
  for merchants and bankers. The City is the general
  name for London within the *gates* and the *bars*.
  Jonathan's Coffee House, Exchange Alley, Cornhill, is
  associated in the 'Tatler' and 'Spectator' with
  'Stock-Jobbers'. Sir Roger de Coverley represents the
  landed gentry in the 'Spectator'. The Lizards appear
  in the 'Guardian'.
10 John Dunton (1659-1733), bookseller and periodical
  writer; George Ridpath (d. 1726), Whig journalist.
11 Steele's Dunkirk pieces were interpreted by Tories as
  an affront to Queen Anne and her ministers.
12 Ovid, *Metamorphoses*, XI, 174-9. (Omitted are
  11.177-8: 'instabilesque imas facit et dat posse
  moveri:/cetera sunt hominis, partem damnatur in
  unam.') 'The Delian God did not suffer ears so dull
  to keep their human form, but lengthened them out and
  filled them with shaggy, grey hair, he also made them

unstable at the base and gave them the power of
motion. Human in all else, in this one feature was
he punished, and wore the ears of a slow-moving ass.'
13   See 'Tatler' 1.
14   'The Dispensary' (1699) was written by Sir Samuel
     Garth (1661-1719); see 'Tatler' 105.
15   The thematic refrain in Steele's Dunkirk pieces.
16   In 1713 and 1714 Steele was often called a Judas by
     Tory pamphleteers.
17   Tory writers frequently saw Steele ending his days in
     either a sponging-house or in Bedlam.
18   The 'Englishman' was a political sequel to the
     'Guardian'.

4.   'JOHN TUTCHIN'S GHOST TO RICHARD ST--LE, ESQ;'

1713

John Tutchin (*c*. 1661-1707) was a Whig pamphleteer. He
published the 'Observator' twice weekly from 1702 until
his death. Often persecuted and threatened for his
Whiggism, he was set upon by a pack of hoodlums in
September 1707 and died within a few days. This anonymous essay, written when Steele was the most visible of
Whig targets, seeks to fix a relationship between Tutchin
and Steele in political madness and may even carry an
implicit threat.

John Tutchin's
GHOST
TO
Richard St--le, Esq;

It is with no small Concern I shall publish the following
Account of the *untimely End* of a Great Man, who, for some
Years past (for his *Gentleman-like* Stile, his *Bright* and
Polite Way of Writing, as well as his *Christian Temper* in
all Controversies) had, with the *Greatest Justice*, gain'd
himself the *Applause* of the best Part of Mankind, as well
as the *Admiration* of the *Fair* Sex, who were grown such
constant Readers of his *Paper*, that you shou'd scarce find
a Lady dressing, or drinking Tea in a Morning with her

Friends, but Mr. St--le's Paper made up the best Part of
the Entertainment. (1)

How then shou'd we all be affected with the Instability·
of all Sublunary Things; or indeed ought we not to be prepar'd, and, with the greatest Presence of Mind, be ready
to encounter the various and dreadful Changes, which a
Day, a Week, or a Year, may bring upon our Temper, Inclination, Reason, or the whole Fabrick it self; when we shall
duly weigh and consider that neither Brightness of Parts,
nor the most Solid Wisdom, which this Gentleman was so
much Master of, cou'd avert his Deplorable Catastrophe.

He had indeed for some Time (almost ever since his
being chosen a M—ber of P—ment) (2) been observ'd by his
nearest Friends, to talk wildly, and wonderfully affect
what we call, Building Castles in the Air: He was continually harping upon, and profess'd himself a real
Admirer of, AEsop's Project, of Boys in Baskets, borne up
by Eagles, assuring his intimate Acquaintance, he would
lay it before the H—se of C—ons, in order to have a
strong Fort built in the Clouds, to secure our Commerce,
and command the Dunkirk Privateers: Thus he went on for
some Time, but was constantly watch'd by his Friends, to
whom in his more Lucid Intervals, he would complain of a
strange Coldness and Dulness in his Brain, often pointing
to the upper Part of his Head; but being, on the 5th of
October last, (3) left accidentally alone in his Chamber,
he fastned the Door on the Inside, and retir'd into his
Closet, where he had not been long before Something gave
three Hollow Knocks at the Door, which stood almost open:
This rous'd our more than Christian Hero; (4)

>   Whose Head right pensively inclined was,
>   On that Right Hand, which both with Sword and Pen
>   Had purchas'd such Immortal Fame;
>   Laurels so many, and Renown so bright,
>   That rais'd, and Stuck his Name among the Stars;
>   When, quite aghast! he Something heard rush in,
>   And by his Side a dismal Ghost he saw;
>   In its Right-Hand a trusty Oaken Plant
>   He grasp'd, and under t'other Arm close hugg'd
>   A Leathern Bottle, corked well, and fill'd
>   With Liquor wondrous strong and strange, he bore;
>   And thus with hollow Voice the Phantom Spoke.
>   'Here Mighty Champion of that Cause renown'd!
>   Which whilom I defended, while alive;
>   Here, drink thy Fill; and to his Mouth he plac'd
>   The Bottle; 'tis Lethe dash'd with Acheron:
>   I here dismiss thy wretched, fluttering Soul,
>   And all its poor depending Faculties,

And in their Room inspire Thee with mine Own.
Be Bold, be Saucy, Arrogant, and Dull,
Let Kiss mine A--se, and *Rogue*, and *Rascal*,
Fill all thy *Glorious* Pithy Lines;
Silence and Vanquish thy obdurate Foes,
Rebellious Thoughts, preluding to the rousing up
The *Good Old Cause*, I need not to inspire;
Thou hast them of Thy own, and rooted deep,
Too deep to be wash'd out by *Lethe*'s Draught;
Nor need I give Thee *Pride*, nor Black *Ingratitude*,
Those Noble Virtues Thou hast practis'd long
Against Thy Q---n and all Thy *Benefactors*;
The Fame of which has long since reach'd the *Nether
    Sky*,
And given Thy Friends below *Immortal* Joy.
Arise, Arise, *Renowned S---tor*,
No more a 'Guardian', 'Tatler', or 'Spectator';
But be like me, Thy Predecessor, Base,
Insipid, Haughty, Infamous, traducing
The Best of *Governments* and *Ministry*
As near Perfection, as you Mortals can be;
And henceforth let it be in *Scorn* and *Irony*,
When Mortals the old Proverb use, and say,
As bright, or true as *Steele*.'
Here paus'd the Sprite; but seeing that the *Hero* lay
A senseless Lump of Flesh, inanimate,
His Oaken Towel to his brauny Back
He thrice apply'd,
And with a Voice, much louder than before;
'Rise up, rise up, rise up, O *Englishman*,'
He cry'd. 'Twas this that gave new Life; why name I
    Life!
New Soul, new Sense, and perfectly *new Man*:
At this the *Hero* op'd his wondring Eyes,
And, as the *Spirit* vanish'd from the Place,
The well-known mighty Back he plainly saw
Of the much fam'd, redoubted TUTCHIN:
He rose, and following cry'd, *My Father*!
Oh! let me press you in my eager Arms;
But Nothing cou'd he grasp but fleeting Air:
A wondrous Change within himself he found;
He set him down, and, at one glorious Heat,
With Inspiration swoln, and staring wild,
Struck out the First, the Conquering 'Englishman'.

I was willing to oblige the Publick with this *Miltonick
Episode* intire, as I had it from a trusty Hand, even
Mrs. *Jenny Bickerstaff* her self: (5) Since it contains
the Authentick Account of a *Transmutation*, or

Metamorphosis, the most amazing perhaps, that any Age can produce, as well as to obviate and expose a fictitious Account, that is publish'd, as if the *Gentleman* we have been speaking of had been dubb'd an *Englishman*, by one *Nestor Ironside*; who, 'tis pretended, only gave him a Knock on the Pate, and stuff'd some *trifling Papers* under his *Wigg*. How strangely must we be impos'd on by Misrepresentations, of what happens at a Distance from us, when an Affair so astonishing and considerable as this, that happen'd even in our *Metropolis* it self, is not only misrepresented, but even credited by Men of *Sense* and *Figure* among us!

Notes

1 A play upon the untimely end of John Partridge,
   almanac-maker.
2 Steele was elected MP for Stockbridge on 25 August
   1713.
3 'Englishman' 1 was published on 6 October 1713.
4 A play upon Steele's first prose tract, 'The Christian
   Hero' (1701).
5 That is, Isaac's half-sister Jenny Distaff.

5. JOHN ARBUTHNOT[?], 'AN INVITATION TO PEACE'

1714

'An Invitation to Peace: or Toby's Preliminaries to Nestor Ironsides, Set forth in a Dialogue between Toby and His Kinsman' was written possibly by Dr John Arbuthnot either in December 1713 or in the first few months of 1714. A sequel to 'The Character of Richard Steele', the prose pamphlet 'An Invitation to Peace' concludes with an address to Mr Ironsides in couplets.

An Invitation to Peace: or Toby's Preliminaries to Nestor Ironsides, Set forth in a Dialogue between Toby and his Kinsman.

To Mr Ironsides

'Twas you who first did put to flight
The Amber Cane of sauntring Knight,
The Shoulder-knot, the Hat and Feather
And Rocklowe worn in sultry Weather.
The SPEC, was you, or Part of you,
Which first subdu'd the red-heel'd Shoe.
The Snuff-box too, with Nun and Priest,
The flutt'ring Coxcomb's nauseous Jest.
The only Object that could suit
The delicate and well-bred Brute.
To Play-house whensoe're you came
To SPEC, to Censure and Reclaim,
The guilty Chloe curtsy'd low,
The Fop his tributary Bow
Submissive paid, and strait would be
Demure, as if he came to see.
To Vice from Folly you could step,
Or rather, if you please, could leap.
Nor Atheist then, that is, Free-drinker;
Nor others tedious to rehearse,
Below the Dignity of Verse;
Howe're, disguis'd in Virtue's Shape,
SPEC'S Guilt-pursuing Pen could scape.
Great was the Dread, all fell before ye;
Tam Fool *quam* Knave, *tam* Whig *quam* Tory.
In vain the Rich your Doors would crowd,
No *Safeguard Money* was allow'd.
The Town and you did long wage War;
That is, 'twas long fight Dog, fight Bear.
But you, at last, did overcome,
And brought th' Eternal Laurel home.
Great was the Glory then, I trow,
As great as that of *Marlborough*.
Nor did you rid us of a lesser Evil,
He beat the Bourbon, you the Devil.

6.   'THE CASE OF RICHARD STEELE, ESQ; BEING AN IMPARTIAL
ACCOUNT OF THE PROCEEDINGS AGAINST HIM'

1714

An excerpt from a Whig pamphlet that begins with a
description of Steele's parliamentary trial and his
subsequent expulsion from the Commons.

March 18th. Mr. *Steele's* Hearing came on, and the Con-
course was very great upon this Occasion. Several Gentlemen who had plac'd themselves in the Galleries, and the
Speaker's Chamber, refusing to withdraw, were by Order of
the House taken into Custody of the Serjeant at Arms.
    The Order of the Day being read, Mr. *Steele* was asked
whether he was the Author of the beforemention'd Pamphlets: (1) He freely own'd, that he wrote and publish'd
them; after which a Debate arose about the Method of Proceeding, and at length Mr. *Steele* was permitted to make
his Defence, which he did accordingly, and then withdrew.
    Many were the Speeches and Debates on both sides, the
House sat till past 12 at Night, and came at last to these
Resolutions, 1. *That* (Two of) *the said Pamphlets* (viz.
The 'Crisis' *and* The Close of the 'Englishman') *were
scandalous and seditious Libels, containing many Expressions highly reflecting upon her Majesty, the Nobility,
Gentry, Clergy and Universities of this Kingdom, maliciously insinuating, That the Protestant Succession in
the House of* Hanover *is in danger under her Majesty's
Administration, and tending to alienate the Affections of
her Majesty's good Subjects, and to create Jealousies
and Divisions among them. 2. That Mr.* Steele*, for his
Offence in Writing and Publishing the said scandalous
and seditious Libels, be Expelled this House.*

    Thus far, Sir, I have given you a summary Account of
the publick Transactions relating to this Affair of Mr.
Steele. I shall add to these a very particular Incident,
which is known to very few. Mr. *Steele* was not expell'd
the House till late in the Night; but the 'Examiner',
which was printed off by 12 the same foregoing Day, gives
an insulting Account of his Expulsion, which was near 12
Hours before it was actually done. I only insert this as
Matter of Speculation, and so leave it to you.
    It is and has been remarkable, that if a Stranger were

to form his Judgment of Men by the Representations of the
Party Writers, he must imagine that there were only Fools
and Knaves that made any Figure on both sides. For it is
sufficient now-a-days to make any Man forfeit his Character of Wit and Honesty, to declare himself on either.
    Mr. *Steele* is a very eminent Instance of this Truth;
for till he declar'd himself on the Side of what the
EXAMINER calls the *Ruin'd Party*, (2) he was cry'd up by
both Sides as the brightest Man that had appear'd in all
the politer Arts. His Wit was grown the Standard of
Excellence, and his Picture bought up and kept in the
Chambers and Closets of the Witty and the Gay, as *Ovid*'s
was worn on the Fingers of those of the same Character in
Rome. But when he had once appear'd in a Cause, which was
not lik'd by many, his Wit as well as his Morals was condemn'd, and he scarce allow'd Sense enough to write his
Name with any tolerable Correctness....

Notes

1 The formal charges on 12 March cited the 'Englishman'
   46 and 57 and 'The Crisis'.
2 The Whigs.

7. JOHN LACY, 'THE STEELEIDS'

1714

In 1714 the pseudonymous John Lacy published 'The Steeleids', a political poem, which has as its plot in the
third canto a 'Tryal of Wit' presided over by Milton, who
holds Ithuriel's 'Wand'.

    SUCKLING (1) was sent *Mercurial* Messenger,
    To Summon all *False Muses* to the Bar;
    When All appear'd, Each Guilty, *Guilty pleads*,
    Hiding red Faces, with their drooping Heads;
    Yet each, to Mollify her Crime, reveals
    The *Wit* was theirs, but the Sedition *St—l's*
    And to gain *Pardon* too, they urg'd beside,
    Their Master lent them out to feed his Pride.

Euterpe was lent out by *Ad——on*
To Him *Thalia*, *Clio* too belong,
And fair *Calliope*'s Harmonious Tongue;
Erato and *Pol'hymnia* humbly hope
They safely may return to little *P——pe*.
Two *Muses* more (I need not write each Name)
To *T---kel*, *G--y*, and *E--den* laid a Claim.
Nor must you, Sacred *Bards*, admire to see
Two Muses that Inspired *Poets Three*;
For where *Melpomene* bewails *St——l's Dun*,
Tames *Shrews*, or does his *Scolding Wife* bemoan
Forty dull *B——dg——lls* clubb'd for her alone; (2)
But *St---le*, when Perfect Dulness he design'd,
Scrawl'd *Bungled Treason*, and all Helps resign'd.
   St——le, that in faction still had led the Van,
Came in the Rear of the Felonious *Clan*.
With Words in Sound *Sublime*, but *Low* in Truth,
Such as too oft, Seduce our *British* Youth:
In Faction's Cause, his loud unweary'd Tongue
Bawl'd out a large Impertinent Harangue,
Short of the Subject, but three Hours long.
Sawcy his Mien, his Looks were set t'affront,
Dogged his Eye, and Brazen was his Front;
He stir'd the Ordure of his Filthy Brains,
And cast a Nuisance about with Pains;
Malice and Study, put him in a Sweat,
And every Pore perspir'd of *Belinsgate*.(3)
   The first he fell upon, was Honest BEN,
That Prince of Poets, and that best of Men:
St——le called him Rascal, Plagiary and Fool,
And all the Lines, that were BEN's own, were Dull;
Did both his Birth and Library Blame,
And call'd him *Brickdust*, to disgrace his Name;
- And deeper to Imprint the vile Disgrace,
Described the Trowel, where the Pen was plac'd.
When the Dull Drolling Scene was made compleat,
He Punn'd, and call'd him *Plaisterer* of Wit.
   POOR PHILIPS, still more bitterly he maul'd,
And *Crab-tree*, from his *Cyder* Poem, call'd;
Then in some Sneering *Ironies*, he Swore,
Pindus was Founded first on *Penmenmaur*.
The Bards that treated him with Christian spleen,
Were once fanaticks, as might full be seen,
Writ in their *Phyz*, Imprinted in their *Mien*.
DRYDEN retain'd a Puritanick Grace,
And wore the *Holy Leer* upon his Face.
   When almost all the Bards in Heav'n had spoke,
And all his Hopes, tho' not Presumptions broke;

OLDHAM, For Keen and Pointed *Satyr* fam'd,　⎫
Stuck every Worded Arrow that he aim'd,　　　⎬
And with an *honest Warmth*, he thus declaim'd.⎭
　False Figures, Warm with *Vicious* Energy,
Sink Authors *low*, to tug their Patrons *high*;
Yet *heavy* Brains, and a too *light* Repute,
When weigh'd together, never fail to do't;
Hyperboles thus Strain'd beyond their Force,
Make both, ill-aiming to be better, worse.
M———o's Blind side, each *Common-Soldier* knows,
Scorns the vile Praise, that from mean *Dulness* grows;(4)
If *Graceful* Flattery adorns the Lines,
Most sneaks the *Bard*, where most the *Patron* Shines.
Since thus this Wicked *Quack* empoisons Sense,
And wraps the Drug in Gilded Eloquence,
Perswades weak cred'lous Leaders of the Crowd,
T'adore and set up this their Popular God;
Whom, did they know, his Godship would be lost,
His *Statue* would be made his *Whipping-Post*;
Such a Mischievous Master in the Art,
Should, in Proportion to his Talent, Smart;
One that's at *Satyr* full as good, as he
Is at his *Panegyrick* Dawbery;
Should in a Travesty of Flat'ry rant,
And kill, with Harshness, the smooth Sycophant.
　E'en you, (5) LORD STEWARD, here had ne'er attain'd,
But Heaven, by lost *Paradise*, you *gain'd*;
And you, great DRYDEN, whose immortal Strains
Gave the Dead *Romans*, Emulating Pains,
Cromwell, that *Glorious Villain*, in thy Lines,
Like Kings, in their Triumphant Justice, Shines;
Here, for that Flat'ring Crime, thou ne'er hadst been,⎫
Hadn't *Applauded* DAVID brought thee in,　　　⎬
And his Superior Merit raz'd that Sin;　　　　⎭
Nor should we, *you*, admired WALLER, see,
If, like a Sea-green *Syren* Deity,
You hadn't Sung YORK's Conquest on the Sea,
In Sounds of more than human Symphony;
If CHARLES had not been more than once thy Choice,
And made thee Strain, t'outdo thy own best Voice,
Like thy great *first-sung* Champion, had'st thou fell,
Bold Urger of his Actions, into Hell.
Since *St———le* then Praises one, whose Horrid Soul
Shares more of the Black Fiend, than *now* does Noll;
I'll for each Praise, a Hearty Curse bestow,　⎫
On *him*, and his *Dark Angel* M——, (6)　　　⎬
Who *both* have *Inspirations* from *below*;　　⎭
May that *foul* Minister, be all his Life
Hated by *all*, and with *himself* at *Strife*;

May *St——le* of Drunken Vapours, void his Brains,
Till of the Cause, his Purse as void remains;
May *he* that Pen'd his Holiness his Fees,
Get none to feed his own Debaucheries;
Let his *keen* Stomach teaze his *blunted* Head,
To venture Nonsense out *in vain* for *Bread*;
Hadn't to that Fat Carcass, Heavenly Art,
St——le's meagre Soul Condemn'd too close to part;
I'd wish, O could that glorious Wish prevail!
His *Soul* to Bedlam, and his *Corps* to *Jail*.
Not at all this, did the Stanch Blockhead Blush,
Then MILTON rose, and spoke his *Sentence* thus;
　　Be St——le Confin'd, for three ensuing Years,
Among the lowest Herd of Pamphleteers;
Let him still mouth *at us, still miss his Aim,* ⎫
For Bread, yet more disgrace a Graceless *Name,* ⎬
And as he gets it, eat that Bread in Shame. ⎭
Be St——le with Ignominious Shame expell'd,
And by TH' EXAMINER *this Seat be Fill'd.* (7)
　　When the last Snatch of Light in rising Spires,
Shall lift his brighter Soul from Funeral Fires,
We'll all descend half way, our Friend *to meet,*
And then attend him to th'adjoyning Seat;
To him, my own I proudly would resign,
For he, as first in Merit, first should shine.
　　St——le and his *Writings* were together hurl'd,
Down into Famous *Grub-street's* Paper World;
Hence *Dunton, Ridpath,* who defend his Cause, (8)
Date the first Ruin of *Poetick Laws.*

Notes

1　'Sir John Suckling, was the most proper Man to pitch
　upon, as a *Summoner of the Muses* to the Bar, and it
　seems to be done in Allusion to that Poem of his,
　call'd "The Session of the Poets"' (Lacy).
2　Joseph Addison, Thomas Tickell, John Gay, Laurence
　Eusden, Eustace Budgell. 'There cannot, I think, be
　any thing more Just than to allow all the *Wits* of
　those *Papers* Mr. *St--le* Publish'd, to the Authors
　thereof; and the *Sedition* to him alone' (Lacy).
3　'This alludes to his *Tryal*, his *Speech* in Defence of
　himself, and his other *Papers* after his Expulsion from
　the *Hon. H.* of *C--ns*, and the Persons he fell upon, he
　treated in the same manner, as he is here Represented
　to treat these Poets, who are themselves not more
　Famous in the way of *Poesie*, than those are for
　Patriots and Statesmen, who agreed to the Shame and

Punishment, justly inflicted upon this wretched
Miscreant' (Lacy).
4   John Churchill (1650-1722), 1st Duke of Marlborough.
5   'All the *Old Poets* mentioned by *Oldham* were *Whigs*; but
they Repented, to a Man, of their Iniquities before
they died' (Lacy).
6   Charles Montagu (1661-1715), 1st Earl of Halifax.
7   The most important Tory periodical (3 August 1710 to
26 July 1714) during Queen Anne's last ministry.
8   George Ridpath's 'Flying Post' (1695-1731) was vigorously Whig; John Dunton's 'Athenian Gazette' (1691-7)
was far less political and Whiggish.

8.   BENJAMIN VICTOR, 'ON THE DEATH OF SIR RICHARD STEELE'

1729

From 'Original Letters, Dramatic Pieces, and Poems', 3
vols (1776), III, pp. 28-30.
    Benjamin Victor (d. 1778) began his career as a barber
'within the liberties of Drury Lane'. In 1722 he met Sir
Richard Steele through Aaron Hill. For his admiration of
'The Conscious Lovers', see No. 26.

On the DEATH of

Sir   R I C H A R D   S T E E L E,

In the YEAR 1729.
Inscribed to Sir ROBERT WALPOLE.
GREAT STEELE, my friend is dead, O, empty name
Of earthly bliss! 'tis all an airy dream!
Receive what tears to friendship's loss belong,
In the sad subject of a mournful song.
Friendship! thou tyranness, whose cruel throne,
Heaps on poor mortals sorrows not their own;
And yet who courts thee not?----who would be free?
Who can be said to live, unbless'd by thee?
To mourn this loss, let *gratitude* impart,
The honest feelings of a faithful heart:
Say, for my theme, what numbers shall I chuse?
Thou first instructor of my infant muse?

Lur'd by the music of thy charming song,
And taught by maxims from thy tuneful tongue.
When STEELE submitted to the pow'r of death,
No common mortal then resign'd his breath.
His charitable acts, profusely kind,
Declar'd the feelings of a humane mind:
There I have seen the various passions move;
Truth, goodness, honour, harmony and love!
At others woe, he sharpest pain has known,
And for another's want, forgot his own.
H——y, and all the inglorious rebel train,
Strove to corrupt his worth, but strove in vain; (1)
He was above their little arts of state;
And would not wound his peace, to mend his fate.
　　Worth, great like his, deserv'd the PATRIOTS
　　　　care!
(For blooming merit must be cherish'd there!)
WALPOLE, to you, he breath'd a lasting flame,
And died with blessings on your noble name:
By YOU distinguish'd, he adorn'd our land;
Honour'd with favours from your bounteous hand:
To YOU his daring LOYALTY was known,
How just and warm his zeal - how like your own! (2)

Notes

1 Robert Harley as Lord Treasurer in 1710-14.
2 Robert Walpole (1676-1745) helped to prepare Steele's
   defence before the Commons in March 1714. Both men
   were closely associated as dissident Whigs in 1717-19.
   For Walpole's plans to memorialize Steele in the autumn
   of 1729, see Mitchell, 'The Monument', No. 9.

9. JOSEPH MITCHELL, 'THE MONUMENT'

1729

Steele died in September 1729. Joseph Mitchell's poem
commemorates that fact. It is also a eulogy of Walpole
for his plan to erect a monument in Westminster Abbey to
Steele. (The plan came to nothing.)

THE

M O N U M E N T:

OR, THE
MUSE's MOTION.

CROWN'D with the Wreath of universal Praise,
In Peace and Honour, and with Length of Days,
The Bard, the Patriot, Soldier, and the Sage,
The Friend of Men, and Glory of our Age,
The peerless STEELE his Spirit hath resign'd,
And left in Tears a wretched World behind.
Yes, He too, subject to imperial Fate,
Is fal'n! Alas! how transient mortal State!
But are the *Muses* all, at once, struck dumb?
Yet unadorn'd remains the silent Tomb?
Is POPE confounded with uncommon Woe?
No more does YOUNG's high Inspiration flow?
Quite is the laurel'd EUSDEN'S Lyre unstrung?
And TICKELL'S Harp on rueful Willows hung? (1)
Ungenerous Tribe! ----- But let the Sons of Verse,
Whose studied *Elegiacs* would prove *Farce*,
Continue silent, as the gloomy Grave -----
WALPOLE, who lives but to support and save,
Alone, will better do the Hero Right,
And fix his Friend in everlasting Light.
    A Monument, becoming thy great Mind,
Wou'd pay, at once, the Vows of All Mankind.
And, while It kept alive his Worth and Fame,
Who wou'd not bless the kind Preserver's Name?
Honours to STEELE wou'd thy own Glory raise,
And grave on every grateful Heart thy Praise:
Faction and Malice Then wou'd turn thy Friends -----
Such Rev'rence on such Godlike Deeds attends!
    And sure, O STEELE, (if Souls from Flesh set free
Their Friends' last, pious, Offices can see)
Thou'dst look on This illustrious Instance, pleas'd;
And boast, among the Shades, that It was rais'd,
(In Honour of thy Merit, Mind, and Pen)
By th'ablest Judge and truest Friend of Men.
Well, to the dead, may WALPOLE stretch his Care,
Whose great Protection all the living share.
    But had'st thou liv'd in letter'd *Greece* of old,
Thy Statue had been form'd of massy Gold,
Thy Self among thy Country's Gods enroll'd!
Nor wou'd the Genius of the ancient *Rome*
Been satisfy'd to lodge Thee in a Tomb,
But, with the Honours due to Patriot Flame,

The Publick had immortaliz'd thy Name.
  Be hush, my Muse, and Providence revere -
STEELE was reserv'd to act the Hero Here,
In doubtful Days for Liberty to stand,
Maintain the *British* Rights, and Save the Land.
Like *Hercules*, to rid our Earth He rose
Of publick Monsters and domestic Foes,
By Reason's Force to vindicate the Law,
And make the Sons of Slavery stand in Awe;
Nor breath'd a Vice or Folly in the Crowd,
By his facetious Satyr unsubdu'd.
When, when again, *Britannia*, wilt thou boast
A Son more Godlike than our *Guardian* lost?
When shall we see so many Virtues met?
Such glorious Gems in one small Circle set?
  Shou'd (Heav'n avert it!) WALPOLE leave us too,
And his lov'd STEELE to Realms of Light pursue,
How soon, *Britannia*, wou'd thy Beauty fade?
What equal Hand wou'd hasten to thy Aid?
Long, very long, Ye Pow'rs, suspend his Fate;
On Him depends the Safety of the State.
While He, our *Atlas*, its vast Burden bears,
What need to fear the Falling of the Spheres?
  Life of thy Country, be it still thy Care;
Long let the Realm thy happy Influence share,
Ev'n in their own Despite make Mortals blest,
Live to conclude thy Schemes, of Schemes the Best!
Then, crown'd with Honour, late retire to Rest.
But, O! amid the Business of the State,
Still may the *Muses* own Thee good as great;
Ev'n to their Dust thy guardian Zeal extend,
And let STEELE'S Shade confess Thee still his Friend.
  Methinks, Already given is thy Command,
And artful GIBBS (2) applys the skilfull Hand!
What mimick Features does the Marble show?
With Life and Beauty how the Figures glow?
Breathes not that Image? seems it not to speak?
Does not this Busto give the 'Tatler' back?
By WALPOLE'S Bounty, BICKERSTAFF revives,
Refines our Language, and reforms our Lives!
Ages, unborn, the Blessing shall enjoy;
Nor, till the Volumes of the spacious Sky
Blaze in one Flame, shall one or t'other die!
  Thrice happy Poets by such Patrons grac'd,
And, after Death, in such Distinction plac'd!
Cou'd I but hope such Honours to obtain,
How eager I'd attempt a nobler Strain,
Make an Eternity of Fame my Strife,
And Spurn, at once, corroding Cares and Life.

But vain th'Ambition! ---- Then be This my Boast,
(So shall my Name be not entirely lost!)
'MITCHELL to WALPOLE first this Motion made,
And first to STEELE Poetic Honours paid.'

Notes

1 Edward Young, Laurence Eusden, and Thomas Tickell had
   all written elegies on the death of Addison. Pope is
   mentioned because of Allan Ramsay's pastoral elegy
   (1719) (No. 59) wherein the lament is sung by 'Richy
   and Sandy', i.e. Steele and Pope.
2 James Gibbes or Gibbs (1682-1754), architect and sculp-
   tor who in the 1720s designed several memorial monuments in the Abbey.

10. CORBYN MORRIS ON STEELE

1744

From the Dedication to Robert Earl of Orford in 'An Essay
towards Fixing the True Standards of Wit, Humour, Raillery, Satire, and Ridicule', pp. xvi-xviii.

THIS Method of tearing from the Senate the most resolute
Patriots, upon any Pretences, was a favorite Scheme with
that shameless Ministry; Your Expulsion was succeeded by
the same ungenerous Treatment of Mr. *Steele*; (1) a Gentleman endeared to the Nation by the Humanity and Politeness
of his Writings; and as generally esteemed, as known, for
the amiable Candour and Softness of his Manners. But when
he saw our Honour abroad abandoned, and our Liberties at
home devoted a Sacrifice, he scorned all Applause upon
lesser Subjects, and generously employed his Pen in Defence of his Country. When he viewed the *Protestant
Succession* at stake, he disdained all Fame for Pieces of
Elegance: And made it the Object of his Public Writings,
to inspire the Sentiments of Freedom, and to rouse the
Virtue of his Country --- THIS was his Crime in those Days
of Fury, and for *this* it was determined to exclude him
from the Senate - When he exposed the Injustice of his

Adversaries, he stood supported between Mr. *Walpole*, and General *Stanhope* (2) - Your Abilities were then honorably employed in his Defence, And if Reason had carried any Weight, or Eloquence Persuasion in that Day, you had saved *him* from the Injury, and his *Enemies* from the eternal Reproach, of his Exclusion.

Notes

1 On 21 December 1711, Walpole, as Secretary of War, was charged by the commissioners of public accounts with mishandling forage contracts for Scotland. He was found 'guilty of high breach of trust and notorious corruption', and on 17 January 1712 was expelled from the House and committed to the Tower. For the account of Steele's expulsion on 18 March 1714, see 'The Case of Richard Steele, Esq;' (No. 6).
2 Supported by Walpole, General Stanhope, and Addison, Steele spoke for three hours in his defence but was judged guilty by what he later called 'the insolent and unmanly sanction of a majority'.

11. LETTERS, CONVERSATIONS, AND RECOLLECTIONS OF
S. T. COLERIDGE

1836

From I, pp. 178-91. The 'I' is Thomas Allsop (1795-1880), who first came to know Coleridge in 1818. After the poet's death Allsop edited and published their exchange of letters, along with conversations and recollections, in 1836. Coleridge once wrote of Allsop, 'Were you my son by nature, I could not hold you dearer.'

It was about this time that I met with an odd volume of the 'Tatler', during a forced stay at a remote and obscure inn in the wilds of Kinder Scout.
    The book opened at a paper (one of Steele's), giving an account of the writer's meeting with an old friend, recalling to his memory their early intimacy, and the services he had rendered him in his courtship, the

delightful pictures which he calls up of the youthful,
animated, and happy lovers, which, with a felicity peculiar to Steele, such was the fineness, the pure gold of
his nature, he associates, rather than contrasts, with
the quiet happiness, the full content and the still devotion (the heart-love), which makes an *Elysium of a home* in
other respects only *home*-ly.

This picture yet I think one of the most pure and most
delightful of that age, for it belongs in its manners and
some of its accessories to the past century, I mentioned
to Coleridge on my return, and had, as I expected, my
pleasure repeated, deepened, and extended. It was a joy
and ever new delight to listen to him on any congenial
theme, on one congenial to *you* as well as to *him*. I was
especially pleased to find that he valued Steele, always
my prime favourite, so much above Addison and the other
essayists of that day; he denied that Steele was, as he
himself said in a pleasantry, 'like a distressed prince
who calls in a powerful neighbour to his aid, and who,
once in possession, became sovereign!' Addison was
necessary to give variety to the papers, but in no other
sense did he give value. Steele's papers are easily
distinguished to this day by their pure humanity springing from the gentleness, the *kindness* of his heart. He
dwelt with much *unction* on the curious and instructive
letters of Steele to his wife; and with much approval
on the manliness with which, in the first letters, he
addressed the lady to whom he was afterwards united....

II Steele the Pamphleteer

12. DANIEL DEFOE, 'THE HONOUR AND PREROGATIVE OF THE
QUEEN'S MAJESTY VINDICATED'

1713

Defoe's pamphlet, sometimes attributed to Mrs Manley,
was published on 13 August in reply to the 'Guardian' of
7 August. Since Steele wrote as 'English Tory', Defoe
(now in Harley's employ) donned the mask of 'Country
Whig'.

...We [in the Country] have Whig and Tory among us as you
have, only I think, if there is any Difference, we are
blessed with a little more Temper here than you are at
London in our Party-Disputes, and we do not let our
Debates of these Matters break into our Conversation,
much less into our Charity and Friendly Neighbourly
Behaviour one to another, as we hear it does among you
at London.

In this mannerly sociable way of Conversing one with
another, we have been very much beholding to your diverting Paper; for frequently, when any two or more of our
Neighbours began to be warm in their settling the State,
and the rest of us have apprehended that it might go too
far; you have been our Cure for those Excursions, and the
rest would cry, Come have done with these Things, adjourn
your Debate till you have more Temper, Come, let us read
the 'Guardian': (1) Then the Musick of your Tongue like
David's Harp has allay'd the Storm, the Sea of Words would
grow Calm, and the Evil Spirit of Contention went out from
among us.
75

Nor, Sir, was it any hindrance to our Edification, that
we knew very well,
1. That the greatest part of the Wit and Humour we find
in your Paper was not your own. (2)   Or,
2. That you were not always an Exemplification of the
Morals you recommended.

We have had Charity enough to hide the Infirmities of
our Instructors, and to take the Benefit of what was
bright, without Searching too far into the Dark side of
him that spoke it.

Thus, Sir, while you preserv'd the Neutrality of your
Paper, and wisely avoiding to engage in the Party-strife
of the Age applyed your self to be both profitable and
pleasant to all sides; every Body valu'd and lov'd you,
and you were made useful, both to the Delight and Instruction of those that read your Papers.

I freely own, I often read you with Pleasure, for we
that were Whigs, as we knew you are also a Whig, valu'd
our selves upon finding the Tories submitting to the Charm
of your Pen, and giving an Authority to what you said,
even because you said it.

But when your 'Guardian' of the 7th of *August* came down
among us, it is impossible to express to you the Confusion
it put us all in, as well Whig, as Tory. (3)

We Whigs were more especially Agitated with the two
tormenting Passions of Shame and Grief, in your behalf.
The Tories, who as I hinted above, were till now Men of
Temper, and mastering themselves by good *Manners* and
Neighbourly Behaviour, would sometimes suffer you to be
Moderator among them; now flew out into a just Rage, and
upbraided us all with what, till now, we had kept them
off from (*viz.*) That it was the Principle of the Whigs
to Insult the Government.

We that are Whigs here in the Country having been
strangers to such things as these, began to question with
our selves, whether we were right Whigs or no. It was
always our Principle, that we had a right to our Constitution. That the just Execution of the Laws was our Property. That to Invade or Dispence with them by Arbitrary
Power was an Act of Tyranny, and might be legally opposed.
We believ'd the Parliamentary Limitation of the Crown,
lawful and just, and that the *Illustrious House* of *Hanover*
are rightfully and legally Heirs *in Tail* of the Imperial
Crown of these Kingdoms, and that by Vertue of this Parliamentary Limitation, the Queen whose Right is also
Hereditary is our only rightful, lawful and undoubted
Sovereign.

Yet it was always our *Practise* as *Whigs*, and we
believ'd it out Duty as *Englishmen* to submit to Her

Majesty's just Government, to recognize Her Authority, and
to pay the utmost Duty and Regard to Her Person. And however we may not have been of those who have the most
approv'd the Measures of the present Managers, or been
glad of the Removal of the last; yet we never thought it
our Business to assault the Ministry, *who act*, in the
publick Administration, much less to attack the Queen's
Person with Indecencies and undutiful Behaviour of any
kind: Submitting to the Government which we live under,
we pray'd for better Times; that God who guides the World
would direct Her Majesty to such Measures as should Issue
in the Good of Her People, the Safety of Religion, and his
own Glory: And tho' we were none of the Forwardest for a
Peace, things standing as we were told in such a Posture,
that a War might have been more to the general Advantage;
yet as Her Majesty thought otherwise, Peace is always
desirable to trading Nations; and trusting in Her
Majesty's Wisdom and Her Care for the good of Her People;
We, tho' *Whigs*, acquiesced in the Peace, always allowing
the Queen had an undoubted Right by the Constitution to
make Peace and War without being accountable for the
Conditions. (4)

The Tories indeed used to upbraid us with being Turbulent, Uneasy under Government, of Commonwealth-Principles,
Lovers of Faction, and I know not what; but our Behaviour
testifying for us, that we liv'd agreeable to the above-
said Principles; we always justified those Principles by
our Practise, and they began to entertain differing
Notions of us, by the Moderation and Temper which they
found we behav'd with; insomuch that many of those who
were call'd Tories became moderate on their side also,
acknowledging that they were no Enemies to Liberty if
rightly stated; that in a due Medium between the Prerogative of the Crown and the Property of the Subject consisted the true Felicity of Government, and that the due
Execution of the Laws was the only Safety of all our
Estates.

Thus Moderation in Principles acting both sides, our
Differences lessen'd every Day, and Charity began to take
place; though we have many Tories, yet we have no Jacobites
among us; and we differ'd with less Heat than we find you
do at *London* by a great deal. Nor, Sir, could all the
Party-writers of the Town enflame us, but we began to look
upon them with the just Contempt which Incendiaries
deserve.

It is you alone that have spoil'd all this Harmony;
you alone, Sir, was able to do it; you that had obtain'd
the good Opinion of both sides, you that were, *as above*,
our constant Moderator, you who our affected Wits and

Polititians stood in awe of, and who we that are Whigs
boasted of; you alone have blown up all our Society, made
your Friends asham'd of you, made the moderate Men hate
you, and the warmer Tories triumph over us in your Infir-
mity. Now they upbraid us with the 'Guardian'; they tell
us 'tis in the Nature of a Whig to be ungrateful, to
insult their Sovereign, to fly in the Face of Government,
and to trample upon the Prerogative of the Crown. Then
they shew us the dreadful Paper you have writ. Here, *say
they*, read your Oracle, your 'Guardian', your Favourite!
see how the Villain treats the best of Sovereigns, the
best Mistress to him, whose Bread he has eaten, and who
has kept him from a Goal! Read it again, say they: Put
it into *English*, said a Neighbour mine to me, come make
the best of it! then he reads the abominable Language as
follows;

'The *British* Nation EXPECT, &c. And again, The *British*
Nation EXPECT the immediate Demolition of *Dunkirk*. And a
third time, with a Tone of threatning, The *British* Nation
EXPECT it.' *See the* 'Guardian', August 7, 1713. (5)

I would fain have pleaded for you, that this was not
to be understood to be spoken to or pointed at the Queen,
but to the People of *Dunkirk*, and I search'd the whole
Paper for something to have brought you off with that way.
But it would not do, they laugh'd at me....

I hope, Mr. *Steele*, by that time you have read thus
far, you will be convinced and own your self in the
Wrong; that you will make *L'amend Honorable*, as far as
you are capable to do it, and humbly fly to Her Majesty's
Clemency for Pardon: But how you can expect it should be
granted, that you know best.

In the mean time you have done an irreparable Injury
to us your Friends; and as to your own Reputation I see no
Remedy or Recovery for that, but in your Repentance.

Indeed I have entertain'd some hopes of you, and have
spoken it in your Favour from that known part of your
Character, (*viz.*) that your Practice is just the reverse
of your Instructions to others; which Character, tho' it
may lose you something in the Article of your Morals, will
make you full amends in that of your Loyalty to your
Prince, and especially of your Gratitude to your Royal
Benefactress.

You have indeed another Plea, how far it may stand you
in stead I cannot judge at this Distance, *viz.* That you
are not the Author of the 'Guardian' only, the hand con-
veying it to the Town, like the Voratious Beast at
Button's, who hands things to you as the old Priests of
Diana did to the Oracle, and by whom again the Devil
answer'd, and deluded the World.

This we always knew, and could easily distinguish by
the Dulness, when Mr. *Steele* spoke in his own Language,
and when another Man's. Now this will excuse you very
much, when you are charg'd with any thing which has too
much Wit to be your own Performance: But in Villainy and
Treason this will not do, since in putting off base Money,
the Coiner indeed is the Original Offender; but the Payer
of it for good Silver is the Criminal, who the Law takes
hold of, and will punish, unless he deliver himself, by
proving who he had it from.

Good Mr. *Steele*, be so just to your Country, as to let
the honest People of *Stockbridge* know who the Gentleman
they are desired to Chuse to Represent them in Parliament
is, and how he has Treated the Queen their Sovereign in
Print; and tho' I know your Election is necessary to you,
to Protect you from your just Debts, which you are or
might be able enough to pay; yet in generous Justice to
your Country, which you have shewn great Inclination to
serve in other Cases, you can do no less than let them
know how the Case stands, and if they will Chuse you
afterwards, none can be blamed but themselves....

Notes

1 The 'Guardian' was begun on 12 March 1713.
2 Addison's involvement in the 'Tatler' and the 'Spectator' was often used by the Tories against Steele.
3 'Guardian' 128 called for the demolition of the port
   facilities and the fortifications of Dunkirk, as sti-
   pulated by the Treaty of Utrecht. See 'The Character
   of Richard Steele, Esq;' (No. 3), n. 11.
4 The War of the Spanish Succession was begun in 1701.
   By 1713 France, England, and Holland signed the Peace
   of Utrecht. (Only Charles VI fought on for another
   year, consenting in 1714 to the treaties of Rastatt
   and of Baden and so ending the war in Europe.)
5 With this statement in mind, Addison laughed at Tory
   writers who found out Treason in the word Expect'
   ('Guardian' 160).

13.   JONATHAN SWIFT, 'THE IMPORTANCE OF THE GUARDIAN
CONSIDERED'

1713

Appearing on 2 November, Swift's pamphlet is an ironical
non-answer to Steele's 'Guardian' 128 and 'The Importance
of Dunkirk Consider'd.'

The PREFACE

MR. Steele *in his Letter to the Bailiff of* Stockbridge
has given us leave to treat him as we think fit, as he is
our Brother-Scribler; but not to attack him as an honest
Man. *That is to say, he allows us to be his* Criticks,
but not his Answerers; *and he is altogether in the right,
for there is in his Letter much to be* Criticised, *and
little to be* Answered. *The Situation and Importance of*
Dunkirk *are pretty well known,* Monsieur Tugghe's *Memorial,
published and handed about by the Whigs, is allowed to be
a very Trifling Paper: And as to the immediate Demolish-
ment of that Town, Mr.* Steele *pretends to offer no other
Argument but the* Expectations *of the People, which is a
figurative Speech, naming the tenth Part for the whole:
As* Bradshaw *told King* Charles I. *that the People of*
England Expected *Justice against him.   I have therefore
entred very little into the Subject he pretends to Treat,
but have considered his pamphlet partly as a* Critick, *and
partly as a* Commentator, *which, I think, is to treat him
only as my Brother-Scribler, according to the Permission
he has graciously allowed me.*

To the Worshipful Mr. *JOHN SNOW.* Bailiff of *Stockbridge.*

SIR,
I have just been reading a Twelve-peny Pamphlet about
Dunkirk, addressed to your Worship from one of your
intended Representatives; and I find several Passages in
it which want Explanation, especially to You in the Country: For we in Town have a way of Talking and Writing,
which is very little understood beyond the Bills of Mortality.   I have therefore made bold to send you here a
second Letter, by way of Comment upon the former.
    In order to this, *You Mr.* Bailiff, *and at the same
time the whole Burrough,* may please to take Notice, that

London-Writers often put Titles to their Papers and Pamphlets which have little or no Reference to the main
Design of the Work: So, for Instance, you will observe in
reading, that the Letter called, *The Importance of Dunkirk*,
is chiefly taken up in shewing you the *Importance* of Mr.
Steele; wherein it was indeed reasonable your Burrough
should be informed, which had chosen him to Represent them.
    I would therefore place the *Importance* of this Gentle-
man before you in a clearer Light than he has given himself the Trouble to do; without running into his early
History, because I owe him no Malice.
    Mr. *Steele* is Author of two tolerable Plays, (or at
least of the greatest part of them) (1) which, added to
the Company he kept, and to the continual Conversation and
Friendship of Mr. *Addison*, hath given him the Character of
a Wit. To take the height of his Learning, you are to
suppose a Lad just fit for the University, and sent early
from thence into the wide World, where he followed every
way of Life that might least improve or preserve the Rudiments he had got. He hath no Invention, nor is Master of
a tolerable Style; his chief Talent is Humour, which he
sometimes discovers both in Writing and Discourse; for
after the first Bottle he is no disagreeable Companion.
I never knew him taxed with Ill-nature, which hath made me
wonder how Ingratitude came to be his prevailing Vice; (2)
and I am apt to think it proceeds more from some unaccountable sort of Instinct, than Premeditation. Being the
most imprudent Man alive, he never follows the Advice of
his Friends, but is wholly at the mercy of Fools or
Knaves, or hurried away by his own Caprice; by which he
hath committed more Absurdities in Oeconomy, Friendship,
Love, Duty, good Manners, Politicks, Religion and Writing,
than ever fell to one Man's share. He was appointed
Gazetteer by Mr. *Harley* (3) (then Secretary of State) at
the Recommendation of Mr. *Mainwaring*, with a Salary of
Three Hundred Pounds; was a Commissioner of Stampt-Paper
of equal Profit, and had a Pension of a Hundred Pound *per
Annum*, as a Servant to the late Prince *George*.
    This Gentleman, whom I have now described to you, began
between four and five Years ago to publish a Paper thrice
a Week, called the 'Tatler'; It came out under the
borrowed Name of *Isaac Bickerstaff*, and by Contribution of
his ingenious Friends, grew to have a great Reputation,
and was equally esteemed by both Parties, because it
meddled with neither. But, sometime after *Sacheverell*'s
Tryal, when Things began to change their Aspect; (4) Mr.
Steele, whether by the Command of his Superiors, his own
Inconstancy, or the Absence of his Assistants, would needs
corrupt his Paper with Politicks; published one or two

most virulent Libels, and chose for his Subject even that
individual Mr. *Harley*, who had made him Gazetteer. But
his Finger and Thumb not proving strong enough to stop the
general Torrent, there was an universal Change made in the
Ministry; (5) and the Two new Secretaries, not thinking it
decent to employ a Man in their Office who had acted so
infamous a Part; Mr. *Steele*, to avoid being discarded,
thought fit to resign his Place of Gazetteer. Upon which
occasion I cannot forbear relating a Passage *to you Mr.
Bailiff, and the rest of the Burrough*, which discovers a
very peculiar Turn of Thought in this Gentleman you have
chosen to Represent you. When Mr. *Mainwaring* recommended
him to the Employment of Gazetteer, (6) Mr. *Harley* out of
an Inclination to encourage Men of Parts, raised that
Office from Fifty Pound to Three Hundred Pound a Year;
Mr. *Steele* according to form, came to give his new Patron
Thanks; but the Secretary, who had rather confer a hundred
Favours than receive Acknowledgments for one, said to him
in a most obliging manner: Pray Sir, do not thank me, but
thank Mr. *Mainwaring*. Soon after Mr. *Steele's* quitting
that Employment, he complained to a Gentleman in Office,
of the Hardship put upon him in being forced to quit his
Place; that he knew Mr. *Harley* was the Cause; that he
never had done Mr. *Harley* any Injury, nor received any
Obligation from him. The Gentleman amazed at this Discourse, put him in mind of those Libels published in his
'Tatlers': Mr. *Steele* said, he was only the Publisher,
for they had been sent him by other Hands. The Gentleman
thinking this a very monstrous kind of Excuse, and not
allowing it, Mr. *Steele* then said, Well, I have Libelled
him, and he has turned me out, and so we are equal. But
neither would this be granted: And he was asked whether
the Place of Gazetteer were not an Obligation? No, said
he, not from Mr. *Harley*; for when I went to thank him, he
forbad me, and said, I must only thank Mr. *Mainwaring*.

But I return, Mr. Bailiff, to give you a further Account of this Gentleman's Importance. In less, I think,
than Two Years, the Town and He grew weary of the 'Tatler':
He was silent for some Months; and then a daily Paper came
from him and his Friends under the Name of 'Spectator',
with good Success: This being likewise dropt after a certain Period, he hath of late appeared under the Style of
'Guardian', which he hath now likewise quitted for that of
'Englishman', but having chosen other Assistance, or
trusting more to himself, his Papers have been very coldly
received, which hath made him fly for Relief to the never-
failing Source of Faction.

On the ..... of *August* last, Mr. *Steele* writes a Letter
to *Nestor Ironside*, Esq; and subscribes it with the Name

of *English Tory*. On the 7th the said *Ironside* publishes
this Letter in the 'Guardian'. How shall I explain this
Matter to you, Mr. *Bailiff*, and your Brethren of the
Burrough? You must know then, that Mr. *Steele* and Mr.
Ironside are the same Persons, because there is a great
Relation between *Iron* and *Steel*; and *English Tory* and Mr.
Steele are the same Persons, because there is no Relation
at all between Mr. *Steele* and an *English Tory*; so that to
render this Matter clear to the very meanest Capacities,
Mr. *English Tory*, the very same Person with Mr. *Steele*,
writes a Letter to *Nestor Ironside*, Esq; who is the same
Person with *English Tory*, who is the same Person with Mr.
Steele: And Mr. *Ironside*, who is the same Person with
English Tory, publishes the Letter written by *English
Tory*, who is the same Person with Mr. *Steele*, who is the
same Person with Mr. *Ironside*. This Letter written and
published by these *Three* Gentlemen who are *One* of your
Representatives, complains of a printed Paper in *French*
and *English*, lately handed about the Town, and given
gratis to Passengers in the Streets at Noon-day; the Title
whereof is, *A most humble Address or Memorial presented to
Her Majesty the Queen of* Great Britain, *by the Deputy of
the Magistrates of* Dunkirk. This Deputy, it seems, is
called the Sieur *Tugghe*. Now, the Remarks made upon this
Memorial by Mr. *English Tory*, in his Letter to Mr. *Ironside*, happening to provoke the 'Examiner', and another
Pamphleteer, they both fell hard upon Mr. *Steele*, charging
him with Insolence and Ingratitude towards the Queen. But
Mr. *Steele* nothing daunted, writes a long Letter *to you
Mr. Bailiff, and at the same time to the whole Burrough*,
in his own Vindication: But there being several difficult
Passages in this Letter, which may want clearing up, I
here send you and the Burrough my Annotations upon it.

Mr. *Steele* in order to display his *Importance* to your
Burrough, begins his Letter by letting you know *he is no
small Man*; because in the Pamphlets he hath sent you down,
you will *find him spoken of more than once in Print*. It
is indeed a great Thing to be *spoken of in Print*, and must
needs make a mighty Sound at *Stockbridge* among the Electors. However, if Mr. *Steele* has really sent you down all
the Pamphlets and Papers printed since the Dissolution,
you will find he is not the only Person of Importance; I
could Instance *Abel Roper*, Mr. *Marten* the Surgeon, Mr.
John Moor the Apothecary at the Pestle and Mortar, Sir
William Read, Her Majesty's Oculist, and of later Name
and Fame, Mr. *John Smith* the Corncutter, with several
others who are *spoken of more than once in Print*. Then he
recommends to your Perusal, and sends you a Copy of a
printed Paper given *gratis* about the Streets, which is the

Memorial of Monsieur *Tugghe* (above-mentioned) *Deputy of the Magistrates of Dunkirk*, to desire Her Majesty not to demolish the said Town. He tells you how insolent a Thing it is, that such a Paper should be publickly distributed, and he tells you true; but these Insolences are very frequent among the Whigs: One of their present Topicks for Clamour is *Dunkirk*: Here is a Memorial said to be presented to the Queen by an obscure *Frenchman*: One of your Party gets a Copy, and immediately Prints it by Contribution, and delivers it *gratis* to the People; which answers several Ends. *First*, It is meant to lay an Odium on the Ministry; *Secondly*, If the Town be soon demolished, Mr. *Steele* and his Faction have the Merit, their Arguments and Threatnings have frighted my Lord Treasurer'. *Thirdly*, If the Demolishing should be further deferred, the Nation will be fully convinced of his Lordship's Intention to bring over the *Pretender*.

Let us turn over fourteen Pages, which contain the Memorial itself, and which is indeed as idle a one as ever I read; we come now to Mr. *Steele*'s Letter under the Name of *English Tory*, to Mr. *Ironside*. In the Preface to this Letter, he hath these Words, *It is certain there is not much danger in delaying the Demolition of* Dunkirk *during the Life of his present most Christian Majesty, who is renowned for the most inviolable Regard to Treaties; but that pious Prince is Aged, and in case of his Decease,* &c. This Preface is in the Words of Mr. *Ironside* a professed Whig, and perhaps you in the Country will wonder to hear a Zealot of your own Party celebrating the *French* King for his Piety and his religious Performance of Treaties. For this I can assure you is not spoken in jest, or to be understood by contrary; There is a wonderful resemblance between that Prince and the Party of Whigs among us. Is he for arbitrary Government? So are they: Hath he persecuted Protestants? So have the Whigs: Did he attempt to restore King *James* and his pretended Son? They did the same. Would he have *Dunkirk* surrendred to him? That is what they desire. Does he call himself the *Most Christian*? The Whigs assume the same Title, though their Leaders deny Christianity: Does he break his Promises? Did they ever keep theirs?

From the 16th to the 38th Page Mr. *Steele*'s Pamphlet is taken up with a Copy of his Letter to Mr. *Ironside,* the Remarks of the 'Examiner', and another Author upon that Letter; the Hydrography of some *French* and *English* Ports, and his Answer to Mr. *Tugghe*'s Memorial. The Bent of his Discourse is in appearance to shew of what prodigious Consequence to the Welfare of *England*, the Surrendry of *Dunkirk* was. But here, Mr. Bailiff, you must be careful;

for all this is said in Raillery; for you may easily remember, that when the Town was first yielded to the Queen,
the Whigs declared it was of no Consequence at all, that
the *French* could easily repair it after the Demolition,
or fortify another a few Miles off, which would be of more
Advantage to them. So that what Mr. *Steele* tells you of
the prodigious Benefit that will accrue to *England* by destroying this Port, is only suited to present Junctures
and Circumstances. For if *Dunkirk* should now be represented as insignificant as when it was first put into Her
Majesty's Hands, it would signify nothing whether it were
demolished or no, and consequently one principal Topick of
Clamour would fall to the Ground.

In Mr. *Steele*'s Answer to Monsieur *Tugghe*'s Arguments
against the Demolishing of *Dunkirk*, I have not observed
any thing that so much deserves your peculiar Notice, as
the great Eloquence of your new Member, and his wonderful
Faculty of varying his Style, which he calls, *proceeding*
like a Man of great Gravity and Business. He has Ten
Arguments of *Tugghe*'s to answer; and because he will not
go in the old beaten Road, like a Parson of a Parish,
First, Secondly, Thirdly, &c. his manner is this,

In answer to the Sieur's *First*.
As to the Sieur's *Second*.
As to his *Third*.
As to the Sieur's *Fourth*.
As to Mr. Deputy's *Fifth*.
As to the Sieur's *Sixth*.
As to this Agent's *Seventh*.
As to the Sieur's *Eighth*.
As to his *Ninth*.
As to the Memorialist's *Tenth*.

You see every Second Expression is more or less diver-
sified to avoid the Repetition of, *As to the Sieur's*, &c.
and there is the Tenth into the Bargain: I could heartily
wish Monsieur *Tugghe* had been able to find Ten Arguments
more, and thereby given Mr. *Steele* an Opportunity of shewing the utmost Variations our Language would bear in so
momentous a Tryal.

Mr. *Steele* tells you, That having now done *with his*
foreign Enemy Monsieur Tugghe, *he must face about to his*
Domestick Foes, who accuse him of Ingratitude and insult-
ing his Prince, while he is eating her Bread.

To do him Justice, he acquits himself pretty tolerably
of this last Charge: For he assures You, he gave up his
Stampt-Paper-Office, and Pension as Gentleman-Usher,
before he writ that Letter to himself in the 'Guardian',

so that he had already received his Salary, and spent the
Money, and consequently the *Bread was eaten* at least a
Week before he would offer to *insult his Prince:* So that
the Folly of the 'Examiner's' objecting Ingratitude to him
upon this Article, is manifest to all the World. (7)

But he tells you, he has quitted those Employments to
render him more useful to his Queen and Country in the
Station you have honoured him with. That, no doubt, was
the principal Motive; however, I shall venture to add some
others. *First*, The 'Guardian' apprehended it impossible,
that the Ministry would let him keep his Place much
longer, after the Part he had acted for above two Years
past. *Secondly*, Mr. *Ironside* said publickly, that he was
ashamed to be obliged any longer to a Person (meaning Lord
Treasurer) whom he had used so ill: For it seems, a Man
ought not to use his Benefactors ill above two Years and
a half. *Thirdly*, the *Sieur Steele* appeals for Protection
to you, Mr. Bailiff, from *others* of your *Denomination*, who
would have carried him *some where else*, if you had not
removed him by your *Habeas Corpus* to St. *Stephen*'s Chapel.
Fourthly, Mr. *English Tory* found, by calculating the Life
of a Ministry, that it hath lasted above three Years, and
is near expiring; he resolved therefore to *strip off the
very Garments spotted with the Flesh*, and be wholly re-
generate against the Return of his old Masters.

In order to serve all these Ends, your Burrough hath
honoured him (as he expresses it) with chusing him to
represent you in Parliament, and it must be owned, he hath
equally honoured you. Never was Burrough more happy in
suitable Representatives, than you are in Mr. *Steele* and
his Collegue, nor were ever Representatives more happy in
a suitable Burrough.

When Mr. *Steele* talk'd of *laying before Her Majesty's
Ministry, that the Nation has a strict Eye upon their
Behaviour with relation to* Dunkirk, Did not you, Mr.
Bailiff, and your Brethren of the Burrough presently
imagine, he had drawn up a sort of Counter-Memorial to
that of Monsieur *Tugghe*'s, and presented it in form to
my Lord *Treasurer*, or a Secretary of State? I am confident you did; but this comes by not understanding the
Town: You are to know then, that Mr. *Steele* publishes
every Day a Peny-paper to be read in Coffee-houses, and
get him a little Money. This by a Figure of Speech, he
calls, *laying Things before the Ministry*, who seem at
present a little too busy to regard such Memorials; and,
I dare say, never saw his Paper, unless he sent it them
by the Peny-Post. (8)

Well, but he tells you, he *cannot offer against the*
'Examiner' *and his other Adversary, Reason and Argument*

without appearing void of both. What a singular Situation
of the Mind is this! How glad should I be to hear a Man
*offer Reasons and Argument, and yet at the same time
appear void of both*! But this whole Paragraph is of a
peculiar strain; the Consequences so Just and Natural, and
such a Propriety in Thinking, as few Authors ever arrived
to. *Since it has been the Fashion to run down Men of much
greater Consequence than I am; I will not bear the Accusation.* This I suppose is, *to offer Reasons and Arguments,
and yet appear void of both.* And in the next Lines; *These
Writers shall treat me as they think fit, as I am their
Brother-Scribler, but I shall not be so unconcerned when
they attack me as an honest Man.* And how does he defend
himself? *I shall therefore inform them that it is not in
the Power of a private Man, to hurt the Prerogative,* &c.
Well; I shall treat him *only as a Brother-Scribler:* And I
guess he will hardly be attacked as an honest Man: But if
his meaning be that his Honesty ought not to be attacked,
because he *has no Power to hurt the Honour and Prerogative
of the Crown without being punished*; he will make an
admirable Reasoner in the House of Commons.

But all this wise Argumentation was introduced, only to
close the Paragraph by haling in a Fact, which he relates
to you and your Burrough, in order to quiet the Minds of
the People, and express his Duty and Gratitude to the
Queen. The Fact is this; That *Her Majesty's Honour is in
danger* of being lost *by Her Ministers tolerating Villains
without Conscience to abuse the greatest Instruments of
Honour and Glory to our Country, the most Wise and Faithful Managers, and the most Pious, disinterested, generous,
and self-denying Patriots;* And the Instances he produces,
are the Duke of *Marlborough*, the late Earl of *Godolphin*,
and about two Thirds of the Bishops.

Mr. Bailiff, I cannot debate this Matter at length,
without putting you and the rest of my Countrymen, who
will be at the Expence, to Six-pence Charge extraordinary.
The Duke and Earl were both removed from their Employments; and I hope you have too great a Respect for the
Queen, to think it was done for nothing. The former was
at the Head of many great Actions; and he has received
plentiful Oblations of Praise and Profit: Yet having read
all that ever was objected against him by the 'Examiner',
I will undertake to prove every Syllable of it true, particularly that famous Attempt to be General for Life. The
Earl of *Godolphin* is dead, and his Faults may sojourn with
him in the Grave, 'till some Historian shall think fit to
revive part of them for Instruction and Warning to Posterity. But it grieved me to the Soul, to see so many
good Epithets bestowed by Mr. *Steele* upon the Bishops:

Nothing has done more hurt to that Sacred Order for some
Years past, than to hear some Prelates extolled by Whigs,
Dissenters, Republicans, Socinians, and in short by all
who are Enemies to Episcopacy. God, in his Mercy, for
ever keep our Prelates from deserving the Praises of such
Panegyrists!

Mr. *Steele* is discontented that the Ministry have not
called the 'Examiner' *to Account as well as the* 'Flying-
Post'. (9) I will inform you, Mr. Bailiff, how that
Matter stands. The Author of the 'Flying-Post' has thrice
a Week for above Two Years together, published the most
impudent Reflections upon all the present Ministry, upon
all their Proceedings, and upon the whole Body of *Tories*.
The 'Examiner' on the other side, writing in Defence of
those whom Her Majesty employs in her greatest Affairs,
and of the Cause they are engaged in, hath always borne
hard upon the Whigs, and now and then upon some of their
Leaders. Now, Sir, we reckon here, that supposing the
Persons on both Sides to be of equal Intrinsick Worth, it
is more Impudent, Immoral, and Criminal to reflect on a
Majority in Power, than a *Minority* out of Power. Put the
Case, that an odd Rascally Tory in your Borough should
presume to abuse your Worship who, in the Language of Mr.
Steele, is first Minister, and the Majority of your Brethren, for sending Two such Whig-Representatives up to
Parliament: And on the other side, that an honest Whig
should stand in your Defence, and fall foul on the Tories;
would you equally resent the Proceedings of both, and let
your Friend and Enemy sit in the Stocks together? Hearken
to another Case, Mr. Bailiff; suppose your Worship, during
your Annual Administration, should happen to be kick'd and
cuff'd by a parcel of Tories, would not the Circumstance
of your being a Magistrate, make the Crime the greater,
than if the like Insults were committed on an ordinary
Tory Shopkeeper, by a Company of honest Whigs? What
Bailiff would venture to Arrest Mr. *Steele*, now he has the
Honour to be your Representative? and what Bailiff ever
scrupled it before?

You must know, Sir, that we have several Ways here of
abusing one another, without incurring the Danger of the
Law. First, we are careful never to print a Man's Name
out at length; but as I do that of Mr. *Steele*. So that
although every Body alive knows whom I mean, the Plain-
tiff can have no Redress in any Court of Justice.
Secondly, by putting Cases; Thirdly, by Insinuations;
Fourthly, by celebrating the Actions of others, who acted
directly contrary to the Persons we would reflect on;
Fifthly, by Nicknames, either commonly known or stamp'd
for the purpose, which every Body can tell how to apply.

Without going on further, it will be enough to inform
you, that by some of the ways I have already mentioned,
Mr. *Steele* gives you to understand, that the Queen's
Honour is blasted by the Actions of Her present Ministers;
that *Her Prerogative is disgraced by erecting a dozen
Peers, who, by their Votes, turned a Point upon which
Your All depended;* (10) That *these Ministers made the
Queen lay down Her conquering Arms, and deliver Her Self
up to be vanquish'd; That they made Her Majesty betray
Her Allies, by ordering Her Army to face about, and leave
them in the Moment of Distress; That the present Ministers
are Men of poor and narrow Conceptions, Self-Interested,
and without Benevolence to Mankind; and were brought into
Her Majesty's Favour for the Sins of the Nation, and only
think what they may do, not what they ought to do.*
This is the Character given by Mr. *Steele* of those Persons, whom Her Majesty has thought fit to place in the
highest Stations of the Kingdom, and to trust them with
the Management of Her most weighty Affairs: And this is
the Gentleman who cries out, *Where is Honour? Where is
Government? Where is Prerogative?* Because the 'Examiner'
has sometimes dealt freely with those, whom the Queen has
thought fit to *Discard*, and the Parliament to *Censure*.
  But Mr. *Steele* thinks it highly dangerous to the
Prince, *that any Man should be hindered from offering
Thoughts upon public Affairs*; and resolves to do it, *tho'
with the Loss of Her Majesty's Favour*. If a Clergy-man
offers to preach Obedience to the higher Powers, and
proves it by Scripture, Mr. *Steele* and his Fraternity
immediately cry out, What have Parsons to do with Politicks? (11) I ask, What shadow of a Pretence has he to
offer his crude Thoughts in Matters of State? to Print
and Publish them? *to lay them before the Queen and
Ministry?* and to reprove Both for Male-Administration?
How did he acquire these Abilities of directing in the
Councils of Princes? Was it from Publishing 'Tatlers'
and 'Spectators', and Writing now and then a 'Guardian'?
Was it from his being a Soldier, Alchymist, Gazetteer,
Commissioner of Stampt Papers, or Gentleman-Usher? No;
but he insists it is every Man's Right to find fault with
the Administration in Print, whenever they please: And
therefore you, Mr. Bailiff, and as many of your Brethren
in the Borough as can Write and Read, may publish Pamphlets, and *lay them before the Queen and Ministry*, to
shew your utter dislike of all their Proceedings; and for
this Reason, because you *can certainly see and apprehend
with your own Eyes and Understanding, those Dangers which
the* Ministers *do not.*
  One thing I am extreamly concerned about, that Mr.

Steele resolves, as he tells you, when he comes into the
House, *to follow no Leaders, but Vote according to the
Dictates of his Conscience*. He must, at that rate, be a
very useless Member to his Party, unless his Conscience
be already cut out and shaped for their Service, which I
am ready to believe it is, if I may have leave to judge
from the whole Tenor of his Life. I would only have his
Friends be cautious, not to reward him too liberally:
For, as it was said of *Cranmer, Do the Archbishop an ill
Turn, and he is your Friend for ever:* So I do affirm of
your Member, *Do Mr.* Steele *a good Turn, and he is your
Enemy for ever.*

I had like to let slip a very trivial Matter (which I
should be sorry to have done). In reading this Pamphlet,
I observed several Mistakes, but knew not whether to
impute them to the Author or Printer; till turning to the
end, I found there was only one *Erratum* thus set down,
Pag. 45. *Line* 28. *for* Admonition *read* Advertisement.
This (to imitate Mr. *Steele's* Propriety of Speech) is a
very *old* Practice among *new* Writers, to make a wilful
Mistake, and then put it down as an *Erratum.* The Word is
brought in upon this Occasion: To convince all the World
that he was not guilty of Ingratitude, by reflecting on
the Queen, when he was actually under Sallary, as the
'Examiner' affirms; he assures you, *he had resign'd and divested himself of all, before he would presume to write
any thing which was so apparently an* ADMONITION *to those
employed in Her Majesty's Service.* In case the 'Examiner'
should find fault with this Word, he might Appeal to the
Erratum; and having formerly been *Gazetteer*, he conceived
he might very safely venture to *Advertise.*

You are to understand, Mr. Bailiff, that in the great
Rebellion against King *Charles* I. there was a Distinction
found out between the *Personal* and *Political* Capacity of
the Prince; by the help of which, those Rebels professed
to Fight for the *King*, while the great Guns were discharging against *Charles Stuart.* After the same manner
Mr. *Steele* distinguishes between the *Personal* and *Political* Prerogative. He does not care to trust this Jewel *to
the Will, and Pleasure, and Passion of Her Majesty.* If I
am not mistaken, the Crown-Jewels cannot be alienated by
the Prince; but I always thought the Prince could *wear* them
during his Reign, else they had as good be in the Hands of
the Subject: So, I conceive, Her Majesty may and ought to
wear the Prerogative; that it is Her's during Life; and
She ought to be so much the more careful, neither to soil
nor diminish it, for that very Reason, because it is by
Law unalienable. But what must we do with this Prerogative, according to the notion of Mr. *Steele*? It must not

be trusted with the Queen, because Providence has given
Her *Will, Pleasure, and Passion*. Her Ministers must not
act by the Authority of it; for then Mr. *Steele* will cry
out, What? *Are Majesty and Ministry consolidated? And
must there be no Distinction between the one and the
other?* He tells you, *The Prerogative attends the Crown*;
and therefore, I suppose, must lie in the *Tower* to be
shewn for Twelve pence, but never produced, except at a
Coronation, or passing an Act. Well; but says he, *A whole
Ministry may be Impeached and condemned by the House of
Commons, without the Prince's suffering by it:* And what
follows? Why, therefore a single Burgess of *Stockbridge*,
before he gets into the House, may at any time Revile a
whole Ministry in Print, before he knows whether they are
guilty of any one Neglect of Duty, or Breach of Trust.

I am willing to join Issue with Mr. *Steele* in one Particular; which perhaps may give you some Diversion. He is
taxed by the 'Examiner' and others, for an insolent Expression, that the *British* Nation *Expects* the immediate
Demolition of *Dunkirk*. He says, the word EXPECT, was
meant to the *Ministry,* and not to the *Queen; but that however, for Argument sake, he willl suppose those Words were
addressed immediately to the Queen*. Let me then likewise
for Argument sake, suppose a very ridiculous Thing, that
Mr. *Steele* were admitted to Her Majesty's Sacred Person,
to tell his own Story, with his Letter to You, Mr. Bailiff, in his Hand to have recourse to upon Occasion. I
think his Speech must be in these Terms.

MADAM
I Richard Steele *Publisher of the* 'Tatler' *and* 'Spectator',
late Gazetteer, *Commissioner of Stampt Papers, and Pensioner to Your Majesty, now Burgess Elect of* Stockbridge,
*do see and apprehend with my own Eyes and Understanding,
the imminent Danger that attends the Delay of the Demolition of* Dunkirk, *which I believe Your Ministers, whose
greater Concern it is, do not: For, Madam, the Thing is
not done, My Lord* Treasurer *and Lord* Bolingbroke, *my
Fellow-Subjects, under whose immediate Direction it is,
are careless, and overlook it, or something worse; I mean,
they design to sell it to* France, *or make use of it to
bring in the* Pretender. *This is clear from their suffering Mr.* Tugghe's *Memorial to be published without punish-
ing the* Printer. *Your Majesty has told us, that the
Equivalent for* Dunkirk *is already in the* French King's
Hands; therefore all Obstacles are removed on the Part of
France; *and I, though a mean Fellow, give Your Majesty
to understand in the best Method I can take, and from the*

Sincerity of my GRATEFUL *Heart, that the British Nation*
EXPECTS *the* IMMEDIATE *Demolition of* Dunkirk; *as you hope
to preserve Your Person, Crown, and Dignity, and the
Safety and Welfare of the People committed to Your Charge.*

I have contracted such a Habit of treating Princes
familiarly, by reading the Pamphlets of Mr. *Steele* and
his Fellows, that I am tempted to suppose Her Majesty's
Answer to this Speech might be as follows.

Mr. Richard Steele, *late Gazetteer, &c. I do not conceive
that any of your Titles empower you to be my Director, or
to report to me the Expectations of my People. I know
their Expectations better than you; they love me, and
will trust me. My Ministers were of my own free Choice;
I have found them Wise and Faithful; and whoever calls
them Fools or Knaves, designs indirectly an Affront to my
Self. I am under no Obligations to demolish Dunkirk, but
to the Most Christian King; if you come here as an Orator
from that Prince to demand it in his Name, where are your
Powers? If not, let it suffice you to know, that I have
my Reasons for deferring it; and that the Clamours of a
Faction shall not be a Rule by which I or my Servants are
to proceed.*

Mr. *Steele* tells you; his *Adversaries are so unjust,
they will not take the least Notice of what led him into
the Necessity of writing his Letter to the* 'Guardian'.
And how is it possible, any Mortal should know all his
Necessities? Who can guess, whether this *Necessity* were
imposed on him by his *Superiors*, or by the Itch of
Party, or by the meer want of other Matter to furnish out
a 'Guardian'?
But Mr. *Steele* has *had a Liberal Education, and knows
the World as well as the Ministry does, and will therefore speak on whether he offends them or no, and though
their Cloaths be ever so New; when he thinks his Queen and
Country is,* (or as a Grammarian would express it, *are*) *ill
treated.*
It would be good to hear Mr. *Steele* explain himself
upon this Phrase of *knowing the World*; because it is a
Science which maintains abundance of Pretenders. Every
idle young Rake, who understands how to pick up a Wench,
or bilk a Hackney-Coachman, or can call the Players by
their Names, and is acquainted with five or six Faces in
the Chocolate-House, will needs pass for a Man that *knows
the World*. In the like manner Mr. *Steele* who from some
few Sprinklings of rudimental Literature, proceeded a
Gentleman of the Horse-Guards, thence by several Degrees

to be an Ensign and an Alchymist, where he was wholly conversant with the lower Part of Mankind, thinks he *knows*
the World as well as the Prime Minister; and upon the
Strength of that Knowledge, will needs direct Her Majesty
in the weightiest Matters of Government.

And now, Mr. Bailiff, give me Leave to inform you, that
this long Letter of Mr. *Steele* filled with Quotations and
a Clutter about *Dunkirk,* was wholly written for the sake
of the six last Pages, taken up in vindicating himself
directly, and vilifying the Queen and Ministry by
Innuendo's. He apprehends, that *some Representations have*
been given of him *in your Town, as, that a Man of so small*
a Fortune as he *must have secret Views or Supports, which*
could move him to leave his Employments, &c. He answers,
by owning he *has indeed very particular Views; for he is*
animated in his Conduct by Justice and Truth, and Bene-
volence to Mankind. He has given up his Employments,
because he *values no Advantages above the Conveniencies*
of Life, but as they tend to the Service of the Publick.
It seems, he could not *serve the Publick* as a Pensioner,
or Commissioner of Stamp'd Paper, and therefore gave them
up to sit in Parliament out of *Charity to his Country,*
and *to contend for Liberty.* He has transcribed the common
Places of some canting Moralist *de contemptu mundi, & fuga*
seculi, and would put them upon you as Rules derived from
his own Practice.

Here is a most miraculous and sudden Reformation, which
I believe can hardly be match'd in History or *Legend.*
And Mr. *Steele,* not unaware how slow the World was of
Belief, has thought fit to anticipate all Objections; he
foresees that *prostituted Pens will entertain a Pretender*
to such Reformations with a Recital of his own Faults and
Infirmities, but he is prepared for such Usage, and gives
himself up to all nameless Authors, to be treated as they
please.

It is certain, Mr. Bailiff, that no Man breathing can
pretend to have arrived at such a sublime pitch of Virtue
as Mr. *Steele* without some Tendency in the World, to suspend at least their Belief of the Fact, till Time and
Observation shall determine. But I hope few Writers will
be so *prostitute* as to trouble themselves with *the Faults*
and Infirmities of Mr. *Steele*'s past Life, with what he
somewhere else calls *the Sins of his Youth,* and in one of
his late Papers confesses to have been *numerous* enough.
A shifting scambling Scene of Youth, attended with
Poverty and ill Company, may put a Man of no ill Inclinations upon many Extravagancies, which as soon as they are
left off, are easily pardoned and forgot. Besides, I
think Popish Writers tell us, that the greatest Sinners

make the greatest Saints; but so very quick a Sanctifica-
tion, and carried to so prodigious a Height, will be apt
to rouze the Suspicion of Infidels, especially when they
consider that this Pretence of his to so Romantick a
Virtue, is only advanced by way of Solution to that difficult Problem, *Why has he given up his Employments?* And
according to the new Philosophy, they will endeavour to
solve it by some easier and shorter way. For example, the
Question is put, Why Mr. *Steele* gives up his Employment
and Pension at this Juncture? I must here repeat with
some Enlargement what I said before on this Head. These
unbelieving Gentlemen will answer, First, That a new Commission was every day expected for the Stamp'd Paper, and
he knew his Name would be left out; and therefore his
Resignation would be an Appearance of Virtue cheaply
bought.

Secondly, He dreaded the Violence of Creditors,
against which his Employments were no manner of Security.

Thirdly, being a Person of great Sagacity, he hath
some Foresight of a Change from the usual Age of a Ministry, which is now almost expired; from the little Mis-
understandings that have been reported sometimes to happen
among the Men in Power; from the Bill of Commerce being
rejected, and from some *HORRIBLE EXPECTATIONS,* wherewith
his Party have been deceiving themselves and their
Friends *Abroad* for two Years past.

Fourthly, He hopes to come into all the Perquisites
of his Predecessor *RIDPATH*, and be the principal Writer
of his Faction, where every thing is printed by Subscrip-
tion, which will amply make up the Loss of his Place.

But it may be still demanded, Why he affects those
exalted Strains of Piety and Resignation? To this I
answer, with great probability, That he hath resumed his
old Pursuits after the *Philosopher's Stone*, towards
which it is held by all *Adepts* for a most essential
Ingredient, that a Man must seek it meerly for the Glory
of God, and without the least Desire of being rich.

Mr. *Steele* is angry that some of our Friends have been
reflected on in a Pamphlet, because they left us in a
Point of the greatest Consequence; and upon that Account
he runs into their Panegyrick against his Conscience,
and the Interest of his Cause, without considering that
those Gentlemen have reverted to us again. The Case is
thus: He never would have praised them, if they had
remained firm, nor should we have railed at them. The
one is full as honest, and as natural as the other:
However, Mr. *Steele* hopes (I beg you Mr. Bailiff to
observe the Consequence) that notwithstanding this Pamphlet's reflecting on some Tories who opposed the Treaty

of Commerce, (12) *the Ministry will see* Dunkirk *effectually demolished.*

Mr. *Steele* says something in Commendation of the Queen;
but stops short, and tells you (if I take his meaning
right) that he *shall leave what he has to say on this
Topick; till he and Her Majesty are both dead.* Thus, he
defers his *Praises* as he does his *Debts,* after the manner
of the *Druids,* to be paid in another World. If I have ill
interpreted him, it is his own Fault, for studying Cadence
instead of Propriety, and filling up Niches with Words
before he has adjusted his Conceptions to them. One part
of the Queen's Character is this, *that all the Hours of
her Life, are divided between the Exercises of Devotion,
and taking Minutes of the Sublime Affairs of Her Government.* Now, if the Business of *Dunkirk* be one of the *Sublime Affairs of Her* Majesty's *Government,* I think we ought
to be at ease, or else she *takes Her Minutes* to little
Purpose. No, says Mr. *Steele,* the Queen is a *Lady,* and
unless a Prince will now and then get drunk with his
Ministers, *he cannot learn their Interests or Humours*;
but this being by no means proper for a *Lady,* she can know
nothing but what they think fit to tell her when they are
Sober. And therefore *all the Fellow-Subjects* of these
Ministers must watch their Motions and *be very solicitous
for what passes beyond the ordinary Rules of Government;*
For while we are foolishly *relying upon Her Majesty's
Virtues;* These Ministers are *taking the Advantage of
encreasing the Power of* France.

There is a very good Maxim, I think it is neither *Whig*
nor *Tory,* that the Prince can do no wrong; which I doubt
is often applied to very ill Purposes. A Monarch of
Britain is pleased to create *a Dozen Peers,* and to make a
Peace; both these Actions are, (for instance,) within the
undisputed Prerogative of the Crown, and are to be reputed
and submitted to as the Actions of the Prince: But as a
King of *England* is supposed to be guided in Matters of
such Importance, by the Advice of those he employs in his
Councils; whenever a Parliament thinks fit to complain of
such Proceedings, as a publick Grievance, then this Maxim
takes Place, that the Prince can do no wrong, and the
Advisers are called to Account. But shall this empower
such an Individual as Mr. *Steele* in his *Tatling* or *Pamphleteering* Capacity, to fix *the ordinary Rules of Government,* or to affirm that *Her Ministers, upon the Security
of Her Majesty's Goodness, are labouring for the Grandeur
of* France? What ordinary Rule of Government is transgressed by the Queen's delaying the Demolition of *Dunkirk?*
Or what Addition is thereby made to the Grandeur of
France? Every Taylor in your Corporation is as much a

Fellow-Subject as Mr. *Steele*, and do you think in your
Conscience that every Taylor of *Stockbridge* is fit to
direct Her Majesty and Her Ministers in *the sublime
Affairs of her Government?*

But He *persists in it, that it is no manner of Diminution of the Wisdom of a Prince, that he is obliged to act
by the Information of others.* The Sense is admirable;
and the Interpretation is this, that what a Man is forced
to *is no diminution of his Wisdom:* But if he would conclude from this Sage Maxim, that, because a Prince *acts
by the Information of others*, therefore those Actions may
lawfully be traduced in Print by every Fellow-Subject;
I hope there is no Man in *England*, so much a *Whig*, as to
be of his Opinion.

Mr. *Steele* concludes his Letter to you with a Story
about King *William* and his *French Dog-keeper, who gave
that Prince a Gun loaden only with Powder, and then pretended to wonder how his Majesty could miss his Aim:
Which was no Argument against the King's Reputation for
Shooting very finely.* This he would have you apply, by
allowing Her Majesty to be a Wise Prince, but deceived by
Wicked Counsellors, who are in the Interest of *France*.
Her Majesty's Aim was Peace, which, I think, She hath
not miss'd; and, God be thanked, She hath got it, without
any more Expence, either of SHOT or POWDER. Her *Dog-
keepers*, for some Years past, had directed Her *Gun*
against Her *Friends*, and at last *loaded* it so deep, that
it was in danger to *burst* in Her Hands.

You may please to observe, that Mr. *Steele* calls this
Dog-keeper a *Minister*, which, with humble Submission, is
a gross Impropriety of Speech. The Word is derived from
Latin, where it properly signifies a *Servant;* but in *English* is never made use of otherwise, than to denominate
those who are employ'd in the Service of Church or State:
So that the Appellation, as he directs it, is no less
absurd, than it would be for you, Mr. Bailiff, to send
your 'Prentice for a Pot of Ale, and give him the Title
of your *Envoy*; to call a Petty-Constable a *Magistrate*, or
the Common Hangman a *Minister* of Justice. I confess, when
I was choqued at this Word in reading the Paragraph, a
Gentleman offer'd his Conjecture, that it might possibly
be intended for a Reflection or a Jest: But if there be
any thing further in it, than a want of Understanding our
Language, I take it to be only a Refinement upon the old
levelling Principle of the Whigs. Thus, in their Opinion,
a *Dog-keeper* is as much a *Minister* as any Secretary of
State: And thus Mr. *Steele* and my Lord *Treasurer* are both
Fellow-Subjects. I confess, I have known some *Ministers,*
whose Birth, or Qualities, or both, were such that

nothing but the Capriciousness of Fortune, and the
Iniquity of the Times, could ever have raised them above
the Station of *Dog-keepers*; and to whose Administration
I should be loath to entrust a Dog I had any Value for:
Because, by the Rule of Proportion, they who treated their
Prince like a *Slave,* would have used their *Fellow-Subjects*
like *Dogs;* and how they would treat a *Dog,* I can find no
Similitude to express; yet I well remember, they maintained a large Number, whom they taught to *Fawn* upon themselves, and *Bark* at their Mistress. However, while they
were in Service, I wish they had only kept Her Majesty's
DOGS, and not been trusted with Her GUNS. And thus much
by way of Comment upon this worthy Story of King *William*
and his *Dog-keeper.*

I have now, Mr. Bailiff, explained to you all the
difficult Parts in Mr. *Steele*'s Letter. As for the
Importance of *Dunkirk*, and when it shall be Demolished,
or whether it shall be Demolished or not, neither he, nor
you, nor I, have any thing to do in the Matter. Let us
all say what we please, Her Majesty will think Her self
the best *Judge*, and Her Ministers the best *Advisers;*
neither hath Mr. *Steele* pretended to prove that any Law
Ecclesiastical or Civil, Statute or Common, is broken,
by keeping *Dunkirk* undemolished, as long as the Queen
shall think best for the Service of Her Self and Her
Kingdoms; and it is not altogether impossible, that
there may be some few Reasons of State, which have not
been yet communicated to Mr. *Steele*. I am, with Respect
to the Borough and Your self,

> SIR,
>> Your most Humble
>>> and most Obedient Servant,
>>>> &c.

> FINIS.

Notes

1 'The Funeral' and 'The Lying Lover'.
2 The Tories charged that Steele's pieces on Dunkirk
   revealed ingratitude to the Crown.
3 Probably Addison mentioned Steele's name to Sunderland, Secretary of State for the Southern Department.
   His Lordship then sent his nomination of Steele as
   Gazetteer to Harley, Secretary of State for the Northern Department since 1704. Harley approved it.
4 The trial of the High Churchman Henry Sacheverell
   (*c.* 1674-1724) occurred from 27 February to 23 March
   1710.

5 The Godolphin ministry, which in eight years altered
   from Tory to Whig, began to crumple in June 1710.
   Sidney Lord Godolphin (1645-1712) was dismissed as
   Lord Treasurer on 8 August. His ministry was
   succeeded by that of Harley-St. John.
6 Arthur Maynwaring (1668-1712) was the intermediary
   between Sunderland and Harley.
7 For 14-21, 21-24 August 1713.
8 The 'Englishman'.
9 The 'Flying-Post' was founded in 1696 and ran with
   brief interruptions until 1731.
10 See Steele's 'Letter to Sir M.[iles] W.[arton] Concerning Occasional Peers' (1713).
11 This was a typical Whig argument during the Sacheverell trial.
12 In the House the 'Hanover Tories', led by Sir Thomas
   Hanmer, voted against the trade clauses in the Peace
   Treaty and made possible their defeat in June 1713.

14. JONATHAN SWIFT, 'THE FIRST ODE OF THE SECOND BOOK OF
HORACE PARAPHRAS'D'

1714

Printed on 6 or 7 January 1714, this was another of
Swift's contributions to the Tory war against Steele.
On 22 October 1713 Steele in the 'Englishman' advertised
a newly conceived pamphlet 'The Crisis', which was not
printed until 19 January 1714. Swift used this delay to
mock 'The Crisis', and its author's political pretensions.

    Dick, thou'rt resolv'd, as I am told,
    Some strange *Arcana* to unfold,
    And with the help of *Buckley*'s Pen (1)
    To vamp the *good Old Cause* again,
    Which thou (such *Bur——t*'s shrewd Advice is) (2)
    Must furbish up and Nickname *CRISIS*.
    Thou pompously wilt let us know
    What all the World knew long ago,
    (Ere since Sir *William G——e* was May'r, (3)
    And *HAR——Y* fill'd the *Commons* Chair) (4)
    That we a *German* Prince must own

When *A—N* for Heav'n resigns Her Throne.
But more than that, thou'lt keep a rout
With - who is *in* - and who is *out*,
Thou'lt rail devoutly at the *Peace*,
And all its secret *Causes* trace,
The *Bucket-play* 'twixt Whigs and Tories,
Their ups and downs, with fifty Stories
Of *Tricks*, the Lord of *Ox——d* knows,
And *Errors* of our *Plenipoes*.
Thou'lt tell of *Leagues* among the Great
Portending ruin to our State,
And of that dreadful *coup d'eclat,   *(*Vide* 'En-
Which has afforded thee much Chat,   glishman',
The *Q——n* (*forsooth, Despotick*) gave   No. 36.)
Twelve *Coronets*, without *thy* leave!
A Breach of Liberty, 'tis own'd,
For which no Heads have *yet* aton'd!
Believe me, what thou'st undertaken
May bring in Jeopardy thy Bacon,
For Madmen, Children, Wits and Fools
Shou'd never meddle with Edg'd Tools.
But since thou'rt got into the Fire,
And canst not easily retire,
Thou must no longer deal in *Farce*,
Nor pump to cobble wicked Verse;
Untill thou shalt have eas'd thy Conscience,
Of Spleen, of Politicks and Nonsense,
And when thou'st bid Adieu to Cares,
And settled *Europe's Grand* Affairs,
'Twill then, perhaps, be worth thy while
For *Drury-lane* to shape thy Stile: (*This is*
'To make a pair of Jolly Fellows,   *said to be*
The Son and Father, join to tell us,   *the Plot of*
How Sons may safely disobey,   *a Comedy*
And Fathers never shou'd say nay,   *with*
By which wise Conduct they grow Friends   *which Mr.*
At last' - and so the Story ends.   St--le *has*
                                                long
    When first I knew thee, *Dick*, thou wert *threatned*
Renown'd for Skill in *Faustus* Art, (5)   *the Town.*)
Which made thy Closet much frequented
By buxom Lasses - Some repented
Their luckless Choice of Husbands - others,
Impatient to be like their Mothers,   *Vide*
Receiv'd from thee profound Directions   Tatlers.
How best to settle their Affections;
Thus thou, a Friend to the Distress'd,
Didst in thy calling do thy best.

But now the *Senate* (if things *hit*
And thou at *Stockbridge* wert not *bit*)
Must feel thy Eloquence and Fire,
Approve thy Schemes, thy Wit admire,
Thee with *Immortal Honours* crown,
Whilst *Patr'ot-like* thou'lt strut and frown.

What, tho' by Enemies 'tis said,
The *Lawrel*, which adorns thy Head;
Must one Day come in competition,
By vertue of some sly *Petition:* (6)
Yet *Mum* for that, hope still the best,
Nor let such Cares disturb thy Rest.

Methinks I hear thee loud, as Trumpet,
As bagpipe shrill, or Oyster-Strumpet,
Methinks I see thee, spruce and fine,
With Coat embroider'd richly shine,
And dazzle all the *Idol-Faces*
As thro' the *HALL* thy Worship paces:
(Tho' this I speak but at a venture,
Supposing thou hast *Tick* with *Hunter*)
Methinks I see a *black-guard Rout*
Attend thy Coach, and hear them shout
In Approbation of thy Tongue,
Which (in their Stile) is *purely* hung.
Now, now you carry all before ye,
Nor dares one *Jacobite* or *Tory*
Pretend to answer one Syl--lable,
Except the Matchless Hero *Abel.* (7)
What tho' her *Highness* and her *Spouse*
In *Ant——rp* keep a frugal House, (8)
Yet not forgetful of a Friend
They'll soon enable thee to spend,
If to *Macc--rt--y* thou wilt toast, (9)
And to his *Pious Patron's Ghost.*
Now manfully thou'lt run a Tilt
'On *Popes*, for all the Blood they've spilt,
For Massacres, and Racks, and Flames,
For Lands enrich'd by crimson Streams,
For inquisitions taught by *Spain,*
Of which the Christian World complain.' (10)

Dick, we agree - all's true, thou'st said,
As that my Muse is yet a Maid,
But, if I may with freedom talk,
All this is foreign to thy Walk:
Thy *Genius* has perhaps a knack
At trudging in a beaten Track,

> But is for *State-Affairs* as fit,
> As mine for Politicks and Wit.
> Then let us both in time grow wise,
> Nor higher, than our Talents, rise,
> To some snug Cellar let's repair
> From Dunns and Debts, and drown our Care;
> Now quaff of honest Ale a Quart,
> Now venture at a Pint of Port,
> With which inspir'd we'll club each Night
> Some tender Sonnet to indite,
> And with *Tom D'urf--y, Phill-ps, D--nnis*, (11)
> Immortalize our *Dolls* and *Jenneys*.

Notes
1   Samuel Buckley published 'The Crisis' and the
    'Spectator'.
2   Gilbert Burnet (1643-1715), Bishop of Salisbury
    and Whig polemicist.
3   Sir William Gore, Lord Mayor of London in 1702.
4   Harley, Speaker of the Commons, 1701-5.
5   Bickerstaff's interest in astrology and Steele's in
    alchemy.
6   To declare his election invalid as the member from
    Stockbridge.
7   Abel Roper (1665-1726), a Tory journalist.
8   Having been dismissed from his offices in December
    1711, Marlborough lived for a time in Antwerp.
9   George Maccartney (c. 1660-1730), second to Charles
    Lord Mohun in his duel with the Duke of Hamilton.
    Accused of giving the Duke a fatal stab wound when
    he had already fallen, General Maccartney fled to
    Holland.
10 A parody of Steele's pamphleteering style.
11 Thomas D'Urfey (1653-1723), poet and dramatist;
    Ambrose Philips (c. 1675-1749), poet; John Dennis
    (1657-1734), critic and dramatist.

15.   STEELE AND ADDISON ON THE PEERAGE BILL

1719

On 28 February 1719 Stanhope and Sunderland had the Duke
of Somerset bring to the Lords a special committee's

resolutions for the reform of the peerage. These resolutions became the basis of the peerage bill, which intended
to limit the number of newly created English and Scottish
peers.

The bill was introduced to the Lords on 14 March and
the Whigs, already divided, split on the issue. Addison
supported the bill and the ministerial Whigs who introduced it. Steele, now a follower of Walpole and other
dissident Whigs, argued against the measure as both MP
and pamphleteer. The two former friends fought each other
in the 'Plebeian' and the 'Old Whig', Addison being so ill
that he could not continue his journal beyond the second
number.

The bill was defeated on 8 December. Addison never
knew the outcome; he had been dead for six months when the
vote was counted.

Steele's 'Plebeian' ran for four numbers (14 March to
6 April 1719) and Addison's 'Old Whig' for two (19 March
to 2 April).

From the 'Plebeian' 2

Those who are not particularly acquainted with the Vocation of *Pamphlet-Writing*, have very much wonder'd that a
Matter of so great Consequence, as the Affair of the
PEERAGE, and espous'd by such Persons as are very well
known to be its Patrons, cou'd have been so long a while
upon the Stage, and no Champion appear for it: but others,
who are more vers'd in this kind of Business, know, there
cou'd not be wanting Persons enough to make their Court,
by producing their Lucubrations on this Head. But as it
is a Subject that will not very well bear debating, their
Masters, without doubt, were of opinion, that the best way
was, to let all manner of Writing alone, and keep all that
cou'd be said on that Subject, for the Time and Place
where it was absolutely necessary to say something.

The Agitators for the Bill assur'd themselves, that no
body wou'd be so bold as to attack first; and consequently
judg'd themselves out of all danger. (1) But the PLEBEIAN
starting forth unexpectedly, they were forc'd, like People
in a Surprize, or on an Invasion, to march immediately any
Troops they had: and indeed, these are some of the most
tatter'd I ever saw.

The first Champion that appear'd for this Bill, was a
Person who exhibited himself in the 'St. James's-Post' of
Wednesday, March 18. in this Advertisement: *Some Consider-
ations relating to the Peerage of* Great Britain. *Wherein*

the Arguments for *the Reasonableness and Expediency of a Bill said to be depending, are stated* Pro *and* Con.

This Performance, I have not been able to venture upon; for He that can state Arguments *for* the Bill, both *Pro* and *Con*, is too slippery a Person for any body to lay hold of.

The next that enter'd the Lists, on the same side of the Question, having been more fortunate than to discover *himself beforehand*, I have perus'd his Labours.... (2)

The next that follows these two Combatants for this Bill, is somebody or other that is us'd to Masquerading, as I suppose; and indeed he is so well disguis'd, that 'tis impossible to know him. When I first read the Title, 'The Old Whig', I expected no less than the utmost Wrath and Indignation against the House of Lords. I could not help thinking but he would have been for *Voting them* useless at least, as his Ancestors did formerly: but I was extremely surpriz'd to find just the contrary; that he was for giving them such a Power, as would soon make the *House of Commons useless*: and therefore he might as well have taken any other Title in the World, as 'The Old Whig'. I am afraid he is so *old a Whig*, that he has quite *forgot his Principles*....

[Steele proceeds to debate the arguments set forth by the 'Old Whig'.]

From the 'Old Whig' 2

The Author of the 'Plebeian', to shew himself a perfect Master in the *Vocation of Pamphlet Writing*, begins like a Son of *Grubstreet*, with declaring the great Esteem he has for himself, and the Contempt he entertains for the Scribblers of the Age. One wou'd think, by his way of representing it, that the unexpected Appearance of his Pamphlet was as great a Surprize upon the World as that of the late Meteor, or indeed something more terrible, if you will believe the Author's magnificent Description of his own Performance. *The* Plebeian, says he, *starting forth unexpectedly, they were forced like People in a Surprize, or on an Invasion, to March immediately any Troops they had*. If Cardinal *Alberoni*'s Attempt, which furnishes the Allusion, succeeds no better than that of his Friend the Pamphleteer, he won't have much to boast of. (3)

Our Author in his triumphant Progress, first animadverts on a Writer, whom he says he never read, which being my own Case, I shall leave that Writer to defend himself. The second he mentions, considering the Strength

of his Arguments, and the Closeness of his Reasoning,
deserved a little more regard from the 'Plebeian', who, it
seems, *with much ado went thro' the Performance*. This
would certainly have been true, had he gone through it
with a design to answer it.

Having routed Baronius, *and confounded* Bellarmine, *pass
we on the next,* said the Country Curate to his admiring
Audience. (4) Our Author pursues his Conquests with the
same Satisfaction and Intrepidity. In the first place he
is angry with a Writer for assuming the Name of the *Old
Whig*, who may more recriminate upon this Author for taking
that of the *Plebeian*, a Title which he is by no means fond
of retaining, if we may give Credit to many shrewd Gues-
sers. But he tells the Old Whig, that he *expected* from
that Title *no less than the utmost Wrath and Indignation
against the House of Lords.* How does this agree with the
Censure he passes upon him afterwards, for *treating that
Species in such a manner as he dares not venture to
repeat!* I must however remind this Author of the *Milk*
with which he *nurses our Nobles*, not to omit his stagnated
Pool; (5) Passages of such a Nature, that in Imitation of
the Author, I shall dispatch them with an *Horresco referens!*... (6)

From the 'Plebeian' 3

The PLEBEIAN expected before now to have heard again from
the 'Old Whig', especially as to his making good the last
Particular taken notice of in the Paper, *Numb*. II. which
relates to the Part he was pleas'd to affirm his Majesty
had already taken in this Affair; and for which there does
not seem to be any Foundation. However, as *Age is apt to
be slow*, the PLEBEIAN is willing to wait some time longer
to be satisfied in that point....

From the 'Plebeian' 4

The PLEBEIAN has been oblig'd to object to the 'Old Whig'
one of the *Infirmities* of *Age*, viz. *Slowness*; and he must
now take notice of another, tho he does it with great
Reluctance, that is, *Want of Memory*: for the *Old Gentleman* seems to have forgot, that at his first Appearance he
promis'd the Publick a particular Treatise on the Subject
of the *Peerage*, as it relates to *Scotland*....

Notes

1 The dissident Whigs began the paper war on 14 March
   1719 with Steele's 'Plebeian' 1 and Walpole's 'Thoughts
   of a Member of the Lower House'.
2 On 19 March appeared Robert Molesworth's 'Letter from a
   Member of the House of Commons to a Gentleman without
   Doors'.
3 Guido Alberoni (1664-1752), Italian statesman in Spanish service, Cardinal of the Roman Catholic Church.
4 Caesar Baronius (1538-1607), Italian ecclesiastical
   historian, Cardinal of the Roman Catholic Church.
   Saint Roberto Bellarmine (1542-1621), Italian theologian, Cardinal, Doctor of the Church, and a major
   influence in the Catholic reformation.
5 Steele's pamphlet 'An Account of the Fish-Pool' (1718).
6 Virgil, 'Aeneid', II, 204: 'I shudder as I remember.'

III Steele the Dramatist

'THE FUNERAL', 1701

16. CHARLES GILDON, 'A COMPARISON BETWEEN THE TWO STAGES'

1702

Published anonymously on 14 April 1702, the pamphlet has
been attributed to Charles Gildon. This excerpt (pp.
145-71) provides one of the earliest comments on Steele as
moralist and dramatist. Specifically it discusses 'The
Funeral' and in cursory fashion 'The Christian Hero'.
For an account of Gildon, see No. 41·

...Let's talk of something else.
  Ramble. Of the Play ['The Funeral'] we are come from,
or of any other: We'll be ty'd to no Subject.
  Sullen. 'Tis a dangerous Matter to talk of this Play;
the Town has given it such applause, 'twill be an ungrateful undertaking to call their Judgments in question.
  Ramb. Sure you won't condemn what so many good Judges
have approv'd.
  Sull. Not directly condemn it: We count that Horse a
good Racer that comes within distance: I shall agree with
the Opinion thus far, that it is a diverting Play, and
that it is writ with Care and Understanding; that the
Author's Intentions are noble, and that it is in many
places a just and lively Satyr.
  Ramb. I hear the Gentleman is a fine Companion, and
passes for a Wit of the first Rank.

Sull. By his Play I shall never allow you that: I can allow you this, that he seems a good judge of Comedy; that he has touch'd some things very justly; that his Vices are new, and his Characters not ill drawn.

Ramb. And the contrivance admirable?

Sull. By no means: Tho' he seems to know how to form a Play, yet his Play does not appear very much to justifie it: I don't think his Contrivance within the compass of humane Policy; one Turn in it especially, which is indeed the only turn in the Play....

Ramb. And what do you infer from all this?

Sull. I infer, that notwithstanding some Beauties in it, this is not a just Comedy; some things are very well, but the Principal very much amiss.

Ramb. Sure thou art out o'thy Senses; we shall certainly have thee affronted for thy Heresie: Can you pretend to make out what you say?

Sull. Ay, indeed can I, and am ready with my Evidence when you will.

Ramb. Are you of that Opinion too, *Critick?*

Crit. I am directly of Opinion, that the Town is sometimes the worst Judge in the World; 'tis like the monster *Polyphemus* with one Eye, that sees everything imperfectly: If this is not so, I wonder how it cou'd applaud a Play with so many Deformities.

Ramb. Hye day! I have mended the matter finely; why, you rail worse than he, but positively you are both Mad.

Crit. I hate railing; but speaking Truth is often now a days so call'd: I am directly of *Sullen*'s Judgment in what he says: Many exceptions may be made against it, some of no very considerable moment, but some of 'em fundamental and irreconcilable.

Ramb. Better and better I'faith; I shall have a fine time on't between you.

Crit. But the better to judge of it, it will be convenient first to take a general survey of it, and then putting the several parts together, sum up the Fable in few Words.

Sull. Pray let us beg that favour of you.

Crit. I observ'd it so attentively, that it's still fresh in my Memory: As well as I can, take the Fable thus.

Lord Brumpton *having lately had a Lethargic Fit, and supposed by all the Family, but* Trusty, *to be dead, because of that Fit; is desired by* Trusty *to make use of their Opinion of his Death, to observe the Sentiments and Behaviour of his Family, but especially of his Wife, who had been long suspected by* Trusty. *Accordingly* Sable *the Undertaker is retain'd in the Secret, and the Plot is carry'd on against* Lady Brumpton: Lord Hardy *and* Campley

are intrigued with Sharlot and Harriot, two Orphans in
ward with Lord Brumpton, which Ladies live in the House
with him, and without any knowledge of the Plot pursue
their own Affairs: Cabinet is an old Crony of Lady Brumpton's and still her Creature; the Lawyer and Waiting-
woman are little to the purpose. Lord Brumpton takes the
hint from Trusty, does as he advises, and continues to let
them believe him dead: This gives him oportunities of
seeing his Wife's Behaviour, and being at length convinc'd
of her Hypocrisie, reveals himself, and after some per-
plexity about a Settlement, she is found to ha' been
formerly marry'd to Cabinet, and so dismist with shame.
This is the Plot and the chief Argument; the Amours and
the rest are of inferiour consideration, and in the
Author's own Phrase, Subaltern.

    Sull. You have sum'd it up right, so that the Play
runs on the supposition of a Man's death, and under that
Circumstance the several pranks are perform'd: Now that
which seems incredible, is, that a Man of any Rank or
Relations, shou'd lye dead so long, and no body see him;
that neither his Wife (whose desire of his Death required
as full assurances as 'twas possible to get) shou'd not
gratifie her cruel Curiosity in viewing him, and confirm-
ing her Security; that neither of the Orphan Sisters, who
liv'd in the Family, and who were well affected to him,
shou'd be desirous to look on him, nor for Satisfaction
nor for Sorrow; that a Man of his Quality shou'd be Coffin'd up, and all things provided for the Interment, and
not so much as a Friend, a Servant, or the common
Searchers inquire after his Death, 'tis strange.

    Crit. 'Tis so; but I will tell you what is stranger;
and that is, that immediately upon his Death, and all the
while the Corps is supposed to lye in the House, the several Intrigues of the Play are carry'd on: First Sharlot
and Harriot, under the same Roof, and at the Moment of
his death, are openly drolling and raillying each other
about their Sweethearts; but that is not enough, presently
Fardingale, a Servant in the House, comes in with a Song,
and squeals it to the Lute, while Campley's Hat serves for
a Desk to lay it on: Is not this an odd Prologue to a
Funeral?

    Sull. The most absurd contrivance that ever was; and
I thank you for the hint; it had escap'd me truly.

    Crit. Horace says,

    Infelix operis Summa, qui ponere totam,
    Nesciat——— ———, Epist. ad Pison. (1)

And what shall we say to the rest when the Foundation is

so ill laid! Well, the old Woman not singing it to their
Minds, *Campley*, who is a Gentleman of Sense and Manners,
is desired to sing it; he presently does it without any
excuse or regard to the sad occasion that requir'd another
sort of Behaviour, and no sooner is that over, but he Gal-
lants her with his Love in an Air of the greatest Levity,
and she hears him with all the Pleasure he cou'd desire!
then to compleat the Scene, the Widow her self rushes in,
and helps out the Conversation and Drollery.

Sull. That was an unhappy oversight: I have not read
any thing so guilty.

Crit. Most abominable: I do not insist upon the Widow's
Humour, but her Conduct; as the Character is to render her
a Hypocrite, so she ought to have dissembled her Joy in
the presence of those who were her Enemies: The Ladies had
violent suspicion of her Falshood, therefore she shou'd
have put on a Face of gloom and melancholy; nor was there
in this Scene any occasion to shew her self, much less to
display her Joy at such a juncture: This is bad enough,
but that the Persons of Probity, as *Sharlot, Harriot, Campley*; nay even the Lord's *own Son*, signal for his Vertue
and Sincerity, shou'd forget such a doleful Moment, and
Burlesk away the Days of Mourning in Mirth and Fooleries
of Love, is disagreeable and monstrous.

Ramb. I am of Opinion with you in that; but the Audience was in too great a hurry to mind it.

Crit. The whole Oeconomy of the Play runs on this very
point: As I told you, the *Lord Hardy*, who was the
Deceased's Son (and by the way, has all advantages of
Piety and Honour that the Poet cou'd give him) I say, even
he too instead of lamenting his Father's suddain Death,
(tho' he had reason enough, for he was to fall into worse
Hands) never shews the least concern, nor mentions it but
once, and that is, when he remembers he is now cut off
from his hopes of the Estate; but instead of sighing for
his Father, he only Sighs for his Mistress, and within a
Wanscoat of his Father's Corps, with all the gaiety imaginable pursues his Intrigues: The rest of the Action is
of a piece, and altogether is unseasonable, barbarous and
shocking.

Ramb. I don't know what to say to't; you have reason
on your side; for considering the Circumstances every way,
it seems a little too much strain'd.

Crit. This reduces this so celebrated Comedy to the
indignity of the vilest Farce; and which renders it still
more unlike Comedy, is the manner of *Sharlot's* escape out
of the House.

Sull. I had that in my Eye with the first appearance
of the *Catastrophe*; I thought it too gross for humane
Faith.

Crit. You remember how it is: *Lord Hardy*'s Men are to
set on the Corps as it is to be carried out to the Grave,
under a weak pretence of claiming the Administration:
Hardy does as he is directed, and having seiz'd the Herse,
he goes to open it, expecting to see his Father, but out
jumps *Lady Sharlot*: This is surprizing beyond all belief,
that a Lady of her delicacy shou'd be Coffin'd up, and
kept close some Hours, without the relief of one gasp of
Air; that she shou'd be carried out in such solemnity, and
by all the terrible Equipage of Death to be put into a
condition of dying in good earnest, only to make her
escape to her Lover————if that be *Comedy*, I have done with
the Stage.

Sull. It's forc'd for a surprize without any manner of
provocation; she might have got out o'Doors in such a Confusion without studying that Artifice.

Crit. Nor has *Cabinet*'s discovery of his prior Marriage with *Lady Brumpton* a sufficient Cause; *Trusty* says,
he discover'd it because he was frighted with the imagination of seeing *Lord Brumpton*'s Ghost; What can be more
childish? for a Fellow of his stubborn wickedness to be
bubbl'd with the Notion of a Spirit; 'tis boyish and
ridiculous.

Sull. One thing more I observ'd: *Sable* the Undertaker,
who in the *second Act* was menac'd by *Trusty* for his
Roguery and Extortion, goes off unpunish'd, contrary to
the Law of *Comedy*.

Ramb. The Poet reckon'd him sufficiently punish'd in
having his Men beaten, and the Funeral Procession interrupted.

Sull. How can that be any punishment to him, when he
was in that Scene of the *second Act* promised the same Reward for keeping the Secret, as he was to receive for the
Funeral? and without doubt the Money was paid.

Ramb. How do you know that?

Sull. Because we hear nothing to the contrary: if
Trusty, who had the management of the Plot had a mind to
bilk him, he shou'd ha' told us so.

Crit. This being the Foundation of the Play, it admits
of an imputation very different from the Character it has
obtain'd: But to make the Author amends, we must own he
has touch'd the Humour of some of our modern Widows, and
the Knavery of those Undertakers very luckily; this latter
is a new Satyr, but the first has once before, and but
once successfully, been upon the Stage; as I remember 'tis
Shakespear's Puritan, or *Widow of* Watling-street, (2)
where the dissimulation of these Widows is pleasantly
describ'd....

Ramb. If you will not allow the *Plot*, pray what do you

think of the *Language?*

Crit. For ought I know the Author may value himself on
that Talent; nay, perhaps that sort of writing may in some
Mens Opinions be best: but I must acknowledge, whether it
be the misfortune of my Ignorance, or love of another kind
of Stile, I have no relish for his; nay, I think it altogether improper for Comedy.

Ramb. That's very hard.

Crit. It may be my single Opinion, but it seems to me
too concise and stiff: I declare for the plain and easie
way of Conversation, where a Man's Mind may be understood
without telling his Story twice: and I think such a Dialogue ought to be in *Comedy,* especially in such places
where the Hearers are to be prepar'd for some great Undertaking, as in the Scene between *Lord Brumpton* and *Trusty*
in the first, and between *Trusty* and *Cabinet* in the fourth
Act.

Ramb. You mean that of the Letter which *Cabinet* is
supposed to have sent to him.

Crit. The same: I wou'd have you apprehend me right,
I do not arraign the Poet for shadowing his Plot; but I
may justly blame him for delivering himself so enigmatic-
ally as he meant to puzzle us with a Riddle; his Words do
not so much as squint on the Design, nor indeed are they
to be well understood; as I remember they are these –
Cabinet says I *Being born a Gentleman and bred out of all
Roads of Industry, I fell into the narrow mind to do so
and so - Road of Industry* is an odd Phrase, and *falling
into the narrow mind,* is Nonsense: I observ'd afterwards
that Interview was to back the Letter, which I suppose
contain'd the discovery of his Marriage with *Lady Brumpton.* Again, the chief Scene in the Play, which is the
opening of the first Plot between the *Lord* and *Trusty,* is
obscure; nor cou'd I with all my attention understand what
they meant till the Play was almost over, and several
Gentlemen who sat near me were perplext with the same
doubt. Again, *Trim* tells *Trusty,* that his Lord will *wait
him immediately* – Why not wait on him? I hate that affectation of gelding a Sentence, 'tis too starcht and *Laco-
nick* for *Comedy.* Again, *You are the Man who look'd so
pleas'd to see me look so fine to go to Court,* which is
ill expres't by all the *so's* and *to's,* and a childish
Thought to boot, from a Man of so solemn a Mien as *Trusty.*
The Examples are innumerable ——— take these two out of
the *Prologue* for all the rest.

    Our Author made, a full House to invite
    A Funeral a Comedy to Night.

The Words are writ and pointed in the Prologue as I speak
'em. The next is ——

No in old England *nothing can be won,*
Without a faction good or ill be done.

What a forc'd transposition of Words here is! If any Man
understands 'em at first hearing, I'll forfeit my Ears for
deceiving me.
Sull. What think you of several of his long *Parenthe-*
ses?
Crit. In Discourse they are highly improper, because
the *Parenthesis* being of a distinct Sense from the rest of
the Speech, and having no Mark in speaking to divide one
from the other, as there is in writing, they must be confounded together: But there is no need of using any at all;
for I'll undertake to talk a whole Day together, and not
use one.
Ramb. Nay, now you assume; do you compare your self
with the Author?
Crit. I understand my Mother Tongue well enough to
talk it with the Author, or any body else; I hope there's
no great vanity in saying I can talk *English.*
Ramb. If your Vanity ends there, 'tis nothing; but
when you undertake to Correct, you must be upon your
Guard, and keep your self out of Censure.
Crit. I affirm no more than you, or any body may do
in this matter of the *Parenthesis*: I believe I can shew
you forty good Plays without one, and you will hardly
shew me one good Play that uses them....
Ramb. Did you every read the *Christian Hero*?
Crit. Yes, what do you mean by asking me?
Ramb. Pray don't be angry. Is it not an extraordinary
thing?
Crit. You're enough to make a Man mad: *Grande Sopho-*
cleo carmen bacchamur hiatu. (3) Nothing but Rapture both
in Poetry and Prose.
Ramb. How very waspish! Good lack! a Man cannot have
a civil Answer to a civil Question.
Crit. Your Question is impertinent, and I begin to be
sick o' the Office: But let me hear it again.
Ramb. Not from me Faith, I'm as sick of your Surliness,
as you can be of my Impertinence.
Sull. Pray Gentlemen, let me stickle; I must have no
civil Wars; good *Trinculo* and *Stephano*, (4) share the
Island betwixt you, and let me be your Embassador of Peace:
I'll propose the Question again; Don't you think the *Chris-*
tian Hero an extraordinary thing?
Crit. Look ye Sir——to answer you Dogmatically, and

in few words. No.
  Ramb. Very Dogmatically truly!
  Sull. Come, your reason *Chagrin*, your reason.
  Crit. Thus then briefly: 'Tis a Chaos, 'tis a confusion of Thoughts, rude and indigested; tho' he had the
advice of an ingenious Man to put it into Method.
  Ramb. Say you so? that's more than I heard.
  Crit. 'Tis Dated from the Tower-guard, as a Present
to his Colonel, (5) that his Colonel might think him even
in time of Duty a very contemplative Soldier, and I sup-
pose by the roughness of the Stile, he writ it there on
the Butt-end of a Musquet. (6)
  Sull. Hush! no Reproaches; the Gentleman has done very
well, and chose a worthy Subject.
  Ramb. It bore two Editions. (7)
  Crit. It did not; it was but once printed, nor is all
that Impression sold; 'tis a Trick of the Bookseller's to
get it off.
  Ramb. Well, I'm sorry I can't bring you to my good
Opinion of the Author.
  Crit. And perhaps I don't think much worse of him than
you do: I wou'd not take every thing on trust from common
Fame; I will exercise my Sense in all things, and that
shall be to me a law....

[Sullen, Ramble, and Critick return to a discussion of 'The
Funeral', finding its witticisms deficient and its grammar
faulty.]

  Crit. But the Author hits a notable piece of Gallantry
in the *Three hundred Pound Bill*: But why payable to the
Man? In all Sense and Reason, that made it a Gift to the
Man, and not to the Master; if honest *Trim* had kept the
Money, no common Law in *England* cou'd ha' taken it out of
his Hands. Then, in the beginning of the *third Act, Trim*,
in the narration of his success with *Mademoiselle*, says,
That she being mov'd by these Promises - wou'd do such and
such matters for them, *&c.* but we hear of no Promises, nor
any thing like 'em; it's just become an Intrigue between
Trim and her, but we hear of no Love nor Lover's Promise.
  Ramb. Perhaps it shou'd ha' been *Premises*, and then it
had been Sense.
  Crit. In the same Act the Lady in her Conversation
with Lord *Hardy*, talks of a Brother's Death, whose Memory
is dear to her; it seems he dy'd abroad, and she condoles
her Misfortune in the resemblance there is between her
Lord and her Brother: This, in my Opinion, is not only impertinent, but by no means to be admitted into *Comedy*; such
Images are too afflicting, and do not agree with the

Nature and Gayety of that kind of Drama: All *Ideas* of distress are to be banish'd, and our Lives only to be represented, with the Humours, Vices, and Vicissitudes of 'em:
but our Deaths not to be mention'd, not so much as by
Similitude. But as what *Trusty* says afterwards, that his
Father had taught Lord *Brumpton*, the Exercise of Arms,
tho' the Lord was a Colonel, and t'other only a Captain
in his Lordship's Regiment--- I say, as the Author is a
better Soldier than I, it becomes me to submit that controversy to him.

  Sull. It seems to me too a little preposterous, but
we must acquiesce in that point to the Men of Discipline.

  Ramb. But pray resolve me one fair Question, and without Passion: Has he not describ'd the Sextons and Grave-
diggers to the Life?

  Crit. I believe these Fellows bad enough; and that
practice of removing dead Bodies from one place to
another, is a most unchristian Roguery; I know it to be
true in several Parishes at this end of the Town, and it
is a deplorable shame that such Rascals are suffer'd to
do so: But I never knew till now, that the *Undertakers*
had Farm'd the Church-yards, and bought the Dominion of
the Graves and the Dead: I thought their Attendance had
ended at the laying down of the Coffin; and that the
stripping and shifting the Carcasses from place to place,
had been the sole Inheritance of the Officers of the
Church. But to proceed....

  Sull. But pray let us turn the other end of the Glass,
and see what prospect that gives us: And as you have been
stringing up his Faults, so give me leave to reckon some
things that are well in him: First, he has variety of
Characters, and even in the same Character variety of
Humour: *Harriot* is a Lady of a spruce Wit, and fiery
Mettal: *Sharlot* is Grave and Methodical; the first interview between *her* and Lord *Hardy*, is very Courtly and
Passionate: 'Tis true, she degenerates in that Scene of
Billingsgate with the *Widow,* but 'tis a contrivance for
Revenge and Mirth. Lord *Hardy* is a Character of a Noble
kind; there's the Duty of a Son, the Faith of a Lover,
the Integrity of a Debtor, and the Bravery of a Soldier,
all comprehended in him: That of *Campley*, has the Air of a
Man of Sense, a sincere Lover, and a hearty Friend: *Trim*
has the true Impudence of a Man o'Quality's Favourite
Servant: *Puzzle* is a general Representative of the Inns o'
Courts; and *Trusty*, a fine Example of Fidelity in Servants; the waiting Women in their several Faculties, are
good Copies of all that Sisterhood; and to conclude all---
Lord *Brumpton* is a just Example of a doating, uxorious
Husband, and *Lady Brumpton* an Epitome of most of the Sex

when they become Widows.

    Ramb. Ay, this is Civil Mr. *Sullen*; let's have as much of this as you please.

    Sull. Then take two or three more: The Visiting Scene is a Master-piece; I prefer it to that in *The Lady's visiting Day* by great odds: (8) The Incidents are many, and all arise naturally from the Business of the Play; there's not one broken Scene in the whole; that Incident of the *Lawyer*, and that of the *Recruits*, I like extremely; and Lord *Brumpton*'s Advice to his Son and *Campley* in the last Scene admirable. To all this, the Moral is the true result of the Play, not in the least strain'd, as many are.

    Ramb. And now you have both given your Judgments, pray take mine: I think the Gentleman who writ this and the *Christian Hero*, to be indued with singular Honesty, a noble Disposition, and a conformity of good Manners; and as he is a Soldier, these Qualities are more conspicuous in him, and more to be esteemed: He has a Heart fit for his Imployment, and where he touches the Government, which he is a Servant to, his Lines shine with Loyalty and good Instruction: My Prayer for him is, That on all occasions he has to exert his Courage in the Service of her Majesty, and the Nation, his Sword may be as successful as his Muse.

    Sull. I commend your conclusion *Ramble*, and joyn with you in it; it's fit every Gentleman shou'd be incourag'd that writes with so good an Intention; and I commend the good Nature of the Town, that gave his first Essay such Approbation; notwithstanding the Errors we have mention'd.

    Crit. I neither envy him, nor reproach the Town for their Applause; and I am apt to think we have not nam'd any of his Errors which he himself was not conscious of: He does not want that Understanding which some of his Brethren do, and I hope, if he will divert us with another, to find it more correct.

    Ramb. I'll answer for him....

Notes

1 'Ars Poetica', or 'Epistle to the Pisos', 34-5: 'He
   [the craftsman] is dissatisfied with the sum of his
   work because he does not know how to represent the
   whole figure.'
2 Among Shakespeare apocrypha is an anonymous comedy
   'The Puritan, or The Widow of Watling Street' (1607).
3 Juvenal, VI, 636: 'Think you...I am mouthing in
   Sophoclean tones a grand theme [unknown to the
   Rutulian hills and skies of Latium?].'

4 Low characters in 'The Tempest'.
5 John Lord Cutts, 'Colonel of His Majesty's Cold-Stream
   Regiment of Guards, &c.'
6 It was written while Steele was actively engaged in and
   near London as an Ensign of the Guards.
7 First edition, 15-17 April, 1701; second edition, 17-19
   July of the same year.
8 A comedy by William Burnaby, presumably first acted in
   late 1700 or early 1701. It was published 27 February
   1701.

17. RICHARD STEELE, 'SPECTATOR' 51

28 April 1711

The letter-writer was probably Steele himself, finding
fault with an isolated line in 'The Funeral' in order to
denounce the comedies of Etherege for smuttiness and to
urge the reformation of the stage in the interest of
'Chastity and Modesty'.

Saturday, April 28, 1711

Torquet ab Obscenis jam nunc Sermonibus Aurem!
                                        Hor. (1)

Mr. SPECTATOR,
'MY Fortune, Quality and Person, are such as render me as
Conspicuous as any Young Woman in Town. It is in my Power
to enjoy it in all its Vanities, but I have, from a very
careful Education, contracted a great Aversion to the forward Air and Fashion which is practised in all Publick
Places and Assemblies. I attribute this very much to the
Stile and Manners of our Plays: I was last Night at the
'Funeral', where a Confident Lover in the Play, speaking
of his Mistress, Cries out - *Oh that* Harriot! *to fold
these Arms about the Waste of that Beauteous strugling,
and at last yielding Fair! (2)* Such an Image as this
ought, by no means, to be presented to a Chaste and Regular Audience. I expect your Opinion of this Sentence,
and recommend to your Consideration, as a SPECTATOR, the
Conduct of the Stage at present, with Relation to Chastity

and Modesty.

> I am, *SIR*,
> Your Constant Reader,
> and Well-Wisher.' (3)

The Complaint of this Young Lady is so just, that the Offence is gross enough to have displeased Persons who cannot pretend to that Delicacy and Modesty, of which she is Mistress. (4) But there is a great deal to be said in Behalf of an Author; if the Audience would but consider the Difficulty of keeping up a sprightly Dialogue for five Acts together, they would allow a Writer, when he wants Wit, and can't please any otherwise, to help it out with a little Smuttiness. I will answer for the Poets, that no one ever writ Bawdry for any other Reason but Dearth of Invention. When the Author cannot strike out of himself any more of that which he has superior to those who make up the Bulk of his Audience, his natural Recourse is to that which he has in common with them; and a Description which gratifies a sensual Appetite will please, when the Author has nothing about him to delight a refined Imagination. It is to such a Poverty we must impute this and all other Sentences in Plays, which are of this kind, and which are commonly term'd Luscious Expressions.

Notes

1 Horace, 'Epistles', II. i. 127: 'Even then he turns the ear from obscene words.'
2 From the first edition (II. i).
3 Probably Steele himself. See 'The Spectator', ed. Donald F. Bond (1965), I, p. 216.
4 'The Funeral' had been performed at Drury Lane on 26 April 1711. The second edition of the play, published in September of that year, revised the offending passage: 'O that Harriot! to Embrace that Beauteous--'.

'THE TENDER HUSBAND', 1705

18.   PAMELA ON 'THE TENDER HUSBAND'

1741

From vol. IV, Letter 15 of Samuel Richardson's 'Pamela'
[1740, 1741], 4 vols, 1742.
   'The Tender Husband' opened on 23 April 1705.   Its
first run alone was disappointing.   By 1793-4 it had been
performed 165 times and on 8 occasions by royal command.
It was particularly popular during the 1730s.

Mrs. B—— to Lady Davers.

MY DEAR LADY, - I gave you, in my last, my bold remarks
upon a tragedy - 'The Distressed Mother'. (1)   I will now
give you my shallow notions of a comedy - 'The Tender
Husband'.
   I liked this part of the title; though I can't say I
was pleased at all with the other, explanatory of it; or,
- 'The Accomplished Fools'.   But when I was told it was
written by Sir Richard Steele, and that Mr. Addison had
given some hints towards it, if not some characters, Oh
dear sir! said I, give us your company to this play; for
the authors of the 'Spectators' cannot possibly produce
a faulty scene. (2)
   Mr. B—— indeed smiled; for I had not then read the
play: and the Earl of F——, his countess, Miss Darnford,
Mr. B——, and myself, agreed to meet with a niece of my
lord's in the stage box, which was taken on purpose.
   There seems to me, my dear lady, to be a great deal of
wit and satire in the play: But, upon my word, I was
grievously disappointed as to the morality of it: nor, in
some places, is *probability* preserved; and there are
divers speeches so very free, that I could not have expected to meet with such, from the names I mentioned.
   I should be afraid of being censured for my presumption, were I to write to anybody less indulgent to me than
your ladyship.   But I will make no apologies to you,
madam. - Let me see, then; can I give you the brief
history of this Comedy, as I did of the Tragedy? - I profess I hardly know whether I can or not; at least, whether
I should or not. - But I'll try.

The tender husband, Mr. Clerimont, has for his wife a
lady who has travelled, and is far gone in all the French
fashions: 'She brought me,' says he, 'a noble fortune;
and I thought she had a right to share it; therefore
carried her to see the world, forsooth, and make the tour
of France and Italy, where she learned to lose her money
gracefully, to admire every vanity in *our* sex, and contemn
every virtue in *her own*; which, with ten thousand other
perfections, are the ordinary improvements of a travelled
lady.' (3)

Tender as the husband was to be supposed to the wife,
which, by the way, is not extremely apparent, in *proper* or
right instances of tenderness, I presume to think he shows
no great politeness to the sex in general in this speech;
and the poet will be the less excusable for it, if he has
not drawn a general character of travelled ladies; and
much less still, if it shall appear, that that of Mrs.
Clerimont, on which this general reflection is founded,
is carried beyond nature and probability too.

But what is the method the tender husband takes to reclaim the lady? - Why this: he sets a former mistress of
his own to work, in man's clothes, to insnare her: and
thus he declares himself: - 'Now I can neither mortify her
vanity, that I may live at ease with her, nor quite *discard* her, till I have catched her a little enlarging her
innocent freedoms, as she calls them. For this end I am
content to be a French husband, though, now and then, with
the secret pangs of an Italian one; and therefore, sir,
or madam' (to his mistress Lucy, under the name of Mr.
Fainlove, in the dress of a young coxcomb), 'you are thus
equipped to attend and accost her ladyship.' A speech
unnecessary to Fainlove, who was dressed before for that
purpose, and had actually won money, in that character,
of Mrs. Clerimont. But the poet had no other way to let
the audience know it, as it should seem - 'It concerns
you,' continues he, 'to be diligent: if we (*i.e.*, himself
and his lady) wholly part - I need say *no more*: if we do
not - I'll see thee *well provided for*.'

Here's a fine moral scene opened, my lady, with regard
to Mr. Clerimont, his lady, and his kept mistress! Mr.
Fainlove, alias Mrs. Lucy, undertakes the task, in hopes
to live with Mr. Clerimont, in case of a divorce from his
wife; or to be provided for in case the plot does not
succeed; which makes it apparent, that, to say nothing of
his morality, poor Lucy had not met with a generous man
in Mr. Clerimont; since, after the forfeiture of her
honour, she was still to do a more infamous job, if possible, to procure for herself a provision from him.

Then Mr. Clerimont proceeds to instruct the new-made

man how to behave like a coxcomb, in order to engage his
lady's attention, and to join in all her foibles, till she
can furnish him with an opportunity to detect them in such
a way, as shall give a pretence for a divorce (a hint that
has been scandalously improved, and made *more* fashionable,
since this play was written); and this he does in such
free language and action, as must disgust any modest
person of either sex.

Then the poet causes this faithful mistress, in order
to make her character shine above that of the wife, and
indeed above his own likewise, to present her employer
with bills for five hundred pounds, which she tells him
she won of his wife the preceding night; and makes up two
thousand pounds which, Mr. Clerimont says, this unpro-
vided-for mistress of his has won from his lady, and
honestly given him; or else he could not, he owns, have
supplied her gaming losses. And Lucy declares, she will
gain him for ever from his lady, if she can: Yet, you'll
see by and by, that it is not love to his particular
person, more than *any* other, that is Lucy's inducement:
of course, then, it must be wickedness for wickedness'
sake.

The next character is Captain Clerimont, brother to the
other gentleman, a man of fashion and of the world, who,
being a younger brother, has his fortune to make; and we
shall see presently how he proposes to make it.

The next is Pounce, an infamous jobber or broker of
stocks, marriages, or anything – whose character be
pleased to take in his own words: 'Now 'tis my profession
to assist a *free-hearted* young fellow against an *unnatural
long-lived* father – to disencumber men of pleasure of the
vexation of unwieldy estates; to support a feeble title
to an inheritance!' – One that, Mr. Clerimont says, by way
of *praise,* he has seen prompting a stammering witness in
Westminster Hall, that wanted instruction; and could venture his ears with great bravery for his friend!

A worse character than this, can there be? Yet is it
not produced to be punished, neither.

The next person introduced is Hezekiah Tipkin, a banker
in Lombard Street, a man of an infamous and sordid character, and a vile usurer; who has a beautiful niece, Miss
Bridget Tipkin, over-run with affectation and romance;
with a great fortune in money, which so attracts the captain, that he supposes, in a sordid but witty manner
enough, all imaginable perfections in her person, before
he has a sight of it. This young lady, by a treaty between her uncle Tipkin and Sir Harry Gubbin, a tyrannical,
positive, hot-headed country gentleman, is designed to be
married to Humphrey, the son of Sir Harry, a creature so

savage, so rough, and so stupid, that there cannot be
drawn a stronger contrast than between his character and
that of Miss Bridget.

Mr. Pounce, who is employed as a broker in *their* match,
is, for a reward of one thousand pounds, to cheat them and
poor Humphrey, and to procure this young lady for Captain
Clerimont. Admirable justice and morality, all round!
you'll say, my lady. - For this purpose, it was necessary
that Mr. Pounce should find Mr. Humphrey so great a fool,
that, though he never saw him before, he very easily sets
him against his father, and against his cousin Bridget;
and all this on the wedding-day, in order to induce him to
make court to a person he tells him of, but never saw: And
who should this person be, as he tells him, but the sister
of Fainlove, Clerimont's man-dressed mistress? Which
sister, however, was to be Fainlove or Lucy herself, with
a worthy intent to impose upon poor Humphrey, as a wife,
this cast-off mistress of Clerimont. A just, a generous,
an exemplary plot this!

The next character is an old maiden gentlewoman, aunt
to Miss Bridget, an antiquated virgin, who, as Pounce
says, has a mighty affectation for youth, and is a great
lover of men and money - and she is set over her niece as
a promoter of the match with Humphrey. - Over this lady
Mr. Pounce has a great ascendant, half for sordid reasons, and half for amorous ones; and she makes a thorough
ridiculous and improbable character. Pounce introduces
Captain Clerimont into the company of the aunt and her
niece; and entertains the former, while the captain
engages the latter on the subject of her beloved romance.
These, with Mrs. Clerimont's maid Jenny, are the principal
characters.

I need not, my lady, take up much of your time or my
own, to tell you how they proceed.

Mr. Clerimont, then, after bearing from his wife what
hardly any gentleman could bear, surprises Fainlove, as a
man (and a very wicked scene it is, in every part), taking
shocking freedoms with her: and falling into a feigned
rage, threatens to kill Fainlove. The lady at first
menaces, and is haughty and arrogant; but finding by her
husband's behaviour to Lucy, whom he then addresses with
fondness before her face, that she is tricked by a woman
in man's habit, in her turn would kill the impostor as
Lucy, whom as Fainlove she tried to save; and a scene on
this occasion occurs, to my thinking, very ridiculous.
Mr. Clerimont then upbraids her with her guilt; and what
was hardly ever known in nature, she reforms *instantly* on
the spot, and expresses all the signs of contrition
imaginable. He forgives and receives her, guilty as she

is in her intention, her person only untainted, and an
adulteress in her mind, as she would have been in fact,
had Fainlove been a man: and a moving scene, had it been
from proper motives, follows. *Yet* (still more preposterous - excuse me, madam) afterwards she resumes all her
travelled and nonsensical airs, all her improbable follies, to help to support the plot in favour of Captain
Clerimont upon Miss Bridget, and the infamous one of
Pounce's and Mr. Clerimont's against poor Humphrey, the
only *innocent* character in the play, and the only *suffering* one: And this latter, as well as the former plot,
being brought about, a laughing scene is produced, by Sir
Harry's soundly cudgelling his stupid son, for permitting
himself to be so foolishly drawn in.

Now, my good lady, can you see one character, and I
think, I have given them justly, fit to be set up for an
example in this celebrated play of an author so celebrated? I must own, as I said before, I was greatly disappointed in my expectations of it. There is indeed a
great deal of sprightly wit, and knowledge of the wicked
part of the world, displayed in it, as it seems to me, by
what I have heard Mr. B——— talk sometimes; but there is
not one character in it but what is shockingly immoral,
and at the same time, either *above* or *below* nature; so
that the ridicule which is intended in it, on the bad
characters, cannot, in my poor opinion, be just or effi-
cacious.

For first, there never, I believe, could be a gentleman so foolishly tender, yet so plottingly cruel, to his
lady, as Mr. Clerimont.

There never could be such a very fantastical lady as
Mrs. Clerimont. - And there is such an improbability in
the intimate access, which Lucy in man's clothes has to
her; in that creature's lewd views, yet faithful and
generous conduct, in giving back to Clerimont, who had
not provided for her, two thousand pounds, won of the
fantastical lady; and yet in her being so little delicate
in her *love* to Clerimont, which one would expect should
be her motive, as to join to trick and marry one of the
greatest fools in the world; that it was surprising to
me, that it could pass either author or audience.

Then Tipkin's character is unnaturally, stupidly,
yet knavishly bad.

Sir Harry Gubbin is a father who never could have his
fellow; and after furiously beating his son, is reconciled to his marriage, as instantly as Mrs. Clerimont is
converted; and that to an unknown person, who appears to
him in man's clothes, for the sake of three thousand
pounds fortune only, although he had been quarrelling

with Tipkin about one thousand pounds, which he would not
give up, out of ten thousand pounds which his son was to
have had with Bridget.

Numps, his son, is a character, take it altogether,
quite out of nature and probability. 'Tis hardly possible, that a savage, brought up in a wood, who never conversed with man or woman, could be so stupid; and easily
might a poet form a plot for a play, if such a character
could be admitted as Numps's.

The aunt is credulous, and affected beyond probability
also.

Miss Bridget delicately indelicate in many places, and
improbably fantastic in all.

Pounce shamelessly glorying, and *succeeding* in his villany, and deeming the imputation of the worst rogueries
to him, as a panegyric: and such immoralities, mingled
with obscenities, all through, that I was glad when the
play was over.

But yet, to say truth, there are very pretty descriptions, and a great deal of wit and humour in it. The
dialogue is lively; the painter's scene entertaining;
and that between Sir Harry and Tipkin, diverting, though
low; which, together with the fantastic airs of Mrs.
Clerimont, and Miss Bridget, and the farcical humours of
Numps, make it the less wonder, that such as did not
attend to nature, probability, and morality, were struck
with the life and spirit of the performance: and especially as Mr. Wilks, who acted Captain Clerimont, and Mrs.
Oldfield, who acted Miss Bridget, so incomparably performed their parts, as must have saved a play even of a
worse tendency than 'The Accomplished Fools'. (4)

The moral I will transcribe, although I doubt it is a
very inapplicable one to the characters; and so is far
from making amends for a long performance that in such a
variety of characters has not *one* moral in it; nor indeed
is there so much as one just or generous design pursued
throughout the play.

You've seen th'extremes of the domestic life,
A son too much confined - too free a wife.
By gen'rous bonds you either should restrain,
And only on their inclinations gain.

This I call inapplicable, because it was needless
advice to such husbands as Mr. Clerimont, for whom it
seems designed; for he was generous to excess, carrying
her abroad to Italy and France, and paying all her debts
of honour implicitly: whence the name of the play, 'The
Tender Husband'.

Wives, to obey, must love. -

Clerimont did everything to make a grateful woman love
him, before his strange plot to reclaim her.

- Children revere,
While only slaves are governed by their fear. (5)

Mrs. Clerimont was not treated like a slave, yet is
reclaimed only by *fear*. So that the moral seems to be
calculated for the Numpses (the fools and idiots) and the
Sir Harries; two characters that, as I humbly apprehend,
never were in nature, any more, it is to be hoped, than
are the rest.

It looks to me, in short, as if the author had forgot
the moral all the way; and being put in mind of it by some
kind friend (Mr. Addison, perhaps), was at a loss to draw
one from such characters and plots as he had produced; and
so put down what came uppermost, for the sake of custom,
without much regard to propriety. And truly I should
imagine likewise, that the play was begun with a design to
draw more amiable characters, answerable to the title of
'The Tender Husband'; but that the author, being carried
away by the luxuriancy of a genius which he had not the
heart to prune, on a general survey of the whole, distrus-
ting the propriety of that title, added the under one:
with an - OR, 'The Accomplished Fools', in justice to his
piece, and compliment to his audience. And, pardon me,
madam, had he called it 'The Accomplished Knaves', I
would not have been angry at him, because there would have
been more propriety in the title.

I wish I could, for the sake of the authors, have
praised every scene of this play: I hoped to have reason
for it. Judge then, my dear lady, what a mortification it
was to me, not to be able to say I liked above one, the
painter's scene, (6) which too was out of time, being on
the wedding-day; and am forced to disapprove of every
character in it, and the views of every one. I am,
dearest madam,

Your most obliged sister and servant,
P.B.——.

Notes

1 Written by Ambrose Philips, the play was first acted
   on 17 March 1712. Steele wrote the Prologue, and
   Eustace Budgell, probably assisted by Addison, the
   Epilogue.

2 For Steele's statement of Addison's help in the composition of 'The Tender Husband', see 'Spectator' 555.
3 The next three quotations are from this same act and
   scene.
4 Robert Wilks (*c*. 1665-1732); Anne Oldfield (1683-1730).
   Pamela probably derived their names from the cast
   listed in the edition of 1705.
5 The last six lines of 'The Tender Husband', spoken by
   Captain Clerimont.
6 'The Tender Husband', IV. ii.

19. DANIEL DEFOE, 'THE FEARS OF THE PRETENDER'

1715

This is an excerpt from Defoe's pamphlet 'The Fears of the
Pretender Turn'd into the Fears of Debauchery....with a
Hint to Richard Steele, Esq;'. Representative of an
extremist position, Defoe argued against the theatre as a
place of sin and indicted Steele for promoting attendance
at the playhouses.

...and it is Vain for Men to say, we are true to the
Protestant Succession, we are Enemies to the *Pretender*,
if they are, at the same Time, void of Religion, aban-
don'd to Immorality, press'd to Debauch the Morals of the
People, they are Enemies to God; and it must be granted,
That overballances all the Merits of their being Enemies
to the *Pretender*. No Church can be out of Danger in the
Hands of those, who act against the Interest of God and
Religion in the World.
    The fam'd Writer of the 'Tattlers' and 'Spectators' is
an eminent Example of the Case now in Debate, and let the
best of his Eloquence Defend it, if he is able; his
Genius, Humour and Learning are Inimitable. He recommended himself to every Degree and Capacity. It was a Reflection on a Man's Understanding, to detract from his
Character; (1) and the bright Things written by him, will
be valuable to Posterity. He exposed many a bad Custom
to an eternal Ridicule, and deliver'd us from a Load of
Habits, which in our Speech and Manners, Writing and Conversation, help'd to make us Ridiculous. The Absurdities

of Speech, of Gesture, of Behaviour; the Rudeness of Men,
the Immodesty of Women, Legitimated by Custom, receiv'd
admirable Reproof from his Pen; and he ought to be forgiven a Thousand Miscarriages of an ordinary Nature, for
the sake of these Things, whether in his own Practice, or
in his Writing; but it can never be forgiven him, either
by God, or Man, till he Repents of, and Reforms it; that
he did more by recommending the Play-Houses, to promote
the present Madness of the Age, in running up the Humour
of following Plays to such an Extream, as we now see it,
than all the Agents Hell ever employed before.

In this he has assisted to Debauch the Morals of the
People, especially about the Court, more than all the
Regulations of Conduct, owing to his other Writings, can
ballance; and indeed he surfeited good Men, even with the
rest of his Writings, and caused his Paper exceedingly to
decline, by making its Works a meer Abridgment of the Play-
House, a Compliment upon the Performance, and in short, a
Broker to the Actors.

Here, what he pleas'd to mention, was ever admir'd;
and for the 'Spectator' to give a good Word to a Play,
was to fill the House. In process of Time, his Name was
put to the Prologue and Epilogue, to push a Play into
the World; and for a grave Person, in an Antick Dress,
with a Comick Gravity, to sit in a Box, and suppos'd,
tho' but in Banter, to be the 'Spectator', was sufficient
to draw the whole Town to the Theatre.

By these Things, it is not to be imagined, what Number
of People, from City and Country, (who could Entertain
themselves before, with Innocent Diversion, and good Company, and had no Opinion of the Play-Houses,) were drawn
in by Crowds, to follow the Stage; and Plays were represented in such a Manner, in so many Particulars, as that
it was not doubted, but the Stage would go farther to
settle our Vertue than the Pulpit, and we should be
Play'd out of Vice and Prophaneness, sooner than Preach'd
out of it. God forbid we should have no better Arguments
against the Danger of the Church, than what may be drawn
from these Maxims.

From these beginnings, (*such was the Witchcraft of his
Perswasions*,) the present Humour of the Town, in their
flocking to the Stage, took their rise, and an innumerable Crowd of *Italian* Actors flock'd daily over to *London;*
and for a Test of the advances in Vertue and Piety, these
would Inspire us with the most Celebrated Play; and That
which seized the Humour of the Town with an Irresistible
Magick, was particularly Eminent for recommending the
Vertue *of Self-Murther*, to the Practice of a Christian
Country, and exalting the Character of *Cato* as an

inimitable Hero, who laid violent Hands upon himself to
preserve his Liberty, when he ought, would he have been a
Pattern of Vertue and Gallantry, with the Bravery of a
true Hero, never to have abandon'd the Liberty of his
Country, which he Notoriously did, but to have fought for
it to the last Gasp; and according to that truly Heroick
Expression of King *William*, mentioned by Sir *William
Temple, Have dy'd in the last Ditch*. (2) To bring this
back to the Thing, for which it was mentioned, it must be
acknowledged, that this Recommending the Stage by the
Writer of the 'Spectator', has had a fatal Effect upon the
People of this Kingdom, and especially on the Court and
City; and how far Circumstances have concurr'd since that,
to make this Humour of following the Play-Houses Univer-
sal, is left to common Observation.

It is true, the Queen, upon many Occasions, did not
fall in with the Humour; Her Majesty was a Pattern of
Vertue, and of strict Piety, and gave no Encouragement
to the Vices of her People, especially by her own Example;
but on the contrary, embrac'd, with Chearfulness, every
Occasion of restraining the Excursions of others, and
shewing her Dislike of the Atheism, Prophaneness, Immoralities and Debaucheries of her Subjects: Hence we found
That growing Lay-Stall of Lewdness and Filthiness, call'd
May-Fair, (3) suppress'd by her especial Command; all the
private Play-Houses, which used to be Built there, were
forbidden; the like was done at *Bartholomew-Fair* and
Southwark-Fair, (4) all these were suppress'd in her
Reign; nor could all the Solicitations of her Ladies, and
the Recommendations by Mr. *Steel* of this or that Play, or
part of a Play, prevail upon Her Majesty once to oblige
them, or give Encouragement to any of her Subjects to
follow, or Visit them by her Example.

Custom may have made these Things less scandalous
abroad than here; and perhaps His Majesty, and the Royal
Family, who see the Torrent of the Peoples Humours, and
not yet being fully informed of the fatal Consequences of
Play-Houses to the People of *Great Britain*, have not yet
thought fit to shew that Dislike and Resentment of their
Behaviour, which in Time, the Players, and Hunters of
Play-Houses also, will give them Cause to do.

Yet even already, we find, His Majesty has been
obliged to give strict Orders that all offensive Expressions shall be carefully Censur'd, and taken out of
them. (5) Time, no doubt, will shew, that not the Lewdness of Words only will be needful to be expung'd from
the Play-Houses, but when the People shall, by their
Excesses (*for the* English *pursue no Vice with Moderation*)
convince the King and Royal Family, that the Play-Houses

are the Receptacles of the Scandalous, the Nests of Rakes,
Bullies, &c. that Fightings, Whorings, Murthers, are the
common Practice of these Places; that the Plays grow Lewd
in spight of Laws and Regulations, the Players scandalous
and Lawless, and in short, that the Youth of the Kingdom
receive there a general Tincture of Debauchery, and Wickedness, when His Majesty shall be told, that it was so in
King *Charles* IId's Time, and that 173 Murthers and Duels
were committed and occasion'd at the several Play-Houses,
on Quarrels commenc'd there, within 19 Years of that
Reign; and that great Progress is already made in the like
Mischief, upon this new Encrease of the People's Humour
to follow those Play-Houses: I say, when His Majesty shall
be rightly and fully inform'd of these Things, there is no
Question but his Zeal for Religion, and Concern for the
Good of his People, will move him to put an effectual Stop
to this growing Evil, and let the Nation know, that it is
their Reformation, not their universal Destruction that is
the Thing desired by him; and that he can by no means
gratify them in a Liberty so fatal to themselves as this
will be.

It is no Ill-will to the Writer of the 'Spectator',
that occasions this Remark: Whether it is just or not, it
is left, I say, to common Observation; and if just, I
think it must be granted, that is more than necessary to
mention it, that those People may see how easily, and by
what insensible Degree they are drawn to a general Defec-
tion of Vertue, and to follow a Practice, which in time
will be the Ruin, not of the Church only, but even of
Religion it self in the Nation.

Notes

1 But see Defoe's 'Honour and Prerogative of the Queen's
   Majesty Vindicated' (No. 12).
2 Sir William Temple (1628-99), statesman, author,
   ambassador to the Hague. In the dispatches sent by
   Temple, Prince William made a number of such assertions, albeit in diplomatic language ('The Works of
   Sir William Temple' [1720], II, pp. 391, 429, 446,
   448).
3 May-fair, so called from a *fair* originating in King
   Charles's reign and held in Brook Field (the present
   Curzon and Hertford Streets). In 1708 the fair was
   declared 'a public nuisance and inconvenience' and
   suspended for several years. See 'Tatler' 4, 20.
4 Both fairs were held in September and offered freak
   and puppet-shows, drolls, rarities, operas, tight-rope

walking, etc.

5 When Steele became a licensee of the Theatre Royal in
   Drury Lane in October 1714, he was charged by the
   King's ministers to prohibit the performance of those
   plays containing 'any passages or expressions offensive
   to piety and good manners, until the same be corrected
   and purged'.

20. COLLEY CIBBER, DEDICATION TO 'XIMENA'

1719

Colley Cibber (1671–1757) dated his dedication to Steele
29 September 1719. Long associated with the Theatre Royal
as actor, dramatist, and manager, Cibber worked hard to
see his friend Steele become governor of the Drury Lane
Theatre. For two years there was harmony. With the
appointment of Lord Newcastle as Lord Chamberlain in
April 1717, however, peace gave way to discord as Steele
and Newcastle fought for control of the theatre. Tension
increased but before any punitive action was taken against
Steele, Cibber wrote his dedication in which he pointed
out his friend's great service to his country and the ill-
usage he received for his efforts. After the publication
of 'Ximena', Cibber was silenced and by January 1720
Steele was expelled from the governorship.

To Sir *RICHARD STEELE*.

While the World was under the daily Correction and Authority of your *Lucubrations*, their Influence on the Publick
was not more visible in any one Instance, than the sudden
Improvement (I might say Reformation) of the Stage, that
immediately follow'd them: From whence it is now apparent,
that many Papers, (which the Grave and Severe then
thought were thrown away upon that Subject) were, in your
speaking to the *Theatre,* still advancing the same Work,
and instructing the same World in Miniature; to the end,
that whenever you thought fit to be silent, the Stage, as
you had amended it, might, by a kind of substituted
Power, continue to Posterity, your peculiar manner of
making the Improvement of their Minds their publick
Diversion.

Nothing but a Genius so universally rever'd could, with
such Candor and Penetration, have pointed out its Faults
and Misconduct; and so effectually have redeem'd its Uses
and Excellence from Prejudice and Dis-favour. How often
have we known the most elegant Audiences drawn together at
a Day's Warning, by the Influence or Warrant of a single
'Tatler', in a Season, when our best Endeavours without
it, could not defray the Charge of the Performance? This
powerful and innocent Artifice soon recover'd us into
Fashion, and spirited us up, to think such new Favour of
our Auditors worthy of our utmost Industry; and 'tis to
that Industry so instructed, the Stage now owes its Reputation and Prosperity: And therefore, as I have heard you
say, (which I hope will justify my repeating it) *viz*. To
talk of suppressing the Stage, because the Licentiousness,
Ignorance or Poverty of its former Professors may have
abus'd the proper Ends of its Institution, were, in Morality, as absurd a Violence, as it would be in Religion to
silence the Pulpit, because Sedition or Treason has been
preach'd there: And tho' for the same Reason our ancient
Legislature may have been justly provok'd to mention such
Actors in Terms of Ignominy, yet that ought no more to be
a Reproach to his Majesty's present Company of Comedians, than it is to the Patriots of old *Rome*, that their
first Founders were Robbers and Outlaws.

After such Benefits receiv'd, what less return could
the Gratitude and Interest of the Actors think of, than
to intreat you to join in their Petition to the Crown, to
set you at their Head, that you might as justly partake
of the Profits, as the Praise and Merit of Supporting
them? How much you have done for us was visible to all
the World, what Sense we have of it is yet known to few;
I therefore take this Occasion to make our Acknowledgments, if possible, as publick as our Obligations.

The good you have done Mankind gives every sensible
Heart a double Delight; that of the Benefit it self, and
the Pleasure of thanking you: And yet, if we consider the
World, as one Person, we cannot but say it has been
ungrateful to you: ...

But I am not to forget, there has been a Circumstance
in your Merit too, that could have happen'd to no Man but
your Self: To say you had hazarded your Life, or Fortune,
for the Service of your Country, were but to allow you
Praise in common with Thousands, that have done the same:
But when we consider how *Amiable a Fame* you sacrific'd to
its Interests, it would be barbarous not to inquire into
the Value of it: How long, and happily did *Old Isaac* triumph in the universal Love, and Favour of his Readers?
The Grave, the Chearful, the Wise, the Witty, Old, Young,

Rich and Poor, all Sorts, though never so opposite in
Character, whether Beaux or Bishops, Rakes or Men of
Business, Coquets or Statesmen, Whigs or Tories, All were
equally his Friends, and thought their Tea in a Morning
had not its Taste without him: Thus, while you appear'd
the *Agreeable Philosopher* only, Mankind by a general
Assent came into your Applause, and Service: And yet, how
in a Moment was this calm, and unrivall'd Enjoyment blown
into the Air, when the Apprehension of your Country's
being in a Flame called upon you to resign it, by employ-
ing the same Spirit of Conviction, in the restless Office
of a *Patriot*? For no sooner did you rise the Champion of
our insulted Constitution, than one Half of the Nation
(that had just before allow'd you the proper *Censor* of our
Morals) in an Instant deny'd you to have had either *Wit,
Sense* or *Genius*; the Column they had been two Years
jointly raising to your Reputation, was then, in as few
Days, thrown down by the implacable Hands that rais'd it.
But when they found no Attacks of Prejudice could deface
the real Beauty of your Writings, and that they *still*
recover'd from the Blow, their Malice then indeed was
driven to its last Hold, of giving the Chief Merit of them
to another great Author, (1) who they allow'd had never so
audaciously provok'd them: This was indeed turning your
own Cannon upon you, and making use of your private Vertue
to depreciate your Character; for had not the diffusive
Benevolence of your Heart thought even *Fame* too great a
Good to be possess'd *alone*, you would never (as you confess'd in the *Preface* to those Works) have taken your
nearest Friend into a Share of it: A Man of Modern Prudence would have consider'd a *Fame* so *peculiar*, as a
Mistress, whom *his* Services only had deserved; and would
have maturely deliberated, before he trusted her Constancy
in private, with the dearest Friend upon Earth: Your
Enemies therefore thus knowing that your own Consent had
partly justify'd their Insinuations, saved a great deal
of their Malice from being ridiculous, and fairly left you
to apply to such your singular Conduct, what *Mark Antony*
says of *Octavius* in the Play---

> *Fool that I was! upon my Eagle's Wings
> I bore this Wren, 'till I was tir'd with soaring,
> And now, he mounts above me----*   Dryd. (2)

Nothing is more common among the prudent Men of this
World, than their Admiration that you will not (with all
your Talents) be guided to the proper Steps of making
your Fortune: as if that were the *non ultra* of Happiness:
Can they suppose that Flattery, Deceit and Treachery, or

the perpetual Surrender of our Reason, Will, and Freedom
to the Convenience, and Passions of others, with a Train
of the like abject Servilities, if your Spirit could stoop
to them, are not as soon attain'd to, as their contrary
Vertues? And that consequently it is much easier to *make*
a Fortune, than to *deserve* One? Such Men can never know
how much the Conscious Transport of having done their
Duty, is preferable to all the mean, unwieldy Pomp of
arrogant, and unmerited Prosperity--- But let them hug
themselves, and count their Happiness by their Sums of
Gold; yours is to know, the Service you have done your
Country has contributed to their being secure in the
Possession of it, and that such (however unfashionable
Actions) are (like their Gold) intrinsically valuable
only for their Weight, which can neither rise or fall
from the Stamp of Favour, or Discouragement....

Notes

1 Addison.
2 Dryden, 'All for Love' (1678), II. i.

21. JOHN DENNIS, 'THE CHARACTERS AND CONDUCT OF SIR JOHN
EDGAR', LETTERS I, IV

1720

From 'The Critical Works of John Dennis', ed. E. N.
Hooker (1939-43), II, pp. 181-92, 213-16.

Letter I

Sir JOHN,
The World has a long Time wonder'd that you, who have so
many Years endeavour'd to pass for a Person of the greatest Probity of the Age, should constantly chuse to go by
an *Alias*, which is almost always an infallible Sign of a
Knave. (1) But notwithstanding your setting forth in
Disguise, during this Season of *Masquerades*, I no sooner
took up your Paper, but I found several as distinguishing
Marks of your Mind, as your Black Peruke, and your Dusky

Countenance are of your Right Worshipful Person. The
Pedantry of your *Motto*, (2) The Singularity of your Style,
which has a Smack of *Tiperarian*, as *Livy*'s had of *Patavin-
ity*; your impertinent Praise of your Son, your diffuse
Description of him, of his Person, his Parts, his Address
(*id populus curat scilicet*) (3) and above all, that
Characteristical Stroke of Vanity, where you tell us,
that you are very well entertain'd in an Assembly, where
those who in other Conversations pass for fine Gentlemen,
and fine Ladies, would be uninform'd Savages; all these
denote you to be a certain Person, whom the King has
graciously vouchsaf'd to Knight; and who has since with
wonderful Goodness, Modesty, Wisdom, and Gratitude,
bewail'd in Publick, that his Majesty has been so
Gracious.

Well! my dear Knight, thou seest I have found thee
out; and having found thee to be my old Acquaintance, I
may make a little more free with thee, than if thou wert
a meer Stranger. (4) Yet however I may mislike thy
Design, I cannot but commend the Greatness of thy Spirit,
who being a Knight in Reality, wilt no longer be a Squire
not even in Masquerade; which has more than once oblig'd
a Dutchess to dwindle into a Dairy Maid; but art resolv'd,
like a true Man of Honour, to be tenacious of it alone and
in the Dark.

But 'tis Time to come to the Business. You say you are
engaged, by the generous Concern of an old Lady, to undertake in this publick Manner, the Preservation and Improvement of the *English* Stage. If I presume now to give you a
little wholesome Advice, will not you be Angry?

Lay aside this foolish Design. You have neither
Capacity, nor Learning, nor Authority, for such an Undertaking. What! Do you pretend to set up for a Preserver
and Improver of the publick Tast? You, who have done
more to corrupt it, and to destroy it, than any Hundred
Men in all *England*? You, of whose Errors in Judgment in
your Lucubrations and Speculations, one might compile
whole Volumes? You, who by your Criticisms, and by your
Conduct, have brought the Stage to a Sort of a *Loosing
Loadum*, where they who write worst, are sure to succeed
best. Once more, I say, lay aside this foolish Design,
or rather this foolish Pretence, for 'tis not your Design
to improve any Thing, but your own Privy-Purse, Sir *John*;
and you have been Twenty Years in improving that, and are
just where you begun; so unlucky you are at improving,
Sir *John*. The Truth of the Matter is this. You, and
your Viceroy, *C*———*r*, (5) and the rest of your Deputy
Governors, have got the Ill-will of the Court, and Town,
by exerting several noble Qualities, too well known both

to Court and Town, to be mentioned here. Now your Interests being dependant on each other, and as it were the
same, you have concerted and contrived between you, like
to *Bessus*, (6) and the Brothers of the Sword, to play the
Game into each others Hands; so to retrieve your Interests, and your false Reputations, and to cast a Mist before the Eyes of those who never were clear-sighted. In
order to this, you are to cry them up for accomplish'd
Actors, and for inoffensive irreproachable Persons; and
they are to extol you to the Skies, for a noble-minded,
bright, and most generous Patron; and *C——r* is to place
you among the Gods, as the *Romans* did their Emperors, by
making you fly like an Eagle to them. (7)

There is not one of those few Readers, who have vouchsaf'd to read the Papers call'd the 'Theatre', but see
through the Design of them. While you and your Deputies,
like Four Babies, put your Fingers before your Eyes, and
being Blind your selves, fancy that no body else can See.

For do but consider with what intolerable Blunders you
begin. You doubt not, you say, but you shall bring the
World into your Opinion, that the Profession of an Actor,
who in the other part of his Conduct is irreproachable,
ought to receive the same kind Treatment, which the World
is ready to pay all other Artists. I will not quarrel
with you about your *English* here. I shall let that alone
till the end of the Letter. At present I shall only take
Notice of Things. You must give me Leave at present only
to tell you, that you are running a Way that is quite
Counter to the Improvement of the Stage. For to improve
the Stage, it would be necessary to admonish your Deputies to mend their Faults, and to augment their Talents;
whereas you are for annihilating the first, and magnify-
ing to such a Degree the last, as to imply that there is
no Room for improving them. But the Truth of the Matter
is, that tho' the Conduct of your Actors were Irreproachable, which no body will affirm but your self; and their
Talents in their Kind incomparable, which neither they
nor you believe; yet would they by no Means be equal to
some other Artists.

Yet this Paradox you pretend to maintain by the
Authority of *Cicero*. As if the greatest Authority in the
World could signify any Thing against Reason and Experi-
ence, which are both against you, as we shall shew anon.
I shall at present maintain, that the Authority of *Cicero*
is as much against you, as either Reason, or Experience.

To shew you that I am resolved to agree with you, as
much as I possibly can, I will not quarrel with the Sense
of your pretended Quotation from *Cicero*. I will only
quarrel with the Application of it. *Cicero*, you say,

observes, in the first Book of his Offices, *That Persons
are to be esteemed Genteel, or Servile, according as the
Arts or Capacities in which they are employed, are
Liberal, or Mechanical.* He esteems those Liberal, in
which the Faculties of the Mind are chiefly employed, and
those Mechanical, in which the Body is the more laborious
Part. Now from hence you are pleased to infer, that the
Employment of an Actor depending upon the Labour of the
Mind, more than upon that of the Body; a good Actor ought
as much to be valued and esteem'd as any other Artist
whatever. A very surprizing Inference! For to convince
you that this Passage of *Cicero* can never be scrued nor
tortur'd to the Advantage of Actors; that Orator, in his
Oration for *Archias* the Poet, (8) asserts in the Compass
of four Lines, what is contradictory of each of the
Branches of the foresaid Inference....

Now here the *Roman* Orator plainly asserts two Things:
First, That the Employment of an Actor depends more upon
the Body than upon the Mind: And, Secondly, That the
Esteem which we ought to have, ev'n for an excellent,
inoffensive, irreproachable Actor, is infinitely less
than what we ought to have for several other Artists.
By the way, we shall take Occasion to convince you anon,
that excellent, inoffensive, irreproachable Actors, are
now-a-days black Swans.

But suppose we should allow, that the Employment of an
Actor depends more on the Mind than it does on the Body;
is it not monstrous to conclude from thence, that an
Actor ought to be as much esteem'd as any other Artist
whatever? The Employment of a Pedant certainly depends
more upon the Mind than it does on the Body: But shall we
infer from thence, that a Pedant ought to be as much
esteem'd, as an accomplish'd Divine, or a consummate
Statesman?

But you are pleas'd, Sir *John*, to proceed to still
greater Wonders. *For*, say you, *if there be no Objection
against what the Orator says, that Men are to be consider'd only from their Abilities,* (by the way, the
Orator never said any thing like it;) *let their severest
Enemies name the Profession, which requires Qualifications for the Practice of it, more elegant, more manly,
more generous and more ornamental, than that of a just
and pleasing Actor.* That is to say in plain *English*,
That a just and pleasing Actor has Qualifications as
elegant, as manly, as generous, and as ornamental, as
any one of any Profession whatever. That is to say
that *Dogget* and *Ben Johnson*, being just and pleasing
Actors, have Qualifications as elegant, as manly, as
generous, as ornamental, as ever had formerly Archbishop

Tillotson, or my Lord Chancellor *Bacon*.

Now, Sir *John*, can you forbear laughing, upon the reading this, at the Repetition of your own Extravagance?
But besides that all this is monstrously and ridiculously
false, and the reverse of common Sense; you knock your
own pretended Design on the Head, which is the Improvement
of the *British* Stage; and are the very worst Enemy that
the Actors can possibly have. For by augmenting the Pride
of these People by your vain Assertions, you are sure at
the same time to augment their Insolence, their Impudence,
their Ignorance and their Arrogance; which will render
them absolutely unimproveable, and bring them further into
Disgrace with the Court and Town, till they become at last
insupportable. Therefore 'tis plain, from your taking
this Method, that either you do not design the Improvement
of the Stage, notwithstanding your Pretence; or that you
do not understand it.

But I, who really and sincerely intend the Improvement
of the Stage, will shew that I understand it better than
you; and will be a better Friend to these People, by
shewing them what They really are, and by that means rendring them humble, and consequently docile and improve-
able. For I pretend to shew both you and them, that
Actors are so far from having the great Qualities of
extraordinary Men, that they have not the Understanding
and Judgment of ordinary Gentlemen; because they have not
had their Education.

I defy any one to name so much as one great Actor in
my Time, who had had a generous Education; that is, who
had from his Youth been train'd up to Arts and Sciences.
Nor do I know of any one great Actor, since the Establishment of the Stage in *England*, who had extraordinary
Parts.

Shakespear, indeed, had great Parts; but he was not a
great Actor.

Otway and *Lee* had both Education and Parts; but they
were wretched Actors; which soon oblig'd them to quit the
Stage, and take up a nobler Employment.

There cannot be a more certain Sign of the Meanness of
Actors Capacities, than their being the worst Judges in
the World of the very Things about which they are eternally employ'd. And the present Actors, who are the
Managers of the Play-House, (9) have given all the World
an irrefutable Proof, that they have still less Knowledge
of Plays than had any of their Predecessors. For have not
they turn'd Booksellers *mal à propos*, and given a Hundred
and twenty Pound for the Copy of a Play, for which none
of their Predecessors would have given Five Pound? (10)
Perhaps they may say, that they depended upon the Interest

of the Author, and a numerous Cabal. A very foolish
Dependance! and which sets in a full Light their want of
Understanding. For tho' the Interest of an Author, and
a numerous Cabal, may go a great way towards a Theatrical
Success; they will be so far from availing a Bookseller,
that on the contrary, the Publishing of a damn'd Play,
which has had Success upon the Stage, is very certain to
put an End ev'n to that Success.

The very Employment of an Actor makes him less capable
of understanding Plays, than those who have other Affairs,
and other Diversions. For as a Sot and a Rake, who runs
from Tavern to Brandyshop, from Brandyshop to Tavern, and
is continually swilling, deadens his Palate, and depraves
his Taste to that degree, that he is utterly incapable of
distinguishing between brew'd and sophisticated Liquors,
and the pure and generous Juice of the Grape: So Players,
who are always swallowing their Parts, and getting by
Rote with equal Application, and equal Earnestness, what
a Person who has a noble Genius produces, and what a
wretched Poetaster scribbles; become utterly incapable
of distinguishing between the pure and golden Stream that
flows from the immortal Fountain of *Hippocrene*, and that
which springs from a muddy Source.

Their sordid Love and Greediness of Gain, contributes
not a little to the corrupting their Understandings. For
when a foolish Play happens to have a Run, as they call
it, their sordid Temper inclines them to believe it good:
It immediately becomes what they call a Stock Play; and
is regarded as a Standard.

If you can gain so great a Point, as to make Players
pass for Men of great Abilities, and for inoffensive,
irreproachable Persons, you will stem a strong Current,
which has prevail'd in the World for above Two Thousand
Years. At *Rome*, during the Purity of the Commonwealth,
they were accounted infamous; and the *Censors* of the
Republick never fail'd to remove them from the Tribe in
which they found them, to a lower. In *France* they are
always excommunicated; and no Priest will, or dares to
absolve them, till they are in the Article of Death.
Here in *England*, they have always been look'd upon as
Vagabonds and Rogues by Statute; unless they have been
under the Protection of our Kings, or of some of our
English Peers. Yet in this last Case, I have been
credibly inform'd, that, for great Misdemeanors, they
have been sent to *Whitehall*, and whipt at the Porter's
Lodge. And I have heard *Jo. Haines* more than once
ingenuously own, that he had been whipt twice there.

If *C———r*, in the Days of King *James*, or King *Charles*
the First, had dar'd to treat a Lord Chamberlain with

half the Insolence that he has lately done the present,
(11) he would have been made an errant Bullbeggar: His
Bones would have been as bloody, as his Head is raw.

I have now shewn you, what the Sense of the best and
wisest Nations is, and has been, with relation to Actors.
If I may be allow'd to speak my own, I am inclin'd to
believe that good Actors, as long as they are irreproachable in the rest of their Conduct, ought to be encourag'd
and esteem'd; yet to be encourag'd and esteem'd as Actors,
not as Gentlemen, nor as Persons who have a Thousand
times their Merit: But that ev'n the best Actors, with
the most unblameable Conduct, are never to be trusted
with Power. The trusting People with Power, who have
neither Birth nor any Education, is sure to make them
insolent, not only to Poets by whose Labours they live,
but to Persons of the very first Quality in *England*.

Besides what has happen'd lately, I remember the Time
in a former Reign, when Three Peers of *England*, a Duke
and Two Earls, both the one and the other some of the
most Illustrious of their respective Benches, wanted
Power to get one poor Comedy acted; a certain insolent
impertinent Actor, who has lately reviv'd his Insolence
with large Additions, had (thro' old *Rich*'s Weakness,
whom he led by the Nose) Power to withstand them all.

Well then, Sir *John*, I would have good Actors, as long
as they are inoffensive, esteem'd and encourag'd as
Actors; that is, as the Tools and Instruments, and
Machines of the Muses, as the Apes of a Poet's Meaning,
and the Eccho's and Parrots of his Voice. But if they
once dare to grow insolent, if they behave themselves
like Beggars on Horseback, and not only ride furiously
as soon as they are up, but endeavour to ride over those
very Persons who but the Moment before mounted them; they
ought to be us'd like *Indians* who run a-muck in their own
Country, or like Dogs who run mad in ours.

I come now to consider Actors in particular, as they
are at present upon the *English* Stage; which you say you
prefer to any other in *Europe*. I will not dispute that
with you, because it signifies nothing to the Purpose.
But has the *English* Stage made any Improvement, since it
has been under the Intendency of this separate Ministry?
(12) Has it not vilely degenerated? Are there either
the great Actors that were upon it Thirty Years ago; or
any such new entertaining Comedies as from Time to Time
appear'd upon it? Is there any Promise of a future Poet?
Is there any Promise of a future Actor? No; all is going
to Ruin: The Stage is sinking under you; and there is no
Hope of saving it, but by getting it out of the Hands of
the Separate Ministry.

I know very well, that the present Managers of the
Stage, empty by Nature, and vain by Success, value themselves abundantly upon their crowded Audiences. But how
little Discernment, nay, how little common Sense is requir'd to know, that their full Audiences are only the
Effects of the Numbers of their Spectators, increas'd by
several great Events which have happen'd of late Years;
as, the Revolution, the Union, the King's Accession to the
Crown, and the Return of our Armies from the Continent?
This is the only Reason why the Audiences are fuller than
they were formerly, when they were far better entertain'd.

But while the Stage is thus sinking under you, by the
Conduct of your Deputies, and your own, you are bragging
that they will exalt it higher than those of the *Grecians,*
and *Romans*; like a frank Godfather, you Promise and vow
strange Things in their Names, which like most other God-
fathers, and other Godchildren, neither they nor you will
ever keep, or perform. But is there any Thing in the
Course of Nature, that can encourage you to make such a
Promise? For you may take my Word for it, the World has
done taking you for a Conjurer, and is come to believe
that you deal with the Devil only, like other Sinners.
Is there then any Thing in the Course of Nature, that can
encourage you to make such a Promise? Is Ruin become the
Road to Exaltation? Or must the Stage be buried like a
Plant, in order to rise and Flourish?

But, Sir *John,* I am heartily sorry, for your Sake, that
you made any Mention of the *Grecian* Stage. You had better
have stuck to that of *Rome.* For if we may judge of the
future by the past, you will be much more AEmulous of the
Roman Stage, than the *Grecian.* The *Grecian* Stage was
supported by great Originals. The *Roman* Stage, for the
most Part, by Copies of those Originals. The *Romans* had
very few Plays that were worth one Farthing, but what they
borrow'd from the *Grecians*, as you, and your Deputy
Governor, borrow from the *French.* The Romantick Lady, in
the 'Tender Husband', (13) is taken from the *Precieuses
Ridicules* of *Moliere.* But there is this Difference between *Moliere*'s Comedy and yours:

Moliere's Comedy was very seasonable; And for that very
Reason, among others, was very entertaining and instructive. It appeared at a Time, when the Family of the *Precieuses* was as numerous at *Paris*, as that of the *Coquettes*
is at present in this wicked Town. But that Large and
Fantastick Family disappear'd at once upon the Acting of
that Comedy, like Nocturnal Vapours upon the rising of the
Sun. But the Romantick Lady, in the 'Tender Husband', is
so singular a Monster, that she can neither be instructive
nor delightful. For if a Comick Poet does not Paint the

Times in which he lives, he does nothing at all. But the
Reading Romances, and Books of Knight Errantry, had long
been out of Fashion, before the 'Tender Husband' appear'd.
   'The Lying Lovers' is made up of Two Plays of *Corneille*, 'The Lyar', and 'The Sequel of the Lyar'. I shall
say no more of it, than that it is a very wretched Copy of
a very indifferent Original. For Comedy was not the
Talent of *Corneille*. Your Champion, and your Deputy
Governor, has made as bold with the *French*, as you, and
to as good a Purpose; he has bravely turn'd the 'Tartuffe'
of *Moliere* out of Ridicule. But then to commute for that
Offence, he has with equal Bravery Burlesqu'd the 'Cid' of
Corneille. We may guess, as I said before, at your future
Conduct, by your past. You, and your Deputy Governor,
will go on to borrow from the *French*, and continue to rail
at them. (14) 'Tis not enough for some People to Rob,
unless they likewise Murder. But how generous was the
conduct of the old *Romans*, when compar'd with yours? They
borrow'd from the *Grecians*, as you do from the *French*, and
came short of the *Grecians* in what they Borrow'd, as you
Two do of the *French*. But then they frankly own'd the
Obligations they had to them, and own'd them their Superiors. If *Horace* imitated *Pindar*, as he did very much, He
had the Modesty and the Prudence to affirm, that *Pindar* is
Inimitable. (15)
   But the Mention of the *Grecian* and *Roman* Stage, recalls
to my Remembrance, that neither the *Athenians*, nor the
Romans, would by any Means suffer their Actors to have the
Management of their Stage; nor would it ever be suffer'd
in *France*, if the Actors were not all Excommunicated; who
being consequently look'd upon as a living Portion of the
Damn'd, and the Devil's advanced Guard, no Man of Condition dares appear at the Head of them.
   That Players shou'd have the Management of the Stage,
you see was contrary to the Sense of the Ancient *Grecians*
and *Romans*; and is suffer'd by the *French*, only on the
Account of their being under Excommunication. How it was
managed among us, before the Reign of King *Charles* II. I
will not pretend to tell exactly: But I have strong Reasons to believe, that it was always under the Inspection
and Regulation of the Court. For Forty Years after the
Restoration, it was always under the Regulation of my
Lord Chamberlain. And during those Forty Years, it
flourish'd exceedingly; and was illustrious for Great
Wits, and famous for Great Actors. The great Writers have
disappear'd, and the few good Actors who remain, are like
to have no Successors. The Muses have abandon'd it with
Disdain, as scorning to be controll'd by Wretches, who
neither know nor value their Merit; and who, like the

Dunghill-Cock in *AEsop*, when they find a Jewel, reject it
for a Barley-Corn: Yet you, forsooth, pretend to make it
outvy all that ever appear'd at *Athens*, by running counter
to those very Methods, which rais'd the *Athenian* Stage so
high....

[Deleted are four paragraphs in which Dennis attacks
Colley Cibber.]

I believe I have hit the Mark. This last is certainly
the Thing. There are several extraordinary Qualities
which are common to both of you, which have caus'd this
Union of Affections, and this Sympathy of Souls.

In the first place, you have both of you risen from
very inconsiderable Beginnings. You; Sir *John*, if I have
not been misinform'd, are descended from a Trooper's
Horse; and your Deputy Governor was begot by a Cane-Chair
upon a Flower-Pot. There is no great Harm in all this:
But then you have both of you shamelessly flown in the
Faces of the very Persons who rais'd you.

In the Second place, You are both of you great Squand-
erers; one of you an avaritious Squanderer, and the other
both an avaritious and a vain-glorious one. His Purse and
yours seem to be contriv'd, like a certain Knight's Fish-
Pool; the Purses let out Gold, as the Fish-Pool does
Water, as fast as they take it in.

Your Deputy, in the Compass of two Years, has thrown
away Six Thousand Pounds at the *Groom-Porter's*, (16)
without making the least Provision for his Family; yet
Hope still remains at the Bottom of the Box for him; for
which Reason, he is hopelessly undone.

You, Sir *John Edgar*, have been a Squanderer in Three
Elements. Some of your Gold has been consum'd in *Rosycru-
cian* Fire. When you, and *Burnaby* the Poet, and *Tilly*, the
late Warden of the *Fleet*, enter'd into an Indenture Tripartite, as *Face*, and *Subtle*, and *Doll Common* (17) had
done before you; but with this Difference, that these last
were Cheats, whereas you and your Brethren were Gulls.
With an Eagerness, like that of Sir *Epicure Mammon*, (18)
were you embark'd in the Search of your *Aurum potabile*;
when you us'd to say to one another, over your Midnight
Suppers, *Drink, and be Rich.*

Some of your Pelf has been wasted in the Smith's Forge;
not out of any sordid Desire of Gain, but Zeal for the
Service of the Ladies Petticoats. (19)

More has been lost in the vast Depths of the Ocean, in
Quest of Cod-Fish and old Ling.

What noble Designs, and what glorious Projects for the
Censor of *Great Britain*, and for the Auditor General of

the Universe? (20)   Still more of your Money has been
scatter'd in Air; where for so many Years you have been
building Castles, and will continue to build, to squander,
and to consume, till the Earth gets the better of her
Sister Elements, and you and your Projects disappear
together.

There is a Third extraordinary Quality, Sir *John*, which
is common to you and your Viceroy; which is, That you have
both of you, for several Years together, been the celebrated Authors of other People's Works. Your Muses have a
pretty near Resemblance with a Certain Comedian's Wife,
who passing with the Cully who married her for a Virgin,
had several Children by other Persons, before her Husband
lay with her. I make no doubt but that your Muses are the
more agreeable to both of you, because they are so very
prolifick without any Trouble of yours. For you are sure
of the Profit; and you have both of you enough of that
Sort of Philosophy which is of the natural Growth of *Tipperary*, to despise the Infamy. Which puts me in mind of a
notorious Tragedian, who being admonish'd by his Friends
not to marry a certain Strumpet, of whose acquir'd Attractions he was grown very fond; because such a Marriage
would bring Shame and Infamy upon him; swore by *G——*, that
he lik'd her the better for it. (21)

With how great Satisfaction, nay, with how great Joy,
with how great Transport have I often reflected, that you
and your Viceroy have infinitely surpass'd old *Villers
Bays* of *Brentford*! (22) That he has entirely submitted to
his two younger Brothers; *Dicky Bays*, and *Colley Bays*, of
the Hundred of old *Drury*! You are come to contemn his
obsolete Rules, his *Regula Duplex*, his Rule of Transvers-
ing and Transposing: (Tho' I think, by the way, Sir *John*,
you were formerly often in at the latter.) You are come
to despise his Rule of Record, his Rule by way of Table-
talk. You have shewn, that you look with Scorn on his
Rule of Invention, and his *Drama* Common-Place-Book. He,
poor Mortal, was contented to glean here and there a
Sentence, sometimes from *Plutarch*, sometimes from *Seneca*,
and sometimes from modern *Montaign*. Whereas you have
found a shorter way to *Parnassus*. You and your Viceroy
bravely and boldly seize upon other Men's Plays; cause
new Title-Pages to be printed; and so, to the Amazement
of some few Readers, they pass with the rest for your own.

I was formerly so weak as to think, that nothing was
more a Man's own than his Thoughts and Inventions. Nay,
I have been often inclin'd to think, that a Man had absolute Property in his Thoughts and Inventions alone. I
have been apt to think, with a great Poet, that every
Thing else which the World calls Property, is very

improperly nam'd so:

> tanquam
> *Sit proprium quidquam, puncto quod mobilis Horae,*
> *Nunc prece, nunc pretio, nunc vi, nunc sorte suprema,*
> *Permutet Dominos, & cedat in altera Jura.* (23)

The Money that is mine, was somebody's else before, and
will be hereafter another's.

Houses and Lands too are certain to change their Land-
lords; sometimes by Gift, sometimes by Purchase, and sometimes by Might; but always, to be sure, by Death. But my
Thoughts are unalterably and unalienably mine, and never
can be another's. They are out of the Reach of Fortune,
that disposes of all Things else. 'Tis not in the Power
of Fate it self, to alienate, or transfer them; it can
only make them pass for another's, or annihilate them,
and cause them to be swallowed and lost in the Abyss of
Time.

I have therefore formerly been inclin'd to think,
That nothing ought to be so sacred as a Man's Thoughts
and Inventions: And I have more than once observ'd, That
the impudent Plagiary, who makes it the Business of his
Life to seize on them, and usurp them, has stuck at no
other Property, but has dar'd to violate all that is
Sacred among Men.

But here of late, the wonderful Operations of your
self and your Viceroy, and your more wonderful Success
upon them, have so confounded me, that I know not what
to think.

As I have wonder'd at the noble Assurance with which
you and your Deputy Governor have surpass'd your Elder
Brother of *Brentford* in the Quickness of becoming an
Author; so, Sir *John*, if you will pardon a little Digression, I will felicitate you upon those dextrous Politicks,
by which you have so much refin'd upon his; and by which,
when you bring any Thing upon the Stage, you secure
Success to your Works. For old *Bays* was contented with
the Printing a Hundred Sheets, in order to insinuate his
Play into the Boxes: But you, Sir *John*, upon the like
Occasion, have, by way of Lucubration and Speculation,
printed a Hundred Thousand Sheets. He, poor Wretch, was
satisfy'd with placing a Dozen or two of his Friends in
the Pit, who were instructed to do their Duty: But you,
Sir *John*, upon such an Occasion, have order'd a Thirty
Pound Dinner to be got ready at the *Rose*; where, like
another *Arthur*, you and your Knights of the Round Table,
have eat and drunk your selves up to Success; and have
become invincible. In short, you have almost fill'd the

Pit and Galleries with your own Creatures; who have been
order'd, at some certain Signals, to clap, laugh, huzza,
to clatter their Canes and their Heels to such a degree,
that the Hissing of a Hundred Snakes could no more be
heard, than in the Uproar and Din of a Battel.

I begin to perceive, that, before I was aware, I have
run into too great a Length for a Letter; for which I
heartily beg your Pardon. I shall finish your Viceroy's
Picture in a Second Letter, which shall follow immediately
upon the Heels of this; and afterwards I shall proceed to
the rest.

I am,

SIR,

Yours, &c.

From Letter IV

The PICTURE OF Sir *John Edgar*.

SIR *John Edgar*, of the County of —— in *Ireland*, is of a
middle Stature, broad Shoulders, thick Legs, a Shape like
the Picture of *somebody* over a Farmers Chimney, a short
Chin, a short Nose, a short Forehead, a broad flat Face,
and a dusky Countenance. He us'd to compare himself to
an *Eagle*; and to oblige the first Fool that he met with,
to give it under his Hand that he was so. But neither
his Nose, nor his Eyes, nor his Discernment, nor his broad
flat Face, nor his dusky Countenance were held to be Aqui-
line. He was believ'd to be in all these more like to
another Bird than an *Eagle*. Yet with such a Shape, and
such a Face, he discover'd at Sixty that, he took himself
for a Beauty, and appear'd to be more mortify'd upon his
being told he was Ugly, that he was by any reflection that
was ever made upon his Honour or his Understanding. (24)

He is a Gentleman born, Witness himself: of a very
Honourable Family, certainly of a very Ancient one. For
his Ancestours flourish'd in *Tipperary* long before the *English* ever set Foot in *Ireland*. He has Testimony of this
more Authentick than the *Heralds* Office, or than any Human
Testimony; for God has mark'd him more abundantly than he
did *Cain*, and stamp'd his Native Country upon his Face,
his Understanding, his Writings, his Actions, his Passions, and above all his Vanity. The *Hibernian* Brogue is
still upon all these, tho long Habitude and length of Days
have worn it from off his Tongue.

He is the greatest Pretender but one, of the Age in
which he lives; a Pretender both to Understanding and
Virtue, but especially to the latter. But some malicious

People have thought, that he made constant Court to that
venerable Lady, not out of any Affection which he had for
her Person, but because he was struck by the Charms of the
Joynture which he believ'd might follow her. And they
were confirm'd in this Opinion, by observing the Quarrels,
which he had every Day with one or other of her four
Daughters. Yet this pretended Passion did him great Service. It was to him *Major Domo, Factotum, Housekeeper,
Cook, Butler, Taylor* and *Sempstress*; because we live in a
noble Climate, where Persons who are universally known to
be Cheats and Sharpers, keep their Coaches by being so.(25)
     Yet to one of the Daughters of that venerable Lady, he
paid great respect in Publick, *videlicet*, to Madam *Justice*.
And to gain her Favour, and obtain her Protection, he
thought it not beneath him, to admit the meanest of her
Servants and Officers into the greatest familiarity with
him. So that there was no respect of Persons among them.
But it was *Jack* and *Tom*, and *Will* and *Hal*, and *Dick* with
them. But he always combin'd with these her Servants to
injure and abuse her in Private, and unknown to her play'd
a hundred Pranks with them to the prejudice of her Interest
and Reputation; which were not long kept so very Private,
but the World took notice that neither he nor the Servants
car'd one Farthing for the Mistress they pretended to
serve. He would very often do Extravagant things, very
seldom Generous ones, and never by his good-will Just
ones. Yet was he a great pretender to Generosity; but
Generosity with him was squandring away his Money upon
Knaves and Fools who flatter'd him. Thus a Bubble is a
very generous Creature to the *Shark* who preys upon him;
and a Beggar is generous to the Vermin that feed upon him.
     He had that seeming respect for the Laws of his Country,
and appear'd to be so delighted with them, that tho' he had
the Happiness of enjoying them as much as the most zealous
of his Fellow Subjects, even as those to whom one may say,
the Zeal of the Law hath eaten them up; yet that he might
be sure the Correspondence between them might be for Life,
he had, thro' a greatness of Soul peculiar to him, assum'd
a noble Resolution that would never suffer him to pay any
one a Farthing, 'till it came to Execution. Yet notwithstanding all this he was not satisfy'd; but was always
crying out Law, Law, more Law, more Law. (26)
     He appears to be mighty zealous for the Rights of the
People, and to be terribly afraid of the return of the old
Aristocracy, by which he has got the nick Name with some
of *Aristocracy Edgar*. No Man had ever so much in his
Mouth, Benevolence and Beneficence to Mankind, as he;
which to his Creditors seems a great fable: For, say they,
since he hates us who have most oblig'd him, to that

degree, that he cannot endure to see our Faces, how can he
possibly love the rest? He us'd one while to call himself the *Christian Heroe*, till it grew a publick Jest.
For the People would not allow him to be a Heroe, because,
tho he had been a Soldier so many Years in the time of a
Bloody War, he never had been present either at Siege or
Battle; and he could not possibly, they us'd to say, be a
Christian, because he us'd constantly to spend the
Mornings in Cursing *the Houshold of Faith*, tho' they came
in shoals to his Levees, out of pure Zeal to exhort him
to do his Duty.

He valued himself exceedingly, upon being a great
Improver, and a great Reformer, tho' the truth of the
matter is, that he never had half Skill enough to improve
any thing, nor half Virtue enough to reform any thing.
During the time that he was Governour of the *Bear-Garden*,
the Diversions of that place were more Stupid and Barbarous than ever they were known to be before, and the wild
Beasts more mischievous and untractable. And he was
especially so far from Reforming any thing, that it was
generally observ'd, that the greater part of those who
had been most intimate with him, were very far from being
more Virtuous than their Neighbours: tho' he never fail'd
of doing one thing in order to the making them so, and
that is, entring them in the School of Adversity.

Now as for *Temperance*, another Daughter of the above-
mentioned venerable Lady, he caresses and courts her all
the live-long Day; and compliments her as the Queen of
Morals, and the Empress of Life. But as soon as the Night
approaches, then sparkling Champaign puts an end to her
Reign.

He judiciously believes, that by preaching Abstinence
up by Day-light, he has made an honourable Composition
for his drinking three Bottles by Candle-light·

We may say of his Fortitude, what *Butler* said of *Hudibras*'s Wit; He may be Master of a very great deal, but
thro' abundance of Modesty is shie of making any Parade of
it, but reserves it for an occasion which no body can
divine. For he has declar'd against single Combat by his
Writings, and against Siege and Battle by his Conduct and
Actions, that is, by staying at home in a time of War,
with a Commission in a Pennyless Pocket, and choosing
rather to run the Risk of being taken Prisoner by the
English, than of being kill'd by the *French*.

Now as for *Prudence*, the fourth Daughter, he has a
Magnanimity which teaches him utterly to despise her,
and to regard her as an abandon'd Person, that prostitutes her self to the lowest Mechanicks. He therefore
makes it the business of his Life to Affront her, and

abuses her in all his Conversation, his Writings and his
Actions; of which there can be no stronger Testimony,
than his mortally disobliging his cordial tho' partial
Friends who rais'd him, and going over to a Party whom he
had exasperated beyond any possibility of a sincere
Reconcilement.

He is so great a Friend to Union, that almost all
Orders and Ranks of Men are united in his Person. For he
has been Poet, Orator, Soldier, Officer, Projector, Newsmonger, Casuist, Scribe, Politician, Fish-monger, Knight
and Gold-finder; and what is never enough to be admir'd,
he has been all these, by virtue of other Mens capacities.
Like a very Patentee, he has perform'd the Functions of
all these by Proxy, and by Deputy. As an Author he Writ
by Proxy; as a Soldier by Proxy he fought; he is so given
to do every thing by Proxy and by Deputy, that one would
swear he lies with his Mistress by Proxy and by Deputy, as
several honest worthy Gentlemen of his Antiquity are us'd
to lie with theirs.

Tho no Man in *Great Britain* is so fit a Subject for
Satire as himself, yet has he been always writing waggish
Lampoons upon others. And whenever he exposes a Lord in
one of his Libels, he has got a trick of affronting him
ten times more by way of begging his Pardon.

He has been always begging something of the Government;
and tho he has obtain'd ten times more of it than he
deserv'd, yet he grumbling thinks they have given him
nothing, because he has retain'd nothing; and is outragiously angry with some of the great Officers of the
Crown, because they have refus'd to wast the whole time of
their Administration in *pouring Water into a Sieve*.

He had one while, as I hinted above, obtain'd a Patent
to be Governour of the *Bear-garden*; tho that Patent was
invalid and void, by vertue of a previous Statute. Yet
when he thought himself establish'd in that Post, he chose
a *Bear*, a *Baboon*, and a *Wolf* for his Deputy Governours;
but partly growing Lazy, and being partly convinc'd, that
the Deputies were fitter for Government than the Principal, he abandon'd all to them; who conducting themselves
by their Bestial Appetites, play'd such Pranks, that both
Governours and Deputies were all remov'd, and the *Bear-
Garden* turn'd into a *Theatre*. Which Conduct of his puts
me in mind of one *Sempronius* a *Roman* Knight, who was made
Director of the *Ludi Fescennini*, a rough sort of *Bear-
Garden* Drama, in use among the uncultivated *Romans*, before
they were polish'd by the *Grecian* Arts; into which Employment he introduc'd three Wretches as his Deputies, who
were the utter ruin of that Diversion. For these four
Persons had not among them all as much Judgment as a

Ballad maker. And yet upon having this paultry Office
conferr'd upon him, *Sempronius* most vainly and imperti-
nently usurp'd the name of *Censor*; which coming to alarm
the true *Censors*, they enquir'd into his Life, upon which
finding him to be the greatest *Fourbe*, and the greatest
Impostor, that had appear'd among them since the Foundation of the City, they turn'd him with Disgrace out of
his Government, dismounted him and took his Horse from
him; and not contented with this, banish'd him from *Rome*
itself; and upon his Departure, caus'd the same general
Lustration to be made, that was us'd, when a certain bod-
ing, broad, flat, dusky-fac'd Prodigy had been hooted from
out the Walls.

Notes

1   Sir John Edgar, the persona of the 'Theatre'.
2   The motto, inaccurately quoted, is from Virgil,
    'Georgics', IV, 3-5.
3   Terence, 'Andria', I. ii. 14: 'Oh to be sure, the
    world makes that its business.'
4   See Dennis's earlier attacks: 'To the Spectator, on
    Poetical Justice'; 'To the Spectator, on Criticism
    and Plagarism'. Both were printed in 1712.
5   Colley Cibber.
6   A cowardly braggart in Beaumont and Fletcher's 'King
    and no King' (acted in 1611, printed in 1619).
7   Citing Dryden's 'All for Love', Cibber had compared
    Addison to a wren and Steele to an eagle bearing the
    smaller bird on its back (see No. 20).
8   'Pro Archia', VIII, 17.
9   Barton Booth (1681-1733), Thomas Doggett (d. 1721),
    Robert Wilks, and Colley Cibber.
10 A reference to the fact that Thomas Southerne (1660-
    1746), actor and playwright, received £120 for the
    copyright of 'The Spartan Dame' from William Rufus
    Chetwood (d. 1766), a publisher and prompter at the
    Drury Lane Theatre.
11 Thomas Pelham-Holles, first Duke of Newcastle (1693-
    1768).
12 In refusing to heed a request of the Lord Chamber-
    lain, Cibber argued that the governor and his mana-
    gers were 'a sort of separate ministry'.
13 Biddy Tipkin.
14 Steele railed at French drama in 'Theatre' 2.
15 Horace, 'Odes', IV. ii. 1-32.
16 The Groom Porter's was a gambling house where Cibber
    played and lost heavily.

17 Characters in Jonson's 'Alchemist' (1610).
18 Sir Epicure Mammon, a caricature of greed and arro-
    gance in 'The Alchemist'.
19 Steele was reputed to have helped in the design for a
    folding petticoat.
20 Bickerstaff was Censor and Sir John Edgar Auditor-
    General.
21 A possible allusion to Booth's marriage to the former
    mistress of the Duke of Marlborough and James Craggs
    the younger.
22 Bayes, the name under which Dryden is mocked in 'The
    Rehearsal' (1672) by George Villiers, Duke of Bucking-
    ham.
23 Horace, 'Epistles', II. ii. 171-4: 'just as though
    anything were one's own, which in a moment of flitting
    time, now by prayer, now by purchase, now by force,
    now - at the last - by death, changes owners and
    passes under the power of another.'
24 Like Mrs Manley in 'The New Atalantis', Dennis
    delighted in mocking Steele's physical appearance.
    See the first paragraph in Letter I of 'The Charac-
    ters and Conduct of Sir John Edgar'.
25 Often given to self-righteousness, Steele irritated
    several readers of his periodicals, particularly of
    the 'Theatre', with avowals of his rectitude and vir-
    tuous intentions.
26 The beginning of this paragraph paraphrases a state-
    ment by Steele in 'Theatre' 11: 'Let the Gentleman
    have but the freedom of the Laws, and be permitted to
    do good to himself and others, and his condition is
    as happy as that of any subject the King has.'

22. LETTERS OF THOMAS RUNDLE TO MRS SANDYS

1789

Thomas Rundle (*c*. 1688-1743) took holy orders in 1716 and
became Bishop of Derry in 1735. This letter, written
after 5 April 1720, was addressed to the widowed Barbara
Sandys (1685-1746). It appears in the two-volume 'Letters
of Thomas Rundle ... to Mrs. Barbara Sandys' ... with
Introductory Memoirs by James Dallaway (Dublin, 1789).

I am sorry I could not get for you a whole set of
'Theatres'; the very best are wanting. The demand for
them was so great, that even his fiercest enemies bought
them up, and enjoyed the author, while they persecute the
man. The Plays though neither excellent, yet will divert
a dull hour in the country; and may be esteemed as tolerable as any that have appeared these last seven years.
But that is but a poor compliment to be made them; for, in
this midnight of dramatic wit, a thing that shines no
brighter than a glow worm, will call our eyes to it, and
amuse a spectator. Tho' Sir R. Steele is not permitted to
act his play, (1) yet he is resolved to entertain us every
way he can; and his favourite, Sir John Edgar, is to be
published very quickly: (2) if while I am in *London*, I'll
take care to send it; if not, Knapton shall have orders to
do it. (3)

Notes

1 'The Conscious Lovers'.
2 The 'Theatre', published twice weekly from 2 January to
   5 April 1720, was to be collected and reprinted by John
   Nichols.
3 James Knapton, a bookseller in Ludgate Street.

23. [JOHN DENNIS?], 'THE BATTLE OF THE AUTHORS LATELY
FOUGHT IN COVENT-GARDEN'

1720

The pamphlet may have been written by John Dennis or someone close to him. This excerpt (pp. 21-41) describes a
mock-heroic battle 'between Sir John Edgar, Generalissimo
on one side, and Horatius Truewit, on the other'. Sir
John [Steele] is the loser.

...AS the Enemy march'd up with undaunted Hearts, and in
perfect Order, it was propos'd by *Th--b--ds*, (1) that they
should at once Bray all their Instruments of War, and make
all their Assinine Supporters Bray loud at the same time.
For he told them that he had read that on a certain time

the God *Baccus* with all his drunken Crew marching thro'
India, an Army of the Natives was gather'd together to
Oppose, and Destroy them, but that the Braying of the Ass
of old *Sileneus* put that Army to flight, no sooner said,
but done, and there was streight rais'd such a horrible
Noise by the Asses, their warlike Instruments, and the Mob
of *Scribblers*, as must have driven away all Creatures of a
fine Ear, that were not secur'd against this horrible Din
by the force of their own Harmony.

AT this time happen'd two fatal Omens, which gave a
certain Presage of the Evil Fortune that was to befall Sir
John and his Party: The first was this, *C---r* (2) being
dissatisfy'd with his former Post of *Adjutant* General, as
thinking it too hazardous, and likewise remembring that
they had no Banner to Fight under, very wisely Petition'd
the Goddess, that he might be *Standard-bearer,* which being
granted, he immediately advanc'd the Head of *Shakespear*,
and fix'd himself in the Center of the Rabble, as the most
secure Place that he could chuse; by him stood his Friend
Major General *Drum*, but of a suddain, the Head of *Shakespear* was remov'd by some invisible Agent, and that of his
Godson Sir *William* put in his Room; how this was brought
about was uncertain, there being two different Accounts of
it, one is, that *Shakespear*'s Ghost disdaining to see his
Head made use of as a protection to Fools and Scribblers,
who only admir'd his Faults, and knew nothing of his Perfections, had taken away his *Picture*, and transported it
to the Enemy, who paid a due Homage to his real Excellencies, and with himself condemn'd his irregularities. The
other Account is, that the *Muses* out of their respect to
Shakespear, that his Image might not be among those whom
Apollo had devoted to Ruin, and likewise to deprive the
Enemy of their *Paladium*, in which they put a wonderful
Confidence, transported it to a Place of more Safety;
but then the Goddess of Ignorance finding her Friends
without any *Standard*, immediately clap'd the Phiz of Sir
William in its place; but this was not sufficient to raise
that Courage, which the Loss of the former had depress'd,
tho' now they fought under the Banner of one Knight, as
well as under the Command of another; the other ill Omen,
was the Lieutenant General *The—b—ds*, either diffident
of his Cause, or as some say, won over by the immortal
Harmony of the Enemy jumping from his *Assinego*, fled over
to the contrary Party, for it is a very uncommon thing to
find Lieutenant Generals among Deserters; but all these
evil Omens could have no effect upon the Courage of Sir
John Edgar, nor his Lieutenant General *De—F—e*, (3) but
Steel'd with invincible Ignorance to prevent any farther
Desertion, they immediately order'd their whole Army to

Discharge all their Artillery of Sound, Smoke, and the
Atramentus Missives; but *Apollo*, brought a South wind up
the Street, and drove it all back upon themselves, and so
wounded abundance of their own People.

BY this time *Apollo*'s Army was come up to the End of
the Street, and *S———l* on one Side, full of his beloved
God *Baccus*, and *Y———g* (4) on the other, joyn'd them, tho'
neither of 'em without receiving a wound from the Enemy.
When Sir *John* and his Party beheld the small Number of the
Foe, their Courage reviv'd, and they promis'd themselves
a certain Victory, for their dull Sight could only discover the mortal Warriors, which were indeed few in Number,
without seeing the least of those immortal Hero's and
Demi-Gods, who attended, and supported them.   First,
there was *Horatius Truewit*, Generalissimo mounted upon
Pegasus, with a flaming Sword in his right Hand, whose
Name is *Logos*, which by Interpretation is Reason. From
his Shoulders in a golden Ribband, hung a Quiver full of
Darts or Javlins, fatal to Ignorance and Pretenders; above
him in the Air, and hovering over him, was the most beauti-
tiful Goddess call'd Art, wonderfully Charming, and exact
in all her Proportions; a silent Harmony issuing from her
Eyes and a Vocal one from her Mouth; on each side of him
were *Homer, Virgil, Sophocles, Euripides, Aristotle,
Horace*, and several other Artful Heroes of Antiquity; in
his Eyes, shone Judgement, and Fancy, harmoniously blended together.   After him, follow'd a Rank of mortal
Heroes in their proper Chariots of War, in a most exact,
and regular Order; there was *Ambrosius* clad all in Green,
except a Tragick *Mantle*, which hung down behind him, with
a Shepherd's Crook in one Hand, and a Scrip by his Side,
with the Rural Pipe hanging before him; there was good
Nature and calmness in his Face, with a glimpse of Majesty, which in a proper Place his Performances have discover'd; by his Side hung likewise a Quiver of those
fatal Javlins, which however he never made use of, but
upon this Occasion; on one Side of him was the *Greek Theo-
critus*, on the other, the *Roman Varrius*; but not to describe every one in particular, I shall only say, there
was besides these two *Thomas Tastewell*, Esq; *Anthony Artlove*, Esq; *William Whitlove*, on whom attended *Aristophanes, Menander, Terence,* and *Ben Johnson*, and lastly
Anonimus.   *Th——b——ds, ——Y——g* and *S——ll* being now furnish'd with Arms by *Apollo*, march'd to the Encounter on
Foot.

THE Army's now joyning Battle, *Truewit* on his *Pegasus*
makes directly to Sir *John Edgar*, but the Fight was mon-
sterously unequal. *Truewit* gave no blow in vain, the
Knight none that could hurt his Opponent.   The first

stroke of *Truewit* had certainly cleft *Sir John* to the
middle, had not the Goddess Ignorance dexterously turn'd
it aside; but it fell not in vain, for it cut off his
Asses Head entirely. The *Knight* undaunted fought now on
Foot with a Courage worthy of a nobler Cause, if it may
not properly be call'd Fool hardiness; and now having
receiv'd many desperate Wounds every where, but in his
Face, for having a peculiar Opinion of his Beauty, he
chiefly guarded that. The finishing blow coming now down
upon him from *Truewit's* thundering Arm, *Apollo* arrested
his Sword in the Air, and cry'd out: No my Son he shall
not have the Honour of falling by thy right Hand, take
him Prisoner, I preserve him to a more infamous Fate;
Truewit perfectly obedient to the God, seiz'd his now
resistless Antagonist Prisoner. *Anonimus* in the mean time
had not less Success against Lieutenant General *De——*
F——e, but in Imitation of his Leader spar'd his Life, and
took him Prisoner: Whilst the Fate of these two Generals
were thus deciding, *Ambrosius* in spight of the Humanity of
his Temper, spying his old Servant Major General *Drum* in
Arms against him, drew a Javlin, and sent it with such unerring force, that it transfix'd his Body, and that of
C—— C——r, who stood close to him, and so both fell to
the ground together. What shall I say of the prowess of
William Whitlove, who slew at least ten Scribblers of what
they now call *Comedy*, in which Number were *Ch——r B——ok*
Jack —— L—— and *G——f——h* and several others of equal
Infamy, tho' of Names less known; in short every one did
their part, but *Th——b——ds, S——ll* and *Y——g* exerted
themselves in a wonderful manner by vast slaughters of
the common People, in hopes by that means to wash out
their former Stains, and Ingratiate themselves with
Apollo by the present Vigour of their Actions. To come
to a Conclusion of this Battle, the Generals being thus
taken, the *Standard-Bearer*, and his Comrade Major General
Drum being kill'd, and the whole Field of Battle strow'd
with the Bodies of slain Scribblers; the Auxillery Rabble
soon fled away, and left an entire Victory to *Truewit*,
and his Party.

THE Field of Battle being thus clear'd of the living
Enemy, the next thing that was to be done, was to remove,
if not bury the Slain: But to make that Matter easy, and
Expedious, *Apollo* immediately Metamorphos'd them all into
so many *Maggots*, which being swept together into a Heap,
they were presently thrown into the *Dust Cart* that was
coming by, in order to be carryed out of the Town to the
first *Laystall*, with the rest of the Dust and Rubbish of
the Place;...

AND now *Covent Garden* (5) being clear, there was in a

moment Erected under a rich Pavilion, a Court of Judicat-
ure, with proper Seats for *Apollo*, the *Muses*, and the
immortal Heroes of *Parnassus*, and the two vanquish'd
Generals were set to the Bar. Lieutenant General *De F-e*
unwilling to detain the Court, modestly pleaded Guilty to
the Indictment, which was only for *Nonsense* and *Dullness*;
Sir *John Edgar* being of a more turbulent Nature, stood
upon his Justification, the Heads of his Indictment were,
First, *That not having the fear of* Apollo *before his*
Eyes, he had presum'd to set up for an Author, without
either Learning, Judgment or Genius, contrary to the
express Laws of Parnassus; Secondly, *That having stolen a*
popular Applause from the Writings of other Men, he, with
an unusual Assurance, had arrogated their Merit to him-
self; Thirdly, *That he had not only broken all the Laws*
of Parnassus, *but had traiterously endeavour'd to under-*
mine and destroy the very Laws themselves, by that means
to introduce Anarchy and Confusion into the Kingdom of
Order *and* Harmony; to which Articles and several others
not here mention'd, the *Knight* of the *Dusky Countenance*,
very boldly pleaded *Not Guilty*. Upon which *Anthony Art-*
love Esq; stood up to make good the Charge. The *First*
Article he prov'd, by showing that all Learning consisted
either in the Knowledge of Arts and Sciences, or of Languages, but that Sir *John* was so far from having any share
in the knowledge of Arts and Sciences, that he did not so
much as know in what they consisted; to Instance only in
Poetry, 'tis true he has call'd it the *Art of Poetry*, but
uses the Word Art without any manner of meaning, for an
Art must purpose to itself a certain End, and must by
Consequence have some certain means of arriving at that
End, which means are what is call'd the Rules, to deny
which, to *Poetry*, is to deny it to be an Art, and to make
it a meer Whimsy, of no Use or intrinsick Value; and this
I take to be little less than High-Treason against the
very Constitution of *Parnassus*, and its Sovereign Lord
Apollo; this false and traytorous Position he has endeavour'd to recommend and insinuate into the People, by
scandalous and odious Reflections and false imputations
thrown every where thro' his Writings, on the true Judges
and Defenders of the Laws of *Parnassus*, by turning the
Name of *Critic* into Ridicule, and several times asserting,
especially in one of his late 'Theatres', (6) that he
never knew a *Critic* write any thing well himself, contrary
to the known fact of all Ages and Nations, since it is
evident, that there never was any thing in any Language
or Time, of any Value and Esteem written, but by the most
perfect Judges or *Critics* in, and the most exact Observers of the Rules or Laws of *Parnassus*;...

AS to the Second Article of Indictment, I have Witnesses here to produce, that will make it out beyond Contradiction, that what goes under his Name, is so far from being his, that if we take away what belongs to other People, there would not remain ten tollerable Papers to himself; but hear the Evidence.

IN this place appear'd near a Hundred Witnesses, from whom he had receiv'd a Support to his Purse, and his Reputation; in his 'Tatlers', 'Spectators', 'Guardians', and the rest, except his 'Theatres', which are all his own, as *Pope, Hughes, Eusden, Tickell, Clay, Ambrose Phillips,* Dr. *Swift, Budgell,* and above all *Addison*; besides, near a hundred others who had Contributed either single Papers entire, or parts of Papers, which the *Knight* had fill'd up.

AS for a Proof of the last Article, I think that is sufficiently made out, by what I have said upon the *first*, and by the whole Course and Series of his Papers, which tend to persuade the World, that all Laws and Rules of *Poetry* are Confinement and Constraint, not to be borne; and indeed only worthy Laughter. As if Learning, Knowledge and Art were mere Pedantry, and that ignorance only could distinguish a fine Gentleman, and a polite Writer (as he calls himself) from other Men. I shall take no Notice of the boasts of his Beauty, but leave your Eyes to be judges how far his Claims are more just to that, than to Wit, and Poetry. His guilt being thus made out, I do demand Judgment against him.

ARTLOVE having done, the *Knight* was order'd to reply to his Charge; rising up with a *Handkerchief* in his Hand, he put it to his Eyes, and wiping away the falling Drops, he thus begun.

'WHAT has been said, I confess has touch'd me very nearly, and the latter part of it, which relates to the beauty of my Person has drawn, even Tears from my Eyes: My Adversary, indeed only says, that I have a *dusky Countenance*, and leaves the determination of the Merits of my Beauty to the Beholders Eyes; but I take that to be a Point to be so far already decided, that it cannot now come into Dispute: 'Tis ten Years since, and more, that in one of my 'Tattlers', I declar'd my self a Handsome black young Fellow, for then, you must know, I was not much above five and forty Years of Age, that I am still thus Handsome. I have not only asserted in my THEATRES, but have produc'd a fair Lady's Letter to confirm my Opinion; and since the *Ladies are the best Judges of Man's Beauty*; I have here a whole Packet of Billets to produce from the fair Sex.'

UPON which, he pull'd out a Handful of Letters, which

being taken from him, were found to be all written with
his own Numerical Fist, to his dear self, which caus'd a
sufficient Laughter in the Court.

'YOU may Laugh Gentlemen, *continu'd he*, but I ought not
to be Treated in this manner, who am the *Cato*, and *Socrates* of the Age; who am the greatest *Patriot*; the greatest Statesman; the finest Gentleman; the most facetious
and witty Companion; that this Age has produc'd; and whose
Wit, if it were not for a Company of dull Fellows about a
certain great Person, that shall be Nameless, and who for
fear of it, keep me from him, I should soon be at the Head
of the Ministry: If you doubt of this, or any other of the
Praises I have here given my self, do but peruse my
'Theatres', and you will find them all confirm'd under my
Hand in Print, which I think is proof enough of their
Validity.'

SIR *John*, Sir *John*, interrupted the Court, leave off
your Bouncing, your intolerable Vanity, and Answer to the
Charge that is brought against you.

'WHY,' reply'd Sir *John*, 'I think I am answering to
that Charge, whilst I am speaking in my own Praise; for if
I can persuade you, as I hope I have the World, that I am
the Best, the most Honourable, the Wisest, the most Beautiful, and the wittiest Man of my time: What signifies reply-
ing to the Objections of a dull ill-natur'd Critic: Who
dares call in Question the Merits of Pen? Of that Pen,
which has demolish'd *Dunkirk*, destroy'd the *Tory Ministry*,
set up that of the *Whigs*, secur'd the *Protestant Succession*, thrown out the *Peerage Bill*, and brought in that of
the *Weavers*, (7) and establish'd a Fame and Reputation
among all the *Lady's* and *Beaus* of this large City; arriv'd
at by none but my self? It is true, that the Adversary
has endeavour'd to lessen my Merit, by proving that I have
had great helps in all my Writings; but that I take to be
rather a proof of my Excellence, for they were but my
Journeymen; and if they perform'd well, it necessarily
added to my Reputation; for imploying such skilful Work-
men.... But if this will not do here, I must plainly tell
you, that I do absolutely disown the Jurisdiction of this
Court, and Appeal only to my favourable Readers and
Admirers.'

THE Court having over-rul'd his Plea of *Non Coram
Judice*, and told him plainly, that if he had nothing else
to urge, they should proceed to Judgment. He cry'd out,
'*I am an Englishman*, and as such insist upon my Privilege,
of saying and writing what I please. I follow my own
Opinion without regard to what any body else thinks of the
matter, and in that show my self a Man of Honour; for a
Man of Honour, is only to be true to his own Opinion,

whether right or wrong. I say, again, I am an *Englishman*,
and therefore insist upon being Try'd by the Laws of my
Country; for what have I to do with a Company of Foreign-
ers, such as your *Aristotles*, and *Horace*, your *Homers* and
Virgils, and the like Exotics, who understood not one word
of *English*: Wherefore I say, *Law, Law*, English *Law*, by
nothing else will I be Try'd and Judg'd.'
     UPON this, *Artlove* rose up, and thus Address'd himself
to the furious Knight....
     'YOUR present Case Sir *John*, comes under the Head of
Immemorial Custom, for, ever since Learning has been
fix'd, and encourag'd in this Nation, the Authors who have
Taught this Learning, have likewise been fix'd, and
establish'd by the general Consent of all those who have
either Taught, or Apply'd themselves to obtain it: Now,
this Learning consists in the Knowledge of Arts and Sciences, which only can distinguish the *Learn'd* from the
Vulgar; but all Arts and Sciences, as I have before
observ'd, consisting of certain Rules, peculiar to each
Art. Whoever offend against these Rules must be Judg'd
by them, and whoever would destroy them, plainly endeavours to destroy all manner of Learning, and so to level
the Learn'd, and the Vulgar: Nay, to give the Vulgar the
Advantage above the Learn'd, directly contrary to that *Law*
of Immemorial Custom, which has Establish'd Schools and
Universities in this Nation; for the Teaching of those
very Arts and Sciences.
     'FROM all this, Sir *John*, it is Evident that you are
Try'd by the *Law* of *England*, both for your Offences
against the Rules of Art, and your Traiterous endeavours
to destroy, even Art it self, Establish'd, as I have
shown by the Customary *Law* of this Nation; and it would
be no hard matter to prove that this Customary *Law* is
confirm'd, likewise by Acts of Parliament: If therefore
you have no more to plead, but your empty Clamour about
Law, that being thus remov'd, the Court will proceed to
your Sentence.' *Artlove* having done, the *Knight*, without
taking Notice of any one of his Reasons, continu'd still
to cry out, '*Law, Law*, I am an *Englishman*, and a Man of
Honour'; but being with much difficulty Silenc'd.
     THE Court proceeded to Judgment, as follows: *Daniel*
was condemn'd to write nothing for the future, but *News
Papers*, or Letters to, and in Praise of Mr. *Mist*. (8)
     THE *Knight's* Sentence, was immediately to have his
Eyes pick'd our by the *Pen* of the vilest *Ballad-maker* in
Town. This Sentence affecting in a particular manner
those lights of his valu'd Beauty, his Eyes: It caus'd
great Emotions in him, both of Rage and Grief, Exclamations, and Tears; till *Truewit* mov'd with his Agony,

interced'd with the Court for a mitigation of his Sentence, which the Court granting, Order'd *Truewit* to pronounce what Doom he pleas'd upon him, which was this.

*THAT he should Write on still, just as he had done,
till then, with the same majesterial Pride and Vanity;
the same Verbosity; the same want of Sense and Understanding; till he had no Body to buy and read his Papers;
but this Condition was added, That he should never mention
the words* Arts, Athens *or* Rome, *and that* Th---b--ds
*should be set as a Watch upon him, to see that he
observ'd, exactly these Conditions; and then the Court
broke up.* Apollo *and the* Muses *went directly for* Parnassus. *The living Heroes, pleas'd with the happy Event of
this Day's Encounter, retir'd to that Pleasure, or Study,
to which his Inclination led him; and the Knight even
satisfy'd with his Infamy, made his way directly Home to
be cur'd of his Wounds; write a* 'Theatre', *and rejoyce
with the* Printer *and* Bookseller, *that he was come off so
well, and had the Liberty to write on just as he had done
before, without ever hoping, or desiring to write better.*

Notes

1 Lewis Theobald (1688–1744), poet, critic, and dramatist; the first hero of Pope's 'Dunciad'.
2 Colley Cibber.
3 Long a foe of Steele, Defoe was introduced because of
   his reputation as a party hack.
4 Edward Young (1683–1765), well known as Addison's
   disciple.
5 An area where prostitutes gathered and which served
   generally as a centre of dissipation.
6 'Theatre' 12.
7 'The Spinster. In Defence of the Woollen Manufac-
   tures' (19 December 1719), 1.
8 Nathaniel Mist (d. 1737), printer often tried for
   libels against the government.

'THE CONSCIOUS LOVERS', 1722

24.   JOHN DENNIS, 'A DEFENCE OF SIR FOPLING FLUTTER'

1722

Dennis published his pamphlet on 2 November 1722. As part
of his continuing quarrel with Steele, he was further
enraged by the advance publicity for the reception of 'The
Conscious Lovers' on 7 November. By defending Etherege's
'Man of Mode', which Steele had disparaged as early as
1711, Dennis hoped to repudiate the moral principle on
which 'The Conscious Lovers' was built.

THE PREFACE

THE following Defence of the Comedy of Sir *Fopling Flutter,*
not only contains several Remarks upon Comedy in general;
Remarks that are equally necessary for the Writing it
sucessfully, and for the Judging of it surely; but every
Article of that Defence, is a just Censure of a certain
Comedy now in Rehearsal, (1) if I can depend upon the
Account which I have had of it, from several who have read
it, or to whom it has been read. And that the Account
which I have had of it is very just, I am apt to believe,
not only from the Judgment and Sincerity of the Persons
from whom I had it, but likewise from the scandalous
Methods that are us'd, to give it a false and a transitory
Reputation. (2)
     I have formerly made Mention of Poetical Mountebanks.
The Author of the Comedy now in Rehearsal, has all the
Marks of an Empiric of *Parnassus*: His Play has trotted as
far as *Edinburgh* Northward, and as far as *Wales* Westward,
and has been read to more Persons than will be at the
Representation of it, or vouchsafe to read it, when it is
publish'd.
     Another certain Sign that a Man is an Empiric, is,
when he gives high *Encomiums* to himself, and his *Nostrums*,
and pretends at the same Time, that those *Encomiums* are
given by others. Now, Advertisements have been sent to
the News-Papers to this Effect, That the Comedy now in
Rehearsal, is, in the Opinion of excellent Judges, the
very best that ever came upon the *English* Stage. (3) Now,

no Body could send that Advertisement but the Author, or
one of his *Zany's*, by his own Contrivance, or, at least,
Connivance. No one could send such an Advertisement, or
give such a Judgment, but a Fool, or a Knave; a Knave, if
he did it with a Design to impose on the World, and a Fool
if he did it in the Sincerity of his Heart. For, to
declare with Judgment, that a Play is the very best that
ever came upon the *English* Stage, requires vast Consideration, profound Reflection, and a long, long Comparison.
And what Mortal is qualify'd to pass such a Judgment upon
a single momentary Reading? He who sent those Advertisements then, sent them with a Design to impose upon the
World, or is an arrant Ass. But 'tis highly improbable,
that a Fool who knows nothing of the Matter, should give
himself the Trouble to send such an Advertisement; or that
any one else should do it but the Author, or the Author's
Zany's by his Subornation. For whose Interest could it be
but theirs, to endeavour to impose upon the World? But
now, if it shall appear by the following Treatise, that
the Author of the Dramatick Piece in Rehearsal, knows
nothing of the Nature of True Comedy, then how foolishly
arrogant are those insolent and impudent Advertisements?
These very Ways of Proceeding, sufficiently declare the
Author's Consciousness of his own Incapacity; for a noble
Genius will scorn such infamous Methods, and will resolve
to owe his Reputation to his Merit, and not to tricking
Artifice. These are some of the Methods which the present
Managers of the Stage have us'd to ruine the *Dramas*, and
with it all other Human Learning, which is in some Measure
dependant on it. For since Cabal and Trick, and the
Favour and Interest of three or four sordid Wretches, have
been found necessary for the obtaining Success; every one
who is duly qualify'd to write for the *Stage*, has either
with a just Disdain refus'd it, or has undertaken it with
extream Reluctancy. The *Drama* therefore is like to be
lost, and all the Arts dependent on it; therefore every
one who is concern'd for the Honour of his Country, ought
to do his utmost Endeavour to prevent a Calamity which
will be so great a Disgrace to it: And all who are concern'd for the Honour of the *KING*, ought to reflect with
Indignation, that by the Malice, and the basest *Breach of
Trust* of Persons whom His MAJESTY has appointed to encourage Literature, all the gentle Studies of Humanity are
like to be either entirely lost, or extreamly impair'd,
in his otherwise auspicious Reign.

A DEFENCE OF Sir *Fopling Flutter*.

A Certain Knight, who has employ'd so much of his empty
Labour in extolling the weak Performances of some living
Authors, has scurrilously and inhumanly in the 65th 'Spectator', (4) attack'd one of the most entertaining Comedies
of the last Age, written by a most ingenious Gentleman,
who perfectly understood the World, the Court, and the
Town, and whose Reputation has now for near thirty Years
together, surviv'd his Person, and will, in all Probability, survive it as long as Comedy shall be in vogue; by
which Proceeding, this worthy Knight has incurr'd the
double Censure, that *Olivia* in the 'Plain-Dealer' has cast
upon a certain Coxcomb, *Who rather*, says she, *than not
flatter, will flatter the Poets of the Age, whom none will
flatter; and rather than not rail, will rail at the Dead,
at whom none besides will rail.* (5)
    If other Authors have had the Misfortune, to incurr the
Censure of ill-nature with unthinking deluded People, for
no other so much as pretended Reason, than because to improve a noble Art, they have expos'd the Errors of popular
Writers, who ow'd their Success, to the infamous Method of
securing an ignorant or a corrupt Cabal; when those Writers were not only living, but in full Prosperity, and at
full Liberty to answer for themselves; what Appellation
must he deserve, who has basely and scurrilously attack'd
the Reputation of a Favourite of the comick Muse, and of
the Darling of the Graces, after Death has for so many
Years depriv'd him of the Means of answering for himself?
    What the Knight falsely and impudently says of the
Comedy, may be justly said of the Criticism, and of the
whole 65th 'Spectator', that 'tis a perfect Contradiction
to good Manners and good Sense. He allows this Comedy, he
says, to be in Nature, but 'tis Nature in its utmost
Corruption and Degeneracy.
    Suppose this were true, I would fain know where he
learnt, that Nature in its utmost Corruption and Degeneracy, is not the proper Subject of Comedy? Is not this a
merry Person, who, after he has been writing what he calls
Comedy for twenty Years together, shews plainly to all the
World, that he knows nothing of the Nature of true Comedy,
and that he has not learnt the very first Rudiments of an
Art which he pretends to teach? I must confess, the Ridicule in Sir *Fopling Flutter*, is an Imitation of Corrupt
and degenerate Nature, but not the most corrupt and the
most degenerate; for there is neither Adultery, Murder,
nor Sodomy in it. But can any Thing but corrupt and
degenerate Nature be the proper Subject of Ridicule? And
can any Thing but Ridicule be the proper Subject of

Comedy? Has not *Aristotle* told us in the Fifth Chapter of
his Poeticks, that comedy is an Imitation of the very
worst of Men? Not the worst, says He, in every Sort of
Vice, but the worst in the Ridicule. And has not *Horace*,
in the Fourth Satyr of his First Book, reminded us, that
the old *Athenian* Comick Poets made it their Business to
bring all Sorts of Villains upon the Stage, Adulterers,
Cheats, Theives, Murderers? But then they always took
Care, says a modern Critick, that those several Villanies
should be envelop'd in the Ridicule, which alone, says he,
could make them the proper Subjects of Comedy. If this
facetious Knight had formerly liv'd at *Lacedemon* with the
same wrong turn'd Noddle that he has now among us, would
he not, do you think, have inveighed against that People,
for shewing their drunken Slaves to their Children? Would
he not have represented it as a Thing of most pernicious
Example? What the *Lacedemonians* did by Drunkenness, the
Comick Poet does by that and all other Vices. He exposes
them to the View of his Fellow Subjects, for no other
Reason, than to render them ridiculous and contemptible.

But the Criticism of the Knight in the foresaid 'Spectator', is as contrary to good Manners, as it is to good
Sense. What *Aristotle* and his Interpreters say of Tragedy,
that 'tis infallibly good when it pleases both the Judges
and the People, is certainly as true of Comedy; for the
Judges are equally qualify'd to judge of both, and the
People may be suppos'd to be better Judges of Comedy than
they are of Tragedy, because Comedy is nothing but a Picture of common Life, and a Representation of their own
Humours and Manners. Now this Comedy of Sir *Fopling
Flutter*, has not been only well receiv'd, and believ'd by
the People of *England* to be a most agreeable Comedy for
about Half a Century, but the Judges have been still more
pleas'd with it than the People. They have justly believ'd (I speak of the Judges) that the Characters, and
especially the principal Characters, are admirably drawn,
to answer the two Ends of Comedy, Pleasure and Instruction; and that the Dialogue is the most charming that has
been writ by the Moderns: That with Purity and Simplicity,
it has Art and Elegance; and with Force and Vivacity, the
utmost Grace and Delicacy. This I know very well, was the
Opinion of the most eminent Writers, and of the best
Judges contemporary with the Author; and of the whole
Court of King *Charles* the Second, a Court the most polite
that ever *England* saw.

Now, after this Comedy has pass'd with the whole People
of *England*, the knowing as well as the Ignorant, for a
most entertaining and most instructive Comedy, for fifty
Years together, after that long Time comes a Two-Penny

Author, who has given a thousand Proofs thro' the Course
of his Rhapsodies, that he understands not a Tittle of all
this Matter; this Author comes and impudently declares,
that this whole celebrated Piece, that has for half a
Century, been admir'd by the whole People of *Great Britain*, is a perfect Contradiction to good Sense, to good
Manners, and to common Honesty. *O Tempora! O Mores!*

The Knight certainly wrote the foremention'd 'Spectator', tho' it has been writ these ten Years, on Purpose
to make Way for his fine Gentleman, (6) and therefore he
endeavours to prove, that Sir *Fopling* is not that genteel
Comedy, which the World allows it to be. And then,
according to his usual Custom, whenever he pretends to
criticise, he does, by shuffling and cutting and confound-
ing Notions, impose upon his unwary Reader; for either Sir
George Etheridge, did design to make this a genteel
Comedy, or he did not. If he did not design it, what is
it to the Purpose whether 'tis a genteel Comedy or not?
Provided that 'tis a good one: For I hope, a Comedy may be
a good one, and yet not a genteel one. The 'Alchimist' is
an admirable Comedy, and yet it is not a genteel one. We
may say the same of 'The Fox', and 'The silent Woman', and
of a great many more. (7) But if Sir *George* did design to
make it a genteel one, he was oblig'd to adapt it to that
Notion of Gentility, which he knew very well, that the
World at that Time had, and we see he succeeded accordingly. For it has pass'd for a very genteel Comedy, for
fifty Years together. Could it be expected that the
admirable Author, should accommodate himself, to the
wrong headed Notions of a would be Critick, who was to
appear fifty Years after the first Acting of his Play.
A Critick, who writes Criticism, as Men commit Treason or
Murder, by the Instigation of the Devil himself, whenever
the old Gentleman owes the Knight a Shame?

To prove that this Comedy is not a genteel one, he endeavours to prove that one of the principal Characters, is
not a fine Gentleman. I appeal to every impartial Man,
if when he says, that a Man or a Woman are genteel, he
means any Thing more, than that they are agreeable in
their Air, graceful in their Motions, and polite in their
Conversation. But when he endeavours to prove, that *Dorimont* is not a fine Gentleman, he says no more to the Purpose, than he said before, when he affirm'd that the
Comedy is not a genteel Comedy; for either the Author
design'd in *Dorimont* a fine Gentleman, or he did not. If
he did not, the Character is ne'er the less excellent on
that Account, because *Dorimont* is an admirable Picture of
a Courtier in the Court of King *Charles* the Second. But
if *Dorimont* was design'd for a fine Gentleman by the

Author, he was oblig'd to accommodate himself to that
Notion of a fine Gentleman, which the Court and the Town
both had at the Time of the writing of this Comedy. 'Tis
reasonable to believe, that he did so, and we see that he
succeeded accordingly. For *Dorimont* not only pass'd for a
fine Gentleman with the Court of King *Charles* the Second,
but he has pass'd for such with all the World, for Fifty
Years together. And what indeed can any one mean, when he
speaks of a fine Gentleman, but one who is qualify'd in
Conversation, to please the best Company of either Sex?

But the Knight will be satisfy'd with no Notion of a
fine Gentleman but his own. A fine Gentleman, says he, is
one who is honest in his Actions, and refin'd in his Language. If this be a just Description of a fine Gentleman,
I will make bold to draw two Consequences from it. The
first is, That a Pedant is often a fine Gentleman. For I
have known several of them, who have been Honest in their
Actions, and Refin'd in their Language. The second is,
That I know a certain Knight, who, though he should be
allow'd to be a Gentleman born, yet is not a fine Gentleman. I shall only add, that I would advise for the future,
all the fine Gentlemen, who travel to *London* from *Tipperary*, to allow us *Englishmen* to know what we mean, when we
speak our native Language.

To give a true Character of this charming Comedy, it
must be acknowledg'd, that there is no great Mastership
in the Design of it. Sir *George* had but little of the
artful and just Designs of *Ben Johnson*: But as Tragedy
instructs chiefly by its Design, Comedy instructs by its
Characters; which not only ought to be drawn truly in
Nature, but to be the resembling Pictures of our Contemporaries, both in Court and Town. Tragedy answers to
History-Painting, but Comedy to drawing of Portraits.

How little do they know of the Nature of true Comedy,
who believe that its proper Business is to set us Patterns for Imitation: For all such Patterns are serious
Things, and Laughter is the Life, and the very Soul of
Comedy. 'Tis its proper Business to expose Persons to
our View, whose Views we may shun, and whose Follies we
may despise; and by shewing us what is done upon the
Comick Stage, to shew us what ought never to be done upon
the Stage of the World.

All the Characters in Sir *Fopling Flutter*, and especially the principal Characters, are admirably drawn, both
to please and to instruct. First, they are drawn to
please, because they are drawn in the Truth of Nature; but
to be drawn in the Truth of Nature, they must be drawn
with those Qualities that are proper to each respective
Season of Life.

This is the chief Precept given for the forming the
Characters, by the two Great Masters of the Rules which
Nature herself dictated, and which have been receiv'd in
every Age, for the Standards of writing successfully, and
of judging surely, unless it were with Poetasters, and
their foolish Admirers....

[Dennis quotes from Horace, 'Ars Poetica', 153ff., 161ff.,
and from Aristotle's 'Rhetoric', II, 14.]

A Comick Poet, who gives to a Young Man the Qualities
that belong to a Middle Ag'd Man, or to an Old Man, can
answer neither of the Ends of his Art. He cannot please,
because he writes out of Nature, of which all Poetry is
an Imitation, and without which, no Poem can possibly
please. And as he cannot please, he cannot instruct;
because, by shewing such a young Man as is not to be seen
in the World, he shews a Monster, and not a Man, sets
before us a particular Character, instead of an allegorical and universal one, as all his Characters, and especially his principal Characters, ought to be; and therefore
can give no general Instruction, having no Moral, no
Fable, and therefore no Comedy.
Now if any one is pleased to compare the Character of
Dorimont, to which the Knight has taken so much absurd
Exception with the two forementioned Descriptions, he will
find in his Character all the chief distinguishing Strokes
of them. For such is the Force of Nature, and so admirable a Talent had she given Sir *George* for Comedy, that,
tho' to my certain Knowledge he understood neither *Greek*
nor *Latin*, yet one would swear, that in drawing his *Dorimont*, he copy'd the foresaid Draughts, and especially
that of *Aristotle*. *Dorimont* is a young Courtier, haughty,
vain, and prone to Anger, amorous, false, and inconstant.
He debauches *Loveit*, and betrays her; loves *Belinda*, and
as soon as he enjoys her is false to her.
But 2dly, The Characters in Sir *Fopling* are admirably
contriv'd to please, and more particularly the principal
ones, because we find in those Characters, a true Resemblance of the Persons both in Court and Town, who liv'd at
the Time when that Comedy was writ: For *Rapin* tells us
with a great deal of Judgment, *That Comedy is as it ought
to be, when an Audience is apt to imagine, that instead
of being in the Pit and Boxes, they are in some Assembly
of the Neighbourhood, or in some Family Meeting, and that
we see nothing done in it, but what is done in the World.
For it is,* says he, *not worth one Farthing, if we do not
discover our selves in it, and do not find in it both our
own Manners, and those of the Persons with whom we live
and converse.* (8)

The Reason of this Rule is manifest: For as 'tis the
Business of a Comick Poet to cure his Spectators of Vice
and Folly, by the Apprehension of being laugh'd at; 'tis
plain that his Business must be with the reigning Follies
and Vices. The violent Passions, which are the Subjects
of Tragedy, are the same in every Age, and appear with the
same Face; but those Vices and Follies, which are the
Subjects of Comedy, are seen to vary continually: Some of
those that belonged to our Ancestors, have no Relation to
us: and can no more come under the Cognisance of our present Comick Poets, than the Sweating and Sneezing Sickness
can come under the Practice of our contemporary Physicians. What Vices and Follies may infect those who are to
come after us, we know not; 'tis the present, the reigning
Vices, and Follies, that must be the Subjects of our present Comedy: The Comick Poet therefore must take Characters from such Persons as are his Contemporaries, and are
infected with the foresaid Follies and Vices....

But the Characters in this Comedy are very well form'd
to instruct as well as to please, especially those of
Dorimont and of *Loveit*; and they instruct by the same
Qualities to which the Knight has taken so much whimsical
Exception; as *Dorimont* instructs by his Insulting, and his
Perfidiousness, and *Loveit* by the Violence of her Resentment and her Anguish. For *Loveit* has Youth, Beauty,
Quality, Wit, and Spirit. And it was depending upon
these, that she repos'd so dangerous a Trust in *Dorimont*,
which is a just Caution to the Fair Sex, never to be so
conceited of the Power of their Charms, or their other
extraordinary Qualities, as to believe they can engage a
Man to be true to them, to whom they grant the best
Favour, without the only sure Engagement, without which
they can never be certain, that they shall not be hated
and despis'd by that very Person whom they have done
every Thing to oblige.

To conclude with one General Observation, That Comedy
may be qualify'd in a powerful Manner both to instruct and
to please, the very Constitution of its Subject ought
always to be Ridiculous. Comedy, says *Rapin*, is an Image
of common Life, and its End is to expose upon the Stage
the Defects of particular Persons, in order to cure the
Defects of the Publick, and to correct and amend the
People, by the Fear of being laugh'd at. That therefore,
says he, which is most essential to Comedy, is certainly
the Ridicule. (9)

Every Poem is qualify'd to instruct, and to please most
powerfully by that very Quality which makes the Fort and
the Characteristick of it, and which distinguishes it from
all other Kinds of Poems. As *Tragedy* is qualify'd to

instruct and to please, by Terror and Compassion, which
two Passions ought always to be predominant in it, and to
distinguish it from all other Poems; *Epick Poetry* pleases
and instructs chiefly by Admiration, which reigns throughout it, and distinguishes it from Poems of every other
Kind. Thus *Comedy* instructs and pleases most powerfully
by the Ridicule, because that is the Quality which distinguishes it from every other Poem. The Subject therefore of every Comedy ought to be ridiculous by its Constitution; the Ridicule ought to be of the very Nature and
Essence of it. Where there is none of that, there can be
no Comedy. It ought to reign both in the Incidents and
in the Characters, and especially in the principal Characters, which ought to be ridiculous in themselves, or so
contriv'd, as to shew and expose the Ridicule of others.
In all the Masterpieces of *Ben Johnson*, the principal
Character has the Ridicule in himself, as *Morose* in 'The
Silent Woman', *Volpone* in 'The Fox', and *Subtle* and *Face*
in 'The Alchimist'. And the very Ground and Foundation of
all these *Comedies* is ridiculous. 'Tis the very same
Thing in the Master-pieces of *Moliere*; The 'Misanthrope',
the 'Impostor', the 'Avare', and the 'Femmes Savantes'.
Nay, the Reader will find that in most of his other
Pieces, the principal Characters are ridiculous; as,
'L'Etourdi', 'Les precieuses Ridicules', 'Le Cocu Imagin-
aire', 'Les Facheux', and 'Monsieur de Pourceaugnac',
'Le Bourgeois Gentilhomme', 'L'Ecole des Maris', 'L'Ecole
des Femmes', 'L'Amour Medecin', 'Le Medecin Malgré luy',
'Le Mariage Forcé', 'George Dandin', 'Les Fourberies de
Scapin', 'Le Malade Imaginaire'. The Reader will not only
find, upon Reflection, that in all these Pieces the
Principal Characters are ridiculous, but that in most of
them there is the Ridicule of *Comedy* in the very Titles.
'Tis by the Ridicule that there is in the Character of
Sir *Fopling*, which is one of the principal ones of this
Comedy, and from which it takes its Name, that he is so
very well qualify'd to please and to instruct. What true
Englishman is there, but must be pleas'd to see this
ridiculous Knight made the Jest and the Scorn of all the
other Characters, for shewing, by his foolish aping
foreign Customs and Manners, that he prefers another
Country to his own? And of what important Instruction
must it be to all our Youth who travel, to shew them,
that if they so far forget the Love of their Country,
as to declare by the espousing foreign Customs and Manners, that they prefer *France* or *Italy* to *Great Britain*,
at their Return, they must justly expect to be the Jest and
the Scorn of their own Countrymen.
  Thus, I hope, I have convinc'd the Reader, that this

Comical Knight, Sir *Fopling*, has been justly form'd by the
Knight his Father, to instruct and please, whatever may be
the Opinion to the contrary of the Knight his Brother.
Whenever 'The Fine Gentleman' of the latter comes upon
the Stage, I shall be glad to see that it has all the
shining Qualities which recommend Sir *Fopling*, that his
Characters are always drawn in Nature, and that he never
gives to a young Man the Qualities of a Middle-aged Man,
or an old one; that they are the just Images of our Contemporaries, and of what we every Day see in the World;
that instead of setting us Patterns for our Imitation,
which is not the proper Business of *Comedy*, he makes those
Follies and Vices ridiculous, which we ought to shun and
despise; that the Subject of his *Comedy* is comical by its
Constitution; and that the Ridicule is particularly in
the Grand Incidents, and in the principal Characters.
For a true Comick Poet is a Philosopher, who, like old
Democritus, always instructs us laughing.

Notes

1   'The Conscious Lovers'.
2   According to E. N. Hooker, 'The Critical Works of John
    Dennis' (II, p. 495), 'no English play had ever
    received half of the advance publicity which "The
    Conscious Lovers" enjoyed.'
3   The newspaper advertisement (2 October 1722) of the
    play concluded in that manner.
4   'Spectator' 65 (15 May 1711) contains Steele's attack
    on Etherege's 'The Man of Mode, or Sir Fopling Flutter'
    (1676).
5   An inaccurate quotation from William Wycherley's 'The
    Plain Dealer', I. i.
6   'The Fine Gentleman' was the original title of 'The
    Conscious Lovers'.
7   Plays by Ben Jonson: 'The Alchemist' (1610); 'Volpone,
    or the Fox' (1606); 'Epicoene, or The Silent Woman'
    (1609).
8   René Rapin's 'Reflections on Aristotle's Treatise of
    Poesie' (1674), tr. Thomas Rymer, pt. II, sect. xxv.
9   Ibid.

25.   'FREEHOLDER'S JOURNAL'

1722

This review of 'The Conscious Lovers' appeared on 14
November 1722, just a week after its first appearance at
Drury Lane Theatre.

From My Own Apartment

The Play of the 'Conscious Lovers' had such a Reputation
before it was known, that a Man of no very great Curiosity
would have ventur'd to squeeze into the Crowd that went to
see it the first Night. The Reputation of the Author, who
has wrote more, (at least has been read more, and that is
writing to purpose) than any Man now amongst us, might, I
believe, bring great Numbers there; and indeed I had great
Hopes that we should see the *Christian Hero* as truly
represented in the *Drama*, as in another Piece of the same
Author's, which I think, deserves the highest commendation. But I must say, my Expectations were not answered,
and that this may not seem only an ill natur'd Assertion,
I shall give my Reasons for it.
    The Representation of a *Gentleman* (a Character that
comprehends all Religious as well as Moral Virtues) is
confessedly the laboured Design of the Poet in this Play;
but because I remembered a much finer *Gentleman*, represented in a Play, written in the darkness of *Paganism*, therefore I was out of Humour with his. I need not acquaint my
learned Readers, that the principal Characters of the
'Conscious Lovers', as well as the whole Plot, are taken
from the most celebrated Play of Antiquity; from the
finest Play of the finest Age; in a Word, from a Play
written by the most polite Pens of the *Augustan* Age. They
know that I mean the 'Andria' of Terence. After this
then, would not one expect, that a Play copy'd after so
excellent a Model, should answer our Hopes? Would not one
expect, that the Picture of the *English Gentleman*, would
be finely drawn, when the Roman sat for him? Nay, when
the light of Christianity was made use of to beautify the
Piece, and add substantial Ornaments to it, which could not
be expected to be found in the other? If therefore the
Roman Gentleman appears upon Examination, for to transcend
the *Christian*, the Poet surely hath not alone that Honour
to his Religion, which he ought, however good his Intentions might be.

I suppose it will be allow'd me, that a Man's Virtue
is the greater, the more powerfully he is tempted, or
threatened to give it up. The ancient Poet lays his *Pamphilus* under much greater Difficulties than our Modern
does his *Bevil*, and therefore his Virtue is the brighter,
and he the *finer Gentleman*. For, *Pamphilus* had a more
suspicious Father to deal with. *Simo*'s Character is more
morose, and not mix'd with that Affection as old *Bevil*'s.
From the Behaviour and Disposition of *Simo*, one must
imagine that he would never have forgiven his Son, had he
discover'd his Marriage; and his Son thro' the whole Play
expects no better Usage. Besides, *Simo* suspects *Glycerium*
for an Harlot, and indeed with great Reason too, and
therefore might justly be thought more irreconcileable,
whereas old *Bevil* has nothing to object to *Isabella*; and
seems only to prefer *Lucinda* to her, because she had so
great a Fortune.

But to add to this, *Pamphilus* had his whole Dependence
upon his Father, but *Bevil* had not, who was then actually
in Possession of a great Estate left by his Mother.
Pamphilus is distracted not only with the Prospect of
certain Poverty, but with his more particular Necessities
at that Juncture, when his Mistress was lying in. He considers, that if he should leave her, and marry the proposed Bride, he might then maintain her; but if he should
refuse, he must infallibly starve with her. Here his
Virtue was at its last Crisis, and notwithstanding this,
he resolves not to abandon his Mistress, let what would
happen. But nothing near so unhappy a Dilemma appears in
Bevil's case.

Again, *Pamphilus* was firmly betroth'd, but so was not
Bevil: The former had the Heart of his Passion cool'd by
Enjoyment, but *Bevil* had still all the Violence of Love
upon him. So that *Pamphilus* his Perseverance, flows from
Reason, and the Remembrance of his plighted Vows, which
Bevil's cannot do, because he never made any; and there-
fore there is greater mixture of self Love in *Bevil*'s
Character, and I cannot but think him a Man of greater
Merit, who will not leave his Mistress, when he can, nay,
when he, has the strongest Temptations to it; than he, who
will stick to a Woman he had never made any open Proffers
of Love to. *Pamphilus* would have been esteemed a profli-
gate *Scoundrel*, had he left his Mistress, but so would not
Bevil, had he left *Arabella*, that was not even his
Mistress.

I shall only add, that *Bevil* makes no Conscience of
telling a lie to his Father, that he would marry Lucinda,
which is inconsistent with his great Declarations of
filial Duty. If this be blameable in a *Pagan*, how much

more in a *Christian*? But *Pamphilus* makes no such mighty
Profession of Obedience, but thinks that if his Father
should command him to marry the Woman he did not love, he
ought to be disobey'd, so that if the Event had been unhappy, he would be much more excusable in not obeying,
than *Bevil* who must have forfeited his declared Character
thereby.

Upon the whole, then, *Bevil*'s Merit amounts to no more
than this, that he relieved a fine Woman he fell in Love
with, maintained her with the greatest Elegance, and never
made use of those Obligations to him, as a means to
debauch her. So that all that can be said is, that he
was not vicious, when a fair Opportunity invited. But
Pamphilus was actually virtuous, and resolved that no Misfortune should make him otherwise. My Lord *Bacon*'s Observation will decide which of these two Characters is the
most amiable; *Certainly,* (says he) *Virtue is like precious
Odours, most fragrant when they are incens'd or crush'd:
For Prosperity doth best discover Vice, but Adversity doth
best discover Vertue.* (1)

I think therefore our modern Poet, shou'd have laid this
Gentleman under greater Difficulties, thereby to shew how
much more powerful the Precepts of Religion are in the support of Virtue [*sic*], than those of Morality. But he seems
to be cautious of transcribing *Pamphilus*'s Character too
near, for fear the Play should not be esteem'd his own. It
may therefore be said in his Excuse, That it is no wonder
he should fail in his Attempt of shewing a perfect *Gentleman*, when he has deviated from a Character, than which 'tis
impossible humane Wit can form a finer. This is but a poor
Excuse. His Boldness is highly censurable, in placing his
Hero near so glaring a Light, and thus bringing him within
the View of a Comparison.

But pray, may not the *Christian Hero* be drawn with as
noble, or nobler Qualifications, than the *Roman* has been?
Hath not the Poet greater Advantages? Are not the Rewards
proposed by Religion, stronger Motives to just and good
Actions, than the Dictates of Morality? But the finest
Colours do but make the unskilfulness of the Painter more
apparent, and the more they shine, the more they shew the
Disproportion and the Daub.

There is one Scene indeed, wherein the Poet raises his
Hero far above any thing that Morality can dictate. I
mean that in the fourth Act, wherein *Bevil* cools himself
by the Sentiments of Religion, and the Prospect of a
future State, in the midst of a violent Passion, raised by
the ungrateful Provocation of a Friend, whose Injuries
must be more afflicting, and his Taunts of Cowardise more
pungent. The unlawfulness as well as the madness of

Duelling, is here finely exposed, by a Way of Reasoning
which Christianity only could dictate. The Poet makes a
proper Use of those Advantages, which his Religion
afforded him, and if he had done so through the whole
Play, we should not now complain, that the *Roman* so far
exceeds the *English Gentleman*.

Note

1 Francis Bacon, Of Adversity, in 'The Essays'.

26. BENJAMIN VICTOR, 'AN EPISTLE TO SIR RICHARD STEELE'

1722

An excerpt (pp. 11-17) from 'An Epistle to Sir Richard
Steele, on his Play, call'd The Conscious Lovers'. It is
an answer to the 'Freeholder's Journal' and Dennis's 'A
Defence of Sir Fopling Flutter'.
Victor's 'Epistle' was published on 29 November.

It was the Opinion of all the Antients, that Love (the
usual Argument of all Comedies) is there best written
where it is most distress'd, and in despairing Passion;
that Part of Comedy seeming best which is nearest
Tragedy. It is also mention'd in many Places that there
were banish'd from the Theatre at *Athens*, and hiss'd from
Rome, that brought Parasites on the Stage with Apish
Actions, Fools with uncivil Habits, or Cortesans with
immodest Words. It is plain, Sir, you have taken the
best Method to move the Audience to the suppression of
Vice by presenting 'em with such a Worthy Noble Character
as *Bevil*, a Man full of Mercy, Beneficence, Affability,
Mildness, and Compassion.
    His affable Behaviour to Seignior *Carbonelli* in the 3d
Act.... This is a Beauty, whereby every one may distin-
guish a well bred Gentleman from a proud Upstart.
    Notwithstanding the Author of the 'Freeholder's
Journal' has taken upon him to degrade the Character of
Bevil, I am certain it infinitely exceeds that of *Pam-
philus* in the 'Andria' of *Terence*, which he prefers so

much before it, if (as he allows) he is the finest Gentleman, whose Virtues are most permanent.

He alledges, that Bevil is not under such Difficulties
as *Pamphilus*, and that therefore, not falling from his
Duty, was not so great a Virtue in him as in *Pamphilus*.
But if the greatest Part of the learn'd World are not mistaken in their Opinions, *Bevil*'s is much the more dangerous Circumstance, for it has been generally agreed, that
Superfluity, and Ease, are the Decay of Reason, and
Virtue, and allowing Poverty, and Want, to have their
Temptations, yet our Judgment is in a much better Condition than when we abound, and consequently our Virtue is
in less Danger. If this be true, (As I think it's undis-
putable) how Glorious a Character is that of *Bevil*'s, who
in the Heat of Youth, omits gratifying the most natural
Passion of his Age, *viz.* the possessing himself of a
Lady, who had Wit and Beauty to engage, and gratify every
Sense, a Person whom he passionately lov'd, and that he
was convinc'd had a Value for him; and this Restraint was
not from a Fear of being disinherited, for he had an
independant Sufficiency, but from the most generous
Motion of the Mind, a Resignation of his Will to that of
a kind beneficent Parent. *Pamphilus* was betrothed to his
Glycerium, so that he could not have ·abandon'd her, without the utmost Villainy; besides he had an Inducement to
this Duty, if the Enjoyment of a Person whom he lov'd may
be esteem'd so: Therefore all that this Resolution amounts
to is, the preserving the Mistress of his Affections with
an indigent low Fortune, to Infamy and Plenty, which, if
it was a vertuous Choice, was not a very extraordinary one
in a Person of his Age: But *Bevil*'s Merit has no Allay,
since the Promise he makes to his Father, of marrying
Lucinda, (which is the only Imperfection this Critick
finds in his Integrity) is no Reflection, for he never
made the least Overture of his amorous Passion to *Indiana*,
because he would have it absolutely in his Power to discharge this Duty to his Father, without Injustice to her.

In short, if polite Language, noble Sentiments, and
the subjecting every Passion to the Law of Reason, are the
essential Parts of a fine Gentleman, *Bevil*'s is a perfect
Character.

I can't help telling you, Sir, with what sensible
Pleasure I observ'd the chief Part of the Audience
receive your Hero's Behaviour in the first Scene of the
fourth Act, where his Friend *Myrtle* challenges him upon a
Suspition of Treachery, and being of a warm hasty Temper,
he endeavours to provoke him to a Duel.

It has been the Custom of almost every Author of Comedy,
to draw the Gentleman a Man of such Courage as not to

evade a Fight, tho' upon ever so slight an Occasion: Now,
Sir, you have dar'd to give us an Example of a very un-
polite Gentleman, one who these Beaus call a preaching
Dervise, who, instead of the Sword's Point, gives his
Antagonist moral Sentiments, by saying, *You know, Sir, I
have often dar'd to disapprove of the Decisions a Tyrant
Custom has introduc'd, to the Breach of all Laws both
divine and human....* (1) Is it possible, Sir, that
De----s can be so void of Shame to attempt to prove, that
vicious Characters is the only Business of Comedy, and
that their corrupt Examples have the same design'd Effect
upon the Audience as the virtuous honourable Character;
he might as well say, it is in the Power of a handsome
young wanton Woman of the Town to reclaim a wild whoreing
young Fellow from that Faculty; or, that a Baudy-house is
a fitter Place for the Improvement of Virtue, than a
Church....

Note

1 'The Conscious Lovers', IV. i.

27. 'SIR RICHARD STEELE, AND HIS NEW COMEDY'

1722

The title page states the pamphlet's purpose: 'Sir Richard
Steele, and his New Comedy, call'd, The Conscious Lovers,
Vindicated, from the malicious Aspersions of Mr. John
Dennis.' It appeared on 13 December.

THERE is not a Thing attendant on Life, more Pernicious
and Destructive to Society than the Spirit of *Ill Nature*:
It renders a Man uncapable to be a Friend, unqualified for
a Companion, and unfit for all the good Offices of Humanity. Where this is prevalent, Judgment, Sense, Learning
and Ingenuity suffer; and 'tis impossible he can be either
a good Judge, or a good Critick, who permits this Spirit
to reign in him; for it leads Men to Partiality, to Envy,
Hatred, and every Thing obnoxious to Mankind.
    BUT yet so little is this regarded in the present Age,

that we have Men who set up for Criticks and Judges of the
Performances of others, who have no other Qualification to
recommend them. They snarl like mungrel Curs at their Contemporaries, and as a Whelp that is often whipp'd, the
more they are under Correction the more they *bark*; and if
they cannot themselves *sing* melodiously, they are fully
resolv'd to *howl* outragiously.

AMONGST these Criticks, so remarkable in the World, the
most considerable is Mr. *John Dennis*: A Man famous for his
Ill Nature, more than for his Poetry; a Person that pretends to be a Critick, who knows not the Office of a Critick; and who rather than he will not be read, will descend to write to the *Worthies* of *Billingsgate*, with whom
only his Language and his Manners can be match'd.

THIS Gentleman has for almost Fifty Years past constantly declar'd War against Merit; and 'tis no Wonder
that *He*, who has profess'd himself an Enemy to Religion
and common Humanity, should now take to his Arms, and
attack the Promoter and Encourager of them; by endeavouring (tho' impotently) to censure a Play the most virtu-
ously elegant that this, or perhaps any Age has produc'd,
and, with his usual Candour, before he has seen it, give
it the Stamp of Damnation.

SINCE Ill Nature, Envy and Inveteracy have so large a
Share in his 'Defence of Sir Fopling Flutter', and he has
therein given the greatest Scope for an Answer to him, I
shall briefly go thro' this *vile Heap of Scandal*, with
Observations and Remarks, whereby it will appear that the
great Critick of this Age (in his own Opinion) is no Critick at all, but, to speak in his own eloquent Language,
a *Fool* and an *Owl*.

IN the beginning of the Preface to his *Extraordinary
Labours*, this Author presumes to instruct us how to
write successfully, which he proposes by the Observation
of his Rules; but unless he can bring Testimonies of his
own Success, by the Pursuit of those Rules, Are those
Rules to be follow'd? Can his Rules be of any Use to
Poets, which have always damn'd the Author of them? Or
are they preach'd up to others, that by enforcing the
Practice of them, they may be equally damn'd with Mr.
Dennis? - I take it the latter is the Design of this
Author.

THEN he goes on, and pretends to shew, that scandalous
Methods have been us'd to give the 'Conscious Lovers' a
false Reputation; and insinuates, that the Author of it
is a Poetical Mountebank. I would here willingly ask
him, Whether scandalous Methods are any ways necessary to
recommend Virtue, which this Play manifestly does? Or,
whether it is possible that scandalous Methods can

recommend what is Virtuous? I am very sure of the contrary; and one might as well allow that the Praises of a
Knave should imbellish the Character of an honest Man,
which all Men can contradict. And as to the *Knight*'s
being a Poetical Mountebank, and an *Emperick of Parnassus*,
this Appellation belongs only to Mr. *Dennis*, who is
undoubtedly a *Quack of Parnassus*, because all his Productions have *fail'd of Success*, which is the true and infallible Characteristick of an ignorant Emperick.

HE says, Advertisements have been sent to the News-
Papers, to publish to the World, that this Comedy is, in
the Opinion of excellent Judges, the very best that ever
came upon the *English* Stage: And he says, None could send
those Advertisements but the Author. This is judging so
uncharitably and enviously, without knowing the Certainty
of it, that I am very confident none but Mr. *Dennis* would
so much as have imagin'd it.

THE Conduct, under this Head, relating to a certain
Comedy lately acted, may be conjectur'd to be as the
Well-natur'd Mr. *Dennis* affirms, because it stood in need
of some Helps of this Kind; but every one will allow that
the 'Conscious Lovers' has no Occasion for Props beyond
its own Merit: But admitting it had, Is it not more
Rational to suppose that some of the Gentlemen who had
the Favour of perusing this Play, before it was brought
on the Theatre, would be the first, if not the only Persons, that should give it any extraordinary Assistance of
this Nature?

NEXT he says, That those Persons are *Fools*, or *Knaves*,
as *differ from him*. This is very decent and mannerly Language, becoming a Gentleman of Mr. *Dennis*'s Talents; and
I am surpriz'd he has not gone on and told us, That they
are *Flaming Jacobites*, and Friends to the *Pretender*, and
deserve to be hang'd for not bringing in the *Protestant
Succession* into every new Play.

HE blames Persons for passing Judgment upon this Play,
on a single momentary Reading; and yet he judges himself
with a Vengeance, *without reading it*. - But this is Mr.
Dennis; and none but Mr. *Dennis* could be guilty of such a
Conduct.

THEN says he, A noble Genius will scorn any infamous
Methods to raise his Reputation: Which is most certainly
true; and it is likewise true, that a noble Genius will
scorn *infamous Reflections* on others. He tells us, That
all Human Learning is in some Measure dependant upon
Plays, and yet he says, That nothing but *Ridicule* is the
Comic Drama; but surely *Ridicule* is not *all* Human Learning, unless he means the Ridicule of some of his *Learned
Criticisms*.

THIS is follow'd with a manifest Falsity, when he declares, that by the Management of the *Players*, every one who is duly qualified to write for the Stage, has either with Disdain refus'd it, or has undertaken it with extream Reluctancy. - Indeed I cannot say but Mr. *Dennis* may have undertaken to write for the Stage with Reluctancy, because he has so often *wanted Success*, and, what is a great Mortification, in the general Opinion, that *justly* too: But this is not the Case of our other Poets. And if he now refuses it, 'tis because his Works are written with so much Art, and extraordinary Judgment, that no one can find out their Beauties but himself, and they would be *refused to be acted* at both the Theatres.

'TIS the fear of being disdain'd, which makes him disdain those sordid Wretches (as he is pleas'd to call them, the Managers of the Theatre) his greatest Benefactors; and least he should write on with further Damnation, he has at last, it seems, resolv'd not to write for the Stage at all. A Glorious Resolution! I hope he will keep it; and then I am sure the Players, the Town, his Friends, and Acquaintance, will think themselves so far oblig'd to him, as even to *subscribe* to their *own Abuse*, in a private Way, where *he* only is the Printer and Publisher of his own excellent Productions.

HE concludes his Preface, with telling us, that base Breaches of Trust are committed by Persons who are appointed by his Majesty to encourage Literature; and that all the gentle Studies of Humanity are like to be lost. - Here I am to ask him, who 'tis he means by the Persons appointed by his Majesty to encourage Literature? If he means, amongst them, a Noble D-ke at their Head, it is no less than *Scan. Mag.* (1) and ought to be taken Notice of as such: And I would propose to him this familiar Question, Whether Mr. *Dennis* knows any Thing of the gentle *Studies of Humanity*, who has made it the whole Business of his Life to trample under Foot all Human Learning, and been the most violent and turbulent Oppressor of it that ever liv'd? Or, Whether, if he is acquainted with them, they are not, by his uncommon Treatment, in the greatest Danger of being lost and eraz'd?

THUS much for the Preface. I now come to the Book itself, entitled, '*A Defence of Sir* Fopling Flutter, *a Comedy.*' *Written by Sir* George Etheridge. *In which Defence is shewn, that Sir Fopling, that merry Knight, was rightly compos'd by the Knight his Father, to answer the Ends of Comedy; and that he has been barbarously and scurrilously attack'd by the Knight his Brother, in the Sixty fifth 'Spectator': By which it appears, that the latter Knight knows nothing of the Nature of Comedy.*

IN this Book he tells us, That Sir *Fopling Flutter* was
written by a most ingenious Gentleman, who perfectly understood the World, the Court, and the Town, and whose Reputation has surviv'd his Person: To all which I agree with
this Critick; but I may, without the Spirit of Prophecy,
pronounce, that the same will not appear to be the Case of
Mr. *Dennis*.

HE then attacks the latter Knight in a very barbarous
manner, and charges him with Impudence, a want of Manners,
and of Sense; a Charge which was never imputed to Sir
Richard Steele till now, and which is so very Groundless
and Malicious, that it leaves not the least Impression
behind it. And I appeal to the World, at least that small
Part of it which has read the Writings of Mr. *Dennis*,
whether in any one Piece he has writ, he has acquitted
himself with *Modesty*, and consistent with *good Manners*?
The Contrary is so Notorious, that the distinguishing Mark
of his Performances, by which his Pieces are known more
than by their Learning, is personal Scandal, unmannerly
Reflections, and outragious Abuse, very unbecoming any
Man of Sense.

BUT to proceed to his Criticisms, he mentions what
Aristotle, and his Interpreters, say of Tragedy, and
that it is certainly as true of Comedy, that 'tis infallibly Good when it pleases both the *Judges* and the *People*;
and that the People may be suppos'd to be better Judges of
Comedy than they are of Tragedy, because Comedy is nothing
but a Picture of Life, and a Representation of their own
Humours and Manners. – Here he allows the *People to be
Judges* of Comedy; and if so, is not the 'Conscious Lovers'
an Excellent Comedy, which has gain'd upon the People
beyond any Comedy that has been brought on the Stage for
this Twenty Years past, and been acted for three Weeks
together with the most universal Applause?

WHAT he says from *Aristotle*, that Tragedy is Good when
it pleases the *Judges* and the *People*, is incontestably
true: Now his Tragedies never pleas'd the People, and
seldom any Judges; and therefore, by *Aristotle*'s Rules,
they cannot be good.

HE tells us, that the Ends of Comedy are Pleasure and
Instruction; which all Men allow; and that Sir *Fopling*'s
Character is pleasing by the Ridicule; but not so Instructive as a more serious Character: For Vice represented,
the Virtuous will say, cannot be so truly Instructive as
Virtue. People indeed may be laugh'd out of some Follies
and Vices; but laughing at Vice and Folly does not set to
the People Examples of Virtue.

AS this Play of Sir *George Etheridge*, was writ in the
Reign of King *Charles* II. it was very much applauded; for

though the Court of that Prince was perhaps the most
polite that ever *England* saw, it was not the most Virtuous: There were then a great many Sir *Fopling Flutters*,
who could not help being fond of their own Pictures, at
a Time Vice was countenanc'd, and Folly in fashion: But
since those Days it has not been so.

IN another Place Mr. *Dennis* takes Pains to point out
a Critick, who (he says) writes Criticism, as Men commit
Treason or Murder, by the *Instigation of the Devil.* - If
he has any Meaning here, I am confident it is so applic-
able to himself, that the *Critick*, in the Esteem of Mankind, will belong to no other Person.

THEN, says this Critick, *Dorimont* not only pass'd for
a Fine Gentleman with the Court of King *Charles*, but he
has pass'd for such with all the World for fifty Years
together: And what indeed can any one mean, when he speaks
of a Fine Gentleman, but one who is qualified in Conversation to please the best Company of either Sex. This
excellent Observation intimates, that a *Fine Gentleman*
must be a *Rake*, a *Beau*, an *Inconstant*, and *debauch'd
Person*, or he cannot be qualified in Conversation to
please; otherwise he must allow that a Virtuous, Moral,
Constant Person, of the opposite Character, may please:
But such Characters he every where owns he is a Stranger
to, and knows nothing of them.

HE goes on, towards the End of his Pamphlet, and tells
us, that the Principal Characters of Comedy should be
always ridiculous, and gives some Instances to prove it:
But if this were granted, where the finest Gentleman is
to be expos'd to View in a Character upon the Stage, how
ridiculous must it make a Fine Gentleman appear to the
World. To my Understanding, a Fine Gentleman, and a
Ridiculous Character, are wholly inconsistent, so that
this Character must be banish'd the Stage: Or you may as
well make a Buffoon a Fine Gentleman, as a Fine Gentleman
a Buffoon.

THE only good Observation he has made in his Book is,
*That Tragedy instructs chiefly by its Design, and Comedy
instructs by its Characters.* - But cannot Comedy instruct
by Virtuous Characters? Will nothing but Vice and Ridicule please; and shall Ridicule only be the Standard of
Wit? I desire Mr. *Dennis* to answer me this; and whether
the Town is not to be entertain'd with Virtue; and if it
is, Whether *Entertainment be not one of the Ends of
Comedy*.

THE last Thing I have to observe is, where he affirms,
that whenever a Poet shews a Man that is not to be seen
in the World, he shews a Monster; and insinuates from
hence that the Principal Character in the 'Conscious

Lovers' is a Monster, for that there is no such Person,
at least in *England*, where the Author has laid his Scene.
But I know of no Monster, but the Critick who asserts it.
If Sir *Richard Steele*'s Fine Gentleman be a Monster,
because he has Prudence enough not to be a Buffoon,
Virtue enough not to ravish a young Lady, and Conduct
enough to refuse a rash Challenge; I am sure he is a
Beautiful One; and how a *Monster* can be *Beauteous* I don't
understand.

IF the Character of *Bevil*, in the 'Conscious Lovers',
be drawn by the Poet somewhat beyond Life, if it is possible for Life to come to it, he is certainly to be justified as a Fine Gentleman, and not stil'd a Monster: And
we have the Authority of *Aristotle*, that Poets and Pain-
ters may be allow'd to draw Characters *stronger than Life*,
which incontestably decides all Controversies that may
arise on this Head.

INDEED I must own, that to very *Vicious Persons* Virtue
is monstrous, because it differs so vastly from Them and
their Practice. And to deal plainly with our malicious
and unmannerly *Critick*, I must tell him 'tis he is the
Monster, by differing from all his Contemporaries: And
that *He*, like a Man who fires a Blunderbuss that is over-
charg'd, instead of demolishing others, has knock'd down
himself.

THERE are some Persons who object to the Title of this
new Play, and would impose on the World a new Etymology to
the Word *Conscious*, that its Meaning is confin'd only to
Guilt; but let these Gentlemen, if they understand him,
look into *Virgil*, and they will find this Word more frequently apply'd, by that elegant and judicious Poet, to
Virtue, than to point out the Actions of the Guilty.

THERE are others, who say it is not a Comedy, but a
Tragedy. But these Persons happen not to know the Difference between Tragedy and Comedy; that all Tragedies have a
fatal Catastrophe essential to them; and that the 'Conscious Lovers', as all Comedies should do, ends successfully. I confess the safe Return of a Friend or Relation,
after all Expectations are given over, to a tender and
affectionate Breast is exceedingly moving; But from where
does it proceed? Does it not proceed from Joy? The
Answer is, Yes! And can Joy be Tragedy? The Reply is,
No. This is so very obvious, that all Men of Sense and
Learning will joyn with me in it, and that Sir *Richard
Steele*'s new Play, if it be not in the strictest Sense
throughout a Comedy, it is an Entertainment superior to
it.

SOME Criticks also tell us, that the Character of the
Fine Gentleman, in this new Comedy, is taken from

Terence, who was the Original of Comedy; (notwithstanding
Mr. *Dennis* won't allow it be Comedy) and censure the
Author for not making his Gentleman more Virtuous, at the
same time Mr. *Dennis* blames him for having too much
Virtue - Such is the hard Fate of Writers for the Stage.
- But what can we expect when so many ignorant and illit-
erate Persons take upon themselves to be Criticks and
Censors?

WHAT I have said shall at present serve as an Answer
to Mr. *Dennis*, and the Popular Objections injudiciously
rais'd against the 'Conscious Lovers': I shall now examine
into the true Business of a Critick, and prove that Mr.
Dennis, as appears by his Writings, knows nothing of it,
tho' he assumes the Title of *Critick-General of Great-
Britain*.

DRYDEN remarks that we are fallen into an Age of illiterate, censorious and detracting People; and takes leave
to tell them, that they wholly mistake the Nature of Criticism, who think its Business is principally to find
Fault. Criticism, as it was first instituted by *Aristotle*,
was meant a Standard of judging well. The chiefest Part
of which is, to observe those Excellencies which should
delight a reasonable Reader. If the Design, the Conduct,
the Thoughts, and the Expressions of a Poem, be generally
such as proceed from a true Genius of Poetry, the Critick
ought to pass his Judgment in favour of the Author. 'Tis
malicious and unmanly to snarle at the little Lapses of a
Pen, from which *Virgil* himself stands not exempted.
Horace acknowledges that *Homer* nods sometimes: (2) He is
not equally awake in every Line: But he leaves it also as
a standing Measure for our Judgment,

> *Non, ubi plura nitent in Carmine, paucis*
> *Offendi Maculis, quas aut incuria fudit*
> *Aut Humana parum cavit Natura.* (3)

TO this we may add, that the Office of a Critick, as
Originally understood, is to illustrate obscure Beauties;
to place some Passages in a better Light; to help out an
Author's Modesty, and shield him from Ill Nature.

NOW whether Mr. *Dennis*, in any of his Criticisms, has
answer'd this Character, I appeal to himself, and his most
candid and unprejudic'd Readers. I believe it must be
allow'd that he has made it his principal Study not only
to find Fault, but maliciously to find Fault, and with
some of the greatest Poems of the Age, without allowing
them one single Beauty; (4) and he has been so far from
shielding the Ill Nature of others, that nothing but Ill
Nature has appear'd against them.

Mr. *RIMER* tells us, that 'till of late Years *England* was as free from Criticks as from Wolves: (5) That they who are the least acquainted with the Game, are the aptest to bark: And that our modern Criticks are like Wasps, rather annoy the Bees than terrify the Drones.

THIS is so very Just, as to our present great Critick, that I take upon me most humbly to inscribe it to him; and I dare say, whoever is acquainted either with him, or his Writings, will own it belongs to him. His greatest Genius is Personal Scandal, and he will admit of nothing else to be represented upon the Theatre.

POPE's Back has been with this Critick a Greater Subject of Criticism, than the largest and most swelling Volume of his Poetry: But if the decent and mannerly Words, *Scoundrel, Rascal, Fool, Blockhead,* and *Owl* are Language Essential to a Critick, I must confess he has excell'd not only his Contemporaries, but all that have gone before him.

AND to conclude, who is the *Owl* (a Title which he has liberally conferr'd on all his Brother Poets) by the Features of his Countenance, his very timorous Temper, and never venturing himself Abroad but at Night, or in Dark Allies in the Day, (Marks which bear the strongest Description) is very well known to all such Persons as have the Honour to know Mr. *Dennis.*

Notes

1 *Scandalum magnatum* was a term used in early English law to designate words spoken in derogation of a peer or other great officer of the realm. Such slander was regarded as a more heinous offence than that spoken of a common person.
2 The whole passage is a paraphrase from The Author's Apology for Heroic Poetry and Poetic Licence (1677), in 'The Essays of John Dryden', ed. W. P. Ker (1926), I, pp. 179-80.
3 An inaccurate version of 'Ars Poetica', 351-3.
4 E.g., Sir Richard Blackmore, Joseph Addison, Alexander Pope.
5 Thomas Rymer, The Preface of the Translator, to Rapin's 'Reflections on Aristotle's Treatise of Poesie'.

28   JOHN DENNIS, 'REMARKS ON THE PREFACE TO THE CONSCIOUS LOVERS'

1723

From 'Remarks on the Conscious Lovers' in Hooker, II, pp. 257-62.
    Steele's comedy was first produced on 7 November 1722. Having already attacked it in 'A Defence of Sir Fopling Flutter' prior to its production, Dennis was surprised by the vigour of Steele's adherents and the success of the play.
    The 'Remarks' were published on or about 24 January 1723.

THE Author tells us in the Beginning of his Preface, That *'this Comedy has been receiv'd with universal Acceptance'*. Whether he is in the Right, or not, I appeal to the World. The Reason which he gives for this universal Acceptance is very extraordinary: *'It has been receiv'd'*, says he, *'with universal Acceptance, for it was in every Part excellently perform'd'*. Is it not a pleasant Humility in a Dramatick Writer, to affirm, that he is indebted for his whole Success to the Actors? I was apt to believe, at the first Sight, that this was an affected Modesty, and a counterfeit Humility. But when I went a little further, I began to think I was mistaken, and that the Author was in earnest; for he seems to be apprehensive, that the Applause of the Reader would hardly be so general as was that of the Spectator; and he does his Endeavour to induce the Reader not to pass a Judgment of the Play, till he has seen it acted: *'It must be remembred,'* says he, *'that a Play is to be seen, and is made to be represented with the Advantage of Actors, nor can appear but with half the Spirit without it.'* Now there have been several Plays writ in several Languages, which were never design'd to be seen. There are two of our own: The Tragedy of 'Sampson', by *Milton*; and the 'State of Innocence', by *Dryden*. 'Tis true, indeed, most Plays are design'd by their Authors to be seen, but that is not the chief Design of a Dramatick Writer, who has a good Genius. For such an Author writes to all Countries, and to all Ages, and writes with the lively Hope, that his great Master-pieces shall outlive the very Language in which they are compos'd. When Sir *Richard* says, That a Play can appear but with half the

Spirit, unless we see it acted, I would fain ask, on whom
he designs to impose this? If he who reads a Play is
qualified to read and to judge, he reads it with a truer
and juster Spirit than can be supplied by any Company of
Actors. If such a Reader happens at any Time to be better
pleased with the Representation of a Play than the reading
it, 'tis an infallible Sign, that such a Play is a very
wretched Performance.

But let us see how Sir *Richard* goes on. *'The greatest
Effect,'* says he, *'of a Play in reading it, is to excite
the Reader to go see it; and when he does so, it is then a
Play has the Effect of Precept and Example.'* Good God! is
it possible that this could come from any one but a Man
who is resolv'd to shew that he takes all his Readers to
be Ideots? When we read the Tragedies of *Sophocles* or
Euripides, or the Comedies of *Aristophanes, Plautus,* or
Terence, is the greatest Effect they have upon us, the
exciting us to go to see them acted? When Sir *Richard*
read the 'Andria' of *Terence*, was the exciting him to go
to see it acted the greatest Effect that it had upon him?
No, the greates Effect that it had upon him, was the
Desire to se another Play acted, and that was his own
deplorable Imitation of the 'Andria'.

'But a Play,' says he, *'has only, in the Representation, the Effect of Example and Precept.'* So that 'tis
not the Dramatick Persons, it seems, 'tis not *Timoleon,
Scipio, Bontus,* who are to be the Examples of Virtue to
us; no, 'tis the Players, I warrant, who represent them;
'tis Mr. *Booth*, Mr. *Robert Wilks*, and Mr. *Colley Cibber*,
whose Heroick Virtue we are to imitate, and by whose
Actions we are to be instructed.

But Sir *Richard* goes on, and tells us, That the chief
Design of the 'Conscious Lovers' was to be an innocent
Performance. Now there are a hundred innocent Performances upon the *British* Stage: But perhaps he meant a Performance that should have nothing but its Innocence to
recommend it, and should, by consequence, be thought the
only Play of its Kind. But in that he is mistaken, for
there is one more, and that is, the Performance of *Bays*
in the 'Rehearsal', which is, indeed, incoherent, incon-
gruous, impertinent, insipid, and ridiculous; but certainly a very innocent Performance. I am afraid it will
appear by the following Sheets, that the 'Conscious
Lovers' has no small Share of some of these Qualities, and
has nothing valuable but barely the Catastrophe. And here
I cannot but observe, that Sir *Richard*, who has upon so
many Occasions inveigh'd against the Rules, and particularly, in that notable Paper call'd the 'Theatre', owes
the only entertaining Scene of his Play to the Observation

of a Rule of *Aristotle*, which is, That the Discovery should
be immediately follow'd by the Change of Fortune, that is,
by the Catastrophe. Sir *Richard*, indeed, without ever
dreaming of *Aristotle*, had it from *Terence*, who took it
from *Menander*, who had it from the Precept of that great
Philosopher, and from the Practice of *Sophocles* and *Euripides*. For the tragick and comick Poets frequently borrow'd their Hints from one another; but, at the same time,
took Care to do it with Judgment, and not to intrench upon
each other's Province. And therefore we see, that the
Discovery in *Terence*, and the Reconciliation of *Simo* to
Pamphilus, is comprehended in a narrow Compass, and has
nothing in it of those violent Transports of Grief which
are inconsistent with Comedy.

Versibus exponi Tragicis res comica non vult, (1)

says *Horace* in his 'Art of Poetry', which *Boileau* has
imitated in the two following Lines of his:

*Le Comique ennemi des soupirs & des pleurs
N'admet point en soi des Tragiques Douleurs*. (2)

But I beg the Reader's Pardon for this Digression, and
now return to the Preface.

As to the Quarrel in the fourth Act, I shall speak to
it in its Place. In the mean time I am of the Number of
those, who believe that this Incident, and the Case of
the Father and Daughter, are not the proper Subjects of
Comedy. When Sir *Richard* says, that any thing that has
its Foundation in Happiness and Success must be the Subject of Comedy, he confounds Comedy with that Species of
Tragedy which has a happy Catastrophe. When he says,
that 'tis an Improvement of Comedy to introduce a Joy too
exquisite for Laughter, he takes all the Care that he can
to shew, that he knows nothing of the Nature of Comedy.
Does he really believe that *Moliere* understood the Nature
of it: I say *Moliere*, who, in the Opinion of all *Europe*,
excepting that small Portion of it which is acquainted
with *Ben Johnson*, had born away the Prize of Comedy from
all Nations, and from all Ages, if for the sake of his
Profit, he had not descended sometimes too much to Buf-
foonry. Let Sir *Richard*, or any one, look into that
litle Piece of *Moliere*, call'd 'La Critique de l'Ecole des
Femmes', and he shall find there, that in *Moliere*'s
Opinion, 'tis the Business of a Comick Poet to enter into
the Ridicule of Men, and to expose the blind Sides of all
Sorts of People agreeably; that he does nothing at all, if
he does not draw the Pictures of his Contemporaries, and

does not raise the Mirth of the sensible Part of an Audience, which, says he, 'tis no easy Matter to do. This is
the Sense of *Moliere*, tho' the Words are not his exactly.

When Sir *Richard* talks of a Joy too exquisite for
Laughter, he seems not to know that Joy, generally taken,
is common like Anger, Indignation, Love, to all Sorts of
Poetry, to the Epick, the Dramatick, the Lyrick; but that
that kind of Joy which is attended with Laughter, is the
Characteristick of Comedy; as Terror or Compassion,
according as one or the other is predominant, makes the
Characteristick of Tragedy, as Admiration does of Epick
Poetry.

When Sir *Richard* says, That weeping upon the Sight of a
deplorable Object is not a Subject for Laughter, but that
'tis agreeable to good Sense and to Humanity, he says nothing but what all the sensible Part of the World has already
granted; but then all that sensible Part of the World have
always deny'd that a deplorable Object is fit to be shewn
in Comedy. When Sir *George Etherege*, in his Comedy of
'Sir Fopling Flutter', shews *Loveit* in all the Height and
Violence of Grief and Rage, the Judicious Poet takes care
to give those Passions a ridiculous Turn by the Mouth of
Dorimant. Besides that, the Subject is at the Bottom
ridiculous: For *Loveit* is a Mistress, who has abandon'd
her self to *Dorimant*; and by falling into these violent
Passions, only because she fancies that something of which
she is very desirous has gone beside her, makes herself
truly ridiculous. Thus is this famous Scene in the second
Act of 'Sir Fopling', by the Character of *Loveit*, and the
dextrous handling the Subject, kept within the Bounds of
Comedy: But the Scene of the Discovery in the 'Conscious
Lovers' is truly Tragical. *Indiana* was strictly virtuous:
She had indeed conceiv'd a violent Passion for *Bevil*; but
all young People in full Health are liable to such a Passion, and perhaps the most sensible and the most virtuous
are more than others liable: But besides, that she had
kept this Passion within the Bounds of Honour, it was the
natural Effect of her Esteem for her Benefactor, and of
her Gratitude, that is, of her Virtue. These Considerations render'd her Case deplorable, and the Catastrophe
downright tragical, which of a Comedy ought to be the most
comical Part, for the same Reason that it ought to be the
most tragical Part of a Tragedy.

Before I take my Leave of Sir *Richard*'s Preface, I
cannot help saying a Word to his Song, which he has
brought in here by Violence, to the great Surprize of
the Reader, for no other End, than to shew that he is as
notable at Metre as he is at Prose. He seems as much concern'd for the Omission of it in the Representation of

his, as *Bays* in the third Act of the 'Rehearsal' is for
the Neglect of his; nay, and to have as high an Opinion of
it, as that merry Bard discovers that he has of his, when
he says to *Johnson*, *'What! are they gone without singing my
last new Song?'* *'s Bud, would it were in their Bellies.
I'll tell you, Mr.* Johnson, *if I have any Skill in these
Matters, I vow to Gad this Song is peremptorily the very
best that ever yet was written: You must know it was made
by* Tom Thimble*'s first Wife, after she was dead.'*

So that this Song of Mr. *Bays* too, as well as his
Brother Sir *Richard*'s, is a Love-Song, design'd just as
judiciously, express'd just as passionately, but more harmoniously, more freely, and better contriv'd for Melody.
And yet from the Omission of this Song of his, does Sir
Richard take an occasion to affront the finest Artist of
his kind in the World, and to treat Signor *Carbonelli* like
a Country Fidler, who sings 'John Dory' at Wakes and Fairs
to Hobnail'd Peasants and Milk-Maids.

I thought here to take my Leave; but the Sight of *Terence* and *Cibber* together provokes me to go a little farther.

> *Jungentur jam gryphes equis: aevoque sequenti
> Cum canibus timidi venient ad pocula damae.*
>
> Virg. (3)

Sir *Richard* says, that he is extremely surpriz'd to find
what *Cibber* told him prove a Truth, that what he valued himself so much upon, the Translation of *Terence*, should be imputed to him as a Reproach. Sir *Richard* knew very well, that
Cibber had said so many false Things with relation to this
Play, that he might be very well surpriz'd to find Truth
come from him, especially upon that Subject. But Sir *Richard* is mistaken; *Cibber* is constant to himself, and does
not deviate from Falshood upon this Occasion. No Mortal
reproaches Sir *Richard* with his Translation of *Terence*. He
has shewn clearly, that he is not capable of translating
any one Scene of him. But tho' he had been never so capable, he ought to have known that a Translation of *Terence*,
by the best Hand in the World, would not succeed upon the
English Stage. He ought to have known the Defect, that
the *Romans* themselves, who liv'd some time after him, and
especially *Caesar*, found in that Comick Poet. The great
Objection to him was, that he wanted the comick Force,
that is to say, that he had not in his Comedies that
Humour and Pleasantry which are so agreeable to the
Nature of Comedy. For the Force of any kind of Writing
consists chiefly in that which distinguishes it from all
other Kinds. Now the Ridicule being that which distinguishes Comedy from every other kind of Poetry, the *Comick*

Force must consist in that. But how came it to pass then,
that five of the six Comedies of *Terence* succeeded upon
the *Roman* Stage? The Answer is plain, because the Gener-
ality of the *Romans*, at the Time they were writ, knew no
better. The *Roman* Comedy in general had but little of
that agreeable Pleasantry that is fit to divert Men of
Sense, which occasion'd the following Censure of *Quintil-
ian*.(4)....And therefore, when *Shadwell* undertook to write
a Comedy upon the Plan of the 'Adelphi', he, who very well
knew the Nature of his Art, and by consequence knew what
was defective in the *Roman* Comedy, took particular Care
to supply from his own Invention the Ridicule that was
wanting in that; and it was by using that Method that he
made the 'Squire of Alsatia' a very good and very entertaining Comedy. *Moliere*, who writ upon the same Plan, has
done the very same Thing in his 'L'Ecole des Maris'. He
has done the very same in his 'Fourberies de Scapin',
which is writ upon the Plan of the 'Phormio'; but in the
latter, he has gone too far, and shamefully, to use the
Expression of *Boileau*, coupled *Terence* with *Jack-Pudding*;
a Conjunction as scandalous as Sir *Richard* had made of
Terence and his Friend *Cibber*: I heartily congratulate
both of them upon this their mutual Friendship. They are
par nobile fratrum, a Pair so pious, so good, so human, so
virtuous, so religious, that they are perfectly secur'd,
even in the midst of a treacherous World, of each other's
mutual Fidelity; because there is not in the World that
Third Person who is fit to be a Friend to either. The
Knight was too humble, when he attributed the great
Success of his Play to the Players in general; the Success
is only due to himself, and to his virtuous Friend; that
is, to that Cabal which was so industriously conven'd by
them, and to those Artifices which were with so much Skill
conducted by them. They have done greater Services than
this for each other, and have secured the Stage to themselves alone, which they regard as their proper *Domain*,
and therefore every Stranger who for the future comes upon
their Ground, is to be esteem'd a Trespasser. In the mean
Time, they have resolved between themselves, to make the
Town swallow any Entertainment which they shall think fit
to provide for them; and they seem agreed to vouch for
each other. *Cibber* is to make Affidavit, that the
Knight's Gudgeons are Cod-Fish and Sea-Carp, that arriv'd
by the last Fish-Pool; (5) and the Knight is to give it
upon his immaculate Honour, that *Cibber*'s Strickle-Bats
and Millers-Thumbs are either Mullets or Turbuts. And
they seem to have made a formal Order, That the Town shall
believe them, under the Penalty of being treated with the
same Anathema's that *Martin* and *John* were treated by *Peter*

in the 'Tale of a Tub'; that is, if you will not give
Credit to what we tell you, rather than believe your
Senses, G——d eternally damn you. *Cibber* indeed has
receiv'd some transitory Rebukes upon taking this Resolution; (6) but he still keeps firm to his Point, and is
resolv'd to carry it.

Notes

1   'Ars Poetica', 89.
2   Boileau, 'L'Art Poëtique' (1671), III, 401-2.
3   Virgil, 'Eclogues', VIII, 27-8: 'Griffins now shall mate
    with mares, and, in the age to come, the timid deer
    shall come with hounds to drink.'
4   'Institutio Oratoria', X. i. 99-100. In this pas-
    sage Quintilian finds Roman comedy inferior to that of
    the Greeks.
5   A reference to Steele's unsuccessful project for bring-
    ing fish from foreign waters alive to Great Britain.
6   On 19 December 1719, the Duke of Newcastle, as Lord
    Chamberlain, had ordered Cibber off the stage of the
    Drury Lane Theatre.

29.   'THE CENSOR CENSURED'

1723

This excerpt contains the Preface, which delineates the
anonymous author's intention, and the first dialogue
(pp. 1-13). The theme and subject of this detailed and
lengthy pamphlet (88 pages) are explained in the sub-
title: 'Or, The Conscious Lovers Examin'd: in a Dialogue
between Sir Dicky Marplot [Steele] and Jack Freeman. Into
which Mr. Dennis is introduced by way of Postscript; with
some observations on his late Remarks.'

THE PREFACE

ONE of the greatest Advantages an Author can gain from the
World, is to spread an universal Prejudice in Favour of
his Work before it appears. The Mind so prepossess'd, will

struggle hard to reconcile the Performance to the first
Impression; either because it does not care to have the
Expectation balk'd, or for fear the Judgment should be
call'd in question, for rashly giving into the Common
Vogue, without a due Examination. An Author, however, on
both these Considerations, stands fair for gaining many
strenuous Advocates, if his Piece is not altogether unworthy.

Under these happy Circumstances the CONSCIOUS LOVERS
first appear'd; and we were taught to expect, that
Vertue, long banish'd the Scenes, was once more to make
a flourishing Figure on the Stage, adorn'd with all the
gay Simplicity of sprightly Innocence. Thus she was to
have the Force of *Precept* and *Example* too; and thus at
once she was to instruct and please.

'Twas no small Delight to those who retain a Regard
for Vertue, to find the general Inclination of the Town
was to applaud so glorious an Undertaking. Even surly
Devots were prepared to brighten up their Countenances,
and appear in the Theatre, to give Encouragement to such
a wish'd-for Reformation. What a noble Opportunity was
here for the Poet (had he been equal to the Task) to have
convinced the Hypocritical Tribe, that Vertue was not
confined to a sanctified Face, a stiff Air, or a formal
OEconomy of Dress; but that she could shine in the
Splendor of a fine Gentleman, without suffering the least
Stain on her innate Purity! and then appear brightest,
when she seem'd to lie under the strongest Temptations!
How beautiful must the Behaviour of that Person be,
whose Wit, good Sense, and Vertue could assist and adorn
each other!

This was what the Town expected from the CONSCIOUS
LOVERS; and with this View they entertain'd the favourable Prejudice. But how fallen from their Hopes are they,
to find the *Fine Gentleman*, thus greatly design'd to
recommend, particularly, some extraordinary Vertues,
remarkably infamous for the contrary Vices! So entire was
the Dependence of the Audience on the Intention of the
Poet, that they gave him the *Plaudite*, without taking Time
to sift the several Characters, and examine whether they
fully answer'd their Expectations, or not.

I declare myself one of those who went advantageously
prepared to join in the Applause; but when I heard *Terence* abused in a Translation; his Characters murder'd;
and such as were design'd Patterns of Vertue, recommending
Vice by their Actions; when I found Dramatick Rules
infringed; the Unity of Characters broken; Persons introduced, of monstrous Shape and Birth, and of no Use towards
the grand Action; the Likeness to Human Nature destroy'd,

without any View, that I could discern, either of Instructing or Pleasing: In short, when instead of a Comedy just
in its Rules, and nobly instructive in its Morals; diverting with chast Wit, free from Obscenity and Profaneness;
when, I say, I heard the Contrary of all this, fired with
a just Indignation at such a flagrant Abuse, I could not
forbear exclaiming with *Juvenal*,

> *Impune ergo recitaverit ille togatas?*
> *- Stulta est clementia cum tot unique*
> *Vatibus occurras, periturae parcere chartae.* (1)

The most partial Eye cannot wink at such Absurdities
as these; from one especially who has published those
admirable Essays justly admired by all the World, for
tracing Human Nature thro' all the various Shapes and
Turns of Vice and Folly, and for laying down such Rules
as may serve to regulate the Conduct of Life in every
Degree and Station. There we find the true Representation of Nature, described with solid Sense, chast Wit,
and sprightly, diverting Humour. From such an Author,
the World had good Reason to expect the like Entertainment.

'Tis much to be fear'd, the superficial Judges among
both Sexes, lured by the plausible Appearance of several
Persons of the *Drama* (who have many good Precepts in their
Mouths, tho' their Practice contradicts 'em all) will
implicitly follow their Examples: Besides, many well-
meaning People, upon the bare Credit of the Author, will
conclude he could not err so grossly as to run counter to
those Rules, so beautifully display'd in the foremention'd Essays. Thus great Numbers are liable to be
seduced by this treacherous Comedy; the Gentlemen to be
undutiful to their Parents, false to their Friends, *&c.*
the Ladies to despise their Mothers, to be abusive in
their Language, and (what is of the utmost Consequence) by
being like *Indiana*, fondly credulous, and by trusting
rashly to a fair Face and smooth Promises (depending on
their own *Conscious Innocence*, and the Mens *Conscious
Honour*) are like to lose their Vertue, and all that Reputation which a modest Lady ought to prize above her Life.

Here, then, is the Snake in the Grass, who, by lurking
under such a specious Character, may slily give the fatal
Sting, the mortal Stab to Vertue and Honour. The Masque
of Goodness is the securest Cheat to play the D---l in,
while the alluring Form renders the black Design unsuspected.

I have endeavour'd, in a chearful Dialogue, to detect
the foul Hypocrisy, and destroy the Venom of this deadly

Snake: If I have not quite deprived him of his Sting, I
have at least lash'd him from his Concealment into Sight
and Observation, and leave him to be cured by an abler
Scourge.

THE
Censor Censured,
IN A
DIALOGUE
BETWEEN
Sir *DICKY MARPLOT*
AND
JACK FREEMAN.

Dicky.
My worthy Friend *Jack Freeman* come to Town! This is
Matter of Joy, indeed, to all your Acquaintance, but more
especially to your humble Servant.
    Jack. Sir *Dicky* -
    Dick. Nay, my Friend, that's ungenerous! - *Now I am
a Knight, that's true; and every body knows I'm a Knight,
and I can't help it* - But prithee don't upbraid me.
    Jack. Dear *Dick*, then, your friendly Salute is most
welcome, because I know your Heart dictates to your
Tongue. After declaring this Opinion, I need not tell
you that I'm overjoy'd at meeting you. But, Ceremony
apart, how goes the World?
    Dick. Why, much after the old Rate, I think: Fools
talk Politicks, and rail themselves into a Prison;
Atheists blaspheme, Free-thinkers are a numerous and a
thriving Tribe; Profaneness and Immorality were never
more flourishing, nor the Parsons more lazy and indolent -
    Jack. Hold, hold, *Dick*; I know you bear the Clergy no
very good Liking; and as for the Progress of Vice, 'twas
not what I meant by my Enquiry: However, if that is the
Case, why don't you take up your Rod again, and lash the
Nation into a Sense of their Impieties. I think you have
not appear'd very considerable a great while; and the
World may reasonably expect, from that publick Spirit you
have so much boasted of, that you'll never cease to promote the Reformation of Mankind.
    Dick. To convince you then that I have always had that
laudable Design at Heart, I shall shew you a Piece worthy
my three Years Labour and Industry. Now, Sir, I can say
with Sir *Richard Blackmore, I have rescued the Muses out
of the Hands of Ravishers, to restore them to their sweet
and chast Mansions, and to engage 'em in an Employment
suitable to their Dignity.* (2)

Jack. However, lay aside your Self-Commendation for
the present, (for you have already gone as far, at least,
as Modesty can allow) and let me plainly understand what
this mighty Performance is.

Dick. I confess, a Man should not run too great a
Length in his own Praise; but sure my Friend will allow
me to rejoice at the Service I have done my Country: 'Tis
that Reflexion inspires my Raptures; and if *Horace* may be
indulged in his Self-Satisfaction and Sufficiency to cry
out,

Exegi monumentum aere perennius, &c. (3)

I think I have an equal Pretence at least to exclaim with
him,

>   *Usque ego postera*
> *Crescam laude recens.* (4)

As for your *livor edax,* I despise it, I defy it; and am
now got beyond the Reach of Criticism and Malice.

Jack. Prithee, *Dick,* don't be so extravagant; besides,
thou hast all the Joy to thyself; 'tis impossible I should
assist in the Triumph, till I'm acquainted with thy Victory. Truce with the rapturous Exclamations for a while,
and tell me what thou hast done that thus transports thee.

Dick. O *Freeman!* the true Spirit of Comedy was
never touch'd so happily before, by either Ancient or
Modern! The best are dull, flat, and insipid to mine!
Mine has the *utile dulci* in Perfection! The Characters
so admirably design'd, so nobly instructive; such Symmetry and Exactness in the Features and Lineaments; so
regularly proportion'd, heighten'd after the Copy of the
most perfect Nature; - In short, Sir, you'll find the
Titian Stroke in every Part. Let the malicious World pursue their splenetick Humour, and deny me the Credit due to
my other Writings; I don't care if I am ingenuous for
once, and confess, whatever Touch met with Applause, ow'd
its Success to foreign Assistance; yet this, this finish'd
Piece is all my own, - the legitimate Offspring of this
happy Brain. For this, I freely strip myself of all my
borrow'd Laurels, and expect *Apollo* should take the Crown
from his own Head, and adorn my Temples with it.

Jack. I acknowledge, *Dick,* you have been a little
roughly treated in your Time: But since you have been
ingenuous in your Confession, prithee be as free in your
Answer to the following Question: In the mean while, this
little Digression will give you Time to cool, and recover
your Sedateness, that you may be the better enabled to
give me an Account of the applauded Work with which you

are so enamour'd. - Was you really the Author of those Remarks on a Declaration, publish'd some few Years since?(5)

Dick. I could wish, my Friend, you had not revived my
Shame and Confusion on that Score; tho' I declare sincerely to you, I did it with an Intention different from
what was imputed to me. Believe me, I had no more Design
to disperse and recommend the Thing, than I had to blast
my own Praise. And, indeed, I was not sensible of my
Error, till a non-juring Parson stopt me in the Street
soon after the Publication, and whisper'd me - Mr. *Short-
Face*, I congratulate you on your Conversion! What News
from *Avignon*? I don't doubt you you'll discharge the
Post of S——y of S——te to the general Satisfaction. -
Immediately a snarling Cynick, less credulous, fell foul
on me for the Want of Grammar in my Remarks, and many
other Faults, which I don't care to hear of, much less to
enumerate. However, I was no so much shock'd at that, as
at the Parson's Address, which had like to have spoil'd my
Preferment.

Jack. To tell you the Truth, *Dick*, I believe you lost
a great deal of Reputation by that Jobb; and many, who
before had cry'd you up for a Man of Wit and Judgment,
were obliged to retrace, to preserve their own Reputations.

Dick. Well, dear *Freeman*, don't be too unkind in the
Remembrance of past Faults, for which I have undergone a
sorrowful Penance. I confess I was too forward, and left
off my Leading-Strings too soon; but now, Sir, I have
learnt to go alone, and I question not but this Play of
mine will convince you of the Truth of it.

Jack. I must own, you have rais'd my Curiosity; but
prithee, when am I to see it?

Dick. I have a Copy in my Pocket; and because I know
you have Judgment, temper'd with Candour and Good-Nature,
I shall be pleas'd to have you peruse it; that if you
should observe an accidental Slip, which the best Writers
are apt to overlook, you may advertise me, and prevent
the Critick's little Malice. - But first give me Leave to
inform you of my Design.

Jack. Ay now, *Dick*, you seem to be coming to your
Temper, and the Business; and I shall listen attentively
to you.

Dick. Come on then. - My Plot, you must know, is that
of *Terence*'s 'Andria'.

Jack. How, Sir! Can a Man of your boasted Capacities
stoop so low as to build on another's Foundation, and not
make use of your own Invention.

Dick. Patience, Patience, my Friend! Why, I have so
turn'd the Characters, that *Terence* himself, was he now
living, I'll be bold to say, would not lay any Claim to

'em. 'Tis true, I borrow great Part of his first Act;
but then, the Beauty of my Translation (upon which I
highly value myself) so far exceeds the Original, that
every body will be sensible I've done the old *Roman* an
Honour, in bestowing so fine a Dress on his naked Thoughts.

Jack. Have a care, *Dick*; they have pleas'd for a great
many Generations, even to Admiration; and none of the
Judicious have dar'd to undertake the New-modelling of 'em.
They shine so bright in such an unaffected Nobleness and
Simplicity of Dress, that all People have thought it an
Injury either to add or diminish. I'll venture to say,
'tis a hazardous Undertaking!

Dick. The greater then will be my Reputation, if I do
it successfully: And in that Particular my Confidence
anticipates the Praises of my Country, and cries, Bravely
attempted, and nobly executed.

Jack. Well, *Dick*, I must suspend my Judgment till I
read your Play, and then——You know my frank Disposition
so well, that you have no Reason to doubt but I'll speak
my simple Thoughts.

Dick. That Knowledge makes me exult in this Manner,
being well assured of your Approbation. You are sensible
I have one great Advantage over the Heathen, in having the
Christian Pattern to finish the Character of my fine
Gentleman! 'Tis there I triumph! there I quite eclipse
old *Terence*!

Jack. Prithee, *Dick*, learn some Decency and Moderation
in thy Transports; and don't insult that excellent Author
on an Advantage which is owing to your good Fortune, not a
Superiority of Genius over him.

Dick. I don't design so much to trample on *Terence*, as
to rejoice at my own Felicity, in having been the glorious
Instrument of reconciling these two seeming Contradic-
tions, Christianity and Gallantry.

Jack. I must confess, *Dick*, 'tis an Undertaking well
worthy the ablest Pen: For as the two Characters are
the most sublime, it requires the utmost Skill to blend
'em so handsomely together, that neither the Christian may
lose ought of the Strictness of his Principles, by the
additional Gayety of the fine Gentleman; nor the latter
abate of his facetious, chearful Humour, by the restraining Severity of the Christian. And then again, as they
are the most exalted Representations in Life, and describe
the utmost Degree of Perfection Human Nature can arrive
at; what an Exactness of Thought and Contrivance, what an
harmonious Delicacy of Style is requisite to form this
sprightly, solid, gay, religious, Christian Gentleman!

Dick. Truly, *Freeman*, I was well aware of all this
Difficulty, and therefore have spent three whole Years in
Touching and Retouching, to finish all my Characters, but

this principal one especially, after *Aristotle*'s Model; which instructs us, either in Poetry or in Painting, to describe Men, not as they really are, but as they ought to be. Thus, to make my fine Gentleman complete, I have collected all the scatter'd Beauties appertaining to either Character, without their Deformities or Faults; and thus array'd, my finish'd Hero shines.

Jack. But give me leave to take notice, that our great Criticks have thought it faulty to make a good Character wholly perfect; lest it should give Cause, tho' not a just one, to impious People to arraign the Justice of Heaven, for laying such exquisite Perfection under any Difficulties or Misfortunes: Besides, it would destroy its Likeness to Human Nature, which is by no means able to arrive at that consummate Height.

Dick. I confess there is some Truth in that Observation: However, it may serve as a Pattern for Mankind; and they will readily be brought, from the Amiableness of Vertue, to think it their Duty, as well as Glory, to come as near that Example as may be. Truly, I'm afraid, if I have transgress'd any Dramatick Rule, 'tis that: But then, I have this to urge in my Defence; transported by a true Religious Zeal, I could not bear to think my Favourite Character should have one Blot.

Jack. But pray, Sir, what may be the Title of this finish'd Piece?

Dick. Why, I'll tell you; I have been this Twelve-month in fixing it. At first I came to a sort of a Resolution to call it 'The Fine Gentleman'.

Jack. Very well; a Noble Title indeed! and how came you to alter it?

Dick. I consider'd that would be too plain: For tho' few can arrive at the Character, yet most People know what is meant by it; and you must understand, we deep Writers hold this a constant Maxim and a Rule to walk by, *Ars est celare artem.* (6) 'Tis too vulgar to let every body know one's Meaning: Besides, 'twould prevent the agreeable Surprize of being let into it by Degrees. Add to this, the Obscurity of the Title carries a sort of a Secret with it, which pleases the curious *Goût* of most part of my Audience, especially those of the Feminine Gender.

Jack. Yet after all, *Dick*, this appears but trifling, to pretend to make (as you properly call'd it) a sort of a Secret of that which you design all the World shall understand. Tho' deep, yet clear, is a very fine Rule. But, to be free with you, you seem to misunderstand that admirable Instruction of *Ars est celare artem*: It does not mean you should be dark, or aenigmatical; but that you should conceal your Fiction so well, that it may pass for Nature;

that you should work up your Piece with such a Stretch of
Imagination, such a Delicacy of Fancy (which depend on the
Sublimity of your Genius) that it may bear a second and a
third View, and so on, and still discover fresh Beauties:
—That's the Glory of hiding Art with Art.

Dick. Alas! Sir, were we to follow those Rules altogether, how many of us Moderns, do you think, would bear
reading? No, no; our Business is to perplex the Argument,
and then many of our Readers will imagine there may be
something in our Works, because they don't know what to
make of 'em. Besides, Party Spleen, Prejudice and Ill-
Nature, with many other necessary Qualifications, have an
admirable Influence over the Minds of our Readers, and
serve us in very good stead, when a sound Judgment and
ready Wit are wanting. Thanks to my Stars, I'm not unpro-
vided.

Jack. Why, *Dick*, have you lost all Grace? and can you
glory in those Vices which are the Stain and Scandal of a
Rational Being? If you design to recommend your Play by
these Methods, I shall not think it worth my while to read
it.

Dick. No; what I have now urged, may serve as a sufficient Apology for many other of my genuine Writings; but
my Play is entirely free from the least Taint. Tho' I can
assure you, if I thought the World would forget to apply
the Character of my fine Gentleman, which I am so fond of,
I would take the Pains to write a long Preface to prove
him an exemplary Whig.

Jack. Prithee, *Dick*, lay aside thy peevish Notions of
Party-Distinctions; thou hast not had extraordinary
Success that Way; witness thy Remarks before-mention'd.
I know thou hast a rancorous Disposition, which thou
wouldst fain have construed as a devoted Zeal. But let
me advise thee to leave off, and not persist in furnishing
wrangling Fools in Coffee-Houses with Matter of Dispute
and Squabble. All thinking Men despise thy unreasonable
Methods to set them at Variance, and are humbly content to
be sociable and good-natur'd, in spight of thy Endeavours
to the contrary. — But all this while you have forgot to
inform me what the Real Title of this notable Dramatick
Performance is.

Dick. In a word then, I call it the 'Conscious
Lovers'.

Jack. 'The Conscious Lovers'? I protest I'm at a loss
to guess what can be meant by it.

Dick. Ha! ha! ha! There's the Joke and the Secret I
told you of before. Why, Sir, 'tis so delicately
abstruse, that no Man in *England* could have conceal'd the
Design better.

Jack. But since you rely in some measure on my

Judgment, prithee explain your Meaning.

Dick. You are to understand, then, these two Lovers
are so desperately enamour'd, that with all their good
Sense they dare not trust each other with the Secret.

Jack. Why so, pray? Is it above the Dignity of their
Sense, or is it criminal to be in Love?

Dick. No, no; you are wide of the Mark: They are too
well-bred to confess it.

Jack. Is it a Sign of Good Breeding, then, to hide the
generous Passion of an honest Heart?

Dick. Not so, neither; but being so refin'd in their
Manners, they scorn to tread in the Steps of others, and
be so blunt as to speak their Thoughts: Ev'ry 'Prentice
can do as much.

Jack. And, truly, I don't see what the best-bred
Gentleman in the Universe can do more; but express himself in better Terms.

Dick. O fie, *Jack Freeman,* I'm asham'd of you! What?
a fine Gentleman tell a Lady he's in Love with her; to
call all her modest, *conscious* Blushes into her Cheeks,
and put her into extreme Disorder and Confusion?

Jack. Really, *Dick,* I don't apprehend any great Violence done to her Modesty; nor an Occasion for any Confusion, but a very agreeable one, upon hearing an Offer of
Love made from the Person she most admires.

Dick. 'Tis true, she approves the Love; but the
Manner — the Manner, Sir; —there's the Nicety.

Jack. I profess, I cannot but approve the Manner that
has been in Use in all polite Ages and Nations; and that
is, an ingenuous Declaration in the Terms of Decency and
Respect, making proper Allowances for the coy Restraints
which Custom has impos'd on the Fair Sex.

Dick. No, Sir, that won't do. My Model is more delicate than that comes to: Instead of squeezing their Words
thro' the Organs of common Sense, I make my Lovers converse by Intuition.

Jack. A very abstracted Notion! but how is it possible to understand one another at that rate?

Dick. Their Souls have a perfect good Understanding
all the while, and are (as I call it) *conscious*; tho'
neither of the Lovers can express the Assurance of a reci-
procal Passion. Their Souls feast luxuriously upon Sublime Ideas (a Banquet too refin'd for common Sense) so
that the poor Lady is strangely perplex'd to know what my
fine Gentleman intends; and he's too much of a Gentleman
to tell her: Nor is she ever like to know it from his
Mouth.

Jack. How then? how will they ever be able to come
together?

Dick. Pho! that's a Question indeed; — Now observe —
In the Fifth Act I make the two old Fathers (who by that
time become *conscious* too) thrust 'em together. — There's
Fancy! — there's Imagination! ——There's Genius for you! —
Ah! *Freeman*, 'twould do your Heart Good to hear, what
pretty, soft Contrivances, what ready Turns of Thought she
has to draw him, if possible, into a Confession of Love;
and to observe how artfully he turns 'em all off, without
clearing up the Doubts of her Mind. I profess, 'tis
incomparably fine!

Jack. And so — she, as it were, courts him to a Confession, which he industriously avoids, tho' he has a
mutual Passion for her? and waits till the two old
Fellows tack 'em together, without satisfying the Lady
from his own Lips, that he really loves her? — Methinks,
that's not altogether so complaisant to the Lady, nor so
kind to himself, as one might reasonably expect from a Man
in his Circumstances: For the mutual Pleasure of declaring
an honourable Passion, is not the Least Delight in Love.

Dick. That's true; but you may suppose my fine
Gentleman has very good Reasons for not coming to an
Eclaircissement so readily as she would have had him;
which you'll be convinced of, when you read the Play.

Jack. Till then, I shall suspend my farther Judgment
on the Case.

Dick. Let me inform you of one dexterous Masterpiece
of Cunning, to secure myself against the under Class of
Criticks, who must be appeas'd, or my Play might run the
Risque of being damn'd, in spight of all my Labour, and
its Perfection.

Jack. That, I confess, seems to be a very material
Consideration, and worth guarding against: For the Great
Vulgar and the Small make up, for ought I know, nine
Parts in ten of your Audience. But the Method to silence
'em? ——

Dick. You must know, I have got a clever Prologue,
wrote by a *Cunning Shaver*, which frightens 'em out of
their Wits (and in smooth Language too) by telling 'em,
that as I've been so bold as to correct the Viciousness
of the Stage, and present a Play perfectly clean, and
free from all Obscenity, I challenge an Applause from all
those who have any Regard for Vertue and their own Reputations. (7)

Jack. That, perhaps, may have some present Influence;
tho' 'tis ten to one but they grumble in their Gizzards,
and depart dissatisfy'd for Want of a luscious Refresh-
ment.

Dick. Nay, I've a Salvo for that too; for to secure
a *Plaudite* at last, I have a bawdy Epilogue.

Jack. How, how, *Dick*? a bawdy Epilogue to a vertuous
Play!

Dick. Ay, marry Sir, and an admirable Contrivance too!
And to give it the heightening *Goût*, I bring out my very
fine Lady to laugh at my very fine Gentleman, for not
making better Use of his Opportunities, &c.

Jack. This appears to me to be turning your Play into
Ridicule, and only setting up Vertue for the Mobb to throw
Stones at.

Dick. You are to take Notice, Sir, *Indiana* means no
more than to describe the Behaviour of a modern fine
Gentleman in such a Case.

Jack. That will not excuse her, *Dick*: For if, as
Horace says, a Satyr, who comes staring from the Woods,
must not be allow'd to be obscene and impudent; (8) how
monstrously vile is it, to suffer a fine Lady to talk at
that rate, or to give the most distant Hint of any thing
that bears a Relation to Immodesty! What do you think the
Judicious and the Grave will say to this?

Dick. Pho! I have an Answer ready for them: The Epilogue is not Part of my Play.

Jack. But 'tis Part of the Entertainment, *Dick*; and
being the last, is the most likely to leave the deepest
Impression. 'Tis true, 'tis altogether Modern, and therefore not treated of by the Ancients; but as 'tis generally
the most witty Part of the whole Performance, it will be
the most prevalent.

Dick. But I've yet another Trick, which I'm sure can't
fail: That same *Cunning Shaver*, you must know, who wrote
my Prologue, has furnish'd me with an Epilogue too; which
I design to print, and omitt the Bawdy one. (9)

Jack. And do you expect thus to get clear of the
Imputation, after you have entertain'd the whole Town with
it for a Fortnight, or more?

Dick. Never fear; — If I am press'd hard upon that
Head, 'tis but abusing my Arraigner, bespattering him with
a little *Billingsgate*, and setting him in the Class of
Small Criticks: Or suppose I confidently give the Town the
Lye, and declare there was no such Thing? Or, if that
won't do, I'll swear I was *Sick,* and knew nothing of the
Matter, and throw the Crime upon the Licentiousness of the
Players: The D——l's in't, if I want an Assurance to go
thro' with either of these Methods to screen myself.

Jack. Well, *Dick*, thou art an Original, I confess! ——
But the Play.

Dick. Here 'tis; and when you have perus'd it, I shall
expect to see you again....

Notes

1   Juvenal, I. 3, 17-18: 'Shall this one have spouted to
    me his comedies, and that one his love ditties, and I
    be unavenged?' 'It is a foolish clemency when you
    jostle against poets at every corner, to spare paper
    that will be wasted anyhow.'
2   The Preface to 'Prince Arthur' (1695).
3   'Odes', III. xxx. 1: 'I have finished a monument more
    lasting than bronze.'
4   'Odes', III. xxx. 7-8: 'On and on shall I grow, ever
    fresh with the glory of after time.'
5   'An Account of the State of the Roman-Catholick
    Religion Throughout the World' (1715, 1716).
6   From Dryden's Examen of the Silent Woman, in 'An
    Essay of Dramatic Poesy' ('The Essays of John Dryden',
    ed. W. P. Ker (1926), I, p. 92).
7   The Prologue was written by Leonard Welsted.
8   'Ars Poetica', 220-30.
9   The Epilogue by Benjamin Victor, spoken during the
    first run, was not published with the play. Welsted's
    Epilogue was substituted.

30.   JOSEPH MITCHELL, 'TO SIR RICHARD STEELE ON ... THE
CONSCIOUS LOVERS'

c. 1723

From 'Poems on Several Occasions', 2 vols (1729), II,
pp. 255-8.

TO Sir *RICHARD STEELE;*
On the successful Representation of his
excellent COMEDY, call'd, *The
CONSCIOUS LOVERS.*

In ancient Times, before a *Pulpit-Throne,*
Or *Preaching,* was, at ROME and ATHENS, known,
Virtue and *Wit,* on *Theatres,* were bred,
And *People* follow'd, as the *Poets* led.
These publish'd nothing, but what Heav'n inspir'd,
And all their Dictates were, by *Those,* admir'd.

Heroes, whose Bravery bought immortal Fame,
Were deem'd a *Second*, and less sacred Name.

But Vice crept in, as *Priestcraft* got the Sway,
Down fell the *Stage*, and *Poets* went astray.
For several Ages, and, in every Land,
The *Muse* has drudg'd, beneath a *Tyrant*'s Hand;
Old *Sterling Wit* been chang'd for mungrel Rhime,
And all the *Drama* turn'd into a Crime.
The tuneful Tribe, condemn'd to mean Regard,
Just *Rules* and *Morals* barter for Reward.
And so debauch'd the *general Taste* appears,
That all is damn'd, that native Beauty wears.

To mend the Manners of the *madding* Age,
And model new the Conduct of the Stage,
For vulgar *Genii*, is a Task too high;
A Task, that claims approv'd Authority!
'Tis yours, O STEELE, in conscious Virtue bold,
To show the *Drama*, as it was of old;
To please the Eye; and practise on the Heart;
With Force of Reason, and the Flowers of Art!
Be this the Praise of your last, lov'd, Essay,
Where Wit and Honour all their Charms display;
The Stage is conquer'd to its first Intent,
Labour is Gain, and Pleasure innocent.
What BRITON, now, will reckon Virtue dull?
Shall Morals more to sleep the Hearer lull?
No longer, Fops, make Ridicule of Truth,
Nor blush to grow politely sage, in Youth,
By BEVIL's Conduct regulate your Life,
And make good Sense the *Fashionable* Strife.

And, ye, sow'r (1) *Criticks*, to our *Poet* bow,
And bind the Laurel, on his sacred Brow;
In all he writes, superior Worth confess;
Detraction cannot make his Glory less.
The worthy Sage, whose publick Spirit long
Has stood *Director* of our Taste and Song;
Whose generous Labours, yet unrival'd, frame
Our *Style* and *Manners*, for his Country's Fame,
He will, in spite of Envy, ever rise,
Belov'd of *All*, but *Those*, whom *All* despise.

Notes

1 An adjective frequently applied to Dennis.

IV The 'Tatler'
1709-11

31.   'THE CHARACTER OF THE TATLER'

[*c.* 1709]

'The Character of the Tatler',[*c.* 1709] is a broadside,
'Printed, and Sold by *Benj. Bragg*, at the *Black-Raven* in
Pater-Noster-Row'.   Much indebted to Mrs Manley's attacks
on Steele, it not only indulges in *ad hominem* criticism
but exposes the 'Tatler' as an adjunct of party.

SIR,
As to that Part of your Letter wherein you lay your
Commands upon me, to give you some Account of the Author
of a Paper call'd, 'The Tatler', and who he is, I have
taken what Care I can to gratifie your Curiosity in this
Point, tho' to little or no Purpose, for after the most
diligent Enquiry I cannot find him: I thought I had had
him once, coming to the House where he was said to be at
Dinner; but as I entered the Room he disappear'd; whether
he flew out of the Window, or up the Chimney, or what
other Way he escaped, I cannot say: But I am informed he
is very much like *Will in the Whisp*, he is always farther
off when you conceive you have him in your Hand.   The most
I can learn of him is that his True Name is *Abednego
Umbra*; (1) he was formerly in the Reign of King *Thoris-
mond* the Second a Member of the Colledge in the University
of —; (2) I am acquainted with a Fellow of the same House
with him, his Contemporary, who remembers *Nego*, as they
us'd to call him, perfectly well, who gives me this
Description of him, That he is a Tall, Short, Lean, Fat,

Black, Fair, Dull, Witty, Somebody, Nobody, and so forth;
from whence you may guess whence he was Born, that is,
what Countryman he is, without a Pair of Spectacles. He
was Born of Christian Parents, (as 'tis whispered, for
'tis said he denies it,) whose Nativity was Calculated by
Prophet *Partridge* a little before his Death; but he would
not speak out what Destiny the Stars had assigned him to,
but he left it in Shorthand, as a Legacy to his Wife— ,
but never to be Publish'd till after his Resurrection
which is to be on the same Day with Monsieur the *French*
Chymical Prophet, some Time since also Deceas'd, at least
he disappear'd. Here are strange Stories go of this
'Tatler': He so often varies his Shape, that *Proteus*,
Posture *Clerk* and *Gerkin*, are but Tom Fools to him. But
what is most surprizing, is that he can change others
also as well as himself into what Forms he pleases; which
Operation he performs by a new-invented Sort of Mathe-
matical Mill, call'd, *Whimsie*, into which he puts the
Subject Matter he is to work upon. And tho' the Persons
he seizes go into the Whimsical Mill never so Beautiful,
Wise, Prudent, Learned, &c. they immediately come out
again the most Hideous, Deformed, Ignorant, Foolish,
Ridiculous, Animals imaginable; (3) not fit to be Ambas-
sadors to Scare-Crows, or to the King of *Bantam*. (3)
This Engine, I mean the *Whimsie Mill*, is managed by a
limited number of Performers, called Directors, (4) who
meet so many Times a Week to consider with great Deliberation about the Method of carrying on this Grand Affair of
so much Consequence to the Sleepy World; no one is to be
entered into this Society but under the Sacred Seal of
Secresie, and signing a Paper, whereby they oblige themselves to call every Thing by a Wrong Name, take every
Thing in a Wrong Sense, and put False, and Rude, New and
Unheard-of, Interpretations upon Nature, Manners, and
Religion. Two of these most Famous Directors are Dr.
T--------l, an Old Fumbling Pedlar, a Seller of Small
Wares to Poor, Silly, People, who have bad Eyes. Mr.
H----y, that Famous Polemical Knight Errant, who has
challenged all the Race of *Nimrod*, the great Hunter, to
show a better Title to their own Dominions than he can to
them, for himself, *L----y*, (5) he is now entering the
Lists against *Gog*, *Magog*, and vows he will not leave a
Giant living upon Earth. But of this Class I am assured
you will hear more hereafter. But to return to the Esq;
strongly presumed to be Seignior *Chalybo*; Captain *S----l*,
that mighty Wit, who surpasses all Mens Understanding,
and knows Nobody, even not himself: For tho' there was a
Time when he was Poor Seignior *Chalybo*, he now, I say, is
willing to change his Name, and to be I.B. Esq; with a

seeming great deal of Entreaty; tho' I must confess I
fancy *Fame* is mistaken in the Name, for Seignior *Chalybo*
is all Perfection, all Humane, all Polite; he is Somebody,
and his Jests and Turns are all very Natural, but Esq; *B*
alias *Abednego Umbra*, scorns to be confined to Civility of
Nature; he Soars above common Thoughts and Actions; he
turns all the Creatures he Transmutes into Figures, the
most unlike Nature possible, and to what they were before
in themselves. He turns a pretty Parrot into a Rhinocer-
os, an humble Bee into an Elephant, for the Service of
Aurenge Zebe, (6) &c. But how comes this to be discover'd? Why, they say one *Tonsonius*, (7) a Sorcerer, is
conveyed into his Presence every Night, riding upon the
Back of a *Palantine* (but he must be Hoodwinkt,) where
without saying one Word upon Forfeiture of his Life and
Fortune, there is put into his Hand an Engine, called a
Clavis, which goes by the Name of *The Modern Interpreter
of Metamorphoses*. Mrs. *Crackenthorpe* (8) hearing that
Esq; *B*, was acquainted with Mr. *Flamsted*, writ an Ingenious Letter to him by the Peny-Post, to meet her at the
said Philosopher's House in *Greenwich-Park* at the Hour
One, by Moon-light, (knowing the Esq's; Bashfulness, how
loth he was to be seen Publickly and Barefac'd,) that
they Three might be Merry together, and Dance the Hay.
She comes to the Place appointed, when behold who should
she meet there but the Devil upon Two Sticks; the poor
Lady fell in Fits, and from that Fright has never been
able to write Sense, of which sad Mischance her Printer
gives the World an Account Three Times a Week.
    In short, I. B. Esq; is resolved, in Person, not to be
discovered, and therefore some are contented if you will
but allow them to be on his Family; which since the
Blazing Star of last *Monday* was Sevennight is grown very
Numerous, not a Constable in the Parish but pretends to be
near allied to him; and if you dare to question him his
Assertion, he lays you over the Pate with his Staff Authority to make out his Relations.
    Every Master of the most Noble Science of Defence lays
in a Claim, and proves it by Quarter-Staff, Drum-Stick,
Hazelwood and Crabtree, with a huge Number more that shall
be Nameless are in hopes of not being disown'd by him.
    Even *Jenny Cutbeard* says, that though her Father was a
Razor, her Mother was a Staff.
    There is a strong Rumour that he has been in *Holland,
Rome, Geneva,* and *England*, at the same Time, and that
there are those will make Affidavits of the Truth of the
Fact; but at this Report the Backs of the Metaphysicians
are up; and to overthrow this wild Opinion, some of the
Refined Virtuoso's undertake to maintain that I. B. Esq;

is nowhere at all; and this they do by a Machine,
Entituled, *Demonstration*, a Property peculiar to their
Institution, by which they make out Impossibilities as
plain as any Sort of Director in the Universe; but to
overthrow this Demonstration, Unfortunate as it is, in the
next Tuesday's 'Gazette' (9) *viz*. the ——Instant there
will be inserted among the Advertisements, by one who
knows (and there are not many that do) a Full, True, and
Impartial, Account of I. B. Esq; alias A. U. of his Parentage, Birth, Education, Place of Abode, Company, Office,
Manner of Life, Acquaintance, Adventures, with the Faithful History of his Invisible Ring, and how he came to
write the 'Tatler' by Inspiration; with some Merry Remarks
of his being taken in Bed with the ——'s Wife, his Escape,
and Resolutions thereupon, together with his Manual
Prayers and Pindaricks, &c. to be used upon several
Occasions.

To which will be added a Philosophical Transaction of
the paring of Turnips, and an Astonishing Piece or Discovery of a Trap for Slander, which (after the Manner of
the Modern Rabby, or Mystical Theologists, who find the
Revelation, and illustrate Paradoxes by Paradoxes,)
proves Mechanically the Lawfulness of a Layman's playing
a Prize with a Bishop, By an Author who is everywhere and
nowhere, I. B. Esq; Adieu.

I am Your's, &c.

Notes

1   A parody of Shadrach, Meshach, and Abednego in the
    fiery furnace (Daniel, 3. 11-30). Unlike them Steele
    emerges scorched from his alchemical furnace.
2   In the Hilary term of 1690 Steele matriculated at
    Christ Church, Oxford, and in August 1691 migrated to
    Merton.
3   An allusion to Steele's satire on Tory leaders: e.g.,
    Harley ridiculed as Polypragmon and Hanno in the
    'Tatler'.
4   Perhaps Charles Lord Sunderland (1674-1722), Arthur
    Maynwaring, and Addison. For others, see note 5.
5   An allusion to the 'Tatler's' alleged free-thinking
    or religious errors, personified in Matthew Tindal
    (1657-1733), deist; Benjamin Hoadly (1676-1761), low-
    church cleric; John Lacy (1664-*post* 1737), pseudo-
    prophet.
6   From Dryden's last rhymed drama (1676) and contemporary
    history, Aureng-Zebe was the conqueror of the empire
    of India from Shah Jehan, his father, and his brothers.

7   Jacob Tonson the elder (*c*. 1656-1736), bookseller and
    a member of the Kit-Cat club.
8   The persona of the 'Female Tatler' (1709).
9   The 'Gazette' was the government's official newspaper;
    Steele functioned as Gazetteer while he wrote the
    'Tatler'.

32.   THE 'EXAMINER' ON THE 'TATLER'

1710

These two issues of the 'Examiner' represent typical Tory
attacks on what was becoming more visibly a Whig journal.
The number for 24-31 August 1710 ridicules Steele's
slanted news reporting, the material that issues from
'St. James's Coffee House'.   The number for 5-12 October
engages in *ad hominem* criticism of Steele and belittles
him as an ineffectual but pretentious party hack.

24-31 August 1710

I have been so engaged of late with Mr. *Pett--m*, (1) and
other Persons of Rank and Figure, that I had not time to
pay my Respects to two Writers of my own Form.   This
should have been done sooner; because 'tis the Misfortune
of us *Half-Sheet* Authors, that one of our Productions is
in danger of being forgotten, before another appears.   We
are like those little Animals (mention'd by grave Writers)
that are born, and live, and dye within the Compass of a
Day.   If we please or amuse our Readers at *Tom*'s or at
Will's, (2) between Sun and Sun, 'tis sufficient; but our
Fame seldom lasts till late in the Evening; and the very
Remembrance of us is usually lost by the next Morning.
However, 'tis not I hope too late to take Notice of *two*
Papers, that are now above a Fortnight old, since the
Subject on which they are written is considerable enough,
to keep them in being a little longer, than their ordin-
ary Term of Life.
    We had lately News of a great Action in *Spain*, where
for some Years the War has been carry'd on very *calmly*,
and we were overjoy'd with the Success that attended Her
Majesty's Arms there.   I had the Curiosity to read all

the Accounts that were given of it; but was more particularly pleas'd with the Relation, which the 'Gazetteer'
and the 'Tatler' (3) of the same Day (as indeed these *two*
Authors are never asunder) oblig'd us with.

Nothing can be more Instructive or Entertaining than to
see in how different a Manner, and with what a variety of
Stile, two eminent Pens may employ themselves on the same
Subject. We equally admire the same *Catiline*, as he is
drawn either by *Cicero* or *Salust*: And after we have read
that fine Description of the Battle of *Cannae* in *Polybius*,
we are not less pleas'd to read it over again in *Livy*.
Nay, the different Portraitures of King *CHARLES* I. done
by the same masterly Hand of *Vandyke*, are more entertaining to a judicious Eye, than the Figures of two several
Persons, that have no manner of Resemblance. The happy
Mixture of Diversity and Agreement, the Art of so drawing
the same Piece, as that it shall be both like and unlike
it self, conveys an exquisite Pleasure to him, whose
Taste is nice enough to relish it. Something of this
Delight I found in comparing my two weekly Friends: And
because the best way of improving a Pleasure is to communicate it, I will give my Reader a Specimen of those different Beauties, with which they have described the same
Action.

[Gaz.] *Five thousand Men of his Catholick Majesty's Troops, under General* Wesel, *in the* Lampourdan, *were on their march.* —	[Tat.] *Five thousand Men were on their march, in the* Lampourdan, *under the Command of Gen.* Wesel, *having receiv'd Order from his Catholick Majesty.* —
[Gaz.] *His Catholick Majesty order'd General* Stanhope *to march with* 14 *Squadrons of Horse.* —	[Tat.] *The King of* Spain *commanded General* Stanhope *with a Body of Horse consisting of* 14 *Squadrons.* —
[Gaz.] *To disturb the Enemy in their Passage of the River* Segra *and* Noguera, *between* Lerida *and* Balaguer —	[Tat.] *To prevent their Passage over the River* Segra *and* Noguera, *between* Lerida *and* Balaguer. —
[Gaz.] *All the Horse on both sides came to a general Engagement.*	[Tat.] *The Battle improv'd to a general Engagement of the Cavalry of both Armies.* —
[Gaz.] *The Duke of* Anjou *retir'd to* Lerida. —	[Tat.] *That Prince was retiring towards* Lerida. —

When I reflect upon these different Turns of Expression, equally Graceful, equally Numerous, I cannot but
condemn the Judgment of *Longinus*, and the rest of the

Greek Criticks, who would persuade us, that after a correct Writer has adjusted the due Order of his Words,
there can be no Change of 'em but for the worse. We have
here before us a plain Instance to the contrary, of two
polite Authors, who relating the same Action have fallen
upon much the same Words, and yet have been so happy in
the different way of ranging them, as to make it doubtful, whose Periods are most Harmonious, whose Narrative
most Beautiful.

Whether *Lampourdan* sounds best at the Beginning or End
of the Sentence? Whether 14 *Squadrons of Horse* or *a
Body of Horse consisting of* 14 *Squadrons*, has a better
Cadence? Whether their Passage *OF the River*, or their
Passage OVER the River, is more Elegant and Tuneful, I
defy any Critick living to determine. Many Observations
might be made on these parallel Places; I satisfy my self
in giving the Hint, but I will leave my Reader the Pleasure of pursuing and improving it.

We see how exactly these two Genius's agree in their
Narrative: They move together in an amicable Way, Hand in
Hand, and like the *Two Kings in the* 'Rehearsal', smell to
the same *Nosegay*. (4) But their different Characters
oblige them to part here: The 'Gazetteer', after the
Matter of Fact is over, goes off the Stage; He is a
judicious Historian; The 'Tatler' must stay to refine a
little and reflect; he is a *diverting Wit*: And the
Heroick Scene being over, he enlivens you with a little
Farce in the *Postscript*. The *Favourers*, says he, *of the
House of* Bourbon *amongst us*, (*i.e.* those of them that
live at *Milan*, whence this Letter is dated) *affirm, That
this* Stanhope, *that could as it were get out of his Sick
Bed, to Fight against the King of* Spain, *must be of the
Antimonarchical Party*. (5)

Cou'd as it were get out of his Sick-Bed, is very
Elegant; but might have misled us to think, that he did
not get out of his Bed, if we had not been told before,
that *his Joy surmounted his Weakness*. It puts me in mind
of an *Epitaph* upon the old *Organist* at *Lincoln,*

———— *Jacet hic Ioannes,*
Organa namque loqui fecerat ille Quasi.

Which was thus translated in those Days,

———— John *lyes here,*
Who made the Organ for to speak, or as it were.

But this General we allow, did get out of his Bed and
Fight; and we shou'd be ready to give him the Praises due

to so gallant an Action: But that the 'Tatler' seems to
insinuate, That none but the *Whigs* have any Right to commend him.   The *Favourers of the House of* Bourbon *affirm*,
That this Action must be done by *one of the Antimonarchical Party*.   Is every one *Antimonarchical*, that beats these
Bourbonites?   For what a rigid *Republican* must they take
him, who gave *France* that terrible Blow at *Wynnendale*? (6)
And what a *Monarchical High-Flyer* must he be reckon'd,
who was pleas'd to lose *Spain* at *Almansa*? (7)   But why
must Mr. *Stanhope* be of the *Antimonarchical Party*? (8)
because he Fights by the Commission of one *Monarch*, for
the Establishment of another upon his Throne?   I dare say,
King *Charles* has no Design of setting up a *Republick* in
Spain; and I guess by some late *Phaenomena* (for I deal
with the Stars too, *Isaac*) that Her Majesty will be able
to *prevent* one here.

But let General *Stanhope*'s Principles be what they
will, Are you sure he will thank you for making so free
with them in his Absence?   Methinks no good Servant of the
Queen's shou'd be pleas'd with being thought an Enemy to
Monarchy.   Or if you have leave to call him what *Names* you
please (which I very much question) why are his Politicks
brought in upon this Occasion?   What have Notions of
Government to do with Conduct and Courage in the Field?
If we had had, during this War, twenty thousand more
English-men in *Spain*, I am of Opinion the *Favourers of the
House of* Bourbon wou'd have run away long ago, without
asking what *Party* they were of.   I fancy too, if the
Muster-Rolls of these 14 Squadrons at the *Segra* were
view'd, they wou'd not *All* be found *Antimonarchical*: I
dare answer for the *German Horse*, that they have never
thoroughly consider'd this Point.

I have enquir'd of *Jacob* and *Kidney*, (9) and two or
three more of your Friends, and they tell me that the
only Reason, why you give Mr. *Stanhope* this Title of
Antimonarchical, is, because he quoted a *Republican*
Author in the Trial last Winter. (10)   But perhaps the
General is not highly oblig'd to you for going so much
out of your way, to put us in mind of the *Orator*.   I
can't think he wou'd take it ill, if a Man shou'd venture
to say, That he makes a better Figure in the *Field* than
at the *Bar*, and can lead Troops with more Success than he
can plead a Cause.   Wou'd Sir *Simon Harcourt*, or if you
had rather, Sir *James Mountague*, be angry, were it said,
That they are not so well vers'd in *Battles* and *Sieges*, as
they are in *Eloquence* and *Argument*? (11)   Or that either
of them cou'd defend a Town, or manage a Campaign, with
that Dexterity and presence of Mind, as one of them vindicated the *Rights of the Crown*, and the other complemented

the Noble Lord upon the WOOLPACK!

The Earl of Rochfort *and Count* Nassau *fell in this Action*: And for fear no Body in *England* shou'd know it, we are told from *Milan* whose Sons they were: *And that their Fathers had a great place in the Confidence of the late King* William, *by whom they were Enobled*. We remember very well their Titles, and when they had them; and because your Talent lies more in foretelling what *shall* be, than in recording what *has* been, let me inform you, 'twas under a *Tory Ministry*, and while several Great Men were in the Confidence of King *William*, who were afterwards supplanted by some of your *Antimonarchical* Gentlemen. In one Word, a Son of Mr. *Overkirk* must be universally lamented, as well for his Father's Merit as his own. We are sorry too for the loss of the Earl of *Rochfort*; but I am afraid, *Isaac Bickerstaff*, who now complements him with the Title of *Heroick Youth*, has forgot the 'Tatler' of *Tun*, *Gun*, and *Pistol*.

After all, *Isaac*, tho' I have us'd this Freedom with you, I wou'd not have you take me for your Enemy; I am one of your *two Guinea Subscribers*, and consequently (if I may take your Word for it in your *Dedication*) am a Person *eminent* for *Wit*, *Beauty*, *Valour*, or *Wisdom*, some one or more of 'em. And if you in your turn will take my Word, I assure you, I have been very well entertain'd with several of your Papers; and have given them their just Commendation to many of my Ingenious and Learned, but I must own, *Monarchical* Friends. No Body desires more than I do, that you shou'd go on to expose Vice and Folly, and recommend Morality and Virtue, as agreeably as you can, and as often as you please. My Advice to you is only this, That you wou'd still appear in your proper Sphere; and not quit a Character which has giv'n you some Credit, to take up another that does not in the least become you. Give me leave to tell you, you mistake your Talent, whenever you meddle with Matters of *State*; your Jest pleases no Body, when it reflects upon the *Constitution*, under which you live. Don't magnify your *Constellation* of Worthies to that degree, as if the World were to be left in Darkness, if any of those *Shining Lights* shou'd be withdrawn. *Eclipses* you see have happen'd, which you did not foretel: Begin to take care of your self; remember the Fate of one of your Predecessors, and don't gaze at Your *Stars*, 'till you fall into a *Ditch*. No more of your *Politick Lucubrations*; put out your Candle; favour your Age; and go to Bed sooner.

—— *Nam TUA Caelo*
Praecipitant, suadentq; Cadentia sydera somnos. (12)

P.S. The 'Tatler', in his last, promises us, that as
the Town fills he will be *Wittier*: I am sorry, for his
sake, it has been empty so long. I believe he will be
shortly as good as his Word, for his Friends, I hear, are
coming from *Ireland*. I expect too, some of my Friends
from the same Country; and as he is to be New-rigg'd out
for a Wit, so I don't question but that there will from
thence too come fresh Materials for an 'Examiner'.

Notes

1   For Mr Petticum, see 'Tatler' 136.
2   Both were coffee-houses. Tom's was in Russell Street,
    opposite Button's, and was named after the landlord
    Thomas West. Will's, named after its owner Will Urwin,
    was also in Russell Street.
3   'Tatler' 210, published as was the 'Gazette' on 12
    August 1710.
4   In 'The Rehearsal', the mock-heroic Two Kings of
    Brentford think and do alike, 'And like true brothers
    walk still hand in hand' (II. ii).
5   The conclusion of 'Tatler' 210.
6   The victory of General John Webb (*c.* 1667-1724) and
    6,000 infantry at Wynendael (28 September 1708).
7   The defeat of British forces led by Henry de Massue,
    Earl of Galway (1648-1720) on 25 August 1707.
8   James Stanhope (1673-1721), 1st Earl Stanhope;
    general and statesman.
9   Jacob apparently refers to the owner of Jacob's
    Coffee-house ('Tatler' 224); Kidney the waiter at St.
    James's Coffee-house appeared in the 'Tatler'.
10 The impeachment proceedings of Henry Sacheverell in
    February-March 1710.
11 Simon Harcourt (*c.* 1661-1727), 1st Viscount Harcourt,
    who succeeded Sir James Montagu (1666-1723) as
    attorney-general in 1710.
12 A revised quotation from the 'Aeneid', II, 8-9:
    'Now too *your* night is speeding from the sky and the
    setting stars invite to sleep.'

5-12 October 1710

Among all the ill Qualities in Mankind, I know none that
makes a worse Figure, than *Excess of Vanity*: 'Tis disagreeable wherever we meet with it; but no where so much
as in a Writer. A little *extempore* Conceitedness may be
endur'd; but a meditating lucubrating Fop is intolerable.

A *vain* Coxcomb in Company may, under good Management, be
made diverting for a quarter of an Hour; and a *vain*
Officer in an Army, may have the luck to succeed in some
rash Enterprize: In such Cases as these it often falls
out, that *Something is produc'd out of Nothing.* Nay, I
have known one of these *Thraso*'s, celebrated by a judicious Author for a Hero, and propos'd as a Pattern of
Military Virtue to the Men of Arms: But the same Spirit
of *Vanity*, that made this Gentleman pass with *some* for a
Hero, cou'd never make him pass with *any* for a *Poet*. An
Author cannot take a surer way of lessening the Reputation of his Performances, than by over-valuing them. But
little Writers are betray'd into this Folly, by an indiscreet Imitation of Great Ones. They that are acquainted
with my Lord *Bacon*'s Essays will easily pardon him for
saying, *He conceives they will last as long as Books
last.* (1) They that read the Episode of *Nisus* and
Euryalus, would give *Virgil* leave to boast,

> *Nulla dies unquam memori vos eximet aevo;*
> *Dum Domus AEneae Capitoli immobile saxum*
> *Accolet, imperiumq; Pater Romanus habebit.*

And yet he modestly introduces it with

> ——*Si quid mea carmina possunt.* (2)

Writers of the first Rank, in Works design'd for Eternity,
may be allow'd to have a due Sense of their own Excellencies: But for a weekly Retailer of loose Papers, one of
which is still dying before the next is born, to assume
the same Privilege, is perfectly ridiculous. I must
observe farther, That the *Ancients* (I wish I cou'd say
a *Modern* too, whom I am by and by to Examine) where they
are guilty of this Ostentation, seem sensible of the
risque they run, and take pains in those very places to
excel, and to out-write themselves. That *Vain* Epistle of
Tully to *Lucceius*, is one of the best in the whole Collection. And the two last *Odes* of the 2d and 3d Books of
Horace, where he promises himself Fame and Immortality,
are wrought up with exquisite Skill and Care: And yet when
he comes to

> —— *Sume Superbiam*
> *Quaesitam meritis,* (3)

he dares not venture to speak it in his own Person, but
with a fine turn of Thought applies it to his *Muse*. 'Tis
plain that *Horace* saw 'twas too much to take to himself:

They must have great Modesty and Judgment; who, after
this, can chuse it for their *Motto*. I have never heard of
any but one *Scholar* and the 'Tatler', that cou'd think it
became 'em. Men that have this Satisfaction in their own
Merit, wou'd enjoy it with more quiet, if they did not
provoke People to disturb them; but the Itch of being very
Abusive is almost inseparable from *Vain-Glory*. *Tully* has
these two Faults in so high a degree, that nothing but his
being the best Writer in the World, can make amends for
them: And yet the 'Tatler' in his Paper of *September* 26.
has out-done him in Both; he speaks of himself with more
Arrogance, and with more Insolence of others. (4)
     First, he sets himself out as a *Noble Creature that
is*, as it were, *the Basis and Support of Multitudes*:
Meaning, I suppose, *John Nutt, John Morphew, Charles
Lilly, &c*. (5) This indeed is very great; but it often
happens, that Supporters, which have such a Weight upon
them, are scarce able to support themselves. I am in no
Critical Humour at present; or else I should ask him, what
sort of *Basis* it is that *supports* something *below* it, as I
take an *Inferior* to be? I know he will have recourse
again to his *saving* Expression, that did him some Service
once before, and tell me, that he does not call it a
Basis, but a *Basis* as it were: And this will, *as it were*,
be as good as writing correctly: Tho' in this Paper he
does not seem so much to aim at being correct, as copious.
He is so intent upon being something Extraordinary, that
he scarce knows what he would be; and is as fruitful in
his Similes, as a Brother of his whom I lately took notice
of. In the compass of a few Lines he compares himself to
a *Fox*, to *Daniel Burgess* (6) to the *Knight of the Red
Cross*, to an *Oak with Ivy about it*, and to a *Great Man
with an Equipage*: But at last he rises in his Images, and
nothing will satisfie him but the *Sun*. He has taken, it
seems, the Device of the King of *France*, and, I suppose,
'twill not be long before he has his Motto too, *Nec pluri-
bus impar*. And truly 'twill suit well enough, if those he
has to deal with, are what he in his great Civility and
good Breeding, represents them, *Owls, Bats, Fleas, Lice,
Vermin, small Wits, Scriblers, Niblers, &c*. After this
List of Names, I was surpriz'd to hear him say, That *he
has hitherto kept his Temper pretty well*. I wonder how
he will write, when he has lost his Temper. I suppose, as
he now is very angry and unmannerly, he will then be
exceeding courteous and good-humour'd.
     I had a Curiosity to know where his *Apartment* was on
the 25th of *September*, when he talk'd so much of *Fleas*,
and *Lice*, and *Vermin*; or what place cou'd fill his Head
with such Ideas. I have heard some Criticks say that *Lee*

cou'd have writ his 'Constantine'·no where but in *Bedlam*;
(7) and that 'twas easy to discover a Scene in *Otway*, that
smelt of the *Spunging-House*. (8) But I forbore this
Inquiry, and went on to the next Simile which he honours
himself with: *His Antagonists*, he says, *are like a great
Man's Equipage, who do Honour to the Person on whom they
Feed*. This is something more gentile: I am glad he has
an Equipage that gratifies his *Vanity*: But there is an
Equipage that does no great *Honour to the Person on whom
they Feed*. l have heard of a certain Illustrious Person,
who having a *Guard du Corps*, that forc'd their Attendance
upon him, put them into a Livery, and maintain'd them as
his Servants: Thus answering that famous Question,

Quis Custodiet ipsos Custodes?

For he, I think, might properly be said to keep his
Keepers, in *English* at least, if not in *Latin*. If you
intend, Mr. *Tatler*, to keep your Attendants, you must be
a little more punctual in your Payments: They complain
that they have nothing to feed upon, and are in great
danger of Starving. (9)
 You gave them your Word long since, that you wou'd
begin to be *Witty* in *October*; and in this modest Essay
upon your self, that lies before me, you promise to *Shine*.
I have heard some that have waited upon you this Fortnight, say, they no more can perceive any Sparks of Wit
or Light to break from you, than they did when you was
Dull by Design.
 I seldom read such idle Papers: The flaming one with
Quaesitam meritis, (10) &c. in the Front, fell into my
Hands by chance; but seeing there that you were so bent
upon *excelling* and *shining*, I was tempted to look into
what you have writ since, and that has quite cur'd my
Curiosity for the future.
 When I read your Account of the *Pillion*, drawn out
into two Pages, how tedious, thought I, are old Men in
telling old Stories; and how much better was this told by
Mrs. *Andrea Polhill* at her Maid's Wedding?
 I hop'd, as you did, that your Friend the *Upholsterer*
had been Dead: He was of a very low Character at first;
but after we had had his Company so often, a long Letter
from him was extremely insipid. (11)
 I perus'd your History of *Joseph*. (12) Do you intend
to go through the *Old Testament*? If you do, let me recommend a Book that may be of use to you: I found *Blome*'s
History of the Bible in my Maid's Hand, and turn'd to the
Story of *Joseph*: He tells it more pathetically than you
do, and gives us a pretty Picture of it besides. (13)

If you *shine on* at this rate, your Antagonists, as you
call 'em, are safe; you'l *scorch* nothing but Turkies and
Capons.

You produc'd a Stanza or two out of the *Red-Cross*
Knight, that did not suit your Performances so well, as
another Passage of *Spencer*'s that I refer you to.

The Gentle Usher VANITY by Name, (14)

whom you have chosen for your Guide, will show you the
way to a House thus describ'd:

> *A stately Palace built of squared Brick,*
> *Which cunningly was without Mortar laid;*
> *Whose Walls were high, but nothing strong nor thick,*
> *And golden foil all over them display'd.*
> *It was a goodly Heap for to be behold,*
> *But full great pity that so fair a Mold,*
> *Did on so weak Foundation ever sit:*
> *For on a sandy Hill that still did flit*
> *And fall away, it mounted was full high,*
> *That ev'ry breath of Heaven shaked it.*
> *Great Troops of People travell'd thither-ward,*
> *Both day and night of each degree and place;*
> *But few returned, having scaped hard,*
> *With baleful Beggary, or foul Disgrace.* (15)

Notes

1 The Epistle Dedicatory to the 'Essays, or Counsels
   Civil & Moral'.
2 'Aeneid', IX, 446-9: 'If aught my verse avail, no day
   shall ever blot you from the memory of time, so long
   as the house of Aeneas shall dwell on the Capitol's
   unshaken rock, and the Father of Rome hold sovereign
   sway.'
3 'Odes', III. xxx. 14-15: 'Accept the proud honour won
   by thy merits.'
4 'Tatler' 229.
5 The three men were involved in the printing and/or the
   distribution of the 'Tatler'.
6 'Merry' Daniel Burgess (1645-1713), minister to a con-
   gregation in Carey Street, Lincoln's Inn. His
   meeting-house was wrecked by a Sacheverell mob in
   1710.
7 Nathaniel Lee (c. 1653-92), dramatist. According to
   William Oldys's manuscript notes to Gerard Langbaine's
   'An Account of the Dramatic Poets', Lee - who drank

too much wine one night - 'was killed or stifled in
the snow'.
8 Thomas Otway (1652-85), dramatist. Again, according
to Oldys, Otway died in a sponging-house, although
Giles Jacob described it as a public house.
9 Steele in May 1709 and April 1710 was briefly
arrested for debt.
10 The motto of 'Tatler' 229.
11 The Upholsterer, who was devoted to politics rather
than his shop, was a character frequently seen in the
'Tatler', especially 155, 160, 178.
12 'Tatler' 233.
13 Richard Blome (d. 1705) first published in 1691 'History of the Old and New Testament' from the French of
Nicolas Fontaine.
14 'The Faerie Queene', I. iv. 13.
15 A non-sequential quotation (lines from stanzas 3,4,5)
from 'The Faerie Queene', I. iv.

33. 'A CONDOLING LETTER TO THE TATTLER'

c. 1710

This Tory pamphlet is as much an attack on Richard Steele
as it is on the 'Tatler'. Steele himself had read it.
In 'Tatler' 228 he wrote, 'I have been *annotated*,
retattled, *examined*, and *condoled*; but it being my standing maxim never to speak ill of the dead, I shall let
these authors rest in peace and take great pleasure in
thinking that I have sometimes been the means of their
getting a bellyful.'

SIR,
Nothing is more remarkable in the Nature of Man, and
nothing exposes him more, to the just Satyr of his Wiser
Fellow-Creatures, *the Brutes*; than that he never fails to
commit that Crime himself, which he reproves in another;
and never fails Reproving in another, what he commits
himself.
    A Time of Affliction is a Proper Time for Reflection:
In the Days of Prosperity (Tattling) *rejoyce; but in the
Day of Adversity* (Prison) *consider.* Eccles. vii. 14.
    It is true, That as no Man is without Sin, and so it

is not necessary to the Qualification of *a Censor* of Mankind, that he shou'd be what Human Nature does not afford;
viz. Spotless and Perfect: But it is certainly necessary,
he shou'd be as clear a Man as possible, and especially
clear of those particular Follies he reproves. *Cato* was
chosen *Censor* of *Rome*, for the Reputation of his own Austerity, and the known Practice of a Rigid Vertue.

And here, Sir, the Word, *Chosen*, seems to throw in
another Clause in the Indictment; The Grave and Venerable
Office of a Censor, *Anglice*, a Judge and Reprover of
Manners, which was in *Rome*, one of the most Honourable
Places among the Magistracy, and of Greatest Authority;
was always in the Choice of the People, or at least
Senatus Populusq; Romae were the Choosers. But when a
Man, who has no such Choice fix'd upon him, but (as some
say Mr. *Bickerstaff* has done) usurps that Office, and
gives himself that Title; besides the Stock of Face
requisite to the Usurpation, and besides the Crime of the
Usurpation it self; such a Man shou'd have had a special
Regard to his own Reputation, and unless he was resolv'd
to court the worst of Characters, ought to have been
careful to merit the best.

And here we cannot but pay Homage to the Goddess *Fortune*; it's true, you Christians, have Un-Deify'd that Old
Dutchess, and giv'n, all that former Ages ador'd Her for,
to *Providence*, but as for us honest Heathens, we must
talk to one another in our own Dialect, and to Mr. *Bickerstaff*, who is now, *he knows*, in his Decrepit Age; it
wou'd be very absurd to talk, at this Time of Day, of
Turning *Christian*.

I say, therefore, we cannot but acknowledge the Justice of *Fortune*, who in all her Tossings and Wheelings of
Mankind about the World, observes still a certain Law,
famous among the Ancients, and which always carries a
great Deal of Self-Reflection in it, I mean, *RETRIBUTION*,
or, *Lex Talionis*.

Here's Poor Mr. *Bickerstaff*, it is not many Months
since he incarcerated honest *Partridge*, and laid him,
dead or alive, in the Earth without any Crime; of which
the Living Spectrum of *John Partridge*, which *they say*, is
all of him, that has ever since appear'd in the World,
made loud Complaints; protested against the Injustice,
and declar'd he receiv'd an Inexpressible Injury; having
been murther'd a Way that no Man was ever kill'd before;
contrary to the known Laws of *Man-Slaughter*, and the
Laudable Usage and Custom of *Assassination*. But the Man
complain'd in vain, Mr. *Bickerstaff*, protected by the
Mob, continu'd to justify the Crime; and to this Day made
him no Reparation: But now 'tis come Home to him, and the

Alternative is visible: *Fortune* having turn'd her Wheel
round, and the True Reverse of Things now appearing;
Behold! He that imprisoned *Partridge* in the Grave, is
himself bury'd in that worst of Graves, a Jail; (1) as
Partridge was mercifully admitted to walk about after he
was dead, so *Bickerstaff* is kindly suffer'd to *Tattle*
after he is bury'd; *Partridge* had a Death without a Grave,
Bickerstaff a Grave without Death.

See the Justice of *Fortune* (a Tattling Phrase). Mr.
Bickerstaff will, I hope, make a good Use of the Observation, and Moralize upon the Subject like a good Philosopher.

Retaliation *is a Hint*,
The Gods *for* Mankind's *Good appoint*,
In which the Circumstances *chime*,
That Punishment *may show the Crime*.

Nor is the Case of Poor *Partridge* singly upon your
Friend Mr. *Bickerstaff*, But he is desir'd to reflect upon
his Treatment of the Author of the *Post-Man*, who he unjustly opprest in the too Critical Handling a Word in the
English Tongue, and very unmercifully treated that Gentleman; (2) when at the same Time, the Words, tho' not, perhaps, so Polite, were just in Signification, and legitimated by Custom, *The Best Judge of Language*; but all this
While Mr. *Bickerstaff* forgat to do a Piece of Justice,
which no Man of Honour cou'd have satisfy'd himself in
the Omission of; *viz*. To have Own'd, that Mr. *Fonvive* (3)
is a Foreigner, and has obtain'd the Just Character of
Writing the best *English* of any Stranger in *Britain*....

Now, there are two Sorts of General Language in the
World: The Language of *our Words*, and the Language of *our
Actions*: Our *Words* speak, and our *Deeds* speak; and Wise
Men take as much Care to have their Actions speak Sence,
as their Tongues; nay, the Nonsence of our Behaviour, is
every Jot as ridiculous, and as justly exposes us to Cen-
sure, as the Nonsence of our Speech. And is it possible!
that Mr. *Bickerstaff*, who has assum'd the Office of
Censor, *(as before)* and expos'd the Nonsence spoken by the
Canes, the *Snuff-Boxes*, the *Farthingales*, the *Stripe
Garters*, &c. Trifles in the Nation's Morals, should himself talk the Nonsence of *Intemperance, Drunkenness,
Immense Prodigality,* and *Unaccountable Profusion*.

Pray Sir, Be pleas'd to ask Mr. *Bickerstaff*, a few
Questions from me, as a Friend; which, perhaps, in his
present Retirement, he may think worth answering, at
least, to himself.

1. *Whether it is not palpable Nonsence, for a Man, who
   has a Plentiful Income, no great Family, no Necessary Expensive Port to maintain, or Charge to support, to run himself in Debt, meerly by Luxury,
   and Profuse Living?*

2. *Whether a Man of Thought, thus not to think, is not
   unsufferable Nonsence?*

3. *Whether Mr. Bickerstaff, who, all Men know, has a
   large Sallary, a Good Profit for Tatling; and who
   has receiv'd Large Bounties from the Generous Part
   of Mankind, could go to the Gate-House, or any
   House, for Debt, without being guilty of Great
   Nonsence?*

4. *Whether on these Accounts, he has not unqualify'd
   himself, to reprove any Man for Nonsence; and
   ought not by Way of Penance, to confine himself from
   it, for a certain Time; viz. 'Till the Happy Day
   of his own Reformation?*

Mr. *Bickerstaff* has been very diverting of Late, in the
Account he has given us of his *State-Barometers*, and his
Church-Thermometers, and such Kind of Weather-Glasses; and
Useful Things they are, indeed, of their Kind; but, I
wonder, how he came to make no Mention of a certain
Oeconomical Barometer, or, *a Family Weather-Glass*;... (4)
But, however, as I have study'd the Thing pretty well, and
have made some visible Improvements in this most useful
Engine, I cannot but recommend it to Mr. *Bickerstaff*, both
for his own Use, and his making farther Improvements upon
—in his Solitudes; according to the just Character of our
Country-Men, that we are better to improve than to invent.
   The Tube of this Glass is of the Usual Size, 32 Inches;
the *Liquid* within, compounded of certain Exquisite Extrac-
tions, drawn from the most Refin'd Principles, such as
Spirit of Brain, Tincture of Thought, Salt of Prudence,
and many more, the Rarest and most Admirable Principles in
the World, the *Flegmatic* or *Humid*, is sometimes *Patriar-
chal*, sometimes *Filial*, sometimes *Conjugal*, sometimes
Personal; but being mixt together make the best Preparation in the World.
   The Lines to mark the Ascent, or Descent of the *Liquid*,
are at proper Distances, and the Measures are thus:

Madness,

Poverty,

Extravagance,

Excess or Profusion,

Waste,

Generous Liberality,

Plenty,

FAMILY,

Frugality,

Parsimony,

Niggardliness,

Covetous,

Sordidly Covetous,

Wretchedness or Rich Poverty,

Madness....

Now I need not direct Mr. *Bickerstaff*, to Examine how high his *Family-Weather-Glass* has risen; but must humbly recommend it to him, as he is *Censor* of *Great-Britain*, whether justly or assum'd, to give us some of the Reproaches due to that Man, who having a plentiful Revenue, and no Family-Charge, profusely wasts it in Extravagances and Excess, and goes to Jail for Debt, and desire him to tell us, Sir,
1. What Honesty he can pretend to in it?
2. What Pity he can expect?
These few Observations, Sir, are humbly recommended to Mr. *Bickerstaff* to take Notice of, or to let alone, as he shall think fit.

Your Humble Servant

Censor Censorum

Notes

1 See the 'Examiner' for 5–12 October 1710 (No. 32) note 9.
2 'Tatler' 212.

3   Jean de Fonvive wrote the 'Post-Man', judged a Whig
    paper by the Tories.
4   A Political Barometer or State Weather-Glass appears
    in 'Tatler' 214; the Ecclesiastical Thermometer in
    'Tatler' 220.

34.   WILLIAM COWPER, 'A LETTER TO ISAAC BICKERSTAFF'

1710

The pamphlet was written by William Cowper (d. 1723),
first Earl Cowper. It was 'Occasion'd by the Letter to
the Examiner'.

SIR,
I Am not apt to judge too fondly of Men by their first
Appearance; else, as the Writer of the 'Letter to the
Examiner' (1) has treated that Author, I might have
been tempted long since, and when I had seen little more
than the Introduction to your 'Tatlers', to compliment
you on your Abilities.
    I own that from your setting out, I hop'd for great
Benefit to the Publick from your Lucubrations; but before
you had pass'd a reasonable time of Probation, one could
not absolutely assure one's self, that you would make a
right use of that excellent Genius which Heaven has given
you. Wit had so long and so generally been made to serve
the vilest Purposes, on pretence its end is to please,
that the plainest Truth in Nature, namely, that Honesty
and Pleasure are inseparable, seem'd irrecoverably sunk
into Oblivion, till you undertook to bring it up again
into clear day, not by Argument, but Example, by numerous
Sketches and some finish'd Pieces drawn with irresistible
Strength and Beauty.
    As you disclos'd your Design by degrees, you had my
Esteem in proportion; and you will allow me to say you
had it not intire, till in the course of your Papers I
had observ'd, that as you could discern and describe,
much better than our *Drydens* and *Lestranges*, the true
Springs of private and domestick Happiness; (2) you had
likewise so much Generosity of Spirit and Benevolence
for Mankind than they, as to insinuate gradually into the

Publick, that as acting with all the noble Simplicity of
Nature and common Reason carries a Man with Ease and
Honour thro' all the Scenes and Offices of ordinary Life;
so the same Principles, which in Friendship, Love, and
common Converse and Society, go to the Composition of the
Person, whom both Sexes agree to call by the good natur'd
name of *the generous honest-Man*, must necessarily contribute to the forming of the best Servants of a Prince, and
the truest Patriots.

But as in doing this you took a proper Season to expose
some of those brutish Notions of Government, and vile Arts
of wretched Pretenders to Politicks, which are the certain
Bane of National Felicity; you have provok'd your Adversaries (while I was studying a Compliment of Thanks to
you) to give you so high an Encomium, that 'tis impossible
for me, with all the Affection and Veneration I have for
you, to go beyond them. The Writer of the 'Letter to the
Examiner' comparing you to *Cato* the Censor, and forgetting
(as Men of his Vivacity of Imagination may be allow'd to
do, without bringing their reading in question) that there
were two *Catos*, applies to you *Lucan*'s fam'd Saying of the
last.

Victrix causa Diis placuit, sed victa Catoni. (3)

*That however Providence dispos'd of Events, he adher'd to
the just, tho' vanquish'd Cause.* And the 'Examiner' pursuing the same Thought, reminds you, by a sneering Application of some words of *Virgil*.

*——Tua Caelo
Praecipitant, Suadentque cadentia Sydera somnos.* (4)

*That you have chosen a time to declare your Sentiments,
when the Patrons of both them and you are removing from
Court.*

Thus, Sir, I have staid till nothing is left me but
only to congratulate you on the very great Honour they
have done you: And to confess the Truth, I am glad I can
so easily acquit my self of the most troublesome Part of
a Visit, Salutes and Compliments.

Notes

1 'A Letter to the Examiner' (1710) was written by Henry
   St John (1678-1751), later first Viscount Bolingbroke.
2 Their names were often so coupled; see, e.g., Swift,
   An Apology in 'A Tale of a Tub'.

3 'De Bello Civili', I, 128: 'For, if the victor had the
   gods on his side, the vanquished had Cato.'
4 See 'Examiner', 24-31 August 1710 (No. 32), note 12.

35. JOHN GAY, 'THE PRESENT STATE OF WIT'

1711

Dated by Gay as of 3 May 1711, 'The Present State of Wit'
was probably the first non-political statement of the
'Tatler's' innovative performance and literary excellence.

The 'Examiner' is a paper which all men, who speak without prejudice, allow to be well written. Though his subject will admit of no great variety; he is continually
placing it in so many different lights, and endeavouring
to inculcate the same thing by so many beautiful changes
of expression, that men who are concerned in no Party,
may read him with pleasure. His way of assuming the
Question in debate is extremely artful; and his 'Letter
to Crassus' (1) is, I think, a masterpiece. As these
Papers are supposed to have been written by several
hands, (2) the critics will tell you that they can discern a difference in their styles and beauties; and pretend to observe that the first 'Examiners' abound chiefly
in Wit, the last in Humour.
    Soon after their first appearance, came out a Paper
from the other side, called the 'Whig Examiner', written
with so much fire, and in so excellent a style, as put
the Tories in no small pain for their favourite hero. (3)
Every one cried, 'BICKERSTAFF must be the author!' and
people were the more confirmed in this opinion, upon its
being so soon laid down: which seemed to shew that it was
only written to bind the 'Examiners' to their good behaviour, and was never designed to be a Weekly Paper....

    Before I proceed further in the account of our Weekly
Papers, it will be necessary to inform you that at the
beginning of the winter [on Jan. 2, 1711], to the infinite surprise of all men, Mr. STEELE flang up his
'Tatler'; and instead of ISAAC BICKERSTAFF, Esquire, sub-
scribed himself RICHARD STEELE to the last of those

Papers, after a handsome compliment to the Town for their
kind acceptance of his endeavours to divert them.

The chief reason he thought fit to give for his leaving
off writing was, that having been so long looked on in all
public places and companies as the Author of those papers,
he found that his most intimate friends and acquaintances
were in pain to speak or act before him.

The Town was very far from being satisfied with this
reason, and most people judged the true cause to be,
either

That he was quite spent, and wanted matter to continue
his undertaking any longer; or

That he laid it down as a sort of submission to, and
composition with, the Government, for some past
offences; or, lastly, (4)

That he had a mind to vary his Shape, and appear again
in some new light. (5)

However that were, his disappearance seemed to be bewailed
as some general calamity. Every one wanted so agreeable
an amusement, and the Coffee-houses began to be sensible
that the *Esquire's Lucubrations* alone had brought them
more customers, than all their other News Papers put
together.

It must indeed be confessed that never man threw up his
pen, under stronger temptations to have employed it
longer. His reputation was at a greater height, than I
believe ever any living author's was before him. It is
reasonable to suppose that his gains were proportionably
considerable. Every one read him with pleasure and good-
will; and the Tories, in respect to his other good
qualities, had almost forgiven his unaccountable imprudence in declaring against them.

Lastly, it was highly improbable that, if he threw off
a Character the ideas of which were so strongly impressed
in every one's mind, however finely he might write in any
new form, that he should meet with the same reception.

To give you my own thoughts of this Gentleman's
Writings, I shall, in the first place, observe, that there
is a noble difference between him and all the rest of our
Polite and Gallant Authors. The latter have endeavoured
to please in their fashionable vices and false notions of
things. It would have been a jest, some time since, for a
man to have asserted that anything witty could be said in
praise of a married state, or that Devotion and Virtue

were any way necessary to the character of a Fine Gentleman.   *BICKERSTAFF* ventured to tell the Town that they were
a parcel of fops, fools, and coquettes; but in such a
manner as even pleased them, and made them more than half
inclined to believe that he spoke truth.

Instead of complying with the false sentiments or vicious tastes of the Age - either in morality, criticism, or
good breeding - he has boldly assured them, that they were
altogether in the wrong; and commanded them, with an authority which perfectly well became him, to surrender themselves to his arguments for Virtue and Good Sense.

It is incredible to conceive the effect his writings
have had on the Town; how many thousand follies they have
either quite banished or given a very great check to! how
much countenance, they have added to Virtue and Religion!
how many people they have rendered happy, by shewing them
it was their own fault if they were not so! and, lastly,
how entirely they have convinced our young fops and young
fellows of the value and advantages of Learning!

He has indeed rescued it out of the hands of pedants
and fools, and discovered the true method of making it
amiable and lovely to all mankind.   In the dress he gives
it, it is a most welcome guest at tea-tables and assemblies, and is relished and caressed by the merchants on
the Change.   Accordingly there is not a Lady at Court, nor
a Banker in Lombard Street, who is not verily persuaded
that Captain STEELE is the greatest Scholar and best Casuist of any man in England.

Lastly, his writings have set all our Wits and Men of
Letters on a new way of Thinking, of which they had little
or no notion before: and, although we cannot say that any
of them have come up to the beauties of the original, I
think we may venture to affirm, that every one of them
writes and thinks much more justly than they did some time
since.

The vast variety of subjects which Mr. STEELE has
treated of, in so different manners, and yet ALL so perfectly well, made the World believe that it was impossible they should all come from the same hand.   This set
every one upon guessing who was the *Esquire*'s friend? and
most people at first fancied it must be Doctor SWIFT; but
it is now no longer a secret, that his only great and constant assistant was Mr. ADDISON. (6)

This is that excellent friend to whom Mr. STEELE owes
so much; and who refuses to have his name set before those
Pieces which the greatest pens in England would be proud
to own.   Indeed, they could hardly add to this Gentleman's
reputation: whose works in Latin and English Poetry long
since convinced the World, that he was the greatest Master

in Europe of those two languages.

I am assured, from good hands, that all the visions, and other tracts of that way of writing, with a very great number of the most exquisite pieces of wit and raillery throughout the *Lucubrations* are entirely of this Gentleman's composing: which may, in some measure, account for that different Genius, which appears in the winter papers, from those of the summer; at which time, as the 'Examiner' often hinted, this friend of Mr. STEELE was in Ireland.

Mr. STEELE confesses in his last Volume of the 'Tatlers' that he is obliged to Dr. SWIFT for his 'Town Shower', and the 'Description of the Morn', with some other hints received from him in private conversation. (7)

I have also heard that several of those *Letters*, which came as from unknown hands, were written by Mr. HENLEY:(8) which is an answer to your query, 'Who those friends are, whom Mr. STEELE speaks of in his last "Tatler"?'

But to proceed with my account of our other papers. The expiration of *BICKERSTAFF's Lucubrations* was attended with much the same consequences as the death of *MELIBOEUS's Ox* in VIRGIL: as the latter engendered swarms of bees, the former immediately produced whole swarms of little satirical scribblers.

One of these authors called himself the 'Growler', and assured us that, to make amends for Mr. STEELE's silence, he was resolved to *growl* at us weekly, as long as we should think fit to give him any encouragement. Another Gentleman, with more modesty, called his paper, the 'Whisperer'; and a third, to please the Ladies, christened his, the 'Tell tale'.

At the same time came our several 'Tatlers'; each of which, with equal truth and wit, assured us that he was the genuine *ISAAC BICKERSTAFF*.

It may be observed that when the *Esquire* laid down his pen; though he could not but foresee that several scribblers would soon snatch it up, which he might (one would think) easily have prevented: he scorned to take any further care about it, but left the field fairly open to any worthy successor. Immediately, some of our Wits were for forming themselves into a Club, headed by one Mr. HARRISON, (9) and trying how they could shoot in this Bow of ULYSSES; but soon found that this sort of writing requires so fine and particular a manner of Thinking, with so exact a Knowledge of the World, as must make them utterly despair of success.

They seemed indeed at first to think, that what was only the garnish of the former 'Tatlers', was that which recommended them; and not those Substantial Entertainments

which they everywhere abound in. According they were continually talking of their *Maid*, *Night Cap*, *Spectacles*, and
CHARLES LILLIE. However there were, now and then, some
faint endeavours at Humour and sparks of Wit: which the
Town, for want of better entertainment, was content to
hunt after, through a heap of impertinences; but even
those are, at present, become wholly invisible and quite
swallowed up in the blaze of the 'Spectator'.

You may remember, I told you before, that one cause
assigned for the laying down the 'Tatler' was, Want of
Matter; and, indeed, this was the prevailing opinion in
Town: when we were surprised all at once by a paper called
the 'Spectator', which was promised to be continued every
day; and was written in so excellent a style, with so nice
a judgment, and such a noble profusion of Wit and Humour,
that it was not difficult to determine it could come from
no other hands but those which had penned the *Lucubrations*.

This immediately alarmed these gentlemen, who, as it is
said Mr. STEELE phrases it, had 'the Censorship in Comis-
sion'. They found the new 'Spectator' came on like a torrent, and swept away all before him. They despaired ever
to equal him in Wit, Humour, or Learning; which had been
their true and certain way of opposing him: and therefore
rather chose to fall on the Author; and to call out for
help to all good Christians, by assuring them again and
again that they were the First, Original, True, and
Undisputed *ISAAC BICKERSTAFF*.

Meanwhile, the 'Spectator', whom we regard as our Shelter from that flood of false wit and impertinence which
was breaking in upon us, is in every one's hands; and a
constant topic for our morning conversation at tea-tables
and coffee-houses. We had at first, indeed, no manner of
notion how a diurnal paper could be continued in the
spirit and style of our present 'Spectators': but, to our
no small surprise, we find them still rising upon us, and
can only wonder from whence so prodigious a run of Wit and
Learning can proceed; since some of our best judges seem
to think that they have hitherto, in general, outshone
even the *Esquire*'s first 'Tatlers'.

Most people fancy, from their frequency, that they must
be composed by a Society: I withal assign the first
places to Mr. STEELE and his Friend.

I have often thought that the conjunction of those two
great Geniuses, who seem to stand in a class by themselves, so high above all our other Wits, resembled that
of two statesmen in a late reign, whose characters are
very well expressed in their two mottoes, viz., *Prodesse
quam conspici*, (10) and *Otium cum dignitate*. (11)

Accordingly the first [ADDISON] was continually at work
behind the curtain, drew up and prepared all those
schemes, which the latter still drove on, and stood out
exposed to the World, to receive its praises or censures.

Meantime, all our unbiassed well-wishers to Learning
are in hopes that the known Temper and prudence of one of
these Gentlemen will hinder the other from ever lashing
out into Party, and rendering that Wit, which is at present a common good, odious and ungrateful to the better
part of the Nation. (12)

If this piece of imprudence does not spoil so excellent
a Paper, I propose to myself the highest satisfaction in
reading it with you, over a dish of tea, every morning
next winter.

As we have yet had nothing new since the 'Spectator',
it only remains for me to assure you, that I am

> Yours, &c.,
> J.G.

Westminster, May 3, 1711.

Notes

1   'Examiner' (8 February 1710), by Swift.
2   Conceived probably by Henry St John, the 'Examiner'
    enlisted the help of William Oldisforth, Mrs Manley,
    Jonathan Swift, Matthew Prior, and others.
3   Written by Addison.
4   The rumour had it that Steele agreed in early October
    1710 to neutralize or end the 'Tatler' in exchange
    for the right to continue in the Stamp Office.
5   See John Oldmixon, 'The Life and Posthumous Works of
    Arthur Maynwaring' (1715), p. 193.
6   Steele acknowledged Addison's help in 'Tatler' 271.
7   'Tatler' 9, 238. Swift contributed to about a dozen
    numbers.
8   Anthony Henley (d. 1711) may have contributed to vari-
    ous essays in the 'Tatler': e.g., 11, 26, 193.
9   William Harrison (1685–1713) began a continuation of
    the 'Tatler' on 13 January 1711, probably at the sug-
    gestion of St John and Swift. It lasted until May
    1711. For other 'continuations', see R. P. Bond, 'The
    Tatler', pp. 204–5.
10 'To be useful rather than to be conspicuous': the
    motto of Lord Somers.
11 'Leisure with dignity': the motto of Lord Halifax.
12 To the Tories.

36. HENRY FELTON, 'A DISSERTATION ON READING THE
CLASSICS'

[1713], 1715

From the second edition (1715) of 'A Dissertation on Reading the Classics, and Forming a Just Style. Written in
the Year 1709'.

Upon this Occasion, my Lord, (1) I cannot pass by Your
Favourite Author, the grave and facetious 'Squire *Bickerstaff*, who hath drawn Mankind in every Dress, and every
Disguise of Nature, in a Style ever varying with the Humours, Fancies, and Follies he describes. He hath showed
himself a Master in every Turn of his Pen, whether his
Subject be light, or serious, and hath laid down the Rules
of common Life with so much Judgment, in such agreeable,
such lively and elegant Language, that from him Your Lordship at once may form Your Manners and Your Style.

Notes

1 John Manners (1696–1779) styled (erroneously) Lord
  Roos (1703–11); Marquess of Granby (1711–21); 3rd
  Duke of Rutland (1721–79).

V The 'Spectator'
1711-12, 1714

37.   'A SPY UPON THE SPECTATOR'

1711

The Preface from an unsigned pamphlet, 'A Spy Upon the
Spectator'.

There may be some more than ordinary Reasons to look
narrowly into the 'Spectator's' Designs and Management.
The Tyranny that he pretends to exert over the Sense and
Reason of his Countrymen; and the small Stock of Discretion with which he lays his Daily Burthen of *Speculations*
upon them, makes it necessary to stop him in the beginning, and let him know, that the Foundations of his Power
are only imaginary, and his Notions are of the same
Nature, as the Clouds and Mist that he pretends to cast
over his Actions.

   Care should be taken, lest by following him, we lose
our Wit, Morality and Religion: For should we look upon
him to be the Touchstone of Wit, and the Rule and Standard
of Judgment; and afterwards find that he is flat in the
one, and exercises the other upon Trifles, (Num. 10.) it
may at last make us have a contemptible Opinion of Ingenuity and Learning.

   Morality is a serious thing, and of too much value to
be lost; and therefore, altho' the 'Spectator' at present,
under the pretence of enlivening it by *Wit*, (N. 10.) may
impose only the Shadow of it upon us instead of the Substance; yet he should not be permitted to proceed so far,
as to make a Buffoon of *Aristotle*, and write a Burlesque

upon *Epictetus.*

The Profession, as well as Character of the Clergy, are
too sacred for the trivialness of such Papers; and who
knows but the 'Spectator', who expresst his aversion to
Bells at two Months old (N. 1.) and has contracted a
Friendship with a *Divine*, that under the shelter of a weak
Constitution, has laid aside the *Cares* and *Business* of his
Function, to attend upon *Clubs* and *Chamber-Council* (N. 2.)
may have some design against the fifty new Churches, at
least will be against having any *Steeple-houses* and *Bel-
fries* to them.

It may easily be shown, That it would be no pity, *If
all the Discoveries he has made were still in the possession of a silent Man*, (N. 1.) for the World would be no
great Loser: And whereas he says, *He'll publish a Sheet-
full of Thoughts every Morning*, (N. 1.) that he often
publishes his Half-sheet with little or no Thinking.

The several 'Spectators' being a disjoyn'd and confused
huddle of unmethodiz'd Notions, I do not look upon my self
oblig'd to take them in order: However (notwithstanding
his Magisterial Authority) every one of them, in proper
time and place, may meet with due Correction: And perhaps
he shall shortly find, he has not Art enough to disguise
himself; and that a Net is too thin a *Cloak* for a *Party-
Man* to dance in.

38. WILLIAM WAGSTAFFE, 'A COMMENT UPON ... TOM THUMB'

1711

William Wagstaffe (1685-1725), a physician, wrote 'A
Comment upon the History of Tom Thumb' in 1711 in order
to ridicule the 'Spectator's' ballad criticism and its
use of epic rules and poetry to measure the literary
value of 'Chevy Chase' and 'Two Children in the Wood'.
He mistakenly assumed the essays were written by Steele.

It is a surprising Thing that in an Age so Polite as
this, in which we have such a Number of Poets, Criticks
and Commentators, some of the best things that are extant
in our Language shou'd pass unobserv'd amidst a Croud of
inferior Productions, and lie so long buried as it were,

among those that profess such a Readiness to give Life to
every thing that is valuable. Indeed we have had an
Enterprising Genius of late, that has thought fit to dis-
close the Beauties of some Pieces to the World, that might
have been otherwise indiscernable, and believ'd to have
been trifling and insipid, for no other Reason but their
unpolish'd Homeliness of Dress. And if we were to apply
our selves, instead of the Classicks, to the Study of Ballads and other ingenious Composures of that Nature, in
such Periods of our Lives, when we are arriv'd to a
Maturity of Judgment, it is impossible to say what
Improvement might be made to Wit in general, and the Art
of Poetry in particular: And certainly our Passions are
describ'd in them so naturally, in such lively, tho'
simple, Colours, that how far they may fall short of the
Artfulness and Embellishments of the *Romans* in their Way
of Writing, *yet cannot fail to please all such Readers*
as are not unqualify'd for the Entertainment by their
Affectation or Ignorance.

It was my good Fortune some time ago to have the
Library of a School-Boy committed to my Charge, where
among other undiscover'd valuable Authors, I pitch'd upon
'Tom Thumb' and 'Tom Hickathrift', Authors indeed more
proper to adorn the Shelves of *Bodley* or the *Vatican*,
than to be confin'd to the Retirement and Obscurity of a
private Study. I have perus'd the first of these with an
infinite Pleasure, and a more than ordinary Application,
and have made some Observations on it, which may not, I
hope, prove unacceptable to the Publick; and however it
may have been ridicul'd, and look'd upon as an Entertainment only for Children, and those of younger Years, may
be found perhaps a Performance not unworthy the Perusal
of the Judicious, and the Model superiour to either of
those incomparable poems of 'Chevy Chase', or 'The Children in the Wood'.   The Design was undoubtedly to recommend Virtue, and to shew that however any one may labour
under the Disadvantages of Stature or Deformity, or the
Meanness of Parentage, yet if his Mind and Actions are
above the ordinary Level, those very Disadvantages that
seem to depress him, shall add a Lustre to his Character.

There are Variety of Incidents, dispers'd thro' the
whole Series of this Historical Poem, that give an agreeable Delight and Surprise, *and are such as* Virgil *himself*
wou'd have touch'd upon, had the like Story been told by
that Divine Poet, viz. his falling into the Pudding-Bowl
and others; which shew the Courage and Constancy, the
Intrepidity and Greatness of Soul of this little Hero,
amidst the greatest Dangers that cou'd possibly befall
him, and which are the unavoidable Attendants of human
Life.

Si fractus illibatur orbis,
Impavidum ferient ruinae. (1)

The Author of this was unquestionably a Person of an
Universal Genius, and if we consider that the Age he wrote
in, must be an Age of the most profound Ignorance, as
appears from the second Stanza of the first *Canto*, he was
a Miracle of a Man.

I have consulted Monsieur *Le Clerk*, and my Friend *Dr.*
B---ly concerning the Chronology of this Author, (2) who
both assure me, tho' neither can settle the Matter
exactly, that he is the most ancient of our Poets, and
'tis very probable he was a *Druid*, who, as *Julius Caesar*
mentions in his *Commentaries*, us'd to deliver their Precepts in Poetry and Metre. The Author of 'The Tale of a
Tub', believes he was a *Pythagorean* Philosopher, and held
the *Metempsichosis*; and Others that he had read *Ovid*'s
'Metamorphosis', and was the first Person that ever found
out the Philosopher's Stone. A certain Antiquary of my
Acquaintance, who is willing to forget every thing he
shou'd remember, tells me, He can scarcely believe him to
be Genuine, but if he is, he must have liv'd some time
before the *Barons* Wars; (3) which he proves, as he does
the Establishment of Religion in this Nation, upon the
Credit of an old Monument.

There is another Matter which deserves to be clear'd,
whether this is a Fiction, or whether there was really
such a Person as *Tom Thumb*. As to this, my Friends tell
me, 'Twas Matter of Fact, and that 'twas an unpardonable
Omission in a certain Author, (4) never once to mention
him in his 'Arthur's', when nothing is more certain, than
that he was the greatest Favourite of that Prince, and a
Person who had perform's some very eminent Services for
his Country. And indeed I can't excuse his taking no
Notice of our Poet, who has afforded him such Helps, and
to whom he is so much oblig'd for the Model of those Productions: Besides it had been but a Debt of Gratitude, as
Sir *R—— B——* was a Member of the Faculty, to have made
honourable mention of him who has spoken so honourably of
the Profession, on the Account of the Sickness of his
Hero.

I have an old Edition of this Author by me, the Title
of which is more Sonorous and Heroical, than those of
later Date, which for the better Information of the
Reader, it may not be improper to insert in this Place.
'Tom Thumb *his Life and Death, wherein is declar'd his*
many marvellous Acts of Manhood, full of Wonder and
strange Merriment': Then he adds, '*which little Knight*
liv'd in King Arthur'*s Time in the Court of* Great

Britain'. Indeed there are so many spurious Editions of
this Piece upon one Account or other, that I wou'd advise
my Readers to be very cautious in their Choice, and it
would be very wisely done, if they wou'd consult the
curious *AElianus* concerning this Matter, who has the
choicest Collection of any Man in *England*, and understands the most correct Editions of Books of this Nature.

I have took a great deal of Pains to set these Matters
of Importance in as clear a Light as we Criticks generally do, and shall begin with the first *Canto*, which
treats of our Hero's Birth and Parentage, and Education,
with some other Circumstances which you'll find are
carry'd on in a manner not very inelegant, *and cannot fail
to please those who are not Judges of Language, or those
who notwithstanding they are Judges of Language, have a
genuine and unprejudic'd Taste of Nature.*

> *In* Arthur's *Court* Tom Thumb *did live;*
> *A Man of mickle Might,*
> *The best of all the Table round,*
> *And eke a doubty Knight,*
> *In Stature but an Inch in Height,*
> *Or quarter of a Span;*
> *Then think you not this worthy Knight*
> *Was prov'd a valiant Man.*

This Beginning is agreeable to the best of the Greek
and Latin Poets; *Homer* and *Virgil* give an Idea of the
whole Poem in a few of the first Lines, and here our
Author draws the Character of his Hero, and shews what
you may expect from a Person so well qualify'd for the
greatest Undertakings.

In the Description of him, which is very fine, he insinuates, that tho' perhaps his Person may appear despicable and little, yet you'll find him an Hero of the most
consummate Bravery and Conduct, and is almost the same
Account *Statius* gives of *Tydeus*.

> ———— *Totos infusa per artus,*
> *Major in exiguo regnabat corpore virtus.* (5)

If any suppose the Notion of such an Hero improbable,
they'll find the Character *Virgil* gives *Camilla* to be as
far stretch'd:

> *Illa vel Intactae segetis per summa volaret*
> *Gramina, nec teneras cursa laesisset Aristas:*
> *Vel mare per medium, fluctu suspensa tumenti*
> *Ferret Iter: celeres nec tingeret aequore plantas.* (6)

But to proceed,

His Father was a Plowman plain,
His Mother milk'd the Cow,
And yet a Way to get a Son
This Couple knew not how,
Until such time the good old Man
To learned Merlin *goes,*
And there to him in deep Distress
In secret Manner shows,
How in his Heart he wish'd to have,
A Child in time to come,
To be his Heir, tho' it might be
No bigger than his Thumb;
Of which old Merlin *was foretold,*
That he his Wish shou'd have,
And so a Son of Stature small
The Charmer to him gave.

There is nothing more common throughout the Poets of
the finest Taste, than to give an Account of the Pedigree
of their Hero. So *Virgil*,

——*Aeneas quam Dardanio Anchisae*
Alma Venus Phrygii genuit Simoentis ad undas. (7)

And the Manner of the Countryman's going to consult
Merlin, is like that of *Aeneas*'s approaching the Oracle
of *Delphos*.

——*Egressi veneramur Apollinis Urbem.*(8)

And how naturally and poetically does he describe the
Modesty of the Man, who wou'd be content, if *Merlin* wou'd
grant him his Request, with a Son no bigger than his
Thumb.
The two next Stanza's carry on the Idea with a great
deal of Probability and Consistence; and to convince the
World that he was born to be something more than Man, he
produces a Miracle to bring him into it.

Begot, and born in half an Hour,
To fit his Father's Will.

The following Stanza continues the Miracle, and brings
the *Fairy Queen* and her Subjects, who gives him his Name,
and makes him a Present of his Apparel.

Whereas she cloath'd him fine and brave,
In Garments richly fair,
The which did serve him many Years
In seemly sort to wear.

So *Virgil* of Queen *Dido*'s Present to *Ascanius*:

Hoc Juvenem egregium praestanti munere donat. (9)

And again,

—— *Quem candida Dido*
Esse sui dederat Monumentum & pignus Amoris. (10)

The Description of his Dress is very agreeable, and is
not unlike what I have met with somewhere of a Giant going
a Fishing, with an Account of his Implements equal to his
Proportion.

His Hat made of an Oaken Leaf,
    His Shirt a Spider's Web,
Both light and soft for these his Limbs
    That were so smally bred.
His Hose and Doublet Thistle Down,
    Together weav'd full fine;
His Stockings of an Apple green,
    Made of the outward Rind;
His Garters were two little Hairs
    Pluck'd from his Mothers Eye;
His Shooes made of a Mouse's Skin,
    And Tann'd most curiously.

The next Stanza's relate his Diversions, bearing some
Analogy to those of *Ascanius* and other Lads in *Virgil*:

Thus like a valiant Gallant He
    Adventures forth to go,
With other Children in the Street,
    His pretty Tricks to show.

Una Acies Juvenum ducit quam Parvus Ovantem
Nomen Avi referens Priamus. (11)

There is a Piece of Revenge our little Hero took upon a
Play-fellow, which proves, to what an Height Mechanical and
Experimental Philosophy was arriv'd to, in that Age, and
may be worth while to be consider'd by the *Royal Society*.

> *Of whom to be reveng'd, he took*
> *In Mirth and pleasant Game,*
> *Black Pots and Glasses, which he hung*
> *Upon a bright Sun-Beam.*

The third Line is a Demonstration of the Antiquity of
Drinking out of black Pots, which still prevails in most
Counties of this Nation, among the Justices of Peace at
their Petty and Quarter Sessions.

The last four Lines of this Canto, and the beginning of
the next, contain the miraculous Adventure of the Pudding-
Bowl; And by the bye, we may observe, That it was the
Custom of the *Christians* at that time, to make Hog-
Puddings instead of Minc'd-Pies at *Christmas*; a laudable
Custom very probably brought up to distinguish 'em more
particularly from the *Jews*.

> *Whereas about a* Christmas *time,*
> *His Father an Hog had kill'd,*
> *And* Tom *to see the Pudding made,*
> *Fear that it should be spill'd;*
> *He sat the Candle for to Light,*
> *Upon the Pudding-Bowl:*
> *Of which there is unto this Day*
> *A pretty Pastime told:*
> *For* Tom *fell in* ——

Perhaps some may think it below our Hero to stoop to
such a mean Employment as the Poet has here enjoyn'd him,
of holding the Candle, and that it looks too much like a
Citizen, or a *Cot*, as the Women call it: But if we reflect
on the Obedience due to Parents, as our Author undoubtedly
did, and the Necessities those People labour'd under, we
cannot but admire at his ready Compliance with what could
by no Means be agreeable to the Heroical Bent of his Inclinations, and perceive what a tender Regard he had for
the Wellfare of his Family, when he took the strictest
Care imaginable for the Preservation of the Hog-Pudding.
And what can be more remarkable? What can raise the
Sentiments of Pity and Compassion to an higher Pitch, than
to see an Hero fall into such an unforeseen Disaster in
the honourable Execution of his Office? *This certainly is*
conformable to the Way of Thinking among the Ancient
Poets, and what a good-natur'd Reader cannot but be affec-
ted with.

The following Part of this Canto is the Relation of our
Hero's being put into a Pudding, and convey'd away in a
Tinker's Budget; which is design'd by our Author to prove,
if it is understood literally, That the greatest Men are

subject to Misfortunes. But it is thought by Dr. *B——tly*
to be all Mythology, and to contain the Doctrine of the
Transmutation of Metals, and is design'd to shew, that
all Matter is the same, tho' very differently Modified.
He tells me, he intends to publish a distinct Treatise of
this Canto; and I don't question, but he'll manage the
Dispute with the same Learning, Conduct and good Manners,
he has done others, and as Dr. *Salmon* uses in his Correc-
tions of Dr. *Sydenham* and the 'Dispensatory'. (12).

The next Canto is the Story of *Tom Thumb*'s being
swallow'd by a Cow, and his Deliverance out of her, which
is treated of at large by *Giordano Bruno* in his 'Spaccio
de la Bestia trionfante'; which Book, tho' very scarce,
yet a *certain Gentleman*, who has it in his Possession, has
been so obliging as to let every Body know where to meet
with it. After this, you find him carried off by a Raven,
and swallow'd by a Giant; and 'tis almost the same Story
as that of *Ganimede* and the Eagle in *Ovid*.

> *Now by a Raven of great Strength,*
>   *Away poor* Tom *was born.*

> *Nec mora: percusso mendacibus aere pennis*
> *Abripit Iliaden.* (13)

A certain great Critick and *School-master*, who has publish'd such Notes upon *Horace* as were never seen before,
is of Opinion, and has very good Authority for what he
says, that 'twas rather an Owl than a Raven; for, as he
observes with a wonderful deal of Penetration and Sagacity, our Hero's Shoes were made of a Mouse's Skin, which
might induce the Owl to run away with him. The Giant, he
owns, looks very probable, because we find 'em swallowing
People very fast in almost all Romances.

This Canto concludes with our Hero's Arrival at Court;
after he had spent a considerable Part of his Youth in
Labours and Fatigues, had been inur'd to nothing else but
Hardships and Adventures, we see him receive the Recom-
pense of his Merit, and become the Favourite of his
Prince: And here we may perceive all the Fineness of the
Gentleman, mixt with all the Resolution and Courage of the
Warriour; We may behold him as ready to oblige the Ladies
with a Dance, as he was to draw his Sword in their
Defence.

> *Amongst the Deeds of Courtship done,*
>   *His Highness did command,*
> *That he shou'd dance a Galliard brave*
>   *Upon the Queen's Left Hand.*
> *The which he did ——*

This shews he had all the Accomplishments of *Achilles* who was undoubtedly one of the best Dancers in the Age he liv'd, according to the Character *Homer* gives him so frequently of the Agility of his Feet. I have consulted a Master of the Profession of Dancing, who is excellently vers'd in the Chronology of all Dances, he tells me that this *Galliard* came into Vogue about the latter End of the Reign of *Uter Pendragon*, and continu'd during that of King *Arthur*, which is Demonstration to me that our Poet liv'd about that Age.

It is asserted very positively in the latter Editions of this Poem, that the four following Lines are a Relation of the King and *Tom Thumb*'s going together an Hunting, but I have took indefatigable Pains to consult all the *Manuscripts* in *Europe* concerning this Matter, and I find it an *Interpolation*. I have also an *Arabick Copy* by me, which I got a *Friend* to translate, being unacquainted with the Language, and it is plain by the Translation, that 'tis there also *interpolated*.

> *Now after that the King wou'd not*
>   *Abroad for Pleasure go,*
> *But still* Tom Thumb *must go with him*
>   *Plac'd on his Saddle Bow.*

> —— *Ipse Uno graditur comitatus Achate.* (14)

There is scarcely any Scene more moving than this that follows, and is *such an one as wou'd have shin'd in* Homer *or* Virgil. When he was favour'd with his Prince's Ear, and might have ask'd the most profitable and important Posts in the Government, and been indemnify'd if guilty of a *Peculatus*; He only us'd his Interest to relieve the Necessities of his Parents, when another *Person* wou'd have scarcely own'd 'em for his *Relations*. This discovers such a Generosity of Soul, such an Humility in the greatest Prosperity, such a tender Affection for his Parents, as is hardly to be met with, but in our Author.

> *And being near his Highness Heart*
>   *He crav'd a wealthy Boon,*
> *A noble Gift, the which the King*
>   *Commanded to be done;*
> *To relieve his Father's Wants,*
>   *And Mother being old.*

The rest of this Canto relates the Visit to his Father, in which there is something very soft and tender, something *that may move the Mind of the most polite Reader,*

with the inward Meltings of Humanity and Compassion.
The next Canto of the Tilts and Tournaments, is much
like the Fifth Book of *Virgil,* and tho' we can't suppose
our Poet ever saw that Author, yet we may believe he was
directed to almost the same Passages, *by the same kind of
Poetical Genius, and the same Copyings after Nature.*

> *Now he with Tilts and Tournaments,*
>   *Was entertained so,*
> *That all the rest of* Arthur's *Knights*
>   *Did him much Pleasure show;*
> *And good Sir* Lancelot *of* Lake,
>   *Sir* Tristram, *and Sir* Guy;
> *But none like to* Tom Thumb
>   *For Acts of Chivalry.*

> *Longeque ante omnia Corpora Nisus*
> *Emicat ———— (15)*

And again,

> *Post Elymus subit, & nunc tertia palma Diores.* (16)

> *In Honour of which noble Day,*
>   *And for his Lady's Sake,*
> *A Challenge in King* Arthur's *Court,*
>   Tom Thumb *did bravely make.*

> *Talis prima Dares caput altum in proelia tollit,*
> *Ostenditq; humeros latos, alternaq; jactat*
> *Brachia portendens, & verberat ictibus auras.*
> *Quaeritur huic alius: ——*

> *'Gainst whom those noble Knights did run,*
>   *Sir* Chion *and the rest,*
> *But still* Tom Thumb *with all his Might*
>   *Did bear away the best.*

> *Et primum ante omnes victorem appellat Acesten.* (18)

At the same time our Poet shews a laudable Partiality
for his Hero, he represents Sir *Lancelot* after a manner
not unbecoming so bold and brave a Knight.

> *At last Sir* Lancelot *of* Lake,
>   *In manly sort came in,*
> *And with this stout and hardy Knight*
>   *A Battle to begin.*

Huic contra AEneas, speculatus in agmine longo
Obvius ire parat ——— (19)

Which made the Courtiers all aghast.

Obstupuere animi ——— (20)

This Canto concludes with the Presents made by the King
to the Champion, according to the Custom of the *Greeks* and
Romans in such Cases; only his tumbling thro' the Queen's
Ring is observable, and may serve to give some Light into
the Original of that ingenious Exercise so much practis'd
by the Moderns, of tumbling thro' an Hoop.

The last Canto treats of the Champion's Sickness and
Death, and whoever considers the Beauty, Regularity and
majestick Simplicity of the Relation, cannot but be surpris'd at the Advances that may be made in Poetry by the
Strength of an uncultivated Genius, and may see how far
Nature can proceed without the Ornamental Helps and Assistances of Art.   The Poet don't attribute his Sickness to a
Debauch, to the Irregularity or Intemperance of his Life,
but to an Exercise becoming an Hero; and tho' he dies
quietly in his Bed, he may be said in some measure to die
in the Bed of Honour.   And to shew the great Affection the
King had for him, he sends for his Physicians, and orders
all the Care imaginable to be taken for the Conservation
of his Life.

He being slender and tall,
*   This cunning Doctor took*
A fine perspective Glass, with which
*   He did in Secret look.*

It is a Wonder that the learned World shou'd differ
so in their Opinions concerning the Invention and Antiquity of Optic Glasses, and that any one should contend
for *Metius* of *Alcmaer*, or, as Dr. *Plot* does for *Fryar
Bacon*, when, if this Author had been consulted, Matters
might have been so easily adjusted.   Some great Men
indeed wou'd prove from hence, our Knight was the Inventor
of 'em, that his Valet might the more commodiously see to
dress him; but if we consider there were no Beaus in that
Age, or reflect more maturely on the Epithet here given to
the Doctor, we may readily conclude, that the Honour of
this Invention belongs more particularly to that ingenious
Profession.

How lovely is the Account of the Departure of his Soul
from his Body:

And so with *Peace* and *Quietness*
   He left the World below.

Placidaq; ibi demum morte quievit. (21)

And up into the Fairy Land,
   His Soul did fleeting go.

——*At AEthereas repetit mens ignea sedes.* (22)

Whereas the Fairy Queen receiv'd
   With happy Mourning Cheer
The Body of this valiant Knight,
   Whom she esteem'd so dear;
For with her dancing Nymphs in Green
   She fetch'd him from his Bed,
With Musick and with Melody,
   As soon as Life was fled.

——*Et fotum gremio Dea tollit in altos*
Idaliae lucos ——(23)

So one of our Modern Poets;

Thither the Fairies and their Train resort,
And leave their Revels, and their midnight Sport.

We find in all the most celebrated Poets, some Goddess
that takes upon her to be the peculiar Guardian of the
Hero, which has been carry'd on very elegantly in this
Author.
   But again;

For whom King Arthur *and his Knights,*
   Full forty Days did mourn,
And in Remembrance of his Name,
   Who was so strangely born,
He built a Tomb of Marble grey,
   And Year by Year did come,
To celebrate the mournful Day,
   And Burial of Tom Thumb;
Whose Fame lives here in England *still,*
   Among the Country sort,
Of whom their Wives and Children small,
   Tell Tales of pleasant Sport.

So *Ovid*;

————*Luctûs monumenta manebunt*
Semper, Adoni, mei, repetitaq; mortis Imago
Annua plangoris peraget simulamina nostri. (24)

Nor is this Conclusion unlike one of the best Latin
Poems this Age has produc'd.

Tu, Tassi, aeternum vives, tua munera Cambri
Nunc etiam celebrant, quotiesq; revolvitur Annus
Te memorant, Patrium Gens tota tuetur Honorem,
Et cingunt viridi redolentia tempora Porro. (25)

And now, tho' I am very well satisfied with this Performance, yet, according to the usual Modesty of us
Authors, I am oblig'd to tell the World, *it will be a*
great Satisfaction to me, knowing my own Insufficiency,
if I have given but some Hints of the Beauties of this
Poem, which are capable of being improv'd by those of
greater Learning and Abilities. And I am glad to find
by a Letter I have receiv'd from one of the *Literati* in
Holland, That the learned *Hussius,* a great Man of our
Nation, is about the Translation of this Piece into *Latin*
Verse, which he assures me, will be done with a great deal
of Judgment, in case he has enough of that Language to
furnish out the Undertaking. I am very well appris'd,
That there has been publish'd two poems lately, intituled,
The Second and Third Parts of this Author; which treat of
our little Hero's rising from the Dead in the Days of
King *Edgar*: But I am inform'd by my Friend the *School-*
master, and others, That they were compos'd by an Enthusiast in the last Century, and have been since printed
for the Establishment of the Doctrine of Monsieur *Marion*
and his Followers, and the Resurrection of Dr. *Ems.*
    I hope no Body will be offended at my asserting Things
so positively, since 'tis the Privilege of us *Commenta-*
tors, who understand the meaning of an Author seventeen
hundred Years after he has wrote, much better than ever
he cou'd be suppos'd to do himself. And certainly, a
Critick ought not only to know what his Author's Thoughts
were, when he was Writing such and such Passages, but how
those Thoughts came into his Head, where he was when he
wrote, or what he was doing of; whether he wrote in a
Garden, a Garret, or a Coach; upon a Lady, or a Milkmaid;
whether at that Time he was scratching his Elbow, drinking a Bottle, or playing at Questions and Commands.
These are material and important Circumstances so well
known to the *True Commentator,* that were *Virgil* and *Horace*
to revisit the World at this time, they'd be wonderfully
surpris'd to see the minutest of their Perfections

discover'd by the Assistances of *Modern Criticism*. Nor
have the Classicks only reap'd Benefit from Inquiries of
this Nature, but Divinity itself seems to be render'd more
intelligible. I know a Divine, (26) who understands what
St. *Paul* meant by *Higher Powers*, much better than that
Apostle cou'd pretend to do; and another, That can unfold
all the Mysteries of the *Revelations* without Spectacles.

I know there are some People that cast an Odium on me,
and others, for pointing out the Beauties of such Authors,
as have, they say, been hitherto unknown, and argue, That
'tis a sort of Heresie in Wit, and is like the fruitless
Endeavours of proving the Apostolical Constitutions *Genuine*, that have been indisputably *Spurious* for so many
Ages: But let these Gentlemen consider, whether they pass
not the same Judgment on an Author, as a Woman does on a
Man, by the gayety of his Dress, or the gaudy Equipage of
his Epithets. And however they may call me *second-sighted*,
for discerning what they are blind to, I must tell them
this Poem has not been altogether so obscure, but that the
most refin'd *Writers* of this Age have been delighted with
the reading it. Mr. *Tho. D'Urfey*, I am told is an Admirer,
and Mr. *John Dunton* has been heard to say, more than once,
he had rather be the Author of it than all his Works.

How often, *says my Author*, have I seen the Tears
trickle down the Face of the Polite *Woodwardius* upon reading some of the most pathetical Encounters of *Tom Thumb!*
How soft, how musically sorrowful was his Voice! How good
natur'd, how gentle, how unaffected was the Ceremoniale of
his Gesture, and how unfit for a Profession so Merciless
and Inhumane!

I was persuaded by a Friend to write some Copies of
Verses, and place them in the Frontispiece of this Poem,
in Commendation of my self and my *Comment*, suppos'd to be
compos'd by *AG. FT. LM. RW.* and so forth. *To their very
worthy and honour'd Friend* C.D. upon his admirable and
useful *Comment* on the History of *Tom Thumb*; but my Bookseller told me the Trick was so common, 'twould not
answer. Then I propos'd a Dedication to my Lord *such an
One,* or Sir *Thomas such an One*; but he told me the Stock
to be rais'd on Dedications was so small now a Days, and
the Discount to my Lord's Gentleman, *&c.* so high, that
'twould not be worth while; besides, says he, it is the
Opinion of some Patrons, that a Dinner now and then, with,
Sir, I shall expect to see you sometimes, is a suitable
Reward for a publick Compliment in Print. But if, continues my Bookseller, you have a Mind it shou'd turn to
Advantage, write Treason or Heresy, get censur'd by the
Parliament or Convocation, and condemn'd to be burnt by
the Hands of the common Hangman, and you can't fail having

a Multitude of Readers, by the same Reason, *A notorious
Rogue has such a Number of Followers to the Gallows.*

Notes

1   Horace, 'Odes', III. iii. 7-8: 'Were the vault of
    heaven to break and fall upon him, its ruins would
    smite him undismayed.'
2   Jean Le Clerc (1657-1736), Swiss theologian; Richard
    Bentley (1662-1742), scholar and critic.
3   The War of the Roses (1455-85).
4   Sir Richard Blackmore, author of the epic poem
    'Prince Arthur'.
5   'Thebeid', I, 416-17: 'And though the frame was
    smaller, greater valour in every part held sway.'
6   'Aeneid', VII, 808-11: 'She might have flown o'er
    the topmost blades of unmown corn, nor in her course
    bruised the tender ears; or sped her way o'er mid sea,
    poised above the swelling wave, nor dipped her swift
    feet in the flood.'
7   'Aeneid', I, 617-18: '[Art thou] that Aeneas, whom
    gracious Venus bore to Dardanian Anchises by the wave
    of Phrygian Simois?'
8   'Aeneid', III, 79: 'Landing we do homage to Apollo's
    town.'
9   'Aeneid', V, 361: 'This he bestows on the noble youth,
    a lordly prize.'
10 'Aeneid', V, 571-2: 'That fairest Dido had given as
    memorial of herself and pledge of her love.'
11 'Aeneid', V, 563-4: 'One line of youths in triumphal
    joy is led by a little Priam, renewing his grand-
    sire's name.'
12 William Salmon (1644-1713), a practitioner of medi-
    cine. Of dubious reputation, he was the author of
    'Pharmacopoeia Londinensis, or the New London Dispen-
    satory'. Thomas Sydenham (1624-89), physician.
13 Ovid, 'Metamorphoses', X, 159-60: 'Without delay he
    cleft the air on his lying wings and stole away the
    Trojan boy.'
14 'Aeneid', I, 312: 'Then, Achates, alone attending, him-
    self strides forth.'
15 'Aeneid', V, 318-19: 'Nisus far in front of all darts
    forth.'
16 'Aeneid', V, 339: 'Behind comes Helymus, and Diorès,
    now third prize.'
17 'Aeneid', V, 375-8: 'Such was Dares, who at once
    raises his head high for the fray, displays his broad
    shoulders, stretches his arms, spars right and left,

and lashes the air with blows. For him a match is
sought.'

18 'Aeneid', V, 540: 'And hails Acestes victor, first
above them all.'

19 'Aeneid', X, 769-70: 'On the other side Aeneas, espy-
ing him in the long battle-line, moves to meet him.'

20 'Aeneid', VIII, 530 (inaccurately quoted): 'The rest
stood aghast.'

21 'Aeneid', IX, 445: 'And there at length, in the peace
of death, found rest.'

22 Possibly a variant of Ovid's 'Metamorphoses', XV, 449.
Literally the quoted passage, when translated, reads:
'His fiery soul sought again its aetherial place.'

23 'Aeneid', I, 692-3: 'And fondling him in her bosom,
the goddess uplifts him to Idalia's high groves.'

24 'Metamorphoses', X, 725-7: 'My grief, Adonis, shall
have an enduring monument, and each passing year in
memory of your death shall give an imitation of my
grief.'

25 A poetic joke, penned by Wagstaffe, upon Steele's
boast of being a gentleman from Llangunnor and of
possessing a landed estate (inherited from his
mother-in-law). Literally translated, it reads:
'You, Taffy, will live eternally. Even now the
Welshmen celebrate your rewards. And as often as the
year revolves, they remember you. The whole people of
your fathers cherish the honour and bind your sweet-
smelling temples with the leek.'

26 Benjamin Hoadly, 'St. Paul's Behaviour towards the
Civil Magistrate' (1708).

39. 'A LETTER FROM WILL. HONEYCOMB TO THE "EXAMINER",
OCCASION'D BY THE REVIVAL OF THE "SPECTATOR"'

1714

Will Honeycomb is a character in the Spectator Club.
About sixty, he has devoted his life to the pursuit of
gallant trivia. In 'Spectator' 530 he is 'at length
wedded to a plain country Girl'. He becomes the epitome
of the 'converted rake'.
    The 'Spectator', second series, runs from numbers
556 to 635, 18 June to 20 December 1714.

TO THE EXAMINER

Old Friend,
Reading your Paper of the 18th Instant, and observing
another lie by it with the approv'd Title of 'THE SPECTA-
TOR', it brought to mind those jocund Days we three have
spent together. I felt again the pleasant Evenings we
have pass'd, and the agreeable Company we have often been
at the *Trumpet* in *Sheer-Lane*. 'Twas there we have heard
his *short Face* humourously lampoon both Whig and Tory, and
esteem the Character of his broken Upholsterer and the
Erection of his *Bedlam*, Master-strokes of Invention.

How has he degenerated since then! How many Appear-
ances has he put on, what various Shapes has he been
dress'd in, to serve a ruin'd Party! But now, conscious
of his Fault, *and that 'tis against his Interest*, he endeavours a Return, (1) assumes the neutral State, and
tells us, *It is not his Ambition to encrease the Number
either of Whigs or Tories*; and in order to gain Belief,
assures us, *He is quite another Man than what he was.* (2)

I congratulate you on the Success of your Arguments,
and desire your Admission of the *New Convert*, who can
appear again a 'Spectator' after such an *important* Volu-
bility of Tongue, Whatever Cause of Triumph he had from
your acknowledgment of injuring the Offspring of his
Dismal Favourite; yet certainly this Revival of his taking
Form is a tacit Confession of his long pursu'd Error; and
abundantly evinces, that however he bore it off with the
Gentleman-like Epithets of *Rogue*, *Rascal*, and *Villain*,
yet he secretly had a Remorse for apostatizing from the
Service of the Tea-Table; for which he found himself
better qualify'd than *Expecting* from his Sovereign, or
Advising in a Senate.

You must own, 'twas somewhat hard for a Man who had
boasted himself the Companion of a Lord-Treasurer, had
quitted a Place and Pension to sit *three* Weeks in
P——t: (3) 'Twas difficult, I say, for him, who was *once
possess'd of the general good Opinion of the Town*, and at
whose Entrance the Wits at *Button's* rose up *to do honour*,
to descend from his *exalted Station* to regard *Low-Life*,
or concern himself again with the *Furl of the Fan*, or *Use
of the Snuff-Box*. But he had the old Proverb join'd to
his Conviction; and he has long ago told us, *There are
some People who will not be paid with a Song*.

His Shew of Grandeur, and Long Deviation from himself,
puts me in mind of a known Story in the Country; which
take as follows:

'A neighbouring Nobleman, who was famous for indulging
his Humour with those whom Fortune had cast in an inferior

Station of Life, observ'd a Tinker with neglected Budget
lie fast asleep at his Gate. He immediately order'd him
to be carry'd into the Hall; where awaking, he was
directly taken into the Cellar, and after hard Drinking
saluted with the Title of *Your Grace*. The Tinker grew
big with the Repetition of the Sound, and with a rais'd
Voice turns to his Lordship with a *Here's t' ye, Robin*.
When he had drank, the servant neglecting to take the
Cup, in a violent Passion bauls out, *Ye Dog, ye Rascal,
how ye mind US Noblemen*. The Pageantry was carry'd on
some time, and the Head of the Miscreant kept warm: He
lay in a fine Bed, dress'd according to his fancy'd
Quality, sat as Chief at Table, and bore Command in the
Family; 'till the Amusement growing dull, my Lord order'd
his imaginary Peer to be made drunk, cloath'd in his
Tinker's Habit, and plac'd asleep where he was taken up
at his Lordship's Gate.'

In such a Dream of Life has poor *Dic* pass'd these last
two Years, and such a Delirium of Greatness has possess'd
him ever since he enter'd into the Service of the Whigs.
He talks no more of *fine Taste* and *Sentiments, Delicacy
of Stile, Turn of Thought, Beauty of Expression*, and
other beaten Epithets and Phrases, with which the Papers
he furnish'd out us'd so liberally to abound; but is
transform'd from Censor of the Manners, to 'Guardian' of
the Liberties of *Great Britain*. The first Exercise of
his assum'd Power is his 'Letter to Sir M[iles] W[arton]';
wherein he complains bitterly of the Stretch of the Prerogative in the Creation of the new Peers; but 'tis a
doubt among the Learned, whether his not being of the
Number might not occasion the Complaint. In this Character of 'Guardian' the disorder rages violently; he is in
Danger, and cannot be at Ease for *Dunkirk*; and as a
Representative of the clamorous Body *expects* and *demands*
its *immediate* Demolition. At one time he appears in full
Assemblies, stares in the Face of every young Man, and
now and then starts suddenly, and cries out *The Pretender!
The Pretender!* At another, he talks to himself, and has
been overheard to mutter *Commerce, Ballance of Power,
House of Bourbon* and *Spain*: Then on a sudden violently
breaks out, *O Dunkirk! Dunkirk! I EXPECT ye immediately
demolish Dunkirk!*

But he soon quits this Appearance, and in an Instant
(as he himself tells us) *presto pass*, by a kind of magical Stroke is from a Native of *Dublin* turn'd into a True-
born 'Englishman'. Pleas'd with his new Metamorphosis,
he writes and converses with himself, and transcribes old
Bulls and Excommunications more terrible than his Lyon at
Covent-Garden. Nothing will serve him, *good* Man! but his

Religion is in Danger; and in the midst of the Apprehension cries out Popery! Popery! O the Peril of Popery!
The Duke of L[orrain] he is sure is an Overmatch for the
Protestant Powers; (4) and he has heard of *Twenty* Men
listed in *Ireland* for the Service of the Pretender. Now
is the 'Crisis' to gird on the Sword to the Help of the
Lord against the *Mighty*: He hears the Rattling of Drums,
sees Legions engag'd to destroy our Succession, and that
nothing but his Sitting in the *House* can be its Security.
   But by this he rather knows how to *want* than *abound*,
and something must be done to keep up: Some had *sub-
scrib'd* liberally to his Support, and therefore in return
he becomes their *Patriot*: Not a Word shall be spoke
against any of his Friends at J----y M----n's, (5) let
'em never so much libel both Queen and Ministry, but
immediately he stands up in their Defence, and vindicates
in a worse manner all they have said. This is a Shape he
cannot quit 'till the 'Spectator' has made its way into
the Favour of the Town; for I take this to be upheld, and
loaded with Reproaches against the Ministry, for the
Reason assign'd by the *Monitor*, *That it may sell*: And
therefore I desire you would use him gently, and by your
Disregard of whatever he says here, shew you believe he
designs to abandon even this as soon as his *Advantage* is
settled another way.
   He does not stop here: 'Englishman' he'll be no longer;
but transplants *Powell*, (6) and like another Don Quixot
destroys his Puppets, and seizes his *Lodge*. Here he
reviews the past Figure he has made, and in his Melancholy and Dotage turns 'Lover'. However he might now and
then from his inconsistent Way of Talking argue himself
such, yet still he shews his Retirement proceeds from
another Cause; and hearing but a neighbouring Quack pronounce the Word *Expel*, tho' Poison follow'd immediately
after, brought so to mind his late Punishment, that he
told his Friend Tom D'urfey, That as soon as he had recommended him to the World, and prepossess'd an Audience
for his Benefit, he'd abandon Politicks, quit the
borrow'd Form of Love, and either retire, or triflingly
spend the latter as the former of his scribbling Days, by
complying with the Designs of Nature, who had only mod-
ell'd him to discuss 'The Importance of a Petticoat', or
'Crisis of a Mode'.
   While he is courting the good Graces of the Town with
the Air of a 'Lover', he with Intellects as decay'd as he
tells us were his Eyes, appears a 'Reader'; (7) but with
so untuneable a Voice, that few listen'd to the Melody of
such a Charmer; and I am credibly inform'd there are
Reams of this Production to be dispos'd of for the

Service of the Pastry-Cooks.

I was thinking the other Day, had Sir *Roger de Coverly*
liv'd while now, and seen him gone thro' so many Changes,
he would have been more puzzled to have known 'The Spectator' than the Company at *Jonathan*'s: (8) 'Twould have
stagger'd the good old Man, to have seen him so long pursuing in Practice what he had so often inveigh'd against
over a Bottle; and he would rather have believ'd (so well
he knew the Man) the *Rosicrucian* System, than that *Dic
S---le* should be a Politician.

At first, I confess, I imagin'd some invidious Wag had
endeavour'd to foister upon him, and believ'd the Letter
incerted in the 'Guardian' came there thro' Mistake: (9)
But I was too soon undeceiv'd, by his appearing Candidate
at an Election, and afterwards fixing his Name to his
Epistles to himself; the first time I ever saw it with so
much Dislike.

As you have *Examin'd* with Success his mercenary Essays,
and shew'd how far his *Publick Spirit* was concern'd in the
publication of his late Writings, 'Importance of Dunkirk',
'Crisis', and 'Ecclesiastical History', (10) &c. so in
order to re-establish his Credit, and rescue him from the
gross Appearance of being wholly guided by Vanity and
Interest, warn him against praising his own Works, and
telling *Canterbury* Tales to recommend whatever's publish'd
by *J[acob] T[onson]*, or any body else who with a neat
bound Book conveys a Piece or two.

I know I need not entreat you'd forbear Reprisals;
'twould be impossible for you to use an equal Redundancy
of ill Language with him, since he engag'd in a Cause
where it always supplies the Want of Argument.

But he has beat a Parley, laid down his Arms, and begs
a Peace; and,

He that repents of what he'as done amiss,
Stands next to him that never did offend.

While he acts as such, I perswade my self you'll treat him
with Lenity: but the *Rod for the Fool's Back*, says *Solo-
mon*; (11) when he recedes from this Behaviour, and dares
again to affront his Superiors, in using your Endeavours
to vindicate them, and recover him, you'll oblige.

                    Your Constant Friend
                    and Humble Servant,

Middle-Temple,
June 25. 1714

                         Will. Honeycomb.

Notes

1 The contemporary view was that Steele was largely
   responsible for the new series of the 'Spectator'.
2 'Spectator' 556.
3 Parliament opened on 16 February 1714 and Steele was
   expelled on 18 March.
4 See 'Englishman' 57 and 'Mr. Steele's Apology for
   Himself and His Writings'.
5 Jenny Man's Coffee House, Charing Cross; mentioned
   in 'Spectator' 403.
6 Steele attacked Offspring Blackall, Bishop of Exeter,
   and named Powell the puppet-master, in 'Tatler' 44,
   45, 50, 51.
7 The 'Lover', 1-40 (25 February to 27 May 1714); the
   'Reader', 1-9 (22 April to 10 May 1714).
8 Jonathan's Coffee House, Exchange Alley, Cornhill,
   existed from 1680 to 1778, when it was destroyed by
   fire.
9 The Letter by 'English Tory' in 'Guardian' 128.
10 'The Importance of Dunkirk Consider'd' (September
   1713); 'The Crisis' (January 1714); 'The Romish
   Ecclesiastical History of Late Years' (May 1714).
11 Proverbs, X. 13.

40. SIR RICHARD BLACKMORE, 'AN ESSAY UPON WIT'

1716

Sir Richard Blackmore's statement on wit appeared in
'Essays upon Several Subjects' (1716). Educated in
medicine, Sir Richard (d. 1729) was appointed physician
in ordinary to William III and later one of Queen
Anne's doctors. He managed to write large quantities of
poetry, the best of which - according to the 'Spectator' -
was 'Creation' (1712). See also 'Freeholder' 45.

...And many more Books on other moral Subjects have been
compos'd with much Wit and Vivacity in our own and foreign
Countries, to expose Vice and Folly, and promote Decency
and Sobriety of Manners. But the Productions of this
Nature, which have of late appear'd in this Nation,

whether we regard the just and generous Sentiments, the
fertile Invention, the Variety of Subjects, the surprizing Turns of Wit and facetious Imagination, the genteel
Satire, the Purity and Propriety of the Words, and the
Beauty and Dignity of the Diction, have surpass'd all the
Productions of this kind, that have been publish'd in any
Age or Country. The Reader no doubt is before-hand with
me, and concludes, that I mean the 'Tatler' and 'Spectator', which for the greatest Part, have all the Perfection
of Writing, and all the Advantages of Wit and Humour, that
are requir'd to entertain and instruct the People: And it
must chiefly be owing to the great Depravity of Manners in
these loose and degenerate Times, that such worthy Performances have produc'd no better Effects.

41. CHARLES GILDON, 'THE COMPLETE ART OF POETRY'

1718

Charles Gildon (1665–1724) was, as Abel Boyer described
him, a person of 'great literature but mean genius'. Born
a Catholic, he had by the age of thirty become a deist and
shortly thereafter a High Churchman. He was for a while
one of the writers in the Whig stable when Addison was its
overseer. This fact accounts for the fulsome 'Cato
Examin'd' in 1713. Presumably the two men quarrelled:
hence Gildon's attack on the 'Tatler' and 'Spectator' and
his spiteful use of Dennis's 'To the Spectator, on Poetical
Justice' (1712) to refute Addison on the same subject.

...It is a particular Observation I have always made
(said Tyro), that of all Mortals, a Critic is the silliest.
    That is (interrupted *Laudon*) of all Mortals, a Man of
Judgment and *Skill* in *Art* is the silliest. For if you
mean pretended *Criticks*, you shou'd have told us so. Now
as to *Pretenders* to any *Art*, or *Thing*, without Foundation, they are equally silly, for it is want of Understanding in them all. The drawing a ridiculous Character,
and then calling it a *Critic*, is of no manner of Force
against the *Thing*.
    Ah! my Dear Friend *Laudon* (reply'd *Tyro*) you have

intercepted what I had to say from the charming 'Tatler'
on this Head; for when he has told you that a *Critic* is
the silliest of Mortals, he adds his Reason; *for* (says he)
by inuring himself to examine all Things, whether they are
of Consequence or not, he never looks upon any thing, but
with a Design of passing Sentence upon it; by which means
he is never a Companion, but always a Censor. This makes
him earnest upon *Trifles*, and *Dispute* on the most indifferent *Occasions* with *Vehemence.* If he offers to speak or
write, that Talent, which shou'd approve the Work of the
other Faculties prevents their Operation. He comes upon
Action in Armour, but without Weapons; he stands in Safety,
but can gain no Glory....

   You need go no farther (said *Laudon*) 'tis only a very
dry ridicule on the Character, without the least Shadow of
Reason. But Mr. *Isaac*, notwithstanding his Passion
against *Critics*, has play'd the *Critic* himself, not only
in his eighth and ninth 'Tatler', but in several others;
nay, indeed his whole Business seems to be a *Critic* on the
Manners of Men; a harder thing to determine, than the
Rules of Art; unless he wou'd shelter himself under the
Name of *Censor*, which is one, who passes Judgment on something, and so comes to the same Point. But here I cannot
omit one thing, which I find he attacks more than once in
the Course of his Writings; and which I am afraid his
Enemies will say discovers him to be a most abandoned
Pedant. And this is that our *Critics* guide themselves by
what they find in the *French* Writers, without being capable of going so high as the Original *Greek* or *Latin* Masters. (1) This I am sorry I must allow to be a sort of
Refuge of *Pedantry*, as if there were really any *singular*
Merit as to the *Art*, to understand *Greek* or *Latin*. No Man
certainly can condemn the Reason of what we find in
French; and yet it is the *Reason* of the thing, and not our
consulting the *French* Authors, when he, or his Colleagues,
shall write like them: I dare engage the Ingenious will be
oblig'd to them, and consult them without the *French*.
There is nothing so trifling and ridiculous as the Praises
given *Homer*, *Virgil*, &c. By the *Dutch*, most of the
Italian, and *English* Writers; but *Bossu* and *Dacier*, (2)
to the Honour of their Country, enter'd into the true
Merits of those great Poets in their Design, &c. *Dionysius*
Halicarnassaus (3) indeed, so long ago has hit right in
praising *Homer*'s Contrivance, and Design, as well as the
Greatness, and Majesty, of his Expression, and the lively
and passionate Motions of the Sentiments....

   As for what Tongue it is in (assum'd *Manilia*) it matters not, but Criticism it self is the thing that the
'Tatler' falls upon; and good Lord, indeed, what a Figure

does Sir *Timothy Tittle* make in the 'Tatlers'? One would
think, that no Man of *Wit*, wou'd ever after that, have
descended to own the Name of a *Critic*.

Oh! Madam (said Laudon) there is nothing more easie,
than for a Grotesque Painter to clap Asses Ears on the
Head of a *Socrates*, yet that wou'd betray the *Ignorance*,
Folly, or *Impudence* of the Painter, but not any Defect in
that wise *Athenian*. If the 'Tatler' design'd by those,
and some other Stroaks of the like Nature, to ridicule
Criticasters, and impudent Pretenders to *Judgment*, he
shou'd not have endeavour'd to affix the Infamy he
design'd to the Name of *Critic*, but have plainly, and
evidently distinguish'd between them; otherwise the
Asses Ears will cleave to his own Head, for ridiculing
Judgment, without which nothing ever was, or ever can be,
well and justly perform'd either in *Painting* or *Poetry*.

Bless me! (cry'd Manilia) you infinitely surprize me to
hear you oppose the Sentiments of a Paper that so ravish'd
the Town, and almost reconcil'd *Parties* in its Praise,
that were opposite in every thing else. How shall we,
poor Women, Madam (reply'd *Laudon*) for it is only when
these Authors desert them, that they become contemptible
to the *judicious*....

[Laudon continues his refutation of the position of both
the 'Tatler' and the 'Spectator'.]

But to answer all these Difficulties by an Example
against which there will be no Exception, let us look
over the Examen or Criticism of the brightest Person concern'd in the 'Tatlers' and 'Spectators', in his Observations on *Milton*'s 'Paradise Lost', and see if there be
any need of *Greek* or *Latin*, or the understanding of so
many Arts and Sciences, to apprehend what he says on this
Subject. No, it is all plain and easy to an *English*
Reader; he had else miss'd his Aim, the Praise of that
exalted Author, which he has made out with a great deal of
Clearness and Ease.

Passing therefore all this Clamour over as mere Clamour
indeed, and Affectation of being thought singular, and
above the Censure of all but the *Linguists*, I shall proceed to another Error of this Author you have mention'd;
and that is, that he excludes all finding fault from the
Duty of a *Critic*; (4) though it be as plain as any thing
can be, that *Aristotle* in his 'Art of Poetry' has not one
Chapter in which he does not expose and condemn some Fault
of one Poet or other. But then he says the Beauties were
likewise shewn, and had their due Praise; I grant it, but
that was because the Poets he consider'd had their

Beauties. If any *Critic* in our Age should fall on a
celebrated Poem, and expose the Faults in it, without
pointing out the Beauties, he may well be excused; since
in many of them there is not to be found so much as one
beautiful Line; as I cou'd easily prove, were this a Place
and Time.

I shall join with him in declaring against those false
Critics, who are fond of finding, and exposing Pecca-
dillo's, and of turning any valuable Thing into Ridicule.
I am as much against that unfair Mirth as he, and allow
that the Critics of Reputation of all Countries, have
treated the Authors, who fall under their Consideration,
in another Manner. And yet I must needs say, that if a
Man were to write on some Mens Performances, it wou'd be a
hard Matter to avoid being Merry at their taking Absurdities....

I shall only add one Remark more, that by this Gentleman's instancing *Passages*, *Words*, and the like, he seems
to refer all *Criticism* to the *Diction*, without regard to
the more important Parts of Poetry. So that when he talks
of *Critics* finding out *Beauties* in the authors they consider, he means only Commentators, Makers of Notes,
Explainers of Expressions, of which we have said sufficient already, but may perhaps *en passant* add something
more hereafter. Such was *Scaliger* on *Homer*, (5) and most
of those *Critics*, against whom *Aristotle* defends *Homer*'s
Words and Expressions.

Having thus, Madam, I hope answer'd your Quotations
from the 'Spectator' in all its Points, and shewn you,
that you may be a very good Judge of an *English* Poem of
any Kind, without the knowledge of Greek and Latin, or
being conversant with the Authors in those Languages,
whether Poetical or Critical....

Notes

1   See, e.g., 'Tatler' 165, wherein Sir Timothy Tittle
    appears.
2   René Le Bossu (1631–80), author of 'Traité du Poème
    épique' (1675); Anne Lefèvre Dacier (*c*. 1651–1720),
    translator of 'The Iliad' (1711) and 'The Odyssey'
    (1716).
3   Dionysius of Halicarnassus (*fl*. 30 BC), rhetor and
    historian, who wrote on 'The Odyssey'.
4   See, e.g., 'Spectator' 285, 291.
5   Julius Caesar Scaliger (1484–1558), author of
    'Poetices libri septem' (1561).

42.   THEOPHILUS CIBBER, 'THE LIFE OF ADDISON'

1753

An excerpt (III, pp. 311-12, 319-20) from 'The Lives of
the Poets of Great Britain and Ireland'. Theophilus
Cibber (1703-58), an actor, playwright, and son of Colley
Cibber, brought out 'The Lives' (5 vols.) in 1753. Aided
by Robert Shiels, Cibber added little new information to
the biographies. The statement on Addison is, however,
the first extended critical statement since 1734. It
draws from Tickell's 'Preface to the Works' (1721);
Steele's 'Dedication to Congreve' in the second edition
of 'The Drummer' (1722); and the entries in 'The General
Dictionary' (1734) and 'The Biographia Britannica' (1747).

...While he was in Ireland, his friend Sir Richard Steel
published the 'Tatler', which appeared for the first time,
on the 12th of April 1709: Mr. Addison (says Tickell) discovered the author by an observation on Virgil he had communicated to him. This discovery led him to afford farther assistance, insomuch, that as the author of the
'Tatler' well exprest it, he fared by this means, like a
distrest prince, who calls in a powerful neighbour to his
aid: that is, he was undone by his auxiliary.
    The superiority of Mr. Addison's papers in that work is
universally admitted; and being more at leisure upon the
change of the ministry, he continued assisting in the
'Tatler' till 1711, when it was dropt.
    No sooner was the 'Tatler' laid down, but Sir Richard
Steel, in concert with Mr. Addison, formed the plan of the
'Spectator'. The first paper appeared on the first of
March 1711, and in the course of that great work, Mr.
Addison furnished all the papers marked with any Letters
of the Muse CLIO; and which were generally most admired.
Tickell, who had no kindness for Sir Richard Steel,
meanly supposes that he marked his paper out of precaution
against Sir Richard; which was an ill-natur'd insinuation;
for in the conclusion of the 'Spectators', he acknowledges
to Mr. Addison, all he had a right to; and in his letter
to Congreve, he declares that Addison's papers were marked
by him, out of tenderness to his friend, and a warm zeal
for his fame. Steel was a generous grateful friend; it
therefore ill became Mr. Tickell in the defence of Mr.
Addison's honour, which needed no such stratagem, to

depreciate one of his dearest friends; and at the expence
of truth, and his reputation, raise the character of his
Hero. Sir Richard had opposed Mr. Addison, in the choice
of Mr. Tickell as his secretary; which it seems he could
never forget nor forgive.

In the 'Spectators', Sir Roger de Coverly was Mr. Addison's favourite character; and so tender was he of it,
that he went to Sir Richard, upon his publishing a 'Spectator', in which he made Sir Roger pick up a woman in the
temple cloisters, (1) and would not part with his friend,
until he promised to meddle with the old knight's character no more. However, Mr. Addison to make sure, and to
prevent any absurdities the writers of the subsequent
'Spectators' might fall into, resolved to remove that
character out of the way; or, as he pleasantly expressed
it to an intimate friend, killed Sir Roger, that no body
else might murther him. (2) When the old 'Spectator'
was finished, a new one appeared; but, though written by
men of wit and genius, it did not succeed, and they were
wise enough not to push the attempt too far. Posterity
must have a high idea of the taste and good sense of the
British nation, when they are informed, that twenty-
thousand of these papers were sometimes sold in a
day.... (3)

Thus we have gone through the most remarkable passages
of the life of this great man, in admiration of whom, it
is but natural to be an Enthusiast, and whose very enemies expressed their dislike with diffidence; nor indeed
were his enemies, Mr. Pope excepted, (if it be proper to
reckon Mr. Pope Mr. Addison's enemy) in one particular
case, of any consequence. It is a true, and an old observation, that the greatest men have sometimes failings,
that, of all other human weaknesses, one would not suspect them to be subject to. It is said of Mr. Addison,
that he was a slave to flattery, that he was jealous, and
suspicious in his temper, and, as Pope keenly expresses it,

Bore, like the Turk, no rival near the throne. (4)

That he was jealous of the fame of Pope, many have
believed, and perhaps not altogether without ground. He
preferred Tickel's translation of the first book of Homer,
to Pope's. His words are, 'the other has more of Homer',
(5) when, at the same time, in a letter to Pope, he
strenuously advises him to undertake it, and tells him,
there is none but he equal to it; (6) which circumstance
has made some people conjecture, that Addison was himself
the author of the translation, imputed to Mr. Tickell: Be
this as it may, it is unpleasing to dwell upon the

failings, and quarrels of great men; let us rather draw a
veil over all their errors, and only admire their virtues,
and their genius; of both which the author, the incidents
of whose life we have now been tracing, had a large possession. He added much to the purity of the English stile
in prose; his rhime is not so flowing, nervous, or manly
as some of his cotemporaries, but his prose has an original excellence, a smoothness and dignity peculiar to it.
His poetry, as well as sentiments, in 'Cato', cannot be
praised enough.

Mr. Addison was stedfast to his principles, faithful
to his friends, a zealous patriot, honourable in public
stations, amiable in private life, and as he lived, he
died, a good man, and a pious Christian.

Notes

1 'Spectator' 410.
2 Eustace Budgell, the 'Bee' (February 1733), no. 1.
3 As reputedly stated by Tickell. For the best statement of the periodical's circulation figures, see
   Bond's Introduction to 'The Spectator' (1965), I,
   pp. xxv-xxvii.
4 Pope's 'Epistle to Dr. Arbuthnot', 198.
5 John Gay to Pope (8 July 1715), in 'The Correspondence
   of Alexander Pope', ed. George Sherburn (Oxford, 1956),
   I, p. 305.
6 See, e.g., Addison to Pope (26 October and 2 November
   1713), I, pp. 196-7.

43. 'ROBERT HERON', 'LETTERS OF LITERATURE'

1785

'Robert Heron' was in fact John Pinkerton (1758-1826), a
Scottish antiquary and historian. Using his mother's sur-
name, Pinkerton in 1785 published a volume of perverse
opinions called 'Letters of Literature'. In that work he
recommended a new system of orthography, and derided the
writers of classical Greece and Rome. The book, however,
led to his acquaintance with Horace Walpole and more
importantly Gibbon, who thought him learned in history.
   This statement appears as Letter 49.

Letter XLIX

In the course of our correspondence, I believe more than
one occasion hath arisen of placing the critical abilities
of Mr. Addison in no high estimation. But as perhaps
stronger proofs may be required in the most innocent
attack upon the slightest talents of a writer so deservedly eminent, I shall, if you please, in this Letter produce these stronger proofs. There is another reason which
induces me to this disagreeable talk, and it is, that the
most minute failings of such an author deserve animadversion, for the rocks that have injured a vessel of such
supreme rate, would doubtless, if not avoided with caution,
prove of immediate fatality to critical adventurers of
small size.
   The only writings of Mr. Addison, worthy to be considered as pieces of criticism, occur in the 'Spectator'.
This view of his critical errors shall therefore be re-
stricted to that work, and taken in the order in which
they arise. It might be made ten times as long; but I
hurry thro it, being sensible that the task is invidious,
and feeling it disagreeable.

SPECT. No. 5. Addison hath given more proofs than one of
his very slight acquaintance with the Italian language.
Armida is, in the opera of Rinaldo, called an Amazonian
enchantress, or more properly an enchanting Amazon,
(taking *enchanting* in rather an uncommon acceptation) not
from her being of the nation of the Amazons, as Addison
strangely misunderstands it; but from her being an
enchantress and *virago*. The remark on the Christian Magician is equally absurd. The Magician doth not deal with
the devil, as Addison misrepresents it much in the spirit
of an old woman, but with angels, the daemons of Plato-
nism; who were thought the servants of good men, and none
but the good. Before such criticisms no work can stand.
The critic totally misrepresents the meaning, and then
writes criticisms upon his own misrepresentations. The
noted attack on Tasso, which follows these odd blunders,
is dismissed in pity and silent contempt. Tasso is innocent of the charge, and must be honourably acquitted. The
English of Mr. Addison's violent hatred of the opera is,
that he wrote for the English theatre, and was mortified
to see it neglected for the Italian.

No. 18. 'Phaedra and Hippolitus' is so woful a tragedy,
that I know no Italian opera that would not prove a far
higher entertainment.

No. 39. A perfect tragedy, the noblest production of
human nature! Where is epic poetry? but Addison was
writing 'Cato'; and his rules of criticism are always for
his own advantage.
    His praise of Lee on this occasion, and of Blackmore
on another, proves sufficiently the depth of his critical
abilities.

No. 40. The tragicomedy is the most natural, and, of
consequence, the most proper, style of the drama. Very
little learning is required to know that it is not the
product of the English stage, but of every stage, ancient
and modern; except the French, which is sacred to Sleep.

No. 44. Orestes's plea for not killing the Usurper
instantly I believe strikes every reader as futile, and
a mere ancient stage-trick.

No. 62. The praise of Bouhours by Addison and Chesterfield will never rescue him from the contempt of every man
who hath read or thought much. (1) Good stomachs cannot
be satisfied with syllabubs. The critique on Gothic
architecture shews the pitiful *gout de comparaison*. Addison did not know that every Art admits of infinite modes
of beauty; and that to confine it to one of these modes
is the reverse of an attempt to enlarge human knowledge
and enjoyment.

No. 160. This essay on Genius cannot be read without
laughter, and a certain assurance that the author knew not
what it was.

No. 267. What critic ever heard of an *heroic* poem? Why
examine a poem upon principles utterly inanalogous to it?

    I REMEMBER not that Aristotle allows that Homer's fable
wants unit. If he doth, he is a poor critic; if he doth
not, Addison is a poorer.
    THE perpetual quotations of Aristotle give digust. Why
doth he never quote Nature?

No. 273. A Greek's regard for Achilles must have been
very small; like the regard of a Spaniard for a Portu-
guese.

No. 285. That the names of figures of speech were invented to palliate *defects* of speech, is perhaps the only new
critical remark Addison hath ever made; and it is un-
happily quite void of foundation. Mr. Addison forgot that

grammar was invented for speech, not speech for grammar.

No. 297. There is no occasion in Nature for an epic poem
always ending happily. If such a rule existed in the
foolish axioms of criticism, Milton knew to despise it.
Addison should have drawn new rules from Milton, and not
have pretended to judge him by foreign laws, as he doth all
along.

No. 315. The criticism on the Third Book of 'Paradise
Lost' is not sufficiently severe. It is all beneath the
middling from beginning to end.

No. 321. The device of Uriel's descent on a sunbeam is
almost praised in Milton: in Tasso it would have been
tinsel. Tasso hath nothing so tinsical: but thus it is
when critics are ruled by prejudice and not by investi-
gation.

No. 339. The *golden compasses* ought to have been repro-
bated. All metaphors applied from Art to Nature are the
very reverse of sublime.

No. 305. 'The first original of the drama was a religious
worship consisting only of a Chorus, which was nothing
else, but an hymn to a deity.' There are rather more
errors in this sentence than words, as I believe you will
judge from former Letters. The deity was Bacchus, yet we
are told in the next sentence of *innocence and religion*.
Was Mr. Addison so very entire a stranger to Greek science as not to know that the worship of Bacchus was
utterly inconsistent with innocence and religion?

No. 412. We are now arrived at the greatest critical
effort of Addison; that on the pleasures of imagination.
One of the three causes which he lays down as productive
of these pleasures is of no foundation. Novelty never
pleases, except when accompanied with the other causes
Grandeur or Beauty. The first sight of an ugly object
only makes it more disgusting than when use hath in some
measure reconciled us to it. Dr. Akenside, (2) you will
observe from a communication I made to you some time ago,
had struck it out of his Poem, very justly, upon more
mature consideration.
   It is not novelty, but beauty, that makes natural
objects more pleasing in the spring. Beside, they are
new to no man. Mr. Addison surely did not mean his
criticisms for those who had never seen the beauties of
Spring before.

No. 413. Mr. Addison is the first writer who discovered
that *final causes lie bare to our observation*. Bacon
would have said that final causes are utterly unknown to
man. (3) Such is the difference between deep and superficial science. Ignorance is always rash. Knowlege
doubts and trembles.

No. 415. 'For every thing that is majestic imprints an
awfulness and reverence on the mind of the beholder, and
strikes in with the natural greatness of the soul.'
Bravissimo! Cheese is cheese! This is a lively instance
of what they call criticism.

I question if it was Phidias who proposed to cut Mount
Athos into a statue of Alexander. But I beg pardon for
such a remark, for nothing is more pardonable than a slip
of this kind. Indeed they who remember names and dates
seldom remember any thing else.

No. 420. Mr. Addison tells us of the most agreeable
talents of an historian; and seems to think they consist
in entertaining his reader. If so, fabulous historians
are best. The most *agreeable* talent of an historian is
to *instruct*. This is done by discussion of human actions,
and of the characters who were their agents.

Such are the brief remarks which at present occur to
me upon the critical errors of Addison. Volumes might
have been written to refute several of them; but I know
that to you they need only be hinted. Besides I was
quite impatient to get rid of this ungrateful task; for
Addison is one of my most favorite writers, and nothing
but my sacred love of critical equity could have been an
inducement to its execution.
   The best writers are perhaps the most liable to faults
of a certain kind, in like manner as fertile ground is,
where no grain is sown, fertile of weeds. Strong weeds
speak a rich soil, nearly as much as strong corn; yet
they ought to be rooted up that they may not injure the
harvest.

Notes

1 Dominique Bouhours (1628–1702), author of 'Manière de
   bien penser dans les ouvrages d'esprit' (1687). See
   the statement of Philip Dormer Stanhope, 4th Earl of
   Chesterfield (1694–1773) in a letter to his son
   (1 February 1754).

2 Mark Akenside (1721-70), author of 'Pleasures of
   Imagination' (1744).
3 A commonplace of the 'Novum Organum' (1620) was its
   rejection of an inquiry into final causes.

44. JANE AUSTEN, 'NORTHANGER ABBEY'

1818

From 'The Novels of Jane Austen', ed. R. W. Chapman
(Oxford, 1933), V, pp. 37-8.
   In Chapter V of 'Northanger Abbey', Jane Austen mocks
the clichés of contemporary literary tastes.

Yes, novels; - for I will not adopt that ungenerous and
impolitic custom so common with novel writers, of
degrading by their contemptuous censure the very performances, to the number of which they are themselves
adding - joining with their greatest enemies in bestowing
the harshest epithets on such works, and scarcely ever
permitting them to be read by their own heroine, who, if
she accidentally take up a novel, is sure to turn over
its insipid pages with disgust. Alas! if the heroine of
one novel be not patronized by the heroine of another,
from whom can she expect protection and regard? I cannot
approve of it. Let us leave it to the Reviewers to abuse
such effusions of fancy at their leisure, and over every
new novel to talk in threadbare strains of the trash with
which the press now groans. Let us not desert one
another; we are an injured body. Although our productions
have afforded more extensive and unaffected pleasure than
those of any other literary corporation in the world, no
species of composition has been so much decried. From
pride, ignorance, or fashion, our foes are almost as many
as our readers. And while the abilities of the nine-
hundredth abridger of the History of England, or of the
man who collects and publishes in a volume some dozen
lines of Milton, Pope, and Prior, with a paper from the
'Spectator', and a chapter from Sterne, are eulogized by
a thousand pens, - there seems almost a general wish of
decrying the capacity and undervaluing the labour of the
novelist, and of slighting the performances which have

only genius, wit, and taste to recommend them. 'I am no
novel reader - I seldom look into novels - Do not imagine
that *I* often read novels - It is really very well for a
novel.' - Such is the common cant. - 'And what are you
reading, Miss ———?' 'Oh! it is only a novel!' replies
the young lady; while she lays down her book with affected
indifference, or momentary shame. - 'It is only "Cecilia",
or "Camilla", or "Belinda";' (1) or, in short, only some
work in which the greatest powers of the mind are displayed, in which the most thorough knowledge of human
nature, the happiest delineation of its varieties, the
liveliest effusions of wit and humour are conveyed to the
world in the best chosen language. Now, had the same
young lady been engaged with a volume of the 'Spectator',
instead of such a work, how proudly would she have produced the book, and told its name; though the chances must
be against her being occupied by any part of that volumi-
nous publication, of which either the matter or manner
would not disgust a young person of taste: the substance
of its papers so often consisting in the statement of
improbable circumstances, unnatural characters, and topics
of conversation, which no longer concern any one living;
and their language, too, frequently so coarse as to give
no very favourable idea of the age that could endure it.

Notes

1 'Cecilia' (1782) and 'Camilla' (1796) are novels by
   Fanny Burney (1752-1840); 'Belinda' (1801) by Maria
   Edgeworth (1767-1849).

VI Addison the Dramatist

45. THE 'EXAMINER'

27 April–1 May 1713

In this essay, the Tory 'Examiner' responded to the popular
success of Addison's 'Cato' and Whig efforts to make it a
party play. Unable to minimize its significance, the
'Examiner' thought it politically wise to applaud the
tragedy and its author as one who stood above faction.

Among the *Arts of Peace*, that deserve the Notice and Care
of a Government, the *Drama* is not the least considerable.
Tragedy, in particular, when in pursues the great Ends
of its institution, and shews us *Heroick Life* in perfect
Majesty, when by the Beauties of Dress, Scenary, Action,
and Elocution, in themselves empty and artificial, it produces in us real and lasting Vertues, when it turns our
Passions to Objects that may deservedly employ them, is an
Entertainment worthy a polite People, and by the help of a
tolerable Tast and some Attention, may insensibly win upon
our Gay, Idle Youth, and raise the Pleasure up to Instruction. I will not call those Poets, who have corrupted
this Art: For the farther it deviates from its proper End,
the more it loses of its Nature. But the best Reformation
of the Stage is Example, and ought to begin among those,
whose *Genius* and great Names are able to bear them up
against degenerate Custom, and set them at the Head of a
Fashion, which may be so much to the Advantage of Vertue. ·
For this Reason I cannot enough commend the Excellent
Author of 'Cato', who has convinc'd us, in· so happy a

Manner, that the Affections may be moved, and the Passions actuated, by a Distress arising from a Principle
of Honour, as well as Love. Such an Example, so deservedly crown'd with Success, will, I hope, engage others to
join in the Attempt of restoring the *Stage* to its antient
Use, and firing our Youth with high Sentiments of Vertue,
and a generous Passion for their Country.

   Whatever hath been said to prove, That a *Dramatick* Poet
is restrain'd to Persons of a middle Character, neither
perfectly Vertuous, nor Vicious to an Extremity, appears
to have had no more weight with the *Author* of 'Cato', than
with Monsieur *Corneille*. For the *English Cato* is represented more strictly Vertuous, and, if possible, of a more
Godlike Nature than the *Roman*. All the *Underparts* conspire to extol him: Even the *Love-Scents* are made conducive to his Glory; and he is set above *Caesar*, above *Fate*,
above *Jupiter*, nay above *Rome* and *Liberty* it self, as if
the Cause were of less regard than the *Hero*. But the
worst, or rather only bad Action of his Life, is the Last.
Here the *Historian* must justifie the *Poet*, for making a
Self-murder, infamous in it self, and done in Violation of
the Law of Nature and *Pagan* Morality, the *Catastrophe* of a
Character otherwise perfect, and raised to the highest
Dignity of human Nature. I know not whether *Cato* might
not have kill'd himself with a better Grace, as a *Stoick*,
than as a *Platonick*: For *Plato* positively condemns this
way of Dying, but the *Stoicks* allow'd of it, upon a Prin-
ciple of *absolute Freedom*, which is most consistent with
Cato's Character, who, as *Rapin* observes, was a *Stoick* by
Constitution, and expired with an obstinate Resolution
becoming that *Sect*, that his Life and Death might be consistent, and the Unity of *Decorum* kept up in his History.
On the other hand, *Stoicism* was a Corruption of the *Roman*
Morals, and came in with the *Eastern* Fashions, after the
Expedition into *Macedonia*. Hence *Virgil*, *Cicero*, *Macro-
bius*, and others of the purer Age, condemn'd this sort of
Death, as highly Criminal, an act of Cowardice, contrary
to true Liberty, and Offensive to the Gods; but *Tacitus*,
Paterculus, *Seneca*, *Lucan*, and *Valerius Maximus* maintained
the contrary; and the later *Romans*, who had imbib'd the
pernicious Principle from *Greece*, found great ease by it
under the dreadful *Proscriptions* and Massacres of *Marius*,
Sylla and *Cinna*. Perhaps the Horror of a *Stoical* Death,
such as *Cato*'s appears to be in History, who is said to
have torn out his own Bowels in a Frantick manner, after
he had given the fatal Stab, might have been too shocking
upon the *English* Stage, even to have born a Rehearsal; and
therefore the *Poet* chose rather to let him expire upon a
prospect of Immortality, however dark and doubtful, and

divested him, in his last Moments, of that savage unrelen-
ting Temper, which he appears in upon the sight of his
Son's Body: Tho' *Plutarch*, on these Occasions, as at the
Death of his Brother *Caepio*, represents him full of
Grief, and liable to Tears. (1) He is now no longer Stubborn and Inflexible, but expresses the utmost Diffidence
and Uncertainty.

> ————*Why shrinks the Soul*
> *Back on her self, and startles at Destruction?*
> *What means this Heaviness, that hangs upon me?*
> ———— *Alas! I fear*
> *I've been too hasty.*
> *If I have done amiss, impute it not:*
> *The best may erre.* (2)

These Sentiments agree well enough with one, who had no
Call from the Gods; since a little before he had declared
in the *Senate*, that their Cause was not yet Desperate, and
that they might retire and recruit their Forces in *Numidia*. He fell indeed with his Country, but not for it;
and by dying, effectually deserted her Interests. For,
as a Judicious *Writer* observes, had He surviv'd the Murder
of *Caesar*, his popular Character might at that juncture
have retriev'd the Commonwealth, tho' *Brutus* fail'd in the
Attempt, who was detested for his Ingratitude. These
Straights, in Point of *History*, oblig'd the *Tragedian* to
desert *Cato* after his Fall; and therefore he forms his
Moral upon quite another Turn than the Imitation of his
Hero, and only warns us to avoid *Civil Discord*, a Topick
not touch'd upon in the Body of the *Play*, and not
directly arising from his main Design. (3) But these, and
other Niceties, such as the Character of *Juba*, directly
opposite to what he has in *History*, the *Simplicity* of the
Plot, the *Facility* of the *Incidents*, and the judicious
Design of *Underwriting* the *Love-Parts*, are lesser Lights
made to set off the greater, those fine Descriptions of
the Passions of a *Publick Spirit*, its Emotions, Resentments, and Searches after Glory, those exalted Principles
of *Roman* Honour, those just and glowing Images of Liberty,
Vertue, Truth, Valour, and all the Excellencies that human
Nature can display, when it expands it self for the good
of Societies; which makes a *Unity* in the *Dialogue*, as well
as *Action*, and are work'd up with all the Beauties and
Purity of *Classical* Learning; as if there had been no
great Necessity for Adorning the *Theatre* of *Augustus* with
a *Latin Tragedy* of any tolerable Character, when their
noblest Patriots were reserved for our Age, to speak more
like themselves in *English*.

I was so well pleased with 'Cato', that I had no
thoughts of mentioning him in the Language of a *Critick*;
but I would be understood to commend with a little Judgment; and my Aim is to prevent the Folly of one or two
Dablers, who may perhaps mistake a *Flatus* of *Party* for
Genius, and expose themselves by Attacking, what it would
be more for their Advantage to Study, than Censure. They
may think they are provok'd to it, by the Insolence of the
Whigs, who tried to make this a *Party Play*; but their
Clamours and Impertinence deserve no other Notice, on
this occasion, than Contempt and generous Indignation.
What a Misfortune is it for a *Gentleman* of *Wit* and *Vertue*
to be suspected of favouring their Side, with whom Sense
is of no more value than Honesty, unless they can Corrupt
it. Had not a Majority of *better Judges* stept to his
Relief, 'Cato' had been damn'd by the infamous Applauses
of a *Faction*; and instead of keeping his Ground by his own
intrinsick Merit, had subsisted upon their infectious
Breath, which has Tainted every Thing. The Character and
declar'd Opinion of the *Author*, with the Judgment of his
many happy Friends of both *Parties*, were of no Weight with
them; but they resolved to make *Cato* a *Whig*; as if they
intended to crown his Death with a greater Grace of
Poetick Justice. This Indignity rouz'd so many Publick
Spirits, and called them to assistance of 'Cato', who perfectly understand the Arts they mean to encourage, and
redeem'd him out of their Hands, who after being routed
upon every other *Stage*, must not be allow'd to Shine any
where, but at a *Farce*.
    Could a Man, at such a time, be suppos'd capable of
admitting any Diversion from the *Actors* in the *Pit* and
Boxes, the Distress of *Cato* had been merrily temper'd with
an Interlude, which part of the Audience were pleased to
entertain us with the *first Night*, when a Croud of silly
People, Creatures, who wear the Ornaments of the head altogether on the out-side, were drawn up under the Leading of
the Renown'd *Ironside*, (4) and appointed to Clap at his
Signals. I will not suppose them quite so Stupid and
Senseless, but 'Cato', and a little Attention, might have
warm'd them, without the *Word of Command*. The 'Spectator'
never appear'd in Publick with a worse Grace. I remember
Mr. *Bickerstaff* at the *Playhouse*, and with what a modest,
decent Gravity he behav'd himself: Hence he was so well
supported in his Decline, and so heartily pitty'd at his
Death. He would have us'd the Grandson of the *Great
Censor* better. Mr. *Add--on* has so often sav'd him from
exposing himself in the Service of a Faction, that he
would never have requited his Friend, by an attempt to
engage him, against his Will, in the same drudgery.

Sir *Gibby*, and his Band of *Little Criticks* from *Change
Alley*, (5) ought to be Pardon'd, on another Account, for
giving their Zeal an Advantage over their Understanding,
when they Clapt with so much awkward Fury, those Parts in
the Character of *Sempronius*, where he Mouths for *War* and
Liberty. Sympathy is a powerful Motive; and I believe it
was no Surprize to them, to find their own *Cant* put into
the Mouth of a Villain, who profanes the Name of Liberty,
and under that disguise, betrays *Cato* and his own Country.
But the *Old Viceroy*, and his *Embroider'd Underlings*,
should have been the only part of the *Audience* who sate
unconcerned at those fine Lines,

> *When Vice prevails, and impious Men bear sway,*
> *The Post of Honour is a private Station.* (6)

Plunderers of the Publick, and Debtors to the *Senate*'s
Justice, cannot without an egregious *Banter*, apply this to
themselves.

Nothing could have more expos'd the despicable Ignorance and extream Folly of the *Whigs*, than their imagining
there was any thing in this *Tragedy*, which favour'd their
wretched Schemes, or the Characters of their Leaders.
Were a Man to supply the Place of the *Chorus*, and explain
upon *Cato*, he might tell the Audience, how he is represented as contending to the last for the Cause of true
Liberty; a *Liberty* consistent with the Constitution of his
Country; contending

> *For the Laws, the Rights,*
> *The gen'rous Plan of Power, deliver'd down*
> *From Age to Age, by his renown'd Forefathers.* (7)

This Cause he maintains against a few *Mercenary* Wretches
at home, who were Inspir'd, not with the Love of Liberty,
or Thirst of Honour.... This Cause he maintains against
Caesar, the *General for Life*, the *Perpetual Dictator*....(8)
This is the *Caesar* whom Cato oppos'd, the Patron of
War, the fomenter of Civil *Discord*, who was at the Head of
a *Factious Army*, had aw'd and corrupted the *Senate*, forti-
fied himself with Foreign Bands, and made the Ruin of his
Country the Aim of his Ambition. I'll venture the
Parallel, let the *Whigs* apply it where they please.

Was *Cato* for a *Republick*, and will the *Whigs* presume to
own they love him on this Account? But was not that
Republick the *Constitution*? *Machiavil* commends it as a
noble Scheme, because it comprehended the *Three* several
Sorts of Government in an admirable Temperature: The *Con-
sular* Dignity resembled *Monarchy*, the *Senate Aristocracy*,

and the *Tribunes Democracy*. In this it comes near our
Three Legislative Powers; and then there is no manner of
doubt, but if *Cato* had been born in our Age, he would have
liv'd and dy'd a *Briton*.

What a Picture have we of a noisie seditious Medler in
the Person of *Sempronius*? He bauls loudest for *Liberty*,
and yet betrays it. He breaths nothing but Blood and *War*,
and then joins with a treacherous Foreigner *Syphax*, in
conspiring the Ruin of *Cato* and of *Rome*. Whilst *Lucius*,
who is for *Peace*, is represented Mild, Temperate and Wise,
and has *Cato*'s dying Approbation, as a faithful Friend to
his Country. Even *Marcia* and *Lucia* are made to bestow
their Charms only on the Lovers of the Constitution and
to give this as one Reason of their Choice.

In short, nothing belonging to this Play ought to be
the *Whigs*, but only the *Epilogue*.... (9)

Notes

1 'Cato the Younger', in 'Plutarch's Lives' (Dryden's
   translation corrected and revised by A. H. Clough,
   1905), IV, p. 380.
2 'Cato', V. i. 5-6, 32; V. iv. 95-6, 98-9.
3 'Cato', V. iv. 107-112.
4 Steele in the Dedication of 'The Drummer' admits 'that
   he brought together so great an Audience on the first
   Days' of 'Cato's' performance that its success would be
   guaranteed.
5 Sir Gilbert Heathcote (*c*. 1651-1733), Lord Mayor of
   London (1710-11); member of the first board of directors of the Bank of England (1694); Whig MP for the
   City (1700-10).
6 'Cato', IV. iv. 141-2.
7 'Cato', III. v. 73-5.
8 The Tory interpretation of the play equated Marlborough and Caesar.
9 The Epilogue was written by the Whiggish Dr Garth.

46. 'CATO' REVIEWED

2 May 1713

A laudatory review of 'Cato', as it appeared in the

'Flying Post', 30 April–2 May 1713. The reviewer's judgments are all Whig-oriented. In part, they answer the
'Examiner's' comments on 27 April–1 May.

London, May 2.

Sir,
The Tragedy of 'Cato', just published, has met with so
favourable a Reception from the Town, that from thence we
may conclude the Glorious Principles of the Roman Hero to
be more favour'd and approv'd of, than before could be
imagin'd. The Author has taken the most effectual Method
to make his Audiences in Love with Liberty, Virtue, and
their Country, by representing One struggling hard in
maintaining them; One, tho' driven to the greatest
Straits, yet still opposing Tyranny, and an unjust Usurpation. For what is represented on the Stage, if artfully manag'd, and nicely perform'd, makes a deeper Impression on the Mind, and affects one more, than any
other Art or Method possibly can. In short, without
flattering the Poet, it may justly be esteemed the best
Finish'd Piece in its kind that ever appeared in Print.
    'Tis true, the 'Examiner' is already let loose to
trample on the Epilogue, and to worry the Reputation of
the most Ingenious Author; but who could not imagine that
he would *shew his Teeth*, when the Subject is the praise of
Liberty and Virtue? Then let him Snarl (while he cannot
Bite) but take care he does not betray as much Ignorance
in mangling *Dramatick Poetry*, as he lately did in
Heraldry, lest he render himself too obnoxious to such a
Character as the ancient Poets gave Momus, who, Lucian
says, did nothing else but *examine* the Works and Actions
of the Gods and Men, on purpose to rebuke and deride
them. (1)
    I have, for the Benefit of some of your Readers,
collected together a few of those Thoughts which inspir'd
the Breasts of Romans, that if it be possible, those base
degenerate Wretches who pursue no other Interest but their
own, and neglect that of their Country, may be ashamed
and confounded.
    In the first Scene of the Play, the Sons of Cato are
introduced as despairing of their own Success, and tortur'd with that of Caesar's, whose Ambition had made such
dreadful Havock in the Commonwealth. Marcus breaks out.

    Oh Portius, is there not some Chosen Curse,
    Some hidden Thunder in the Stores of Heaven,
    Red with uncommon Wrath to blast the Man
    Who owes his Greatness to his Country's Ruin? (2)

I shall forbear to make any Application here, which
some are very forward to do; it would be an Injustice to
the Author, to wrest his Meaning, by applying it to any
particular Person.

'Tis worth observing how Cato, at the meeting of the
little Senate, moderates the Heat of one, and removes the
Diffidence of another, by telling them, that after Caesar
had forced them to yield, then they might sue for Chains.

And let me perish, but in Cato's Judgment,
A Day, an Hour of virtuous Liberty,
Is worth a whole Eternity in Bondage. (3)

After Orders were given for the executing the base
Villains who conspired Cato's Death, he thus advises his
Friends.

Remember, O my Friends, the Laws, the Rights,
The Gen'rous Plan of Power deliver'd down
From Age to Age by your renown'd Forefathers,
(So dearly bought, the Price of so much Blood)
O let it never perish in your Hands! (4)

The Scene, where Cato meets the Corps of his Son
Marcus, is very moving. He's overjoy'd that his Son died
so gloriously in the Service of his Country: He repri-
mands his Friends for mourning a private Loss;

——— 'Tis Rome requires our Tears:
The Mistress of the World, the Seat of Empire,
The Nurse of Heroes, the Delight of Gods,
That humbled the proud Tyrants of the Earth,
And set the Nations free, Rome is no more.
O Liberty! O Virtue! O my Country! (5)

How wonderfully must this Example work up the Passions
of a generous Briton, and animate him to undergo any Hardships with pleasure, for the Defence of his Country? But
alas! such are these unhappy Times, that with too many
does the Character of Sempronius agree, who shall out-
wardly pretend mighty Zeal for Liberty, but inwardly are
willing for a Popish Pretender, and an Arbitrary Government.

                              Yours, &c.

Notes

1 Lucian, 'Zeus Rants', sects. 19ff.; 'Nigrinus', sect.
   32.

2 'Cato', I. i. 21-4.
3 II. i. 98-100.
4 III. v. 73-7.
5 IV. iv. 90-6.

47. CHARLES GILDON, 'CATO EXAMIN'D'

1713

Published anonymously but written by Charles Gildon,
'Cato Examin'd' was one of the two pamphlets that provoked Dennis to write his attack on the play and reduce
it to an absurdity. For an account of Gildon, see Nos 16,
41.

Having laid down these Certain and Undoubted Rules of
Writing, and Judging of a Tragedy, in a very narrow Compass, for the Variety of the Matter, and the Shortness of
the Time that my Affairs allow me; I shall now venture to
examine, how far the Author of *CATO* has comply'd with them,
and where he has been guilty of any Offence against *Art*.
For let the *ignorant Million* exclaim as they please
against the Rules, and Art, and make a senseless Clamour
about *Nature*, without giving us any Account what they mean
by the Word; the Judicious of all Ages and Nations, where
the Politer Studies have made any Progress, have allow'd
not much more to an Uncultivated Genius, than to mere Art.
Horace, who is own'd a Competent Judge, even by these
Noisy Favourers of Confusion, tells us, That to make a
Great and Just Poet, *Nature* must be instructed, or guided
by *Art*. Indeed, without the Rules, there is no Standard
of Excellence: And the most wretched Poetaster, that has
ever met with Success, has as just a Claim to Merit, as
the most Consummate Writer that ever ennobled the Scene.
    I shall therefore begin with the Plot, or Fable, of the
Tragedy of *CATO*.

    We have seen, that the *Action* to be imitated in a
Tragedy must be One and not Many, it must be Grave and
Serious, not Merry or Ridiculous; it must be entire and
of a just Length, that is, have a *Beginning*, *Middle*, and
End. The Time ought not to exceed the Representation, or

at least what Incidents extend farther ought to fall between the Acts, and the Place for that Reason must be confined to a narrow Compass; Lastly, it ought to be General
or Allegoric, and the Incidents that compose this *Action*
ought to be fitted for the moving of *Terror* and *Compassion.*

The *Fable* or *Action* of *CATO* is plainly *simple*, for there
is no Discovery producing a Change of Fortune in any of
the principal Characters from their knowing one another.
If we make the *Action* of this Play to be the Death of
Cato, it may seem to be with more difficulty preserved
from a Breach of *Unity*, which by the Rules of Art, we have
shewn to be essential to a *Dramatic Action.* But if we
make the Action of the Play to be expressed in the *Moral*
from the Mouth of *Lucius*:

> *From hence let fierce contending Nations know*
> *What dire Effects from Civil Discord flow, &c.* (1)

then the Unity will be most manifest, from every Character
in the Play, from *Cato* himself even to *Syphax* and *Sempron-*
ius. To this, *Cato* owes his Misery and his Death; to this
Marcus his Slaughter, and to this *Syphax* his Destruction
as well as *Sempronius.* It was the *Civil Discord* that
cooped them all up in *Utica* together; that set *Syphax* and
Sempronius to work in forming new Divisions and Civil Discord among that Remnant of *Romans*, which produced the
Death of *Marcus* and *Syphax* directly, and that of *Sempron-*
ius circumstantially, and hastened on that of *Cato* himself.

But not to strain where there is no Necessity, we will
make the *Action* of this Tragedy what, I believe, the Poet
meant it, and that is the Death of *Cato*; by which means
its *Unity* will be yet more clear. Thus the *Fable* is still
of the *Simple* not *Implex* Kind: It is first entire and of a
just Length, has a *Beginning*, *Middle* and *End*; the *Unity* of
Time is preserved by the express Words of the Play...

> Portius: *The Dawn is over-cast; the Morning lowers:*
> *And heavily in Cloud, brings on the Day, &c.* (2)

which shews the Beginning of the Play to open with the
Day, and how it concludes with the Setting Sun.... This
is but Eighteen Lines before the Groans of dying *Cato* are
heard. (3) So that it is plain, that the Time of this
Play is within the allowed Compass of a Day; and it is as
plain, that all that is represented exceeds not the Time
of the Representation, the Overplus of Time being artfully thrown into the Intervals according to the Rules
already laid down.

The Unity of Place, tho' much less considerable, is observed to the greatest Nicety, it being confined to *a large Hall in the Governor's Palace of* Utica.

Sure after this, our Enemies to Regularity will no more object, that a Play written according to the Rules can never please; they must at last own, that if such have ever miscarry'd where the Rules have been justly followed (which I can never grant) it has been the faulty Management of a little *Genius* in the Author, not of the Rules.

That the *Action* is of a just Length, that is, has a *Beginning*, *Middle*, and *End*, we shall shew by the following Examination. The Cause or Design of undertaking an *Action*, we said, is the *Beginning*; the Effects of those Causes, or that Cause, and the Difficulty we find in the Execution, are the *Middle*; and the unravelling or dissolving those Difficulties the *End*. Thus we have shewn, that the Anger of *Achilles* is the Action of the *Ilias*; the Quarrel betwixt him and *Agamemnon* is the Beginning; the Evils this Quarrel produced is the *Middle*; and the Death of *Hector* reconciling *Achilles* by the Tears and Prayers of *Priam*, the *End*.

The *Action* of this *Tragedy* is the Death of *Cato*, the Cause is the Extremity of his and the *Roman* Affairs in his being besieg'd in the City of *Utica*, which is the Beginning; the Delays of his Death were his Hopes of Success, and the Care of his Friends embark'd with him, are the Middle; the utter Disappointment of all in the Treachery of *Sempronius* and *Syphax*, and the Inclinations of *Lucius* and others to try the Clemency of *Caesar*, produc'd his Death, which was the *End*.

The *Beginning*, I have said, is supposed to be the Sequel of something going before, but not dependent on it. Thus *Cato*'s being confin'd to *Utica* was the Consequence of the Civil War, but not depending upon it, since *Cato* might have been elsewhere, as in *Numidia* or any other Place; but being there, the Place and Circumstances were the Cause of his Resolution of dying with the Liberty of his Country, when he had no farther Means of supporting it.

As the Confinement to this City was the Cause of *Cato*'s Fatal Resolution, so it produc'd the Necessities of his Friends, and their Struggle to win him to listen to *Caesar*, and the Conspiracy of *Sempronius* and *Syphax*, and the Death of *Marcus*, which produc'd the *End*, in *Cato*'s Death; for after that we have nothing to expect, the *Action* is at a full Period; and to have gone farther, had been to have begun a new Action, a Defect that our Poet had too much Judgment to be guilty of.

Lastly, The Action ought to be *Allegorical*, not *Particular*. Thus it is with 'Cato'; for it not only shews what

Cato did, but what any other Hero with his *Manners*, and
Qualifications, in the same Circumstances, Notions, and
Passions, wou'd have done: Which will appear plainer, when
we come to examine the *Manners*.

The Incidents which compose this *Fable*, are such as are
fitted to move Terror and Compassion. For what nearer
Relation can there be, than that of a Man to himself? It
is true, this grand Incident is of the first Sort of those
Incidents enumerated, that is, it is done with a perfect
Knowledge of the Fact he commits; yet the Pity is heightened when we find it free from Inhumanity or Malice to any
one, and purely the Effect of an Heroic Frailty of Temper,
that wou'd not think of surviving the Loss of his Country's
Liberty, or of meanly craving the Clemency of the Destroyer
of the *Roman* Liberty.

As for the other *Episodical* Incidents of this Play, we
must look back to the Cause of *Action*, the Confinement to
Utica; this brought all his Family, Children, with *Juba*,
Sempronius, *Syphax*, *Lucius*, and the rest, to the same
Place; and every one of them are one way or other concern'd in the Main *Action*, the Death of *Cato*: So that the
several *Episodes* of Love, and its Effects, plainly proceed from the Cause or *Beginning*, and had a Hand in delaying or farthering the End, according to their several
Inclinations and Interests.

Thus I have as briefly as possible, gone through the
most important Part of the Tragedy of 'Cato', the Plot or
FABLE; and shewn by the Rules themselves, how justly they
have been observ'd by our Author; which alone is a sufficient Justification of the Applause the Town has given it;
since in that is the Supreme Mastery of a *Tragic* Writer,
and in which so many of our Taking Poets have so very much
fail'd. I confess, that this Tragedy has not that Wonderful *Perepetie* or Change of Fortune, and Discovery, which we
find in the *Oedipus* of *Sophocles*. But then it must be
said, that no other Poet but *Sophocles* had them so perfect; and that the Noble Design of shewing us, at this
time, the Fatal Effects of Faction, and Domestic Feuds,
which are at so great and desperate a Height in our Days,
is a Balance for it. Besides, taking his Fable from so
known a History, it was impossible to furnish it either
with a just *Perepetie*, or *Discovery*, which is an Advantage
that the *Greek* Poets had, in building on the Fabulous
Part of *Grecian* Story; of which, through the various
Accounts of their blind and uncertain Tradition, they were
entirely Masters of their *Fables*, and might form them
according to their Pleasure, or the Skill of the Poet, to
render them delightful.

Thus the Common Fable of *Helena* was, that she was

tal:en away to *Troy* by *Paris*; yet *Euripides* has made a very
Beautiful *Discovery* and *Perepetie*, by asserting that *Paris*
carry'd only away a *Phantom*, form'd by *Venus*, to impose on
him, while the true *Helena* was conveyed to *Pharos*, and
shelter'd there in the Temple from the Love of *Theo-
clymenes*, till the Arrival of *Menelaus* on that Coast,
with his Followers, and the Phantom of *Helena*, which
vanishes away, and he finds the real *Helena*, and makes
his Escape with her for *Greece*. (4)

I have often thought, that if our Poets wou'd study the
Nature and true Beauties of Tragedy something more, the
uncertain Part of our own History wou'd be as advantageous
to them; and *Milton* seems of the same Mind in the Writing
of his *English* History. Besides, the Nation being the
same, the Customs and Manners wou'd have a more Natural
Influence on the Audience, and the Poet wou'd avoid some
Absurdities in the *Manners*, which many have been guilty
of, by placing their Scenes in Foreign Countries; for
tho' the Scene be at *Indostan*, or *Constantinople*, the
Manners are all *Northern*, *English*, &c. But of all
Foreign Stories those of *Greece* and *Rome* are the most
valuable; because our common Liberty has given us Senti-
ments, in many things, common with them. I know not but
if we shou'd ever out-live our *Liberties*, but then the
Seraglio may afford us as useful Examples; but as long as
'Cato' pleases, it does not appear that we are much in
Love with Slavery.

I come next to the *Manners*, which has the second Place
in Eminence to the *Plot* or *Fable*. I know it has been
objected, and I my self was once of that Opinion, that
Cato was by no means a proper Hero for Tragedy; a Stoic
by Profession, and therefore supposed to be without Passions, whereas Passion is the very Characteristic of that
Poem, *Violenta Tragedia*.

But in reviewing the Life of that *Roman*, I found that
his Love for his Country was not without Passion, and that
of great Violence, as his bursting into Tears in going
over the Field where the Conflict of *Dyrrachium* was;
and his doing the same whenever Mention was made of the
Battle of *Pharsalia*. (5) His Sword being conveyed away
privately the Night of his Death by the Order of his
Friends, on missing it he called one of his Slaves and bid
him fetch it, but not being obeyed he grew so angry, that
he struck his Slave with such Force that he hurt his own
Hand, crying out he was betray'd, and should be deliver'd
to the Enemy Naked and Unarmed. And his after Words to
his Sons and Friends shew plainly, that he was not so much
a Stoic as to be void of Passion, especially in the Cause
of his Friends and his Country.

This being thus plain, let us examine his *Manners* as a
Dramatic Person, for as such only we have to do with him
here.

The *Manners*, as we have shewn, should have Four Qualities, which all meet in 'Cato'. They must be *good*, that
is, well mark'd; they must be *like*, they must be *convenient* and *equal*. Thus the *Manners* of *Cato* are poetically
good, that is, well marked; for his Discourse makes us
clearly see his Inclinations, and what Resolutions he will
be certain to take. The *Manners* of the Poetical *Cato* are
like; that is, they are conformable to those, which true
History gives this *Roman*.

In History, he was of a Sedate, but Stern Inflexible
Temper, a constant Lover of his Country and its Laws; he
was of singular Integrity, and thought no Cause good, that
was not founded on Justice; incapable of Corruption; and
an irreconcileable Enemy to those, he thought Enemies to
his Country; and of unquestionable Courage both in the
Field and the Senate. Now there is not one of these Qualities but are visible in our Poetic *Cato*, even in the First
Scene of his Appearance. As his Conduct between *Sempronius* and *Lucius*, and to *Decius*, on his Message from *Caesar*,
make it evident.

The *Manners* of our *CATO* are likewise *Convenient*, that
is, every where consistent: As they begin, so they end;
and He is always the Same, which makes Them also *Equal*.

Thus we have seen the *Manners* of our Tragic Hero to
be *Good*, *Like*, *Convenient* and *Equal*; and we shall soon
find that they are also *Necessary*, for the Carrying on
the Action. I have laid it down as a Rule, that there are
Three Sorts of Qualities, that compose the Character of a
Hero. First, Such as are absolutely *Necessary* for the
Fable or *Action*; and those are most to appear, and prevail
above the rest, since the Hero is to be known by them: The
Second are to Embellish the First; and the Third, to
Sustain Both.

The First of these in our *CATO,* is, the *Love of his
Country*, which appears wherever he is seen: And this is
set off by an invincible *Resolution*; and Both are sustain'd by a very uncommon *Fortitude*.

Thus I have likewise gone thro' my Examination of the
Manners of *CATO*, by the Just Rules of *Aristotle* himself;
and shown, beyond Contradiction, that Mr. *Addison* has
arriv'd at a Perfection in this Particular; in which he is
also almost singular among his Contemporary Tragic Writers, (if we add those of King *Charles* II.'s Reign to
them) except *Otway*, some of *Lee*'s Plays, and One or Two
of Mr. *Dryden*'s.

It may perhaps be expected, that having gone thro' the
Plot, and the Principal Character, I should likewise say
something of the other *Dramatick Persons*, that fill up
this Play: But having already shown, that they are all
dependent on the Main *Action*, and produc'd by the Beginning of it; I shall only say, that they are perfectly distinguish'd: The Sedateness of *Portius*, is sufficiently
distinct from the Fiery Temper of *Marcus*. The Two Characters of *Sempronius* and *Syphax*, are distinguish'd in themselves, tho' Carrying on the same Treacherous Cause, nor
are they furnish'd with *Manners*, that are not necessary
to the Business they are engag'd in. They are not made
more wicked, than they shou'd be, merely to introduce a
Villain; but as Love or Lust, and a Fear below a Friend
of *Cato's*, engag'd *Sempronius* in his Treachery, so overcome by such Passions, in this Age, they wou'd almost be
pity'd. More may be said for *Syphax*, no Subject of *Rome*,
nor indu'd with those Principles, that were worn out then
in the *Romans* themselves; a *Numidian*, an *African*, that was
not willing to perish in a Cause, in the Success of which
he cou'd expect to be no Gainer. In short, he is what we
may call Wicked, but not guilty of such Breaches of common
Honesty or confirm'd Villany, as are too frequent on our
Stage, and have nothing Dramatic in them. The Character
of *Womanhood* is every where preserv'd in the Ladies, in
whom Modesty shines, and Virtue is always conspicuous.
Juba is every where honourable, and a true Pupil of *Cato*,
and promising that Man, that he afterwards was in Reality;
he does nothing unworthy a Prince, nor indeed of a *Roman*.
   All I have to say of the *Sentiments* is, that I cannot
find any, but what are the Natural Product of the *Manners*,
the *Occasion*, and *Passion*. And I am satisfy'd, that every
one will excuse my saying nothing of the Diction, since
that is what every one will allow to be Just and Dramatic,
vary'd according to the Subject. The Passions are not
clogg'd with insipid sounding Epithets, that make the
Passion languish, that is, when they have any Passions to
express.
   I shall here conclude, That as this Celebrated Tragedy
of 'Cato' has receiv'd the general Applause of the Town;
the Reader may judge, by the Examination I have made, by
the known and allow'd Rules of the *Drama*, how much Justice
there was in that Applause.

   Est ubi recte judicat est ubi peccat.   Hor. (6)

Notes

1 'Cato', V. iv. 107ff.
2 I. i. 1ff.
3 Juba's reference to the setting sun is in V. iv. 40-5;
   Cato's groan, line 60.
4 'Helena' (412 BC).
5 'Cato the Younger', in 'Plutarch's Lives', ed.
   Clough (1905), IV, pp. 424, 428.
6 Should read 'Interdum volgus rectum videt, est ubi
   peccat' ('Epistles', II. i. 63): 'At times the public
   sees straight; sometimes they make mistakes.'

48. GEORGE SEWELL, 'OBSERVATIONS UPON CATO'

1713

A poetic eulogy which appears at the end of the 'Observations'.

George Sewell (d. 1726), a Cantabrigean, was a bookseller's hack who was adept at linking his name to some
of the illustrious writers of the reigns of Anne and
George I. Despite his own Toryism (at least until 1718),
he twice defended Addison's 'Cato', first in 1713 and then
in 1716 (see No. 52).

Upon Mr. ADDISON'S CATO

Long had the *Tragic Muse* forgot to Weep,
By modern *Operas* quite lull'd a-sleep:
No Matter what the Lines, the Voice was clear,
Thus Sense was sacrific'd to please the Ear.
At last, *One Wit* stood up in our Defence,
And dar'd (O Impudence!) to publish ——Sense.
Soon then as next the just *Tragoedian* spoke,
The *Ladies* sigh'd again, the *Beaux* awoke.
Those Heads that us'd most indolent to move
To *Sing-song*, *Ballad*, and *Sonata* Love,
Began their buried Senses to explore,
And found they now had Passions as before:
The Power of *Nature* in their Bosoms felt,

In spite of Prejudice compell'd to melt.
   When *CATO*'s firm, all Hope of Succour past,
Holding his stubborn Virtue to the last,
I view, with Joy and conscious Transport fir'd,
The *Soul* of *Rome* in One Great Man retir'd:
In Him, as if She by Confinement gain'd   ⎤
Her Pow'rs and Energy are higher strain'd   ⎬
Than when in Crowds of *Senators* she reign'd! ⎦
CATO well scorn'd the Life that CAESAR gave,
When *Fear* and *Weakness* only bid him save:
But when a Virtue like his own revives
The *Hero*'s Constancy —— with Joy he lives.
   Observe the Justness of the Poet's Thoughts
Whose smallest Excellence is want of Faults:
Without affected Pomp and Noise he warms;
Without the gaudy Dress of Beauty charms.
Love, the old Subject of the Buskin'd Muse,
Returns, but such as *Roman Virgins* use.
A *Virtuous Love*, chastis'd by purest Thought,
Not from the Fancy, but from Nature wrought.
   Britons, with lessen'd Wonder, now behold
Your former Wits, and all your Bards of old;
JOHNSON out-vy'd in his own way confess;
And own that SHAKESPEAR's self now pleases less.
While PHAEBUS binds the Laurel on his Brow,
Rise up, ye *Muses*, and ye *Poets* bow:
Superiour Worth with Admiration greet
And place him nearest to his PHAEBUS Seat.

49. JOHN DENNIS, 'REMARKS UPON CATO'

1713

Dennis, 'Remarks Upon Cato, A Tragedy' (1713), in 'The
Critical Works of John Dennis', ed. E. N. Hooker, II,
pp. 41-80.
   This pamphlet is Dennis's critical refutation of
Gildon's and Sewell's eulogistic treatments of 'Cato'.

INTRODUCTION.

'Tis now for some Weeks that my Friends have been urging

me to make some Remarks upon the Tragedy of 'Cato', and
'tis for some Weeks that I have deliberated, whether Prudence would allow me to take such a Step as that is. (1)
I have maturely consider'd both the general and the violent Applause with which that Tragedy has been receiv'd;
That it was acted Twenty Days together; That Ten thousand
of 'em have been sold since the Time it was printed; (2)
That ev'n Authors have publish'd their Approbation of it,
who never before lik'd any thing but themselves; That
Squire *Ironside*, that grave Offspring of ludicrous Ances-
tors, has appear'd at the Head of them; (3) and, That
things have been carry'd to that amazing Height, either by
French Extravagance, or by *English* Industry, that a *Frenchman* is now actually translating this Play into *French*,
which is a thing beyond Example; (4) That a great deal of
Deference is to be paid to a general Applause; That a
Writer can expect nothing by attacking so successful a
Piece, but the Character of an envious and an ill-natur'd
Man, and perhaps of an arrogant, an insolent and presumptuous one; That it would look with a worse Grace in me
than in most People, in me, who have all my Life-time been
an Assertor of Liberty, to endeavour to ruin the Reputation of a Play, which seems writ with a Design to augment
the Love of Liberty; That what would make it look still
worse is, that it has been my Misfortune more than once to
have been engag'd in Disputes of this Nature formerly, by
which, tho' I had Reason still on my Side, I have made my
self numerous Enemies; That Truth now a-days is but a very
feeble Defence against Passion and Prejudice; That I pass
for a Man, who is conceitedly resolv'd to like nothing
which others like, and that I have still endeavour'd to
undeceive others at too cruel an Expence of my own.

To all which my Friends have reply'd, That they are
willing to own that a Deference is to be paid to a general
Applause, when it appears that that Applause is natural
and spontaneous, but that little Regard is to be had to it
when it is affected and artificial; That they have a long
time made this unlucky Remark, that of all the Tragedies
which in their Memory have had vast and violent Runs, not
one has been excellent, few have been tolerable, most have
been scandalous; That there is a Reason to be given for
this in the Nature of the thing; That when a Poet writes a
Tragedy, who knows he has Judgment, and who feels he has
Genius, that Poet presumes upon his own Merit, and scorns
to make a Cabal; That People come coolly to the Representation of such a Tragedy, without any violent Expectation,
or delusive Imagination, or invincible Prepossession; That
such an Audience is liable to receive the Impressions
which the Poem shall naturally make in them, and to judge

by their own Reason and their own Judgments, and that Reason and Judgment are calm and serene, not form'd by Nature to make Proselytes, and to controul and lord it o'er the Imaginations of others: But that when an Author writes a Tragedy, who knows he has neither Genius nor Judgment, he has Recourse to the making a Party, and endeavours to make up in Industry what is wanting in Talent, and to supply by Poetical Craft the Absence of Poetical Art; That such an Author is humbly contented to raise Mens Passions by a Plot without Doors, since he despairs of doing it by that which he brings upon the Stage; That Party, and Passion and Prepossession are clamorous and tumultuous things, and so much the more clamorous and tumultuous, by how much the more erroneous; That they domineer and tyrannize over the Imaginations of Persons who want Judgment, and sometimes too of those who have it, and like a fierce outrageous Torrent, bear down all Opposition before them; That a Man of Judgment is calm and patient under Contradiction, because he knows he is in the right, while Passion, Prejudice and Prepossession grow violent and furious by being oppos'd, because then they begin to doubt that they are in the wrong; That Audiences are often pack'd as well as Juries, (5) and that therefore it sometimes happens, that while the Innocent are condemn'd, the Guilty are acquitted by a Verdict of *Ignoramus*.

That as for the Authors who have publish'd their Encomiums of 'Cato', which they nickname Criticisms, those Authors appear to have been retain'd; and so, like conscientious Lawyers, believe it their Duty to say all that they can for their Client, and not one Word against him, that they may honestly earn their Fees; but that the Author of 'Cato Examin'd' has behav'd himself like an errant Wag, and at the same time that he has prais'd him expresly, has implicitly damn'd him to the Pit of Hell, and has acted the Part of *Sempronius*, who while he openly bullies for *Cato*, is his mortal Enemy in his Heart. (6)

That as for Squire *Ironside*, he comes of a Race that has been most unfortunate in their Talents for Criticism; That his Grand-Father, Squire *Bickerstaff*, who was sometimes entertaining in other things, was almost never in the right when he pretended to judge of Poetry; That his Father, Mr. 'Spectator', had been so merrily in the wrong, as to take Pains to reconcile us to the old Doggrel of 'Chevy-Chase' and the 'Three Children', (7) and to put Impotence and Imbecillity upon us for Simplicity; That he had publish'd a certain Criticism upon *Milton*, in which the Reverse of almost every thing that he has affirm'd is true; That he has had the Assurance to say in it, That 'The Paradise Lost' of *Milton* has an Unity of Action,

whereas in that Poem there are most apparently two Actions, the War of the Angels being an Action by it self,
and having a just Beginning, a Middle and an End; That he
has affirm'd with still greater Assurance, That the
'Ilias' of *Homer* has a Duplicity of Action, and has cited
the Authority of *Aristotle* as a Proof of that Assertion;
whereas *Homer* in that Poem has given the World a Pattern,
which for Unity and Simplicity of *Epick* Action never had
any Parallel, and that *Aristotle* has commended him for it
no less than three times in his little Treatise of
Poetry; (8) That the said Mr. 'Spectator' had arraign'd
and condemn'd the Poetical Justice of the Stage, and had
publish'd a great deal of false and abominable Criticism,
in order to poison his gentle Reader, and prepare the way
for 'Cato'. (9)

That the Attempt of that undertaking *Frenchman*, who is
at present translating 'Cato', has made the writing of a
Criticism upon it necessary, which before was highly
reasonable, because the translating this Play into *French*
being without Precedent or Example, will, together with
the violent and general Applause it has met with, make it
pass for our Nonparello among foreign Nations; which will
expose our own to the Rallery of all *Europe*, unless we
shew, at the same time, that we are not all so ignorant
or mistaken.

That as for the Objection of ill Nature, if I am in the
right in my Criticisms, I may laugh at those who make it;
That right Reason can never pass for ill Nature, unless
with those who are destitute of right Reason; That 'tis
a senseless thing to cherish Libellers and Lampooners,
who defame the Virtues of others to the publick Detriment,
and at the same time to brand those with the Character of
ill Nature, who discover the Errors of an Author's Understanding, only in order to that Author's Improvement, and
the Advancement of a noble Art; That those fulsome Panegyrists are rather to be esteem'd envious and ill-natur'd,
who by nauseously flattering a very defective Author, and
soothing him in his Errors and in his Ignorance, do, as it
were, politickly fix him in his Follies, and render him
proud and incorrigible.

That 'Cato's' being writ with a Design to support
Liberty, is an Objection of no manner of Force; That let
the Design be what it will, the Effect is sure to be contrary; That the shewing a Man of consummate Virtue unfortunate only for supporting Liberty, must of Necessity in a
free Nation be of pernicious Consequence, and must justly
raise the highest Indignation in all true Lovers of
Liberty.

That my having made a great many Enemies by former

Disputes of this Nature, is a certain Proof that I have
been in the right in those Disputes, and that they who hate
me for asserting Truth are resolv'd to remain in the wrong;
That I enter'd into those Disputes, partly to advance the
publick Good by advancing a noble Art, and partly to
retort private Injuries; That either Cause in it self is
good and just, and that both together are strong and
powerful, and that I shall have both together to apologize
for my present Undertaking.

That if I have made numerous Enemies, I have made a few
Friends, of which each singly will outweigh all those numerous Enemies; That all reasonable Men, who by others Artifices, and their own Indolence, have been surpriz'd into
an Approbation of this Play, will be glad to be undeceiv'd,
as knowing well that 'tis their own Reason and their own
Discernment that makes another Man's take Place with them;
That the very Tragick Stage appears to be sinking, since
the great Success of one very faulty Play prognosticates
its Ruin more than the Miscarriage of twenty good ones;
That a good Tragedy may miscarry by the ill Performance of
the Actors, by Prejudice, by Malice, by Squeamishness, but
that a very faulty one can have great Success from almost
nothing but the general Interest of the People; That this
general ill Taste is partly the Effect of the *Italian*
Opera; that a People accustom'd for so many Years to that,
are as ill-prepar'd to judge of a good Tragedy, as Children that are eating Sugar-plumbs are to taste *Champaign*
and *Burgundy*; That nothing but a wholesome Criticism can
have Power to retrieve our Taste; and, That the Errors of
'Cato' must be set in a true Light by me or by some other
Person, or the Tragick Muse must be banish'd from this
Island; That it is set up for a Pattern, and extoll'd by
some Authors, who are famous for their want of Judgment,
not only before all our own, but above all ancient Tragedies; That the Interest of the Common-wealth of Learning
lies at Stake, and the Reputation of *Great-Britain*; and,
That he must be a pleasant Lover of his Country, and a
worthy Member of the Common-wealth of Learning, who is
afraid to assert the Interest of the one, and to defend
the Reputation of the other, least he should make some
mistaken Men his Enemies.

That as to my Resolution to approve of nothing which is
lik'd by others, 'tis a Falshood which carries its own
Evidence with it; that I have writ whole Volumes which
may shew the contrary, and that the contrary may easily be
made to appear in the Remarks which I may make upon 'Cato'.

Remarks upon 'CATO'.

THE 'foresaid Remonstrances of my Friends have at length
so far prevail'd with me, that I have taken a resolution
to make some Remarks upon this Tragedy in the following
Method.

First, I shall endeavour to shew the Faults and Absurdities which are to be found in this Tragedy.
Secondly, I shall attempt to expose the Artifices which
made way for its great Success.

First, I shall endeavour to shew its Faults and Absurdities, and here I design to do Three Things.
1. I shall shew what perfections are wanting to it,
thro' the not observing several of the Rules of *Aristotle*.
2. I shall shew with what Absurdities it abounds, thro'
the observing several of the Rules without any manner of
Judgment or Discretion.
3. I shall shew some Faults and Absurdities, which are
such in Themselves, without any relation to the Rules.

Among the perfections which are wanting to this Tragedy, thro' the not observing the Rules, is first and
chiefly the Fable, there being no Fable to this Tragedy.
The Action of it which is the Death of *Cato*, is a particular Historical Action, a relation of something which *Cato*
did and suffered, and not an action Allegorical and Universal. That it is not Allegorical, appears from hence,
that it carries no moral Instruction with it. For the
Moral which is foisted in at the latter end of this Play,
is wholly Foreign to it, and is not deriv'd from the
Action of it, which is the Death of *Cato*.

From hence let Fierce contending Nations know,
What dire effects from civil Discord flow,
'Tis this that shakes our Country with Alarms,
And gives up Rome *a Prey to* Roman *Arms,*
Produces Fraud, and Cruelty, and Strife,
And Robs the guilty World of Cato's *Life.* (10)

Let us suppose for once, that the Action of this Tragedy is the whole Civil War it self; yet I cannot discern
what knowledge Moral or Intellectual can be drawn from the
'foregoing Lines. The dire effects of Civil discord were
known to all Mankind, long before 'Cato' was writ; and the
only instruction that can be drawn from them, since in
this Tragedy, the Invaders of Liberty are seen to Triumph,

and the Defenders of it to Perish, must be this, That
Fools and Knaves should have a care how they invade the
Liberties of their Country, lest Good and Wise Men suffer
by it, or that Good and Wise Men should have a care how
they defend those Liberties, lest Fools and Knaves should
Triumph.

As the Action of this Play is the Death of *Cato*, no
Instruction but one of these Three can be possibly drawn
from it.   That a Man of consummate Virtue, must expect to
end unfortunately: Or that if a Man of an accomplish'd
virtue, happens to be unfortunate, 'tis his duty to put an
end to his Misfortunes by a Dose or a Dagger, or that if
such a one presumes to resist the Invaders of his
Country's Liberties, he must expect to fall in the Attempt.

Thus, the Action of this Play is so far from carrying a
Moral, that it carries a pernicious instruction with it.
Now I appeal to the Reader, which is most commendable, to
make a Poetical Person of consummate Virtue end unfortunately, and by that means of discourage People from aiming
at Perfection; or to shew a Man of accomplish'd Virtue
driven to lay violent Hands upon himself, only for supporting Liberty, which must needs be a notable Lesson to
People in a free Country, or to an Island so notorious as
ours for the frequency of self Murder.

As the Action of this Tragedy cannot be Allegorical,
because it is not Moral; so is it neither General or Poetical, but Particular and Historical.   A general thing,
says *Aristotle*, is what ev'ry Man of such and such a
Character, would do upon such and such an occasion; as a
particular thing is what such a particular Person, as for
Example *Alcibiades*, did and suffer'd.   Now that a Tragical Action ought at the Bottom to be thus general, ev'n
after the Poet has nam'd his Characters, is the Doctrine
of the same Philosopher.   The principal quality of *Cato*'s
Character, is the Love of his Country, as has been
observ'd by others.   Now the question is, whether 'tis
necessary or probable, that a Man, the predominant quality
of whose Character is the Love of his Countrey, should
fall by his own Hand, as long as his Life is necessary to
the good of his Countrey.   Now that this was the Case of
Cato, may be prov'd from what the Poet has put into the
Mouths of the other Dramatick Persons.   For says *Portius*
to his Sister in the Fifth Act.

> O Marcia, *O my Sister, still there's hope*
> *Our Father will not cast away a Life*
> *So needful to us all and to his Countrey.* (11)

Nay, if we believe what *Lucius* says in the Fourth Act,

the Life of *Cato*, nay, not only his Life, but his submitting to *Caesar* was necessary, not only for the good of his
Country, but for the welfare of Mankind. [Quotes IV. iv.
25-8.]
   So that *Cato*, the Predominant quality of whose Character, was the Love of his Country, killing himself at a
time, when his Life was necessary to the good of his
Country, and to the welfare of Mankind, did not do, what
any Man of the same Character would necessarily or probably do upon the like occasion, and therefore *Cato*'s killing himself, is not a general and Tragical Action, but a
particular thing which *Cato* did and suffer'd.
   Now since 'tis undoubtedly the Fable, which is of the
greatest importance in Tragedy, for as some body has well
observ'd, 'tis the making of the Fable alone, which
belongs peculiarly to the Art of the Poet; for 'tis History and Philosophy which teaches him to form his Characters, and Rhetorick and Grammar, his Sentiments and
Expressions; and since there can be no Fable where the
Action is neither Allegorical nor Universal; and the
Action in this Tragedy of 'Cato', is neither Allegorical
nor Universal; I appeal to the Impartial Reader, whether
this Tragedy of 'Cato' having no Fable, can justly be said
to be a fine Tragedy.
   As the Action of this Tragedy is neither Allegorical
nor Universal, so neither can it be said to be one. The
Action of this Play is the Death of *Cato*; and the Time of
that Action is a natural Day, during which Day the Sons
of *Cato* knew very well, that their Father's Life and the
Liberty of *Rome*, were in the utmost Danger, as appears by
the first four Lines of the Play....
   Now the Question is, whether the Amorous Passions of
Two such noble *Romans* and such dutiful Sons, as *Marcus* and
Portius are describ'd to be, upon that very Day, which in
their own Opinions is like to be the last both of *Rome*'s
Liberty and of their Father's Life, are either necessary
or probable Parts of the Action of the Play, which is the
Death of their Father, and whether if they are neither
necessary nor probable Parts of it, they do not corrupt
the Unity of that Action, and not only corrupt its Unity,
but render it improbable, Romantick and incredible.
   The Rivalship between the Two Brothers, has no manner
of Influence upon the Action of the Play, and therefore
corrupts its Unity, nor has it any Consequence in its
self, but the Author to make way for one of the Rivals
knocks the other on the Head, and kills Him not by any
Effect of his Rivalship, but by the common Fortune of
War. How gross a Copy of the celebrated Rivalship of
Polidor and *Castalio*, which has such a fatal Influence

upon the Action of the Play, and causes such a moving Distress, and such a Deplorable and truly Tragical Catastrophe. (12)

Probability ought certainly to reign in every Tragical Action, but tho' it ought every where to predominate, it ought not to exclude the wonderful; as the wonderful which ought every where to predominate in *Epick* Poetry, ought not to exclude the probable. We shall then treat of the Improbabilities of this Tragedy, when we come to speak of the Absurdities with which it throughout abounds, from the indiscreet and injudicious Observance of some of the Rules of *Aristotle*. We are at present shewing what Beauties are wanting to it from the not observing others of those Rules. Here then are none of those beautiful Surprizes which are to be found in some of the *Grecian* Tragedies, and in some of our own; and consequently here is nothing wonderful, nothing terrible, or deplorable, which all three are caus'd by Surprize. Now as Tragedy is the Imitation of an Action which excites Compassion and Terror; and as that alone can be justly accounted a very fine Tragical Scene, which excites one of those two Passions, or both, in a very great Degree, and as it is impossible either of 'em can be excited in a very great Degree, without a very great Surprize, and there is in this Tragedy no very great Surprize, we find there is not in this Tragedy, no not so much as one very fine Tragical Scene, no not so much as one Scene with which we are extremely mov'd. I sit with Indolence from the opening of the Play to the very Catastrophe; and when at length the Catastrophe comes, instead of vehemently shaking with Terror, or dissolving with melting Pity, I rather burn with Indignation, and I shudder with Horror. When I behold *Cato* expiring by his own Hand, 'tis difficult to tell at which Indecency and which Inconsistency I am shock'd the most, at a Philosopher's acting against the Light of Nature, or at a *Stoick*'s yielding to ill Fortune without the last Necessity, or at the unjust and unfortunate End of a Man of accomplish'd Virtue, or at a Lover of Liberty and of his Country deserting both by his Death.

That Esteem which we conceiv'd for *Cato* at the reading of the ancient Poets, immediately vanishes when we behold his Death, and I begin to wonder what those Poets meant: I begin to think that their Encomiums arose from want of considering this Matter aright; and I find, upon Reflection, that the greatest of them all, both for Genius and Judgment, tho' in his *8th Aeneid* he places *Cato* at the Head of his Demi-Gods, in the *Elysian* Fields, yet he damns him in his *6th*, in the Number of those who fall by their own Hands.

We are enclin'd to believe, that it was rather a Mix-
ture of Pride and Ignorance, than any Degree of Heroick
Virtue, that induc'd *Cato* to be his own Destroyer. We
cannot understand the Suicide of one, who was under no
Necessity to die; for the Cause of Liberty was as yet not
entirely lost, and it appears from the Beginning of the
Second Act, that a Way lay open to him and his for their
Escape by Land.

Numidia's spacious Kingdom lies behind us,
Ready to rise at its young Prince's Call.

And 'tis manifest from the latter End of the *Fourth*,
that the Sea lay open to his Passage; 'tis *Cato* himself
that tells us so. [Quotes IV. iv. 145-9.]
Who then can extremely pity a Man, who rashly dy'd by
his own Hands, when there was no Necessity for Dying,
and who deserted the Cause of Liberty and of his Country,
thro' Stubborness and thro' Ignorance, or sacrifis'd them
to his Stoical Pride? If the Sons of the Great *Pompey* had
follow'd the Example of *Cato*, had there ever been that
noble Contention that there was afterwards in *Spain* for
Liberty, which was within an Ace of reducing *Caesar* to
follow the Example of *Cato*? And what might not have been
the happy Event of that desperate Conflict, had *Cato* animated those Troops by his Presence, and sustain'd them by
his Authority? Even *Portius* takes Notice, in the *Fifth
Act*, of the auspicious Influence that his Father's Presence might have o'er those Assertors of Liberty.
[Quotes V. v. 52-9.]
I am apt to think that *Brutus* and *Cassius* shew'd more
Spirit and more Wisdom, by the magnanimous Choice which
they made to destroy *Caesar*, rather than kill themselves;
and when those two last of the *Romans* were constrain'd to
do at last what *Cato* had done before them, I find their
Deaths to be much more excusable than his; for they were
compell'd by dire Necessity to do what *Cato* had done by
Choice; for they who were the principal Conspirators
against *Caesar*, might expect to be us'd with Severity, if
not with the utmost Cruelty, by *Anthony* and *Octavius*, who
had sworn to revenge his Death. Besides, *Brutus* and
Cassius did not fall, 'till the Cause of Liberty was
utterly and entirely lost; whereas we have shewn that
there were two noble Conflicts for it after the Death of
Cato.
I am apt to think that this Action of *Cato* would not
have had the Approbation even of those *Romans* themselves,
who liv'd in the Vigour of the Commonwealth, and in the
Height of the *Roman* Virtue, and who, after the deplorable

Rout at *Cannae*, caus'd publick Thanks to be return'd to
Terentius Varro, for not despairing of the Common-wealth.
    'Tis certainly the Duty of every Tragick Poet, by an
exact Distribution of a Poetical Justice, to imitate the
Divine Dispensation, and to inculcate a particular Providence. 'Tis true indeed upon the Stage of the World the
Wicked sometimes prosper, and the Guiltless suffer. But
that is permitted by the Governour of the World, to shew
from the Attribute of his infinite Justice that there is
a Compensation in Futurity, to prove the Immortality of
the Human Soul, and the Certainty of future Rewards and
Punishments. But the Poetical Persons in Tragedy exist
no longer than the Reading or the Representation; the
whole Extent of their Entity is circumscribed by those;
and therefore during that Reading or Representation,
according to their Merits or Demerits, they must be
punish'd or rewarded. If this is not done, there is no
impartial Distribution of Poetical Justice, no instructive Lecture of a particular Providence, and no Imitation
of the Divine Dispensation. And yet the Author of this
Tragedy does not only run counter to this, in the Fate of
his principal Character, but every where throughout it,
makes Virtue suffer, and Vice triumph; for not only *Cato*
is vanquish'd by *Caesar*, but the Treachery and Perfidiousness of *Syphax* prevails over the honest Simplicity and
the Credulity of *Juba*, and the sly Subtlety and Dissimulation of *Portius* over the generous Frankness and Open-
heartedness of *Marcus*
    But setting aside for a Moment the Rules of the *Drama*,
which are the Rules of exact Reason, there is not with all
its Improbability so much as any thing in this Tragedy of
that Art and Contrivance, which is to be found in an
entertaining Romance or agreeable Novel; that Art and Contrivance, by which their Authors excite our Curiosities,
and cause those eager Longings in their Readers to know
the Events of things, those Longings, which by their
pleasing Agitations, at once disturb and delight the Mind,
and cause the prime Satisfaction of all those Readers who
read only to be delighted. Instead of that this Author
has found out the Secret, to make his Tragedy highly improbable, without making it wonderful, and to make some
Parts of it highly incredible, without being in the least
entertaining.
    But now let us come to the Characters, and let us shew
that they are not proper for Tragedy. *Cato* himself, who
is the principal Person, is a *Stoick*, and therefore a
very improper Heroe for Tragedy. The Author of 'Cato
Examin'd' says; 'That he was once of the same Opinion,
because being a *Stoick* by Profession, he is suppos'd to

be without Passion; for Passion, says he, is the very
Characteristick of that Poem, *violenta Tragedia*; but, says
he, in reviewing the Life of that *Roman*, I found that the
Love for his Country was not without Passion, and that of
great Violence, as his bursting into Tears, in going over
the Field where the Conflict of *Dyrrachium* was, and in
doing the same whenever Mention was made of the Battel of
Pharsalia.'

But here the Mistake of this Gentleman lies, *viz*. in
affirming that therefore a *Stoick* is an improper Heroe for
Tragedy, because he is suppos'd to be without Passion; for
who ever doubted that a *Stoick* is a Man, and consequently
that he has Passions; even Grace it self does not go so
far as to divest a Man wholly even of worldly Passions,
much less can any Philosophical Discipline pretend to
reach that Length. A *Stoick* is therefore an improper
Heroe for Tragedy, not because he is suppos'd to be actually without Passion, but because he is believ'd to do his
utmost Endeavours to be without them; because he places
his Pride, his Glory, his Excellence in subduing them;
because his great and principal Aim is to make his Reason,
not only the Ruler, but the very Tyrant of them; because
his chief Design is not to regulate, but to extirpate and
extinguish them. From which it is manifest, that an old
Stoick, as *Cato* was, has by long Exercise got some Habits
which make him a very improper Hero for Tragedy. For his
Philosophy has taught him to check his Passions, to conceal them, and to shorten them; so that a *Stoick*, if his
Manners are made convenient, can never be shewn, as *Oedipus* and some other principal Characters of Tragedy are
shewn, *viz*. agitated and tormented by various violent
Passions, from the opening of the Scene to the very Catastrophe.

Besides, 'tis to no purpose to affirm, that *Cato* had
Passions, and violent ones, because he is no where in this
Tragedy drawn in a violent Passion, as this Author has
himself observ'd, ... where he tells us, 'That he finds by
History that *Cato* was of a sedate Temper, and at the same
time finds by the Tragedy that the Poet has every where
drawn him so.' So that here is another Reason why *Cato* is
an improper Hero for the Stage, because his natural
Temper, as well as his Philosophy, was repugnant to Passion. And this Author, ... has given another Reason why
Cato is an improper Heroe for Tragedy. 'Because, says he,
the Characters that are to compose a Tragick Fable or Plot
must not be sovereignly virtuous or innocent; for to make
a perfect virtuous and innocent Character unhappy excites
Horror, not Pity nor Terror.'

If this Author by these perfect Characters, means the

principal Characters of such Tragedies, as end unfortunately with relation to those principal Characters, he
is in the right of it, or *Aristotle* must be in the wrong.
But then I appeal to the impartial Reader, what this
Author would get by it, if I should allow that a *Stoick*
may be a proper Heroe for Tragedy.

Besides this, there is an Inequality in the Manners of
Cato, and therefore they are ill mark'd likewise; for his
Behaviour in the Fourth Act, is by no means answerable to
that Character that is given of him, and that Expectation
that is rais'd of him by *Portius* in the First.

> *How does the Lustre of our Father's Actions,*
> *Thro' the dark Clouds of Ills that cover him,*
> *Break forth, and burn with more triumphant Brightness!*
> *His Sufferings shine, and spread a Glory round him,*
> *Greatly unfortunate he fights the Cause*
> *Of Honour, Virtue, Liberty and* Rome. (13)

And afterwards by *Juba* in the same Act. [Quotes I. iv.
77–82.] And by what he says himself in the Second Act.
[Quotes II. i. 84–100.]

Let us now see whether his Behaviour in the Fourth Act
is answerable to all this.

When the Conspiracy of *Syphax* and *Sempronius* broke out,
by the Mutiny of those *Romans*, who had been seduced by
Sempronius, tho' that part of the Conspiracy was quickly
quell'd, by the general Repentance of those engag'd in it,
by the Deaths of the Leaders, and of *Sempronius* himself;
Cato, as soon as he hears of the Death of the latter,
cries out,

> *O* Lucius, *I am sick of this bad World,*
> *The Day-light and the Sun grow painful to me.* (14)

Now what Reason has a Man of his Character to exclaim
thus, and to fall into Desperation, because Heaven has
discover'd his secret Enemy, and Divine Vengeance has
overtaken a Villain? His Affairs, as yet, are not in a
jot worse Posture than when he shew'd so much Resolution
in the Second Act.

And when he hears of the other part of the Conspiracy,
which is the Attempt of *Syphax* to force his way with his
Numidians thro' the Southern Gate; as soon as he hears of
this Attempt, without expecting the Success, or in the
least waiting for the Event, he cries out,

> Lucius, *the Torrent bears too hard upon me,*
> *Justice gives way to Force: The conquer'd World*
> *Is* Caesar's, Cato *has no Business in it.*

Is this, after all, his boasted Firmness? Is this the
Courage of a valiant Soldier, or the Magnanimity of a
Roman General, or the Impassiveness of an habitual *Stoick*,
or the undaunted invincible Resolution of an admired
Assertor of Liberty? Did ever weak Woman despair sooner,
or yield more tamely to a threatning Accident, before she
knew the Event of it?

There seems likewise to be an Inequality in the Manners
of *Cato*, from the Advice which he gives to *Portius*, in the
latter End of the Fourth Act. [Quotes IV. iv. 130-42.]

Does this look like the Advice of a Man, the predominant Quality of whose Character is the Love of his Country,
and who in the preceding Page saw with Tranquility his
other Son actually dead, and wept immediately afterwards
at the bare Prospect of his Country's Ruin? Is such a Man
consistent with himself, when he advises this Son to desert
his Country while 'tis in the utmost Danger, and instead of
joining the young *Pompey*, and the Remainder of the Republican Party, basely to retire to Solitude, and to submit to
the Conqueror?...

When ever could *Rome* demand more loudly that *Portius*
should venture his Life for her, than at this present Juncture? *Portius* himself is so sensible of his Duty in this
Case, that he makes his Father a fitting Answer, which
leaves no room for a Reply.

> *I hope my Father does not recommend*
> *A Life to* Portius *which he scorns himself.* (16)

The Father actually dies rather than take that Advice
which he gives to his Son; and he would have his Son so
base as to take that Advice, rather than bravely venture
his Life for his sinking Country.

Thus it is plain that there is an Inconsistency and an
Inequality in the Manners of *Cato*: And for the same Reason
too there is an Inconvenience; for the foresaid Advice is
by no means becoming of a faithful Lover of his Country.
Besides, as we observ'd above, if the Manners of *Cato* are
unequal, they are for that Reason ill mark'd: And if the
Manners in so known a Character are ill mark'd, it follows
that they are not resembling. But if 'tis objected here,
That there really was this Inconsistency and this Inequality in the Character of *Cato*, that he did actually give
that Advice to his Son, and therefore that the Character
is resembling: To that I answer, That the Poet either
ought not to have brought that Character on the Stage, or
to have sunk that Quality, or those Qualities in it which
made the Manners inconvenient.

As the Character of *Cato* is too virtuous for perfect

Tragedy, those of *Sempronius* and *Syphax* are too scandalous
for any Tragedy, Perfect or Imperfect. (17) The Author of
'Cato Examin'd', says after *Aristotle*, 'That there is a
sort of Satisfaction in the Punishment of the Wicked; but,
says he, 'it is neither Terror nor Pity, and therefore not
Tragical'. He complains that such scandalous Villanies
are brought upon our Stage, as are fitter for the Hangman's Correction than that of the Muse. I would fain know
whether the Villanies of *Sempronius* and *Syphax*, which are
Mutiny, Desertion and Treason are not of that Number....

Besides, The Character of *Sempronius* is an Usurpation
upon Comedy. For as Hypocrisy it self is by its Nature
Comical, and must be nicely manag'd at any Time to be
otherwise, the Counterfeiting a great Passion after *Sempronius* his manner, *viz.* with Mouthing and Bellowing ...
is undoubtedly very Ridiculous; and then for a Villain to
charge the Treason which he is apparently guilty of himself, upon one whom he and every one knows to be Honest,
as *Sempronius* in the second Act does his upon *Lucius*, is
certainly the very Height of Impudence, and is therefore
perfectly Comical.

Now that which aggravates the Faults of this Character
is, that the gross Dissimulation, join'd to the gross
Affectation that appears in *Sempronius*, is so far from
being necessary to the carrying on the Action of the Play,
that it has directly a Tendency to the producing an
Effect quite contrary to that for which *Sempronius* designs
it, which is to conceal himself from the *piercing Eyes of
Cato*. For gross Dissimulation join'd to gross Affectation
is enough to discover the Hypocrite, not only to *piercing
Eyes*, but even to common Discernments.

Nor is the Transcendent Villany of his Behaviour in the
third Act, towards the Leaders of the Mutiny, in the least
necessary for carrying on the Action of the Play, but has
so direct a Tendency to the discovering the Villany, that
one would think it impossible it should have any other
Effect; so that there are two gross Faults apparent in
this one Character, the Manners of it being in some Places
unnecessarily Villanous, and in others perfectly Comical.

As we have shewn above, that *Cato* is not the fittest
Character for Tragedy, because he is an old *Stoick*, so I
would fain know whether *Portius*, *Marcus*, *Juba*, and *Marcia*,
are so very proper for it, because they are young ones, or
at least are introduc'd as such....

Now I should be apt to think, that a Nest of *Stoicks*
could supply us, with no more proper Persons for an excellent Tragedy, than a Nest of Fools can do for an excellent
Comedy. But here if any of the Author's Friends should
urge in his Behalf, that tho' these Persons are introduc'd

as *Stoicks*, yet the Poet has given them nothing but the
Name, and that in the Sequel, they act more Termagantly,
than any Persons in the World besides themselves, *Stoicks*
or others, would do in their Circumstances, I must allow
that they are in the Right, but then this Question is
liable to be ask'd, Is there not upon this account, some
Inequality, some Inconsistency, and some Poetical badness
of the Manners in them? Is it convenient, is it consistent, or is it expected, that Persons who at first are
introduc'd as Philosophers, as *Romans*, as Lovers of their
Country, as dutiful and affectionate Children to the best
of Fathers, should play the whining Amorous Milk-Sops,
upon that very Day, when Reason is about to yield to
Force, Liberty to Tyranny, *Rome* to *Caesar*, and the sacred
Life of their Father to that universal Tyrant, Death?
when *Portius* in the first Act of this Play, gives *Sempronius* so good a Character of his Sister *Marcia*'s Dutiful-
ness, and her filial Affection and Tenderness. [Quotes I.
ii. 26-9.]

Does he not at the same time give a very wretched one
of his own and his Brother *Marcus*'s? Was it not their
Duty to shew as much Concern for their Father's Danger as
their Sister *Marcia* did? Was it not their Duty at the
same time to shew that they were still less than their
Sister in the Pow'r of soft effeminate Passions; as being
stronger both by Education and Nature, and far more capable both of *Roman* Resolution and of *Graecian* Philosophy....

But as *Marcia* is thus Different from her self, there is
still another strange Inequality, and a whimsical Inconsistency in her lusty Lover *Sempronius*, which we forgot
when we mention'd his Character before. The first time
Sempronius appears he discovers himself to be a Traytor
and a Lover. At his first Entrance he says,

Conspiracies no sooner should be form'd
Than executed.

In the next Page, he shews himself a Lover.

    O my Portius!
Could I but call that wond'rous Man my Father,
Would but thy Sister Marcia *be propitious*
To thy Friends Vows, I might be bless'd indeed. (18)

But Love appears to be his predominant Inclination.
For when he is alone, he declares that the chief Reason
why he is a Traytor is, because he is a Lover....
Thus we see to our great Surprize that *Sempronius* is no

Lover at last, that he is and ever has been incapable of the Soft

Unmanly Warmth, and Tenderness of Love. (19)

And 'tis very much for the Credit of the God of Love that he is so. But would any one have thought when he said to her Brother in the first Act,

> O my Portius!
> *Could I but call that wond'rous Man my Father,*
> *Would but thy Sister Marcia be propitious*
> *To thy Friends Vows, I might be bless'd indeed.*

That he aim'd at nothing but a single Assignation with her? Would one have Thought that by being *bless'd indeed*, he meant nothing, as Mrs. *Frail* said to Mrs. *Foresight*, but the being happy in a Hackney-Coach with her? Is this the Blessing that *Cato*, as he tells us in the first Act, had refus'd to his ardent Vows? Is it for the refusal of this Blessing that he turns Traytor to *Cato* and to his Country? And is this the Trifle which *Syphax* tells him in the second Act, that *Caesar* would not refuse him? Is it not strange, since Bully *Sempronius* was so rampant, that nothing but *Cato*'s Daughter would serve his Turn? And that no less a Pimp would serve him than *Caesar* and her own Father? *Syphax* and *Sempronius* have worthy Sentiments of the great *Caesar* indeed; who expected that he should abandon the Daughter of *Cato*, to be ravish'd by the very Villain who had betray'd her Father; that would have been wonderfully agreable to that Popularity which *Caesar* so much affected, and which was so much his Interest. *Lucius* it seems, and the rest of his Enemies, had more advantag-ious Opinions of *Caesar*, than his two worthy Friends here. For see what he says to *Cato*.

> *The Victor never will impose on Cato*
> *Ungenerous Terms, his Enemies confess*
> *The Virtues of Humanity are Caesar's.* (20)

Sempronius and his Friend *Syphax* seem very inconsistent with themselves, and with the other Characters in what they say or do in relation to *Juba* in the several Parts of this Tragedy. In the third Scene of the first Act *Sempronius* says to *Syphax*,

> *But tell me, hast thou yet drawn o'er young Juba?*
> *That still would recommend thee more to Caesar,*
> *And challenge better Terms.*

To which *Syphax* answers,

Alas! he's lost,
He's lost, Sempronius, *all his Thoughts are full*
Of Cato's *Virtues, but I'll try once more.*
    Semp. *Be sure to press upon him ev'ry Motive.*
Juba's *Surrender since his Father's Death*
Would give up Affrick *into* Caesar's *Hands,*
And make him Lord of half the burning Zone. (21)

And *Cato* says in the second Act, in order to animate
the assembled Senate,

Numidia's *spacious Kingdom lies behind us,*
Ready to rise at its young Prince's Call.
While there is Hope do not distrust the Gods. (22)

And *Syphax* likewise tells *Juba* in the same Act.

Juba *commands* Numidia's *hardy Troops,*
Mounted on Steeds unus'd to the restraint
Of Curbs or Bits, and fleeter than the Winds.
Give but the Word we'll snatch this Damsel up,
And bear her off. (23)

By all this now would not one imagine that this *Juba*
was a mighty Prince, of most formidable Interest, and
able to raise up a very powerful Confederacy against
Caesar? And yet this very *Sempronius* in the second Act,
tho' nothing had happen'd since his high Opinion of
Juba's Power, that could weaken his Interest, mentions
him as one of no Significancy. [Quotes II. vi. 21-6.]
    And *Syphax* treats him with the utmost Contempt, upon
which *Juba* puts this Question to him,

Is it because the Throne of my Fore-fathers
Still stands unfix'd, and that Numidia's *Crown*
Hangs doubtful yet whose Head it shall enclose;
That thou presum'st to treat thy Prince with Scorn? (24)

So that here not only *Syphax* considers him, but he re-
gards himself as a King *de Jure* only, and of no manner of
Power. How unlike to him, who was describ'd before in the
First Act as the Prince. [Quotes I. iii. 29-31.]
    And I would fain know whether *Sempronius* does not treat
him as a Wretch of no manner of *Consequence*, when in the
Fourth Act he attempts to kill him with his own Guards,
in the very Hall of the Governour; and yet in that very
Place, when *Sempronius* lies dead in *Juba*'s Garb, *Marcia*

mistakes him for that young Prince, because of his Regal
Ornaments. [Quotes IV. iii. 7-10.]
    And *Cato* expiring has the same Opinion of him that he
had in the assembled Senate.

> *A Senator of* Rome, *while* Rome *surviv'd,*
> *Would not have match'd his Daughter with a King,*
> *But* Caesar's *Arms have thrown down all Distinction.* (25)

Nor is *Juba* more consistent with himself in the Scene
between him and *Cato* in the Second Act, where he says to
Cato,

> *I'm charm'd whene'er thou talk'st, I pant for Virtue,*
> *And all my Soul endeavours at Perfection.*

By the way, *panting for Virtue* is a pretty brisk Metaphor. Virtue, they say, lies in the Middle; now the
Question is, whether the Virtue for which *Juba* pants is
not in the Middle of *Cato*'s Daughter? But that we shall
see immediately, *Cato* answers,

> *Dost thou love Watching, Abstinence and Toil,*
> *Laborious Vertues all, learn them from* Cato,
> *Success and Fortune must thou learn from* Caesar. (26)

Cato, who does not in the least dream that *Marcia* is
the Virtue that *Juba* pants for, immediately gives him
Charte Blanche. [Quotes II. iv. 71-2.]

> Cat. *What wou'dst thou say?*
> Jub. Cato, *thou hast a Daughter.*

Thus we see that *Juba* is for a Virtue that is not very
consistent with Abstinence; some Watching, indeed, and
Toil there may be in it: But *Cato*, in my Opinion, makes
him a very reasonable Reply. [Quotes II. iv. 75-8.]

> *It is not now a time to talk of ought*
> *But Chains or Conquest, Liberty or Death.*

This *Numidian*'s Desire to solace himself with the
Daughter, at a Time when the Knife was at the Throat of
the Father, is, methinks, something absurd; but the doing
a thing that is something absurd is one certain Sign of a
Lover.
    Thus have we endeavour'd to shew, That the Characters
in this Play are not proper for Tragedy; That the Manners
of them are for the most part ill mark'd, inconvenient,

inconsistent and unequal; and, That the Passions are
sometimes not agreeable to the Characters. We now come
to shew, That the Passions for the most part are not
Tragical, and that they are sometimes false.

And first we shall shew, That the Passions in this
Play, for the most part, are not Tragical. No Passion can
be justly esteem'd a Tragical Passion, but what is the
Cause or the Effect of a real Tragical Distress; that is,
of something which is in it self terrible or deplorable.
The Love therefore that reigns throughout the Tragedy of
Cato is not a Tragical Passion, because it produces no
real Tragical Distress, but a Distress which proceeds only
from the Whimsies or extravagant Caprices of the Lovers.

We have made it appear above, that *Sempronius* is no
Lover; and the Death of *Marcus* is by no means to be impu-
ted to Love, but to his Duty, to his Bravery, to his
Thirst of Glory....

From all which 'tis plain, that Love had not the least
Influence upon the Death of *Marcus*, nor is it mention'd,
or suppos'd, or so much as suspected to have had, by any
of the other Poetical Characters. If here it should be
objected, That the Parting of Lovers is deplorable, and
that consequently every thing that has a Tendency to that
Parting must excite Compassion, and that therefore the
Scene between *Portius* and *Lucia* in the Third Act is truly
Tragical: To that I answer, That I own the Parting of
Lovers to be deplorable, and that consequently every thing
that has a Tendency to that Parting must excite Compassion; but then that Parting must have a real compulsive,
or at least a reasonable Cause, and not proceed like
Lucia's Resolution to part with *Portius*, from Whimsey and
Fantasticalness; for in that Case we cannot believe that
the Lovers will really part, but that they will come to
their Senses again. Now we shall shew immediately, that
not only *Lucia*'s Resolution is fantastical, but that the
Passion in the Scene between her and *Portius* in the Third
Act, and that in the foregoing Scene between *Portius* and
Marcus, has not the least Foundation in Nature.

Marcus, who is represented so warm and so violent a
Lover, yet does not speak one Word to his Mistress thro'
the whole Play; and in the Beginning of the Third Act, he
who is by Nature bold and undertaking, applies himself to
Portius, who is cool and modest, to speak for him....

How dull is this young *Stoick* to believe, that any one
can plead for a Lover like himself, and not to know that
one Glance of a Lover is more capable of going to the
Heart of his Mistress, than all the Art and all the Genius
of the most accomplish'd Orator, and that the little blind
Boy-God is more eloquent and more persuasive than all the

rest of the Gods and Men together; for as to the Reason
that he alledges for this Desire....

But this absurd Petition of *Marcus* is necessary to
draw on the following fantastical Scene. (27)...

Now what can be the Meaning of all this? to make his
Mistress compassionate to his Rival? That for ought I
know may be very Heroick, but of this I am sure that there
is not one jot of Nature in it; for Lovers are jealous,
Women are inconstant, and Pity is often the Fore-runner
of Love....

The plain Meaning ... is, That *Portius* desires his
Mistress to play the Jilt either with himself or his
Brother. Upon which the Lady takes up an extraordinary
Resolution, and says to *Portius*,

> *I see thy Sister's Tears,*
> *Thy Father's Anguish, and thy Brother's Death,*
> *In the Pursuit of our ill-fated Love.*
> *And,* Portius, *here I swear, to Heav'n I swear,*
> *To Heav'n, and all the Pow'rs that judge Mankind,*
> *Never to mix my plighted Hands with thine,*
> *While such a Cloud of Mischiefs hangs about us;*
> *But to forget our Loves, and drive thee out*
> *From all my Thoughts, as far as I am able.* (28)

Which is as much as to say, That she resolves to leave
her Lover to hang himself, for fear his Rival should
drown himself. *Portius* shews in his Answer that he is
quick of Apprehension, and takes it so. [Quotes III. ii.
37-52.]...

And now I desire to ask the Reader, whether *Lucia*'s
Swooning upon *Portius*'s resolving to comply with her
Desire, does not shew more of an Histerical Fit, than of
the magnanimous Spirit of a *Roman* Lady, and of a Mind that
is constant and consistent with it self. For my part, I
always thought that the Passions in Tragedy were to be
produc'd by the Force of the Incidents, and not by the
Weakness of the Dramatical Persons. But *Portius* does not
come one jot behind her in Weakness.

> Ha! she faints.
> *What has my Rashness done? Wretch that I am!*
> Lucia, *thou injur'd Innocence! Thou best*
> *And loveliest of thy Sex! Awake my* Lucia,
> *Or* Portius *rushes on his Sword to join thee.*
> *Her Imprecations reach not to the Tomb,*
> *They shut not out Society in Death.* (29)

He fancies that she's gone for good, and resolves to

overtake her, when her Ladyship luckily recovers.

> O Portius, was this well, to frown on her,
> That lives upon thy Smiles, to call in doubt
> The Faith of one expiring at thy Feet,
> That loves thee more than ever Woman lov'd. (30)

But now she falls into a Relapse of her Histerical
Passion.

> What do I say! my half recover'd Sense
> Forgets the Vow in which my Soul is bound;
> Destruction stands betwixt us, we must part.
>   Port. Name not the Word, my frighted Thoughts run
>   back,
> And startle into Madness at the Sound,

And yet but a Moment pass'd he himself propos'd it.

>   Luc. What would'st thou have me do? consider well
> The Train of Ills our Love would draw behind it.
> Think, Portius, think, thou seest thy dying Brother
> Stab'd at his Heart, and all besmear'd with Blood,
> Storming at Heaven and thee. (31)

This visionary Conceit has taken strong Hold of her
Fancy, and now it seizes upon the Imagination of Portius.

>   Port. To my Confusion and eternal Grief,
> I must approve the Sentence that destroys me. (32)

Well! This is the first time that ever I knew that a
Fit of the Mother was catching. In the next Page her
Ladyship is at it again.

>   Port. Stay, Lucia, stay, what do'st thou say? for
>   ever!
>   Luc. Have I not sworn? If, Portius, thy Success
> Must throw thy Brother on his Fate, farewell,
> Oh! How shall I repeat the Words for ever?
>   Port. Thou must not go, my Soul still hovers o'er
>   thee,
> And can't get loose.
>   Luc. If the firm Portius shake
> To hear of parting, think what Lucia suffers!
>   Port. 'Tis true, unruffled and serene I've met
> The common Accidents of Life, but here
> Such an unlook'd for Storm of Ills falls on me,
> It beats down all my Strength, I cannot bear it,
> We must not part. (33)

Now the common Accidents of Life, which we have seen
him meet *unruffled and serene*, are, the Destruction of his
Country, the Ruin of Liberty, and the probable Approach of
his Father's Death.   And the *Storm of ills that beats down
all his Strength* is this Histerical Fancy of *Lucia*, that
Marcus will be forc'd, by the resistless Power of her
Beauty, to lay dead-doing Hands upon himself.
Thus do these two ingenious Persons contrive to torment
and plague one another, upon an Event which a thousand to
one is imaginary, and which, should it really happen, is
most certainly at a distance, and that is the Self-Murder
of *Marcus*, while they shew no Concern for the Death of
Cato, which they know is likely to happen that very Day,
and which they ought to be studying to prevent; nor for
the Approach of *Caesar*'s Army, which is expected at *Utica*
that very Night, whose Arrival may not improbably be
attended with the Death of *Portius* and *Lucius*; and upon
whose Arrival likewise her whimsical Ladyship her self may,
for any thing she knows, have a delicate green Gown given
her, by some rampant Tribune, or some brawny Centurion.
Of the very few excellent Tragedies which we have upon
our *English* Stage, the 'Orphan' is that which the Author
of 'Cato' seems to have had most an Eye to.   There is in
the 'Orphan' an old moralizing Gentleman, who has two Sons
and a Daughter; there is likewise in the Family another
Lady, who is not a Relation but in their Affections, to
whom the Brothers, tho' Friends, are Rivals.   So that
there is a Resemblance we see between both the Subject
and Characters of the 'Orphan' and 'Cato'.   But now let
us see the Difference that is to be found in the Conduct
of them.   The Passions of *Castalio* and *Polidor* for *Monimia*,
a charming Maid, in the Flower of Youth and Beauty, and
of *Monimia* for *Castalio*, an agreeable Youth; these Passions in the above-nam'd Persons, who are all of them in
the same Family, in the Quiet and Retirement of a Country
Life, and in full Ease and Prosperity, are very natural,
and in high probability; whereas the Passions of *Marcus*
and *Portius*, and of *Marcia* and *Lucia* are unseasonable,
and highly improbable.   The Rivalship in 'Cato' produces
nothing, whereas that in the 'Orphan' is the Cause of a
most deplorable Distress, and a most moving Catastrophe;
for tho' *Castalio* and *Polidor* are represented to be as
warm Friends as *Marcus* and *Portius* can be, yet each of
them strives to succeed in his Love, to the Disadvantage
of the other, which is acting according to Nature, for
Love, like Ambition, can endure no equal, whereas in
'Cato', as we have seen above, a Lover pleads for his
Rival.   In 'Cato', *Marcus* knows nothing of his Brother's
Passion, which is very improbable, since that *Portius* had

been some time in Love with *Lucia* as well as *Marcus*; that
they are all three, as far as we can see, in the same
House; and that Love, tho' he is painted blind, yet has
Eyes as sharp as an Eagle. Nor is it only improbable,
this Ignorance of *Marcus*, but it has likewise no manner
of Consequence. In the 'Orphan', *Castalio* boasts of his
Passion, and is resolv'd to maintain the Birth-Right of
it; that which he conceals is his Intention of Marriage,
which is a great deal more easy to be conceal'd than Love,
and which it is highly probable that one in *Castalio*'s
Circumstances would conceal, least it should come to his
Father's Ear by his Brother's Resentment; but that pro-
able Concealment has a surprizing and dreadful Consequence, which plunges all three into an Abyss of Woe. The
Characters in 'Cato' are represented as Philosophers all;
whereas in the 'Orphan' they are in that Mediocrity which
is requir'd by *Aristotle*, neither wicked and profligate,
nor sovereignly Virtuous, but rather good than wicked.
And the Calamities of all three are occasion'd by Faults
which *Aristotle* terms involuntary, that is, by Faults
occasion'd by the Force of an outrageous Passion. The
Fault of *Castalio*, is dissembling with his Brother, and
marrying *Monimia*, without the Knowledge or Consent of his
Father; that of *Monimia* is the marrying *Castalio*, without
the Knowledge and Consent of his Father, who was her
Benefactor; that of *Polidor*, is dissembling with his
Brother, and the debauching *Monimia* without her Consent,
contrary to the Rights of Hospitality, and that Veneration that was due to his Father's Protection and Guardian-
ship; which Faults in all of them proceed from the Violence of a Passion, which is admirably painted by the most
ingenious Author. And the Moral, tho' not express'd at
the End of the Play, yet most intelligibly implied, is a
wholesome, but terrible Instruction to an Audience to
beware of clandestine Marriages, which involv'd a Family
so happy before in such fatal Disasters. I know very well
that there are Faults in the Conduct of the 'Orphan', but
its Faults are light in Comparison of its Justness and
Beauties. And as there are few Tragedies upon any Stage,
ancient or modern, in which Compassion is mov'd to a
greater Degree, 'tis a sure Sign that it has its Foundation for the most part in Nature.

Nor is the Grief of *Cato* in the fourth Act, one Jot
more in Nature than that of his Son and *Lucia* in the
Third: *Cato* receives the News of his Sons Death not only
with dry Eyes, but with a sort of Satisfaction, and in
the same Page sheds Tears for the Calamity of his
Country, and does the same thing in the next Page, upon
the bare Apprehension of the Danger of his Friends. Now,

since the Love of one's Country is the Love of one's
Countrymen, as I have shewn upon another Occasion, I
desire leave to ask these Questions, Of all our Countrymen which do we love most, those whom we know, or those
whom we know not? And of those whom we know, which do we
cherish most, our Friends, or our Enemies? And of our
Friends, which are the dearest to us, those who are related to us, or those who are not? And of all our Relations, for which have we most Tenderness, for those who
are near to us, or for those who are remote? And of our
near Relations which are the nearest and consequently the
dearest to us, our Offspring or others? Our Offspring
most certainly, as Nature, or in other Words, Providence
has wisely contriv'd for the Preservation of Mankind. Now,
does it not follow from what has been said, That for a Man
to receive the News of his Son's Death with dry Eyes, and
to weep at the same time for the Calamities of his Country, is a wretched Affectation and a miserable Inconsistency? Is not that in plain *English* to receive with dry
Eyes the News of the Deaths of those, for whose Sake our
Country is a Name so dear to us, and at the same time to
shed Tears for those for whose Sakes our Country is not a
Name so dear to us? Upon the Danger of a Man's Country or
his Friends, Reason and Duty require that he should appear
concern'd. Upon the untimely Death of a brave Son,
Nature and Instinct require that he should shed Tears, or
at least that he should feel a Grief great enough to produce that Effect. Now, is not this a pleasant Conduct,
and a merry Philosophy, when a Man appears melting into
Tears where only a bare Concern is requir'd; and appears
with dry Eyes and a calm Heart, where Nature requires a
Flood of Tears, and the most moving Tenderness? If this
were Nature in *Cato*, it would be Nature in other Men.
For tho' we should grant that *Cato* had more Virtue than
other Men, yet great Virtue is in no Men express'd and
shewn by Passion, and in Philosophers less than others,
and least of all in *Stoicks*. One Man indeed may have more
Virtue than another, by the Rigour of his Discipline, or
by the Excellence of his Nature; but the Springs of Passion are the same in all. Philosophy indeed may help to
restrain our Passions, but it never pretended to make them
rise. 'Tis only Nature that can do that, and Nature is
the same in all.
      But granting that 'tis commendable for a Man to shed
Tears for the Danger of his Country, and to behold with
dry Eyes a gallant Son lying dead before him of an untimely Fate, yet, why Tears for his Friends, and none for
his Son? Tears for the bare Prospect of their Calamity,
and none for the certain Destruction of a gallant Son.

There may be Stoicism and Romantick Honour in this for
ought I know, but is there Reason, is there Nature in it?
Is not this a downright Rebellion against Reason, against
Nature, against Providence? Is not this bringing an artificial Character upon the Stage, instead of a natural one?
And is an artificial Character proper for Tragedy, which
is an Imitation of Nature, and whose chief Excellence consists in describing a natural Sorrow?

We have hitherto shewn the Faults that this Author has
committed for want of observing the Rules. We shall now
shew the Absurdities with which he abounds thro' a too
nice observing some of them, without any manner of Judgment or Discretion. The Unities of Time and Place are
mechanick Rules, which, if they are observ'd with Judgment,
strengthen the reasonableness of the Incidents, heighten
the probability of the Action, promote the agreeable
Deceit of the Representation, and add Cleanliness, Grace,
and Comeliness to it. But if they are practis'd without
Discretion, they render the Action more improbable, and
the Representation more absurd, as an unworthy Performance
turns an Act of the highest Devotion into an Act of the
greatest Sin.

I have already mention'd some Indecencies and Improbabilities which are in the Conduct of this Play, which,
tho' I have mention'd them upon other Occasions, yet are
chiefly deriv'd from the indiscreet Observance of the
Unity of Time. 'Tis the Unity of Time that makes the
Manners of the Dramatick Persons very indecent, and the
Passions very improper and unbecoming. But this will
appear more clearly, when we come to consider the Unity
of Time and the Unity of Place together, and to give the
Reader a View of the Scenery as far as is consistent with
the Compass which I have prescrib'd to my self.

Aristotle tells us, that a Tragick Poet ought to take
care, that there be no Incident in his Tragedy which is
without Reason: From whence it follows, that there ought
to be a clear Reason for the Entrance or Exit of each
Dramatick Person, at that particular Time when he enters
upon, or leaves the Place of Action, which is so far from
being observ'd in this Tragedy, that there are often the
strongest Reasons why the Persons of it ought to be in
another Place, than in that in which we behold them. In
order to the making this appear, let us consider the Time
and Place at which the Action of the Play begins. The
Action of this Play is in the great Hall of the Governor
of *Utica*'s Palace, and it begins at the Point of Day....

Portius tells us this, who appears in this great Hall
with his Brother *Marcus* at that early Hour; the Question
is, what they came for? As I did not see the Play acted,

I want to know in what Posture the Brothers appear'd
first, and whether there was upon the Stage a Table with
Candles on it, for as it was but just Dawn, and that Dawn
was over-cast, it must be very Dark in the Hall, so dark,
methinks, that it should be impossible for People within
Doors, to tell whether it were Dawn or no; unless they
talk'd to one another with their Heads out at the Window.
For my part, if I had not seen the Governour of *Utica*'s
large Hall underneath the *Dramatis Personae*, I should have
imagin'd by the two first Lines of the Play that the Scene
had lay'n without Doors; but this is a Trifle in Comparison of what follows. The two Persons who open this Play
are the Sons of *Cato*, two young Men, who profess a great
Love for their Country, and a high Esteem for their
Father; and who besides are by Birth *Romans*, and by Discipline *Stoicks*; and who tell us in the very fourth Line
of the Play, that that Day is like to be the last of their
Father's Life, and of their Country's Liberty.

> *The Dawn is over-cast, the Morning low'rs,*
> *And heavily in Clouds brings on the Day;*
> *The great, th' important Day, big with the Fate*
> *Of* Cato *and of* Rome.

The Question is, whether after they have begun the
Play by declaring this, the Transition to Love is not very
forc'd and unnatural. No noble *Roman* who had been concern'd for his Country, would have thought of Love on that
Day, on which he expected that his Country would lose its
Liberty, much less ought two Persons to have done it, who
at the same time that they were *Romans*, were the Sons and
Disciples of *Cato*. The Place was, as it were, a publick
Place, the Hall of their Father's Palace, where they did
not know but their Indecencies might be over-heard,
especially when it was yet but Dusk, and they could
hardly see one another; and their Father us'd to be an
earlier Man than his Children....
Now I appeal to the Reader, whether *Cato*, if he had
over-heard them, would not have thought them fine *Romans*,
fine *Stoicks*, and delicate dutiful Children? *Marcus*, at
the latter End of this first Scene, says to *Portius*.

> Marc. *A Brother's Sufferings claim a Brother's*
> > *Pity.*
> Port. *Heav'n knows I pity thee! Behold my Eyes.*
> *Ev'n whilst I speak - Do they not swim in Tears?*
> *Were but my Heart as naked to thy View,*
> Marcus *would see it bleed in his Behalf.* (34)

Were ever Tears so wrongly plac'd before? When he told
us above, that that Day was like to be the last of his
Father's Life, and his Country's Liberty, we then neither
saw nor heard of his swimming Eyes, or his bleeding Heart;
and yet that sure was a juster Occasion for them, than the
untimely, unworthy effeminate Passion of *Marcus*. Are
these *Romans*? Are these Philosophers? Are these the
Sons and Disciples of *Cato*?

Nor is there a better Reason to be given, why *Marcus*
leaves the Stage at present, than why he and his Brother
enter'd upon it. For the Reason which he gives for it
himself is much stronger, why *Portius*, who stays, should
do the same.

> Marc. Sempronius *comes.*
> *He must not find this Softness hanging on me.* (35)

Now *Marcus* had nothing to do to hide his Softness, but
to hold his Tongue, whereas *Portius* had swimming Eyes,
and a bleeding Heart. The true Reason why the Author
makes *Marcus* leave the Stage here, is, that he wanted to
be rid of him upon any frivolous Pretence.

Well! But what brings *Sempronius*, who now enters the
Hall of the Governor's Palace, so early? why, he comes to
meet old *Syphax*, as is plain from his Soliloquy. [Quotes
I. ii. 48-50.]

Well! but for what does *Sempronius* come to meet old
Syphax? Why to conspire, to plot! Against whom?
Against the Governor and the Senate. Where? In the
Governour's Hall. When? Just before the meeting of the
Senate, because then there were sure to be People there.
I appeal to the Reader now if these are not close poli-
tick Persons; and if an Author, who makes his Characters,
carry on a Conspiracy against a Governour in his own Hall,
had not need to be as dexterous as Mr. *Bays* is at the
penning a Whisper. (36)...

Upon the Departure of *Portius*, *Sempronius* makes but one
Soliloquy, and immediately in comes *Syphax*, and then the
two Politicians are at it immediately. They lay their
Heads together, with their Snuff-boxes in their Hands, as
Mr. *Bays* has it, and fegue it away. But in the midst of
that wise Scene, *Syphax* seems to give a seasonable Caution to *Sempronius*.

> *But is it true,* Sempronius, *that your Senate
> Is call'd together? Gods! Thou must be cautious,*
> Cato *has piercing Eyes.* (37)

There is a great deal of Caution shewn indeed, in

meeting in a Governour's own Hall to carry on their Plot
against him. Whatever Opinion they have of his Eyes, I
suppose they had none of his Ears, or they would never
have talk'd at this foolish rate so near him.

> *Gods!   Thou must be cautious*

Oh! Yes, very cautious; for if *Cato* should over-hear
you, and turn you off for Politicians, *Caesar* would never
take you, no, *Caesar* would never take you.

Thus have we laid before the Reader some of the Conduct, and some of the Sentiments in the first Act, which
are relatively absurd, that is with Relation to Time and
Place. There are Sentiments in it which are absolutely
so, to which perhaps we may return, when we come to treat
of the Sentiments. But let us now proceed to the second
Act.

When *Cato* in Act 2 Turns the Senators out of the Hall,
upon pretence of acquainting *Juba* with the Result of
their Debates, he appears to me to do a thing which is
neither reasonable nor civil. *Juba* might certainly have
better been made acquainted with the Result of that
Debate in some private Apartment of the Palace. But the
Poet was driven upon this Absurdity to make way for
another, and that is to give *Juba* an Opportunity to
demand *Marcia* of her Father. But the Quarrel and Rage of
Juba and *Syphax*, in the same Act, the Invectives of
Syphax against the *Romans* and *Cato*, the Advice that he
gives *Juba*, in her Father's Hall, to bear away *Marcia* by
Force; and his brutal and clamourous Rage upon his Refusal, and at a time when *Cato* was scarce out of Sight, and
perhaps not out of hearing; at least some of his Guards
or Domesticks must necessarily be suppos'd to be within
hearing, is a Thing that is so far from being probable,
that it is hardly possible.

But because the Quarrel and Reconcilement between *Juba*
and *Syphax*, the Prince and the General, in this Scene of
'Cato', seems to be an Imitation of the Quarrel and
Reconcilement in the Scene between *Anthony* and *Ventidius*,
the Prince and the General, in the First Act of 'All for
Love', I shall endeavour to shew how infinitely short the
Copy comes of the Original. The Quarrel and Reconcile-
ment between *Anthony* and *Ventidius* are pleasing for the
following Reasons. *Ventidius* appears to be perfectly hon-
est, and perfectly a Friend to *Anthony*; he begins the
Scene with an unfeigned Declaration of his Affection and
Tenderness for *Anthony*, which is prepar'd to make the
greater Impression, by the noble Character which even
Alexas, *Ventidius*'s greatest Enemy, gives of him.

Ventidius gives the greatest Proof of his Zeal for
Anthony's Service, and a Proof of the greatest Importance
to him in his present Emergency, in the twelve Legions he
brings to him. The naming of that Proof naturally brings
him to the Mention of *Cleopatra*, and to the telling
Anthony a little too roughly of his greatest Fault, which
had brought him to the very Brink of Ruin, and would infallibly plunge him into the Abyss of it, if he persever'd in
it. And yet the very Rudeness of this Remonstrance proceeds from the Zeal and Affection of *Ventidius*, and aims
at the true Interest and the Honour of *Anthony*. But
Anthony, too warm to make these Reflections, wholly mistakes him, and calls him Traytor upon it, which gives the
justest Occasion in the World for a Turn towards a Reconcilement; for upon that *Ventidius* gives an undeniable
Proof of his Fidelity, by putting him in Mind, that had he
been a Traytor, he had certainly carry'd his twelve
Legions to *Octavius*'s Camp. Upon this *Anthony* relents,
and the Reconcilement is as warm as the Quarrel had been
violent, and is upon this Account delightful, because 'tis
entirely to both their Satisfactions, and for both their
Interests. And as the Conduct thro' the whole Scene is
very just, the whole Scene is writ with a Warmth and a
Spirit, and with a Strength and a Dignity of Expression
that are worthy of the noble Occasion.

The Scene between *Juba* and *Syphax* has in it the very
counterpart of every thing which recommends the other.
The Audience before it begins knows *Syphax* to be a Traytor to *Juba*, and a Villain. *Syphax* begins it like a
Clown and a Brute, with Rallery too low and too gross for
Comedy. The Advice that he gives to *Juba* tends to his
Infamy, if it does not tend to his Ruin. Because *Juba*
will not take that Advice, *Syphax*, like a true Villain,
enrag'd at the Virtue and Integrity of his Master,
affronts him in the grossest manner. *Juba* truly and
justly calls him Traytor upon it; whereas *Anthony*, when he
gave that Language to *Ventidius*, said in his Passion what
he did not think. *Syphax*, upon hearing that terrible Reproach, is not concern'd as *Ventidius* was, for his own
Honour, or for his Master's Unkindness; for *Syphax* knew
himself to be ten times more a Villain than *Juba* believ'd
him to be; but for the vile Safety of his superannuated
Carcass, which obliges him to dissemble a Submission,
which brings on the Appearance of a Reconcilement, that
causes Indignation instead of Satisfaction to the sensible part of an Audience; which must know it to be per-
fidious on the part of *Syphax*, and like to prove fatal
to the Imbecillity of *Juba*. Now add to all this, that Air
of Affectation with which the whole Scene is writ, and

that Absurdity of Sentiments with relation to Time and
Place, which we mention'd above, and then let the Reader
consider what an Imitation this is of the noble Scene
between *Anthony* and *Ventidius*.

Sempronius, in the Second Act, comes back once more in
the same Morning to the Governour's Hall, to carry on the
Conspiracy with *Syphax* against the Governour, his Country
and his Family; which is so stupid, that 'tis below the
Wisdom of the *O——'s*, (38) the *Mac's*, and the *Teague's*;
even *Eustace Commins* (39) himself would never have gone to
Justice-Hall, to have conspir'd against the Government.
If any Officers at *Portsmouth* should lay their Heads
together, in order to the carrying off *J—— G——'s* (40)
Niece or Daughter, would they meet in *J—— G——'s* Hall
to carry on that Conspiracy? There would be no Necessity
for their meeting there, at least till they came to the
Execution of their Plot, because there would be other
Places to meet in. There would be no Probability that
they should meet there, because there would be Places more
private and more commodious. Now there ought to be nothing in a Tragical Action but what is necessary or probable.

But Treason is not the only thing that is carried on in
this Hall. That and Love and Philosophy take their Turns
in it, without any manner of Necessity or Probability,
occasion'd by the Action, as duly and as regularly without
interrupting one another, as if there were a triple League
between them, and a mutual Agreement, that each should
give place to and make way for the other in a due and
orderly Succession.

We come now to the Third Act. *Sempronius* in this Act
comes into the Governour's Hall with the Leaders of the
Mutiny. I have already mention'd that the unparallel'd
Villany of his Behaviour, while *Cato* is with them, is no
way necessary for the carrying on the Action of the Play.
But as soon as *Cato* is gone, *Sempronius*, who but just
before had acted like an unparallel'd Knave, discovers
himself like an egregious Fool to be an Accomplice in the
Conspiracy.

> *Know, Villains, when such paltry Slaves presume*
> *To mix in Treason, if the Plot succeeds*
> *They're thrown neglected by; but if it fails,*
> *They're sure to die like Dogs, as you shall do.*
> *Here, take these factious Monsters, drag them forth*
> *To sudden Death.* (41)

'Tis true, indeed, the second Leader says there are
none there but Friends; but is that possible at such a

Juncture? Can a Parcel of Rogues attempt to assassinate
the Governour of a Town of War in his own House, in Mid-
day, and after they are discover'd and defeated? Can
there be none near them but Friends? Is it not plain
from these Words of *Sempronius,*

> *Here, take these factious Monsters, drag them forth*
> *To sudden Death.*

And from the Entrance of the Guards upon the Word of Command, that those Guards were within Ear-shot? Behold
Sempronius then palpably discover'd. How comes it to
pass then, that instead of being hang'd up with the rest
he remains secure in the Governour's Hall, and there carries on his Conspiracy against the Government, the third
time in the same Day, with his old Comrade *Syphax?* who
enters at the same time that the Guards are carrying away
the Leaders, big with the News of the Defeat of *Sempronius*; tho' where he had his Intelligence so soon, is difficult to imagine. And now the Reader may expect a very
extraordinary Scene: There is not abundance of Spirit
indeed, nor a great deal of Passion, but there is Wisdom
more than enough to supply all Defects.

> Syph. *Our first Design, my Friend, has prov'd*
> *abortive,*
> *Still there remains an After-game to play;*
> *My Troops are mounted, their* Numidian *Steeds*
> *Snuff up the Winds, and long to scour the Desart;*
> *Let but* Sempronius *lead us in our Flight,*
> *We'll force the Gate where* Marcus *keeps his Guard,*
> *And hew down all that would oppose our Passage;*
> *A Day will bring us into* Caesar's *Camp.*
> Semp. *Confusion! I have fail'd of half my Purpose:*
> Marcia, *the charming* Marcia's *left behind.* (42)

Well! but tho' he tells us the half Purpose that he
has fail'd of, he does not tell us the half that he has
carried. But what does he mean by

Marcia, *the charming* Marcia's *left behind?*

He is now in her own House, and we have neither seen
her, nor heard of her any where else since the Play began.
But now let us hear *Syphax.*

> Syph. *How! will* Sempronius *turn a Woman's Slave?*
> Semp. *Think not thy Friend can ever feel the soft*
> *Unmanly Warmth and Tenderness of Love.*

> Syphax, *I long to clasp that haughty Maid,*
> *And bend her stubborn Virtue to my Passion;*
> *When I had gone thus far, I'd cast her off.*
>   Syph. *Well said! That's spoken like thy self,*
>   Sempronius.
> *What hinders then but that thou find her out,*
> *And hurry her away by manly Force.* (43)

But what does old *Syphax* mean by finding her out? They
talk as if she were as hard to be found as a Hare in a
frosty Morning.

>   Semp. *But how to gain Admission?*

Oh! She is found out then, it seems. She is at Home
at last. The subtle Toad, it seems, has been in her Bed-
chamber with her; and that makes him talk of his having
left her behind. And now we have both Halves of his Purpose, both that which he has carried, and that which he
has fail'd of. He has had *Marcia*, and he has left her
behind. But I am afraid that *Sempronius* had not behav'd
himself so vigorously as he ought to have done, and that
makes him doubt of a second Admission.

> *But how to gain Admission? for Access*
> *Is giv'n to none but* Juba *and her Brothers.* (44)

But raillery a part, why Access to *Juba*? for he was
own'd and receiv'd as a Lover neither by the Father,
nor by the Daughter. Well! but let that pass, *Syphax*
puts *Sempronius* out of Pain immediately, and being a
Numidian, abounding in Wiles, supplies him with a Stratagem for Admission, that I believe is a *non pareillo*.

>   Syph. *Thou shalt have* Juba's *Dress, and* Juba's
>   Guards,
> *The Doors will open, when* Numidia's *Prince*
> *Seems to appear before them.* (45)

Sempronius is, it seems, to pass for *Juba* in full Day,
at *Cato*'s House, where they were both so very well known,
by having *Juba*'s Dress and his Guards; as if one of the
Marshals of *France* could pass for the Duke of *Bavaria* at
Noon-Day at *Versailles*, by having his Dress and his Liv-
eries. But how does *Syphax* pretend to help *Sempronius* to
young *Juba*'s Dress? Does he serve him in a double Capacity, as General and Master of his Wardrobe? But why
Juba's Guards? For the Devil of any Guards has *Juba*
appear'd with yet. Well! Tho' this is a mighty politick

Invention, yet methinks they might have done without it.
For, since the Advice that *Syphax* gave to *Sempronius*, was

   To hurry her away by manly Force. (46)

In my Opinion the shortest and likeliest Way of coming at
the Lady was by demolishing, instead of putting on an impertinent Disguise to circumvent two or three Slaves.
But *Sempronius*, it seems, is of another Opinion. He
extols to the Skies the Invention of old *Syphax*.

   Heavens! What a Thought was there? (47)

   Now I appeal to the Reader, if I have not been as good
as my Word. Did not I tell him that I would lay before
him a very wise Scene?

   Dixi in his esse Elegantiam Atticam? (48)

   But I have one Remark more to make, before I take my
leave, for the present, of this third Act, and that is,
that I have not often met with, a more civil, officious,
obliging Person to his Friend than old *Syphax*. He is for
helping his Friends to Diversion, with as little Ceremony
as may be. First he offers his Service to *Juba*; and now
he is for obliging his Friend *Sempronius*. He appears to
have an extraordinary regard for the Daughter of *Cato*,
and is resolv'd that she shall have it one way or other,
at any rate. And because he wisely considers, that
Women are to be struggl'd with to bring them to what they
desire, he, that he may lay a double Obligation upon her,
is resolv'd, both to help her to pleasure, and to a just
Apology for it.
   But now let us lay before the Reader that part of the
Scenary of the fourth Act, which may shew the Absurdities
which the Author has run into, thro' the indiscreet
Observance of the Unity of Place. I do not remember that
Aristotle has said any thing expresly concerning the
Unity of Place. 'Tis true, implicitely he has said
enough in the Rules which he has laid down for the Chorus.
For by making the *Chorus* an essential Part of Tragedy,
and by bringing it upon the Stage immediately after the
opening of the Scene, and retaining it there till the
very Catastrophe, he has so determin'd and fix'd the
Place of Action, that it was impossible for an Author
upon the *Graecian* Stage to break thro' that Unity. I am
of Opinion, that if a modern Tragick Poet can preserve
the Unity of Place, without destroying the Probability of
the Incidents, 'tis always best for him to do it, because

by the Preservation of that Unity, as we have taken
notice above, he adds Grace and Cleanness, and Comeliness
to the Representation. But since there are no express
Rules about it, and we are under no Compulsion to keep
it, since we have no Chorus, as the *Graecian* Poet had; if
it cannot be preserv'd without rendring the greater Part
of the Incidents unreasonable and absurd, and perhaps
sometimes monstrous; 'tis certainly better to break it.

But to come close to our Business, *Lucia* and *Marcia*
are the two Persons who open the fourth Act; *Lucia*, with
the Relicks of her Histerical Fit on her.

> *Now tell me*, Marcia, *tell me from thy Soul,*
> *If thou believ'st it possible for Women*
> *To suffer greater ills than* Lucia *suffers.*

So that we see she is still possess'd with the Vision
of what her Beauty will drive poor *Marcus* to. But while
she is tormented with one Vision her self, she is
resolv'd to Plague her Friend *Marcia* with another.

> *I know thou'rt doom'd alike to be belov'd*
> *By* Juba, *and thy Father's Friend* Sempronius;
> *But shou'd this Father give you to* Sempronius,

Upon which *Marcia* uses a pertinent Expostulation with
her.

> *Why wilt thou add to all the Griefs I suffer*
> *Imaginary Ills and fancy'd Tortures?*

And afterwards makes her a very reasonable Proposal,

> *Let us retire, and see if we can drown*
> *Each softer Thought in Sense of present Danger.* (49)

Had she but made this Proposal to her, before *Lucia's*
meeting with *Portius* in the Third Act, it might have
sav'd her a dreadful Fit of the Vapours. But they
depart, and now comes Bully *Sempronius*, comically
accoutred, and equip'd with his *Numidian* Dress and his
Numidian Guards. Let the Reader attend to him with all
his Ears, for the Words of the Wise are precious.

> *The Deer is lodg'd, I've tracked her to her Covert.*

Now I would fain know, why this Deer is said to be
lodg'd, since we have not heard one Word since the Play
began of her being at all out of Harbour; and if we consider

the Discourse with which she and *Lucia* begin the Act, we
have Reason to believe that they had hardly been talking
of such Matters in the Street. However, to pleasure
Sempronius, let us suppose for once that the Deer is
lodg'd.

   The Deer is lodg'd, I've track'd her to her Covert.(50)

   If he had seen her in the open Field, what Occasion had
he to track her, when he had so many *Numidian* Dogs at his
Heels, which with one Halloo he might have set upon her
Haunches? If he did not see her in the open Field, how
could he possibly track her? This Metaphor *track* is of
the Number of those, that render a Discourse both obscure
and ambiguous. But Rhetorick apart, if he had seen her in
the Street, why did he not set upon her in the Street,
since thro' the Street she must be carry'd at last? Now
here instead of having his Thoughts upon his Business, and
upon the present Danger, instead of meditating and con-
triving how he shall pass with his Mistress thro' the
Southern Gate, where her Brother *Marcus* is upon the Guard,
and where she would certainly prove an *Impediment* to him,
which is the *Roman* Word for the Baggage; instead of
doing this, *Sempronius* is entertaining himself with Whimsies.

   How will the young Numidian *rave to see*
   His Mistress lost? If ought could glad my Soul
   Beyond th' Enjoyment of so bright a Prize,
   'T would be to torture that young gay Barbarian.
   But heark! what Noise? Death to my Hopes, 'tis he,
   'Tis Juba's *self! There is but one Way left,*
   He must be murder'd, and a Passage cut
   Thro' those his Guards. (51)

   Pray what are these his Guards? I thought at present
that *Juba*'s Guards had been *Sempronius*'s Tools, and had
now been dangling after his Heels. But now let us see
what *Juba* says upon seeing him,

   What do I see? Who's this that dares usurp
   The Guards and Habits of Numidia's *Prince?*

We see here that *Juba* does but ask him a pertinent
Question, when he very rudely makes him an impertinent
Answer,

   Semp. *One that was born to scourge thy Arrogance,*
Presumptuous Youth.

Now what is this Arrogance, and what this mighty Presumption? Where lies the Arrogance and the Presumption of
a Man's laying claim to his own Cloaths, when he sees them
upon another Man's Back? If the Meaning of the Word
Arrogance is taking to a Man's self what does not belong
to him, the Reader may easily judge on whose side the
Arrogance lies. Well! *Juba* is amaz'd at this Extravagance of *Sempronius*, and so I make no doubt is the Reader.

> Jub.   *What can this mean*, Sempronius?

Sempronius, who is but for a Word and a Blow, replies,

> Semp.   *My Sword shall answer thee, have at thy*
> *Heart.*
> Jub.   *Nay then beware thy own, proud barbarous Man.*
> (52)

Upon which *Juba* kills him, and upon that *Juba*'s own
Guards surrender themselves Prisoners to *Juba*; when that
Paper-Serpent *Sempronius* goes off with the following
Bounce.

> *Curse on my Stars! Am I then doom'd to fall*
> *By a Boy's Hand? Disfigur'd in a vile*
> Numidian *Dress? And for a worthless Woman?* (53)

'Tis not twenty Lines above, that this worthless
Woman was a bright Prize. But Loss of Blood may pall the
Imagination of the most vigorous Lover. But now let us
sum up all these Absurdities together. *Sempronius* goes
at Noon-day, in *Juba*'s Cloaths, and with *Juba*'s Guards
to *Cato*'s Palace, in order to pass for *Juba*, in a
Place where they were both so very well known; he meets
Juba there, and resolves to murder him with his own
Guards. Upon the Guards appearing a little bashful, he
threatens them,

> *Ha! Dastards, do you tremble?*
> *Or act like Men, or by yon azure Heav'n!* (54)

But the Guards still remaining restiff, *Sempronius*
himself attacks *Juba*, while each of the Guards is
representing Mr. 'Spectator's' Sign of the Gaper, aw'd, it
seems, and terrified by *Sempronius*'s Threats. *Juba* kills
Sempronius, and takes his own Army Prisoners, and carries
them in Triumph away to *Cato*. Now I would fain know if
any part of Mr. *Bay*'s Tragedy is so full of Absurdity as
this.

Upon hearing the Clash of Swords, *Lucia* and *Marcia* come
in. The Question is, why no Men came in upon hearing the
Noise of Swords in the Governour's Hall? Where was the
Governour himself? Where were his Guards? Where were his
Servants? Such an Attempt as this so near the Person of a
Governour of a Place of War, was enough to alarm the whole
Garrison; and yet for almost half an Hour after *Sempronius*
was kill'd, we find none of those appear, who were the
likeliest in the World to be alarm'd; and the Noise of
Swords is made to draw only two poor Women thither, who
were most certain to run away from it. Upon *Lucia* and
Marcia's coming in, *Lucia* appears in all the Symptoms of
an Histerical Gentlewoman....
     She fancies that there can be no cutting of Throats,
but it must be for her. If this is Tragical, I would fain
know what is Comical. Well! upon this they spy the Body
of *Sempronius*, and *Marcia* deluded by the Habit, it
seems, takes him for *Juba*, for, says she,

The Face is muffled up within the Garment. (55)

     Now how a Man could fight and fall with his Face muf-
fled up in his Garment, is, I think, a little hard to
conceive. Besides, *Juba* before he kill'd him knew him to
be *Sempronius*. It was not by his Garment that he knew
this, it was by his Face then; his Face therefore was not
muffled. Upon seeing this Man with the muffled Face,
Marcia falls a raving, and owning her Passion for the
suppos'd Defunct, begins to make his Funeral-Oration.
Upon which *Juba* enters listning, I suppose, on Tip-toe;
for I cannot imagine how any one can enter listning in
any other Posture. I would fain know how it came to pass,
that during all this time he had sent no body, no, not so
much as a Candle-snuffer, to take away the dead Body of
Sempronius. Well! but let us regard him listning.
Having left his Apprehension behind him, he at first
applies what *Marcia* says to *Sempronius*. But finding at
last, with much ado, that he himself is the happy Man,
he quits his Eves-dropping, and discovers himself just
time enough to prevent his being cuckolded by a dead Man,
of whom the Moment before he had appear'd so jealous;
and greedily intercepts the Bliss which was fondly
design'd for one who could not be the better for it. But
here I must ask a Question, How comes *Juba* to listen here,
who had not listned before throughout the Play? Or, How
comes he to be the only Person of this Tragedy who listens, when Love and Treason were so often talk'd in so
publick a Place as a Hall. I am afraid the Author was
driven upon all these Absurdities, only to introduce this

miserable Mistake of *Marcia*, which, after all, is much
below the Dignity of Tragedy, as any thing is which is the
Effect or Result of Trick. This Lamentation over the dead
Body of living *Juba* seems to me to be nearly allied to a
merry Adventure of the same Nature between Sir *Frederick
Frolick* and my Lord *Bevil*'s Sister.

But let us come to the Scenary of the Fifth Act. *Cato*
appears first upon the Scene, sitting in a thoughtful Posture, in his Hand *Plato*'s Treatise on the 'Immortality of
the Soul', a drawn Sword on the Table by him. Now let us
consider the Place in which this Sight is presented to us.
The Place, forsooth, is a large Hall. Let us suppose that
any one should place himself in this Posture, in the midst
of one of our Halls in *London*; that he should appear *solus*
in a sullen Posture, a drawn Sword on the Table by him, in
his Hand *Plato*'s Treatise of the 'Immortality of the Soul',
translated lately by *Bernard Lintott*; (56) I desire the
Reader to consider, whether such a Person as this would
pass with them who beheld him for a great Patriot, a great
Philosopher, or a General, or for some whimsical Person
who fancied himself all these; and whether the People who
belong'd to the Family would think that such a Person had
a Design upon their Midriffs or his own.

In short, that *Cato* should sit long enough in the
aforesaid Posture in the midst of this large Hall, to
read over *Plato*'s Treatise on the Immortality of the Soul;
which is a Lecture of two long Hours: That he should propose to himself to be private there upon that Occasion,
that he should be angry with his Son for intruding there,
then that he should leave this Hall upon the Pretence of
Sleep, give himself the mortal Wound in his Bed-chamber;
and then be brought back into that Hall to expire, purely
to shew his good Breeding, and save his Friends the
trouble of coming up to his Bed-chamber; all this appears
to me to be improbable, incredible, impossible. *Aristotle*
tells us, that there ought to be no Incident in a Tragedy
but what ought to be reasonable. And *Boileau* tells us
after him,

  La Scene Demande une exacte raison. (57)

But this Tragedy of 'Cato', instead of having all its
Incidents reasonable, has hardly one that is so. And I
know no one Tragedy, either Ancient or Modern, *English* or
Foreign, that has a Heroe so famous for Wisdom, or a Conduct so notoriously indiscreet. But so much for the
Faults that are in this Tragedy with regard to the Rules
of *Aristotle*.

Notes

1 Bernard Lintot [Lintott] the printer (supposedly on
  the advice of Pope) urged Dennis to write 'The
  Remarks'. The Duke of Buckingham warned him against
  it.
2 The initial run (14 April-9 May) was for 20 days. In
  1713 there were 8 English, 1 Irish, and 1 Dutch
  editions.
3 John Hughes, Edward Young, Laurence Eusden, Thomas
  Tickell, Digby Cotes, Ambrose Philips, Richard
  Steele (who praised 'Cato' in 'Guardian' 33).
4 Abel Boyer (1667-1729).
5 Steele packed the theatre with Addisonian supporters,
  a fact noted by the 'Examiner' (27 April-1 May 1713).
6 Charles Gildon (see No. 47).
7 Addison examined 'Chevy Chase' in 'Spectator' 70,
  74; and 'Two Children in the Wood' in 'Spectator' 85.
8 Dennis alluded to Addison's 'Spectator' papers on
  'Paradise Lost', which appeared on eighteen successive Saturdays (beginning 5 January 1712).
9 Addison attacked the concept of poetic justice in
  'Spectator' 40.
10 'Cato', V. iv. 107-12.
11 V. iii. 1-3.
12 Otway, 'The Orphan' (1680).
13 'Cato', I. i. 27-32.
14 IV. iv. 7-8.
15 IV. iv. 22-4.
16 IV. iv. 143-4.
17 Certain French critics of the seventeenth century
   (also Dryden and Rymer) argued that totally evil
   characters were inappropriate for tragedy.
18 'Cato', I. ii. 1-2, 22-5.
19 III. vii. 13
20 IV. iv. 32-4.
21 I. iii. 18-20, 21-3, 28-31.
22 II. i. 88-90.
23 II. v. 30-4.
24 II. v. 70-3.
25 V. iv. 88-90.
26 II. iv. 59-63.
27 III. ii.
28 III. ii. 28-36.
29 III. ii. 64-70.
30 III. ii. 73-6.
31 III. ii. 77-86.
32 III. ii. 92-3.
33 III. ii. 107-121.

34   I. i. 99-103.
35   I. i. 112-13.
36   The satirized author (i.e., Dryden) in the mock-heroic
     play within Villiers's 'The Rehearsal'.
37   'Cato', I. iii. 32-34 ('Fegue it away' means 'work at
     full stretch').
38   Titus Oates (1649-1705), the inventor of the Popish
     Plot that took shape in 1678.
39   An informer.
40   Sir John Gibson (1637-1717), from 1710 Lieutenant-
     Governor in the Army.
41   'Cato', III. vi. 7-12.
42   III. vii. 1-10.
43   III. vii. 11-19.
44   III. vii. 20-1.
45   III. vii. 22-4.
46   III. vii. 19
47   III. vii. 25.
48   An inaccurate quotation from Terence's 'Eunuch', V.
     1093, 'Didn't I tell you our soldier had true Attic
     taste?'
49   'Cato', IV. i. 1-3, 8-10, 24-5, 27-8.
50   IV. ii. 1.
51   IV. ii. 5-12.
52   IV. ii. 14-15, 16, 17, 18-19.
53   IV. ii. 20-22.
54   IV. ii. 12-13.
55   IV. iii. 8
56   See 'Plato's Dialogue of the Immortality of the Soul'
     (translated by Mr Theobald and printed for Bernard
     Lintott in 1713).
57   'L'Art Poëtique', III, 122.

50. THE 'GRUMBLER'   *by T. Burnet*

1715

In the issue for 17-20 May 1715, the 'Grumbler' by Squire
Gizzard responded to the published 'Caton d'Utique' by
François Michel Chrétien Deschamps. Printed in Paris
early in 1715, copies had become available in London by
May. 'The Grumbler's' preference for Addison's 'Cato' is
politically oriented, if not Whig-inspired. *feeble*

The Grumbler
by Squire Gizzard

From *Tuesday* May 17. to *Friday* May 20. 1715

Yesterday a Gentleman of my Acquaintance came to make me
a Visit at my new Lodgings, and made me a Present of the
last *French* Tragedy, which (as he said) had been acted at
Paris with good Success. The Title of it is 'Cato of
Utica'. This made me eager to peruse it; which I did, as
soon as my Friend had left me, with a more than ordinary
Diligence and Attention. I had not read quite so far as
the End of the Third Act, when my Patience began to fall,
and my Expectations sunk to nothing. However I was
resolved, since I had gone so far, to see the Conclusion
of it. With much ado I went through the Whole: but do not
remember, that I ever laid a poet out of my Hand in
greater Indignation. This done, I fully purposed in the
warm Resentments of a Critick, to grumble in the Morning
so loud, as to be heard from *London* to *Paris*.
   Upon this I began to examine the whole Performance a-
new; thinking to furnish out this Day's Paper with Remarks
upon it, and to draw a Parallel between this Piece, and
that, which shines so much upon the *British* Stage. But
here I was disappointed again; finding, upon a second
Review, the *French* 'Cato' as much beneath Criticism, as
the *English* 'Cato' is above it.
   I was surprized, that *Monsieur des Champs* should make
Choice of so improper a Story for the Entertainment of
his Yoke-Fellows: Does he not know that *Lucan* was never
published in *France* for the use of the *Dauphin*? Be that
as it will, I am apt to believe the Poet's Want of Genius
upon this Occasion (whether it proceeded from Art or
Nature) has stood him in good stead. It has been Treason
in him to write up to his Subject. I could point out a
great many sublime and beautiful Passages in the *English*
Tragedy, which no Actor would dare to pronounce, nor any
Hearer to applaud, in the Presence of the Grand Monarch.
   The Race of great Poets is quite extinct in *France*.
Racine, *Corneille*, *Boileau* have no Successors. The Muses
will never be prevailed upon to fix their abode but in a
Land of Liberty. The *Parisians* are already come to so
great a Degeneracy of Taste, as to think *Monsieur de la
Motte* a better Poet than *Homer*. (1) The Wits are banded
into Parties: The Factions run high; and it is to be
feared, that the Forces that are assembled at one Coffee-
House to espouse the Moderns, will prove too hard for the
Gentlemen, who rise in Defence of the Ancients. Lampoons
and Satyrs have been plentifully dispersed on both Sides;

and there have been some rougher Skirmishes by way of
Blows....

Note

1   Antoine Houdar de la Motte (1672–1731), poet and
    critic. In 1714 he wrote a verse adaptation of the
    'Iliad' designed to please a polite age.

51. 'A PARALLEL...'

1716

Appended to John Ozell's translation of Deschamps's 'Cato
of Utica. A Tragedy' was 'A Parallel betwixt this Piece
and the Tragedy of Cato written by Mr Addison'.
    The printed version of 'Caton d'Utique' circulated in
London in 1715, and it acquired new interest in 1716 when
Addison's 'Cato' was revived at the Drury Lane Theatre for
intermittent performances between February and May. In
response to this revival Ozell translated the play and
watched the first of its three performances on 14 May
1716.

...I cannot establish the Superiority of the *French* Stage
over the *English* better, than by showing that Mr. *Addison*
must give Mr. *Des Champs* the Precedence. I am so well
persuaded of the Justness of the Cause I defend, and of
your Equity, my Lord, (1) that I thought you the most
proper Judge.
    Cato is a famous Name: That great Man gave such appa-
rent Examples of his Love to his Country and Liberty,
that it is a great Pity that he shou'd never appear in any
Theatre before. The Abbot *Abeille* chose his Death as a
Subject for a Tragedy: (2) All the Learned Men that read,
or heard it read, praise it; but the Author was obsti-
nately resolv'd to deny the Publick it. Mr. *Addison* and
Mr. *Des Champs* form'd at the same time a Design to work
upon this delicate Subject, and they presently perceiv'd
its Driness. *Cato* shut up within the Walls of *Utica*,
kills himself, to avoid falling into *Caesar*'s Hands.

History affords no more; and to extend it to a Tragedy,
there wants Fictions and *Episodes*. Our two Poets have
both, indeed, feign'd, but with this Difference, so much
advantagious to the *French*, that the *Episodes* hold with
the Subject, that they are full of Distress, and discover
the Plot. The *Episodes* of the *English* Poet are absolutely
detach'd from the principal Action, they conceal it; they
make it very often disappear; in short, they serve only
to set it off with Scenes, which make up the Emptiness of
the Tragedy.

A short Analysis of these two Plays will show very much
this Fault in the *English*, that Beauty in the *French*.

In the *English* Play, *Cato* is shut up in *Utica*, with a
few *Romans*, and some *Numidian* Horse, which followed young
Juba. *Caesar* sends to propose Peace, which is refused,
he marches his Troops: *Cato* seeing he was not in a Condition to resist, kills himself.

Portius and *Marcus*, *Cato*'s Sons, are both in Love with
Lucia, the Daughter of a *Roman* Senator. *Portius* is Confident to his Brother, who not knowing he is his Rival,
behaves himself like a generous Man, without stifling his
Passion, or betraying his Brother. *Marcus* is slain,
Portius marries *Lucia*: This is another *Episode*, equally
foreign to the Subject and the first *Episode*.

Young *Juba* loves *Marcia* the Daughter of *Cato*, which
Sempronius, a *Roman*, is likewise in Love with. *Sempronius* is one that attempts to betray *Cato*; *Syphax*, a *Numidian*, conspires with him: They endeavour to make the
Romans mutiny; *Cato* appeases them. *Syphax* proposes to
Sempronius to run away with *Marcia*, and to take upon him
the Royal Habit of *Juba*, to execute the Villainy with
less Difficulty; *Juba* discovering it, kills *Sempronius*,
and *Syphax* flies.

The *English* Poem, as we may observe, is without Unity;
there are three Tragedies, one within another; and the
Author seems to think he miss'd the principal Action: He
is obliged from time to time, by the Reflexions that the
Lovers make, to suppose, that they have something else to
do than make Love, and that in such great Danger, they
shou'd amuse themselves with gallant Conversation. The
French Poet hath feign'd his Fable much better, and dispos'd it with more Art.

Cato is in *Utica*, in a Condition to defend himself, if
an unforeseen Accident had not broke his Measures; and by
his Resolution and Firmness of Mind, is not under greater
Despair than in the *English* Tragedy he may, and ought to
refuse the Peace offer'd by *Caesar*. *Cato* has in the Port
of *Utica*, the King of *Pontus*'s Navy; he has his Troops
encamped with the others near the Port. The Action is not

laid in *Utica*, it is in a Palace of the King of *Numidia*,
some Distance from the Walls, by which Means *Caesar* may
safely conferr with *Cato*, upon his Parole. The Enterprize
between *Caesar* and *Cato* upon the Stage is a bold Undertaking, in which Mr. *Des Champs* has succeeded. *Caesar*
appears as great as he is described in History; incapable
of obeying, worthy to command as the great Master of the
World; very prudent, very happy in Arms; so politick, as
to make others submit without Engagement; an intrepid
Enemy, a generous Conqueror; as Virtuous as his Ambition
would give Leave; sensible of the Passion of Love, but
more sensible of his Greatness than of Love. *Cato* les-
sens him in some Measure, he ought so to do, for Virtue
shines brighter than Vice, and the Support of his Misfortune with Courage, gives a new Lustre to his Virtue.
Pharnaces, the Son of *Mithridates*, so infamous, was proper
to serve as a Foil for *Caesar* and *Cato*, the choice of
these three Characters, so well interwoven, is a great
Master-piece of Art: Beside, the Chain, or Connexion of
the Fable, shews us more the Ability of the Poet.
Pharnaces driven from his Country by *Caesar*, comes to join
the Remainder of *Pompey*'s Party. *Arsenna* believes herself
Queen of *Parthia*, adhering to the same Party, from the
former Engagements of her Father, comes here likewise, to
break off the Match projected with *Pharnaces*, and push'd
on by a secret instinct which she bears to *Cato*; it is by
an Interview with her, that this Piece begins. The pretended Queen of *Parthia* is presently known for *Portia*,
the Daughter of *Cato*.

When an Author has hazarded his Story or Fiction,
without forming to himself an exact likeness to Truth, it
produces not such fine Effects which cannot be condemn'd.
But Mr. *Des Champs*'s fancy is always regulated by a solid
Judgment: All that he supposes is agreeable to what the
Historians give us. He imagines that the Wife of *Crassus*
had with her *Portia*, her Niece, then an Infant; that in
the Defeat of *Crassus*, *Portia* being made a Slave was
presented to the King of *Parthia*; the agreeableness of the
Lines of her Face, with those of the Princess his Daughter, and only Child, inspire him with a Fatherly Affection
for *Portia*. The Princess dies, and the King having no
Heirs remaining, lets *Portia* pass for his Daughter.
Caesar, to whom it was of no small Importance to gain the
King of *Parthia* to his Interest, comes to the Court of
that Prince, without making himself known, to bring him
over from *Pompey*'s Party: He succeeds not in that Affair,
but sees the Princess, and falls in love with her, without knowing that she was *Portia*; she loves him again, yet
did not know it was *Caesar*. The Marriage of the supposed

Princess of *Parthia* with *Pharnaces* is prevented: *Portia*
could not consent; *Pharnaces*'s Crimes, especially the
Assassination of *Pacorus*, Prince of *Parthia*, her Brother,
of whose Murther she finds him the Author, serves her for
a Pretence to break with him: She wanting the Assistance
of the Heads of *Pompey*'s Party, comes to gain them, and
finds her Father in *Cato*, and in *Caesar* her Lover. The
Match being broke off, determines *Pharnaces* to assassinate
Cato; he proposes this to *Caesar*; the Illustrious *Roman*
abhor'd the Treachery of the Son of *Mithridates*, and
informs *Cato* of it. *Pharnaces* in Despair attempts to kill
Cato and *Caesar*, he makes himself Master of their Place of
Conference of *Portia* and *Utica*. The danger that *Caesar*
was in makes him run to succour his Troops; *Pharnaces* is
defeated; but the *Romans* who followed *Cato*, joyn themselves to *Caesar*'s Army; and *Cato* having nothing left to
do, but to submit to *Caesar*, or kill himself; chose to put
himself rather in the latter Circumstance; than that of
Death.

We may observe, that the Contrivance of the Events are
so well manag'd, that all centre themselves in the principal Action. If the Arrival of the Queen of *Parthia* is
the occasion of *Pharnaces*'s Enterprize, which puts *Cato*
under the Necessity of killing himself; it is the Queen
of *Parthia* who detains *Caesar* in the very Place of Conference, and which engages him in the Danger. That Danger
we see stops *Caesar*'s Troops in *Utica*, and takes away
all Assistance from *Cato*: 'Tis not an Event which discovers the Plot, all the Parts of the Actors wait for it,
if I may be allow'd to express my self so.

Mr. *Des Champs* then is to be valued for the Justness
of the *Episodes*; beside, he is to be esteem'd for the
beautiful Effects those *Episodes* produce. The contempt
which *Cato* shews of one of the greatest Kingdoms of the
World, the Horror with which he beholds a Crown in his
Family, are Strokes very proper to let us understand the
greatness of his Soul. The love of *Caesar* and *Portia*, of
the Daughter of *Cato* and a Tyrant of *Rome*, affect us
otherwise than the cold Gallantry of *Portius* and *Lucia*,
of *Sempronius* and *Marcia*, *Cato* oblig'd to *Caesar* for his
Life. *Caesar* fighting for *Cato* in that Situation of
Affairs, must have a great deal more Distress in it, and
engage our Concern more abundantly than for the Love of
Caesar and *Portia*.

You will be convinc'd, my Lord, the Conduct of the
Fable in the *French* Tragedy is regular, wonderful, agreeable to Truth, moving and great. Let us compare our Two
Poets by the manner that they have supported the Character
of *Cato*, and those of the other Parts; let us compare them

afterwards by their Circumstances and Sentiments; for by
the Expression, I shall be so just not to judge of that
of Mr. *Addison* from a Version out of Blank Verse into
Prose. So ought the Critick in this Translation from the
French, to give Grains of Allowance when a Comparison is
made with the Original in his own Language.

Mr. *Addison* and Mr. *Des Champs* have drawn both their
Cato's Natural: In the *English*, the Admiration of *Juba* for
Cato, the Censures which *Sempronius* and *Syphax* make of the
Austerity of his Virtue, gives us a great Idea of him: He
is supported by his Resolution in the midst of the Revolt
of his Troops; and appears great in speaking of his Son's
dying for his Country; But the Opposition of *Caesar* so
necessary to make him shine out is dropt in the *English*
Tragedy; besides *Cato* appears too seldom, and there is too
little Business on the Stage: You scarce lose Sight of him
in the *French* Tragedy: All that he says relates to his
Character, and all that is said of him raises still the
Idea, that is form'd of him in the first Scene. The
Throne of *Parthia* despis'd, the Peace offer'd in vain by
Caesar, *Cato* being abandon'd, and surrounded by *Caesar*'s
Troops, are Occasions given where all his Virtue should
be try'd, and wherein it does appear.

Having finish'd the Parallel of the Two Tragedies, by
the Comparison of the Circumstances and the Sentiments;
let us begin to search for the most beautiful Passages in
the *English* Piece: The first we find is in the Fifth
Entrance in the Third Act, whither we are brought by
Scenes of Gallantry, useless to the Subject, by the moral
Conversations of *Portius* and *Marcus*, *Cato*'s Sons, of *Juba*
and *Syphax*; by a cold Deliberation of the Senate. But it
is to be confess'd, it is surprizing to see the Stage
full of the Chiefs revolted with *Sempronius*, render'd
motionless, disarmed, and attracted by the intrepid Presence, and wise Discourse of *Cato*....

Notes

1 The 'Parallel' is presented 'In a Letter to an English
   Nobleman, now residing at Paris.'
2 Abbé Gaspard Abeille (1648-1718), dramatist. His
   tragedy 'Caton', along with two others, was never
   printed.

52.   GEORGE SEWELL, 'A VINDICATION OF THE ENGLISH STAGE'

1716

The 'Vindication' defends Addison's tragedy from the
animadversions of the 'Parallel'.

I believe, Sir, that our Author, when he wrote this Parallel, had borrowed an *English* 'Cato' of some small Retailer
of Coffee-house *Criticism*, who had mark'd one or two Passages in Mr. *Addison*'s, which he had found generally commended, and passed over the numerous Beauties which strike
upon Men of better Sense, and less Talk. The late Lord
Dorset, (1) it is said, used to double down the the Leaves
of the New-books he had which pleas'd him most, and it so
fell out that a Pretender to Wit usually had the Opportunity of reviewing those his admir'd Passages when his
Lordship was abroad, upon the Credit of which he passed
good a while for a good Judge, and an able Critick. This
great Man being informed of his Friend's Practice resolved
upon a Method of putting his Judgment to a Trial, and
accordingly doubled down abundance of Leaves in a very
dull Book. The Retailer reads it, starts to the Coffee-
house and swells into Raptures in admiration of a Piece
that was generally condemned; but being opposed in his
Extasies, and convinced that he was in the wrong, he
cried out in a Passion, That *my L——d D——t had betrayed
him out of Spite, and Dogs-ear'd the Book in the wrong
Places*. I apply this Story no further, than that it
seems probable that the Writer took those Parts of Mr.
Addison's Play which he commends upon Credit, not upon any
Judgment of his own, for though they are very Beautiful in
their proper Places, yet any one of the least Taste could
not have stop'd his Hand at a single Passage or two of
that incomparable *Tragedy*. All the fine Sentiments of
Liberty, the Effects of *Tyranny* and *Ambition*, and the
noble Passion and Love for ones Country, which reign
through the whole, are passed over in Silence. Sure Signs
that the Play was *Dogs-ear'd for his Use*.
    Observe, Sir, with what an Air he accuses Mr. *Addison*'s
Conduct; The Loves of *Marcus* and *Portia*, of *Juba* and *Sempronius* are *Episodes* that destroy the Unity, and make it
three *Tragedies* in one. Whereas in this Management there
is the most beautiful and probable Simplicity that can be
imagined, the under Parts being artfully connected to the

main Story, and of a Piece with the whole. For it is easy
to imagine a few Noble *Romans*, the two Sons and the Daughter of *Cato*, and a *Numidian Prince* following the Fortunes
of that great Man, and interspersing some Concern for
themselves and their own Success in *Love* amidst a Scene
otherwise full of Misfortunes, and Calamities. On the
contrary, the *French Writer* has picked up a King in one
Country, and a Queen in an another, and so jumbled them
together that they are neither King nor Queen, he has
embarrass'd *Cato*'s Character with unnatural Ornaments, and
sent him out of the World without preparing the Spectators
for so signal a *Catastrophe*. In short, *Cato* is lost and
overshadowed in the Confusion of the other Characters, and
the Play might more justly be called 'Arsenia of Parthia',
than 'Cato of Utica'.

Permit me, Sir, to give you what I think a just Idea of
our English *Cato*, which will easily let you into the meanness of the *French*. *Cato* is drawn, as he really was, a
Lover of Liberty and of his Country, inflexibly good, and
brave, adorned with Virtues that set him above his Misfortunes, strike an awe into his Foes, and give an Example
to his Friends and Followers. He is an avowed Enemy to
Caesar, but it is to *Caesar* as a Tyrant, a Usurper, the
Enemy of his Country, the Foe to Liberty and the Cause of
Justice. Not a Word unbecoming the great Idea we conceive
of *Cato* from the Antients falls from his Mouth, and *Rome*
is always uppermost in the Thoughts. He can condescend to
no Terms but such as secure the Liberties of his Country,
he does not parly, cajole, and play false Rhetoric on
Caesar, but all he says, is nervous, passionate, affecting, and full of the true Roman Spirit. Even when his
Friends mention *Caesar*'s Virtues, how does he return upon
them!

Curse on his Virtues, they've undone his *Country*. (2)

In short, *Cato*, the great Character in the Tragedy, is
always uniform and the same, and as he is the Center of
all the Hopes of his Friends, and the sole Object of the
Conspirator's Villany, every Incident tends only to
illustrate and raise his Character higher.

But *Cato* in the *French* is vastly unlike the *Roman*, that
is, the *English Cato*. *Cato* is there the Friend and Pro-
tector of a King and Queen, and yet an Enemy to *Monarchy*,
he is sullen in one Act, and supplicates in the next, he
speaks of *Caesar* with Contempt, and soon after talks of
him to his Face with a Boyish Eloquence....

All the while I read Mr. *Addison* I see *Cato*, he
answers the Image I have formed to my self of him from

the Draughts of his Character in the best *Latin Authors*;
but I don't know who speaks in the *French*, sometimes I
take him for a Philosopher, sometimes for a Pedant, he is
a Heroe, and a Knight-errant in the compass of two Pages,
and as for his Daughter, *Arsenia* is far the better *Cato*
in *Petticoats*.

Give me leave to transcribe an Objection or two more
from the 'Parallel', and I could tell the Writer where he
stole them too, but they are so pitiful that it is no
matter who is the Owner of them. 'The two first Acts and
half the Third consists of Love-scenes, impertinent to the
Subject, Moral Discourses between *Cato*'s two Sons, and
Juba, and *Syphax*, and lastly, a flat Debate among the
Senators.' Alas! here's one half of *Cato* condemned at
once, and the Play chopped in two in the middle by the
unmerciful Hand of our *Critick*, and truly I wonder his
Cruelty did not extend to the other Parts. Well, but I
will venture to say that this dead-doing Son of the Muses
has only flourished his Flail in the Air, without doing
any manner of hurt to honest 'Cato'.

For the first Act opens the whole View of the Play, it
gives us *Cato* and *Caesar*'s Pictures in the opposite
Lights as they then stood; the Conspiracy of *Sempronius*
begins to work in the second Scene, the Love-scenes are
a proper Part of the Action, and help on the main Design,
and the Discourse between *Syphax* and *Juba* is formed with
the nicest Art to corrupt the Morals of that young Prince,
and make the Conspiracy more general and effectual. And
farther, the Debate among the Senators is just, and
proper, and moving, while it keeps up to the strictness
of *Cato*'s Character, who would not stir in the Cause of
his Country, 'till he had observed the known Maxim of the
Republick in applying first to the *Senate*. But I find
that the *Critick* has mentioned the Impertinence of the
Love-scenes more than once, and the under Dealers in Wit
and Poetry retail this Objection in all their learned
Disputes. (3) I shall therefore shew the Justness and
Propriety of them in particular, and humbly hope that my
Observations will not seem the less true because they are
drawn from Nature it self.

Marcus and *Portius* are both in love with *Lucia*, *Juba*
with *Marcia*, their Passions are supposed to have commenced
long before they were driven to *Utica* with *Cato*; here they
all lie under a general Cloud of Calamity, which threatens
and approaches nearer to them every Minute. In these
Circumstances what could be more natural to brave and gallant Spirits than to endeavour to find out the Fate of
their Passions, when their Lives lie at Stake, that such
a determination might inspire them to tread beyond the

common lengths of Soldiers, in the Cause of their Country, and of Love? A Time of Danger ever makes the Lover think of the Object of his Passion, and when that Object is near, every Minute that his Duty can spare is consecrated by the brave Mind to the Success of his Love. This is so natural, that we find it a common Practice with Men of a serious turn of Mind to write to their Ladies at the approach of a Battle, wherein they are to hazard their Lives. 'Tis true that *Cato* reprehends *Juba* for talking of his Passion for his Daughter at a time of such Extremity, but tho' it became *Cato* to blame him, it as much became *Juba* to love. Both Actions are natural alike, a grave Man could no more help his Rebuke, than a Lover could his Passion. And I hope this will be a sufficient answer, tho' a great deal more might be said to this Objection.

I will not tire you, Sir, with any more of this Critick's Impertinence, but only desire you to observe how differently the Catastrophe is turned in these two *Plays*. *Cato*, in Mr. *Addison*'s, makes the most solemn Preparation for Death imaginable, as a Philosopher he reasons himself out of the Fears of it by a future Prospect, as to a *Roman* he despises Life at the Hand of a Tyrant, and yet he pauses, doubts and struggles under the uncertainty of an un-enlightned Mind, and Principles, that could be but merely conjectural. This is to make *Cato* die like *Cato*, to make Reason get the better of natural Infirmities, Liberty of Slavery, Death attended with the Hopes of a better Existence, preferable to a certain Misery in Life.

In the *French* the Truce between *Caesar* and *Cato* is broke without any Pretence to Reason, an Action entirely abhorrent to a *Roman* Spirit; so true is this Author to himself, all his *Romans* being alike, that is, no *Romans* at all. The Action which follows this Violation of the Truce the Poet lays hold on to send *Cato* out of the World he kills himself in the heat of the Battle with the same Pride as *Ovid* makes stupid *Ajax* do upon the loss of *Achilles*'s Armour.

Ne quisquam Ajacem, *posset superare nisi* Ajax. (4)

The same Childishness *Cato* observes in his Conduct, and dies because *Caesar* should not boast

Of Cato's *Death, or* Cato's *Preservation.* (5)

I should now, Sir, run thro' Mr. *Addison*'s Play, and give you some Reason why it excels not only all the *French* Plays that I have seen, but even those of our own Country-men. But I must defer this to another

Opportunity, when I intend to refute all the Criticisms of this *Parallel-writer*, and those of some other malignant Spirits, who cannot bear to praise any thing which exceeds their own Powers to perform. The *French* Critick, to do him Justice, I believe, judged this best, and told all he knew of the Matter, more to display his Vanity than his Ill-nature. But our *English* ones who envy their Country the Honour of *Cato*, are actuated by a different Spirit, they come with a malicious Resolution of making Faults, where there are none, and a Pride obstinate enough to condemn Beauties, which they cannot but see, and taste. For my own Part I think it easier to forgive a Writer any Fault, than a Design of corrupting our Judgments, or debauching our Principles. And for this Reason it is, that in a short time I intend to publish in a more universal Language, a Vindication of Mr. Addison's 'Cato', and I shall think my self very weak, if I am not able not only to answer the Objections of those Criticks, but to prove the Perfection of that incomparable *Tragedy*.

Notes

1 Charles Sackville, 6th Earl of Dorset and 1st Earl of Middlesex (1638–1706).
2 'Cato', IV. iv. 35.
3 This was standard criticism. Pope, for example, said, 'The love-part was flung in after to comply with the popular taste' (Joseph Spence, 'Observations', ed. James M. Osborn (1966), sect. 154).
4 'Metamorphoses', XIII, 390: '...lest any man save Ajax ever conquer Ajax.'
5 'Caton d'Utique', V. v. The statement is Cato's when 'thro' his Breast he drove his Sword.' The line is reported by Phocas.

53. THE 'FREEHOLDER'S JOURNAL'

1722

Published on 7 February 1722, this issue of the 'Freeholder's Journal' notes the first re-run of 'The Drummer' since Addison's death. The notice is appropriately written as if from Button's, whose patrons, organized by

Steele, had urged the production of the play in 1716.
The notice in the journal, by stressing the moral qualities of 'The Drummer', anticipates the cause of its popularity later in the century.

Button's Coffee-house, *Feb*. 5

On *Friday* Night was Acted at the *Theatre* in Lincoln-Inn-
Fields, the 'Drummer', or the 'Haunted House'. (1) I was
highly delighted to see an Audience so well pleased with
so chast a Play, that their Spirits could be kept up for
five Acts, without any prophane Wit, or ambiguous Obscenity. The Name of Mr. *Addison*, which was put in the Bills,
might have drawn many People there, but certainly the intrinsick Value of the Piece, made them so loudly applaud
it; and though the Characters and Sentiments being so
lively a Transcript of several in the 'Spectator', may
make us just suspect him to be the Author; yet, if it be
not really so, that very Consideration of its being drawn
from the Designings of such an admirable Master, should,
I think, make the Author own it without a Blush, whoever
he be. Our Entertainment here, was closed with some
ridiculous Fooleries of Scaramouch and Harlequin, (2) and
I was very much put out of humour with the Spectators, to
see them so pleased with such an irrational Transition,
from the just Representations of Nature, to the shocking
Distortions of a Human Body. I thought it an Affront to
the Polite Company of a Playhouse, to think to Divert
them with the tumblings of a Merry Andrew, and thus to
level their Taste to that of Clowns and Peasants at a
Mountebank's Show. In my way home from the *Theatre*, I
was taken up with the melancholy Reflection, that no Man
of Learning and Judgment, who considered the uncivil
Treatment this Comedy met with at its first Appearance,
(3) would ever attempt to entertain the Town in this way;
so that in all probability, the Stage must be abandoned
to School-boys, Women, and Players.

Notes

1 The first revival since its opening in March 1716;
   'The Drummer' ran for 7 nights between 2 and 12 February 1722.
2 The farce, 'Harlequin Executed'.
3 It ran only on 10, 13, and 17 March 1716.

54. STEELE ON 'THE DRUMMER'

1716, 1722

Steele's Preface to 'The Drummer' (1716) is followed by
an excerpt (pp. xiv-xvi) from his Dedication to William
Congreve in the 1722 edition of the play. Steele
arranged for the second edition, in part to capitalize on
its successful revival (see No. 53) and in part to retaliate against Tickell, who omitted it from the first collected edition of 'Addison's Works'. Tickell later included
'The Drummer' in a smaller trade edition of 'Addison's
Miscellaneous Works' (3 vols, 1726).

[Steele's Preface to 'The Drummer', 1716]

Having recommended this Play to the Town, and delivered
the Copy of it to the Bookseller, I think my self oblig'd
to give some Account of it.

It had been some Years in the Hands of the Author, and
falling under my Perusal, I thought so well of it, that I
persuaded him to make some Additions and Alterations to
it, and let it appear upon the Stage. I own I was very
highly pleased with it, and lik'd it the better, for the
want of those studied Similes and Repartees, which we,
who have writ before him, have thrown into our Plays, to
indulge and gain upon a false Taste that has prevailed
for many Years in the *British* Theatre. I believe the
Author would have condescended to fall into this Way a
little more than he has, had he before the writing of it
been often present at Theatrical Representations. I was
confirmed in my Thoughts of the Play, by the Opinions of
better Judges to whom it was communicated, who observed
that the Scenes were drawn after *Moliere*'s Manner, and
that an easy and natural Vein of Humour ran through the
whole.

I do not question but the Reader will discover this,
and see many Beauties that escaped the Audience; the
Touches being too delicate for every Taste in a Popular
Assembly. My Brother-Sharers were of opinion, at the
first reading of it, that it was like a Picture in which
the Strokes were not strong enough to appear at a Distance. As it is not in the common way of Writing, the
Approbation was at first Doubtful, but has risen every
time it has been Acted, and has given an Opportunity in

several of its Parts for as just and good Action as ever
I saw on the Stage.
    The Reader will consider that I speak here, not as the
Author, but as the Patentee. Which is, perhaps, the Rea-
son why I am not diffuse in the Praises of the Play, lest
I should seem like a Man who cries up his own Wares only
to draw in Customers.

                                        Richard Steele.

[Steele's Dedication to William Congreve in the 1722
'Drummer']

...Were I now to indulge myself, I could talk a great deal
to you, which I am sure would be entertaining; but as I am
speaking at the same time to all the World, I consider'd
'twould be impertinent: let me then confine my self a
while to the following Play, which I at first recommended
to the Stage, and carried to the Press: No one who reads
the Preface which I publish'd with it, will imagine I
could be induc'd to say so much as I then did, had I not
known the Man I best lov'd had had a part in it, or had I
believ'd that any other concern'd had much more to do
than as an Amanuensis.
    But indeed had I not known, at the time of the Trans-
action, concerning the acting on the Stage and sale of the
Copy, I should, I think, have seen Mr. *Addison* in every
Page of it; for he was above all Men in that Talent we
call *Humour*, and enjoyed it in such Perfection, that I
have often reflected, after a Night spent with him apart
from all the World, that I had had the Pleasure of conversing with an intimate Acquaintance of *Terence* and
Catullus, who had all their Wit and Nature heighten'd
with Humour, more exquisite and delightful than any other
Man ever possessed.
    They who shall read this Play after being let into the
Secret that it was writ by Mr. *Addison*, or under his
Direction, will probably be attentive to those Excellencies, which they before overlook'd, and wonder they did
not till now observe, that there is not an Expression in
the whole Piece which has not in it the most nice Propriety and Aptitude to the Character which utters it; there
is that smiling Mirth, that delicate Satire, and genteel
Raillery which appear'd in Mr. *Addison* when he was free
among Intimates: I say, when he was free from *his remarkable* bashfulness, which is a Cloak that hides and muffles
Merit; and his Abilities were cover'd only by Modesty,
which doubles the Beauties which are seen, and gives

Credit and Esteem to all that are conceal'd.

The 'Drummer' made no great Figure on the Stage, tho
exquisitely well acted; but when I observe this, I say, a
much harder thing of the Stage than of the Comedy. When I
say the Stage in this place, I am understood to mean in
general the present Taste of Theatrical Representations,
where nothing that is not violent, and, as I may say,
grossly delightful, can come on without hazard of being
condemn'd, or slighted. It is here republish'd, and
recommended as a Closet-piece, to recreate an intelligent
Mind in a vacant Hour; for vacant the Reader must be from
every strong Prepossession, in order to relish an Entertainment (*Quod nequeo monstrare & sentio tantum*) which
cannot be enjoy'd to the degree it deserves, but by those
of the most polite Taste among Scholars, the best Breeding
among Gentlemen, and the least acquainted with sensual
Pleasure among Ladies.

The Editor is pleas'd to relate concerning 'Cato', that
a Play under that design was projected by the Author very
early, and wholly laid aside; in advanced Years he re-
assum'd the same design, and many Years after four Acts
were finish'd, he writ the fifth, and brought it upon the
Stage. All the Town knows how officious I was in bringing
it on; and you that know the Town, the Theatre and Mankind
very well, can judge how necessary it was to take measures
for making a Performance of that sort, excellent as it is,
run into popular Applause. I promis'd before it was acted,
and performed by Duty accordingly to the Author, that I
would bring together so just an Audience on the first Days
of it, that it should be impossible for the Vulgar to put
its Success or due Applause to any hazard; but I don't
mention this only to shew, how good an *Aid de Camp* I was
to Mr. *Addison*, but to shew also that the Editor does as
much to cloud the Merit of this Work as I did to set it
forth: Mr. *Tickell*'s account of its being taken up, laid
down, and at last perfected, after such long Intervals
and Pauses, would make any one believe, who did not know
Mr. *Addison*, that 'twas accomplish'd with the greatest
Pain and Labour, and the issue rather of Learning and
Industry than Capacity and Genius; but I do assure you,
that never Play, which could bring the Author any Reputation for Wit and Conduct, notwithstanding it was so long
before it was finish'd, employ'd the Author so little a
time in writing: if I remember right, the fifth Act was
written in less than a Week's time; for this was particular in this Writer, that when he had taken his Resolution,
or made his Plan for what he design'd to write, he would
walk about a Room and dictate it into Language with as
much freedom and ease as any one could write it down, and

attend to the Coherence and Grammar of what he dictated.
I have been often thus employ'd by him, and never took it
into my Head, tho he only spoke it, and I took all the
Pains of throwing it upon Paper, that I ought to call my
self the Writer of it. I will put all my Credit among
Men of Wit for the Truth of my Averrment, when I presume
to say, that no one but Mr. *Addison* was in any other way
the Writer of the 'Drummer'; at the same time I will
allow, that he sent for me, which he could always do, from
his natural Power over me, as much as he could send for
any of his Clerks when he was Secretary of State, and told
me that a Gentleman then in the Room had written a Play
that he was sure I would like, but it was to be a Secret,
and he knew I would take as much Pains, since he recommended it, as I would for him....

VII Addison the Man and Writer

55. MARY DELARIVIERE MANLEY, 'MEMOIRS OF EUROPE'

1710, 1711

Mrs. Manley's first reference to Addison appeared in 'The Memoirs of Europe toward the Close of the Eighth Century' (1710, 1711). This work was subsequently added to 'The New Atalantis' as volumes III and IV. The excerpt printed here is from the 7th edition of 'The New Atalantis' (1736), III, pp. 218-19.

I, who can't be properly named a Judge of the *Greek*, find yet such Inchantment in *Maro*'s Strain, (1) that feeling how I my self, a foreigner, am ravished, must thence conclude his better Judges, the Grecians, entranced by him. I could not behold him in *Julius Sergius*'s Gallery, (2) without something of Ejaculation, an Oblation due to *Maro*'s Shrine from all that can read him. O Pity! that Politicks and sordid Interest should have carried him out of the Reach of Helicon, snatched him from the Embraces of the Muses, to throw him into an old withered artificial Statesman's Arms! (3) Why did he prefer Gain to Glory? Why chuse to be an idle *Spectator*, rather than a Celebrator of those Actions he so well knows how to design and adorn? *Virgil* himself, nor *Virgil*'s greater Master, *Homer*, could not boast of finer Qualifications than *Maro*: *Maro*! who alone of all the Poets, truly inspired, could cease to be himself; could degenerate his godlike Soul, and prostitute that inborn Genius, all those noble Accomplishments of his, for Gold; could turn away his Eyes

from the delicious Gardens of *Parnassus*, of which he was
already in Possession, to tread the wandering Maze of
Business. Farewel *Maro*, till you abandon your artificial
Patron, Fame must abandon you!

Notes

1   As 'Maro', Addison was likened to Virgil.
2   Thomas Wharton, 1st Earl, later Marquis of Wharton.
3   As Lord Lieutenant of Ireland or powerful Whig, Whar-
    ton 'employed' Addison to be first secretary in late
    1708 to 1710, and helped him to be elected MP for
    Malmesbury on 11 March 1710.

56. HENRY FELTON ON ADDISON

[1713], 1715

From 'A Dissertation on Reading the Classics, and Forming
a Just Style', 2nd ed., 1715.
   Addison is recognized only as a poet and in no way
associated with either the 'Tatler' or the 'Spectator'.

And now, my Lord, You see I am entered upon Poetry, where
little need be said after what I have said already. Perhaps I may touch some Characters again; but besides
those I have named, I may recommend Mr. *Addison*, and Mr.
Prior, as perfect Patterns of true poetic Writing. Mr.
Addison is more laboured; like his great Master *Virgil*,
he hath weighed every Word; nor is there an Expression in
all his Lines, that can be changed for any juster, or
more forcible than itself. Mr. *Prior* enjoys the freest
and easiest Muse in the World, and perhaps is the only
Man who may rival *Horace* in an admirable Felicity of Expression, both in the sublime and familiar Way.

57.   LEONARD WELSTED, 'TO THE COUNTESS OF WARWICK ON HER
MARRIAGE WITH MR. ADDISON'

c. 1716

From Leonard Welsted (1688-1747), 'Epistles, Odes, &c.
Written on Several Subjects' (1724), pp. 19-21.

Ambition long has Woman's Heart betray'd,
And Tinsel Grandeur caught th' unwary Maid;
The pompous Stiles, that strike th' admiring Throng,
Have glitter'd in the Eye of Beauty long:
You, MADAM, first the Female Taste improve,
And give your Fellow-Charmers Laws for Love;
A Pomp you covet, not to Heralds known,
And sigh for Vertues equal to your own;
Part in a Man immortal greatly claim;
And frown on Titles, to ally with Fame:
Not *Edward*'s Star, (1) emboss'd with Silver Rays,
Can vie in Glory with thy Consort's Bays;
His Country's Pride does Homage to thy Charms,
And every Merit crowds into thy Arms.

While others gain light Conquests by their Eyes,
'Tis thine with Wisdom to subdue the Wise:
To their soft Chains while courtly Beaux submit,
'Tis thine to lead in Triumph captive Wit:
Her fighting Vassals let *Clarinda* boast,
Of Lace and languishing Cockades the Toast;
In Beauty's Pride unenvied let her reign,
And share that wanton Empire with the Vain:
For Thee, the Arts of *Greece* and *Rome* combine;
And all the Glories, *Cato* gain'd, are thine;
Still *Warwick* in thy boasted Rank of Life,
But more illustrious, than when *Warwick*'s Wife. (2)

Come forth, reveal Thy self, thou chosen Bride,
And shew great *Nassau*'s Poet by the Side; (3)
Thy bright Example shall instruct the Fair,
And future Nymphs shall make Renown their Care;
Embroid'ry less shall charm the Virgin's Eye,
And kind Coquets, for Plumes, less frequent die:
Secure shall Beauty reign, the Muse its Guard;
The Muse shall triumph, Beauty its Reward.

Notes

1 The star of the Order of the Garter.
2 On 9 August 1716 Addison married Charlotte Countess
   Dowager of Warwick and Holland (1679–1731).
3 'A Poem to his Majesty' (William III), written by
   Addison in 1695.

58. NICHOLAS AMHURST, 'A CONGRATULATORY EPISTLE TO THE
RIGHT HONOURABLE JOSEPH ADDISON, ESQ;'

1717

Nicholas Amhurst (1697–1742) was a poet and political
writer. While a student at St John's College, Oxford, he
published this 'Congratulatory Epistle' and a translation
of Addison's Latin poem on the resurrection. Expecting
to move on to a fellowship in 1719, he was expelled from
the predominantly Tory University for libertinism and
misconduct. Amhurst's ardent Whiggism was undoubtedly a
contributory reason.

While Half the Globe is shook with Wars and Arms,
And *Europe* labours with unripe Alarms;
While the mad Suede, (1) with Insolence unknown,
Affects new Kingdoms, and betrays his own:
From Isis' Laurel'd Banks, the Muse reveals
A Joy which ev'ry honest *Briton* feels,
Who sees his Country's and his KING's Commands,
Intrusted to your unpolluted Hands. (2)
Accept, Immortal Sir! an artless Song,
From One, the meanest, of the Vocal Throng,
Who joys to see distinguish'd Merit rise,
Advanc'd the foremost in his PRINCE's Eyes.
From Public Cares One Hour relieve your Breast,
And let the Cause of Warring Nations rest;
While, smote with Glory and Poetic Flame,
Boldly I strive to reach your Deathless Name:
On daring Wings the boundless Height I soar,
Thro' trackless Skies, and Worlds unseen before.
What Tongue so impious to condemn my Pain,
If ADDISON approves the Youthful Strain? (3)

But where shall I begin? - With equal Light,
The POET and the PATRIOT strike my Sight:
Candour unrival'd, and ennobled Love,
Demand the Muse, and her vast Theme improve;
To raise my Verse un-number'd Gifts conspire,
And fill my Bosom with ungovern'd Fire;
For to adorn your Person are combin'd
A piercing Judgment, and unblemish'd Mind:
Each Scheme of Life, with rising Wonders fraught,
Crouds to my View, and swells my lab'ring Thought.
In what you write, the Spirit of the Nine,
And all APOLLO teems in ev'ry Line:
In all you act, transfus'd into your Breast,
Great BRUNSWICK's Soul burns out, (4) in strongest
                                    Light confest.
From WARWICK's Eyes, (5) and Your own spotless Soul,
You MARCIA's Charms, and CATO's Virtues stole. (6)
My grov'ling Fancy sinks beneath your Praise,
And my Breast labours with unequal Lays.

From You the Poet borrows all his Rage,
Unstrung with Years, nor yet matur'd by Age:
Fir'd by Your Numbers, he attempts to write,
That, un-inspir'd, would have declin'd the Flight;
Wrapt and transported with each glowing Line,
In his own Breast he feels the Rage Divine.

How oft, between the Guilty and the Fair,
Hath ROSAMONDA's Blood engag'd my Care? (7)
Forbidden Love, and Majesty betray'd,
By Turns excite my Pity, and upbraid.
How oft have I bewail'd, in CATO's DOOM,
The Fate of *Britain*, and the Fate of *Rome*?

First in Your Page the *British Drama* shone,
And the fam'd *Stagyrite* himself out-done: (8)
Each Scene displays, with matchless Conduct wrought,
The Sweets of Measure, and the Strength of Thought.
By You succeeding Bards shall warm the Age,
And *British* Plans correct the Grecian Stage.

When Churchill, or NASSAU, inspire your Lays, (9)
Dire mingling Hosts are figur'd to the Sight,
And all the dreadful Thunder of the Fight:
My boiling Veins throb with tumultuous Heats,
And ev'ry Pulse with Martial Ardour beats!
Not Your own VIRGIL better sings of Arms,
Nor OVID's Verse can boast such easy Charms.

Nor would the ravish'd Muse alone rehearse

Your fadeless Laurels, and immortal Verse;
More glorious Scenes are open'd to her Eyes,
And unexhausted Funds of Praise arise,
Superior to her Strength; by Heav'n design'd,
At once to profit and delight Mankind;
Adorn'd with Letters, and with Wisdom blest,
The Maker's Image shines upon your Breast.
TICKELL, by your Indulgence, grows to Fame, (10)
And BRUNSWICK borrows Lustre from Your Name.

With the Discernment of *Britannia*'s KING,
The World's remotest sever'd Nations ring:
Who, long for an unshaken Truth renown'd,
To Worth and Merit sheds His Influence round:
Contending Sects applaud their Sov'reign's Voice,
And Factions learn Obedience from His Choice.
The Courtier, thus with ev'ry Grace endow'd,
Hears not the Slanders of th'ill-natur'd Croud:
Greatness henceforth may bear the strictest Test,
Nor Pomp and Virtue be a public Jest.

What may not *Albion* hope in BRUNSWICK's Reign,
BRUNSWICK, the *Neptune* of her ambient Main?
Whilst or a STANHOPE, (11) or an ADDISON,
Directs His Councils, and divides His Throne.
I see the Patriot, big with Albion's Fate,
Oppress'd and struggling with a Kingdom's Weight;
Deep in the close Recesses of whose Soul,
Leagues unconfirm'd, and future Battels roll;
From whom the *Turk* expects the fatal Day, (12)
And ORLEANS by New Schemes is taught to sway: (13)
At his Command, each Nation sheaths the Sword,
And *Europe* leans on each important Word.

The frantick Suede e'er long (tho' drunk with Pride,
He envies Blessings to Himself deny'd,
And rashly aims at Kingdoms, which can boast
A milder Heav'n, and less ungrateful Coast)
Shall see indignant, since averse to Peace,
His Borders lessen'd, as his Foes increase;
And curse, in Wrath, his tow'ring Hopes o'erthrown,
Nor longer swell with Empires not his own:
Shall curse Himself, in his serener Hours,
That rouz'd the Vengeance of the *British* POW'rs:
Shall curse, deluded Prince! but curse too late,
The faithless Main, that bore them to his Fate.

Such is the Harvest, which my Fancy charms,
Of *British* Councils, and of *British* Arms;

When wak'd to Wrath, his Sword AUGUSTUS draws,
And ADDISON deals out his Country's Laws....

   Mean while, great Patron of our *Isis'* Groves,
Whom Brunswick honours, and *Britannia* loves,
Forgive the Rashness of th'advent'rous Muse,
Who your lov'd Name thro Paths unknown persues;
And fondly lifts in un-ambitious Rhymes,
To Hand your Glories down thro After-times;
That Worlds to come, and future Bards may know,
To whom the Beauties of their Verse they owe;
Who first restor'd his Country's injur'd Fame,
And rescu'd from Reproach the Statesman's Name.
Her only Warmth from Zeal innate proceeds,
And a just Knowledge of your Virtuous Deeds;
Content alone, if her unpolish'd Lays,
He deigns to Pardon, whom she strives to Praise.

Notes

1 Charles XII of Sweden (1682–1718), best known for his
resistance in the Great Northern War to Russia,
Denmark-Norway, and Saxony-Poland.
2 In April 1717 Addison was appointed Secretary of State
for the Southern Department.
3 Amhurst was aged 20.
4 George I (1660–1727).
5 Edward Rich (1698–1721), 7th Earl of Warwick, Addison's stepson.
6 Daughter of Cato, in Addison's tragedy.
7 An allusion to Addison's opera 'Rosamond' (1707).
8 Aristotle, born in the Macedonian town of Stageira.
9 John Churchill, 1st Duke of Marlborough; William
Henry (1650–1702), Prince of Orange and Count of
Nassau, King of England (1688–1702).
10 Thomas Tickell (1686–1740) versified his praise of
Addison in his first poem 'Oxford' (1707); also in
'To the supposed Author of the "Spectator"' (in No.
532 of the journal).
11 Active in England's foreign affairs as Secretary of
State for the Southern Department, James Stanhope in
April 1717 became first Lord of the Treasury and
Chancellor of the Exchequer.
12 A reference to the Austro-Turkish War (1716–18).
13 Philip II, Duke of Orléans (1674–1723), regent of
France.

59.   ALLAN RAMSAY, 'RICHY AND SANDY'

1719

Allan Ramsay (1686-1758), a Scottish wig-maker by profession, began to write poetry probably in 1715. About this same time he abandoned his first trade to become a bookseller. In 1717 he met Steele when the latter visited Edinburgh.
In the elegy Richy may be Steele and Sandy Pope.

RICHY

What gars thee look sae dowf, dear *Sandy* say,
Chear up dull Fallow, take thy Reed and play,
My Apron Deary, ——or some wanton Tune,
Be merry Lad, and keep thy Heart aboon.

SANDY

NA, Na! It winna do! Leave me to mane,
This aught Days twice o'er tell'd I'll whistle nane.

RICHY

WOW Man, that's unco' sad, ——is that ye'r Jo
Has ta'en the Strunt? ——Or has some Bogle-bo
Glowrin frae 'mang auld Waws gi'en ye a Fleg?
Or has some dawted Wedder broke his Leg?

SANDY

NAITHING like that, sic Troubles eith were born!
What's Bogles, ——Wedders, ——or what's *Mausy*'s
                                                                    Scorn;
Our Loss is meikle mair, and past Remeed,
EDIE that play'd and sang sae sweet is dead.

RICHY

DEAD sayst thou, Oh! Had up my Heart O *Pan*!
Ye Gods! What Laids ye lay on feckless Man,
Alake therefore, I canna wyt ye'r Wae,
I'll bear ye Company for Year and Day.
A better Lad ne'er lean'd out o'er a Kent,
Or hound a Coly o'er the mossy Bent;
Blyth at the Bought how aft ha we three been,
Hartsome on Hills, and gay upon the Green.

SANDY

THAT's true indeed! But now thae Days are gane,
And with him a' that's pleasant on the Plain.
A Summer Day I never thought it lang
To hear him make a Roundel or a Sang.
How sweet he sung where Vines and Myrtles grow,
And wimpling Waters which in *Latium* flow.
Titry the *Mantuan* Herd wha lang sinsyne
Best sung on aeten Reed the Lover's Pine,
Had he been to the fore now in our Days,
Wi *EDIE* he had frankly dealt his Bays:
As lang's the Warld shall *Amaryllis* ken,
His *Rosamond* shall eccho thro' the Glen;
While on Burn Banks the yellow Gowan grows,
Or wand'ring Lambs rin bleeting after Ews,
His Fame shall last, last shall his Sang of Weirs,
While *British* Bairns brag of their bauld Forbears.
We'll mickle miss his blyth and witty Jest
At Spaining Time, or at our *Lambmass* Feast.
O *Richy*, but 'tis hard that Death ay reaves
Away the best Fouck, and the ill anes leaves.
Hing down ye'r Heads ye Hills, greet out ye'r Springs,
Upon ye'r Edge na mair the Shepherd sings.

RICHY

THAN he had ay a good Advice to gi'e,
And kend my Thoughts amaist as well as me;
Had I been thowless, vext, or oughtlins sow'r,
He wad have made me blyth in haff an Hour.
Had *Rosie* ta'en the Dorts, ——or had the Tod
Worry'd my Lamb, ——or were my Feet ill shod,
Kindly he'd laugh when sae he saw me dwine,
And tauk of Happiness like a Divine.
Of ilka Thing he had an unco' Skill,
He kend be Moon Light how Tydes eb and fill.
He kend, What kend he no? E'en to a Hair
He'd tell O'er-night gin niest Day wad be fair.
Blind *John*, ye mind, wha sang in kittle Phrase,
How the ill Sp'rit did the first Mischief raise;
Mony a Time beneath the auld Birk-tree
What's bonny in that Sang he loot me see.
The Lasses aft flang down their Rakes and Pales,
And held their Tongues, O strange! To hear his Tales.

SANDY

SOUND be his Sleep, and saft his Wak'ning be,
He's in a better Case than thee or me;
He was o'er good for us, the Gods hae ta'en
Their ain but back, ——he was a borrow'd-len.

Let us be good, gin Virtue be our Drift,
Then may we yet forgether 'boon the Lift.
But see the Sheep are wysing to the Cleugh;
Thomas has loos'd his Ousen frae the Pleugh,
Maggy be this has beuk the Supper Scones,
And nuckle Ky stand rowting on the Lones;
Come *Richy* let us truse and hame o'er bend,
And make the best of what we canna mend.

60. TICKELL'S 'ELEGY'

1721

Thomas Tickell (1686-1740), who began to pay homage to
Addison as early possibly as 1707, became Addison's first
editor. In October 1721 he brought out Addison's works
in four quarto volumes. The 'Elegy' was printed in the
first volume and addressed 'To the Earl of Warwick, on
the Death of Mr. Addison'. Of the 'Elegy' Goldsmith
wrote that it 'is one of the finest in our language;
there is so little new that can be said upon a death of
a friend, after the complaints of Ovid and the Latin
Italians in this way, that one is surprised to see so
much novelty in this to strike us, and so much interest
to affect'.
From the first collected edition of 'Addison's Works',
I, pp. xvii-xxi.

To the Right Honourable the
EARL of WARWICK, &c.

If, dumb too long, the drooping Muse hath stay'd,
And left her debt to Addison unpaid
Blame not her silence, Warwick, but bemoan,
And judge, oh judge, my bosom by your own.
What mourner ever felt poetic fires!
Slow comes the verse, that real woe inspires:
Grief unaffected suits but ill with art,
Or flowing numbers with a bleeding heart.

Can I forget the dismal night, that gave

My soul's best part for-ever to the grave! (1)
How silent did his old companions tread,
By mid-night lamps, the mansions of the dead,
Through breathing statues, then unheeded things,
Through rowes of warriors, and through walks of kings!
What awe did the slow solemn knell inspire;
The pealing organ, and the pausing choir;
The duties by the lawn-robe'd prelate pay'd; (2)
And the last words, that dust to dust convey'd!
While speechless o'er thy closing grave we bend,
Accept these tears, thou dear departed friend,
Oh gone for-ever, take this long adieu;
And sleep in peace, next thy lov'd Montagu! (3)

To strew fresh laurels let the task be mine,
A frequent pilgrim, at thy sacred shrine,
Mine with true sighs thy absence to bemoan,
And grave with faithful epitaphs thy stone.
If e'er from me thy lov'd memorial part,
May shame afflict this alienated heart;
Of thee forgetful if I form a song,
My lyre be broken, and untun'd my tongue,
My griefs be doubled, from thy image free,
And mirth a torment, unchastised by thee.

Oft let me range the gloomy Iles alone
(Sad luxury! to vulgar minds unknown)
Along the walls where speaking marbles show
What worthies form the hollow'd mold below:
Proud names, who once the reins of empire held;
In arms who triumph'd; or in arts excell'd;
Chiefs, grac'd with scars, and prodigal of blood;
Stern patriots, who for sacred freedom stood;
Just men, by whom impartial laws were given;
And saints, who taught, and led, the way to heaven.
Ne'er to these chambers, where the mighty rest,
Since their foundation, came a nobler guest,
Nor e'er was to the bowers of bliss convey'd
A fairer spirit, or more welcome shade.

In what new region, to the just assign'd,
What new employments please th' unbody'd mind?
A winged Virtue, through th' ethereal sky,
From world to world unweary'd does he fly?
Or curious trace the long laborious maze
Of heaven's decrees, where wond'ring angels gaze?
Does he delight to hear bold Seraphs tell
How Michael battel'd, and the Dragon fell?
Or, mixt with milder Cherubim, to glow

In hymns of love, not ill essay'd below?
Or do'st thou warn poor mortals left behind,
A task well suited to thy gentle mind?
Oh, if sometimes thy spotless form descend,
To me thy aid, thou guardian Genius, lend!
When rage misguides me, or when fear alarms,
When pain distresses, or when pleasure charms,
In silent whisperings purer thoughts impart,
And turn from ill a frail and feeble heart;
Lead through the paths thy virtue trode before,
'Till bliss shall join, nor death can part us more.

That awful form (which, so ye heavens decree,
Must still be lov'd and still deplor'd by me)
In nightly visions seldom fails to rise,
Or, rous'd by fancy, meets my waking eyes.
If business calls, or crowded courts invite,
Th' unblemish'd statesman seems to strike my sight;
If in the stage I seek to soothe my care,
I meet his soul, which breathes in Cato there;
If pensive to the rural shades I rove,
His shape o'ertakes me in the lonely grove:
'Twas there of Just and Good he reason'd strong,
Clear'd some great truth, or rais'd some serious song;
There patient show'd us the wise course to steer,
A candid censor, and a friend severe;
There taught us how to live; and (oh! too high
The price for Knowledge) taught us how to die. (4)

Thou Hill, whose brow the antique structures grace,
Rear'd by bold chiefs of Warwick's noble race,
Why, once so lov'd, when-e'er thy bower appears,
O'er my dim eye-balls glance the sudden tears!
How sweet were once thy prospects fresh and fair,
Thy sloping walks, and unpolluted air!
How sweet the gloomes beneath thy aged trees,
Thy noon-tide shadow, and thy evening breeze! (5)
His image thy forsaken bowers restore;
Thy walks and airy prospects charm no more,
No more the summer in thy gloomes allay'd,
Thy evening breezes, and thy noon-day shade.

From other ills, however fortune frown'd,
Some refuge in the muse's art I found:
Reluctant now I touch the trembling string,
Bereft of him who taught me how to sing,
And these sad accents, murmur'd o'er his urn,
Betray that absence, they attempt to mourn.
Oh! must I then (now fresh my bosom bleeds,

And Craggs in death to Addison succeeds) (6)
The verse, begun to one lost friend, prolong,
And weep a second in th' unfinish'd song!

These works divine, which on his death-bed laid
To thee, O Craggs, th' expiring Sage convey'd,
Great, but ill-omen'd monument of fame,
Nor he surviv'd to give, nor thou to claim.
Swift after him thy social spirit flies,
And close to him, how soon! thy coffin lies.
Blest pair! whose union future bards shall tell
In future tongues: each other's boast! farewel.
Farewel! whom join'd in fame, in friendship try'd,
No chance could sever, nor the grave divide.

Notes

1 Addison was buried on 26 June 1719 in King Henry VII's
   Chapel in the Albemarle vault, Westminster Abbey.
2 Francis Atterbury (1662–1732), Bishop of Rochester, who
   performed the rites.
3 Addison was buried next to Charles Montagu Lord Halifax, one of his early patrons.
4 Tickell, present at Addison's death-bed, was largely
   responsible for the account of his patron's last words
   to the Earl of Warwick: i.e., 'See in what peace a
   Christian can die.'
5 One of the consequences of his marriage was Addison's
   residence at Holland House in Kensington, which had
   extensive grounds with a 'green lane' comparable to
   the Magdalen College walks along the Isis.
6 Addison had bequeathed his works to James Craggs the
   younger (1686–1721), his literary executor. He died
   of smallpox on 16 February in his 35th year.

61.   THOMAS FITZOSBORNE, 'LETTERS'

1748

Sir Thomas Fitzosborne was the pseudonym of William Melmoth (1710–99), a classicist. 'Letters on Several Subjects' was his first book, published in 1748.

LETTER XVI.

July 3, 1716.

When I mentioned *grace* as essential in constituting a fine
writer, I rather hoped to have found my sentiments reflected back with a clearer light by yours; than imagined you
would have called upon me to explain in form, what I only
threw out by accident. To confess the truth, I know not
whether, after all that can be said to illustrate this
uncommon quality, it must not at last be resolved into the
poet's *nequeo monstrare & sentio tantum.* (1) In cases of
this kind, where language does not supply us with proper
words to express the notions of one's mind, we can only
convey our sentiments in figurative terms: a defect which
necessarily introduces some obscurity.

I will not, therefore, undertake to mark out with any
sort of precision, that idea which I would express by the
word *grace*; and, perhaps, it can no more be clearly described, than justly defined. To give you, however, a
general intimation of what I mean when I apply that term
to compositions of genius, I would resemble it to that
easy air, which so remarkably distinguishes certain persons of a genteel and liberal cast. It consists not only
in the particular beauty of single parts, but arises from
the general symmetry and construction of the whole. An
author may be just in his sentiments, lively in his figures, and clear in his expression; yet may have no claim
to be admitted into the rank of finished writers. Those
several members must be so agreeably united as mutually
to reflect beauty upon each other: their arrangement must
be so happily disposed as not to admit of the least
transposition without manifest prejudice to the entire
piece. The thoughts, the metaphors, the allusions, and
the diction should appear easy and natural, and seem to
arise like so many spontaneous productions, rather than as
the effects of art or labour.

Whatever therefore is forced or affected in the sentiments; whatever is pompous or pedantic in the expression,
is the very reverse of *grace*. Her mien is neither that of
a prude nor a coquet; she is regular without formality,
and sprightly without being fantastical. Grace, in short,
is to good writing, what a proper light is to a fine picture; it not only shews all the figures in their several
proportions and relations, but shews them in the most
advantageous manner.

As genteelity (to resume my former illustration)
appears in the minutest action, and improves the most inconsiderable gesture; so *grace* is discovered in the placing even of a single word, or the turn of a meer

expletive. Neither is this inexpressible quality confined
to one species of composition only, but extends to all the
various kinds; to the humble Pastoral as well as to the
lofty Epic; from the slightest letter to the most solemn
discourse.

I know not whether Sir William Temple may not be considered as the first of our prose authors, who introduced
a graceful *manner* into our language. At least that
quality does not seem to have appeared early, or spread
far, amongst us. But wheresoever we may look for its origin, it is certainly to be found in its highest perfection
in the late essays of a gentleman whose writings will be
distinguished so long as politeness and good sense have
any admirers. That becoming air which Tully esteemed the
criterion of fine composition, and which every reader, he
says, imagins so easy to be imitated, yet will find so
difficult to attain, is the prevailing characteristic of
all that excellent author's most elegant performances. (2)
In a word, one may justly apply to him what Plato, in his
allegorical language, says of Aristophanes; (3) that the
Graces, having searched all the world round for a temple
wherein they might for ever dwell, settled at last in the
breast of Mr. Addison. Adieu. I am, &c.

Notes

1 'I do not know how to demonstrate it, and I feel it
   deeply.'
2 Possibly 'De Oratoria', III. 179-80; 'Ad Herrenium',
   IV. 17.
3 Plato, 'Symposium', sects. 189ff.: 'The Speech of
   Aristophanes.'

62. JOSEPH WARTON, 'AN ESSAY ON THE WRITINGS AND GENIUS
OF POPE'

1756

Joseph Warton (1722-1800) published his 'Essay' in 1756.
He regarded Pope as 'the great Poet of Reason, the *First*
of Ethical authors in verse'.

This is an excerpt from the first edition, pp. 159,
260-2, 265-72.

The arts used by Addison to suppress the rising merit of
POPE, which are now fully laid open, give one pain to
behold, to what mean artifices envy and malignity will
compel a gentleman and a genius to descend. It is certain, that Addison discouraged POPE from inserting the
machinery in 'The Rape of the Lock': that he privately
insinuated that POPE was a Tory and a Jacobite; and had
a hand in writing the 'Examiners': that Addison himself
translated the first book of Homer, published under
Tickell's name: (1) and that he secretly encouraged
Gildon to abuse POPE in a virulent pamphlet, for which
Addison paid Gildon ten guineas. This usage extorted
from POPE the famous character of Atticus, (2) which is
perhaps the finest piece of satire extant....

The tragedy of 'Cato' itself, is a glaring instance of
the force of party; (3) so heavy and declamatory a drama
would never have met with such rapid and amazing success,
if every line and sentiment had not been particularly
tortured, and applied, to recent events, and the reigning
disputes of the times. The purity and energy of the diction, and the loftiness of the sentiments, copied in a
great measure from Lucan, Tacitus, and Seneca the philosopher, merit approbation. But I have always thought,
that those pompous Roman sentiments are not so difficult
to be produced, as is vulgarly imagined; and which,
indeed, dazzle only the vulgar. A stroke of nature is, in
my opinion, worth a hundred such thoughts, as,

When vice prevails, and impious men bear sway,
The post of honour is a private station. (4)

'Cato' is a fine dialogue on liberty, and the love of
one's country; but considered as a dramatic performance,
nay as a model of a just tragedy, as some have affectedly
represented it, it must be owned to want, ACTION and
PATHOS; the two hinges, I presume, on which a just
tragedy ought necessarily to turn, and without which it
cannot subsist. It wants also CHARACTER, although that
be not so essentially necessary to a tragedy as ACTION.
Syphax, indeed, in his interview with Juba, (5) bears
some marks of a rough African: the speeches of the rest
may be transferred to any of the personages concerned.
The simile drawn from mount Atlas, and the description of
the Numidian traveller smothered in the desert, are indeed
in character, but sufficiently obvious. (6) How Addison
could fall into the false and unnatural custom of ending
his three first acts with similes, is amazing in so chast
and correct a writer. The loves of Juba and Marcia, of

Portius and Lucia, are vicious and insipid episodes,
debase the dignity, and destroy the unity of the fable....
     Having been imperceptibly led into this little criti-
cism on the tragedy of 'Cato', I beg leave to speak a few
words on some other of Addison's pieces. The first of his
poems addrest to Dryden, Sir John Somers, and king
William, are languid, prosaic, and void of any poetical
imagery or spirit. (7) The 'Letter from Italy', is by no
means equal to a subject so fruitful of genuine poetry,
and which might have warmed the most cold and correct
imagination. (8) One would have expected a young traveller in the height of his genius and judgment, would have
broke out into some strokes of enthusiasm. With what
flatness and unfeelingness has he spoken of statuary and
painting! Raphael never received a more flegmatic elogy.
The slavery and superstition of the present Romans, are
well touched upon towards the conclusion; but I will venture to name a little piece, on a parallel subject, that
greatly excells this celebrated Letter; and in which are
as much lively and original imagery, strong painting, and
manly sentiments of freedom, as I have ever read in our
language. It is a Copy of Verses written at Virgil's
Tomb, and printed in Dodsley's Miscellanies. (9)
     That there are many well wrought descriptions, and
even pathetic strokes, in 'The Campaign', (10) it would be
stupidity and malignity to deny. But surely the regular
march which the poet has observed from one town to
another, as if he had been a commissary of the army,
cannot well be excused. There is a passage in Boileau,
so remarkably opposite to this fault of Addison, that one
would almost be tempted to think he had 'The Campaign' in
his eye, when he wrote it, if the time would admit it.

     Loin ces rimeurs craintifs, dont l'esprit phlegmatique
     Garde dans ses fureurs un ordre didactique;
     Qui chantant d'un heros les progrés éclatans,
     MAIGRES HISTORIENS, SUIVRONT L'ORDRE DES
          TEMPS;
     Ils n'osent un moment prendre un sujet de vue,
     Pour prendre Dole, il faut que Lille soit rendue;
     Et que leur vers exact, ainsi que Mezerai,
     Ait fait déja tomber - les remparts de Coutrai. (11)

The most spirited verses Addison has written, are, an
'Imitation of the third ode of the third book of Horace'
which is indeed performed with energy and vigour; and his
compliment to Kneller, on the picture of king George the
first. The occasion of this last poem is peculiarly
happy; for among the works of Phidias which he enumerates,

he selects such statues as exactly mark, and characterise,
the last six British kings and queens.

> Great Pan who wont to chase the fair,
> And lov'd the spreading OAK, was there;
> Old Saturn too, with upcast eyes,
> Beheld his ABDICATED skies;
> And mighty Mars for war renown'd,
> In adamantine armor frown'd:
> By him the childless goddess rose,
> Minerva, studious to compose
> Her twisted threads; the web she strung,
> And o'er a loom of marble hung;
> Thetis the troubled ocean's queen,
> Match'd with a MORTAL, next was seen,
> Reclining on a funeral urn,
> Her short liv'd darling son to mourn.
> The last was HE, whose thunder slew
> The Titan race, a rebel crew,
> That from a HUNDRED HILLS ally'd,
> In impious league their king defy'd. (12)

There is scarcely, I believe, any instance, where mythology has been applied with so much delicacy and dexterity,
and has been contrived to answer in its application, so
minutely, exactly, and in so many corresponding circumstances.

Whatever censures we have here, too boldly, perhaps,
ventured to deliver on the *professed* poetry of Addison, yet
must we candidly own, that in various parts of his prose-
essays, are to be found many strokes of genuine and sublime poetry; many marks of a vigorous and exuberant imagination. Particularly, in the noble allegory of Pain and
Pleasure, the Vision of Mirza, the story of Maraton and
Yaratilda, of Constantia and Theodosius, and the beautiful
eastern tale of Abdallah and Balsora; and many others:
together with several strokes in the Essay on the pleasures of imagination. It has been the lot of many great
names, not to have been able to express themselves with
beauty and propriety in the fetters of verse, in their
respective languages; who have yet manifested the force,
fertility, and creative power of a most poetic genius, in
prose. (13) This was the case of Plato, of Lucian, of
Fenelon, of Sir Philip Sidney, and of Dr. T. Burnet, who
in his 'Theory of the Earth', has displayed an imagination, very nearly equal to that of Milton.

> ────────Maenia mundi
> Discedunt! totum video per Inane geri res! (14)

After all, the chief and characteristical excellency of
Addison, was his HUMOUR; for in humour no mortal has
excelled him except Moliere. Witness the character of Sir
Roger de Coverly, so original, so natural, and so invio-
lably preserved; particularly, in the month, which the
'Spectator' spends at his hall in the country. Witness
also 'The Drummer', that excellent and neglected comedy,
that just picture of life and real manners, where the
poet never speaks in his own person, or totally drops or
forgets a character, for the sake of introducing a brilliant simile, or acute remark: where no train is laid for
wit; no JEREMYS, or BENS, are suffer'd to appear. (15).

Notes

1   John Butt points out ('Poems of Alexander Pope', IV,
    p. 341) that Pope 'perceived a sinister significance
    in Addison's advising him not to alter "The Rape of
    the Lock"; and he believed, not without some justifi-
    cation, that Addison had encouraged Tickell to trans-
    late the "Iliad" in order to injure his translations.'
2   'Epistle to Dr. Arbuthnot', 193-214.
3   'Addison assured Pope he did not bring his tragedy on
    the stage with any party views; nay, desired Pope to
    carry the poem to the Lords Oxford and Bolingbroke,
    for their perusal. The play, however, was always con-
    sidered as a warning to the people, that liberty was
    in danger during that Tory ministry' (Warton).
4   'Cato', IV. iv. 141-2.
5   I. iv.
6   I. vi. 83-7; II. vi. 51-7.
7   'To Mr. Dryden' (1693); 'A Poem to his Majesty',
    presented to Sir John Somers (1695).
8   'A Letter from Italy' (1704).
9   'Virgil's Tomb. Naples 1741', in 'A Collection of
    Poems in six volumes by Several Hands' (printed for
    R. and J. Dodsley, 1758), IV, pp. 110-15.
10 'The Campaign' (1705).
11 'L'Art Poëtique', Chant II.
12 'To Sir Godfrey Kneller on his Picture of the King'
    (1716), 59-76.
13 An allusion to John Hawkesworth and his eastern
    stories in the 'Adventurer' (1753-4).
14 Lucretius, 'De Rerum Natura', III. 16-17: 'The walls
    of the heavens open out, I see action going on
    throughout the whole void.'
15 Characters in Congreve's 'Love for Love'.

63.   EDWARD YOUNG, 'CONJECTURES ON ORIGINAL COMPOSITION'

1759

Edward Young became in 1711 or 1712 a protégé of Addison
through his friendship with Thomas Tickell. Young wrote
one of the adulatory poems prefixed to 'Cato'; and a
poetic epistle to Addison on the death of Queen Anne. His
first literary success came with the publication of 'The
Universal Passion' (1725-8). Taking holy orders, he
became rector of Welwyn, where he wrote 'Night Thoughts'
(1742-5) and 'Conjectures on Original Composition' (1759).
   The extract is from 'Conjectures on Original Composition; in a letter to Sir Charles Grandison', 1st edition,
pp. 86-113.

Among the brightest of the moderns, Mr. *Addison* must take
his place. Who does not approach his character with great
respect? They who refuse to close with the public in his
praise, refuse at their peril. But, if men will be fond
of their own opinions, some hazard must be run. He had,
what *Dryden* and *Johnson* wanted, a warm, and feeling
heart; but, being of a grave and bashful nature, thro' a
philosophic reserve, and a sort of moral prudery, he conceal'd it, where he should have let loose all his fire,
and have show'd the most tender sensibilities of heart.
At his celebrated 'Cato', few tears are shed, but *Cato*'s
own; which, indeed, are truly great, but unaffecting,
except to the noble few, who love their country better
than themselves. The bulk of mankind want virtue enough
to be touched by them. His strength of genius has reared
up one glorious image, more lofty, and truly golden, than
that in the plains of *Dura*, for cool admiration to gaze
at, and warm patriotism (how rare!) to worship; while
those two throbbing pulses of the drama, by which alone it
is shown to live, *terror* and *pity*, neglected thro' the
whole, leave our unmolested hearts at perfect peace.
Thus the poet, like his hero, thro' mistaken excellence,
and virtue overstrain'd, becomes a sort of suicide; and
that which is most dramatic in the drama, dies. All his
charms of poetry are but as funeral flowers, which adorn;
all his noble sentiments but as rich spices, which embalm,
the tragedy deceased.
   Of tragedy, pathos is not only the life and soul, but
the soul inextinguishable; it charms us thro' a thousand

faults. Decorations, which in this author abound, tho'
they might immortalize other poesy, are the *splendida
peccata* which damn the drama; while, on the contrary, the
murder of all other beauties is a venial sin, nor plucks
the laurel from the tragedian's brow. , Was it otherwise,
Shakespeare himself would run some hazard of losing his
crown.

Socrates frequented the plays of *Euripides*; and, what
living *Socrates* would decline the theatre, at the representation of 'Cato'? *Tully*'s assassins found him in his
litter, reading the 'Medea' of the *Grecian* poet, to prepare himself for death. Part of 'Cato' might be read to
the same end. In the weight and dignity of moral reflection, *Addison* resembles that poet, who was called the
dramatic philosopher; and is himself, as he says of *Cato,
ambitiously sententious*. But as to the singular talent so
remarkable in *Euripides*, at melting down hearts into the
tender streams of grief and pity, there the resemblance
fails. His beauties sparkle, but do not warm; they
sparkle as stars in a frosty night. There is, indeed„ a
constellation in his play; there is the philosopher,
patriot, orator, and poet; but where is the tragedian?
And, if that is wanting,

   Cur in theatrum Cato severe venisti? MART.

And, when I recollect what passed between him and *Dryden*,
in relation to this drama, I must add the next line,

   An ideo tantum veneras, ut exires? (1)

For, when *Addison* was a student at *Oxford*, he sent up this
play to his friend *Dryden*, as a proper person to recommend
it to the theatre, if it deserved it; who returned it,
with very great commendation; but with his opinion, that,
on the stage, it could not meet with its deserved success.
But tho' the performance was denied the theatre, it
brought its author on the public stage of life. For persons in power inquiring soon after of the head of his college for a youth of parts, *Addison* was recommended, and
readily received, by means of the great reputation which
Dryden had just then spread of him above.

There is this similitude between the poet and the play;
as this is more fit for the closet than the stage; so,
that shone brighter in private conversation than on the
public scene. They both had a sort of *local* excellency,
as the heathen gods a local divinity; beyond such a bound
they, unadmired; and *these*, unadored. This puts me in
mind of *Plato*, who denied *Homer* to the public; that *Homer*

which, when in his closet, was rarely out of his hand. (2)
Thus, tho' *Cato* is not calculated to signalize himself in
the warm emotions of the theatre, yet we find him a most
amiable companion, in our calmer delights of recess.

Notwithstanding what has been offered, this, in many
views, is an exquisite piece. But there is so much more
of art, than nature in it, that I can scarce forbear calling it, an exquisite piece of statuary,

> *Where the smooth chisel all its skill has shown,*
> *To soften into flesh the rugged stone.* ADDISON. (3)

That is, where art has taken great pains to labour un-
dramatic matter into dramatic life; which is impossible.
However, as it is, like *Pygmalion*, we cannot but fall in
love with it, and wish it was alive. How would a *Shakespeare*, or an *Otway*, have answered our wishes. They would
have outdone *Prometheus*, and, with their heavenly fire,
have given him not only life, but immortality. At their
dramas (such is the force of nature) the poet is out of
sight, quite hid behind his *Venus*, never thought of, till
the curtain falls. Art brings our author forward, he
stands before his piece; splendidly indeed, but unfortunately; for the writer must be forgotten by his audience,
during the representation, if for ages he would be remembered by posterity. In the theatre, as in life, delusion
is the charm; and we are undelighted, the first moment we
are undeceived. Such demonstration have we, that the
theatre is not yet opened, in which solid happiness can
be found by man; because none are more than comparatively
good; and folly has a corner in the heart of the wise.

A genius fond of *ornament* should not be wedded to the
tragic muse, which is in *mourning*: We want not to be di-
verted at an entertainment, where our greatest pleasure
arises from the depth of our concern. But whence (by the
way) this odd generation of pleasure from pain? The
movement of our melancholy passions is pleasant, when we
ourselves are safe: We love to be at once, miserable, and
unhurt: So are we made; and so made, perhaps, to show us
the divine goodness; to show that none of our passions
were designed to give us pain, except when being pain'd is
for our advantage on the whole; which is evident from this
instance, in which we see, that passions the most painful
administer greatly, sometimes, to our delight. Since
great names have accounted otherwise for this particular,
I wish this solution, though to me probable, may not prove
a mistake.

To close our thoughts on 'Cato': He who sees not much
beauty in it, has no taste for poetry; he who sees nothing

else, has no taste for the stage. Whilst it justifies
censure, it extorts applause. It is much to be admired,
but little to be felt. Had it not been a tragedy, it had
been immortal; as it is a tragedy, its uncommon fate somewhat resembles his, who, for conquering gloriously, was
condemn'd to die. Both shone, but shone fatally; because
in breach of their respective laws, the laws of the drama,
and the laws of arms. But how rich in reputation must
that author be, who can spare a 'Cato', without feeling
the loss?

That loss by our author would scarce be felt; it would
be but dropping a single feather from a wing, that mounts
him above his cotemporaries. He has a more refined,
decent, judicious, and extensive genius, than *Pope*, or
Swift. To distinguish this triumvirate from each other,
and, like *Newton*, to discover the different colours in
these genuine and meridian rays of literary light, *Swift*
is a singular wit, *Pope* a correct poet, *Addison* a great
author. *Swift* looked on wit as the *jus divinum* to dominion
and sway in the world; and considered as usurpation, all
power that was lodged in persons of less sparkling understandings. This inclined him to tyranny in wit; *Pope* was
somewhat of his opinion, but was for softening tyranny
into lawful monarchy; yet were there some acts of severity
in his reign. *Addison*'s crown was elective, he reigned by
the public voice:

> ———————— *Volentes*
> *Per populos dat jura, viamque affectat Olympo.* VIRG.(4)

But as good books are the medicine of the mind, if we
should dethrone these authors, and consider them, not in
their royal, but their medicinal capacity, might it not
then be said, that *Addison* prescribed a wholesome and
pleasant regimen, which was universally relished, and did
much good; that *Pope* preferred a purgative of satire,
which, tho' wholesome, was too painful in its operation;
and that *Swift* insisted on a large dose of ipecacuanha,
which, tho' readily swallowed from the fame of the physician, yet, if the patient had any delicacy of taste, he
threw up the remedy, instead of the disease?

Addison wrote little in verse, much in sweet, elegant,
Virgilian, prose; so let me call it, since *Longinus* calls
Herodotus most *Homeric*, and *Thucydides* is said to have
formed his style on *Pindar*. *Addison*'s compositions are
built with the finest materials, in the taste of the
antients, and (to speak his own language) on truly *Classic ground*: And tho' they are the delight of the present
age, yet am I persuaded that they will receive more

justice from posterity. I never read him, but I am struck
with such a disheartening idea of perfection, that I drop
my pen. And, indeed, far superior writers should forget
his compositions, if they would be greatly pleased with
their own.

And yet (perhaps you have not observed it) what is the
common language of the world, and even of his admirers,
concerning him? They call him an *elegant* writer: That
elegance which shines on the surface of his compositions,
seems to dazzle their understanding, and render it a little
blind to the depth of sentiment, which lies beneath: Thus
(hard fate!) he loses reputation with them, by doubling
his title to it. On subjects the most interesting, and
important, no author of his age has written with greater,
I had almost said, with equal weight: And they who commend him for his elegance, pay him such a sort of compliment, by their abstemious praise, as they would pay to
Lucretia, if they should commend her only for her beauty.

But you say, that you know his value already —— You
know, indeed, the value of his writings, and close with
the world in thinking them immortal; but, I believe, you
know not, that his name would have deserved immortality,
tho' he had never written; and that, by a better title
than the pen can give: You know too, that his life was
amiable; but, perhaps, you are still to learn, that his
death was triumphant: That is a glory granted to very
few: And the paternal hand of Providence which, sometimes,
snatches home its beloved children in a moment, must convince us, that it is a glory of no great consequence to
the dying individual; that, when it is granted, it is
granted chiefly for the sake of the surviving world, which
may profit by his pious example, to whom is indulged the
strength, and opportunity to make his virtue shine out
brightest at the point of death: And, here, permit me to
take notice, that the world will, probably, profit more by
a pious example of lay-extraction, than by one born of the
church; the latter being, usually, taxed with an abatement
of influence by the bulk of mankind: Therefore, to smother
a bright example of this superior good influence, may be
reputed a sort of murder injurious to the living, and
unjust to the dead.

Such an example have we in *Addison*; which, tho'
hitherto suppressed, yet, when once known, is insuppres-
sible, of a nature too rare, too striking to be forgotten.
For, after a long, and manly, but vain struggle with his
distemper, he dismissed his physicians, and with them all
hopes of life: But with his hopes of life he dismissed not
his concern for the living, but sent for a youth nearly
related, and finely accomplished, yet not above being the

better for good impressions from a dying friend: He came;
but life now glimmering in the socket, the dying friend
was silent: After a decent, and proper pause, the youth
said, 'Dear Sir! you sent for me: I believe, and I hope,
that you have some commands; I shall hold them most
sacred:' May distant ages not only hear, but feel, the
reply! Forcibly grasping the youth's hand, he softly said,
'See in what peace a Christian can die.' He spoke with
difficulty, and soon expired. Thro' grace divine, how
great is man! Thro' divine mercy, how stingless death!
Who would not thus expire?

What an inestimable legacy were those *few dying words*
to the youth beloved? What a glorious supplement to his
own valuable fragment on the truth of Christianity? What
a full demonstration, that his fancy could not feign
beyond what his virtue could reach? For when he would
strike us most strongly with the grandeur of *Roman* magnanimity, his dying hero is ennobled with this sublime
sentiment,

> *While yet I live, let me not live in vain.* CATO. (5)

But how much more sublime is that sentiment when real-
ized in life; when dispelling the languors, and appeasing
the pains of a last hour; and brightening with illustrious
action the dark avenue, and all-awful confines of an eternity? When his soul scarce animated his body, strong
faith, and ardent charity, animated his soul into divine
ambition of saving more than his own. It is for our honour, and our advantage, to hold him high in our esteem:
For the better men are, the more they will admire him;
and the more they admire him, the better will they be.

By undrawing the long-closed curtain of his death-bed,
have I not showed you a stranger in him whom you knew so
well? Is not this of your favourite author,

> ——— *Nota major imago?* VIRG. (6)

His compositions are but a noble preface; the grand work
is his death: That is a work which is read in heaven: How
has it join'd the final approbation of angels to the previous applause of men? How gloriously has he opened a
splendid path, thro' fame immortal, into eternal peace?
How has he given religion to triumph amidst the ruins of
his nature? And, stronger than death, risen higher in
virtue when breathing his last?

If all our men of genius had *so* breathed their last;
if all our men of genius, like him, had been men of genius
for *eternals*; *then*, had we never been pained by the report

of a latter end —— oh! how unlike to this? But a little
to balance our pain, let us consider, that such reports
as make us, at once, adore, and tremble, are of use, when
too many there are, who must tremble before they will
adore; and who convince us, to our shame, that the surest
refuge of our endanger'd virtue is in the fears and
terrors of the disingenuous human heart.

'But reports, you say, may be false; and you farther
ask me, If all reports were true, how came an anecdote of
so much honour to human nature, as mine, to lie so long
unknown? What inauspicious planet interposed to lay its
lustre under so lasting and so surprising an eclipse?'

The fact is indisputably true; nor are you to rely on
me for the truth of it: My report is but a second edition:
It was published before, tho' obscurely, and with a cloud
before it. As clouds before the sun are often beautiful;
so, this of which I speak. How finely pathetic are those
two lines, which this so solemn and affecting scene
inspired?

> *He taught us how to live; and, oh! too high*
> *A price for knowledge, taught us how to die.* TICKELL.
>   (7)

With truth wrapped in darkness, so sung our oracle to
the public, but explained himself to me: He was present at
his patron's death, and that account of it here given, he
gave to me before his eyes were dry: By what means *Addison
taught us how to die*, the poet left to be made known by a
late, and less able hand; but one more zealous for his
patron's glory: Zealous, and impotent, as the poor *AEgyp-
tian*, who gather'd a few splinters of a broken boat, as
a funeral pile for the great *Pompey*, studious of doing
honour to so renown'd a name: Yet had not this poor plank
(permit me, here, so to call this imperfect page) been
thrown out, the chief article of his patron's glory would
probably have been sunk for ever, and late ages have
received but a fragment of his fame: A fragment glorious
indeed, for his genius how bright! But to commend him for
composition, tho' immortal, is detraction *now*; if there
our encomium ends: Let us look farther to that concluding
scene, which spoke human nature not unrelated to the
divine. To that let us pay the long, and large arrear of
our greatly posthumous applause.

This you will think a long digression; and justly; if
that may be called a digression, which was my chief
inducement for writing at all: I had long wished to deliver up to the public this sacred deposit, which by
Providence was lodged in my hands; and I entered on the

present undertaking partly as an introduction to that,
which is more worthy to see the light; of which I gave an
intimation in the beginning of my letter: For this is the
monumental marble there mentioned, to which I promised to
conduct you; this is the *sepulchral lamp*, the long-hidden
lustre of our accomplished countryman, who now rises, as
from his tomb, to receive the regard so greatly due to
the dignity of his death; a death to be distinguished by
tears of joy; a death which angels beheld with delight.

And shall that, which would have shone conspicuous amid
the resplendent lights of Christianity's glorious morn, by
these dark days be dropped into oblivion? Dropped it is;
and dropped by our sacred, august, and ample register of
renown, which has entered in its marble-memoirs the dim
splendor of far inferior worth: Tho' so lavish of praise,
and so talkative of the dead, yet is it silent on a subject, which (if any) might have taught its unletter'd
stones to speak: If powers were not wanting, a monument
more durable than those of marble, should proudly rise in
this ambitious page, to the new, and far nobler *Addison*,
than that which you, and the public, have so long, and so
much admired: Nor this nation only; for it is *Europe's
Addison*, as well as ours; tho' *Europe* knows not half his
title to her esteem; being as yet unconscious that the
dying Addison far outshines her *Addison immortal*: Would
we resemble him? Let us not limit our ambition to the
least illustrious part of his character; heads, indeed,
are crowned on earth; but hearts only are crowned in
heaven: A truth, which, in such an *age of authors*, should
not be forgotten.

It is piously to be hoped, that this narrative may have
some effect, since all listen, when a death-bed speaks;
and regard the person departing as an actor of a part,
which the great master of the drama has appointed us to
perform to-morrow: This was a *Roscius* on the stage of
life; his exit how great? Ye lovers of virtue! *plaudite*:
And let us, my friend! ever 'remember his end, as well as
our own, that we may never do amiss.' I am,

                         Dear SIR,
                              Your most obliged,
                                  humble Servant.

Notes

1 To Cato, in 'The Epigrams of Martial', Bk. I: 'Why on
   our scene, stern Cato, enter here? / Did you then
   enter only to go out?'
2 'Republic', 607 C-D: 'Homer is the most poetic of poets

and the first of tragedians, but we must know the
truth, that we can admit no poetry into our city save
only hymns to the gods and the praises of good men.'
3   'Letter from Italy', 85-6.
4   'Georgics', IV, 561-2: '...and gave a victor's laws
unto willing nations, and essayed the path to Heaven.'
5   'Cato', V. iv. 82.
6   'Aeneid', II, 773: 'a form larger than her wont'.
7   Tickell's 'Elegy' in the first volume of 'Addison's
Works', (see No. 60).

64.   HUGH BLAIR, 'LECTURES ON RHETORIC AND BELLES LETTRES'

[1760], 1783

Hugh Blair (1718-1800) was a Scottish divine and active in
Edinburgh's literary circle, which included David Hume,
Adam Ferguson, Adam Smith, Henry Home Lord Kames, and
others. On 11 December 1759 he began to read lectures on
criticism in the University of Edinburgh. In August 1760
he was made professor of rhetoric there, and on 7 April
1762 Regius Professor of rhetoric and belles-lettres.

From Lecture 19

Of the latter of these [Archbishop Tillotson, Sir William
Temple], the highest, most correct, and ornamented degree
of the simple manner, Mr. Addison, is, beyond doubt, in
the English Language, the most perfect example; and therefore, though not without some faults, he is, on the whole,
the safest model for imitation, and the freest from considerable defects, which the Language affords. Perspicuous and pure he is in the highest degree; his precision,
indeed, not very great; yet nearly as great as the subjects which he treats of require: the construction of his
sentences easy, agreeable, and commonly very musical;
carrying a character of smoothness, more than of strength.
In Figurative Language, he is rich; particularly, in
similies and metaphors; which are so employed, as to
render his Style splendid without being gaudy. There is
not the least Affectation in his manner; we see no marks
of labour; nothing forced or constrained; but great

elegance joined with great ease and simplicity. He is, in particular, distinguished by a character of modesty, and of politeness, which appears in all his writings. No author has a more popular and insinuating manner; and the great regard which he every where shews for virtue and religion, recommends him highly. If he fails in any thing, it is in want of strength and precision, which renders his manner, though perfectly suited to such essays as he writes in the 'Spectator', not altogether a proper model for any of the higher and more elaborate kinds of composition. Though the public have ever done much justice to his merit, yet the nature of his merit has not always been seen in its true light: for, though his poetry be elegant, he certainly bears a higher rank among the prose writers, than he is intitled to among the poets; and, in prose, his humour is of a much higher, and more original strain, than his philosophy. The character of Sir Roger de Coverley discovers more genius than the critique on Milton.

Such authors as those, whose characters I have been giving, one never tires of reading. There is nothing in their manner that strains or fatigues our thoughts: we are pleased, without being dazzled by their lustre. So powerful is the charm of Simplicity in an author of real genius, that it atones for many defects, and reconciles us to many a careless expression. Hence, in all the most excellent authors, both in prose and verse, the simple and natural manner may be always remarked; although other beauties being predominant, this form not their peculiar and distinguishing character. Thus Milton is simple in the midst of all his grandeur; and Demosthenes in the midst of all his vehemence. To grave and solemn writings, Simplicity of manner adds the more venerable air. Accordingly, this has often been remarked as the prevailing character throughout all the sacred Scriptures: and indeed no other character of Style was so much suited to the dignity of inspiration.

Lecture 20

Critical examination of the style of Mr. Addison, in No. 411. of the 'Spectator'.

I have insisted fully on the subject of Language and Style, both because it is, in itself, of great importance, and because it is more capable of being ascertained by precise rule, than several other parts of composition. A critical analysis of the Style of some good author will tend further to illustrate the subject; as it will suggest observations which I have not had occasion to make, and will show, in

the most practical light, the use of those which I have
made.

Mr. Addison is the author whom I have chosen for this
purpose. The 'Spectator', of which his papers are the
chief ornament, is a book which is in the hands of every
one, and which cannot be praised too highly. The good
sense, and good writing, the useful morality, and the
admirable vein of humour which abound in it, render it one
of those standard books which have done the greatest honour
to the English nation. I have formerly given the general
character of Mr. Addison's Style and manner, as natural and
unaffected, easy and polite, and full of those graces which
a flowery imagination diffuses over writing. At the same
time, though one of the most beautiful writers in the Language, he is not the most correct; a circumstance which renders his composition the more proper to be the subject of
our present criticism. The free and flowing manner of this
amiable writer sometimes led him into inaccuracies, which
the more studied circumspection and care of far inferior
writers have taught them to avoid. Remarking his beauties,
therefore, which I shall have frequent occasion to do as I
proceed, I must also point out his negligences and defects.
Without a free, impartial discussion of both the faults and
beauties which occur in his composition, it is evident,
this piece of criticism would be of no service: and, from
the freedom which I use in criticising Mr. Addison's Style,
none can imagine, that I mean to depreciate his writings,
after having repeatedly declared the high opinion which I
entertain of them. The beauties of this author are so
many, and the general character of his Style is so elegant
and estimable, that the minute imperfections I shall have
occasion to point out, are but like those spots in the sun,
which may be discovered by the assistance of art, but which
have no effect in obscuring its lustre. It is, indeed, my
judgment, that what Quinctilian applies to Cicero, 'Ille
se profecisse sciat, cui Cicero valde placebit,' (1) may,
with justice, be applied to Mr. Addison; that to be highly
pleased with his manner of writing, is the criterion of
one's having acquired a good taste in English Style. The
paper on which we are now to enter, is No. 411. the first
of his celebrated 'Essays on the Pleasures of the Imagination', in the Sixth Volume of the 'Spectator'. It begins
thus:

Our sight is the most perfect, and most delightful
of all our senses.

This is an excellent introductory sentence. It is
clear, precise, and simple. The author lays down, in a

few plain words, the proposition which he is going to
illustrate throughout the rest of the paragraph. In this
manner we should always set out. A first sentence should
seldom be a long, and never an intricate one.
  He might have said, 'Our sight is the most perfect, and
the most delightful'. - But he has judged better, in omit-
ting to repeat the article, *the*. For the repetition of it
is proper, chiefly when we intend to point out the objects
of which we speak, as distinguished from, or contrasted
with, each other; and when we want that the reader's
attention should rest on that distinction. For instance;
had Mr. Addison intended to say, That our sight is at once
the most *delightful*, and the most *useful*, of all our
senses, the article might then have been repeated with
propriety, as a clear and strong distinction would have
been conveyed. But as between *perfect* and *delightful*,
there is less contrast, there was no occasion for such
repetition. It would have had no other effect, but to
add a word unnecessarily to the sentence. He proceeds:

> It fills the mind with the largest variety of ideas,
> converses with its objects at the greatest distance,
> and continues the longest in action, without being
> tired or satiated with its proper enjoyments.

This sentence deserves attention, as remarkably harmonious, and well constructed. It possesses, indeed,
almost all the properties of a perfect sentence. It is
entirely perspicuous. It is loaded with no superfluous
or unnecessary words. For, *tired or satiated*, towards
the end of the sentence, are not used for synonymous
terms. They convey distinct ideas, and refer to different members of the period; that this sense 'continues the
longest in action without being tired', that is, without
being fatigued with its action; and also, without being
'satiated with its proper enjoyments'. That quality of a
good sentence which I termed its unity, is here perfectly
preserved. It is *our sight* of which he speaks. This is
the object carried through the sentence, and presented to
us, in every member of it, by those verbs, *fills*, *converses*, *continues*, to each of which, it is clearly the nomi-
native. Those capital words are disposed of in the most
proper places; and that uniformity is maintained in the
construction of the sentence, which suits the unity of the
object.
  Observe too, the music of the period; consisting of
three members, each of which, agreeably to a rule I formerly mentioned, grows, and rises above the other in
sound, till the sentence is conducted, at last, to one of

the most melodious closes which our Language admits;
'without being tired or satiated with its proper enjoyments'. *Enjoyments*, is a word of length and dignity,
exceedingly proper for a close which is designed to be a
musical one. The harmony is the more happy, that this
disposition of the members of the period which suits the
sound so well, is no less just and proper with respect to
the sense. It follows the order of nature. First, we
have the variety of objects mentioned, which sight furnishes to the mind; next, we have the action of sight on
those objects; and lastly, we have the time and continu-
ance of its action. Nor order could be more natural or
happy.

This sentence has still another beauty. It is figurative, without being too much so for the subject. A metaphor runs through it. The sense of sight is, in some
degree, personified. We are told of its *conversing* with
its objects; and of its not being *tired* or *satiated* with
its *enjoyments*; all which expressions are plain allusions
to the actions and feelings of men. This is that slight
sort of Personification, which, without any appearance of
boldness, and without elevating the fancy much above its
ordinary state, renders discourse picturesque, and leads
us to conceive the author's meaning more distinctly, by
clothing abstract ideas, in some degree, with sensible
colours. Mr. Addison abounds with this beauty of Style
beyond most authors; and the sentence which we have been
considering, is very expressive of his manner of writing.
There is no blemish in it whatever, unless that a strict
Critic might perhaps object, that the epithet *large*, which
he applies to *variety*, - 'the largest variety of ideas',
is an epithet more commonly applied to extent than to
number. It is plain, that he here employed it to avoid
the repetition of the word *great*, which occurs immediately
afterwards.

> The sense of feeling can, indeed, give us a notion of
> extension, shape, and all other ideas that enter at the
> eye, except colours; but, at the same time, it is very
> much straitened and confined in its operations, to the
> number, bulk, and distance of its particular objects.

This sentence is by no means so happy as the former. It
is, indeed, neither clear nor elegant. *Extension and shape*
can, with no propriety, be called *ideas*; they are properties of matter. Neither is it accurate, even according to
Mr. Locke's philosophy (with which our Author seems here to
have puzzled himself), to speak of any sense *giving us a
notion of ideas*; our senses give us the ideas themselves.

The meaning would have been much more clear, if the Author had expressed himself thus: 'The sense of feeling can, indeed, give us the idea of extension, figure, and all the other properties of matter which are perceived by the eye, except colours.'

The latter part of the sentence is still more embarrassed. For what meaning can we make of the sense of feeling being 'confined, in its operations, to the number, bulk, and distance, of its particular objects'? Surely, every sense is confined, as much as the sense of feeling, to the number, bulk, and distance of its own objects. Sight and feeling are, in this respect, perfectly on a level; neither of them can extend beyond their own objects. The turn of expression is so inaccurate here, that one would be apt to suspect two words to have been omitted in the printing, which were originally in Mr. Addison's manuscript; because the insertion of them would render the sense much more intelligible and clear. These two words are, *with regard*: - 'it is very much straitened, and confined, in its operations, with regard to the number, bulk, and distance of its particular objects.' The meaning then would be, that feeling is more limited than sight *in this respect*; that it is confined to a narrower circle, to a smaller number of objects.

The epithet *particular*, applied to *objects*, in the conclusion of the sentence, is redundant, and conveys no meaning whatever. Mr. Addison seems to have used it in place of *peculiar*, as indeed he does often in other passages of his writings. But *particular* and *peculiar*, though they are too often confounded, are words of different import from each other. *Particular* stands opposed to *general*; *peculiar* stands opposed, to what is possessed in *common with others*. *Particular* expresses what in the logical Style is called *Species*; *peculiar*, what is called *differentia*. - *Its peculiar objects* would have signified in this place, the objects of the sense of feeling, as distinguished from the objects of any other sense; and would have had more meaning than *its particular objects*. Though, in truth, neither the one nor the other epithet was requisite. It was sufficient to have said simply, *its objects*.

Our sight seems designed to supply all these defects, and may be considered as a more delicate and diffusive kind of touch, that spreads itself over an infinite multitude of bodies, comprehends the largest figures, and brings into our reach some of the most remote parts of the universe.

Here again the author's Style returns upon us in all
its beauty. This is a sentence distinct, graceful, well
arranged, and highly musical. In the latter part of it,
it is constructed with three members, which are formed
much in the same manner with those of the second sentence,
on which I bestowed so much praise. The construction is
so similar, that if it had followed immediately after it,
we should have been sensible of a faulty monotony. But
the interposition of another sentence between them, prevents this effect.

It is this sense which furnishes the imagination with
its ideas; so that by the pleasures of the Imagination
or Fancy (which I shall use promiscuously), I here mean
such as arise from visible objects, either when we have
them actually in our view; or when we call up their
ideas into our minds by paintings, statues, descriptions, or any the like occasion.

In place of 'It is this sense which furnishes' - the
author might have said more shortly, 'This sense furnishes'. But the mode of expression which he has used,
is here more proper. This sort of full and ample assertion, *it is this which*, is fit to be used when a proposition of importance is laid down, to which we seek to call
the reader's attention. It is like pointing with the hand
at the object of which we speak. The parenthesis in the
middle of the sentence, 'which I shall use promiscuously',
is not clear. He ought to have said, 'terms which I shall
use promiscuously'; as the verb *use* relates not to the
pleasures of the imagination, but to the terms of fancy
and imagination, which he was to employ as synonymous.
'Any the like occasion' - to call a painting or a statue
an occasion is not a happy expression, nor is it very
proper to speak of 'calling up ideas by occasions'. The
common phrase, *any such means*, would have been more
natural.

We cannot indeed have a single image in the fancy, that
did not make its first entrance through the sight; but
we have the power of retaining, altering, and compounding those images which we have once received, into all
the varieties of picture and vision that are most
agreeable to the imagination; for, by this faculty, a
man in a dungeon is capable of entertaining himself
with scenes and landscapes more beautiful than any that
can be found in the whole compass of nature.

It may be of use to remark, that in one member of this

sentence there is an inaccuracy in syntax. It is very
proper to say, 'altering and compounding those images
which we have once received, into all the varieties of
picture and vision'. But we can with no propriety say,
'retaining them into all the varieties'; and yet, according to the manner in which the words are ranged, this construction is unavoidable. For *retaining*, *altering*, and
compounding, are participles, each of which equally refers
to, and governs the subsequent noun, *those images*; and
that noun again is necessarily connected with the following preposition, *into*. This instance shows the importance
of carefully attending to the rules of Grammar and Syntax;
when so pure a writer as Mr. Addison could, through inad-
vertence, be guilty of such an error. The construction
might easily have been rectified, by disjoining the par-
ticiple *retaining* from the other two participles in this
way: 'We have the power of retaining those images which
we have once received; and of altering and compounding
them into all the varieties of picture and vision;' or
better perhaps thus: 'We have the power of retaining,
altering, and compounding those images which we have once
received; and of forming them into all the varieties of
picture and vision.' - The latter part of the sentence is
clear and elegant.

> There are few words in the English Language, which are
> employed in a more loose and uncircumscribed sense than
> those of the Fancy and the Imagination.

'There are few words - which are employed'. - It had
been better, if our author here had said more simply -
'Few words in the English language are employed'. - Mr.
Addison, whose Style is of the free and full, rather than
the nervous kind, deals, on all occasions, in this extended sort of phraseology. But it is proper only when some
assertion of consequence is advanced, and which can bear
an emphasis; such as that in the first sentence of the
former paragraph. On other occasions, these little words
it is, and *there are*, ought to be avoided as redundant and
enfeebling. - 'Those of the Fancy and the Imagination'.
The article ought to have been omitted here. As he does
not mean the powers of *the Fancy and the Imagination*, but
the words only, the article certainly had no proper place;
neither, indeed, was there any occasion for other two
words, *those of*. Better, if the sentence had run thus:
'Few words in the English language are employed in a more
loose and uncircumscribed sense, than Fancy and Imagination.'

I therefore thought it necessary to fix and determine
the notion of these two words, as I intend to make use
of them in the thread of my following speculations,
that the reader may conceive rightly what is the subject which I proceed upon.

Though *fix* and *determine* may appear synonymous words,
yet a difference between them may be remarked, and they
may be viewed, as applied here, with peculiar delicacy.
The author had just said, that the words of which he is
speaking were *loose* and *uncircumscribed*. *Fix* relates to
the first of these, *determine* to the last. We *fix* what
is *loose*; that is, we confine the word to its proper
place, that it may not fluctuate in our imagination, and
pass from one idea to another; and we *determine* what is
uncircumscribed, that is, we ascertain its *termini* or
limits, we draw the circle round it, that we may see its
boundaries. For we cannot conceive the meaning of a word,
nor indeed of any other thing clearly, till we see its
limits, and know how far it extends. These two words,
therefore, have grace and beauty as they are here applied;
though a writer, more frugal of words than Mr. Addison,
would have preferred the single word *ascertain*, which conveys, without any metaphor, the import of them both.
The notion of these words is somewhat of a harsh
phrase, at least not so commonly used, as the *meaning of
these words* - 'as I intend to make use of them in the
thread of my speculations'; this is plainly faulty. A
sort of metaphor is improperly mixed with words in the
literal sense. He might very well have said, 'as I
intend to make use of them in my following speculations'.
- This was plain language; but if he chose to borrow an
allusion from *thread*, that allusion ought to have been
supported; for there is no consistency in 'making use of
them in the thread of speculations'; and, indeed, in ex-
pressing any thing so simple and familiar as this is,
plain language is always to be preferred to metaphorical -
'the subject which I proceed upon', is an ungraceful close
of a sentence; better, 'the subject upon which I proceed'.

I must therefore desire him to remember, that by the
pleasures of the Imagination, I mean only such pleasures as arise originally from sight, and that I divide
these pleasures into two kinds.

As the last sentence began with - 'I therefore thought
it necessary to fix', it is careless to begin this sentence in a manner so very similar, 'I must therefore
desire him to remember'; especially, as the small

variation of using, *on this account*, or, *for this reason*,
in place of *therefore*, would have amended the Style. -
When he says - 'I mean only such pleasures' - it may be
remarked, that the adverb *only* is not in its proper place.
It is not intended here to qualify the verb *mean*, but *such
pleasures*; and therefore should have been placed in as
close connection as possible with the word which it limits
or qualifies. The Style becomes more clear and neat,
when the words are arranged thus: 'by the pleasures of the
Imagination, I mean such pleasures only as arise from
sight.'

> My design being, first of all, to discourse of those
> primary pleasures of the imagination, which entirely
> proceed from such objects as are before our eyes; and,
> in the next place, to speak of those secondary pleas-
> ures of the Imagination, which flow from the ideas of
> visible objects, when the objects are not actually
> before the eye, but are called up into our memories,
> or formed into agreeable visions of things, that are
> either absent or fictitious.

It is a great rule in laying down the division of a
subject, to study neatness and brevity as much as possible. The divisions are then more distinctly apprehended, and more easily remembered. This sentence is not
perfectly happy in that respect. It is somewhat clogged
by a tedious phraseology. 'My design being first of all
to discourse - in the next place to speak of - such
objects as are before our eyes - things that are either
absent or fictitious.' Several words might have been
spared here; and the Style made more neat and compact.

> The pleasures of the Imagination, taken in their full
> extent, are not so gross as those of sense, nor so
> refined as those of the understanding.

This sentence is distinct and elegant.

> The last are indeed more preferable, because they are
> founded on some new knowledge or improvement in the
> mind of man: Yet it must be confessed, that those of
> the Imagination are as great and as transporting as
> the other.

In the beginning of this sentence, the phrase, *more
preferable*, is such a plain inaccuracy, that one wonders
how Mr. Addison should have fallen into it; seeing *preferable* of itself, expresses the comparative degree, and is

the same with more eligible, or more excellent.

I must observe farther, that the proposition contained
in the last member of this sentence, is neither clear nor
neatly expressed - 'it must be confessed, that those of
the imagination are as great, and as transporting as the
other'. - In the former sentence, he had compared three
things together; the pleasures of the Imagination, those
of sense, and those of the understanding. In the beginning of this sentence, he had called the pleasures of the
understanding *the last*: and he ends the sentence, with
observing, that those of the Imagination are as great and
transporting *as the other*. Now, besides that *the other*
makes not a proper contrast with *the last*, he leaves it
ambiguous, whether, by *the other*, he meant the pleasures
of the Understanding, or the pleasures of Sense; for it
may refer to either by the construction; though,
undoubtedly, he intended that it should refer to the pleasures of the Understanding only. The proposition reduced
to perspicuous language, runs thus: 'Yet it must be confessed, that the pleasures of the Imagination, when compared with those of the Understanding, are no less great
and transporting.'

A beautiful prospect delights the soul as much as a
demonstration; and a description in Homer has charmed
more readers than a chapter in Aristotle.

This is a good illustration of what he had been asserting, and is expressed with that happy and elegant turn,
for which our author is very remarkable.

Besides, the pleasures of the Imagination have this
advantage above those of the Understanding, that they
are more obvious, and more easy to be acquired.

This is also an unexceptionable sentence.

It is but opening the eye, and the scene enters.

This sentence is lively and picturesque. By the gaiety
and briskness which it gives the Style, it shows the
advantage of intermixing such a short sentence as this
amidst a run of longer ones, which never fails to have a
happy effect. I must remark, however, a small inaccuracy.
A *scene* cannot be said to *enter*; an *actor* enters; but a
scene *appears*, or *presents itself*.

The colours paint themselves on the fancy, with very
little attention of thought or application of mind in
the beholder.

This is still beautiful illustration; carried on with
that agreeable floweriness of fancy and style, which is
so well suited to those pleasures of the Imagination, of
which the author is treating.

We are struck, we know not how, with the symmetry of
any thing we see, and immediately assent to the beauty
of an object, without enquiring into the particular
causes and occasions of it.

There is a falling off here from the elegance of the
former sentences. We *assent* to the truth of a proposition; but cannot so well be said 'to assent to the
beauty of an object'. *Acknowledge* would have expressed
the sense with more propriety. The close of the sentence
too is heavy and ungraceful - 'the particular causes and
occasions of it' - both *particular*, and *occasions*, are
words quite superfluous; and the pronoun *it* is in some
measure ambiguous, whether it refers to beauty or to
object. It would have been some amendment to the Style to
have run thus: 'we immediately acknowledge the beauty of
an object, without enquiring into the cause of that
beauty.'

A man of a polite imagination is let into a great many
pleasures, that the vulgar are not capable of receiving.

Polite is a term more commonly applied to manners or
behaviour, than to the mind or imagination. There is
nothing farther to be observed on this sentence, unless
the use of *that* for a relative pronoun, instead of *which*;
an usage which is too frequent with Mr. Addison. *Which*
is a much more definite word than *that*, being never
employed in any other way than as a relative; whereas
that is a word of many senses; sometimes a demonstrative
pronoun, often a conjunction. In some cases we are
indeed obliged to use *that* for a relative, in order to
avoid the ungraceful repetition of *which* in the same sentence. But when we are laid under no necessity of this
kind, *which* is always the preferable word, and certainly
was so in this sentence - 'Pleasures which the vulgar are
not capable of receiving', is much better than 'pleasures
that the vulgar, &c.'

He can converse with a picture, and find an agreeable
companion in a statue. He meets with a secret refresh-
ment in a description; and often feels a greater satisfaction in the prospect of fields and meadows, than

another dies in the possession. It gives him, indeed,
a kind of property in every thing he sees; and makes
the most rude uncultivated parts of nature administer
to his pleasures: so that he looks upon the world, as
it were, in another light, and discovers in it a multitude of charms that conceal themselves from the gener-
ality of mankind.

All this is very beautiful. The illustration is happy;
and the Style runs with the greatest ease and harmony.
We see no labour, no stiffness, or affectation; but an
author writing from the native flow of a gay and pleasing
imagination. This predominant character of Mr. Addison's
manner, far more than compensates all those little negligences which we are now remarking. Two of these occur in
this paragraph. The first, in the sentence which begins
with, 'It gives him indeed a kind of property' - To this
it, there is no proper antecedent in the whole paragraph.
In order to gather the meaning, we must look back as far
as to the third sentence before, the first of the paragraph, which begins with, 'A man of a polite imagination'.
This phrase, *polite imagination*, is the only antecedent
to which this *it* can refer; and even that is an improper
antecedent, as it stands in the genitive case, as the
qualification only of a *man*.
The other instance of negligence, is towards the end of
the paragraph - 'So that he looks upon the world, as it
were, in another light.' - *By another* light, Mr. Addison
means, a light different from that in which other men view
the world. But though this expression clearly conveyed
this meaning to himself when writing, it conveys it very
indistinctly to others; and is an instance of that sort
of inaccuracy, into which, in the warmth of composition,
every writer of a lively imagination is apt to fall; and
which can only be remedied by a cool, subsequent review.
- *As it were* - is upon most occasions no more than an ungraceful palliative, and here there was not the least
occasion for it, as he was not about to say any thing
which required a softening of this kind. To say the truth,
this last sentence, 'so that he looks upon the world',
and what follows, had better been wanting altogether. It
is no more than an unnecessary recapitulation of what had
gone before; a feeble adjection to the lively picture he
had given of the pleasures of the imagination. The paragraph would have ended with more spirit at the words
immediately preceding; 'the uncultivated parts of nature
administer to his pleasures.'

There are, indeed, but very few who know how to be

idle and innocent, or have a relish of any pleasures
that are not criminal; every diversion they take, is at
the expence of some one virtue or another, and their
very first step out of business is into vice or folly.

Nothing can be more elegant, or more finely tuned, than
this sentence. It is neat, clear, and musical. We could
hardly alter one word, or disarrange one member, without
spoiling it. Few sentences are to be found more finished,
or more happy.

A man should endeavour, therefore, to make the sphere
of his innocent pleasures as wide as possible, that he
may retire into them with safety, and find in them,
such a satisfaction as a wise man would not blush to
take.

This also is a good sentence, and gives occasion to no
material remark.

Of this nature are those of the imagination, which do
not require such a bent of thought as is necessary to
our more serious employments, nor, at the same time,
suffer the mind to sink into that indolence and remiss-
ness, which are apt to accompany our more sensual
delights; but, like a gentle exercise to the faculties,
awaken them from sloth and idleness, without putting
them upon any labour or difficulty.

The beginning of this sentence is not correct, and
affords an instance of a period too loosely connected with
the preceding one. 'Of this nature,' says he, 'are those
of the imagination.' We might ask of what nature? For it
had not been the scope of the preceding sentence to describe the nature of any set of pleasures. He had said,
that it was every man's duty to make the sphere of his
innocent pleasures as wide as possible, in order that,
within that sphere, he might find a safe retreat, and a
laudable satisfaction. The transition is loosely made,
by beginning the next sentence with saying, 'Of this
nature are those of the imagination'. It had been better,
if, keeping in view the governing object of the preceding
sentence, he had said, 'This advantage we gain,' or,
'This satisfaction we enjoy, by means of the pleasures of
imagination.' The rest of the sentence is abundantly
correct.

We might here add, that the pleasures of the fancy
are more conducive to health than those of the

understanding, which are worked out by dint of thinking, and attended with too violent a labour of the
brain.

On this sentence, nothing occurs deserving of remark,
except that 'worked out by dint of thinking', is a phrase
which borders too much on vulgar and colloquial language,
to be proper for being employed in a polished composition.

Delightful scenes, whether in nature, painting, or
poetry, have a kindly influence on the body, as well
as the mind, and not only serve to clear and brighten
the imagination, but are able to disperse grief and
melancholy, and to set the animal spirits in pleasing
and agreeable motions. For this reason Sir Francis
Bacon, in his Essay upon Health, has not thought it
improper to prescribe to his reader a poem, or a prospect, where he particularly dissuades him from knotty
and subtile disquisitions, and advises him to pursue
studies that fill the mind with splendid and illustrious objects, as histories, fables, and contemplations
of nature.

In the latter of these two sentences, a member of the
period is altogether out of its place; which gives the
whole sentence a harsh and disjointed cast, and serves to
illustrate the rules I formerly gave concerning arrangement. The wrong-placed member which I point at, is this;
'where he particularly dissuades him from knotty and subtile disquisitions'; - these words should, undoubtedly,
have been placed not where they stand, but thus: 'Sir
Francis Bacon, in his Essay upon Health, where he particularly dissuades the reader from knotty and subtile speculations, has not thought it improper to prescribe to him,
&c.' This arrangement reduces every thing into proper
order.

I have, in this Paper, by way of introduction, settled
the notion of those pleasures of the imagination,
which are the subject of my present undertaking, and
endeavoured, by several considerations, to recommend
to my readers the pursuit of those pleasures; I shall,
in my next Paper examine the several sources from
whence these pleasures are derived.

These two concluding sentences afford examples of the
proper collocation of circumstances in a period. I
formerly showed, that it is often a matter of difficulty
to dispose of them in such a manner, as that they shall

not embarrass the principal subject of the sentence. In
the sentences before us, several of these incidental circumstances necessarily come in - 'By way of introduction'
- 'by several considerations' - 'in this Paper' - 'in the
next Paper'. All which are, with great propriety, managed
by our author. It will be found, upon trial, that there
were no other parts of the sentence, in which they could
have been placed to equal advantage. Had he said, for
instance, 'I have settled the notion, (rather, *the meaning*) - of those pleasures of the imagination, which are
the subject of my present undertaking, by way of introduction, in this paper, and endeavoured to recommend the pursuit of those pleasures to my readers by several considerations,' we must be sensible, that the sentence, thus
clogged with circumstances in the wrong place, would
neither have been so neat nor so clear, as it is by the
present construction.

Note

1 'Institutio Oratoria', X. i. 112. '[Let us, therefore,
   fix our eyes on him, take him as our pattern, and] let
   the student realize that he has made real progress if
   he is a passionate admirer of Cicero.'

65.   JOHN GILBERT COOPER, 'LETTERS CONCERNING TASTE'

1755

John Gilbert Cooper (1723-69) published 'Letters concerning Taste' in 1755, a work known to Johnson. It reveals
the influence of Shaftesbury, whose disciple he was.
Cooper's discussion of Addison appears in Letters 5 and 6
(pp. 27-9, 32-4).

From Letter 5

You seem to think, EUPHEMIUS, that I contradicted in Conversation the other Day, in a great Measure what I
advanced in a former Letter to you, by allowing CRONOPHI-
LUS to be a Man of a strong Understanding and great

Erudition, and yet at the same time asserting he had
little or no *Taste*. But according to my Observation,
what I wrote, and what I said, are very reconcileable.
For *Taste* does not *wholly* depend upon the natural Strength
and acquired Improvement of the *Intellectual* Powers; nor
wholly upon a fine Construction of the *Organs* of the Body;
nor *wholly* upon the intermediate Powers of the *Imagination*; but upon an Union of them all happily blended, without too great a Prevalency in either. Hence it falls out,
that one Man may be a very great Reasoner; another have
the finest Genius for Poetry; and a third be blessed with
the most delicate Organs of Sense; and yet every one of
these be deficient in that *internal* Sensation called
Taste. On the contrary, a fourth, in whose Frame indulgent Nature has twisted this *triple Cord*, shall feel it
constantly vibrate within, whenever the same *Unison* of
Harmony is struck from without; either in the original
Works of Nature; in the mimetic Arts; or in Characters and
Manners. That worthy Man, and amiable Writer, Mr. ADDISON,
was no great Scholar; he was a very indifferent Critic,
and a worse Poet; yet from the happy Mixture, just mentioned, he was blessed with a Taste truly delicate and
refined. This rendered him capable of distinguishing
what were Beauties in the Works of others, tho' he could
not account so well *why they were so*, for want of that
deep Philosophical Spirit which is requisite in Works of
Criticism. He likewise translated the Poetical Descriptions of OVID very elegantly and faithfully into his own
Language, tho' he fell infinitely short of them in his own
original Compositions, for want of that *unconstrained* Fire
of Imagination, which constitutes the true Poet. Hence we
may be enabled to account for that peculiar Fatality which
attends Mr. ADDISON's poetical Writings, that his Translations seem Originals, whilst his own Compositions have the
confined Air of Translations.

From Letter 6

I Find, EUPHEMIUS, you do not thoroughly concur with me in
a Remark I made in my last Letter, that 'ADDISON was an
indifferent Critic, and a worse Poet.' But however extensive my Regard to the Memory of that great and good Man
may be, and however inimitable and certainly *justly*
admired he ever will be as a Prose Writer, for those moral
and humorous Essays, but more particularly those delightful Allegories his Muse CLIO has left us; yet true Criticism will never allow him to be at the Head even of the
second Class of our *English* Poets. You answer, that there

are several Passages in some of his poetical Compositions,
which breathe a Spirit of Genius equal to any thing
extant, either among the Moderns or Ancients; and at the
same time point out the famous Simile of the Angel of
Destruction, if I may so call it, in the 'Campaign'; and
another at the Conclusion of the first Act of 'Cato'. Now
tho' selecting *particular* Passages from a Poet is not a
certain Method, nor a fair one, of forming a proper Esti-
mate of his *general* Excellence, yet as you so strongly
urge these two, with an Air of Triumph, to be the Inspiration of *Castalian* Streams, I must desire you to examine
them with me critically Line by Line, and I dare say
you'll own, that both betray a great Poverty of Imagination by an insipid Repetition of one Thought in different
Expressions. To begin then with the celebrated Simile in
the 'Campaign', which, for half a Century, has been undis-
tinguishingly admired.

> So when an Angel, by Divine Command,
> With *rising Tempest shakes a guilty Land*,
> Such as of late o'er pale BRITANNIA past,
> Calm and serene *he guides the furious Blast*,
> And pleas'd th' ALMIGHTY's Orders to perform,
> *Rides in the Whirlwind and directs the Storm*.

Now take the second Line of each Couplet, and examine
whether the Thought is varied. Is not 'shaking a guilty
Land with a rising Tempest', and 'directing the Storm',
and 'guiding the furious Blast', the same Action? Is not
acting by 'Divine Command', in the first Verse, and
'performing the Almighty's Orders', in the fifth, the
same Thought likewise? MARCIA's Simile in 'Cato' abounds
still more with this tiresome Tautology.

> So the pure limpid Stream, when foul with Stains,
> Of rushing Torrents, and descending Rains,
> Works itself clear, and as it runs refines.
> > 'Cato', Act. I.

'Rushing Torrents', and 'descending Rains', 'works itself
clear', and 'as it runs refines'. But now having had the
disagreeable Office of denying, for the sake of Truth,
this excellent Man a Right to a Pretension of being a good
Poet, Justice will exact, and my own Inclination lead me
to take notice, that his Translations of OVID are as
faithful and spirited, and at the same time carry as much
the free unfettered Air of Originals, as any other Translations in the English Language.

66.   VICESIMUS KNOX, 'ESSAYS MORAL AND LITERARY'

1779

While Vicesimus Knox (1752-1821) was a fellow of St John's
College, Oxford, he wrote 'Essays Moral and Literary'. He
sent the manuscript to Charles Dilly anonymously. Upon
Johnson's recommendation, the bookseller published it in
one volume in 1778. The second edition, corrected and enlarged in two volumes, appeared in 1779.
   This is essay 118 (from the 4th ed., 1784, II, pp.
143-5).

No. CXVIII.   On the character of Addison as a poet

The lustre of a great name not only sets off real beauties
to the greatest advantage, but adds a grace to deformity,
and converts a defect to an excellence. The enthusiastical
admirers of a favourite author, like ardent lovers, view
those objects with rapture, which cause in others indifference or disgust. Without considering the inequalities
of the same genius, and the diversities of subjects, they
are led to conclude, from the excellence of one part of an
author's works, that all are excellent; and that whatever
bears his signature, is genuine wit, and just taste.
   I know not whether even Mr. Addison, who is so deservedly esteemed the honour of our nation, was not indebted
for a small part of his reputation to the blind bigotry or
prejudice. On any other supposition, I know not how he
could have been admired as a very eminent poet. The dis-
passionate temperature which constituted a solid judgment,
and qualified him for the cool disquisitions of criticism
and morality, rendered him incapable of that animated
spirit which is the soul of poetry. But the reader is unwilling to believe, that so accurate a critic, and so
correct a writer, is himself faulty; and, therefore, when
he passes from his prose to his poetry, and observes a
manifest inferiority and deficiency of merit in the latter,
he rather inclines to distrust his own judgment than the
abilities of the author. Reader after reader has toiled
through the same dull rhimes, perhaps blind to their
faults, or, if sensible of their defects, yet inclined to
join in their praise, in opposition to conviction, from a
dread of the imputation of a depraved taste. Had not a
veneration for his name prevented critics from speaking

their real sentiments, though Addison would, as a moral essayist, most justly have been called the Socrates, Plato, or Xenophon of his age; yet he would never have been esteemed the first of poets.

It would be injustice, while we inspect these volumes, to pass over in silence, the elegant poem which is pre-fixed to the works of Addison, on the death of their author. The melancholy flow of the verse is well adapted to express the tenderness of the sentiments. The beauty of the imagery, and the energy of the expression, entitle this little piece to a very respectable rank among the elegiac compositions of the English writers. It was for a long time little regarded; but the attention lately paid to it, and the commendations bestowed on it, and proofs that literary merit, however unnoticed for a time, through accident, prejudice, or party, is sure to receive the applause it deserves from impartial posterity.

At the end of the verses of Addison to Mr. Dryden, we are told, that the author was but twenty-two years of age when he wrote them. Whether the age was affixed to exten-uate the imperfections, or to enhance the merits of the poem, certain it is, that both these intentions are frus-trated by its extreme insignificance and futility. The production is unworthy the age of twenty-two. (1) Mr. Pope is known to have written his pastorals, which in-finitely exceed the versification of Addison, at sixteen; (2) and Milton acquired an elegance in Latin verse at an earlier period. (3) The thoughts in this piece are not striking, the style is contemptible, and the negligence in the rhime alone would, in the present refinement of taste, consign the work to oblivion.

That all his pieces are upon a level with this, cannot be asserted. That some of them abound with grand concep-tions, and have many good lines, must be confessed. But allowing Addison all the merit in his poetry, which can-dour, or even partiality in his favour can allow, he never can be justly esteemed one of the first poets of the nation. I never heard that Socrates increased his fame by his poetical version of Aesop's Fables, and the best prose-writer in the best age of Rome wrote the line, 'O fortunatam, natam, me consule, Romam'. (4) The truth is, nature usually bestows her gifts with a prudent liberality even to her favourites. One might on the occasion apply to Addison the passage of Martial, 'Hoc Ciceronis habes'. (5) This character of a bad poet you have in common with the great Cicero.

To oppose opinions universally received, is to incur the imputation of vanity, ignorance, and want of taste. But as every individual has a right to private judgment,

and may offer his sentiments to others, while he does it
with modesty, professes a possibility of mistake, and
keeps his mind open to conviction, I have ventured to
advance an opinion against the poetical merit of Addison;
regardless how it may alarm those who submit their judgments to the direction of others, and who pay an implicit
obedience to authority.

Notes

1   In 'Examen Poeticum: Being the Third Part of Miscellany
    Poems' (1693), To Mr. Dryden by Jo. Addison is dated
    'Mag. Coll. *Oxon.*, June 2 1693.' Addison was 21.
2   'The Pastorals', published in the sixth part of
    Tonson's 'Miscellanies' (1709), were written before
    Pope was 21.
3   Milton indicates that his second Latin elegy was writ-
    ten when he was 17. According to William Riley Parker,
    it was written in 1626, when Milton was 18. See
    'Milton a Biography' (1968), I, pp. 32-3.
4   Juvenal, X, 122: 'O fortunate Rome, whose natal day
    may date from me as consul.'
5   'The Epigrams of Martial', II. lxxxix. 4.

67.   SAMUEL JOHNSON, 'LIVES OF THE POETS' - 'ADDISON'

1781

In his conversations with Boswell, Johnson remained a constant admirer of Addison as a prose stylist. In 1776 he
wrote a brief advertisement for an edition of the 'Spectator' printed in that year. 'The Book thus offered to
the Public is too well known to be praised: It comprizes
precepts of criticism, sallies of invention, descriptions
of life, and lectures of virtue. It employs wit in the
cause of truth, and makes elegance subservient to piety:
It has now for more than half a century supplied the English nation, in a great measure, with principles of speculation, and rules of practice; and given Addison a claim
to be numbered among the benefactors of mankind' ('Public
Advertiser', 14 December 1776).

Of his virtue it is a sufficient testimony, that the
resentment of party has transmitted no charge of any
crime. He was not one of those who are praised only after
death; for his merit was so generally acknowledged, that
Swift, having observed that his election passed without
a contest, adds, that if he had proposed himself for king
he would hardly have been refused. (1)

His zeal for his party did not extinguish his kindness
for the merit of his opponents: when he was secretary in
Ireland, he refused to intermit his acquaintance with
Swift.

Of his habits, or external manners, nothing is so often
mentioned as that timorous or sullen taciturnity, which
his friends called modesty by too mild a name. Steele
mentions with great tenderness, 'that remarkable bashfulness, which is a cloak that hides and muffles merit;' (2)
and tells us, that 'his abilities were covered only by
modesty, which doubles the beauties which are seen, and
gives credit and esteem to all that are concealed.'
Chesterfield affirms, that 'Addison was the most timorous
and aukward man that he ever saw.' (3) And Addison,
speaking of his own deficience in conversation, used to
say of himself, that, with respect to intellectual wealth,
'he could draw bills for a thousand pounds, though he had
not a guinea in his pocket.' (4)

That he wanted current coin for ready payment, and by
that want was often obstructed and distressed; that he was
oppressed by an improper and ungraceful timidity, every
testimony concurs to prove; but Chesterfield's representation is doubtless hyperbolical. That man cannot be supposed very unexpert in the arts of conversation and practice of life, who, without fortune or alliance, by his
usefulness and dexterity, became secretary of state; and
who died at forty-seven, after having not only stood long
in the highest rank of wit and literature, but filled one
of the most important offices of state.

The time in which he lived had reason to lament his
obstinacy of silence; 'for he was,' says Steele, 'above
all men in that talent called humour, and enjoyed it in
such perfection, that I have often reflected, after a
night spent with him apart from all the world, that I had
had the pleasure of conversing with an intimate acquaintance of Terence and Catullus, who had all their wit and
nature, heightened with humour more exquisite and delightful than any other man ever possessed.' (5) This is the
fondness of a friend; let us hear what is told us by a
rival. 'Addison's conversation,' says Pope, 'had something in it more charming than I have found in any other
man. But this was only when familiar: before strangers,

or perhaps a single stranger, he preserved his dignity by
a stiff silence.' (6)

   This modesty was by no means inconsistent with a very
high opinion of his own merit.   He demanded to be the
first name in modern wit; and, with Steele to echo him,
used to depreciate Dryden, whom Pope and Congreve defended
against them. (7)   There is no reason to doubt that he
suffered too much pain from the prevalence of Pope's
poetical reputation; nor is it without strong reason suspected that by some disingenuous acts he endeavoured to
obstruct it: Pope was not the only man whom he insidiously
injured, though the only man of whom he could be afraid.(8)

   His own powers were such as might have satisfied him
with conscious excellence.   Of very extensive learning he
has indeed given no proofs.   He seems to have had small
acquaintance with the sciences, and to have read little
except Latin and French; but of the Latin poets his
'Dialogues on Medals' (9) shew that he had perused the
works with great diligence and skill.   The abundance of
his own mind left him little need of adventitious sentiments; his wit always could suggest what the occasion
demanded.   He had read with critical eyes the important
volume of human life, and knew the heart of man from the
depths of stratagem to the surface of affectation.

   What he knew he could easily communicate.   'This,' says
Steele, 'was particular in this writer, that, when he had
taken his resolution, or made his plan for what he
designed to write, he would walk about a room, and dictate
it into language with as much freedom and ease as any one
could write it down, and attend to the coherence and grammar of what he dictated.' (10)

   Pope, who can be less suspected of favouring his memory,
declares that he wrote very fluently, but was slow and
scrupulous in correcting; that many of his 'Spectators'
were written very fast, and sent immediately to the press;
and that it seemed to be for his advantage not to have
time for much revisal. (11)

   'He would alter,' says Pope, 'any thing to please his
friends, before publication; but would not retouch his
pieces afterwards: and I believe not one word in "Cato",
to which I made an objection, was suffered to stand.' (12)

   The last line of 'Cato' is Pope's, having been originally written

   And, Oh! 'twas this that ended Cato's life.

Pope might have made more objections to the six concluding
lines.   In the first couplet, the words *from hence* are
improper; and the second line is taken from Dryden's

Virgil. Of the next couplet, the first verse being included in the second, is therefore useless; and in the third
Discord is made to produce *Strife*.

Of the course of Addison's familiar day, before his mar-
marriage, Pope has given a detail. He had in the house
with him Budgell, and perhaps Philips. His chief companions were Steele, Budgell, Philips, Carey, Davenant, and
colonel Brett. With one or other of these he always
breakfasted. He studied all morning; then dined at a
tavern, and went afterwards to Button's. (13)

Button had been a servant in the countess of Warwick's
family, (14) who, under the patronage of Addison, kept a
coffee-house on the south side of Russel-street, about two
doors from Covent-garden. Here it was that the wits of
that time used to assemble. It is said, that when Addison
had suffered any vexation from the countess, he withdrew
the company from Button's house.

From the coffee-house he went again to a tavern, where
he often sat late, and drank too much wine. In the bottle,
discontent seeks for comfort, cowardice for courage, and
bashfulness for confidence. It is not unlikely that Addison was first seduced to excess by the manumission which
he obtained from the servile timidity of his sober house.
He that feels oppression from the presence of those to
whom he knows himself superior, will desire to set loose
his powers of conversation; and who, that ever asked succour from Bacchus, was able to preserve himself from being
enslaved by his auxiliary?

Among those friends it was that Addison displayed the
elegance of his colloquial accomplishments, which may
easily be supposed such as Pope represents them. The
remark of Mandeville, who, when he had passed an evening
in his company, declared that he was a parson in a tye-wig,
can detract little from his character; (15) he was always
reserved to strangers, and was not incited to uncommon
freedom by a character like that of Mandeville.

From any minute knowledge of his familiar manners, the
intervention of sixty years has now debarred us. Steele
once promised Congreve and the public a complete description of his character; (16) but the promises of authors
are like the vows of lovers. Steele thought no more on his
design, or thought on it with anxiety that at last disgusted him, and left his friend in the hands of Tickell.

His works will supply some information. It appears
from his various pictures of the world, that, with all his
bashfulness, he had conversed with many distinct classes
of men, had surveyed their ways with very diligent observation, and marked with great acuteness the effects of
different modes of life. He was a man in whose presence

nothing reprehensible was out of danger; quick in discerning whatever was wrong or ridiculous, and not unwilling to expose it. 'There are,' says Steele, 'in his writings many oblique strokes upon some of the wittiest men of the age'. (17) His delight was more to excite merriment than detestation, and he detects follies rather than crimes.

If any judgments be made, from his books, of his moral character, nothing will be found but purity and excellence. Knowledge of mankind indeed, less extensive than that of Addison, will shew that to write and to live are very different. Many who praise virtue, do no more than praise it. Yet it is reasonable to believe, that Addison's professions and practice were at no great variance, since, amidst that storm of faction in which most of his life was passed, though his station made him conspicuous, and his activity made him formidable, the character given him by his friends was never contradicted by his enemies: of those with whom interest or opinion united him, he had not only the esteem but the kindness; and of others, whom the violence of opposition drove against him, though he might lose the love, he retained the reverence.

It is justly observed by Tickell, that he employed wit on the side of virtue and religion. (18) He not only made the proper use of wit himself, but taught it to others; and from his time it has been generally subservient to the cause of reason and truth. He has dissipated the prejudice that had long connected gaiety with vice, and easiness of manners with laxity of principles. He has restored virtue to its dignity, and taught innocence not to be ashamed. This is an elevation of literary character, *above all Greek, above all Roman fame*. No greater felicity can genius attain than that of having purified intellectual pleasure, separated mirth from indecency, and wit from licentiousness; of having taught a succession of writers to bring elegance and gaiety to the aid of goodness; and, if I may use expressions yet more awful, of having *turned many to righteousness*. (19)

ADDISON, in his life, and for some time afterwards, was considered by the greater part of readers, as supremely excelling both in poetry and criticism. Part of his reputation may be probably ascribed to the advancement of his fortune; when, as Swift observes, he became a statesman, and saw poets waiting at his levee, (20) it is no wonder that praise was accumulated upon him. Much likewise may be more honourably ascribed to his personal character; he who, if he had claimed it, might have obtained the diadem, was not likely to be denied the laurel.

But time quickly puts an end to artificial and

accidental fame, and Addison is to pass through futurity
protected only by his genius. Every name which kindness
or interest once raised too high, is in danger, lest the
next age should, by the vengeance of criticism, sink it
in the same proportion. A great writer has lately stiled
him *an indifferent poet, and a worse critick.* (21)

His poetry is first to be considered; of which it must
be confessed, that it has not often those felicities of
diction which give lustre to sentiments, or that vigour
of sentiment that animates diction: there is little of
ardour, vehemence, or transport; there is very rarely the
awfulness of grandeur, and not very often the splendour of
elegance. He thinks justly; but he thinks faintly. This
is his general character, to which doubtless many single
passages will furnish exceptions.

Yet if he seldom reaches supreme excellence, he rarely
sinks into dulness, and is still more rarely entangled in
absurdity. He did not trust his powers enough to be neg-
ligent. There is in most of his compositions a calmness
and equability, deliberate and cautious, sometimes with
little that delights, but seldom with any thing that
offends.

Of this kind seem to be his poems to Dryden, to Somers,
and to the King. His ode on St. Cecilia has been imitated by Pope, and has something in it of Dryden's vigour.
Of his 'Account of the English Poets', he used to speak
as a *poor thing*; (22) but it is not worse than his usual
strain. He has said, not very judiciously, in his character of Waller:

> Thy verse could shew ev'n Cromwell's innocence,
> And compliment the storms that bore him hence.
> O! had thy Muse not come an age too soon,
> But seen great Nassau on the British throne,
> How had his triumph glitter'd in thy page. - (23)

What is this but to say, that he who could compliment
Cromwell had been the proper poet for king William?
Addison however never printed the piece.

The letter from Italy has been always praised, but has
never been praised beyond its merit. It is more correct,
with less appearance of labour, and more elegant, with
less ambition of ornament, than any other of his poems.
There is however one broken metaphor, of which notice may
properly be taken:

> Fir'd with that name -
> I bridle in my struggling Muse with pain,
> That longs to launch into a nobler strain. (24)

To *bridle* a *goddess* is no very delicate idea; but why must
she be *bridled*? because she *longs to launch*; an act which
was never hindered by a *bridle*: and whither will she
launch? into a *nobler strain*. She is in the first line a
horse, in the second a *boat*; and the care of the poet is
to keep his *horse* or his *boat* from *singing*.

The next composition is the far-famed 'Campaign', which
Dr. Warton has termed a 'Gazette in Rhyme', (25) with
harshness not often used by the good-nature of his criticism. Before a censure so severe is admitted, let us consider that War is a frequent subject of Poetry, and then
enquire who has described it with more justness and force.
Many of our own writers tried their powers upon this year
of victory, yet Addison's is confessedly the best performance; his poem is the work of a man not blinded by the
dust of learning: his images are not borrowed merely from
books. The superiority which he confers upon his hero is
not personal prowess, and *mighty bone*, but deliberate
intrepidity, a calm command of his passions, and the power
of consulting his own mind in the midst of danger. The
rejection and contempt of fiction is rational and manly.

It may be observed that the last line is imitated by
Pope;

> Marlb'rough's exploits appear divinely bright -
> Rais'd of themselves, their genuine charms they boast,
> And those that paint them truest, praise them most.(26)

This Pope had in his thoughts, but not knowing how to use
what was not his own, he spoiled the thought when he had
borrowed it:

> The well-sung woes shall soothe my ghost;
> He best can paint them who shall feel them most. (27)

Martial exploits may be *painted*; perhaps *woes* may be
painted; but they are surely not *painted* by being *well-
sung*: it is not easy to paint in song, or to sing in
colours.

No passage in the 'Campaign' has been more often mentioned than the simile of the Angel, (28) which is said in
the 'Tatler' to be 'one of the noblest thoughts that ever
entered into the heart of man', (29) and is therefore
worthy of attentive consideration. Let it be first
enquired whether it be at last a simile. A poetical
simile is the discovery of likeness between two actions,
in their general nature dissimilar, or of causes termi-
nating by different operations in some resemblance of
effect. But the mention of another like consequence from

a like cause, or of a like performance by a like agency, is not a simile, but an exemplification. It is not a simile to say that the Thames waters fields, as the Po waters fields; or that as Hecla vomits flames in Iceland, so AEtna vomits flames in Sicily. When Horace says of Pindar, that he pours his violence and rapidity of verse, as a river swoln with rain rushes from the mountain; (30) or of himself, that his genius wanders in quest of poetical decorations, as the bee wanders to collect honey, (31) he, in either case, produces a simile; the mind is impressed with the resemblance of things generally unlike, as unlike as intellect and body. But if Pindar had been described as writing with the copiousness and grandeur of Homer, or Horace had told that he reviewed and finished his own poetry with the same care as Isocrates polished his orations, instead of similitude he would have exhibited almost identity; he would have given the same portraits with different names. In this poem, when the English are represented as gaining a fortified pass, by repetition of attack and perseverance of resolution; their obstinacy of courage, and vigour of onset, is well illustrated by the sea that breaks, with incessant battery, the dikes of Holland. (32) This is a simile; but when Addison, having celebrated the beauty of Marlborough's person, tells us that 'Achilles thus was form'd with every grace', (33) here is no simile, but a mere exemplification. A simile may be compared to lines converging at a point, and is more excellent as the lines approach from greater distance: an exemplification may be considered as two parallel lines which run on together without approximation, never far separated, and never joined.

Marlborough is so like the Angel in the poem, that the action of both is almost the same, and performed by both in the same manner. Marlborough 'teaches the battle to rage'; the angel 'directs the storm': Marlborough is 'unmoved in peaceful thought'; the angel is 'calm and serene': Marlborough stands 'unmoved amidst the shock of hosts'; the angel rides 'calm in the whirlwind'. The lines on Marlborough are just and noble; but the simile gives almost the same images a second time.

But perhaps this thought, though hardly a simile, was remote from vulgar conceptions, and required great labour of research, or dexterity of application. Of this, Dr. Madden, a name which Ireland ought to honour, once gave me his opinion. (34) 'If I had set', said he, 'ten school-boys to write on the battle of *Blenheim*, and eight had brought me the Angel, I should not have been surprised'.

The opera of 'Rosamond', (35) though it is seldom

mentioned, is one of the first of Addison's compositions. The subject is well-chosen, the fiction is pleasing, and the praise of Marlborough, for which the scene gives an opportunity, is, what perhaps every human excellence must be, the product of good-luck improved by genius. (36) The thoughts are sometimes great, and sometimes tender; the versification is easy and gay. There is doubtless some advantage in the shortness of the lines, which there is little temptation to load with expletive epithets. The dialogue seems commonly better than the songs. The two comic characters of Sir Trusty and Grideline, though of no great value, are yet such as the poet intended. Sir Trusty's account of the death of Rosamond is, I think, too grossly absurd. (37) The whole drama is airy and elegant; engaging in its process, and pleasing in its conclusion. If Addison had cultivated the lighter parts of poetry, he would probably have excelled.

The tragedy of 'Cato', which, contrarily to the rule observed in selecting the works of other poets, has by the weight of its character forced its way into this collection, is unquestionably the noblest production of Addison's genius. Of a work so much read, it is difficult to say anything new. About things on which the publick thinks long, it commonly attains to think right, and of 'Cato' it has been not unjustly determined, that it is rather a poem in dialogue than a drama, rather a succession of just sentiments in elegant language than a representation of natural affections, or of any state probable or possible in human life. Nothing here 'excites or asswages emotion'; here is 'no magical power of raising phantastick terror or wild anxiety'. The events are expected without solicitude, and are remembered without joy or sorrow. Of the agents we have no care; we consider not what they are doing, or what they are suffering; we wish only to know what they have to say. Cato is a being above our solicitude; a man of whom the gods take care, and whom we leave to their care with heedless confidence. To the rest neither gods nor men can have much attention: for there is not one amongst them that strongly attracts either affection or esteem. But they are made the vehicles of such sentiments and such expression, that there is scarcely a scene in the play which the reader does not wish to impress upon his memory.

When 'Cato' was shewn to Pope, he advised the author to print it, without any theatrical exhibition, supposing that it would be read more favourably than heard. Addison declared himself of the same opinion; but urged the importunity of his friends for its appearance on the stage.

The emulation of parties made it successful beyond expectation, and its success has introduced or confirmed among
us the use of dialogue too declamatory, of unaffecting
elegance, and chill philosophy. (38)
    The universality of applause, however it might quell
the censure of common mortals, had no other effect than to
harden Dennis in fixed dislike; but his dislike was not
merely capricious. He found and shewed many faults; he
shewed them indeed with anger, but he found them with
acuteness, such as ought to rescue his criticism from
oblivion; though, at last, it will have no other life than
it derives from the work which it endeavours to oppress.

[Johnson quotes from Dennis's 'Remarks upon Cato'. See
No. 49.]

    Such is the censure of Dennis. There is, as Dryden
expresses it, perhaps 'too much horseplay in his raillery';
(39) but if his jests are coarse, his arguments are strong.
Yet as we love better to be pleased than to be taught,
'Cato' is read, and the critick is neglected.
    Flushed with consciousness of these detections of
absurdity in the conduct, he afterwards attacked the sentiments of 'Cato'; (40) but he then amused himself with
petty cavils, and minute objections.
    Of Addison's smaller poems, no particular mention is
necessary; they have little that can employ or require a
critick. The parallel of the Princes and Gods, in his
verses to Kneller, is often happy, but is too well known
to be quoted. (41)
    His translations, so far as I have compared them, want
the exactness of a scholar. That he understood his
authors cannot be doubted; but his versions will not teach
others to understand them, being too licentiously para-
phrastical. They are however, for the most part, smooth
and easy; and, what is the first excellence of a translator, such as may be read with pleasure by those who do not
know the originals.
    His poetry is polished and pure; the product of a mind
too judicious to commit faults, but not sufficiently
vigorous to attain excellence. He has sometimes a striking line, or a shining paragraph; but in the whole he is
warm rather than fervid, and shews more dexterity than
strength. He was however one of our earliest examples of
correctness.
    The versification which he had learned from Dryden, he
debased rather than refined. His rhymes are often disso-
nant; in his 'Georgick' he admits broken lines. He uses
both triplets and alexandrines, but triplets more

frequently in his translations than his other works. The
mere structure of verses seems never to have engaged much
of his care. But his lines are very smooth in 'Rosamond',
and too smooth in 'Cato'.

Addison is now to be considered as a critick; a name
which the present generation is scarcely willing to allow
him. His criticism is condemned as tentative or experimental, rather than scientifick, and he is considered as
deciding by taste rather than by principles.

It is not uncommon for those who have grown wise by the
labour of others to add a little of their own, and overlook
their masters. Addison is now despised by some who perhaps
would never have seen his defects, but by the lights which
he afforded them. That he always wrote as he would think
it necessary to write, now, cannot be affirmed; his
instructions were such as the character of his readers made
proper. That general knowledge which now circulates in
common talk was in his time rarely to be found. Men not
professing learning were not ashamed of ignorance; and in
the female world any acquaintance with books was distinguished only to be censured. His purpose was to infuse
literary curiosity, by gentle and unsuspected conveyance,
into the gay, the idle, and the wealthy; he therefore presented knowledge in the most alluring form, not lofty and
austere, but accessible and familiar. When he shewed them
their defects, he shewed them likewise that they might be
easily supplied. His attempt succeeded; enquiry was awak-
ened, and comprehension expanded. An emulation of intellectual elegance was excited, and from his time to our own
life has been gradually exalted, and conversation purified
and enlarged.

Dryden had, not many years before, scattered criticism
over his Prefaces with very little parsimony; but, though
he sometimes condescended to be somewhat familiar, his
manner was in general too scholastick for those who had
yet their rudiments to learn, and found it not easy to
understand their master. His observations were framed
rather for those that were learning to write, than for
those that read only to talk.

An instructor like Addison was now wanting, whose
remarks being superficial, might be easily understood, and
being just, might prepare the mind for more attainments.
Had he presented 'Paradise Lost' to the publick with all
the pomp of system and severity of science, he would perhaps have been admired, and the book still have been neglected; but by the blandishments of gentleness and facility, he has made Milton an universal favourite, with whom
readers of every class think it necessary to be pleased.

He descended now and then to lower disquisitions, and

by a serious display of the beauties of 'Chevy Chase'
exposed himself to the ridicule of Wagstaff, who bestowed
a like pompous character on 'Tom Thumb'; and to the contempt of Dennis, who, considering the fundamental position
of his criticism, that 'Chevy Chase' pleases, and ought to
please, because it is natural, observes, 'that there is a
way of deviating from nature, by bombast or tumour, which
soars above nature, and enlarges images beyond their real
bulk; by affectation, which forsakes nature in quest of
something unsuitable; and by imbecility, which degrades
nature by faintness and diminution, by obscuring images
and weakening effects.' (42) In 'Chevy Chase' there is not
much of either bombast or affectation; but there is chill
and lifeless imbecillity. The story cannot possibly be told
in a manner that shall make less impression on the mind.

Before the profound observers of the present race repose
too securely on the consciousness of their superiority to
Addison, let them consider his 'Remarks on Ovid', in which
may be found specimens of criticism sufficiently subtle
and refined; let them peruse likewise his Essays on 'Wit',
and on the 'Pleasures of Imagination', in which he founds
art on the base of nature, and draws the principles of
invention from dispositions inherent in the mind of man,
with skill and elegance, such as his contemners will not
easily attain.

As a describer of life and manners, he must be allowed
to stand perhaps the first of the first rank. His humour,
which, as Steele observes, is peculiar to himself, is so
happily diffused as to give the grace of novelty to domestic scenes and daily occurrences. He never 'outsteps the
modesty of nature', nor raises merriment or wonder by the
violation of truth. His figures neither divert by dis-
tortion, nor amaze by aggravation. He copies life with so
much fidelity, that he can be hardly said to invent; yet
his exhibitions have an air so much original, that it is
difficult to suppose them not merely the product of
imagination.

As a teacher of wisdom he may be confidently followed.
His religion has nothing in it enthusiastic or supersti-
tious: he appears neither weakly credulous nor wantonly
sceptical; his morality is neither dangerously lax, nor
impracticably rigid. All the enchantment of fancy and all
the cogency of argument are employed to recommend to the
reader his real interest, the care of pleasing the Author
of his being. Truth is shewn sometimes as the phantom of
a vision, sometimes appears half-veiled in an allegory;
sometimes attracts regard in the robes of fancy, and sometimes steps forth in the confidence of reason. She wears
a thousand dresses, and in all is pleasing.

Mille habet ornatus, mille decenter habet. (43)

His prose is the model of the middle stile; on grave
subjects not formal, on light occasions not grovelling;
pure without scrupulosity, and exact without apparent
elaboration; always equable, and always easy, without
glowing words or pointed sentences. Addison never deviates from his track to snatch a grace; he seeks no ambitious ornaments, and tries no hazardous innovations. His
page is always luminous, but never blazes in unexpected
splendour.

It seems to have been his principal endeavour to avoid
all harshness and severity of diction; he is therefore
something verbose in his transitions and connections, and
sometimes descends too much to the language of conversation; yet if his language had been less idiomatical, it
might have lost somewhat of its genuine Anglicism. What
he attempted, he performed; he is never feeble, and he did
not wish to be energetic; he is never rapid, and he never
stagnates. His sentences have neither studied amplitude,
nor affected brevity: his periods, though not diligently
rounded, are voluble and easy. Whoever wishes to attain
an English stile, familiar but not coarse, and elegant but
not ostentatious, must give his days and nights to the
volumes of Addison.

Notes

1 See Swift's letter (VI) to Stella, dated 12 October
   1710.
2 Dedication to 'The Drummer', in 'The Works of ...
   Joseph Addison', ed. Bohn (1856), V, 152.
3 In a letter to his godson, dated 2 January 1766.
4 R. Phillips, 'Addisoniana' (1803), I, 3.
5 'Memoirs of the Life and Writings of ... Joseph Addison, Esq; With his Character by Sir Richard Steele'
   (1724).
6 Joseph Spence, 'Observations', ed. James M. Osborn
   (1966), sect. 148.
7 Ibid., sect. 814.
8 Ibid., sect. 828.
9 'Dialogues upon the Usefulness of Ancient Medals'
   (1721).
10 Dedication to 'The Drummer', in 'The Works', V, 153.
11 Spence, sects. 169, 171-2.
12 Ibid., sects. 169, 174.
13 Ibid., sects. 149, 181, 183.
14 Ibid., sect. 68.

15 Sir John Hawkins, 'A General History of the Science
    and Practice of Music' (1776), V, p. 316 *n*.
16 Dedication to 'The Drummer', in 'The Works', V, p. 153.
17 Ibid., V, p. 148.
18 See Tickell's Preface to 'The Works' and his poem 'The
    Prospect of Peace'.
19 Pope, 'Imitations of Horace', Epist. II. i. 26;
    Daniel XII. 3.
20 Swift, 'A Libel on D—— D—— and a Certain Great Lord'
    (1730).
21 See 'Lives of the Poets' (1905), II, 127 n.
22 Spence, sect. 170.
23 'Account of the Greatest English Poets' (1694), 96–100.
24 'A Letter from Italy', 177, 179–80.
25 'An Essay on the Writings and Genius of Pope' (1756),
    p. 30.
26 'The Campaign', 473–6. Johnson omitted 1. 474: 'And
    proudly shine in their own native light.'
27 'Eloisa to Abelard', 365–6.
28 'The Campaign', 287–92.
29 'Tatler' 43.
30 'Odes', IV. 2.5.
31 Ibid., 1. 27.
32 'The Campaign', 181–90.
33 Ibid., 419–24.
34 Samuel Madden, DD (1686–1765), miscellaneous writer
    and philanthropist. Johnson assisted him in preparing
    for publication 'Boulter's Monument, a Panegyrical
    Poem, Sacred to the Memory of Dr. Hugh Boulter ...'
    (Dublin, 1745).
35 'Rosamond' (1707) was his first dramatic composition.
36 The scene is laid in Woodstock Park.
37 'Rosamond', II. vii.
38 Spence, sects. 153, 156.
39 In the 'Preface to the Fables', the phrase is said of
    Jeremy Collier.
40 Dennis, 'Letters upon the Sentiments of the Two First
    Acts of Cato' (1721).
41 'To Sir Godfrey Kneller', 53–76.
42 'Remarks on Cato', II, p. 42; 'To H—— C——Esq; Of
    Simplicity in Poetical Composition', in 'Remarks on
    the 70th Spectator' ([1711], 1721).
43 Tibullus, 'Lygdami Elegiae (De Sulpicia)', III. viii.
    14: '[She] wears a thousand garbs and wears with grace
    the thousand.'

68. THOMAS WALLACE, 'AN ESSAY ON THE VARIATIONS OF
ENGLISH PROSE, FROM THE REVOLUTION TO THE PRESENT TIME'

[1796], 1797

This is an excerpt from a lecture read on 18 June 1796 by
Thomas Wallace, AB and member of the Royal Irish Academy.
It won 'The Gold Prize Medal ... for the best Essay on
that Subject'.
    Printed in 'The Transactions of the Royal Irish
Academy' (1797), VI, pt. 2, pp. 41-70.

With Addison and his contemporaries originated the first
variation that occurred, subsequent to the Revolution, in
the composition of English prose. Though the diffuse
style still continued to prevail, it was no longer the
loose, inaccurate and clumsy style by which the compositions of his predecessors were disgraced. So great,
indeed, was the improvement, and so striking the variation
introduced by Addison, that he who compares the productions of this elegant writer with those of the best
writers of 88, will find it difficult to avoid surprise,
how, with such precedents before him, he could have risen
at once to a degree of excellence in style which constitutes him a model for imitation. The forced metaphor, the
dragging clause, the harsh cadence, and the abrupt close,
are all of them strangers to the works of Addison. In the
structure of his sentences, though we may sometimes meet
marks of negligence, yet we can seldom find the unity of a
sentence violated by ideas crowded together, or the sense
obscured by an improper connection of clauses. Though,
like his predecessors, he frequently uses two words to
express one idea, yet, in this instance, he is less faulty
than they; and, among the variations introduced by him, we
must reckon a more strict attention to the choice of words,
and more precision in the use of them.
    Of figurative language Addison has always been acknow-
ledged the most happy model. He was, indeed, the first of
the English prose writers who were equally excellent in
the choice and in the management of their figures. Of
those who preceded him, it has been observed that they
were frequently unhappy in both instances; that their
metaphors either were such as tended rather to degrade
their subject than to give it dignity and elevation; or
that when they were well chosen, they were spoiled by the

manner in which they were conducted, being detained under
the pen until their spirit evaporated, or traced until the
likeness vanished. Addison avoided both faults: his metaphors are selected with care and taste, or rather seem to
spring spontaneously from his subject; they are exhibited
to the mind but for a moment that the leading traits of
similitude may be observed while minute likenesses are
disregarded - like those flashes of electric fire which
often illumine a Summer's night, they shed a vivid, though
a transient lustre, over the scene, and please rather by
the brightness with which they gild the prospect than the
accuracy with which they shew its beauties.

Should it be doubted, whether the improvement of style
which took place in the time of Addison - that variation
which substituted uniform and correct neatness in composition, for what was loose, inaccurate and capricious, be
justly attributed to him - the doubt will vanish when it
is remembered that in no work prior to his time is an
equal degree of accuracy or neatness to be found, and even
among those periodical papers to which the most eminent of
his cotemporary writers contributed, the CLIO of Addison
stands eminently conspicuous. It was, indeed, from the
productions of that classic and copious mind that the
public seems to have caught the taste for fine writing
which has operated from that time to the present, and
which has given to our language perhaps the greatest
degree of elegance and accuracy of which it is suscep-
tible - for if any thing is yet to be added to the improvement of the English style, it must be more nerve and
muscle, not a nicer modification of form or feature.

───── sectantem levia, nervi
Deficiunt animique: (1)

While Addison was communicating to English prose a
degree of correctness with which it had been, till his
time, unacquainted, Swift was exemplifying its precision
and giving a standard for its purity. Swift was the first
writer who attempted to express his meaning without sub-
sidiary words and corroborating phrases. He nearly laid
aside the use of synonimes in which even Addison had a
little indulged, and without being very solicitous about
the structure or harmony of his periods, seemed to devote
all his attention to illustrate the force of individual
words. Swift hewed the stones, and fitted the materials
for those who built after him; Addison left the neatest
and most finished models of ornamental architecture.

Of the character which is here given of these two
writers it is unnecessary to give proof by quoting

passages from their works, for two reasons; the one is,
that their works are in the hands of every body; the
other, that the qualities which we attribute to their
style are so obvious that it were superfluous to illustrate them.

Besides those first reformers of the style of 1688,
there were others, contemporary with them, who contributed
to promote the work which they did not begin. Bolingbroke
and Shaftsbury, like Addison, were elegant and correct,
and seem from him to have derived their correctness and
elegance. Of this, so far as it concerns Shaftsbury,
there is a most remarkable proof. (2) His Tract, entitled
'An Enquiry concerning Virtue', was in the hands of the
public in 1699, in a state very different indeed from that
in which his lordship published, in the year 1726. (3) It
partook of all the faults which were prevalent in the
style of that day, but particularly in the length of its
periods, and the inartificial connection of them. In the
edition of 1726 those errors were in a great measure corrected; the sentences are broken down, and molded with
much elegance into others less prolix; and sharing in some
degree all the beauties of Addison's style, except those
which perhaps his lordship could not copy, its ease and
simplicity. Indeed Shaftsbury, in the form in which we
now have him, appears to be more attentive than Addison to
the harmony of his cadence, and the regular construction
of his sentences; and certainly if he has less simplicity
has more strength. Bolingbroke, too, participating in
correctness with Addison, has some topics of peculiar
praise; he has more force than Addison - and - what may
appear strange, when we consider how much more vehement
and copious he is, has more precision. The nature of the
subjects on which Bolingbroke and Shaftsbury wrote naturally tended to make them more attentive to precision than
Addison. These subjects were principally abstract morality and metaphysics - subjects of which no knowledge can
be attained but by close and steady thinking, or communicated but by words of definite and constant meaning. The
language of Addison, however elegant in itself, or however admirably adapted by its easy flow to those familiar
topics which are generally the subjects of diurnal essays,
was too weak for the weight of abstract moral disquisition,
and too vague for the niceties of metaphysical distinction.
It was fitted for him whose object was to catch what
floated on the surface of life; but it could not serve him
who was to enter into the depths of the human mind, to
watch the progress of intellectual operation, and embody
to the vulgar eye those ever fleeting forms under which
the passions vary.

It might afford much matter of curious speculation to
the philologist, to enquire whether it was this aptitude
in the language of Addison to those light topics of writing in which he excelled that directed his choice of
subjects, or whether his peculiar cast of style was formed
by his choice of such topics. Probably both operated, or
rather both were effects of the same cause. A man's cast
of thought gives a character to his style, and where
choice is free, the subject for composition is determined
by the complexion of the mind....

Notes

1 Horace, 'Ars Poetica', 26-7: 'Aiming at smoothness, I
   fail in force and fire.'
2 See Blair's 'Lectures on Rhetoric and Belles Lettres'
   (1783), I, pp. 192, 207-8, 220-1, 234, 236, 263, 313;
   and especially 396-7.
3 'An Inquiry concerning Virtue' by Anthony Ashley
   Cooper (1671-1713), 3rd Earl of Shaftesbury, was
   surreptitiously printed by Toland in 1699. It was
   later incorporated into 'The Characteristics' (1711).

69. WILLIAM HAZLITT, 'LECTURES ON THE ENGLISH COMIC
WRITERS'

1819

Written originally as an essay for the 'Round Table'
(coll. ed. 1817), Hazlitt's remarks on the periodical
essayists were slightly expanded for a lecture in a series
on the 'English Comic Writers'. The series was delivered
at the Surrey Institution in 1819 and published in the
same year.
     This is an excerpt from Lecture 5, 'On the Periodical
Essayists'.

The ice being thus thawed, and the barrier that kept
authors at a distance from common sense and feeling broken
through, the transition was not difficult from Montaigne,
and his imitators, to our Periodical Essayists. (1)   These

last applied the same unrestrained expression of their
thoughts to the more immediate and passing scenes of life,
to temporary and local matters; and in order to discharge
the invidious office of *Censor Morum* more freely, and with
less responsibility, assumed some fictitious and humorous
disguise, which however in a great degree corresponded to
their own peculiar habits and character. By thus conceal-
ing their own name and person under the title of the
'Tatler', 'Spectator', &c. they were enabled to inform us
more fully of what was passing in the world, while the
dramatic contrast and ironical point of view to which the
whole is subjected, added a greater liveliness and
piquancy to the descriptions. The philosopher and wit
here commences newsmonger, makes himself master of 'the
perfect spy o' th' time,' and from his various walks and
turns through life, brings home little curious specimens
of the humours, opinions, and manners of his contemporaries, as the botanist brings home different plants and
weeds, or the mineralogist different shells and fossils,
to illustrate their several theories, and be useful to
mankind.

The first of these papers that was attempted in this
country was set up by Steele in the beginning of the last
century; and of all our periodical Essayists, the
'Tatler' (for that was the name he assumed) has always
appeared to me the most amusing and agreeable. Montaigne,
whom I have proposed to consider as the father of this
kind of personal authorship among the moderns, in which
the reader is admitted behind the curtain, and sits down
with the writer in his gown and slippers, was a most magnanimous and undisguised egotist; but Isaac Bickerstaff,
Esq. was the more disinterested gossip of the two. The
French author is contented to describe the peculiarities
of his own mind and constitution, which he does with a
copious and unsparing hand. (2) The English journalist
good-naturedly lets you into the secret both of his own
affairs and those of others. A young lady on the other
side Temple Bar, cannot be seen at her glass for half a
day together, but Mr. Bickerstaff takes due notice of it;
and he has the first intelligence of the symptoms of the
belle passion appearing in any young gentleman at the
West-end of the town. The departures and arrivals of
widows with handsome jointures, either to bury their
grief in the country, or to procure a second husband in
town, are punctually recorded in his pages. He is well
acquainted with the celebrated beauties of the preceding
age at the court of Charles II.; and the old gentleman
(as he feigns himself) often grows romantic in recounting
'the disastrous strokes which his youth suffered' from

the glances of their bright eyes, and their unaccountable
caprices. (3) In particular, he dwells with a secret
satisfaction on the recollection of one of his mistresses,
who left him for a richer rival, and whose constant reproach to her husband, on occasion of any quarrel between
them, was 'I, that might have married the famous Mr.
Bickerstaff, to be treated in this manner!' (4) The club
at the Trumpet consists of a set of persons almost as well
worth knowing as himself. The cavalcade of the justice of
the peace, the knight of the shire, the country squire,
and the young gentleman, his nephew, who came to wait on
him at his chambers, in such form and ceremony, seem not
to have settled the order of their precedence to this
hour; (5) and I should hope that the upholsterer and his
companions, who used to sun themselves in the Green Park,
and who broke their rest and fortunes to maintain the balance of power in Europe, stand as fair a chance for immortality as some modern politicians. Mr. Bickerstaff himself is a gentleman and a scholar, a humourist, and a man
of the world; with a great deal of nice easy naïveté about
him. If he walks out and is caught in a shower of rain,
he makes amends for this unlucky accident by a criticism
on the shower in Virgil, and concludes with a burlesque
copy of verses on a city-shower. (6) He entertains us,
when he dates from his own apartment, with a quotation
from Plutarch, or a moral reflection; from the Grecian
coffee-house with politics; and from Wills', or the
Temple, with the poets and players, the beaux and men of
wit and pleasure about town. In reading the pages of the
'Tatler', we seem as if suddenly carried back to the age
of Queen Anne, of toupees and full-bottomed periwigs.
The whole appearance of our dress and manners undergoes a
delightful metamorphosis. The beaux and the belles are
of a quite different species from what they are at present; we distinguish the dappers, the smarts, and the
pretty fellows, as they pass by Mr. Lilly's shop-windows
in the Strand; we are introduced to Betterton and Mrs.
Oldfield behind the scenes; are made familiar with the
persons and performances of Will Estcourt or Tom Durfey;
(7) we listen to a dispute at a tavern, on the merits of
the Duke of Marlborough, or Marshal Turenne; (8) or are
present at the first rehearsal of a play by Vanbrugh, or
the reading of a new poem by Mr. Pope. The privilege of
thus virtually transporting ourselves to past times, is
even greater than that of visiting distant places in reality. London, a hundred years ago, would be much better
worth seeing than Paris at the present moment.

It will be said, that all this is to be found, in the
same or a greater degree, in the 'Spectator'. For myself,

I do not think so; or at least, there is in the last work
a much greater proportion of common-place matter. I have,
on this account, always preferred the 'Tatler' to the
'Spectator'. Whether it is owing to my having been earlier or better acquainted with the one than the other, my
pleasure in reading these two admirable works is not in
proportion to their comparative reputation. The 'Tatler'
contains only half the number of volumes, and, I will venture to say, nearly an equal quantity of sterling wit and
sense. 'The first sprightly runnings' are there: it has
more of the original spirit, more of the freshness and
stamp of nature. The indications of character and strokes
of humour are more true and frequent; the reflections that
suggest themselves arise more from the occasion, and are
less spun out into regular dissertations. They are more
like the remarks which occur in sensible conversation, and
less like a lecture. Something is left to the understanding of the reader. Steele seems to have gone into his
closet chiefly to set down what he observed out of doors.
Addison seems to have spent most of his time in his study,
and to have spun out and wire-drawn the hints, which he
borrowed from Steele, or took from nature, to the utmost.
I am far from wishing to depreciate Addison's talents, but
I am anxious to do justice to Steele, who was, I think,
upon the whole, a less artificial and more original
writer. The humorous descriptions of Steele resemble
loose sketches, or fragments of a comedy; those of Addison
are rather comments or ingenious paraphrases on the genuine text. The characters of the club, not only in the
'Tatler', but in the 'Spectator', were drawn by Steele.(9)
That of Sir Roger de Coverley is among the number.
Addison has, however, gained himself immortal honour by
his manner of filling up this last character. Who is
there that can forget, or be insensible to, the inimitable nameless graces and varied traits of nature and of
old English character in it - to his unpretending virtues
and amiable weaknesses - to his modesty, generosity, hospitality, and eccentric whims - to the respect of his
neighbours, and the affection of his domestics - to his
wayward, hopeless, secret passion for his fair enemy, the
widow, in which there is more of real romance and true
delicacy, than in a thousand tales of knight-errantry -
(we perceive the hectic flush of his cheek, the faltering
of his tongue in speaking of her bewitching airs and 'the
whiteness of her hand') - to the havoc he makes among the
game in his neighbourhood - to his speech from the bench,
to shew the 'Spectator' what is thought of him in the
country - to his unwillingness to be put up as a sign
post, and his having his own likeness turned into the

Saracen's head - to his gentle reproof of the baggage of
a gypsy that tells him 'he has a widow in his line of
life' - to his doubts as to the existence of witchcraft,
and protection of reputed witches - to his account of the
family pictures, and his choice of a chaplain - to his
falling asleep at church, and his reproof of John
Williams, as soon as he recovered from his nap, for talking in sermon-time. The characters of Will. Wimble and
Will. Honeycomb are not a whit behind their friend, Sir
Roger, in delicacy and felicity. The delightful simplicity and good-humoured officiousness in the one, are set
off by the graceful affectation and courtly pretension in
the other. How long since I first became acquainted with
these two characters in the 'Spectator'! What old-
fashioned friends they seem, and yet I am not tired of
them, like so many other friends, nor they of me! How
airy these abstractions of the poet's pen stream over the
dawn of our acquaintance with human life! how they glance
their fairest colours on the prospect before us! how pure
they remain in it to the last, like the rainbow in the
evening-cloud, which the rude hand of time and experience
can neither soil nor dissipate! What a pity that we cannot find the reality, and yet if we did, the dream would
be over. I once thought I knew a Will. Wimble, and a
Will. Honeycomb, but they turned out but indifferently;
the originals in the 'Spectator' still read, word for
word, the same that they always did. We have only to
turn to the page, and find them where we left them! -
Many of the most exquisite pieces in the 'Tatler', it is
to be observed, are Addison's, as the Court of Honour,
and the Personification of Musical Instruments, (10) with
almost all those papers that form regular sets or series.
I do not know whether the picture of the family of an old
college acquaintance, in the 'Tatler', where the children
run to let Mr. Bickerstaff in at the door, and where the
one that loses the race that way, turns back to tell the
father that he is come; with the nice gradation of
incredulity in the little boy, who is got into Guy of
Warwick, and the Seven Champions, and who shakes his head
at the improbability of Æsop's Fables, is Steele's or
Addison's, though I believe it belongs to the former.(11)
The account of the two sisters, one of whom held up her
head higher than ordinary, from having on a pair of
flowered garters, and that of the married lady who complained to the 'Tatler' of the neglect of her husband,
with her answers to some *home* questions that were put to
her, are unquestionably Steele's. - If the 'Tatler' is
not inferior to the 'Spectator' as a record of manners
and character, it is superior to it in the interest of

many of the stories. Several of the incidents related
there by Steele have never been surpassed in the heart-
rending pathos of private distress. I might refer to
those of the lover and his mistress, when the theatre, in
which they were, caught fire; of the bridegroom, who by
accident kills his bride on the day of their marriage,
the story of Mr. Eustace and his wife; and the fine dream
about his own mistress when a youth. What has given its
superior reputation to the 'Spectator', is the greater
gravity of its pretensions, its moral dissertations and
critical reasonings, by which I confess myself less edi-
fied than by other things, which are thought more lightly
of. Systems and opinions change, but nature is always
true. It is the moral and didactic tone of the 'Spectator' which makes us apt to think of Addison (according to
Mandeville's sarcasm) as 'a parson in a tie-wig'. Many
of his moral Essays are, however, exquisitely beautiful
and quite happy. Such are the reflections on cheerfulness, those in Westminster Abbey, on the Royal Exchange,
and particularly some very affecting ones on the death of
a young lady in the fourth volume. These, it must be
allowed, are the perfection of elegant sermonising. His
critical Essays are not so good. I prefer Steele's
occasional selection of beautiful poetical passages,
without any affectation of analysing their beauties, to
Addison's finer-spun theories. The best criticism in the
'Spectator', that on the Cartoons of Raphael, of which
Mr. Fuseli has availed himself with great spirit in his
Lectures, is by Steele. (12) I owed this acknowledgment
to a writer who has so often put me in good humour with
myself, and every thing about me, when few things else
could, and when the tomes of casuistry and ecclesiastical
history, with which the little duodecimo volumes of the
'Tatler' were overwhelmed and surrounded, in the only
library to which I had access when a boy, had tried their
tranquillising effects upon me in vain. I had not long
ago in my hands, by favour of a friend, an original copy
of the quarto edition of the 'Tatler', with a list of the
subscribers. It is curious to see some names there which
we should hardly think of, (that of Sir Isaac Newton is
among them,) and also to observe the degree of interest
excited by those of the different persons, which is not
determined according to the rules of the Herald's College.
One literary name lasts as long as a whole race of heroes
and their descendants! The 'Guardian', which followed the
'Spectator', was, as may be supposed, inferior to it.

Notes

1 Michel Eyquem de Montaigne (1533-92) completed the
   whole of the 'Essais' (3 books) in 1588.
2 The 'Essais', beginning as Montaigne's commonplace-
   book, developed into studies of the human mind,
   'vain, divers, et ondoyant', as gathered from self-
   examination, social observation, and a long literary
   tradition.
3 'Tatler' 117.
4 'Tatler' 107.
5 'Tatler' 86.
6 'Tatler' 238.
7 Thomas Betterton (c. 1635-1710), actor; Anne Oldfield
   (1683-1730), actress; Richard Estcourt (1668-1712),
   actor and dramatist; Thomas D'Urfey (1653-1723), poet
   and dramatist.
8 Henri de la Tour d'Auvergne, Vicomte de Turenne
   (1611-75), French marshal-general killed near Sasbach
   in repelling the Germans.
9 'Spectator' 2.
10 'Tatler' 157, 250.
11 'Tatler' 95 probably is by Steele.
12 'Spectator' 226.

70. THOMAS BABINGTON MACAULAY, 'LIFE AND WRITINGS OF
ADDISON'

1843

Thomas Babington Macaulay (1800-59) was a historian and
critic. He was first elected to Parliament in 1830 as a
Whig, and worked in India (1834-8) as a member of the
supreme council of the East India Company. Upon his
return to England he served in various governmental
offices and as an MP (1839-47, 1852-6). In 1857 he was
made Baron Macaulay of Rothley. His most significant
work is 'The History of England from the Accession of
James the Second' (5 vols, 1849-61).
   Synthesizing the Victorian evaluation of Addison,
Macaulay's encomium appeared first as a review of Lucy
Aikin's two-volume 'Life of Addison' in the 'Edinburgh
Review' for July 1843.

...To the influence which Addison derived from his literary talents was added all the influence which arises from
character. The world, always ready to think the worst of
needy political adventurers, was forced to make one exception. Restlessness, violence, audacity, laxity of principle, are the vices ordinarily attributed to that class
of men. But faction itself could not deny that Addison
had, through all changes of fortune, been strictly faithful to his early opinions, and to his early friends; that
his integrity was without stain; that his whole deport-
ment indicated a fine sense of the becoming; that, in the
utmost heat of controversy, his zeal was tempered by a
regard for truth, humanity, and social decorum; that no
outrage could even provoke him to retaliation unworthy of
a Christian and a gentleman; and that his only faults were
a too sensitive delicacy, and a modesty which amounted to
bashfulness.

He was undoubtedly one of the most popular men of his
time; and much of his popularity he owed, we believe, to
that very timidity which his friends lamented. That
timidity often prevented him from exhibiting his talents
to the best advantage. But it propitiated Nemesis. It
averted that envy which would otherwise have been excited
by fame so splendid, and by so rapid an elevation. No man
is so great a favourite with the public as he who is at
once an object of admiration, of respect, and of pity; and
such were the feelings which Addison inspired. Those who
enjoyed the privilege of hearing his familiar conversation, declared with one voice that it was superior even
to his writings. The brilliant Mary Montague said, that
she had known all the wits, and that Addison was the best
company in the world. (1) The malignant Pope was forced
to own, that there was a charm in Addison's talk, which
could be found nowhere else. (2) Swift, when burning
with animosity against the Whigs, could not but confess
to Stella that, after all, he had never known any associ-
ate so agreeable as Addison. (3) Steele, an excellent
judge of lively conversation, said, that the conversation
of Addison was at once the most polite, and the most
mirthful, that could be imagined; that it was Terence and
Catullus in one, heightened by an exquisite something
which was neither Terence nor Catullus, but Addison alone.
(4) Young, an excellent judge of serious conversation,
said, that when Addison was at his ease, he went on in a
noble strain of thought and language, so as to chain the
attention of every hearer. (5) Nor were Addison's great
colloquial powers more admirable than the courtesy and
softness of heart which appeared in his conversation. At
the same time, it would be too much to say that he was

wholly devoid of the malice which is, perhaps, inseparable
from a keen sense of the ludicrous. He had one habit
which both Swift and Stella applauded, and which we hardly
know how to blame. If his first attempts to set a pre-
suming dunce right were ill received, he changed his tone,
'assented with civil leer', and lured the flattered coxcomb deeper and deeper into absurdity. That such was his
practice we should, we think, have guessed from his works.
The 'Tatler's' criticisms on Mr. Softly's sonnet, and the
'Spectator's' dialogue with the politician who is so zealous for the honour of Lady Q—p—t—s, are excellent
specimens of this innocent mischief. (6)

Such were Addison's talents for conversation. But his
rare gifts were not exhibited to crowds or to strangers.
As soon as he entered a large company, as soon as he saw
an unknown face, his lips were sealed, and his manners
became constrained. None who met him only in great assemblies would have been able to believe that he was the same
man who had often kept a few friends listening and laughing round a table, from the time when the play ended, till
the clock of St. Paul's in Covent Garden struck four. (7)
Yet, even at such a table, he was not seen to the best
advantage. To enjoy his conversation in the highest perfection, it was necessary to be alone with him, and to
hear him, in his own phrase, think aloud. 'There is no
such thing,' he used to say, 'as real conversation, but
between two persons.' (8)

This timidity, a timidity surely neither ungraceful nor
unamiable, led Addison into the two most serious faults
which can with justice be imputed to him. He found that
wine broke the spell which lay on his fine intellect, and
was therefore too easily seduced into convivial excess.
Such excess was in that age regarded, even by grave men,
as the most venial of all peccadilloes, and was so far
from being a mark of ill-breeding, that it was almost
essential to the character of a fine gentleman. But the
smallest speck is seen on a white ground; and almost all
the biographers of Addison have said something about this
failing. Of any other statesman or writer of Queen Anne's
reign, we should no more think of saying that he sometimes
took too much wine, than that he wore a long wig and a
sword.

To the excessive modesty of Addison's nature we must
ascribe another fault which generally arises from a very
different cause. He became a little too fond of seeing
himself surrounded by a small circle of admirers, to whom
he was as a King or rather as a God. All these men were
far inferior to him in ability, and some of them had very
serious faults. Nor did those faults escape his

observation; for, if ever there was an eye which saw
through and through men, it was the eye of Addison. But
with the keenest observation, and the finest sense of the
ridiculous, he had a large charity. The feeling with
which he looked on most of his humble companions was one
of benevolence, slightly tinctured with contempt. He was
at perfect ease in their company; he was grateful for
their devoted attachment; and he loaded them with benefits. Their veneration for him appears to have exceeded
that with which Johnson was regarded by Boswell, or War-
burton by Hurd. It was not in the power of adulation to
turn such a head, or deprave such a heart, as Addison's.
But it must in candour be admitted that he contracted
some of the faults which can scarcely be avoided by any
person who is so unfortunate as to be the oracle of a
small literary coterie....

At the close of 1708 Wharton became Lord Lieutenant
of Ireland, and appointed Addison Chief Secretary.
Addison was consequently under the necessity of quitting
London for Dublin. Besides the chief secretaryship,
which was then worth about two thousand pounds a year,
he obtained a patent appointing him keeper of the Irish
Records for life, with a salary of three or four hundred
a year. Budgell accompanied his cousin in the capacity
of private Secretary.

Wharton and Addison had nothing in common but Whiggism. The Lord Lieutenant was not only licentious and
corrupt, but was distinguished from other libertines and
jobbers by a callous impudence which presented the
strongest contrast to the Secretary's gentleness and
delicacy. (9) Many parts of the Irish administration at
this time appear to have deserved serious blame. But
against Addison there was not a murmur. He long afterwards asserted, what all the evidence which we have ever
seen tends to prove, that his diligence and integrity
gained the friendship of all the most considerable persons in Ireland. (10)

The parliamentary career of Addison in Ireland has, we
think, wholly escaped the notice of all his biographers.
He was elected member for the borough of Cavan in the
summer of 1709; and in the journals of two sessions his
name frequently occurs. Some of the entries appear to
indicate that he so far overcame his timidity as to make
speeches. Nor is this by any means improbable; for the
Irish House of Commons was a far less formidable audience
than the English House; and many tongues which were tied
by fear in the greater assembly became fluent in the
smaller. Gerard Hamilton, (11) for example, who, from
fear of losing the fame gained by his single speech, sat

mute at Westminster during forty years, spoke with great
effect at Dublin when he was Secretary to Lord Halifax.

While Addison was in Ireland, an event occurred to
which he owes his high and permanent rank among British
writers. As yet his fame rested on performances which,
though highly respectable, were not built for duration,
and which would, if he had produced nothing else, have
now been almost forgotten, on some excellent Latin verses,
on some English verses which occasionally rose above mediocrity, and on a book of travels, agreeably written, but
not indicating any extraordinary powers of mind. These
works showed him to be a man of taste, sense, and learning. The time had come when he was to prove himself a
man of genius, and to enrich our literature with compositions which will live as long as the English language.

In the spring of 1709 Steele formed a literary project,
of which he was far indeed from foreseeing the consequences. Periodical papers had during many years been
published in London. Most of these were political; but
in some of them questions of morality, taste, and love
casuistry had been discussed. The literary merit of
these works was small indeed; and even their names are
now known only to the curious.

Steele had been appointed Gazetteer by Sunderland, at
the request, it is said, of Addison, and thus had access
to foreign intelligence earlier and more authentic than
was in those times within the reach of an ordinary news-
writer. This circumstance seems to have suggested to him
the scheme of publishing a periodical paper on a new plan.
It was to appear on the days on which the post left London
for the country, which were, in that generation, the
Tuesdays, Thursdays, and Saturdays. It was to contain the
foreign news, accounts of theatrical representations, and
the literary gossip of Will's and of the Grecian. It was
also to contain remarks on the fashionable topics of the
day, compliments to beauties, pasquinades on noted sharpers, and criticisms on popular preachers. The aim of
Steele does not appear to have been at first higher than
this. He was not ill qualified to conduct the work which
he had planned. His public intelligence he drew from the
best sources. He knew the town, and had paid dear for
his knowledge. He had read much more than the dissipated
men of that time were in the habit of reading. He was a
rake among scholars, and a scholar among rakes. His style
was easy and not incorrect; and, though his wit and humour
were of no high order, his gay animal spirits imparted to
his compositions an air of vivacity which ordinary readers
could hardly distinguish from comic genius. His writings
have been well compared to those light wines which, though

deficient in body and flavour, are yet a pleasant small
drink, if not kept too long, or carried too far.

Isaac Bickerstaff, Esquire, Astrologer, was an imaginary person, almost as well known in that age as Mr. Paul
Pry (12) or Mr. Samuel Pickwick in ours. Swift had
assumed the name of Bickerstaff in a satirical pamphlet
against Partridge, the maker of almanacks. Partridge had
been fool enough to publish a furious reply. Bickerstaff
had rejoined in a second pamphlet still more diverting
than the first. (13) All the wits had combined to keep
up the joke, and the town was long in convulsions of
laughter. Steele determined to employ the name which this
controversy had made popular; and, in 1709, it was
announced that Isaac Bickerstaff, Esquire, Astrologer, was
about to publish a paper called the 'Tatler'.

Addison had not been consulted about this scheme: but
as soon as he heard of it he determined to give his assistance. The effect of that assistance cannot be better
described than in Steele's own words. 'I fared,' he said,
'like a distressed prince who calls in a powerful neighbour to his aid. I was undone by my auxiliary. When I
had once called him in, I could not subsist without dependence on him.' 'The paper,' he says elsewhere, 'was
advanced indeed. It was raised to a greater thing than I
intended it.' (14)

It is probable that Addison, when he sent across St.
George's Channel his first contributions to the 'Tatler',
had no notion of the extent and variety of his own powers.
He was the possessor of a vast mine, rich with a hundred
ores. But he had been acquainted only with the least
precious part of his treasures, and had hitherto contented
himself with producing sometimes copper and sometimes
lead, intermingled with a little silver. All at once,
and by mere accident, he had lighted on an inexhaustible
vein of the finest gold.

The mere choice and arrangement of his words would have
sufficed to make his essays classical. For never, not
even by Dryden, not even by Temple, had the English language been written with such sweetness, grace, and facility. But this was the smallest part of Addison's
praise. Had he clothed his thoughts in the half French
style of Horace Walpole, or in the half Latin style of Dr.
Johnson, or in the half German jargon of the present day,
(15) his genius would have triumphed over all faults of
manner. As a moral satirist he stands unrivalled. If
ever the best 'Tatlers' and 'Spectators' were equalled in
their own kind, we should be inclined to guess that it
must have been by the lost comedies of Menander.

In wit, properly so called, Addison was not inferior to

Cowley or Butler. No single ode of Cowley contains so
many happy analogies as are crowded into the lines to Sir
Godfrey Kneller; and we would undertake to collect from
the 'Spectators' as great a number of ingenious illustra-
tions as can be found in 'Hudibras'. The still higher
faculty of invention Addison possessed in still larger
measure. The numerous fictions, generally original, often
wild and grotesque, but always singularly graceful and
happy, which are found in his essays, fully entitle him to
the rank of a great poet, a rank to which his metrical
compositions give him no claim. As an observer of life,
of manner, of all the shades of human character, he stands
in the first class. And what he observed he had the art
of communicating in two widely different ways. He could
describe virtues, vices, habits, whims, as well as Claren-
don. But he could do something better. He could call
human beings into existence, and make them exhibit themselves. If we wish to find any thing more vivid than
Addison's best portraits, we must go either to Shakespeare
or Cervantes.

But what shall we say of Addison's humour, of his sense
of the ludicrous, of his power of awakening that sense in
others, and of drawing mirth from incidents which occur
every day, and from little peculiarities of temper and
manner, such as may be found in every man? We feel the
charm: we give ourselves up to it: but we strive in vain
to analyse it.

Perhaps the best way of describing Addison's peculiar
pleasantry is to compare it with the pleasantry of some
other great satirists. The three most eminent masters of
the art of ridicule during the eighteenth century, were,
we conceive, Addison, Swift, and Voltaire. Which of the
three had the greatest power of moving laughter may be
questioned. But each of them, within his own domain, was
supreme.

Voltaire is the prince of buffoons. His merriment is
without disguise or restraint. He gambols; he grins; he
shakes the sides; he points the finger; he turns up the
nose; he shoots out the tongue. The manner of Swift is
the very opposite to this. He moves laughter, but never
joins in it. He appears in his works such as he appeared
in society. All the company are convulsed with merriment, while the Dean, the author of all the mirth, preserves an invincible gravity, and even sourness of aspect,
and gives utterance to the most eccentric and ludicrous
fancies, with the air of a man reading the commination
service.

The manner of Addison is as remote from that of Swift
as from that of Voltaire. He neither laughs out like the

French wit, nor, like the Irish wit, throws a double portion of severity into his countenance while laughing inwardly; but preserves a look peculiarly his own, a look
of demure serenity, disturbed only by an arch sparkle of
the eye, an almost imperceptible elevation of the brow,
an almost imperceptible curl of the lip. His tone is
never that either of a Jack Pudding or of a Cynic. It
is that of a gentleman, in whom the quickest sense of the
ridiculous is constantly tempered by good nature and good
breeding.

We own that the humour of Addison is, in our opinion,
of a more delicious flavour than the humour of either
Swift or Voltaire. Thus much, at least, is certain, that
both Swift and Voltaire have been successfully mimicked,
and that no man has yet been able to mimic Addison. The
letter of the Abbé Coyer to Pansophe is Voltaire all over,
and imposed, during a long time, on the Academicians of
Paris. There are passages in Arbuthnot's satirical works
which we, at least, cannot distinguish from Swift's best
writing. But of the many eminent men who have made Addison their model, though several have copied his mere diction with happy effect, none have been able to catch the
tone of his pleasantry. In the 'World', in the 'Connois-
seur', in the 'Mirror', in the 'Lounger', (16) there are
numerous papers written in obvious imitation of his
'Tatlers' and 'Spectators'. Most of these papers have
some merit; many are very lively and amusing; but there is
not a single one which could be passed off as Addison's on
a critic of the smallest perspicacity.

But that which chiefly distinguishes Addison from
Swift, from Voltaire, from almost all the other great masters of ridicule, is the grace, the nobleness, the moral
purity, which we find even in his merriment. Severity,
gradually hardening and darkening into misanthropy,
characterizes the works of Swift. The nature of Voltaire
was, indeed, not inhuman; but he venerated nothing.
Neither in the masterpieces of art nor in the purest
examples of virtue, neither in the Great First Cause nor
in the awful enigma of the grave, could he see any thing
but subjects for drollery. The more solemn and august the
theme, the more monkey-like was his grimacing and chatter-
ing. The mirth of Swift is the mirth of Mephistophiles;
the mirth of Voltaire is the mirth of Puck. If, as Soame
Jenyns oddly imagined, a portion of the happiness of Sera-
phim and just men made perfect be derived from an exquisite perception of the ludicrous, (17) their mirth must
surely be none other than the mirth of Addison; a mirth
consistent with tender compassion for all that is frail,
and with profound reverence for all that is sublime.

Nothing great, nothing amiable, no moral duty, no doctrine
of natural or revealed religion, has ever been associated
by Addison with any degrading idea. His humanity is without a parallel in literary history. The highest proof of
virtue is to possess boundless power without abusing it.
No kind of power is more formidable than the power of
making men ridiculous; and that power Addison possessed in
boundless measure. How grossly that power was abused by
Swift and by Voltaire is well known. But of Addison it
may be confidently affirmed that he has blackened no man's
character, nay, that it would be difficult, if not impossible, to find in all the volumes which he has left us a
single taunt which can be called ungenerous or unkind.
Yet he had detractors, whose malignity might have seemed
to justify as terrible a revenge as that which men, not
superior to him in genius, wreaked on Bettesworth and on
Franc de Pompignan. (18) He was a politician; he was the
best writer of his party; he lived in times of fierce
excitement, in times when persons of high character and
station stooped to scurrility such as is now practised
only by the basest of mankind. Yet no provocation and no
example could induce him to return railing for railing.

Of the service which his Essays rendered to morality
it is difficult to speak too highly. It is true that,
when the 'Tatler' appeared, that age of outrageous profaneness and licentiousness which followed the Restoration
had passed away. Jeremy Collier had shamed the theatres
into something which, compared with the excesses of
Etherege and Wycherley, might be called decency. Yet
there still lingered in the public mind a pernicious
notion that there was some connection between genius and
profligacy, between the domestic virtues and the sullen
formality of the Puritans. That error it is the glory of
Addison to have dispelled. He taught the nation that the
faith and the morality of Hale and Tillotson might be
found in company with wit more sparkling than the wit of
Congreve, and with humour richer than the humour of
Vanbrugh. (19) So effectually, indeed, did he retort on
vice the mockery which had recently been directed against
virtue, that, since his time, the open violation of decency has always been considered among us as the mark of a
fool. And this revolution, the greatest and most salutary
ever effected, by any satirist, he accomplished, be it
remembered, without writing one personal lampoon.

In the early contributions of Addison to the 'Tatler'
his peculiar powers were not fully exhibited. Yet from
the first, his superiority to all his coadjutors was evident. Some of his later 'Tatlers' are fully equal to
any thing that he ever wrote. Among the portraits, we

most admire Tom Folio, Ned Softly, and the Political
Upholsterer. The proceedings of the Court of Honour, the
Thermometer of Zeal, the story of the Frozen Words, the
Memoirs of the Shilling, are excellent specimens of that
ingenious and lively species of fiction in which Addison
excelled all men. There is one still better paper of the
same class. But though that paper, a hundred and thirty-
three years ago, was probably thought as edifying as one
of Smalridge's sermons, (20) we dare not indicate it to
the squeamish readers of the nineteenth century....

He had one consolation [following the fall of the Whigs
in 1710]. Of the unpopularity which his friends had
incurred, he had no share. Such was the esteem with which
he was regarded that, while the most violent measures were
taken for the purpose of forcing Tory members on Whig
corporations, he was returned to Parliament without even
a contest. Swift, who was now in London, and who had
already determined on quitting the Whigs, wrote to Stella
in these remarkable words: 'The Tories carry it among the
new members six to one. Mr. Addison's election has passed
easy and undisputed; and I believe if he had a mind to be
king he would hardly be refused.' (21)
The good will with which the Tories regarded Addison
is the more honourable to him, because it had not been
purchased by any concession on his part. During the
general election he published a political Journal,
entitled the 'Whig Examiner'. Of that Journal it may be
sufficient to say that Johnson, in spite of his strong
political prejudices, pronounced it to be superior in wit
to any of Swift's writings on the other side. When it
ceased to appear, Swift, in a letter to Stella, expressed
his exultation at the death of so formidable an antagonist.
'He might well rejoice,' says Johnson, 'at the death of
that which he could not have killed.' 'On no occasion,'
he adds, 'was the genius of Addison more vigorously exerted, and on none did the superiority of his powers more
evidently appear.'
The only use which Addison appears to have made of the
favour with which he was regarded by the Tories was to
save some of his friends from the general ruin of the Whig
party. He felt himself to be in a situation which made it
his duty to take a decided part in politics. But the case
of Steele and of Ambrose Phillipps was different. For
Phillipps, Addison even condescended to solicit, with what
success we have not ascertained. Steele held two places.
He was Gazetteer, and he was also a Commissioner of Stamps.
The Gazette was taken from him. But he was suffered to
retain his place in the Stamp Office, on an implied

understanding that he should not be active against the new
government; and he was, during more than two years,
induced by Addison to observe this armistice with tolerable fidelity.

Isaac Bickerstaff accordingly became silent upon politics, and the article of news which had once formed about
one third of his paper, altogether disappeared. The
'Tatler' had completely changed its character. It was now
nothing but a series of essays on books, morals, and
manners. Steele therefore resolved to bring it to a close,
and to commence a new work on an improved plan. It was
announced that this new work would be published daily.
The undertaking was generally regarded as bold, or rather
rash; but the event amply justified the confidence with
which Steele relied on the fertility of Addison's genius.
On the second of January 1711, appeared the last 'Tatler'.
At the beginning of March following appeared the first of
an incomparable series of papers, containing observations
on life and literature by an imaginary 'Spectator'.

The Spectator himself was conceived and drawn by Addison; and it is not easy to doubt that the portrait was
meant to be in some features a likeness of the painter.
The Spectator is a gentleman who, after passing a studious
youth at the university, has travelled on classic ground,
and has bestowed much attention on curious points of antiquity. He has, on his return, fixed his residence in
London, and has observed all the forms of life which are
to be found in that great city, has daily listened to the
wits of Will's, has smoked with the philosophers of the
Grecian, and has mingled with the parsons at Child's, and
with the politicians at the St. James's. In the morning,
he often listens to the hum of the Exchange; in the
evening, his face is constantly to be seen in the pit of
Drury Lane theatre. But an insurmountable bashfulness
prevents him from opening his mouth, except in a small
circle of intimate friends.

These friends were first sketched by Steele. Four of
the club, the templar, the clergyman, the soldier, and the
merchant, were uninteresting figures, fit only for a background. But the other two, an old country baronet and an
old town rake, though not delineated with a very delicate
pencil, had some good strokes. Addison took the rude out-
lines into his own hands, retouched them, coloured them,
and is in truth the creator of the Sir Roger de Coverley
and the Will Honeycomb with whom we are all familiar.

The plan of the 'Spectator' must be allowed to be both
original and eminently happy. Every valuable essay in the
series may be read with pleasure separately; yet the five
or six hundred essays form a whole, and a whole which has

the interest of a novel. It must be remembered, too, that
at that time no novel, giving a lively and powerful picture of the common life and manners of England, had
appeared. Richardson was working as a compositor. Fielding was robbing birds' nests. Smollett was not yet born.
The narrative, therefore, which connects together the
'Spectator's' Essays, gave to our ancestors their first
taste of an exquisite and untried pleasure. That narrative was indeed constructed with no art or labour. The
events were such events as occur every day. Sir Roger
comes up to town to see Eugenio, as the worthy baronet
always calls Prince Eugene, goes with the Spectator on the
water to Spring Gardens, walks among the tombs in the
Abbey, and is frightened by the Mohawks, but conquers his
apprehension so far as to go to the theatre when the 'Distressed Mother' is acted. The Spectator pays a visit in
the summer to Coverley Hall, is charmed with the old house,
the old butler, and the old chaplain, eats a jack caught
by Will Wimble, rides to the assizes, and hears a point of
law discussed by Tom Touchy. At last a letter from the
honest butler brings to the club the news that Sir Roger
is dead. Will Honeycomb marries and reforms at sixty.
The club breaks up; and the Spectator resigns his functions. Such events can hardly be said to form a plot;
yet they are related with such truth, such grace, such
wit, such humour, such pathos, such knowledge of the
human heart, such knowledge of the ways of the world, that
they charm us on the hundredth perusal. We have not the
least doubt that if Addison had written a novel, on an
extensive plan, it would have been superior to any that we
possess. As it is, he is entitled to be considered not
only as the greatest of the English essayists, but as the
forerunner of the great English novelists.

We say this of Addison alone; for Addison is the Spectator. About three sevenths of the work are his; and it
is no exaggeration to say, that his worst essay is as good
as the best essay of any of his coadjutors. His best
essays approach near to absolute perfection; nor is their
excellence more wonderful than their variety. His invention never seems to flag; nor is he ever under the necessity of repeating himself, or of wearing out a subject.
There are no dregs in his wine. He regales us after the
fashion of that prodigal nabob who held that there was
only one good glass in a bottle. As soon as we have
tasted the first sparkling foam of a jest, it is withdrawn, and a fresh draught of nectar is at our lips. On
the Monday we have an allegory as lively and ingenious as
Lucian's 'Auction of Lives'; on the Tuesday an Eastern
apologue, as richly coloured as the 'Tales of Scherezade';

on the Wednesday, a character described with the skill
of La Bruyere; on the Thursday, a scene from common life,
equal to the best chapters in the 'Vicar of Wakefield'; on
the Friday, some sly Horatian pleasantry on fashionable
follies, on hoops, patches, or puppet shows; and on the
Saturday a religious meditation, which will bear a comparison with the finest passages in Massillon.

It is dangerous to select where there is so much that
deserves the highest praise. We will venture, however, to
say, that any person who wishes to form a notion of the
extent and variety of Addison's powers, will do well to
read at one sitting the following papers, the two Visits
to the Abbey, the Visit to the Exchange, the Journal of
the Retired Citizen, the Vision of Mirza, the Transmigra-
tions of Pug the Monkey, and the Death of Sir Roger de
Coverley. (22)

The least valuable of Addison's contributions to the
'Spectator' are, in the judgment of our age, his critical
papers. Yet his critical papers are always luminous, and
often ingenious. The very worst of them must be regarded
as creditable to him, when the character of the school in
which he had been trained is fairly considered. The best
of them were much too good for his readers. In truth, he
was not so far behind our generation as he was before his
own. No essays in the 'Spectator' were more censured and
derided than those in which he raised his voice against
the contempt with which our fine old ballads were regarded, and showed the scoffers that the same gold which,
burnished and polished, gives lustre to the 'AEneid' and
the 'Odes' of Horace, is mingled with the rude dross of
'Chevy Chase'.

It is not strange that the success of the 'Spectator'
should have been such as no similar work has ever
obtained. The number of copies daily distributed was at
first three thousand. It subsequently increased, and had
risen to near four thousand when the stamp tax was
imposed. That tax was fatal to a crowd of journals. The
'Spectator', however, stood its ground, doubled its
price, and, though its circulation fell off, still
yielded a large revenue both to the state and to the
authors. For particular papers, the demand was immense;
of some, it is said, twenty thousand copies were required.
But this was not all. To have the 'Spectator' served up
every morning with the bohea and rolls was a luxury for
the few. The majority were content to wait till essays
enough had appeared to form a volume. Ten thousand copies
of each volume were immediately taken off, and new editions were called for. It must be remembered, that the
population of England was then hardly a third of what it

now is. The number of Englishmen who were in the habit
of reading, was probably not a sixth of what it now is.
A shopkeeper or a farmer who found any pleasure in
literature, was a rarity. Nay, there was doubtless more
than one knight of the shire whose country seat did not
contain ten books, receipt books and books on farriery
included. In these circumstances, the sale of the 'Spectator' must be considered as indicating a popularity quite
as great as that of the most successful works of Sir
Walter Scott and Mr. Dickens in our own time.

At the close of 1712 the 'Spectator' ceased to appear.
It was probably felt that the shortfaced gentleman and his
club had been long enough before the town; and that it was
time to withdraw them, and to replace them by a new set of
characters. In a few weeks the first number of the
'Guardian' was published. But the 'Guardian' was unfortunate both in its birth and in its death. It began in dulness and disappeared in a tempest of faction. The
original plan was bad. Addison contributed nothing till
sixty-six numbers had appeared; and it was then impossible
to make the 'Guardian' what the 'Spectator' had been.
Nestor Ironside and the Miss Lizards were people to whom
even he could impart no interest. He could only furnish
some excellent little essays, both serious and comic;
and this he did.

Why Addison gave no assistance to the 'Guardian',
during the first two months of its existence, is a question which has puzzled the editors and biographers, but
which seems to us to admit of a very easy solution. He
was then engaged in bringing his 'Cato' on the stage.

The first four acts of this drama had been lying in his
desk since his return from Italy. (23) His modest and
sensitive nature shrank from the risk of a public and
shameful failure; and, though all who saw the manuscript
were loud in praise, some thought it possible that an
audience might become impatient even of very good rhetoric,
and advised Addison to print the play without hazarding a
representation. (24) At length, after many fits of apprehension, the poet yielded to the urgency of his political
friends, who hoped that the public would discover some
analogy between the followers of Caesar and the Tories,
between Sempronius and the apostate Whigs, between Cato,
struggling to the last for the liberties of Rome, and the
band of patriots who still stood firm round Halifax and
Wharton.

Addison gave the play to the managers of Drury Lane
theatre, without stipulating for any advantage to himself.
They, therefore, thought themselves bound to spare no cost
in scenery and dresses. The decorations, it is true,

would not have pleased the skilful eye of Mr. Macready.
(25) Juba's waistcoat blazed with gold lace; Marcia's
hoop was worthy of a Duchess on the birthday; and Cato
wore a wig worth fifty guineas. The prologue was written
by Pope, and is undoubtedly a dignified and spirited composition. The part of the hero was excellently played by
Booth. Steele undertook to pack a house. The boxes were
in a blaze with the stars of the Peers in Opposition. The
pit was crowded with attentive and friendly listeners from
the Inns of Court and the literary coffee-houses. Sir
Gilbert Heathcote, Governor of the Bank of England, was
at the head of a powerful body of auxiliaries from the
city, warm men and true Whigs, but better known at Jonathan's and Garraway's (26) than in the haunts of wits and
critics.

These precautions were quite superfluous. The Tories,
as a body, regarded Addison with no unkind feelings. Nor
was it for their interest, professing, as they did, profound reverence for law and prescription, and abhorrence
both of popular insurrections and of standing armies, to
appropriate to themselves reflections thrown on the great
military chief and demagogue, who, with the support of the
legions and of the common people, subverted all the
ancient institutions of his country. Accordingly, every
shout that was raised by the members of the Kit Cat was
echoed by the High Churchmen of the October; and the curtain at length fell amidst thunders of unanimous applause.

The delight and admiration of the town were described
by the 'Guardian' in terms which we might attribute to
partiality, were it not that the 'Examiner', the organ of
the Ministry, held similar language. The Tories, indeed,
found much to sneer at in the conduct of their opponents.
Steele had on this, as on other occasions, shown more zeal
than taste or judgment. The honest citizens who marched
under the orders of Sir Gibby, as he was facetiously
called, probably knew better when to buy and when to sell
stock than when to clap and when to hiss at a play, and
incurred some ridicule by making the hypocritical Sempronius their favourite, and by giving to his insincere rants
louder plaudits than they bestowed on the temperate eloquence of Cato. Wharton, too, who had the incredible
effrontery to applaud the lines about flying from prosperous vice and from the power of impious men to a private
station, did not escape the sarcasms of those who justly
thought that he could fly from nothing more vicious or
impious than himself. The epilogue, which was written by
Garth, a zealous Whig, was severely and not unreasonably
censured as ignoble and out of place. But Addison was
described, even by the bitterest Tory writers, as a

gentleman of wit and virtue, in whose friendship many persons of both parties were happy, and whose name ought not to be mixed up with factious squabbles.

Of the jests by which the triumph of the Whig party was disturbed, the most severe and happy was Bolingbroke's. (27) Between two acts, he sent for Booth to his box, and presented him, before the whole theatre, with a purse of fifty guineas for defending the cause of liberty so well against a perpetual Dictator. This was a pungent allusion to the attempt which Marlborough had made, not long before his fall, to obtain a patent creating him Captain General for life.

It was April; and in April, a hundred and thirty years ago, the London season was thought to be far advanced. During a whole month, however, Cato was performed to overflowing houses, and brought into the treasury of the theatre twice the gains of an ordinary spring. In the summer the Drury Lane company went down to the Act at Oxford, and there, before an audience which retained an affectionate remembrance of Addison's accomplishments and virtues, his tragedy was enacted during several days. The gownsmen began to besiege the theatre in the forenoon, and by one in the afternoon all the seats were filled.

About the merits of the piece which had so extraordinary an effect, the public, we suppose, has made up its mind. To compare it with the masterpieces of the Attic stage, with the great English dramas of the time of Elizabeth, or even with the productions of Schiller's manhood, would be absurd indeed. Yet it contains excellent dialogue and declamation, and, among plays fashioned on the French model, must be allowed to rank high; not indeed with 'Athalie' or 'Saul'; but, we think, not below 'Cinna', (28) and certainly above any other English tragedy of the same school, above many of the plays of Corneille, above many of the plays of Voltaire and Alfieri, and above some plays of Racine. Be this as it may, we have little doubt that 'Cato' did as much as the 'Tatlers', 'Spectators', and 'Freeholders' united, to raise Addison's fame among his contemporaries.

The modesty and good nature of the successful dramatist had tamed even the malignity of faction. But literary envy, it should seem, is a fiercer passion than party spirit. It was by a zealous Whig that the fiercest attack on the Whig tragedy was made. John Dennis published 'Remarks on Cato', which were written with some acuteness and with much coarseness and asperity. Addison neither defended himself nor retaliated. On many points he had an excellent defence; and nothing would have been easier than to retaliate; for Dennis had written bad odes,

bad tragedies, bad comedies: he had, moreover, a larger
share than most men of those infirmities and eccentricities which excite laughter; and Addison's power of
turning either an absurd book or an absurd man into ridicule was unrivalled. Addison, however, serenely conscious
of his superiority, looked with pity on his assailant,
whose temper, naturally irritable and gloomy, had been
soured by want, by controversy, and by literary
failures....

In September 1713 the 'Guardian' ceased to appear.
Steele had gone mad about politics. A general election
had just taken place: he had been chosen member for Stockbridge; and he fully expected to play a first part in
Parliament. The immense success of the 'Tatler' and
'Spectator' had turned his head. He had been the editor
of both those papers, and was not aware how entirely they
owed their influence and popularity to the genius of his
friend. His spirits, always violent, were now excited by
vanity, ambition, and faction, to such a pitch that he
every day committed some offence against good sense and
good taste. All the discreet and moderate members of his
own party regretted and condemned his folly. 'I am in a
thousand troubles,' Addison wrote, 'about poor Dick, and
wish that his zeal for the public may not be ruinous to
himself. But he has sent me word that he is determined to
go on, and that any advice I may give him in this particular will have no weight with him.' (29)
Steele set up a political paper called the 'Englishman', which, as it was not supported by contributions from
Addison, completely failed. By this work, by some other
writings of the same kind, and by the airs which he gave
himself at the first meeting of the new Parliament, he
made the Tories so angry that they determined to expel
him. The Whigs stood by him gallantly, but were unable to
save him. The vote of expulsion was regarded by all dis-
passionate men as a tyrannical exercise of the power of
the majority. But Steele's violence and folly, though
they by no means justified the steps which his enemies
took, had completely disgusted his friends; nor did he
ever regain the place which he had held in the public
estimation. (30)
Addison about this time conceived the design of adding
an eighth volume to the 'Spectator'. In June 1714, the
first number of the new series appeared, and during about
six months three papers were published weekly. Nothing
can be more striking than the contrast between the
'Englishman' and the eighth volume of the 'Spectator',
between Steele without Addison and Addison without Steele.

The 'Englishman' is forgotten; the eighth volume of the
'Spectator' contains, perhaps, the finest essays, both
serious and playful, in the English language.

Before this volume was completed, the death of Anne
produced an entire change in the administration of public
affairs. The blow fell suddenly. It found the Tory party
distracted by internal feuds, and unprepared for any great
effort. Harley had just been disgraced. Bolingbroke, it
was supposed, would be the chief minister. But the Queen
was on her death-bed before the white staff had been
given, and her last public act was to deliver it with a
feeble hand to the Duke of Shrewsbury. The emergency produced a coalition between all sections of public men who
were attached to the Protestant succession. George the
First was proclaimed without opposition. A Council, in
which the leading Whigs had seats, took the direction of
affairs till the new King should arrive. The first act of
the Lords Justices was to appoint Addison their secretary....

George the First took possession of his kingdom without
opposition. A new ministry was formed, and a new Parliament favourable to the Whigs chosen. Sunderland was
appointed Lord Lieutenant of Ireland; and Addison again
went to Dublin as Chief Secretary....

Addison did not remain long in Ireland. In 1715 he
quitted his secretaryship for a seat at the Board of
Trade. In the same year his comedy of 'The Drummer' was
brought on the stage. The name of the author was not
announced; the piece was coldly received; and some critics
have expressed a doubt whether it were really Addison's.
To us the evidence, both external and internal, seems
decisive. It is not in Addison's best manner; but it
contains numerous passages which no other writer known to
us could have produced. It was again performed after
Addison's death, and, being known to be his, was loudly
applauded.

Towards the close of the year 1715, while the Rebellion
was still raging in Scotland, Addison published the first
number of a paper called the 'Freeholder'. (31) Among his
political works the 'Freeholder' is entitled to the first
place. Even in the 'Spectator' there are few serious
papers nobler than the character of his friend Lord
Somers, and certainly no satirical papers superior to
those in which the Tory fox-hunter is introduced. (32)
This character is the original of Squire Western, and is
drawn with all Fielding's force, and with a delicacy of
which Fielding was altogether destitute. As none of
Addison's works exhibit stronger marks of his genius than
the 'Freeholder', so none does more honour to his moral

character. It is difficult to extol too highly the candour and humanity of a political writer whom even the
excitement of civil war cannot hurry into unseemly violence. Oxford, it is well known, was then the stronghold
of Toryism. The High Street had been repeatedly lined
with bayonets in order to keep down the disaffected gownsmen; and traitors pursued by the messengers of the Government had been concealed in the garrets of several colleges.
Yet the admonition which, even under such circumstances,
Addison addressed to the University, is singularly gentle,
respectful, and even affectionate. Indeed, he could not
find it in his heart to deal harshly even with imaginary
persons. (33) His foxhunter, though ignorant, stupid, and
violent, is at heart a good fellow, and is at last reclaimed by the clemency of the King. Steele was dissatisfied with his friend's moderation, and, though he acknowledged that the 'Freeholder' was excellently written, complained that the ministry played on a lute when it was
necessary to blow the trumpet. He accordingly determined
to execute a flourish after his own fashion, and tried to
rouse the public spirit of the nation by means of a paper
called the 'Town Talk', which is now as utterly forgotten
as his 'Englishman', as his 'Crisis', as his 'Letter to
the Bailiff of Stockbridge', as his 'Reader', in short, as
every thing that he wrote without the help of Addison.
    In the same year in which 'The Drummer' was acted, and
in which the first numbers of the 'Freeholder' appeared,
the estrangement of Pope and Addison became complete.
Addison had from the first seen that Pope was false and
malevolent. Pope had discovered that Addison was jealous.
The discovery was made in a strange manner. Pope had
written 'The Rape of the Lock', in two cantos, without
supernatural machinery. These two cantos had been loudly
applauded, and by none more loudly than by Addison. Then
Pope thought of the Sylphs and Gnomes, Ariel, Momentilla,
Crispissa, and Umbriel, and resolved to interweave the
Rosicrucian mythology with the original fabric. He asked
Addison's advice. Addison said that the poem as it stood
was a delicious little thing, and entreated Pope not to
run the risk of marring what was so excellent in trying to
mend it. Pope afterwards declared that this insidious
counsel first opened his eyes to the baseness of him who
gave it. (34)
    Now there can be no doubt that Pope's plan was most
ingenious, and that he afterwards executed it with great
skill and success. But does it necessarily follow that
Addison's advice was bad? And if Addison's advice was
bad, does it necessarily follow that it was given from
bad motives? If a friend were to ask us whether we would

advise him to risk his all in a lottery of which the
chances were ten to one against him, we should do our best
to dissuade him from running such a risk. Even if he were
so lucky as to get the thirty thousand pound prize, we
should not admit that we had counselled him ill; and we
should certainly think it the height of injustice in him
to accuse us of having been actuated by malice. We think
Addison's advice good advice. It rested on a sound principle, the result of long and wide experience. The general
rule undoubtedly is that, when a successful work of imagination has been produced, it should not be recast. We
cannot at this moment call to mind a single instance in
which this rule has been transgressed with happy effect,
except the instance of 'The Rape of the Lock'. Tasso
recast his 'Jerusalem'. Akenside recast his 'Pleasures of
the Imagination', and his 'Epistle to Curio'. Pope himself, emboldened no doubt by the success with which he had
expanded and remodelled 'The Rape of the Lock', made the
same experiment on 'The Dunciad'. All these attempts
failed. Who was to foresee that Pope would, once in his
life, be able to do what he could not himself do twice,
and what nobody else has ever done?
    Addison's advice was good. But had it been bad, why
should we pronounce it dishonest? Scott tells us that one
of his best friends predicted the failure of 'Waverley'.
Herder adjured Goethe not to take so unpromising a subject
as 'Faust'. Hume tried to dissuade Robertson from writing
the 'History of Charles the Fifth'. (35) Nay, Pope himself was one of those who prophesied that 'Cato' would
never succeed on the stage, and advised Addison to print
it without risking a representation. But Scott, Goethe,
Robertson, Addison, had the good sense and generosity to
give their advisers credit for the best intentions.
Pope's heart was not of the same kind with theirs.
    In 1715, while he was engaged in translating the
'Iliad', he met Addison at a coffeehouse. Phillipps and
Budgell were there; but their sovereign got rid of them,
and asked Pope to dine with him alone. After dinner,
Addison said that he lay under a difficulty which he
wished to explain. 'Tickell,' he said, 'translated some
time ago the first book of the 'Iliad'. I have promised
to look it over and correct it. I cannot therefore ask to
see yours; for that would be double dealing.' Pope made a
civil reply, and begged that his second book might have
the advantage of Addison's revision. Addison readily
agreed, looked over the second book, and sent it back with
warm commendations. (36)
    Tickell's version of the first book appeared soon after
this conversation. In the preface, all rivalry was

earnestly disclaimed. Tickell declared that he should
not go on with the 'Iliad'. That enterprise he should
leave to powers which he admitted to be superior to his
own. His only view, he said, in publishing this specimen
was to bespeak the favour of the public to a translation
of the 'Odyssey', in which he had made some progress.

Addison, and Addison's devoted followers, pronounced
both the versions good, but maintained that Tickell's had
more of the original. The town gave a decided preference
to Pope's. We do not think it worth while to settle such
a question of precedence. Neither of the rivals can be
said to have translated the 'Iliad', unless, indeed, the
word translation be used in the sense which it bears in
'The Midsummer Night's Dream'. When Bottom makes his
appearance with an ass's head instead of his own, Peter
Quince exclaims, 'Bless thee! Bottom, bless thee! thou art
translated.' In this sense, undoubtedly, the readers of
either Pope or Tickell may very properly exclaim, 'Bless
thee! Homer; thou art translated indeed.' (37)

Our readers will, we hope, agree with us in thinking
that no man in Addison's situation could have acted more
fairly and kindly, both towards Pope, and towards Tickell,
than he appears to have done. But an odious suspicion had
sprung up in the mind of Pope. He fancied, and he soon
firmly believed, that there was a deep conspiracy against
his fame and his fortunes. The work on which he had
staked his reputation was to be depreciated. The sub-
scription, on which rested his hopes of a competence, was
to be defeated. With this view Addison had made a rival
translation: Tickell had consented to father it; and the
wits of Button's had united to puff it.

Is there any external evidence to support this grave
accusation? The answer is short. There is absolutely
none.

Was there any internal evidence which proved Addison to
be the author of this version? Was it a work which Tickell was incapable of producing? Surely not. Tickell was
a Fellow of a College at Oxford, and must be supposed to
have been able to construe the 'Iliad'; and he was a
better versifier than his friend. We are not aware that
Pope pretended to have discovered any turns of expression
peculiar to Addison. Had such turns of expression been
discovered, they would be sufficiently accounted for by
supposing Addison to have corrected his friend's lines, as
he owned that he had done.

Is there any thing in the character of the accused
persons which makes the accusation probable? We answer
confidently - nothing. Tickell was long after this time
described by Pope himself as a very fair and worthy

man. (38) Addison had been, during many years, before
the public. Literary rivals, political opponents, had
kept their eyes on him. But neither envy nor faction,
in their utmost rage, had ever imputed to him a single
deviation from the laws of honour and of social morality.
Had he been indeed a man meanly jealous of fame, and
capable of stooping to base and wicked arts for the purpose of injuring his competitors, would his vices have
remained latent so long? He was a writer of tragedy: had
he ever injured Rowe? He was a writer of comedy: had he
not done ample justice to Congreve, and given valuable
help to Steele? He was a pamphleteer: have not his good
nature and generosity been acknowledged by Swift, his
rival in fame and his adversary in politics?

That Tickell should have been guilty of a villany seems
to us highly improbable. That Addison should have been
guilty of a villany seems to us highly improbable. But
that these two men should have conspired together to
commit a villany seems to us improbable in a tenfold
degree. All that is known to us of their intercourse
tends to prove, that it was not the intercourse of two
accomplices in crime. These are some of the lines in which
Tickell poured forth his sorrow over the coffin of Addison:

Or dost thou warn poor mortals left behind,
A task well suited to thy gentle mind?
Oh, if sometimes thy spotless form descend,
To me thine aid, thou guardian genius, lend.
When rage misguides me, or when fear alarms,
When pain distresses, or when pleasure charms,
In silent whisperings purer thoughts impart,
And turn from ill a frail and feeble heart;
Lead through the paths thy virtue trod before,
Till bliss shall join, nor death can part us more.

In what words, we should like to know, did this
guardian genius invite his pupil to join in a plan such
as the Editor of the Satirist would hardly dare to propose to the Editor of the Age?

We do not accuse Pope of bringing an accusation which
he knew to be false. We have not the smallest doubt that
he believed it to be true; and the evidence on which he
believed it he found in his own bad heart. His own life
was one long series of tricks, as mean and as malicious
as that of which he suspected Addison and Tickell. He
was all stiletto and mask. To injure, to insult, and to
save himself from the consequences of injury and insult
by lying and equivocating, was the habit of his life. He
published a lampoon on the Duke of Chandos; (39) he was

taxed with it; and he lied and equivocated. He published
a lampoon on Aaron Hill; he was taxed with it; and he lied
and equivocated. (40) He published a still fouler lampoon
on Lady Mary Wortley Montague; he was taxed with it; and
he lied with more than usual effrontery and vehemence.(41)
He puffed himself and abused his enemies under feigned
names. He robbed himself of his own letters, and then
raised the hue and cry after them. Besides his frauds of
malignity, of fear, of interest, and of vanity, there were
frauds which he seems to have committed from love of fraud
alone. He had a habit of stratagem, a pleasure in out-
witting all who came near him. Whatever his object might
be, the indirect road to it was that which he preferred.
For Bolingbroke, Pope undoubtedly felt as much love and
veneration as it was in his nature to feel for any human
being. Yet Pope was scarcely dead when it was discovered
that, from no motive except the mere love of artifice, he
had been guilty of an act of gross perfidy to Bolingbroke. (42)

Nothing was more natural than that such a man as this
should attribute to others that which he felt within himself. A plain, probable, coherent explanation is frankly
given to him. He is certain that it is all a romance. A
line of conduct scrupulously fair, and even friendly, is
pursued towards him. He is convinced that it is merely a
cover for a vile intrigue by which he is to be disgraced
and ruined. It is vain to ask him for proofs. He has
none, and wants none, except those which he carries in
his own bosom.

Whether Pope's malignity at length provoked Addison to
retaliate for the first and last time, cannot now be known
with certainty. We have only Pope's story, which runs
thus. A pamphlet appeared containing some reflections
which stung Pope to the quick. What those reflections
were, and whether they were reflections of which he had a
right to complain, we have now no means of deciding. The
Earl of Warwick, a foolish and vicious lad, who regarded
Addison with the feelings with which such lads generally
regard their best friends, told Pope, truly or falsely,
that this pamphlet had been written by Addison's direction. (43) When we consider what tendency stories have to
grow, in passing even from one honest man to another
honest man, and when we consider that to the name of
honest man neither Pope nor the Earl of Warwick had a
claim, we are not disposed to attach much importance to
this anecdote.

It is certain, however, that Pope was furious. He had
already sketched the character of Atticus in prose. In
his anger he turned this prose into the brilliant and

energetic lines which everybody knows by heart, or ought
to know by heart, and sent them to Addison. One charge
which Pope has enforced with great skill is probably not
without foundation. Addison was, we are inclined to
believe, too fond of presiding over a circle of humble
friends. Of the other imputations which these famous
lines are intended to convey, scarcely one has ever been
proved to be just, and some are certainly false. That
Addison was not in the habit of 'damning with faint
praise' appears from innumerable passages in his writings,
and from none more than from those in which he mentions
Pope. And it is not merely unjust, but ridiculous, to
describe a man who made the fortune of almost every one
of his intimate friends, as 'so obliging that he ne'er
obliged'.

That Addison felt the sting of Pope's satire keenly, we
cannot doubt. (44) That he was conscious of one of the
weaknesses with which he was reproached is highly probable. But his heart, we firmly believe, acquitted him of
the gravest part of the accusation. He acted like himself. As a satirist he was, at his own weapons, more
than Pope's match; and he would have been at no loss for
topics. A distorted and diseased body, tenanted by a yet
more distorted and diseased mind; spite and envy thinly
disguised by sentiments as benevolent and noble as those
which Sir Peter Teazle admired in Mr. Joseph Surface; (45)
a feeble sickly licentiousness; an odious love of filthy
and noisome images; these were things which a genius less
powerful than that to which we owe the 'Spectator' could
easily have held up to the mirth and hatred of mankind.
Addison had, moreover, at his command, other means of
vengeance which a bad man would not have scrupled to use.
He was powerful in the state. Pope was a Catholic; and,
in those times, a minister would have found it easy to
harass the most innocent Catholic by innumerable petty
vexations. Pope, near twenty years later, said that
'through the lenity of the government alone he could live
with comfort.' 'Consider,' he exclaimed, 'the injury that
a man of high rank and credit may do to a private person,
under penal laws and many other disadvantages.' It is
pleasing to reflect that the only revenge which Addison
took was to insert in the 'Freeholder' a warm encomium on
the translation of the 'Iliad', and to exhort all lovers
of learning to put down their names as subscribers. (46)
There could be no doubt, he said, from the specimens
already published, that the masterly hand of Pope would do
as much for Homer as Dryden had done for Virgil. From
that time to the end of his life, he always treated Pope,
by Pope's own acknowledgment, with justice. Friendship

was, of course, at an end.

One reason which induced the Earl of Warwick to play
the ignominious part of talebearer on this occasion, may
have been his dislike of the marriage which was about to
take place between his mother and Addison. The Countess
Dowager, a daughter of the old and honourable family of
the Middletons of Chirk, a family which, in any country
but ours, would be called noble, resided at Holland
House. Addison had, during some years, occupied at
Chelsea a small dwelling, once the abode of Nell Gwynn.
Chelsea is now a district of London, and Holland House
may be called a town residence. But, in the days of Anne
and George the First, milkmaids and sportsmen wandered
between green hedges, and over fields bright with dai-
sies, from Kensington almost to the shore of the Thames.
Addison and Lady Warwick were country neighbours, and
became intimate friends. The great wit and scholar tried
to allure the young Lord from the fashionable amusements
of beating watchmen, breaking windows, and rolling women
in hogsheads down Holborn Hill, to the study of letters
and the practice of virtue. These well meant exertions
did little good, however, either to the disciple or to
the master. Lord Warwick grew up a rake; and Addison
fell in love. The mature beauty of the Countess has been
celebrated by poets in language which, after a very large
allowance has been made for flattery, would lead us to
believe that she was a fine woman; and her rank doubtless
heightened her attractions. The courtship was long. The
hopes of the lover appear to have risen and fallen with
the fortunes of his party. His attachment was at length
matter of such notoriety that, when he visited Ireland
for the last time, Rowe addressed some consolatory verses
to the Chloe of Holland House. (47) It strikes us as a
little strange that, in these verses, Addison should be
called Lycidas, a name of singularly evil omen for a
swain just about to cross St. George's Channel.

At length Chloe capitulated. Addison was indeed able
to treat with her on equal terms. He had reason to expect
preferment even higher than that which he had attained.
He had inherited the fortune of a brother who died Governor of Madras. He had purchased an estate in Warwick-
shire, and had been welcomed to his domain in very tolerable verse by one of the neighbouring squires, the
poetical foxhunter, William Somervile. (48) In August
1716, the newspapers announced that Joseph Addison,
Esquire, famous for many excellent works both in verse
and prose, had espoused the Countess Dowager of Warwick.

He now fixed his abode at Holland House, a house which
can boast of a greater number of inmates distinguished in

political and literary history than any other private
dwelling in England. His portrait still hangs there.
The features are pleasing; the complexion is remarkably
fair; but, in the expression we trace rather the gentleness of his disposition than the force and keenness of his
intellect.

Not long after his marriage he reached the height of
civil greatness. The Whig Government had, during some
time, been torn by internal dissensions. Lord Townshend
led one section of the Cabinet, Lord Sunderland the other.
At length, in the spring of 1717, Sunderland triumphed.
Townshend retired from office, and was accompanied by Walpole and Cowper. Sunderland proceeded to reconstruct the
Ministry; and Addison was appointed Secretary of State.
It is certain that the Seals were pressed upon him, and
were at first declined by him. Men equally versed in
official business might easily have been found; and his
colleagues knew that they could not expect assistance
from him in debate. He owed his elevation to his popularity, to his stainless probity, and to his literary fame.

But scarcely had Addison entered the Cabinet when his
health began to fail. From one serious attack he recovered in the autumn; and his recovery was celebrated in
Latin verses, worthy of his own pen, by Vincent Bourne,
(49) who was then at Trinity College, Cambridge. A
relapse soon took place; and, in the following spring,
Addison was prevented by a severe asthma from discharging
the duties of his post. He resigned it, and was succeeded
by his friend Craggs, a young man whose natural parts,
though little improved by cultivation, were quick and
showy, whose graceful person and winning manners had made
him generally acceptable in society, and who, if he had
lived, would probably have been the most formidable of all
the rivals of Walpole.

As yet there was no Joseph Hume. (50) The Ministers,
therefore, were able to bestow on Addison a retiring pension of fifteen hundred pounds a year. In what form this
pension was given we are not told by the biographers, and
have not time to inquire. But it is certain that Addison
did not vacate his seat in the House of Commons.

Rest of mind and body seems to have re-established his
health; and he thanked God, with cheerful piety, for having set him free both from his office and from his asthma.
Many years seemed to be before him, and he meditated many
works, a tragedy on the death of Socrates, a translation
of the Psalms, a treatise on the evidences of Christianity. Of this last performance, a part, which we could
well spare, has come down to us.

But the fatal complaint soon returned, and gradually

prevailed against all the resources of medicine. It is
melancholy to think that the last months of such a life
should have been overclouded both by domestic and by
political vexations. A tradition which began early,
which has been generally received, and to which we have
nothing to oppose, has represented his wife as an arrogant and imperious woman. It is said that, till his
health failed him, he was glad to escape from the Countess
Dowager and her magnificent diningroom, blazing with the
gilded devices of the House of Rich, to some tavern where
he could enjoy a laugh, a talk about Virgil and Boileau,
and a bottle of claret, with the friends of his happier
days. All those friends, however, were not left to him.
Sir Richard Steele had been gradually estranged by various
causes. He considered himself as one who, in evil times,
had braved martyrdom for his political principles, and
demanded, when the Whig party was triumphant, a large compensation for what he had suffered when it was militant.
The Whig leaders took a very different view of his claims.
They thought that he had, by his own petulance and folly,
brought them as well as himself into trouble, and though
they did not absolutely neglect him, doled out favours to
him with a sparing hand. It was natural that he should be
angry with them, and especially angry with Addison. But
what above all seems to have disturbed Sir Richard, was
the elevation of Tickell, who, at thirty, was made by
Addison Undersecretary of State; while the Editor of the
'Tatler' and 'Spectator', the author of the 'Crisis', the
member for Stockbridge who had been persecuted for firm
adherence to the House of Hanover, was, at near fifty,
forced, after many solicitations and complaints, to content himself with a share in the patent of Drury Lane
theatre. Steele himself says, in his celebrated letter to
Congreve, that Addison, by his preference of Tickell,
'incurred the warmest resentment of other gentlemen';
and every thing seems to indicate that, of those resentful
gentlemen, Steele was himself one.

While poor Sir Richard was brooding over what he considered as Addison's unkindness, a new cause of quarrel
arose. The Whig party, already divided against itself,
was rent by a new schism. The celebrated Bill for limit-
ing the number of Peers had been brought in. (51) The
proud Duke of Somerset, first in rank of all the nobles
whose origin permitted them to sit in Parliament, was the
ostensible author of the measure. But it was supported,
and, in truth, devised by the Prime Minister. (52)

We are satisfied that the Bill was most pernicious;
and we fear that the motives which induced Sunderland to
frame it were not honourable to him. But we cannot deny

that it was supported by many of the best and wisest men
of that age. Nor was this strange. The royal prerogative
had, within the memory of the generation then in the
vigour of life, been so grossly abused, that it was still
regarded with a jealousy which, when the peculiar situation of the House of Brunswick is considered, may perhaps
be called immoderate. The particular prerogative of creating peers had, in the opinion of the Whigs, been grossly
abused by Queen Anne's last Ministry; and even the Tories
admitted that her Majesty, in swamping, as it has since
been called, the Upper House, had done what only an extreme case could justify. The theory of the English constitution, according to many high authorities, was that
three independent powers, the sovereign, the nobility, and
the commons, ought constantly to act as checks on each
other. If this theory were sound, it seemed to follow
that to put one of these powers under the absolute control
of the other two, was absurd. But if the number of peers
were unlimited, it could not well be denied that the Upper
House was under the absolute control of the Crown and the
Commons, and was indebted only to their moderation for any
power which it might be suffered to retain.

Steele took part with the Opposition, Addison with the
Ministers. Steele, in a paper called the 'Plebeian',
vehemently attacked the bill. Sunderland called for help
on Addison, and Addison obeyed the call. In a paper
called the 'Old Whig', he answered, and indeed refuted
Steele's arguments. It seems to us that the premises of
both the controversialists were unsound, that, on those
premises, Addison reasoned well and Steele ill, and that
consequently Addison brought out a false conclusion while
Steele blundered upon the truth. In style, in wit, and in
politeness, Addison maintained his superiority, though the
'Old Whig' is by no means one of his happiest performances.

At first, both anonymous opponents observed the laws of
propriety. But at length Steele so far forgot himself as
to throw an odious imputation on the morals of the chiefs
of the administration. Addison replied with severity,
but, in our opinion, with less severity than was due to
so grave an offence against morality and decorum; nor did
he, in his just anger, forget for a moment the laws of
good taste and good breeding....

The merited reproof which Steele had received, though
softened by some kind and courteous expressions, galled
him bitterly. He replied with little force and great
acrimony; but no rejoinder appeared. Addison was fast
hastening to his grave; and had, we may well suppose,
little disposition to prosecute a quarrel with an old
friend. His complaint had terminated in dropsy. He bore

up long and manfully. But at length he abandoned all
hope, dismissed his physicians, and calmly prepared himself to die.

His works he intrusted to the care of Tickell, and
dedicated them a very few days before his death to
Craggs, in a letter written with the sweet and graceful
eloquence of a Saturday's 'Spectator'. In this, his last
composition, he alluded to his approaching end in words
so manly, so cheerful, and so tender, that it is difficult
to read them without tears. At the same time he earnestly
recommended the interests of Tickell to the care of
Craggs.

Within a few hours of the time at which this dedication
was written, Addison sent to beg Gay, who was then living
by his wits about town, to come to Holland House. Gay
went, and was received with great kindness. To his amazement his forgiveness was implored by the dying man. Poor
Gay, the most good-natured and simple of mankind, could
not imagine what he had to forgive. There was, however,
some wrong, the remembrance of which weighed on Addison's
mind, and which he declared himself anxious to repair.
He was in a state of extreme exhaustion; and the parting
was doubtless a friendly one on both sides. Gay supposed
that some plan to serve him had been in agitation at
Court, and had been frustrated by Addison's influence.
Nor is this improbable. Gay had paid assiduous court to
the royal family. But in the Queen's days he had been the
eulogist of Bolingbroke, and was still connected with many
Tories. It is not strange that Addison, while heated by
conflict, should have thought himself justified in
obstructing the preferment of one whom he might regard as
a political enemy. Neither is it strange that, when
reviewing his whole life, and earnestly scrutinising all
his motives, he should think that he had acted an unkind
and ungenerous part, in using his power against a distressed man of letters, who was as harmless and as help-
less as a child.

One inference may be drawn from this anecdote. It
appears that Addison, on his deathbed, called himself to a
strict account, and was not at ease till he had asked
pardon for an injury which it was not even suspected that
he had committed, for an injury which would have caused
disquiet only to a very tender conscience. Is it not then
reasonable to infer that, if he had really been guilty of
forming a base conspiracy against the fame and fortunes of
a rival, he would have expressed some remorse for so
serious a crime? But it is unnecessary to multiply arguments and evidence for the defence, when there is neither
argument nor evidence for the accusation.

The last moments of Addison were perfectly serene.
His interview with his son-in-law is universally known.
'See', he said, 'how a Christian can die.' The piety of
Addison was, in truth, of a singularly cheerful character.
The feeling which predominates in all his devotional writings is gratitude. God was to him the allwise and all-
powerful friend who had watched over his cradle with more
than maternal tenderness; who had listened to his cries
before they could form themselves in prayer; who had preserved his youth from the snares of vice; who had made his
cup run over with worldly blessings; who had doubled the
value of those blessings, by bestowing a thankful heart to
enjoy them, and dear friends to partake them; who had
rebuked the waves of the Ligurian gulf, had purified the
autumnal air of the Campagna, and had restrained the aval-
anches of Mont Cenis. Of the Psalms, his favourite was
that which represents the Ruler of all things under the
endearing image of a shepherd, whose crook guides the
flock safe, through gloomy and desolate glens, to meadows
well watered and rich with herbage. On that goodness to
which he ascribed all the happiness of his life, he relied
in the hour of death with the love which casteth out fear.
He died on the seventeenth of June 1719. He had just
entered on his forty-eighth year.

His body lay in state in the Jerusalem Chamber, and
was borne thence to the Abbey at dead of night. The choir
sang a funeral hymn. Bishop Atterbury, one of those
Tories who had loved and honoured the most accomplished of
the Whigs, met the corpse, and led the procession by
torchlight, round the shrine of Saint Edward and the
graves of the Plantagenets, to the Chapel of Henry the
Seventh. On the north side of that Chapel, in the vault
of the House of Albemarle, the coffin of Addison lies next
to the coffin of Montague. Yet a few months; and the same
members passed again along the same aisle. The same sad
anthem was again chanted. The same vault was again
opened; and the coffin of Craggs was placed close to the
coffin of Addison.

Many tributes were paid to the memory of Addison; but
one alone is now remembered. Tickell bewailed his friend
in an elegy which would do honour to the greatest name in
our literature, and which unites the energy and magnifi-
cence of Dryden to the tenderness and purity of Cowper.
This fine poem was prefixed to a superb edition of Addison's works, which was published, in 1721, by subcription.
The names of the subscribers proved how widely his fame
had been spread. That his countrymen should be eager to
possess his writings, even in a costly form, is not
wonderful. But it is wonderful that, though English

literature was then little studied on the continent,
Spanish Grandees, Italian Prelates, Marshals of France,
should be found in the list. Among the most remarkable
names are those of the Queen of Sweden, of Prince Eugene,
of the Grand Duke of Tuscany, of the Dukes of Parma,
Modena, and Guastalla, of the Doge of Genoa, of the
Regent Orleans, and of Cardinal Dubois. We ought to add
that this edition, though eminently beautiful, is in some
important points defective; nor, indeed, do we yet
possess a complete collection of Addison's writings. (53)

It is strange that neither his opulent and noble widow,
nor any of his powerful and attached friends, should have
thought of placing even a simple tablet, inscribed with
his name, on the walls of the Abbey. It was not till
three generations had laughed and wept over his pages,
that the omission was supplied by the public veneration.
At length, in our own time, his image, skilfully graven,
appeared in Poet's Corner. It represents him, as we can
conceive him, clad in his dressing gown, and freed from
his wig, stepping from his parlour at Chelsea into his
trim little garden, with the account of the Everlasting
Club, or the Loves of Hilpa and Shalum, just finished for
the next day's 'Spectator', in his hand. Such a mark
of national respect was due to the unsullied statesman,
to the accomplished scholar, to the master of pure
English eloquence, to the consummate painter of life and
manners. It was due, above all, to the great satirist,
who alone knew how to use ridicule without abusing it,
who, without inflicting a wound, effected a great social
reform, and who reconciled wit and virtue, after a long
and disastrous separation, during which wit had been led
astray by profligacy, and virtue by fanaticism.

Notes

1 Joseph Spence, 'Observations', ed. James M. Osborn
   (1966), sect. 744.
2 Ibid., sect. 148.
3 Letter XI, dated 9 December 1710; Letter XXX, dated
   8 September 1711.
4 See Johnson's 'Life of Addison', No. 67, note 5.
5 Spence, sect. 822.
6 'Tatler 163; 'Spectator' 568.
7 Hist. MSS. Com., 'Egmont', I, 105 (dated 6 October
   1730).
8 'Spectator' 68, 93.
9 Swift, 'A Short Character of his Excellency Thomas
   Earl of Wharton' (1710).

10 See his Memorial to George I, printed in Lucy Aikin,
    'The Life of Joseph Addison' (1843), II, pp. 151-3.
11 William Gerard Hamilton (1729-96), known inaccurately
    as 'Single Speech'.
12 'Paul Pry', the title of a farce by John Poole
    (c. 1786-1872), produced in 1825.
13 'Predictions for the Year 1708' (1708); 'The Accom-
    plishment of the First of Mr. Bickerstaff's Predic-
    tions' (1708); 'A Vindication of Isaac Bickerstaff,
    Esq;' (1709); 'A Famous Prediction of Merlin, the
    British Wizard' (1709).
14 The Preface to the fourth volume of the collected
    'Tatler' (1710-11).
15 Possibly an allusion to Thomas Carlyle's 'Past and
    Present' (1843).
16 The 'World' (4 January 1753 to 30 December 1756);
    the 'Connoisseur' (31 January 1754 to 30 September
    1756); the 'Mirror' (23 January 1779 to 27 May 1780);
    the 'Lounger' (5 February 1785 to 6 January 1787).
17 Soame Jenyns (1704-87) published in 1776 'A View of
    the Internal Evidence of the Christian Religion'.
18 Richard Bettesworth (c. 1689-1741), an Irish lawyer,
    was denounced by Swift in a 'Declaration of the
    Inhabitants of St. Patrick's' (1734); Jean-Jacques Le
    Franc (1709-84), Marquis of Pompignan, was satirized
    by Voltaire.
19 Sir Matthew Hale (1609-76), judge and author of trea-
    tises on law and religion; John Tillotson (1630-94),
    Archbishop of Canterbury; William Congreve (1670-
    1729), dramatist; Sir John Vanbrugh (1664-1726),
    dramatist.
20 'Tatler' 260; George Smalridge (1663-1719), Bishop
    of Bristol.
21 See Johnson's 'Life of Addison', No. 67, note 1.
22 'Spectator' 26, 329, 69, 317, 159, 343, 517.
23 Addison probably began 'Cato' at Oxford (c. 1694),
    and worked on it while on the Continent (1699-1703).
    The first four acts were read by Cibber in 1703. The
    last act was quickly written in 1713.
24 Such was Pope's advice (Spence, sect. 153).
25 William Charles Macready (1793-1873), actor and
    manager known for the splendour of his Shakespearean
    productions.
26 Coffee-houses in Change Alley frequented by stock-
    jobbers and merchants.
27 Spence, sect. 156.
28 Three tragedies: 'Athalie' by Racine; 'Cinna' by
    Corneille; 'Saul' by Vittorio Alfieri.
29 Addison to Hughes (12 October 1713), in 'The Letters

of Joseph Addison', ed. Graham (1941), p. 280.

30 Probably in the spring of 1714 Steele was made Deputy-
Lieutenant for Middlesex, Surveyor of the Royal
Stables at Hampton Court, and a Justice of the Peace.
By 18 October 1714 he became a licensee of the Theatre
Royal in Drury Lane. By 19 January 1715, he received
his patent as governor of the same theatre. He was
knighted on 9 April 1715.

31 23 December 1715 to 29 June 1716.

32 For the eulogy of Lord Somers, see 'Freeholder' 39.
For the foxhunter, 'Freeholder' 44, 47.

33 'Freeholder' 33.

34 See Warton, 'An Essay on the Writings and Genius of
Pope', No. 62, note 1.

35 Scott had been discouraged by David Steuart Erskine
(1742-1829), 11th Earl of Buchan, and James Ballan-
tyne (1772-1833); Goethe by Johann Gottfried von
Herder (1744-1803), critic and theologian; William
Robertson (1721-93), author of 'The History of the
Reign of the Emperor Charles V' (1769), by David
Hume (1711-76).

36 Spence, sect. 162.

37 Shakespeare, 'A Midsummer Night's Dream', III. i.

38 Pope, on 9 August 1735; in Spence, sect. 163.

39 'Epistle IV to Richard Boyle Earl of Burlington'.
The assumption that Timon is Chandos has been dis-
proved in the twentieth century.

40 Aaron Hill (1685-1750) appears in 'The Dunciad', Bk
II.

41 'First Satire of the Second Book of Horace,
Imitated'.

42 According to Courthope ('Life of Pope', V, pp. 346-7),
Bolingbroke wished Pope to have printed for him a few
copies of 'Letters on the Spirit of Patriotism: On the
Idea of a Patriot King: and on the State of Parties'.
Presumably Pope meddled with the text, had 1,500
copies printed, and secretly kept. After Pope's
death Bolingbroke had the impression destroyed.

43 Spence, sects 165, 166.

44 For the circulation of the Atticus lines during Addison's lifetime, see Spence, sect. 168.

45 Sheridan's 'School for Scandal'.

46 'Freeholder' 40.

47 'Stanzas to Lady Warwick on Mr. Addison's Going to
Ireland'.

48 William Somerville (1675-1742), a Whig and minor poet.

49 Vincent Bourne (1695-1747).

50 Joseph Hume (1777-1855), MP, a radical in politics,
who opposed what he considered unnecessary public
expenditures.

51 The Peerage Bill of 1719 provided that the actual
    number of English peers should never be increased by
    more than six and that twenty-five hereditary peers
    be substituted for the sixteen elected representatives
    of the Scottish peerage in Parliament.
52 Charles Seymour (1662-1748), 6th Duke of Somerset.
53 An allusion to works omitted from Tickell's edition
    which Steele pointed out in his Dedication to Congreve
    in the second edition of 'The Drummer' (1722).

71. WILLIAM MAKEPEACE THACKERAY ON ADDISON AND STEELE

1853

From 'The English Humourists of the Eighteenth Century'
(1853), pp. 70-137.

We have seen in Swift a humorous philosopher, whose truth
frightens one, and whose laughter makes one melancholy.
We have had in Congreve a humorous observer of another
school to whom the world seems to have no moral at all,
and whose ghastly doctrine seems to be that we should
eat, drink, and be merry when we can, and go to the
deuce (if there be a deuce) when the time comes. We
come now to a humour that flows from quite a different
heart and spirit - a wit that makes us laugh and leaves us
good and happy; to one of the kindest benefactors that
society has ever had, and I believe you have divined
already that I am about to mention Addison's honoured
name.
    From reading over his writings, and the biographies
which we have of him, amongst which the famous article in
the 'Edinburgh Review' (1) may be cited as a magnificent
statue of the great writer and moralist of the last age,
raised by the love and the marvellous skill and genius of
one of the most illustrious artists of our own; looking at
that calm, fair face, and clear countenance - those
chiselled features pure and cold, I cannot but fancy that
this great man, in this respect, like him of whom we spoke
in the last lecture, was also one of the lonely ones of
the world. Such men have very few equals, and they do not
herd with those. It is in the nature of such lords of

intellect to be solitary - they are in the world but not
of it; and our minor struggles, brawls, successes, pass
under them.

Kind, just, serene, impartial, his fortitude not tried
beyond easy endurance, his affections not much used, for
his books were his family, and his society was in public;
admirably wiser, wittier, calmer, and more instructed than
almost every man with whom he met, how could Addison
suffer, desire, admire, feel much? I may expect a child
to admire me for being taller or writing more cleverly
than she; but how can I ask my superior to say that I am
a wonder when he knows better than I? In Addison's days
you could scarcely show him a literary performance, a ser-
mon, or a poem, or a piece of literary criticism, but he
felt he could do better. His justice must have made him
indifferent. He did not praise, because he measured his
compeers by a higher standard than common people have.
How was he who was so tall to look up to any but the lof-
tiest genius? He must have stooped to put himself on a
level with most men. By that profusion of graciousness
and smiles, with which Goethe or Scott, for instance,
greeted almost every literary beginner, every small
literary adventurer who came to his court and went away
charmed from the great king's audience, and cuddling to
his heart the compliment which his literary majesty had
paid him - each of the two good-natured potentates of
letters brought their star and riband into discredit.
Everybody had his Majesty's orders. Everybody had his
Majesty's cheap portrait, on a box surrounded with dia-
monds worth twopence a piece. A very great and just and
wise man ought not to praise indiscriminately, but give
his idea of the truth. Addison praises the ingenious Mr.
Pinkethman: Addison praises the ingenious Mr. Doggett the
actor, whose benefit is coming off that night: Addison
praises Don Saltero: (2) Addison praises Milton with all
his heart, bends his knee and frankly pays homage to that
imperial genius. (3) But between those degrees of his men
his praise is very scanty. I do not think the great Mr.
Addison liked young Mr. Pope, the Papist, much; I do not
think he abused him. But when Mr. Addison's men abused
Mr. Pope, I do not think Addison took his pipe out of his
mouth to contradict them....

But it is not for his reputation as the great author of
'Cato' and the 'Campaign', or for his merits as Secretary
of State, or for his rank and high distinction as my Lady
Warwick's husband, or for his eminence as an Examiner of
political questions on the Whig side, or a Guardian of
British liberties, that we admire Joseph Addison. It is

as a 'Tatler' of small talk and a 'Spectator' of mankind,
that we cherish and love him, and owe as much pleasure to
him as to any human being that ever wrote. He came in that
artificial age, and began to speak with his noble, natural
voice. He came, the gentle satirist, who hit no unfair
blow; the kind judge who castigated only in smiling.
While Swift went about, hanging and ruthless - a literary
Jeffries (4) - in Addison's kind court only minor cases
were tried: only peccadilloes and small sins against
society: only a dangerous libertinism in tuckers and
hoops; or a nuisance in the abuse of beaux' canes and
snuff-boxes. It may be a lady is tried for breaking the
peace of our sovereign lady Queen Anne, and ogling too
dangerous from the side-box: or a Templar for beating the
watch, or breaking Priscian's head: or a citizen's wife
for caring too much for the puppet-show, and too little
for her husband and children: every one of the little
sinners brought before him are amusing, and he dismisses
each with the pleasantest penalties and the most charming
words of admonition.

Addison wrote his papers as gaily as if he was going
out for a holiday. When Steele's 'Tatler' first began
his prattle, Addison, then in Ireland, caught at his
friend's notion, poured in paper after paper, and contributed the stores of his mind, the sweet fruits of his
reading, the delightful gleanings of his daily observation, with a wonderful profusion, and as it seemed an
almost endless fecundity. He was six-and-thirty years
old: full and ripe. He had not worked crop after crop
from his brain, manuring hastily, subsoiling indifferently, cutting and sowing and cutting again, like other
luckless cultivators of letters. He had not done much as
yet; a few Latin poems - graceful prolusions; a polite
book of travels; a dissertation on medals, not very
deep; four acts of a tragedy, a great classical exercise;
and the 'Campaign', a large prize poem that won an enormous prize. (5) But with his friend's discovery of the
'Tatler', Addison's calling was found, and the most
delightful talker in the world began to speak. He does
not go very deep: let gentlemen of a profound genius,
critics accustomed to the plunge of bathos, console themselves by thinking that he *could not* go very deep. There
are no traces of suffering in his writing. He was so
good, so honest, so healthy, so cheerfully selfish, if I
must use the word. There is no deep sentiment. I doubt,
until after his marriage, perhaps, whether he ever lost
his night's rest or his day's tranquillity about any
woman in his life: whereas poor Dick Steele had capacity
enough to melt, and to languish, and to sigh, and to cry

his honest old eyes out, for a dozen. His writings do not
show insight into or reverence for the love of women which
I take to be, one the consequence of the other. He walks
about the world watching their pretty humours, fashions,
follies, flirtations, rivalries; and noting them with the
most charming archness. He sees them in public, in the
theatre, or the assembly, or the puppet-show; or at the
toy-shop higgling for gloves and lace; or at the auction,
battling together over a blue porcelain dragon, or a
darling monster in Japan; or at church, eyeing the width
of their rivals' hoops, or the breadth of their laces, as
they sweep down the aisles. Or he looks out of his
window at the Garter in St. James's Street, at Ardelia's
coach, as she blazes to the drawing-room with her coronet
and six footmen; and remembering that her father was a
Turkey merchant in the city, calculates how many sponges
went to purchase her earring, and how many drums of figs
to build her coach-box; or he demurely watches behind a
tree in Spring Garden as Saccharissa (whom he knows under
her mask) trips out of her chair to the alley where Sir
Fopling is waiting. He sees only the public life of
women. Addison was one of the most resolute clubmen of
his day. He passed many hours daily in those haunts.
Besides drinking, which alas! is past praying for, it must
be owned, ladies, that he indulged in that odious practice
of smoking. Poor fellow! He was a man's man, remember.
The only woman he *did* know, he did not write about. I
take it there would not have been much humour in that
story.

He likes to go and sit in the smoking-roon at the
Grecian, or the Devil; to pace 'Change and the Mall - to
mingle in that great club of the world - sitting alone in
it somehow: having good-will and kindness for every
single man and woman in it - having need of some habit and
custom binding him to some few; never doing any man a
wrong (unless it be a wrong to hint a little doubt about
a man's parts, and to damn him with faint praise); and so
he looks on the world and plays with the ceaseless
humours of all of us - laughs the kindest laugh - points
our neighbour's foible or eccentricity out to us with the
most good-natured, smiling confidence; and then, turning
over his shoulder, whispers *our* foibles to our neighbour.
What would Sir Roger de Coverley be without his follies
and his charming little brain-cracks? If the good knight
did not call out to the people sleeping in church, and
say 'Amen' with such a delightful pomposity: if he did not
make a speech in the assize-court *apropos de bottes*, and
merely to show his dignity to Mr. Spectator: if he did not
mistake Madam Doll Tearsheet for a lady of quality in

Temple Garden: if he were wiser than he is: if he had not
his humour to salt his life, and were but a mere English
gentleman and game-preserver - of what worth were he to
us? We love him for his vanities as much as his virtues.
What is ridiculous is delightful in him: we are so fond of
him because we laugh at him so. And out of that laughter,
and out of that sweet weakness, and out of those harmless
eccentricities and follies, and out of that touched brain,
and out of that honest manhood and simplicity - we get a
result of happiness, goodness, tenderness, pity, piety;
such as, if my audience will think their reading and
hearing over, doctors and divines but seldom have the
fortune to inspire. And why not? Is the glory of Heaven
to be sung only by gentlemen in black coats? Must the
truth be only expounded in gown and surplice, and out of
those two vestments can nobody preach it? Commend me to
this dear preacher without orders - this parson in the
tye-wig. When this man looks from the world whose weaknesses he describes so benevolently, up to the Heaven
which shines over us all, I can hardly fancy a human face
lighted up with a more serene rapture: a human intellect
thrilling with a purer love and adoration than Joseph
Addison's. Listen to him: from your childhood you have
known the verses: but who can hear their sacred music
without love and awe?

> Soon as the evening shades prevail,
> The moon takes up the wondrous tale,
> And nightly to the listening earth
> Repeats the story of her birth;
> And all the stars that round her burn,
> And all the planets in their turn,
> Confirm the tidings as they roll,
> And spread the truth from pole to pole.
> What though, in solemn silence, all
> Move round this dark terrestrial ball;
> What though no real voice nor sound,
> Among their radiant orbs be found;
> In reason's ear they all rejoice,
> And utter forth a glorious voice,
> For ever singing as they shine,
> The hand that made us is divine. (6)

It seems to me those verses shine like the stars. They
shine out of a great deep calm. When he turns to Heaven,
a Sabbath comes over that man's mind: and his face lights
up from it with a glory of thanks and prayer. His sense
of religion stirs through his whole being. In the fields,
in the town: looking at the birds in the trees: at the

children in the streets: in the morning or in the moon-
light: over his books in his own room: in a happy party at
a country merry-making or a town assembly, good-will and
peace to God's creatures, and love and awe of Him who
made them, fill his pure heart and shine from his kind
face. If Swift's life was the most wretched, I think
Addison's was one of the most enviable. A life prosperous
and beautiful - a calm death - an immense fame and affection afterwards for his happy and spotless name....

Posterity has been kinder to this amiable creature; all
women especially are bound to be grateful to Steele, as he
was the first of our writers who really seemed to admire
and respect them. Congreve the Great, who alludes to the
low estimation in which women were held in Elizabeth's
time, as a reason why the women of Shakespeare make so
small a figure in the poet's dialogues, though he can himself pay splendid compliments to women, yet looks on them
as mere instruments of gallantry, and destined, like the
most consummate fortifications, to fall, after a certain
time, before the arts and bravery of the besieger, a man.
There is a letter of Swift's, entitled 'Advice to a very
Young Married Lady', which shows the Dean's opinion of the
female society of his day, and that if he despised man he
utterly scorned women too. No lady of our time could be
treated by any man, were he ever so much a wit or Dean,
in such a tone of insolent patronage and vulgar protection. In this performance, Swift hardly takes pains to
hide his opinion that a woman is a fool: tells her to read
books, as if reading was a novel accomplishment; and
informs her that 'not one gentleman's daughter in a thousand has been brought to read or understand her own
natural tongue'. Addison laughs at women equally; but,
with the gentleness and politeness of his nature, smiles
at them and watches them, as if they were harmless, half-
witted, amusing, pretty creatures, only made to be men's
playthings. It was Steele who first began to pay a manly
homage to their goodness and understanding, as well as to
their tenderness and beauty. (7) In his comedies, the
heroes do not rant and rave about the divine beauties of
Gloriana or Statira, as the characters were made to do in
the chivalry romances and the high-flown dramas just going
out of vogue, (8) but Steele admires women's virtue,
acknowledges their sense, and adores their purity and
beauty, with an ardour and strength which should win the
good will of all women to their hearty and respectful
champion. It is this ardour, this respect, this manliness, which makes his comedies so pleasant and their
heroes such fine gentlemen. He paid the finest compliment

to a woman that perhaps ever was offered. Of one woman,
whom Congreve had also admired and celebrated, Steele
says, that 'to have loved her was a liberal education.'
'How often,' he says, dedicating a volume to his wife,
'how often has your tenderness removed pain from my sick
head, and how often anguish from my afflicted heart! If
there are such beings as guardian angels, they are thus
employed. I cannot believe one of them to be more good
in inclination, or more charming in form than my wife.'
His breast seems to warm and his eyes to kindle when he
meets with a good and beautiful woman, and it is with
his heart as well as with his hat that he salutes her.
About children, and all that relates to home, he is not
less tender, and more than once speaks in apology of what
he calls his softness. He would have been nothing without
that delightful weakness. It is that which gives his
works their worth and his style its charm. It, like his
life, is full of faults and careless blunders; and
redeemed, like that, by his sweet and compassionate
nature....
  The great charm of Steele's writing is its naturalness.
He wrote so quickly and carelessly, that he was forced to
make the reader his confidant, and had not the time to
deceive him. He had a small share of book-learning, but
a vast acquaintance with the world. He had known men and
taverns. He had lived with gownsmen, with troopers, with
gentlemen ushers of the Court, with men and women of
fashion; with authors and wits, with the inmates of the
spunging houses, and with the frequenters of all the clubs
and coffee houses in the town. He was liked in all company because he liked it; and you like to see his enjoyment as you like to see the glee of a box full of children
at the pantomime. He was not one of those lonely ones of
the earth whose greatness obliged them to be solitary; on
the contrary, he admired, I think, more than any man who
ever wrote; and full of hearty applause and sympathy, wins
upon you by calling you to share his delight and good
humour. His laugh rings through the whole house. He must
have been invaluable at a tragedy, and have cried as much
as the most tender young lady in the boxes. He has a
relish for beauty and goodness wherever he meets it. He
admired Shakespeare affectionately, and more than any man
of his time; and, according to his generous expansive
nature, called upon all his company to like what he liked
himself. He did not damn with faint praise: he was in the
world and of it; and his enjoyment of life presents the
strangest contrast to Swift's savage indignation, and
Addison's lonely serenity....
  If Steele is not our friend he is nothing. He is by no

means the most brilliant of wits nor the deepest of
thinkers: but he is our friend: we love him, as children
love their love with an A. because he is amiable. Who
likes a man best because he is the cleverest or the
wisest of mankind; or a woman because she is the most virtuous, or talks French; or plays the piano better than the
rest of her sex? I own to liking Dick Steele the man, and
Dick Steele the author, much better than much better men
and much better authors.

The misfortune regarding Steele is, that most part of
the company here present must take his amiability upon
hear-say, and certainly cannot make his intimate acquaintance. Not that Steele was worse than his time; on the
contrary, a far better, truer, and higher-hearted man than
most who lived in it. But things were done in that
society, and names were named, which would make you shudder now. What would be the sensation of a polite youth of
the present day, if at a ball he saw the young object of
his affections taking a box out of her pocket and a pinch
of snuff: or if at dinner, by the charmer's side, she
deliberately put her knife into her mouth? If she cut her
mother's throat with it mamma would scarcely be less
shocked. I allude to these peculiarities of by-gone times
as an excuse for my favourite, Steele, who was not worse,
and often much more delicate than his neighbours....

Dennis, who ran a muck at the literary society of his
day, falls foul of poor Steele, and thus depicts him, -
'Sir John Edgar, of the County of —— in Ireland is of a
middle stature, broad shoulders, thick legs, a shape like
the picture of somebody over a farmer's chimney - a short
chin, a short nose, a short forehead, a broad flat face,
and a dusky countenance. Yet with such a face and such
a shape, he discovered at sixty that he took himself for a
beauty, and appeared to be more mortified at being told
that he was ugly, than he was by any reflection made upon
his honour or understanding.

'He is a gentleman born, witness himself, of very honourable family; certainly of a very ancient one, for his
ancestors flourished in Tipperary long before the English
ever set foot in Ireland. He has testimony of this more
authentic than the Heralds' Office, or any human testimony. For God has marked him more abundantly than he did
Cain, and stamped his native country on his face, his
understanding, his writings, his actions, his passions,
and above all his vanity. The Hibernian brogue is still
upon all these, though long habit and length of days have
worn it off his tongue.' (9)

Although this portrait is the work of a man who was

neither the friend of Steele, nor of any other man alive;
yet there is a dreadful resemblance to the original, in
the savage and exaggerated traits of the caricature, and
every body who knows him must recognise Dick Steele. Dick
set about almost all the undertakings of his life with
inadequate means, and, as he took and furnished a house
with the most generous intentions towards his friends,
the most tender gallantry towards his wife, and with this
only drawback, that he had not wherewithal to pay the rent
when Quarter-day came, - so, in his life he proposed to
himself the most magnificent schemes of virtue, forbearance, public and private good, and the advancement of his
own and the national religion; but when he had to pay for
these articles - so difficult to purchase and so costly to
maintain - poor Dick's money was not forthcoming: and when
Virtue called with her little bill, Dick made a shuffling
excuse that he could not see her that morning, having a
headache from being tipsy over night; or when stern Duty
rapped at the door with his account, Dick was absent and
not ready to pay. He was shirking at the tavern; or had
some particular business (of somebody's else) at the
ordinary; or he was in hiding, or worse than in hiding,
in the lock-up house. What a situation for a man! - for
a philanthropist - for a lover of right and truth - for
a magnificent designer and schemer! Not to dare to look
in the face the Religion which he adored and which he had
offended: to have to shirk down back lanes and alleys, so
as to avoid the friend whom he loved and who had trusted
him - to have the house which he had intended for his
wife, whom he loved passionately, and for her ladyship's
company which he wished to entertain splendidly, in the
possession of a bailiff's man, with a crowd of little
creditors, - grocers, butchers, and small-coal men,
lingering round the door with their bills and jeering at
him. Alas! for poor Dick Steele! For nobody else of
course. There is no man or woman in *our* time who makes
fine projects and gives them up from idleness or want of
means. When Duty calls upon *us*, we no doubt are always
at home and ready to pay that grim tax-gatherer. When *we*
are stricken with remorse and promise reform, we keep our
promise, and are never angry, or idle, or extravagant any
more. There are no chambers in *our* hearts, destined for
family friends and affections, and now occupied by some
Sin's emissary and bailiff in possession. There are no
little sins, shabby peccadilloes, importunate remembran-
ces, or disappointed holders of our promises to reform,
hovering at our steps, or knocking at our door! Of
course not. We are living in the nineteenth century,
and Poor Dick Steele stumbled and got up again, and got

into jail and out again, and sinned and repented; and
loved and suffered; and lived and died scores of years
ago. Peace be with him! Let us think gently of one who
was so gentle: let us speak kindly of one whose own breast
exuberated with human kindness.

Notes

1 Macaulay's review of Lucy Aikin's 'Life of Addison'
   (1843) (No. 70).
2 Addison writes of William Penkethman (or Pinkethman)
   in 'Spectator' 31; of Thomas Doggett in 235; of Don
   Saltero in 'Tatler' 226.
3 The Saturday papers on Milton appeared from 5 January
   to 3 May 1712.
4 George Jeffreys (1648-89), Baron Jeffreys of Wem
   (1685), Lord Chancellor of England. Particularly
   known for his judicial severity in the 'bloody
   assizes' of 1685, he has become the prototype of the
   brutal English judge.
5 The 'prizes' are as follows: Tonson in the autumn of
   1705 published Addison's 'Remarks on Several Parts of
   Italy', dedicated to Lord Somers. A few months
   earlier it had become known that Addison was to be
   under-secretary to Sir Charles Hedges, Secretary of
   State. He received the appointment in 1706.
6 The last two stanzas of Addison's 'The spacious firma-
   ment on high', his reworking of Psalm XIX. 1-4. See
   'Spectator' 465.
7 See, e.g., 'Tatler' 206.
8 Gloriana (Queen Elizabeth) in Spenser's 'Faerie
   Queene' (1589, 1596); Statira, the wife of Alexander
   the Great, in Nathaniel Lee's 'Rival Queen' (1677).
9 From Letter IV of 'The Characters and Conduct of Sir
   John Edgar' (1720) (No. 21).

Select Bibliography

The items listed in this bibliography are not reproduced in the text.

+ 10 Ax Defence pamphlets in the Text. = 30 overall!!

THE EIGHTEENTH CENTURY

ADDISON, JOSEPH, 'De la Religion chrétienne', ed. Gabriel Seigneux de Correvon, 1757.

AMHURST, NICHOLAS, 'The Christian Poet ... with Memoirs of Mr. Addison's Life and Writings', 1728.

ARBUCKLE, JAMES, 'An Epistle to the Right Honourable Thomas Earl of Hadington, on the Death of Joseph Addison', 1719.

BRADLEY, RICHARD, 'A Philosophical Account of the Works of Nature as founded upon the Plan of the Late Mr. Addison', [1721], 1739.

BUDGELL, EUSTACE, 'A Letter to Cleomenes', 1731.

BURNET, THOMAS, 'Essays, Divine, Moral and Political', 1714.

COBDEN, EDWARD, 'A Poem on the Death of the Right Honourable Joseph Addison', 1720.

'The Crisis of Honesty', 1720.

'The Crisis upon Crisis. A Poem. Being an Advertisement stuck in the Lion's Mouth at Button's: and addressed to Doctor S---t', 1714.

'A Defence of the Crisis', 1714.

'A Dialogue between A. and B., containing some Remarks upon Mr. Steele's Letter to the Englishman. Being a Supplement to the Examiner', 1713.

DU BOS, JEAN BAPTISTE, Réflexions Critiques sur la Poésie & sur la Peinture, I ([1719], 1732), p. 340.

'L'Esprit d'Addisson: ou les Beautés du Spectateur, du Babillard, et du Gardien ... avec un précis de sa vie', 1777.

452

EUSDEN, LAURENCE, 'A Letter to Mr. Addison on the King's Accession to the Throne', 1714.

ROWE, E., 'An Expostulary Epistle to Sir Richard Steele upon the Death of Mr. Addison. By a Lady', 1720.

> 'The False Alarm: or, Remarks upon Mr. Steele's Crisis', 1714.

> F. G., Gent., 'The History of the First and Second Session of the Last Parliament ... in Mr. Steele's Case', 1714.

FOXTON, THOMAS, 'Serino, or The Character of a Fine Gentleman', [1723], 1725.

GILDON, CHARLES, 'The Laws of Poetry', 1721.

GODWIN, WILLIAM, Of English Style, 'The Enquirer', 1797.

GOLDSMITH, OLIVER, 'The Bee', 1759, No. 1.

HUDDESFORD, W., 'A Congratulatory Letter to Addison upon his being appointed one of his Majesty's Principal Secretaries of State', 1717.

> 'Jack the Courtier's Answer to Dick the Englishman's Close of the Paper so Call'd', 1714.

JACOB, GILES, 'Memoirs of the Life and Writings of the Right Honourable Joseph Addison, Esq; with his Character by Sir Richard Steele', 1724.

JONES, R., 'Britannia Triumphans', 1717.

'Journal Littéraire de la Haye', 1717, vol. IX.

> LACY, JOHN [pseud.], 'The Ecclesiastical and Political History of Whigland', 1714.

> 'A Letter to Richard Steele, concerning his Crisis', 1714.

'The Life of Mr. Dennis, the renowned Critick. In which are likewise some Observations on most of the Poets and Criticks, his Contemporaries'. Not written by Mr. [Edmund] Curll, 1734.

> MEREDITH, ROYSTON, 'Mr. Steele Detected', 1714.

MERES, SIR JOHN, 'The Equity of Parliaments, and Publick Faith Vindicated', 1720.

'A New Epilogue to The Conscious Lovers'. Spoken in Dublin, 13 May 1724. Published in the same year.

'Le Paradis perdu de Milton. Poëme heroïque', traduit de l'anglois, avec les remarques de M. Addisson, 1729. There were other French translations with Addison's Paradise Lost papers appended; see, e.g., those of 1748, 1755, 1757, 1782. At the Hague similar editions were printed, e.g., 1730, 1774.

'Il Paradiso perduto; Poema inglese' ... con le annotazioni di G. Addison, 1758; similar editions, e.g., 1791, 1794.

PERCY, THOMAS, 'Reliques of Ancient English Poetry', 1765 (ed. Henry B. Wheatley, 1876), I, pp. 19, 21, 22, 249-51; III, pp. 169-76.

PHILIPS, AMBROSE, 'The Free-Thinker', 11 April 1718.
> PHILO-TEMPLO-BASILEUS [pseud.], 'A Defence of the Church of England and the Clergy, against the Misrepresentations and False Charges of Sir Richard Steele', 1715.
> PRYNN, WILLIAM [pseud.], 'A Second Whigg-letter from William Prynn to Nestor Ironside', 1713.
> 'Remarks upon the Truth, Design and Seasonableness of Sir Richard Steele's Dedication to the Pope', 1715.
> SEWELL, GEORGE, 'Schism, destructive of the Government, both in Church and State', 1714.
> SEWELL, GEORGE, 'Sir Richard Steele's Recantation', 1715.
> SEWELL, GEORGE, 'Upon Mr. Steele's Incomparable Elegy on the Death of Queen Mary', 1715.
> STAINES, T., 'A Defence of Mr. Steele. In a Letter to a Friend in the Country', 1714.
'The State of the Case, between the Lord Chamberlain of His Majesty's Household, and Sir Richard Steele ... Restated, in Vindication of King George, and the Most Noble Duke of Newcastle', 1720.
> SWIFT, JONATHAN, 'The Publick Spirit of the Whigs', 1714.
TICKELL, THOMAS, Preface to 'The Works of the Right Honourable Joseph Addison', 1721.
VICTOR, BENJAMIN, 'The History of the Theatres of London and Dublin from the Year 1730 to the Present Time', 1761, II, pp. 99-101.
> 'A Vindication of Sir Richard Steele, against a pamphlet intituled, A Letter to the Right Worshipful Sir R.S. concerning his remarks on the Pretender's Declaration', 1716.
VOLTAIRE, FRANÇOIS AROUET DE, 'Letters Concerning the English Nation', 1733, Letter 23.
> WAGSTAFFE, WILLIAM, 'A Letter from the Facetious Doctor Andrew Tripe, at Bath, to the Venerable Nestor Ironside', 1714.
YOUNG, EDWARD, 'A Letter to Mr. Tickell', 1719.
YOUNG, R., 'Tentamen de Scriptis Addisonianis', 1725.

THE NINETEENTH CENTURY

AIKIN, LUCY, 'The Life of Joseph Addison', 1843.
AITKEN, GEORGE A., 'The Life of Richard Steele', 1889.
AXON, W. E. A., 'The Literary History of the Drummer', 1895.
BELJAME, A., 'Le Public et les Hommes de Lettres en Angleterre au dix-huitième Siècle 1660-1744, first published 1881; translated 1948.
'Biographia Dramatica', 1812, vol. II ('The Drummer', 'The Conscious Lovers', 'Cato'); vol. III ('Rosamond').

COURTHOPE, W. J., 'Addison', 1884.
DILKE, C. W., 'The Papers of a Critic', 1875.
DOBSON, AUSTIN, 'A Paladin of Philanthropy', 1899.
DRAKE, NATHAN, 'Essays, Biographical, Critical, and
Historical, Illustrative of the Tatler, Spectator, and
Guardian', 1805.
FORSTER, JOHN, 'Historical and Biographical Essays', 1858.
GILFILLAN, G., 'Poetical Works of Addison', 1859.
HARTMANN, H., 'Steele als Drammatiker', 1880.
HUNT, LEIGH, 'A Book for a Corner', 1849.
INCHBALD, ELIZABETH, 'The British Theatre', 1808: vol.
VIII ('Cato'); vol. XII ('The Conscious Lovers').
IRVING, DAVID, Critical Examination of a Passage in the
Writings of Addison, 'The Elements of English Composi-
tion', 1801.
KOCH, M., 'Über die Beziehungen der englischen Literatur
zur deutschen im 18 Jahrhundert', 1883.
MONTGOMERY, HENRY R., 'Memoirs of the Life and Writings of
Steele', 1865.
OGLE, NATHANIEL, 'Spectator' (corrected edition with bio-
graphical preface), 1827.
PAUL, A., 'Addison's Influence on the Social Reform of his
Age', 1876.
PHILLIPS, R., 'Addisoniana', 1803.
TUCKERMAN, HENRY T., 'Essays, Biographical and Critical;
or, Studies of Character', 1857.
ZANELLA, GIACOMO, 'Paralleli Letterari: Studi', 1885.

THE TWENTIETH CENTURY

ACHURCH, ROBERT W., Richard Steele, Gazetteer and
Bickerstaff, 'Studies in the Early English Periodical',
ed. Richmond P. Bond, 1957, pp. 49-72.
AVERILL, JAMES H., The Death of Stephen Clay and Richard
Steele's 'Spectators' of August 1711, 'Review of English
Studies' XXVIII (1977), pp. 305-10.
BAINE, RODNEY M., The Publication of Steele's 'Conscious
Lovers', 'Studies in Bibliography' II (1949-50), pp. 169-73.
BLANCHARD, RAE, 'The Christian Hero', by Richard Steele:
A Bibliography, 'The Library' 4th series, X (1930), pp.
61-72.
BLOOM, EDWARD A. and LILLIAN D. 'Joseph Addison's Sociable
Animal', 1971.
BLOOM, LILLIAN D., Addison's Popular Aesthetic: The
Rhetoric of the 'Paradise Lost' Papers, 'The Author in His
Work: Essays on a Problem in Criticism', eds. Louis L.
Martz and Aubrey Williams, 1978, pp. 263-81.
BOND, DONALD F., Addison in Perspective, 'Modern

Philology' LIV (1956), pp. 124-8.
BOND, DONALD F., Introduction to 'The Spectator', 1965.
BOND, RICHMOND P., 'The Tatler', 1971.
BRAUER, GEORGE C., Jr., Recommendations of the 'Spectator' for Students during the Eighteenth Century, 'Notes and Queries' CC (May 1955), pp. 207-8.
BROADUS, EDMUND K., Addison's Influence on the Development of Interest in Folk-Poetry in the Eighteenth Century, 'Modern Philology' VIII (1910-11), pp. 123-34.
CARDWELL, G. A., Jr., The Influence of Addison on Charleston Periodicals 1795-1860, 'Studies in Philology' XXXV (1938), pp. 456-70.
CONNELY, WILLARD, 'Sir Richard Steele', 1934.
DOBRÉE, BONAMY, The First Victorian, 'Essays in Biography', 1925.
FOÀ, GIOVANNA, 'Two Essayists, Richard Steele and Joseph Addison', 1957.
FURTWANGLER, ALBERT, Mr. Spectator, Sir Roger, and Good Humour, 'University of Toronto Quarterly' XLVI (1976), pp. 31-50.
GAY, PETER, The Spectator as Actor, 'Encounter' XXIX (December 1967), pp. 27-32.
GOLDGAR, BERTRAND, 'The Curse of Party: Swift's Relations with Addison and Steele', 1961.
GUSTAFSON, W. W., The Influence of the Tatler and Spectator in Sweden, 'Scandinavian Studies and Notes', 1932, vol. XII.
HEGNAUER, A. G., 'Der Einfluss von Addisons "Cato" auf die dramatische Literatur Englands und des Continents in der ersten Hälfte des 18. Jahrhunderts', 1912.
HORN, R.D., The Early Editions of Addison's 'Campaign', 'Studies in Bibliography' III (1950-1), pp.256-61.
KENNY, SHIRLEY S., Richard Steele and the 'Pattern of Genteel Comedy', 'Modern Philology' LXX (1972), pp. 22-37.
KENNY, SHIRLEY S., Recent Scholarship on Richard Steele, 'British Studies Monitor' IV (1973-4), pp. 12-24.
LEWIS, C. S., Addison, 'Essays on the Eighteenth Century Presented to David Nichol Smith', 1945, pp. 1-14.
LITTO, F. M., Addison's 'Cato' in the Colonies, 'William and Mary Quarterly' XXIII (1966), pp. 431-49.
LOFTIS, JOHN, 'Steele at Drury Lane', 1952.
LONSDALE, ROGER (ed.), Addison, Steele and the Periodical Essay, 'The Sphere History of English Literature', vol. IV: Dryden to Johnson, 1971, especially pp. 155-9.
MILIC, LOUIS T., The Reputation of Richard Steele: What Happened?, 'Eighteenth Century Life' I (1975), pp.81-7.
MOORE, J.R., Gildon's Attack on Steele and Defoe in 'The Battle of the Authors', 'PMLA' LXVI (1951), pp. 534-8.
NOCE, HANNIBAL S., Early Italian Translations of Addison's

'Cato', 'Petrarch to Pirandello: Studies in Italian Litera-
Literature in Honor of Beatrice Corrigan', ed. Julius A.
Molinaro, 1973, pp. 111-30.

REYNOLDS, RICHARD R., The Fall and Rise of Richard Steele:
A Crossroads of Law and Politics, 'Enlightenment Essays',
IV (1973), pp. 36-41.

ROGAL, SAMUEL J., Joseph Addison (1672-1719): A Check List
of Works and Major Scholarship, 'Bulletin of the New York
Public Library' LXXVII (1974), pp. 236-50.

SCHULZ, DIETER, Richard Steele: 'The Conscious Lovers',
'Das Englische Drama im 18. und 19. Jahrhundert: Interpretationen', ed. Heinz Kosok (1976), pp. 74-86.

SHAWCROSS, I., Addison as a Social Reformer, 'Contemporary
Review' CLIII (May 1938), pp. 585-91.

SMITHERS, PETER, 'The Life of Joseph Addison', 2nd ed.,
1968.

'The Spectator', ed. Donald F. Bond, 1965.

STEELE, RICHARD, 'The Englishman', ed. Rae Blanchard, 1955.

STEELE, RICHARD, 'Occasional Verse', ed. Rae Blanchard,
1952.

STEELE, RICHARD, 'Periodical Journalism, 1714-16', ed. Rae
Blanchard, 1959.

STEELE, RICHARD, 'The Plays of Richard Steele', ed.
Shirley S. Kenny, 1971.

STEELE, RICHARD, 'The Theatre, 1720', ed. John Loftis,
1962.

STEELE, RICHARD, 'Tracts and Pamphlets', ed. Rae Blanchard,
1944.

SUTHERLAND, JAMES, The Last Years of Joseph Addison,
'Background for Queen Anne', 1939, pp. 127-44.

THORPE, CLARENCE D., Addison's Contribution to Criticism,
'The Seventeenth Century: Studies in the History of English
Thought and Literature from Bacon to Pope', by R. F. Jones,
et al., 1951, pp. 316-29.

TODD, W. B., Early Editions of the 'Tatler', 'Studies in
Bibliography', XV (1962), 121-33.

WATSON, MELVIN R., 'Magazine Serials and the Essay Tradition, 1746-1820', 1956.

WATSON, MELVIN R., The Spectator Tradition and the Development of the Familiar Essay, 'ELH', XIII (1946), pp.189-215.

WINTON, CALHOUN , 'Captain Steele', 1964.

WINTON, CALHOUN , 'Sir Richard Steele, M.P.', 1970.

ZAIC, FRANZ, Joseph Addison: 'Cato', 'Das Englische Drama
im 18. und 19. Jahrhundert: Interpretationen', ed. Heinz
Kosok (1976), pp.46-56.

Index

The index is divided into the following categories:

I   Names and titles (other than Addison's and Steele's); places and events.
II   Periodicals written jointly or separately by Addison and Steele; selected characters.
III   Addison: biography and characteristics; reputation; works.
IV   Steele: biography and characteristics; reputation; works.

I NAMES AND TITLES

IV   STEELE